WITH THE CARRIERS IN KOREA

Looking Back

From the files of The Associated Press

TODAY IS MONDAY, *July 3, the 184th day of 2017. There are 181 days left in the year.*

Today's Highlight in History:

On July 3, 1863, the three-day Civil War Battle of Gettysburg in Pennsylvania ended in a major victory for the North as Confederate troops failed to breach Union positions during an assault known as Pickett's Charge.

On this date:

In 1775, Gen. George Washington took command of the Continental Army at Cambridge, Mass.

In 1913, during a 50th anniversary reunion at Gettysburg, Pa., Civil War veterans re-enacted Pickett's Charge, which ended with embraces and handshakes between the former enemies.

In 1938, President Franklin D. Roosevelt marked the 75th anniversary of the Battle of Gettysburg by dedicating the Eternal Light Peace Memorial.

In 1944, during World War II, Soviet forces recaptured Minsk from the Germans.

In 1950, the first carrier strikes of the Korean War took place as the USS Valley Forge and the HMS Triumph sent fighter planes against North Korean targets.

In 1962, French President Charles de Gaulle signed an agreement recognizing Algeria as an independent state after 132 years of French rule.

In 1976, Israel launched its daring mission to rescue 106 passengers and Air France crew members being held at Entebbe Airport in Uganda by pro-Palestinian hijackers; the commandos succeeded in rescuing all but four of the hostages.

In 1987, British millionaire Richard Branson and Per Lindstrand became the first hot-air balloon travelers to cross the Atlantic, parachuting into the sea as their craft went down off the Scottish coast.

In 1992, the first U.S. Air Force C-130 transport planes from Operation Provide Promise arrived in the besieged Bosnian capital of Sarajevo.

Beebe added these are the first wolves with a melanistic — or black — color the facility has received in decades.

The puppies were transported from Predators of the Heart in Anacortes, a nonprofit animal refuge sanctuary that houses nizations.

Erin Hawkins is a reporter with the Olympic Peninsula News Group, which is composed of Sound Publishing newspapers Peninsula Daily News, Sequim Gazette and Forks Forum. Reach her at ehawkins@sequimgazette.com.

ERIN HAWKINS/

Robert Beebe, Olympic Game Farm pr a 6-week-old male timber wolf puppy sister Grace, will soon join the rest o the game farm near Sequim.

WITH THE CARRIERS IN KOREA

THE FLEET AIR ARM STORY, 1950-1953

John R P Lansdown

CRÉCY

Dedicated to those thirty-four aircrew who
gave their lives in operations from the Royal Navy
and Royal Australian Navy aircraft carriers
from June 1950 to July 1953

Pusan Cemetery Commonwealth Memorial

Published by Crécy Publishing Limited in 1997
© John R P Lansdown, 1997

ISBN 0 947554 64 5

Printed and bound in Great Britain by
Biddles Ltd, Guildford and King's Lynn

Crécy Publishing Limited
Southside, Manchester Airport,
Wilmslow, Cheshire SK9 4LL, UK

CONTENTS

ACKNOWLEDGEMENTS

Without the encouragement and assistance of the staff of the Fleet Air Arm Museum — Graham Mottram (Curator), Len Lovell, Anne Bell and Dave Richardson (Librarians) and Peter Chisholm (Engineer) — this whole project would have been impossible; they are the custodians of the Squadron Diaries, Record Books, Line Books and photographs on which this book is based; together with Peter Chisholm's deep technical knowledge of the aircraft, who recalled much that I had forgotten and who put me straight on many occasions.

Many people have helped me, and I am grateful to those who have patiently replied to my letters. Particularly I must thank: W.R. Blackmore, Conway Maritime Press, Lieutenant Commander J.F. Blunden RN, Les Dalton, Captain W.W.F. Chatterton-Dickson RN, M. Cottingham, G.B. Edgeler, Commander R.B.L. Foster OBE RN, Lieutenant Commander R.E. Geale MBE RAN, Curator Australian Naval Aviation Museum, Max Hastings, Commander D.C.V. Isard RN, Lieutenant Commander Fred Lane RAN, Captain A.J. Leahy CBE DSC RN, Lieutenant Commander P.H. London DSC RN, Professor Callum A. MacDonald, Rear Admiral P.N. Marsden RN, Captain D.G. Mather RN, Professor S. McGrail, Commander G.D.H. Sample OBE DSC RN, Captain A.L.L. Skinner RN, John Winton.

FOREWORD

I am sure that when Johnny Lansdown embarked on this venture, to write about the part played by the Fleet Air Arm and the British and Australian carriers in the Korean War, he had no idea just how much time, effort and research it was going to take. Happily he persevered, and now that it is finished he has presented an accurate account of the activities of the British and Commonwealth carriers from information currently available in the public domain.

As is so often the case, this war went on much longer than expected. Experienced aircrew were limited, following World War II demobilisation, so the flying training machine had to be geared up to meet the increased demand. Accordingly more and more young aircrew found themselves going straight from the flying training pipeline to the carriers off Korea, having accumulated some 360 hours and 17 deck landings. It was 'on the job' training after that.

This book covers every day's flying from the British carriers, sometimes very briefly and at other times more fully, as for instance the downing of a MiG by Furies from *Ocean*, which became known as Hoagy's MiG. Similarly 'Pug' Mather's experiences as a PoW deservedly gets fuller coverage — especially as this was the second time that he was shot down!

As it happens, I was flying as Pug's No. 2 when he was shot down the second time. He said 'I have been hit under my seat, please come and have a look'. As I was arriving underneath his aircraft to inspect the damage his Sea Fury broke in half behind his seat. I spent the next few milliseconds avoiding his complete detached tail section. The real story is his own in Chapter 12, and much more worth reading.

Although those involved undoubtedly retain vivid memories, the Korean War was not regular front page news and now, after some forty years, it is almost forgotten. In consequence, a book of this sort is welcome in documenting the very considerable part played by the carrier-borne aircraft throughout the war, and I am sure it will be well received by aircrews, groundcrews and ship's companies alike. It should also appeal to a wider readership and provide a very useful point of reference.

Vice Admiral Sir Edward Anson KCB, FRAeS

INTRODUCTION

The most famous remark about Korea was that made at the MacArthur hearings by General of the Army Omar Bradley; he said it would be 'the wrong war, at the wrong place, at the wrong time, and with wrong enemy.' The statement, which was actually made not about Korea but about enlarging the war by attacking China, has come to sum up the public perception of the Korean War, as if it were somehow a lapse of taste or good judgement which should not have happened, and which should best be forgotten.

At the time, in 1950, the war in Korea was a long way from home, it was only five years from the end of the Second World War, it was during the unpopular period of National Service in Great Britain, the media were not interested and reported it reluctantly — unlike the Falklands and the Gulf. If it was not a forgotten war, then it was almost an ignored one.

It was the first time the United Nations resisted aggression and the Western Powers opposed Communism; although the war ended with no clear victor, it is argued that it gave the Communists cause to think before embarking on acts of aggression in the years that followed; if South Korea had been lost to Communism, what other countries might not rapidly have followed suit?

The war has generated a not inconsiderable literature since its conclusion in 1953. This book records the part played by the Fleet Air Arm during those three years, covering every day when aircraft were airborne; but not in isolation — the Royal and Commonwealth Navies had many other ships involved, all of which are mentioned; as is the United States Navy whose ships carried the principal responsibility for the successful prosecution of the maritime war.

CHAPTER 1

PRELUDE TO WAR

After the end of World War II, Asia was in a state of turmoil. Communist agents were everywhere exploiting local situations in favour of Russia against her erstwhile allies. China was being Communised by Mao Tse-tung, while General Chiang Kai-shek was trying to re-organise his Chinese Nationalist forces on the island of Formosa (Taiwan) under the umbrella of the United States Navy. Moscow was supplying arms and munitions to the Communists, while the United States was doing the same for the Nationalists. But the United States, Britain and the other western powers had their eyes focused on Europe, looking eastwards.

Korea had been a Chinese province until in 1894 Japan landed an army 'to make it part of the Japanese map'. Moscow and Tokyo competed for power and concessions in Seoul, until, following the Japanese victory over the Russian fleet at Tsushima, Korea became a Japanese protectorate in 1905, was annexed outright in 1910, and the story for the next 35 years was one of shameless exploitation by Japan.

Korea is a roughly rectangular peninsula, about 240 miles wide and 550 miles long, in area a little less than England, Scotland and Wales, projecting southward from the mainland of Asia to within 100 miles of Japan, bounded on the north by Manchuria and the Russian Maritime Province.

In the Cairo Declaration of 1943 and the later Potsdam Declaration of 1945, China, the United Kingdom and the United States had expressed their determination that 'in due course Korea shall become free and independent'. Soviet Russia entered the war against Japan a few days before it ended, and thereby gained an opportunity of obtaining a foothold in Korea. Japanese control ended in September 1945, and in order to fill the political vacuum caused by the withdrawal of the Japanese, it was occupied by Russian forces in the north and United States forces in the south, the dividing line between them being fixed by an *ad hoc* arrangement as the parallel of 38° north latitude. The northern part is mountainous, containing most of the industry and mineral deposits of the country, while the south is mainly agricultural and is inhabited by about two-thirds of the population.

It had never been contemplated by the Western Powers that the demarcation line should be anything other than an administrative convenience for rounding up Japanese troops after 14th August 1945 — VJ Day. Once this task had been completed, it had been visualised that all foreign troops would be withdrawn from Korea, and the country allowed to rise again as an independent nation as soon as the people had decided what form of government they wanted.

From 1945 to 1948 the United Nations Assembly made numerous attempts to unite North and South Korea under one central government, but all efforts were baulked by Soviet Russia. The Republic of Korea, headed by President Syngman Rhee, was created in 1948 after an election organised by a United Nations Commission. The Republic was accepted by the United Nations, except for Russia and her satellites, as the lawful government of Korea. North Korea had refused to take part in these elections, and shortly afterwards Soviet Russia announced that they had held their own elections in the North and had formed the Korean People's Democratic Republic which Russia then claimed as the rightful government of Korea.

By 1950, in the North, Communism was firmly in control, while in the South the people demanded a democratic form of government and professed a hatred of Communism.

Soviet troops were withdrawn from the north by December 1948, and by July 1949 the last 500 American troops had left from the south, except for a small staff of advisers who remained at the request of the Government to help train new Republican armed forces, although the American occupation ended officially on 23rd August 1948. This left the Republic of Korea with responsibility for guarding its own frontier along the 38th Parallel. A commission which arrived in Korea in February 1949 made several abortive attempts to unite the two halves of the country. While all this was going on, a tense political atmosphere was established in the approved Hitler/Stalin fashion, leading to a series of border incidents and increased animosity, with each side accusing the other of creating disturbances along the frontier. Quantities of Russian arms were pushed into the country and by June 1950 the North Korean forces had built up to about 90,000 troops, 180 tanks and 175 operational-type aircraft — which compared somewhat unfavourably with the RoK forces of about the same numerical strength but with no armour or heavy artillery and only 13 Piper Cubs and 10 Harvards. In the absence of American forces which had departed 11 months before, Moscow deemed the moment propitious on 25th June 1950 to blow the whistle and the invasion of South Korea was set in motion.

At a meeting with the United Nations Commission on 10th June, the North Koreans protested that they wanted peaceful unification of the country. Fifteen days later, without any declaration of war or other warning, they launched their invasion.

At 4.00 a.m. on Sunday 25th June 1950, the Communist North Korean Armed Forces, after a devastating mortar and artillery barrage, crossed the 38th Parallel, attacked the Republic of Korea, and advanced south. Seoul, capital of South Korea and only about 30 miles south of the 38th Parallel, was the objective of a two pronged attack which included 100 tanks and 100 aircraft. They also attacked towards Chunchon in the centre, and a third column made rapid progress down the east coast. This attack achieved complete strategic and tactical surprise having been masked by a skilful deception plan during the preceding weeks.

The forces of the Republic of Korea, lacking tanks, military aircraft and artillery could do little, the invaders advanced at will during the first four days. On 27th June President Syngman Rhee and his Government moved 100 miles south to Taejon.

To the Communist commanders it must have seemed that the war was already won; but in their preparations they had left one factor out of their calculations which was to prove their undoing — sea power. North Korean naval forces were negligible, consisting of about 50 ships, all small, though probably sufficient to deal with the South Korean Navy of about 40 small ships which were later enhanced with the addition of four frigates and other vessels. The geographical configuration of the Korean peninsula renders it very susceptible to the pressure of sea power. From the moment the United Nations came in, the relentless pressure of sea power clamped down on the Communists; the UN navies were to play a big part in sealing off the Communist coasts from any seaborne supplies, in providing mobility to the armies by amphibious landings, and in bombardment by gun and aircraft. Thanks to it, a foothold was retained around Pusan where the land forces could be built up, which, supplied and supported by the navies, repelled the invasion and would drive the invader back across the frontier.

The United Nations Secretary-General, Mr. Trygve Lie, summoned a meeting of the Security Council on that Sunday afternoon. Earlier, on 13th January, the Soviet delegate, Mr. Yakov Malik, had walked out of the Security Council in protest against the UN's refusal to recognise Communist China in place of the Nationalists. He had not returned to the Security Council on 25th June, so, by a 9-0 vote, with Yugoslavia abstaining, a UN resolution was passed condemning the North Korean attack and calling for the withdrawal of their forces that were south of the 38th Parallel. However, on 29th June, Mr Gromyko, Soviet Foreign Minister, sent a note to Washington alleging that South Korea had provoked the conflict.

This was a unique resolution. For the first time the UN had unequivocally supported one combatant against another. In 1982, after another act of unprovoked aggression, Resolution 502 was passed — with Russia abstaining — instructing Argentina to withdraw her forces from the Falklands Islands. And in 1990 Security Council Resolution 660 unanimously condemned a third act of aggression — the Iraqi invasion of Kuwait.

A second resolution, passed on 27th June, requested UN members to assist the Republic of Korea repel aggression and restore 'peace and security' in the area. Within three days, 32 of the 59 member states of the UN had endorsed this recommendation, and many had offered military assistance: the Canadian, Australian and New Zealand Governments offering naval support and the Australians air support from their RAAF squadrons already based at Iwakuni in Japan.

The US Ambassador in Moscow argued in a telegram of 25th June that the

North Korean aggression represented a clear-cut Soviet challenge that the US must answer firmly and swiftly as it constituted a direct threat to the US leadership of the free world against Soviet Communist imperialism. Stalin's Korean adventure offered Washington the chance to seize the initiative and draw the line against Communist expansion. General Omar Bradley, Chairman of the American Joint Chiefs of Staff, remarked on the same day that American military support could be provided under the guise of aid to the UN.

The dominant Western members of the UN shared the American perspective and regarded the attack as a Soviet probe. Few could credit the Democratic People's Republic of Korea with a capacity for independent action. But it's army was by no means contemptible, consisting as it did of seven infantry and one armoured divisions in the front line with two infantry divisions in reserve.

Immediate military action was taken by President Harry S. Truman in the United States. He ordered US air and sea forces to give South Korean troops cover and support, and the US 7th Fleet to deploy between the Chinese mainland and the island of Formosa to prevent an attack on it by Chinese Communists. Admiral A.W. Radford, CinC US Pacific Fleet based at Pearl Harbour, had been directed to organise another task group for service in the western Pacific. General of the Army Douglas MacArthur, commanding US occupation forces in Japan from his headquarters in Tokyo, was placed in command of US troops in the whole area.

On June 27th Mr. Clement Attlee, British Prime Minister, and his Ministers agreed, without recorded dissent, that 'it was the clear duty of the United Kingdom Government to do everything in their power, in concert with other members of the United Nations, to help the South Koreans to resist aggression'.

By 7th July a Unified Command had been established under the UN flag. Although the war that had now broken out in Korea was formally a UN war the world organization did not attempt to control military operations, turning over the running of the conflict to President Truman, the Joint Chiefs of Staff and General MacArthur in Tokyo.

MacArthur was now wearing two hats. He was Supreme Commander of the United States Forces in the Far East as well as Commander in Chief of the United Nations Forces. In Japan he had three infantry divisions and one (dismounted) cavalry division of the US 8th Army, but at 70% strength, and the armoured units were equipped with light tanks only. Under him Lieutenant General George E. Stratemeyer, CinC US Far East Air Force, had eight-and-one-half combat groups which were responsible for the air defence of Japan, Okinawa, the Philippines and Guam.

The war was to develop into four clear phases — the North Korean invasion, the Allied counter assault in mid-September, Chinese intervention from early November to January 1951 and finally the seesaw war of stalemate until the armistice of July 1953.

The British and Commonwealth carriers were active throughout the war: *Triumph* to the end of September 1950, *Theseus* to April and *Glory* to September 1951, HMAS *Sydney* to January, *Glory* to May, *Ocean* to November 1952, *Glory* to May 1953 and *Ocean* to the end of hostilities in July 1953.

Carrier operations always carry the potential for catastrophe; a flight deck, as anyone who is familiar with naval aviation is aware, is among the most hazardous spots on earth. As demanding as flight deck operations were later in the era of angled-deck carriers equipped with steam catapults and sophisticated landing aids, Korean war operations in the era of straight-deck carriers with hydraulic/pneumatic catapults and an LSO waving paddles at the pilot held even greater danger.

On 16th September 1951 a damaged Banshee, unable to drop its hook, landed on USS *Essex*, leapt the barriers, and trundled forward of the island, on its way to an inevitable collision. Its pilot presumably guessed the deck crews had already re-fuelled and re-armed the fighters neatly parked along the port side of the flight deck, for the aircraft veered sharply to starboard, ramming four unarmed and un-refuelled aircraft and disintegrating in a huge fireball. The pilot's decision plus prompt damage control and swift ship handling that took advantage of the winds localised the damage and *Essex* resumed operations next day. But the accident claimed seven men, injured 27 others and destroyed four aircraft. On the following 4th November an errant Panther bounced over USS *Antietam's* barriers, killing four, injuring ten and leaving two aircraft destroyed and six others damaged.

There was only one major fire in a carrier during operations off Korea. At 0616 on 6th August 1952, after having launched eight pre-dawn hecklers, USS *Boxer* became prey to a portside hangar deck fire. For some reason, an aircraft's fuel tank exploded on the hangar deck, igniting other aircraft; the explosion tossed some on their backs. On the flight deck, 60 more fully fuelled and armed awaited launch. Captain Marshall B. Gurney did not launch them, he reduced speed from 30 knots and directed that as many aircraft as possible be re-spotted forward of the island and to jettison all the ordnance. The fire was attacked with foam and water from number 2 elevator which was lowered with fire control teams and an aircraft with engine running to clear the smoke. The fire drove 63 crewmen over the side, all of whom were picked up by *Boxer's* consorts, trapping others below and forcing the abandonment of some engineering spaces. After five hours the fire was out, at a cost of nine dead, 30 injured and 18 aircraft damaged or destroyed.

Capricious weather added other challenges. From 13th to 15th October 1951 Typhoon Ruth disrupted 7th Fleet air and surface operations in the Formosa/Korea/Japan area. HMAS *Sydney* was hit particularly hard, 50% Fireflies and Sea Furies sustained storm damage.

During the entire war there was no challenge to UN command of the sea, and this fact, which is so easy to mention in passing, was the absolute determinant of the way the war was fought, or indeed the fact that it could be fought at all. Except for its air strikes, the Navies remained something of a 'Silent Service' in the Korean War, but their ubiquitous presence, to bring supplies in, to put soldiers ashore at Inchon or to take them off at Hungnam, to provide coastal gunfire support, was a classic demonstration both of the versatility and the vital nature of sea power.

CHAPTER 2

HMS TRIUMPH

800 and 827 Squadrons
5th June 1950 to 29th September 1950

When the North Koreans invaded South Korea on Sunday 25th. June 1950, *HMS Triumph* (Captain A.D. Torlesse DSO) and her squadrons were enjoying a summer cruise to Japan in company with other ships of the Far East Fleet.

Admiral Sir Patrick Brind, Commander in Chief Far East Station, had kept as many ships as possible in Japanese waters to avoid the heat of Singapore and Hong Kong in the summer. While they were there they formed part of the naval occupation forces commanded by Vice-Admiral C.T. Joy USN. The Japanese government functioned subject to the control of the Supreme Commander Allied Powers, General Douglas MacArthur. Occupation and control were predominantly American, but since September 1945 Commonwealth forces under Australian command had been based at Kure; by June 1950 these were limited to one Australian battalion and a unit of the RAAF at Iwakuni. A Commander RAN controlled Kure dockyard.

On Friday 8th June *Triumph* was at Ominato in northern Japan. She was anchored about two miles from the nearest landing ashore, a gloomy prospect for boats' crews. The town of Ominato was little more than a few ramshackle huts, while the old Japanese air station was in a state of ruin. It had been intended to spend Monday to Friday at sea on exercises and to return to harbour for the weekend before sailing for Hong Kong and return to Chatham by 13th November so that *Glory* could re-commission. At Aden, *Triumph* would hand over to *Theseus* who would join *Unicorn* in 1st Aircraft Carrier Squadron, Far East Fleet.

During the week of 12th to 16th June flying included RATOG for the Seafire pilots of 800 Squadron. Lieutenant Commander P.B. Jackson, the Air Group Commander, and Lieutenant Commander B.C. Lyons, C.O. of 827 Squadron, tested the catapult for use by Fireflies for the first time since recommissioning at Sheerness on 21st April 1949. Two Seafires of 800 Squadron were written off due to landing too far over to port and causing the skin to wrinkle. Another two aircraft were written off during the week, also due to wrinkling.

Skin wrinkling had always been a problem with this delicate aeroplane — 'wrinkled like a prune' was one pilot's expressive description of his aircraft. It could be caused in two ways. The first was by 'splatting' on the deck after a badly judged

Seafire too high – round again!   *(Handley)*

landing approach. The proverbial 'stalled Seafire' dropped heavily tail first from the deck-landing attitude giving excessive up-load on the tail wheel and its supporting structure causing compressive wrinkling of the upper surface skin (which could be seen visually) and tensile separation of the skin from its frames at the lower surface which was detected by using feeler gauges between the rivets. The other cause was off-centre landing, mentioned above. The sting arrestor hook on the aircraft, fitted below the rudder, caught the wire deck span which then brought the aircraft to rest with a deceleration of about 1.5g in a short distance of 60 ft. If the landing was off-centre, the wire pulled the tail over towards the edge of the deck, causing the fragile Seafire fuselage to whip and to wrinkle on one side and to pull the frames from the skin on the other side. In either case there were limits laid down by the manufacturer as to the number of wrinkles and their depth, and to the size of gaps between frames and skin. When the gaps and wrinkles were too wide and deep, the aircraft was no longer safe to fly and had to be taken out of the flying programme and ultimately returned to the United Kingdom for repair.

On Saturday 24th June *Triumph*, with HMS *Cossack* in company, sailed from Ominato for Hong Kong, setting a southerly course through the Sea of Japan between the Korean peninsula and Japan. A warning that typhoon Elsie was in the offing had been received so aircraft lashings were doubled up and the ship secured and made safe. Elsie, however, did not materialise, she had blown herself out before reaching their position.

Rear Admiral W.G. Andrewes, Flag Officer Second in Command Far East Fleet, flying his flag in *Belfast*, heard of the invasion on the Sunday evening and immediately decided to move south from Hakodate in north Japan to Yokosuka. *Triumph* was recalled to Japanese waters from passage to Hong Kong.

News of the North Korean attack reached *Triumph* on Monday, and so a flight of fully armed Seafires was kept on deck in case of emergencies. The Fireflies carried out flight drill and catapulting in place of the previously scheduled exercise attack on the airfield at Iwakuni. On return the CO, Lieutenant Commander Lyons, missed all the arrestor wires and entered both barriers.

Two days later *Triumph* and *Cossack* fuelled and provisioned at Kure where they joined *Jamaica* and *Consort*, HMAS *Shoalhaven* and the RFA Tanker *Wave Conqueror*. *Triumph* secured alongside the jetty and disembarked her unserviceable aircraft — four Seafires and two Fireflies — thereby easing congestion in the hangar.

The next day, 29th June, Admiralty ordered CinCFE to 'place RN at present in Japanese waters at the disposal of the US Naval Commander for Korean operations in support of Security Council resolutions'.

These US naval forces under the command of Vice Admiral C.T. Joy consisted of the cruiser USS *Juneau*, together with four destroyers and six minesweepers; a complete amphibious force was also in the area carrying out exercises. Further afield, but within easy steaming distance, the US 7th Fleet under Vice Admiral A.D. Struble USN, was available for operations in Korea and to patrol off Formosa.

An initial advantage of the Korean War was that a ready made high command already existed — the US occupation forces in Japan. Unfortunately there was no joint headquarters, each of the three services had its own separate organisation.

At Singapore, Admiral Sir Patrick Brind flew his flag as CinCFE; responsible to him, as FO2FE, was Rear Admiral Andrewes.

Admiral A.W. Radford, CinC US Pacific Fleet, was at Pearl Harbour, and his sub-commands consisted of Admiral Struble with the US 7th Fleet — CTF 77 (Commander Task Force) — and Vice Admiral Joy in Japan as COMNAVFE. The 7th Fleet was broken into two Task Groups: Rear Admiral J.M. Hoskins with the fast carriers (CTG 77.4) and Captain C.W. Parker with 8 destroyers (CTG 77.2).

Admiral Joy was also responsible to General MacArthur for the conduct of all naval operations in Korea. In order to achieve his aim of implementing the blockade of North Korea, he decided that Admiral Andrewes with the British Commonwealth and Allied ships should form the West Korean Support Group (CTG 96.8) and Rear Admiral J.M. Higgins with US ships the East Korean Support Group (CTG 96.5), both operating directly under him. Admiral Joy would only issue broad instructions, leaving the details to the two flag officers concerned. For the next three years this policy worked well, with a continual interchange of ships between coasts. In addition to these two groups, four other forces were responsible to Admiral Joy: these were the amphibious force under Rear Admiral Doyle, the minesweepers under Captain R.T. Spofford USN, the RoK Navy under Admiral Sohn with Commander Luosey USN as American liaison officer and the Escort Carrier Group under Rear Admiral R.W. Ruble, this Group later to be dispersed.

These divided responsibilities caused considerable overlapping and Admiral Joy could not give sufficient personal attention to the day-to-day operations and movements of ships. Admiral Andrewes pressed for a co-ordinating naval authority, with an intelligence staff, to be set up in Sasebo, the American naval base at the western end of the island of Kyushu in Japan, about 160 miles from the port of Pusan in South Korea, the nearest point; this in due course was implemented.

The RN command set-up was complicated vis-à-vis the US because Admiral Andrewes had four separate but inter-related duties to perform:

    a) operation of United Nations ships placed under his operational command by Admiral Joy,

    b) logistic support of British Commonwealth and Allied ships forming part of the UN forces,

    c) the organisation in Japan with base and resulting staff,

    d) as FO2FE, the administration of all ships on the station, subject to the general control of the CinC for all matters of policy.

Admiral Brind did all he could to ease the burden on Admiral Andrewes, readily acceding to his requirements and frequently anticipating them. Much of the success of the British Commonwealth's efforts at sea in the Korean War can be ascribed to the happy relationship between the CinC and FO2FE and the trust by the former for the latter's conduct of operations.

Triumph and *Cossack* sailed from Kure at 0530 on 29th June to rendezvous in the afternoon with Admiral Andrewes, flying his flag in *Belfast*, together with *Jamaica* and *Consort*. Throughout the day precautionary anti-submarine patrols were flown by the Fireflies. This British detachment provided a welcome reinforcement to Admiral Joy as they made their way to Okinawa to join the US 7th Fleet.

On passage to Okinawa, *Triumph* had flown dawn to dusk anti-submarine patrols. There were rumours that enemy aircraft had been encountered in the battle zone and that they included Yak-3s, LA-5s and IL-2s (all of Russian manufacture); 10 enemy aircraft were claimed to have been shot down for the loss of one USAF Shooting Star. They also heard that their old friends from Iwakuni, 77 Squadron RAAF, had been ordered to Korea.

The South Korean capital of Seoul had been captured by North Korean forces on 30th June; on the same day, the first American troops landed in Korea from Japan.

The fleet arrived at Okinawa at first light on 1st July to find a very barren and uninteresting looking island. 800 Squadron's Diary recorded 'The American 7th Fleet which is in harbour consists of the carrier USS *Valley Forge*, the cruiser and flagship USS *Rochester*, 9 destroyers and 3 submarines, also a large depot ship. Aircraft on board *Valley Forge* were nearly all on deck and made a very impressive display and included jet Panthers, Skyraiders and a few Corsairs.'

After refuelling at the oiling jetty, *Triumph* sailed during the first dog watch and joined Admiral Andrewes in *Belfast* and they, together with *Cossack* and *Consort*, headed for the west coast of Korea and the Yellow Sea. *Jamaica* and the frigates *Black Swan* and *Alacrity* joined Rear Admiral Higgins USN, flying his flag in *Juneau*, for operations off the east coast.

Next day they joined the US fleet consisting of *Rochester* wearing the flag of Vice Admiral Struble (CTF 77), *Valley Forge*, flagship of Rear Admiral Hoskins (CTG 77.4), and eight destroyers. The British element became TG 77.5. 827 Squadron flew A/S patrols and during the afternoon an aircraft from each squadron was flown round the fleet to familiarise the Americans with Seafires and Fireflies. No difficulty was experienced by British ships working with Americans. 'It all seemed so familiar,' wrote Admiral Andrewes in his Report of Proceedings, 'as it was just what we had done so often during exercises with very similar forces. We didn't feel out of things and were already getting back into the easy use of American signal books.'

Monday 3rd July dawned, the first day of operational flying against an enemy for five years — Hot War. The tension, apprehension and excitement are apparent from 800 Squadron's diary (827's is much more terse!) and it will bear quoting in full:

'D' DAY. The first strike flew off at 0615 and consisted of 12 Seafires and 9 Fireflies. Producing 12 Seafires was a great effort by the ground crews as it meant 100% serviceability.

The target was Kaishu (Haeju) airfield, about 120 miles from the ship; the object of the attack was primarily to destroy aircraft and, secondly, installations. Approach was made at low level, but about 15 miles from the target the fog and low cloud forced the strike up. Luckily the cloud cleared over the target and the attack went in as planned, 71 Flight attacking from the west followed by 73 Flight, then 3 Flights of Fireflies and lastly 72 Flight, all Flights attacking in various sectors from a northerly direction. Unfortunately, no aircraft or movement was observed on the airfield, in fact the place looked deserted. Most of the rockets went into the hangars and administration area and a few on the concrete dispersal, the last Flight to attack found the target completely obscured by black smoke.

The only conclusion that can be drawn from this operation is that a reconnaissance of the intended target must be carried out first, as the primary object of the strike, to destroy aircraft, was not achieved.

In spite of the Air Group Commander's warning about not going below 600 feet in the attack, several aircraft were hit by debris thrown up by the rocket explosions and Lieutenant Lamb got a piece in his radiator. On return to the Fleet both his temperature gauges were off the clock so he stood by to bale out, but as the ship was into wind he decided to land on. By a stroke of luck he made it, and on throttling back after landing the engine came to a grinding halt and is of course a complete write off.

The Americans had better luck on their strike and managed to destroy eight aircraft on the ground at Heiju (Pyongyang) airfield and a further two in the air. They encountered both heavy and light flak but suffered no damage. Their only loss of the day was one of the Corsairs on CAP which caught fire and ditched close by one of the destroyers, which rescued the pilot in very quick time.

Three very boring sorties of CAP were flown during the afternoon and evening, with not even a scare to relieve the monotony.'

Lieutenant Commander Lyons, returned with a hole through his fuselage thought to have been caused by light flak.

On the next day, *Valley Forge* had flown off an early strike which, in the prevailing light southerly winds, had taken the fleet so far to the south that *Triumph's* Fireflies were out of range of any target and so did not launch her first strike until 1100 after some northing had been made. Twelve Fireflies and seven Seafires (one had had to return unserviceable shortly after take off) attacked various targets in the general area of Haeju, Ongjin and Yonan: army bases were strafed, buildings and railway bridges were rocketed and a village fired on with 20 mm cannon fire; two flak trucks mounting some small calibre weapons were hit and gun positions attacked near the coast. There was no enemy air activity and all aircraft returned safely. A Firefly had to make a one wheel landing due to mechanical trouble and a Seafire had a hole in the port combat tank where a cartridge case from the aircraft ahead had penetrated.

Firefly 1 piloted by Lieut. R.D. Forrest.   *(FAAM)*

Valley Forge's strikes had damaged two gunboats in Taedong Bay and had destroyed and damaged railway bridges, locomotives and rolling stock. She celebrated Independence Day to no mean tune. One of her Skyraiders which had been shot up over the target and had no hook or flaps went into the deck park and wrote off eight aircraft, a Corsair made a successful one wheel landing and the air-sea rescue helicopter ditched after engine failure. Fortunately none of these incidents resulted in any loss of life.

Admiral Andrewes subsequently remarked that choice of targets for British aircraft was severely limited by the Firefly's strike radius which could not be planned for more than 120 to 130 nautical miles. The versatility of the American aircraft was marked in comparison with the British; both the Skyraider and the Corsair had better endurance, and could apparently carry mixed loads of bombs, rockets and drop tanks, and could be catapulted with any of them.

Vice Admiral Struble congratulated all hands in the British ships on the way they had 'taken their responsibilities and at the successes already achieved.' 'In fact,' wrote Admiral Andrewes, 'things did work well, thanks very largely to our previous practice and knowledge of American ways, signals and, frequently, language'.

On completion of the day's flying, the force turned to the southward, *Belfast*, *Cossack* and *Consort* heading for Sasebo and the rest of the fleet for Okinawa. The force anchored at 0900 on 6th July and *Triumph* was refuelled and stored from RFA's *Green Ranger* and *Fort Charlotte*. It was rumoured that, on the day before, American and Australian aircraft had flown over 100 sorties, and that enemy losses were 7 aircraft, 7 tanks, 20 locomotives, 5 motor torpedo boats and 6 trawlers.

Triumph stayed in harbour for the next six days, when normal maintenance was carried out on the aircraft and a lecture programme was arranged for the pilots, the emphasis being on bombardment spotting which was seen as their likely future role. Because the Americans considered that the Seafire bore a marked resemblance to the North Korean Yak 9, all the aircraft had broad black and white stripes painted on their wings and fuselage — 'D-Day markings'. On the Saturday evening, 8th July, a contingent of American officers from *Valley Forge* was entertained to drinks on the quarter-deck. An excellent party ensued at which many useful experiences were exchanged; several of *Triumph's* officers were invited to take a look at *Valley Forge* the next day. It was reported that 'other entertainment's have been severely curtailed owing to the fact that we are still restricted to one dollar a week, but in spite of this several people have managed to make their money go a long way at the various American clubs ashore'.

Meanwhile, on the east coast, *Jamaica* and *Black Swan* had joined Rear Admiral Higgins USN (CTG 96.5), flying his flag in *Juneau*, and two destroyers cruising off the coast with the object of preventing North Korean forces and agents from landing south of the 38th Parallel. The patrol lasted for nine days during which time cliff roads, bridges, oil tanks and the harbour of Cumunchin were bombarded. On 8th July the British forces suffered their first casualties. *Jamaica* and the US destroyer *Swenson* were bombarding very attractive cliff road targets, proceeding at six knots and at close range for accuracy, when a shore battery, whose existence was unknown, opened fire at about 3000 yards range. Though promptly taken under fire and silenced, a lucky shot had hit the foot of one of the tripods of *Jamaica's* mast and killed one Able Seaman and wounded five soldiers from Hong Kong who had embarked for the summer cruise and had volunteered to act as supply parties;

several others were wounded from the same shot.

Admiral Andrewes set up a base for his ships at Sasebo — 1,079 miles from Hong Kong and 10,580 from Britain. It has a good harbour, protected from the weather, but it had no defences. Also as a base it was on a small scale and its facilities were fully extended due to the port being used by US warships in unusually large numbers in addition to Admiral Andrewes' squadron and to elements of US army passing through, the US Navy having taken over Army and Air Force transportation from the US Army on 1st July. As regards repair facilities, the base could only cope up to LCT size, but the Sasebo Shipbuilding Company — third largest in Japan and with little work at the time — could take on work on a larger scale.

Amenities for the Fleet were sparse, the two existing clubs for US ratings being too small to absorb the large numbers and also only accepting scrip dollars. Agreement was reached with Commander Whalley USN (Commander, Fleet Activities) for the loan of another building in which to set up a Fleet Canteen, and he was joined by Lieutenant (S) McGoldrick and Lieutenant (E) Pinder as liaison officers from the British side.

SS *Wusueh*, renamed HMS *Ladybird*, was commissioned as Admiral Andrewes headquarters ship from September 1950 until she was relieved by HMS *Tyne* in April 1953.

There was the question of replacement and upkeep of *Triumph's* aircraft. CinC suggested two programmes for *Unicorn* for this purpose, viz.

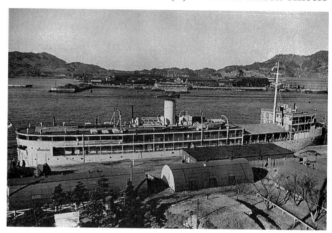

HMS *Ladybird.*   *(Cooper)*

(a) Move to an air station in the forward area (possibly Iwakuni) with all available aircraft and act as an aircraft repair and replenishment ship; or

(b) Disembark the Air Repair Department plus workshops equipment and stores to HMS *Simbang* (air station at Sembawang, Singapore) and act as a replenishment ship only.

Admiral Andrewes and Captain Torlesse preferred the second alternative for the following reasons:

(a) It would not be easy to find *Unicorn* a suitable base for her task. Admiral Joy was averse to basing carriers in Japanese waters, but,

although Okinawa would have been a practicable base, it would have
been unsatisfactory.

(b) Work would progress more surely at *Simbang* and the policy of
manning and, equipping the air station would be maintained.

(c) *Unicorn* would not be a drain on logistics in the forward area.

On 4th July Admiral Andrewes requested co-operation from the RAF
Sunderland squadron with his task group. Though Air Ministry approval had not
been given for RAF operations in Korea, Air Commodore Davies, AOC Hong
Kong, agreed to base one Sunderland at Iwakuni where the US Navy was
concentrating its flying boats.

At the same time, plans for implementing the blockade were being worked out.
Overall instructions on matters of policy were issued by Admiral Joy. These
included notes on the international law governing blockade and directions for the
treatment of ships trying to evade it. The instructions for the USN governing
maritime and aerial warfare were adopted for all United Nations ships participating.
UN warships were enjoined to keep well clear of Manchurian and Russian coasts.

A somewhat ticklish question arose regarding the policy to be adopted towards
unidentified submarines. Admiral Joy, Admiral Brind and Admiral F.P. Sherman
(Chief of Naval Operations, Washington) finally agreed the instructions that were
issued, but in the event no incident arose that could have been an unidentified
submarine. It was also laid down that aircraft endangering ships might be fired
upon at any time.

On 8th July Admiral Andrewes issued the first operational order to his ships —
Task Group 96.8. In it he laid down his objectives:

(a) Enforcement of blockade of the coast occupied by the North Koreans.

(b) Prevention of infiltration by sea on coasts held by South Koreans.

(c) Provision of naval support as required against North Korean maritime
forces or land targets.

The operational area was bounded on the north by the parallel of 39°30'N and on
the east by the west and south coasts of Korea as far as longitude 128°E (55 miles
west of Pusan).

On 13th July *Triumph* sailed from Okinawa and spent half a day flying a small
programme, particularly some talk-down landings as the low sun in the east made
it difficult to see the batsman's signals. In the evening a Sunderland arrived with
some very welcome mail and, after refuelling, spent the night at the seaplane
moorings. After two more days in harbour, including a briefing for an operation
on the east coast in support of landings by an American force, *Triumph* sailed in
company with *Rochester*, *Valley Forge*, *Comus* and eight USN destroyers.

Due to the limited range of the Fireflies, it had been decided that they would provide anti-submarine patrols while four Seafires provided CAP over the fleet.

By this time the prospects of being able to retain a hold on the Korean peninsula seemed slim; the North Korean armies had driven south relentlessly, the port of Pusan was full of shipping and the refugee-packed roads out of Pusan could accommodate no more troops.

The situation was saved on 18th July by the landing, by Rear Admiral Doyle's force, of the US 1st Cavalry Division at Pohang just before the arrival of the North Koreans who had swept down the east coast. The landing was unopposed and by evening 10,000 troops, 2,000 vehicles and 2,700 tons of cargo had been put ashore. By 25th July this force was blunting the enemy's drive down the Taegu/Pusan highway. Because of the lack of opposition during the landing, 21 aircraft from *Valley Forge* attacked Chosin oil refinery (the largest in Korea with an annual output of 1.7 million barrels), completely destroying it with 500 lb. and 1,000 lb. bombs and with rockets.

During the day an arrestor wire unit gave some trouble in *Triumph* which prevented flying for a short time until it was repaired. Mr. Reid, on returning from a CAP sortie, landed-on off-centre to port and his port wing dropped and hit the fore batting position, causing severe damage to the leading edge which meant a main-plane change in *Unicorn*, reducing the number of aircraft in 800 Squadron to ten. 18 CAP and 14 A/S sorties were flown this day.

One of *Valley Forge*'s jet aircraft crashed into the sea immediately after catapulting, but the pilot was picked up by the helicopter in a minute-and-a-half and was back on board in three minutes.

The next day *Triumph* flew 27 CAP sorties by the Seafires and 10 A/S by the Fireflies. On the last land-on of the day, Mr. White, piloting a Seafire, caught number 10 wire and, very gently, engaged the barrier. The engine was not shock-loaded, so after replacing the propeller the aircraft was serviceable again. The fact that he had flown over six hours that day may have been the explanation.

On 19th July, Lieutenant P. Cane made the last recorded operational rescue by Sea Otter. He and his observer, Aircrewman G. O'Nion, were briefed that a Corsair from *Valley Forge* had been hit by light flak and had been forced to ditch about 120 miles north-north-west of their carrier's position, near Wonsan. By the time they took off from *Triumph's* deck they had learned that the Corsair pilot, Lieutenant Wendell R. Muncie USN, was in his dinghy with his aircraft sunk and was being circled by two other aircraft from his own unit.

They established RT contact with the circling Corsairs and were warned that sea conditions would be rough for alighting. By the time they found the dinghy visibility was poor, there were white horses on the sea surface, and conditions were well outside the limits for the Sea Otter, with a steep chop of between four and five feet and a wind of twenty to thirty knots. With a real body in the dinghy, in enemy waters, there was no way they would not have a go at alighting. O'Nion recalls: 'We hit the first wave with a hell of a bang and I thought we would dive into the next one, but with consummate skill Lieutenant Cane held the nose up and we settled into a trough.' Lieutenant Commander Cane, on the other hand, says: 'In fact it's quite straightforward; you set the aircraft in a steep, nose up descent with as low a forward speed as possible and wait until you hit the water, then you close the throttle. It was quite a thump, and one wingtip float was damaged.'

He taxied up to the dinghy as quickly as the sea state would permit, with O'Nion standing up in the forward hatch. He hooked a slip line onto the dinghy and allowed it to float under the wing and alongside the rear hatch. Having secured the line he nipped aft and hoisted the pilot into the aircraft via the rear hatch, then sinking the dinghy with his knife. Muncie was uninjured and pleased to see them, though full of wonder at the Orville Wright machine that had appeared out of the sky.

Cane goes on to say: 'When the hatches were shut, and the two in the back were settled down, I took off. This was very exciting because it consisted of ploughing into the sea, banging from wave to wave, trying not to porpoise, until a wave threw the aircraft into the air with just enough airspeed to enable me to keep it there without hitting the next wave.' O'Nion, on the other hand, recalls: 'I cannot remember how many waves we hit. It felt like being in a roller coaster at a fairground. Seas were breaking over the top mainplane and the engine, which spluttered and caught again. The last wave we hit pushed us staggering into the air.'

Finally they had to contend with a difficult landing back on *Triumph's* deck. The ship had already recovered its Seafires and Fireflies which were all ranged forward so that the crash barrier had to be kept up when the Sea Otter arrived. It was never funny for the pilot of an Otter to land on a carrier with the barrier up since the aircraft design placed the cockpit almost in the nose, thus ensuring that the pilot would probably be decapitated on impact. However Lieutenant Cane did it neatly, and they were immediately struck down the forward lift into 'A' hangar. They clambered out and Muncie took off his Mae West and handed it to Cane — it seemed the take-off from the water had scared him far more than his ditching. For this very gallant rescue Lieutenant P. Cane was awarded the United States Air Medal and CPO O'Nion was Mentioned in Despatches. 'Dumbo', as the Americans called her, had proved her usefulness!

During these operations, *Triumph* had played a strenuous, if unspectacular, part, putting up a total of 140 hours flying. Admiral Andrewes described the restriction of her aircraft to CAP and A/S as 'galling, but unquestionably correct in the circumstances. The Seafire 47 is superior to the Corsair as a defensive fighter, while the strike radius of the Firefly is only half that of a US Skyraider'.

Triumph's starboard stern gland had been causing trouble due to deterioration of the packing. On 21st July Captain Torlesse decided it would be unwise to remain at sea for the further two days of operations then in prospect so *Triumph*

and *Comus* were
detached from the
Task Group and
sailed for Sasebo,
where they arrived
at 1000 next day.

Unicorn and
Fort Charlotte were
already there.
U n i c o r n
disembarked seven
replacement Seafires
and five Fireflies,
and embarked the
two Seafire write-
offs, bringing

About to launch Seafires and Fireflies.   *(Handley)*

Triumph's total of
Seafires to 17, four below complement. *Fort Charlotte* supplied 126 tons of stores.

On 24th July there was an urgent call from the Army for assistance by carrier-
borne aircraft. North Korean Peoples Army (NKPA) units were advancing down the
west coast in force and the US 8th Army was in danger of encirclement. CAS was
imperative, though there were difficulties in the way of its provision.

The Americans had two different systems in use for close support operations —
the US Air Force and the US Navy/Marine.

In the USAF/Army system, command over CAS aircraft was not exercised by
front line units but was jointly co-ordinated at Army level. The Joint Operations
Centre assigned strike aircraft to a particular mission which were then controlled
by a liaison-type aircraft (known as Mosquitoes) airborne in the area in which the
strike had been ordered. CAS targets were those in the battle zone up to ten miles
from the front. There had been no air/ground training between the USAF and US
Army units, nor was a tactical control system in existence.

The USN/Marine system had developed in the Pacific War. The ground
commander could make use of a certain number of aircraft as he saw fit. A few
aircraft constantly orbited the battlefield ready to strike at targets within 50 to 200
yards of the immediate front lines. Pilots received their information and directions
from a trained crew directly in the front line. The efficacy of the support depended
on the efficiency of the ground crew and their communications.

Admiral Struble replied to the Army's request for assistance, but warned that
their value for CAS depended entirely on satisfactory communications and control.
Admiral Joy signalled that 'The calculated risk of damage to friendly forces must

be accepted'. The ground situation was so critical that operations should commence on 25th July.

Triumph and *Comus* sailed to join TF77 that morning and steered for an area north of Quelpart Island. During the day, 28 sorties of Fleet CAP were flown totalling 54 hours, but unfortunately two more Seafires were written off: one due to an off-centre landing causing unacceptable skin-wrinkling, and the other when the tail-wheel was pushed over the edge of the flight deck by the handling party causing damage to two frames that was beyond the ability of the ship's Air Maintenance Department to repair. Firefly operations were limited to A/S patrols.

Valley Forge aircraft operated in the Kunsan/Chonju/Kwangju area for four days, but the results were minor owing to lack of satisfactory air/ground communications.

On 26th July, *Triumph* and *Comus* moved to the east coast where 827 Squadron flew routine A/S patrols and some CAP sorties to relieve their hard-pressed Seafire companions. Some mild excitement was caused on the first day when a US destroyer dropped several depth charge patterns, but it was never known whether there had been a submarine target, there were no signs of oil or other debris afterwards, but there were known to be many whales in the vicinity at the time.

An unfortunate incident occurred on the morning of the 28th. A flight of Seafires had been ordered to investigate a bogey which turned out to be several B-29 Super Fortresses. Mr. White was acting as No.3 as the leader's radio had packed up; he passed an American aircraft at about 300 yards range when, for no apparent reason, it opened fire on him and hit his aircraft in the rear fuel tank with its first burst. He immediately rolled onto his back and baled out. The sea was too rough to

operate the Sea Otter, but he was picked up by the US destroyer *Eversole* after about an hour in the water, suffering from burns to his face, arms and shoulders, his condition otherwise appeared to be satisfactory.

The next day was uneventful, CAP and A/S patrols only being carried out, and two days later,

Sea Otter land-on.   *(Cane)*

on 31st July, *Triumph* secured alongside in Kure. The Air Group Commander congratulated the Air Group on their good work and pointed out that the serviceability over the last month had been higher than ever before and the accident rate lower

The next eight days, until 8th August, were spent in Kure on aircraft maintenance and self-refit, the two unserviceable Seafires being disembarked by lighter to Iwakuni, reducing the number on board to 14. A signal was received from USAF Headquarters, signed Stratemeyer, expressing regret for Mr. White's incident, but suggesting that all aircraft should keep out of gun range of the Superforts. Lieutenant Handley, Senior Pilot of 800 Squadron, left the ship soon after arrival to brief the Americans on bombardment spotting and very soon found himself in a Neptune giving a practical demonstration. He made two trips, the first when he controlled British destroyers bombarding Mokpo and the second with *Belfast* and *Kenya* bombarding Inchon; he reported results as satisfactory, and several targets received direct hits, including two girls' schools thought to be being used as troops' quarters, and damage was caused to factory buildings, oil tanks, railway sidings and rolling stock. Admiral Andrewes considered the operation well planned and executed and he thought that it might discourage the enemy from using Mokpo as a port for shipping supplies eastwards to the front.

Doubts, particularly in General MacArthur's headquarters, were being expressed as to the effectiveness of the blockade. In the six weeks since the start of the war roads, bridges, locomotives and rolling stock had been reported as destroyed *by* US aircraft. The Communists were showing an astonishing aptitude for improvisation in keeping land communications running: trains hid in tunnels by day for night running, and camouflaged railway tracks on log caissons by-passed demolished bridges. This, with many variations, was to be the pattern for the next three years.

Triumph sailed from Kure on 9th August for Sasebo. Three Seafires were catapulted to Iwakuni for compass swinging, returning in the evening, the remainder of the pilots carrying out deck landing practice. 800's diary comments that 'The rest in Kure certainly hasn't improved the DLs, which for the most part were pretty shocking...'; another Seafire was written off after a badly off-centre landing, leaving only 13 available for the flying programme.

After embarking Admiral Andrewes and his staff, *Triumph* joined *Kenya*, *Comus*, *Sioux* and *Athabaskan* for operations on the west coast. The British Fleet had been given the task of blockading this coast and, owing to the numerous islands, inland waterways and areas un-navigable to ships of the fleet it was essential to use aircraft for reconnaissance to see whether the enemy was using these areas for sea transport.

On Sunday 13th August photographic sorties were flown by the Seafires over Mokpo and Kunsan, both of which were found to be deserted, Mokpo having been heavily damaged by bombardment from sea and air. A few small junks were seen and two small coastal ferries were attacked with 20mm cannon fire. Photographic reconnaissance later in the day showed Inchon to have been nearly razed and still smouldering from recent attacks by US carrier borne forces.

The next day's activities were concentrated further north at Chinnampo, the main North Korean naval base. The early morning photographic sorties saw little evidence of movement in the port, but both heavy and light antiaircraft fire was encountered over the town. The photographs had revealed three ships at the mouth of the Taedong estuary which were attacked by a strike of six Seafires and six Fireflies during the afternoon. Hits were obtained with 601b high explosive rockets on a 2,000 ton freighter, an 800 ton coaster and a camouflaged motor minesweeper.

Kunsan from a Firefly of 827 Squadron, 15 August 1950.   *(FAAM)*

Tuesday was comparatively quiet, the Fireflies carrying out their normal daily A/S patrols and the Seafires their CAP. Both squadrons carried out armed reconnaissance of Inchon and the coast, but nothing was attacked. Lieutenant Commander MacLachlan did some bombardment spotting for *Jamaica* whose target was a large factory at Kunsan. This was more in the nature of a practice than anything else, but several hits were obtained in the target area.

The next two days were spent in Sasebo. 827 Squadron's diarist notes with great pleasure 'Just before we arrived in Sasebo, a signal was received from Admiralty which was met with much enthusiasm — "Splice the mainbrace". It marked in time honoured fashion the birth of Princess Anne to HRH Princess Elizabeth…lunchtime was much enlivened by the flow of the golden liquid.'

From 18th to 21st August *Triumph* was operating off the west coast in the Inchon/Kunsan area, escorted and accompanied variously by *Jamaica*, *Kenya*, *Comus*, *Charity*, *Consort*, *Sioux* and *Athabaskan*. The US 7th Fleet was also in the area with its CAP thereby releasing the Seafires from this duty that had absorbed more than half the Seafire effort. One Firefly maintained an A/S and investigation patrol that was useful for examining surface radar contacts and sightings and linking with ships out of VHF contact. The Fireflies, with rockets, sunk a 150 ton gunboat armed with two 3 pounder guns and several light anti-aircraft weapons. Apart from this, no really worthwhile shipping targets were found and pilots were authorised to attack military targets in the port areas. Lieutenant Commander MacLachlan's flight went on an armed photographic mission as far north as Pyongyang, the North Korean capital. Very little movement was observed on the river, but all the factories seemed to be working full blast, and as the flight approached the city it was attacked by fairly heavy flak, later estimated to be 75 mm. This was the first occasion on which the Squadron had been subjected to such heavy opposition. 827 Squadron claimed the sinking of a small war vessel of about 150 tons with 16 rockets. Other targets damaged or destroyed during this patrol included railway trucks near Mokpo, two small motor coasters at Kunsan and oil tanks at Kyomipo. Reconnaissance was carried out as far north as the River Yalu, the Manchurian border, but nothing suspicious was sighted. On the last day of the patrol, a flak position on the

Damaged junks at Mokpo, August 1950.   *(Christmas)*

island of Wolmido, off Inchon, was attacked with good results; and *Consort* carried out a bombardment of a factory at Kunsan, controlled by a Seafire, gaining about 50% hits.

The Seafires were now reduced to an availability of only nine; two aircraft had reached the limit of acceptable cumulative wrinkling and a third was over-stressed due to an off-centre landing on the last day of the patrol. *Unicorn* had only seven replacements left, so the total number available in the Far East was then only sixteen.

On 23rd August *Triumph* entered Sasebo to join the other two large carriers of the United Nations Fleet, *Valley Forge* and *Philippine Sea*; they made an impressive sight and would have been an excellent target had the North Koreans had an air force capable of launching an attack.

The North Korean Air Force was not totally impotent, for while they were in harbour they received the unpleasant news that *Comus* had been attacked *by* two IL-10 Sturmovik aircraft when about 85 miles west of Kunsan. The ship was holed on the port side, one rating being killed and another injured. She was able to steam at 15 knots, and, escorted by *Consort* and covered by aircraft from *Sicily*, she sailed for Kure. The inference drawn by the pilots to this news was that there would be more CAP.

Admiral Andrewes, flying his flag in *Triumph*, and in company with *Kenya Cockade* and HMCSs *Cayuga* and *Sioux*, sailed from Sasebo at 0900 on 26th August for four days of operations off the west coast of Korea. During the afternoon and the dog watches deck landing practice was held for the three 'returned veterans' — Lieutenants Abraham, Reid and Tallin — and three new pilots who had joined 800 Squadron in Sasebo. During this session, one aircraft was written off (leaving only nine available on board) and the three new pilots were taken out of the flying programme until they had had more deck landing training ashore.

As a result of the attack on *Comus*, the Seafires, as surmised, had to concentrate on CAP leaving armed reconnaissance to the Fireflies. The situation in the four ports of Inchon, Chinnampo, Kunsan and Mokpo showed little change: a few junks and sampans were under way, supply craft lay up in creeks during the day but two motor cruisers of about 100 tons were sunk by rockets near Antung as well as various small craft and motor junks lying inshore between Inchon and the south-west point of Korea. A pontoon landing stage at Kunsan was damaged, two or three pontoons being sunk. A contemporary (but anonymous) newspaper cutting reported, in a popular style, '...Drury Lane, Windmill, Apollo, Savoy, Criterion and Coliseum were but nostalgic theatre names for patrol areas among the islands and inlets. Lieutenant Ronald Forrest and CPO

Camouflaged North Korean sampans attacked by Lieut. Forrest and CPO Churlish, 28 August 1950.   *(Forrest)*

Jim Churlish found three green islands were in fact three small camouflaged North Korean gunboats. CPO John Greenfield in an accompanying Firefly with Commissioned Pilot Derek Collingwood said: "They were as full of foliage as a tree. They had something like gorse stuck on every part that would carry it."

On 29th August a Firefly landed-on without an arrestor hook and entered the barrier. A large part of one blade of the propeller, including the root, broke off and, glancing off the lower surface of the Flying Control position, broke the glass in the Operations Room scuttle, entered the Operations Room and struck Lieutenant Commander I.M. MacLachlan, Commanding Officer of 800 Squadron, causing injuries from which he died. He was buried at sea that evening, off the coast of South Korea, with full naval honours.

On the 30th *Triumph* sailed for Sasebo where she met *Unicorn*, lately arrived from Pusan, and embarked *Unicorn's* last 14 aircraft — six Seafires and eight Fireflies. The Seafires would prove to be unsatisfactory and difficult to maintain.

Unicorn and *Ceylon* had arrived in Pusan earlier and had disembarked the 1st Battalion The Argyll and Sutherland Highlanders and the 1st Battalion The Middlesex Regiment from Hong Kong as the British 27th Brigade. On 3rd September they were joined by the 3rd Battalion Royal Australian Regiment, and the force was renamed the 27th British Commonwealth Brigade. The Argylls were to be known throughout their time in Korea as the 'Agile and Suffering Highlanders'.

Two months earlier, on 30th June, the first US troops had landed in Korea in support of the South Korean Army. Having spent nearly five years as the occupying forces of Japan, they were out of practice and training when it came to operational tactical fighting, and in spite of much courageous fighting, the NKPA drove south until the United Nations forces were holding the small area known as the Pusan Perimeter, roughly 60 miles square in the south-east corner of Korea. The port of Pusan had reasonable facilities for disembarking troops and stores and the perimeter was held tenaciously.

During the month of August the carriers of the US 7th Fleet had launched 2,841 strikes from *Valley Forge* and *Philippine Sea* in support of troops holding the Pusan Perimeter; these operations were controlled from the Joint Operations Centre in the style practised by the USAF. The escort carriers *Sicily* and *Badoeng Strait*, carrying US Marine Corps Air Groups, mainly supported the Marine Brigade ashore. Up to 14th September *Sicily* flew 688 sorties and *Badoeng Strait* 671. These strikes from all four carriers resulted in great damage to enemy troops and equipment at and near the front lines and in slowing up the advance on Pusan. 'The Navy carriers were a vital factor in holding the Pusan Perimeter', General MacArthur wrote.

Had it not been for the total domination of the air by the US 5th Air Force and the carriers on both the east and west coasts; by the efficiency of the naval blockade of both coasts; and for the support given to the ground forces by these two arms, there is little doubt that the Communist tide would have rolled on to the Straits of Tsu Shima within the first 60 to 90 days.

800 Squadron's new Flight organisation was:

71 Flight	**72 Flight**	**73 Flight**
Lt. Handley (CO)	Lt. Lamb (SP)	Lt. Abraham
Mr. Peters	Lt. Reid	Lt. Fluker
Lt. Kettle	Lt. Treacher	Lt. Berry
Mr. Warren	Lt. Hanchard-Goodwin	Mr. Reid
	Spare Lt. Tallin	

Triumph sailed from Sasebo on 3rd September for the west coast. On the 4th another Seafire was written off in an unusual accident. The belly-mounted fuel drop-tank came adrift as the aircraft was being launched by the catapult, badly ripping the bottom skin of the fuselage, but luckily the aircraft was landed-on safely. The day's flying consisted of the usual CAP and reconnaissance resulting in two 50 ton motor junks being shot up at Kunsan.

The Fireflies spotted for bombardments of Inchon by *Jamaica* and *Charity* on the 5th, and on the 6th 800 Squadron spotted for *Jamaica* at Kunsan where a railway station and buildings on the airfield were bombarded.

On completion, *Triumph with Athabaskan*, and HMASs *Warramunga* and *Bataan* sailed for the east coast to relieve the US 7th Fleet carriers which had been withdrawn for storing and for maintenance.

Dawn on the 8th found the fleet 50 miles off Wonsan, the main North Korean port on the east coast, 100 miles north of the 38th parallel. The first strike of 6 Fireflies escorted by 6 Seafires rocketed and strafed road and rail communications to the south, damaging a tunnel and blowing up the engine of a train in Shikuogi station with a direct hit from a 60lb. rocket from a Firefly.

During the afternoon's reconnaissance by six Seafires and four Fireflies a concentration of 80 boxcars was attacked in the goods yard at Kowon and another 40 found and attacked at Yonghung. The Fireflies' rockets were very effective against this kind of target, much more so than the 20 mm cannon of the Seafires.

Three aircraft were written off during

Arming a Firefly with 60lb RP; note the 20mm cannon belt feed mechanism.   *(Forrest)*

the day. Lieutenant Abrahams made a one wheel landing in his Seafire which nearly took him over the port side; Lieutenant Mortimer in a Firefly bounced on the deck, missed all the arrestor wires and was only prevented from going into the deck park by the hook catching in the second barrier which then caused both oleos to collapse when the aircraft struck the deck. Lieutenant Berry, on return from the second strike in a Seafire found he could not get his hook down in spite of every manoeuvre. After a long period of tension, while the best course of action was being decided, he finally baled out from about 10,000 feet. The normal method of slow flying and climbing out on the wing was employed, and he was picked up and returned to the ship by HMAS *Bataan*, none the worse for wear. 800 Squadron was now reduced to 10 aircraft.

Bad weather on the 9th reduced flying to only eight sorties in one event in the afternoon, where two Fireflies and two Seafires did considerable damage to Koryo airfield with rockets and cannon. 800 Squadron suffered another blow, which ruined it as an operational unit, when four more aircraft had to be written off due to skin-wrinkling which had reached the limit of safety. Some of these were aircraft received from *Unicorn* only the previous week and had not been subjected to anything out of the ordinary in the way of landings; they were probably a particularly old batch — the bottom of the Seafire barrel.

So ended another patrol. *Triumph* secured in Sasebo at 1000 on Sunday 10th September.

This period saw the start of mine warfare. On 4th September USS *MacKean* reported mines at the entrance to Chinnampo, on the 7th *Jamaica* sighted mines on the surface 25 miles west of Chinnampo and next day *Ceylon* sighted some south of Fankochi Point. They were of a type similar to the British Mk 1 or Russian Mk 26 and could have been laid by any reasonably sized junk and presented a very grave danger to patrolling ships, who, if their patrols were to be effective, had to cover certain focal points that were as well known to the enemy as to the UN ships.

Another of Admiral Andrewes' major anxieties was the possibility of Russian submarines taking a hand. They could have done so very easily, probably without anyone knowing, and their successes would have been attributed to mines laid by Korean fishermen from sampans. Fortunately the threat never materialised during the course of the war, though there were numbers of reported sonar contacts with unidentified submerged objects. Also, no Commonwealth ship ever fell a victim to mines.

Chinnampo, 28 August 1950 – 827 Squadron.

(FAAM)

CHAPTER 3

HMS TRIUMPH

800 and 827 Squadrons
Inchon Landings

The Chairman of the US Joint Chiefs of Staff, General of the Army Omar N. Bradley, had stated, in October 1949, 'I also predict that large scale amphibious operations… will never again occur'. Within less than a year, the US 1st Marine Division was fighting its way ashore over the beaches and sea-walls of Inchon.

On Tuesday 12th September *Triumph*, wearing the flag of Admiral Andrewes, sailed from Sasebo, in company with *Warramunga*, *Concord*, *Charity* and *Cockade*, for the west coast and, though the ships' companies did not know it, for the landings at Inchon.

There was probably no army commander in the world who was more aware of the potentialities of sea power than General Douglas MacArthur, with his unrivalled experience in the war against Japan.

As early as 4th July, only nine days after the opening of hostilities by the North Korean Communists, General MacArthur had convened a conference in Tokyo at which he proposed an amphibious counterstroke at Kunsan or, preferably, Inchon. Operation Bluehearts was to take place on 22nd July.

Bluehearts lasted less than a week; but the seed had been sown, and the US 1st Marine Division, with attached air, was to be brought to war strength in the USA and was to sail from San Diego in mid-August to be

Lieut. Mortimer's Firefly barrier engagement, 8 September 1950.   *(FAAM)*

available for operations in Korea in the autumn — General MacArthur wanted it by 10th September.

There were some advantages for Inchon as the objective for the landings: its harbour was well protected and was ice-free, it was only 25 miles from Seoul, the South Korean capital, and 16 miles from Kimpo, Korea's best airport.

However, Inchon had every natural and geographic handicap to an amphibious landing. Commander Monroe Kelly USN, a member of Admiral Doyle's staff, said 'Make up a list of amphibious "don'ts" and you have an exact description of the Inchon operation'. It had a very high tidal range, of more than 30 feet, with a continual tidal stream in the channel of up to 7 or 8 knots; there were large areas of mud flats at low water; there was very little sea-room for turning or manoeuvre. The waters were eminently mineable and were commanded by heights or islands suitable for sighting batteries to shoot minesweepers; the port was dominated at the entrance by the island of Wolmi-do; and beaches, in the common usage of the word, were non-existent.

Because Inchon was the worst possible place to bring in an amphibious assault, it was, in a sense, the best — by turning disadvantage to advantage. 'Inchon was the jack-pot spot', commented Vice Admiral Struble.

Seoul was reported to contain about 15,000 enemy troops; 19 propeller driven Yak and Stormovick aircraft were at Kimpo; and 2 battalions of raw conscript troops, 2,000 strong, were at Inchon.

General MacArthur's plan for Operation Chromite was:

a) Air attack and naval bombardment of Wolmi-do Island for some days prior to the landing. Other diversionary attacks were to be made on Pyongyang and Kunsan areas.

b) The initial landing on Wolmi-do would be at first high water at 0630 on 15th. September.

c) Landings at Inchon would be at second high water at 1700 on 15th September.

d) Rapid expansion of the beach-head to seize Kimpo airfield and to secure Seoul.

e) Bombardment and fire support to be provided by cruisers and destroyers. Air cover, strikes and close support to be provided by fast carrier and escort carrier aircraft within the objective area.

Brigadier General Thomas J. Cushman USMC was in command of the 1st Marine Air Wing, with the temporary title of Tactical Air Command X Corps. This Wing would be responsible for support for the landings, operating from the small US escort carriers *Sicily* and *Badoeng Strait* with F4U Corsairs. Unlike battles ashore, assault landings have to rely during the most critical phase, that of initial lodgement, on fire support from ships and aircraft. It is only when the beach-head is established can artillery assume its normal role.

Distant view of Sasebo.   *(Stock)*

US Navy and Marine aircraft had to be withdrawn from supporting General Walker's 8th Army in the Pusan perimeter in preparation for Chromite. The US 5th Air Force therefore had to take on the entire support of 8th Army.

France's contribution to the Inchon landings was the ageing frigate *La Grandière*. She had steamed into Sasebo on 29th July, with five months supply of wine — but no coding machine — to find the largest international fleet assembled in the Far East since the days of the Boxer Uprising, there were warships from six foreign powers, and Sasebo had the feel of a regatta. 'Truly the Korean War was *très dare* at Sasebo,' recorded *La Grandière's* captain. 'Drinks flowed without stopping from the moment of arrival. *La Grandière* had to uphold the reputation of France by gulping down great quantities of whisky, gin, horses-neck, and other mixtures, and, above all, by entertaining when our time came. The flowing tide of cocktails and champagne quickly cleared the air of protocol which sometimes prevailed at first…We shall always remember the atmosphere of camaraderie among the Navies of the United Nations.' Besides the usual conviviality whereby bone dry American wardrooms provided steak dinners and foreign ships provided the cocktails, there was, observed the French, 'a lively struggle among the smaller, less dignified, destroyers and frigates to get prints of a certain photograph of Miss Esther Williams, the luscious American starlet, whose charms made her the favourite pin-up of the Korean War.'

In mid August, RoK naval forces had begun a campaign of harassment along the west coast of South Korea. This included raids, the evacuation of loyal South Koreans and the occupation of some of the numerous small islands which girdle the coast. In this, the RoK forces were enthusiastically supported by Admiral Andrewes and ships under his command in those waters. During one of these intelligence and reconnaissance operations, Lieutenant Eugene F. Clark USN repaired the light in the lighthouse on the island of Palmi-do, an island pinnacle jutting up at the junction of two channels in the approaches to Inchon, which had been superficially damaged by a landing party from *Athabaskan* some while earlier.

Admiral Andrewes, as CTF 91, was in command of the Blockade and Covering Force of Commonwealth ships. The tasks assigned to this force wars:

a) to conduct special reconnaissance and covering missions prior to D Day,

b) to provide cover for units of the attack force en route to the Inchon area,

c) to perform interdiction missions on D-Day and thereafter; and air spotting for *Jamaica* and *Kenya*, and

d) to maintain a blockade of the west coast south of latitude 39°35'.

He divided his ships into the larger Northern Group of *Triumph* and her destroyers under Captain Torlesse's command; the Support Element of *Ceylon* under the command of Captain K. Lloyd-Davies; the Screen of *Warramunga*, HMAS *Bataan*, *Charity*, *Cockade* and *Concord* all under the command of Commander Becher RAN in *Warramunga*. The smaller Southern Group consisted mainly of the Escort Element *Cayuga*, *Athabaskan* and *Sioux*. RoKN vessels provided a Coastal Element in both Groups. RFA *Wave Prince* and subsequent relief tankers were attached to the US Mobile Logistic Service Group.

Capt. A.D. Torlesse, Rear-Admiral W.G. Andrewes, Lt Cdr G. Grease (Ops), Cdr M. Bruce (Air).   *(Handley)*

On D-2 and D-1 *Triumph* was to provide air cover to the Attack Force on passage round the south-west corner of Korea to 36°N. From D-day onwards she would be operating with *Ceylon* and three or four destroyers as an A/S screen to the west of Inchon, taking advantage of strong air patrols from US 7th Fleet working in the vicinity. *Triumph's* aircraft were to be available for interdiction and spotting.

During the passage from Sasebo, a warning was received from Japan of typhoon Kezia approaching from the Pacific and typhoon lashings were put on

Triumph's aircraft, but it came to nothing. On 13th September HMAS *Bataan* joined the screen, and the Fireflies provided cover for several large convoys as they moved round the corner of Korea, as well as carrying out armed reconnaissance and search sorties, on a reduced scale, along the coast and over

Planeguard destroyer – probably HMAS *Bataan* with a whaler seaboat manned and swung overboard.   *(ANAM)*

the towns of Kunsan and Mokpo, in order to keep the enemy intelligence guessing and to convince him that all was normal. The air effort of which *Triumph* was capable was severely limited. The number of aircraft serviceable and fully operational was seldom more than a dozen, and the importance of each sortie had to be carefully weighed before it was flown. The maximum that was possible was to keep a small CAP on stand-by, two spotters on station and to fly normal blockade patrols as far north as Chinnampo.

While ship-based US Marine Corps squadrons worked close in, Admiral Ewen's carriers, *Valley Forge* and *Philippine Sea*, commenced sealing off the Inchon/Seoul objective area. Their Panther jets raked every known Communist airfield northward up the coast, within a radius of 150 miles of Inchon. Wide ranging strikes were also carried out against Chinnampo, Ongjin, Inchon and Kunsan, any one of which could be the site of an amphibious descent.

On 10th September the Corsairs from *Sicily* and *Badoeng Strait* dropped 95 tanks of napalm on Wolmi-do, destroying 38 of 44 buildings in the workshop area and during the next two days burnt out the entire dwelling area and 80% of the buildings in the north of the island. At the same time they struck Inchon and Kimpo; and as a dividend, Admiral Ewen's Fast Carrier Force backed them up with three hefty strikes by AD Skyraiders, the superb single-engined carrier attack aircraft that could carry a bigger bomb load than the US Air Force's B-17 Flying Fortress bombers.

On D-1, Admiral Andrewes gave a final briefing to the aircrew disclosing that the location of the invasion was to be Inchon and that the first assault would go in to capture Wolmi-do, the key to the defence system, at 0600 next morning. During the cruiser bombardment of Inchon, *Kenya* was fired on by NKPA guns, but she suffered no hits, and the guns were silenced by a USMC strike.

Kenya and *Jamaica* carried out preliminary bombardments on the 13th, spotted by Corsairs. Floating mines had been seen to the westward which were sunk by gun-fire.

Whitesand Bay had carried out a diversionary operation when she landed US and Royal Marines near Kunsan on the night of 12/13th. They shot up a machine-gun post and re-embarked without loss.

Chromite was essentially a United States Marine Corps operation, planned and carried out against considerable political opposition and no little military misgiving. It was a huge success.

Seven US destroyers led the assault and bombarding fleet up Flying Fish Channel of the Salee River to Inchon. They were followed by three LSMRs loaded with 5 inch bombardment rockets, a further three destroyers, then the Headquarters Ship USS *Mount McKinley* with Rear Admiral J.H. Doyle in command of the amphibious force, Lieutenant General O.P. Smith USMC in command of the 1st US Marine Division, the landing force, and General MacArthur. In the rear, to take up downstream stations, were the cruisers, with Rear Admiral J.M. Higgins leading in Toledo, followed *by* Vice Admiral Struble, on whose shoulders the whole enterprise rested, in *Rochester* and finally *Kenya* and *Jamaica*, described by an American observer as 'the smart, seamanlike British Light Cruisers'.

At first light *Triumph* was 60 miles from Wolmi-do, and flew off her first pair of Fireflies, fitted for these operations with 45 gallon overload fuel tanks to give them two hours over the target, to spot for *Jamaica* and *Kenya*. Good results were obtained throughout the day by these bombardments, and worthy of mention was a particular one by *Jamaica*, assisted by Lieutenant Mortimer, which hit some hidden store of explosives and the whole of the top of a hill disappeared with a column of smoke rising to about 8,000 feet — by far the most

Beached small craft near Chinnampo -direct hit by a Firefly, August 1950. *(Wood)*

spectacular explosion of the day. Both Squadrons were involved in spotting and armed reconnaissance sorties. One section of Seafires found no targets at Haeju, but later both Seafires and Fireflies found targets in the Chinnampo area. Barges and a coaster were attacked, the aircraft being engaged by flak. This flak position was located during a later sortie and successfully attacked with rockets and cannon fire. Unfortunately another Seafire had to be written off as the result of a heavy landing during the day.

British Commonwealth frigates — and *La Grandière* — showed a fine example of endurance and enjoyed none of the excitement of action.

On the conclusion of the day's operations, General MacArthur signalled to Admiral Andrewes 'My heartiest felicitations on the splendid conduct of the Fleet units under your command. They have added another glamorous page to the long and brilliant histories of the Navies of the British Commonwealth.'

From first light USMC Corsairs from *Sicily* and *Badoeng Strait* were attacking Wolmi-do; cruisers and destroyers started their bombardments at the same time; and half an hour later the three rocket ships fired 1,000 rockets each onto the landing beaches and slopes of the island. In less than three hours, by 0800, the island had been secured. At about 1000 one of 800 Squadron's spotting Seafires reported that the Stars and Stripes were flying from the flagstaff at the top of the island.

In Seoul, near panic reigned among the NKPA. They were utterly surprised, in spite of early and accurate warning from Inchon.

Following the capture of Wolmi-do, minesweepers could comb the approach channels to the two landing beaches for the second wave at 1730, the next high tide, and transports and LSTs with the assault Marines followed the minesweepers.

Jamaica and *Kenya* were dropping 6-inch shells on the rear of Blue Beach, to the south of Inchon, and USSs *Gurke* and *Henderson* were working over the beaches with 5-inch shells. Some unsuccessful air spotting a couple of days earlier (caused by muddled communications between ships and aircraft by pilots, supposedly fully trained but who were apparently wholly unfamiliar with the process), prompted the comment from an American that '... using RN FAA spotters from *Triumph*, whose spotting procedure (not to mention their English) was more intelligible...', led to much more successful bombardment.

Both landings at Inchon in the second assaults were successful, though there were some moments of concern when follow-up waves of landing craft did not arrive until somewhat later than their scheduled time. However, those that did land more or less as planned contained the troops and leaders needed for success — they secured the bridge-head.

By the end of D-day Admiral Doyle had landed 13,000 troops and their weapons and equipment. Nineteen more fully loaded transports and cargo ships, and eight more LSTs had arrived on schedule and were being unloaded. The total cost to

Landing tanks at Inchon Blue Beach, 15 September 1950.   *(Christmas)*

the landing force had been 21 killed, 1 man missing and 174 wounded. At least 300 prisoners had been taken.

Much has been made in accounts of Inchon of seeming disorganisation and confusion, (especially the Blue Beach assault to the south of the town), in this unrehearsed landing without parallel. The fact remains that landings were made on time, objectives were captured on schedule, and the enemy was struck so hard and so quickly that he was incapable of organised resistance or reaction until too late. General Smith matter-of-factly put it in his log 'D-day had gone about as planned'.

During the five days following the landings *Triumph's* few remaining aircraft were used in armed reconnaissance north and south of Inchon, and in bombardment spotting for the cruisers.

On the 16th, Lieutenant Treacher section of Seafires attacked gun positions on an airfield in the Haeju area, and Lieutenant Kettle attacked two junks, reported by *Charity* as suspect for the recent mine-laying expeditions; one was destroyed and the other damaged.

Admiral Higgins' Gunfire Support Group fired on targets of opportunity on the 16th, but *Kenya* and *Jamaica were* not called upon that day. *Kenya* took the chance to re-ammunition from US Auxiliary Ryder, loaded with British ammunition.

Early on the 17th the North Korean Air Force delivered its only blow during the campaign. At 0555 a Yak-3 and a Stormovick IL-10, mistakenly taken to be friendly, flew slowly from north to south at a height of about 1000 feet down the line of ships anchored in the approach channel. They dived gently toward Admiral Struble's flagship *Rochester* and dropped two bombs close astern; the second aircraft following also attacked, its bomb hitting the aircraft crane but not exploding. The two aircraft then made for *Jamaica* at anchor 500 yards astern who had her bridge and upper works raked with machine-gun and cannon fire which

HMS *Kenya*, HMAS *Bataan* and *Wave Prince*.   *(Forrest)*

killed one and wounded two members of the ship's company. The British cruiser reacted more quickly to this attack, and with 4 inch and pom-pom fire shot down the Stormovick. This was the first instance in the war of an aircraft being brought down by a ship's anti-aircraft fire. *Rochester* had been caught flatfooted, her anti-aircraft battery did not fire a shot. After this attack *Jamaica* shifted berth to 3,600 yards from Wolmi-do. *Kenya* was at anchor two miles further south. Together they carried out a short bombardment at enemy troops. That night *Jamaica* fired, without spotting, into an area in order to contain enemy formations. These were the last bombardments carried out by British cruisers.

As a result of this attack *Triumph's* CAP was scrambled twice, but both occasions turned out to be false alarms. This was the only flying the Seafire Squadron got during the day. *Charity* and Lieutenant Commander Lyons' section of Fireflies co-operated in bombarding some coastal guns near Haeju.

Only one section of Seafires, led by Lieutenant Tallin, flew on the 18th, attacking two barges in the Haeju area. The Fireflies carried out their normal spotting trips, which were reported as rather dull, being largely conducted tours of the battlefield.

On the next day, a section of Seafires led by Lieutenant Abraham carried out the usual armed reconnaissance in the Chinnampo area. A 500 ton ship was damaged, another smaller one was damaged on the slipway, a floating crane was set on fire and finally a flak position was attacked. On return from this trip, Mr. Warren caught number 10 wire and quite gently engaged the barrier. In the evening three Seafires were scrambled to deal with some rice carrying junks reported by *Concord* in the Haeju area. After a long search two medium sized but fairly innocent looking junks were found and attacked. The Fireflies, in addition to reconnaissance sorties, spotted for *Ceylon* when she proceeded inshore to join the bombarding force. On return from one of these trips Lieutenant Hayes, on a low approach, struck the round-down which knocked up the hook, with the result that he too entered the barrier, but at full speed, with spectacular results.

On 20th September the Seafires made only one armed reconnaissance by the CO and Senior Pilot, damaging a patrol craft in the Chinnampo estuary. With only three aircraft left, this was all they could do. The Fireflies were in little better shape with only eight aircraft, but they carried out a good shoot with *Ceylon* on extensive defence works and gun positions on the coast west of Haeju.

With only eleven obsolescent aircraft, *Triumph* had reached the end of her useful operational life in Korean waters. *Theseus* was due in about a week, and so Admiral Andrewes decided to sail *Triumph* for the United Kingdom.

On 19th September the services of the two British cruisers came to an end. *Jamaica* ammunitioned from USS *Hewett* and then proceeded to Sasebo where she arrived during the following afternoon; *Kenya* relieved *Ceylon* on patrol on the same day.

While *Jamaica* was ammunitioning, a damaged jet aircraft from *Valley Forge* ditched alongside. The pilot was picked up unharmed by one of *Jamaica's* boats which later returned him to USS *Virgo*, at anchor half a mile away.

During the Inchon landings, *Jamaica* fired 1,290 six-inch shells and 393 four-inch; *Kenya* 1,242 six-inch and 205 four-inch. It was a strenuous time for all hands. Ship's companies had to be kept at an abnormally high state of readiness in order to guard against floating mines, air attacks, saboteurs and other threats, as well as having to be ready at all times to meet calls for fire from the army ashore. There was little time for sleep or rest. Captain Salter gave particular credit to the engine room staffs, who kept steam at virtually immediate notice throughout the week, and whose duties kept them down below where they could see none of the excitements going on all around; and to the wireless staffs who were handling exceptional numbers of signals.

Captain J.H. Unwin in *Mounts Bay*, with *Whitesand Bay*, *Morecambe Bay*, HMNZSs *Tutira* and *Pukaki*, USSs *Bayonne, Newport* and *Evansville* with FS *La Grandière* formed a Task Element covering an arc 50 miles long, 40 miles south-west of Inchon, forming the outer screen with RoK vessels forming the inner.

Their functions during, and for a considerable period after, the Inchon landings, included:

a) Action against enemy aircraft, surface craft, submarines, suicide boats and swimmers carrying limpet mines.

b) Prevention of barge and fishing boat movement, and enemy movement between islands, and between islands and the mainland.

c) Detection and destruction of mines.

None of these activities was attempted by the enemy, perhaps due to the screen, but that did not detract from the arduous nature of the task. They were continually under way in narrow waters, close to indifferently charted land and shoals, in very strong tides. The strain imposed on Captains, Navigating Officers and Officers of the Watch was considerable. Traffic in and out of Inchon was heavy, every ship entering the patrol area had to be challenged and identified. Advance information of movements was seldom available. The reluctance of merchant ships and darkened RoK patrol vessels to answer challenges added to the difficulties. The danger of air attack was always present though none of the screen was attacked; there were generally a great many aircraft, each of which had to be identified. For the first eight days, anti-aircraft armament was manned in two watches day and night.

Constant vigilance was called for in case the enemy strewed mines in the only two main channels to the port.

The only direct contact with the enemy was when *Mounts Bay* fired 118 four-inch shells at a party of Koreans constructing gun emplacements on the south shore. During this bombardment *Mounts Bay* grounded for 20 seconds on a mudbank in a charted depth of seven fathoms, fortunately no damage was sustained.

After ten days, *Rowan* and *Newport* were detached, and on 30th September the US minesweepers were withdrawn. Captain Unwin was then left with *Mounts Bay*, *Whitesand Bay*, *Tutira*, *Pukaki*, *La Grandière* and two RoK motor minesweepers to provide the screen until 14th October. After 25th September each ship was allowed a three day maintenance period, either alongside or at anchor near the US repair ships *Hector* and *Piedmont* who were extremely helpful and co-operative.

The whole operation provided valuable experience in screening and patrolling with long periods of sea-keeping without recourse to base facilities. The work of the engine room departments was particularly noteworthy; ships were continually under way for 28 or 29 days out of 32 with frequent bursts of high speed. Not a single ship suffered any breakdown at all. Communications departments were called upon to handle an exceptionally heavy volume of signals. Hands were closed up in two watches by night and in two or four by day. For both officers and men it was a prolonged and wearying experience. Captain Unwin noted 'And beyond fatigue, there was always the danger of boredom to combat; though something was always happening, the scene changed not. But like his predecessors over many centuries, the sailor of today obviously enjoys being at sea; the spirit of all ships, British, Commonwealth and French remained splendid throughout...'

On 14th October the 'Iron Ring' round Inchon, as the screen was known by the Americans, was discontinued.

On 17th September, Kimpo and its airfield were occupied by US Marines, capturing an intact Yak-3 and two Stormovicks. The Yak was repainted in US markings and flown to Japan for technical and intelligence evaluations. The first aircraft to land at Kimpo was a Sikorsky HO3S-1 helicopter (later known in the UK by its British designation as the S-51 Dragonfly) from Marine Observation Squadron 6. This Marine detachment of eight aircraft was the first helicopter unit to be flown in combat operations.

Rather than break up a going concern on the two US escort carriers, *Sicily* and *Badoeng Strait*, which had so far provided tactical air support for the landing forces, General Cushman's shore-based Marine air component, Air Command X Corps, flew into Kimpo on 19th and 20th with two day and one night fighter Corsair squadrons. In less than two days after its capture, General Cushman had Kimpo in full operation, with 2,051 people and three tactical squadrons.

During the 18th and 19th, over 50 requests for air support, mainly from the Marines, had been met by the carrier-borne squadrons of *Sicily* and *Badoeng Strait*. These experienced squadrons reported and attacked North Korean tanks near Yongdung-po as well as large accumulations of supplies on a sandspit of the river between Yongdung-po and Seoul.

A week after Inchon, Lieutenant General Walton H. Walker's 8th Army, as the hammer, began to make real headway toward the link-up with X Corps as the anvil, an essential part of General MacArthur's strategy. By 23rd September the Communists were in evident retreat from the Pusan perimeter, being harried up the central corridor towards X Corps beachhead. On the 27th, at a bridge above Osan, the hammer struck the anvil, when L Troop of the 7th Cavalry driving north made contact with a 31st Infantry outpost.

The 1st US Marine Division, supported by their comrades from the carriers, swept on to Yongdung-po and Seoul, which fell after much bitter fighting, on 28th September.

On 29th September, General MacArthur and President Syngman Rhee arrived at the South Korean capital of Seoul. MacArthur, in restoring Rhee as President, said 'Mr. President, my officers and I will resume our military duties and leave you and your government to the discharge of civil responsibility'.

In his report to the United Nations after the capture of Seoul, General MacArthur stated

'Events of the past two weeks have been decisive...A successful frontal attack and envelopment has completely changed the tide of battle in South Korea. The backbone of the North Korean army has been broken and their scattered forces are being liquidated'.

Operation Chromite changed the entire course of the war. In immediate results the fortnight's campaign accomplished the following:

1. It caused the disintegration of the North Korean perimeter about Pusan.

2. By liberating the national capital and dislocating the logistical system

of the Communists it brought about the destruction of the In Min Gun.

3. It returned the United Nations to the 38th parallel and thus preserved the Republic of Korea. In so doing — for the first and only time since 1945 — it restored freedom to a capital city conquered by Communists.

4. It retrieved the honour of American arms so smirched in the retreats, surrenders and ineptness of the fighting in the south since 25th June.

More important than these military results, Inchon underscored what had nearly been forgotten since 1945, that the United States, Britain and the Commonwealth are maritime powers. Only through the sure and practised exercise of seapower could this awkward war in a remote place have been turned upside down in a matter of days.

Chromite was probably General MacArthur's greatest feat of generalship; it was certainly his last victory, and the irony was that it bore the seeds of his own downfall. He had prevailed over the doubters on his own staff and other Naval and Marine experts, and over the Joint Chiefs of Staff. He had President Truman's approval to permit operations north of the 38th parallel.

Unknown to the West, Red China had determined that crossing of the 38th parallel by United Nations troops was the contingency that would precipitate Chinese intervention in Korea.

Triumph arrived at Sasebo on 21st September where she entered dry dock for two days for temporary repairs to her starboard stern gland.

Before sailing for Hong Kong on the 25th, she received this signal:

TO: TRIUMPH   FROM: ADMIRAL JOY

ON THE DEPARTURE OF HMS TRIUMPH FROM THE COMMAND OF THE NAVAL FORCES FAR EAST, I TAKE PLEASURE IN SAYING TO THE CAPTAIN, THE OFFICERS, THE FLYING PERSONNEL AND THE CREW OF THIS SPLENDID FIGHTING SHIP — WELL DONE. YOUR ENTHUSIASTIC AND EFFECTIVE EFFORTS HAVE CONTRIBUTED IMMEASURABLY TO THE UNITED NATIONS CAUSE IN KOREA.

While General Walton Walker's 8th US Army was fighting its rearguard, defensive, actions southward from Seoul, concerned with bringing to safety American and other civilians, the forces that could be used in an offensive role were the UN navies and air forces.

The US Navy's 7th Fleet, commanded by Vice Admiral Struble, assigned its major tactical element, TF 77, to the job of blockading the Korean coastline, after destroying whatever minor enemy naval forces existed. The chronicles of the Korean War concern themselves largely with the bitter fighting on the ground. This is only just, for the ground forces had to slug it out night and day with a resourceful and (for a long time) numerically superior foe. But the men of all the navies afloat and aloft fought with characteristic gallantry and effectiveness, carrying out interdiction missions along the Korean coast, grimly devoting themselves to the thankless and dangerous job of sweeping mines out of the channels, or engaging in underwater demolition tasks, often in sub-zero weather.

As for the airmen, without them the war would have been over in 60 days with all Korea in Communist hands. Handicapped in their task of reconnaissance by a lack of trained photographic interpreters, the fliers of all the units involved, British, Australian and American, and the ground crews, working round the clock in every kind of weather, operating from scanty runways or slippery decks, managed to eliminate the North Korean Air Force early in the battle, destroyed much of the NKPA armour, and transported critically needed men and supplies to spots of greatest danger. With the navies controlling the shipping lanes and preventing even small hostile forces from side-slipping along the coast, while transporting the bulk of supplies and equipment needed for rapid build up of the 8th Army, and the Air Force providing complete mastery of the skies, our ground forces managed to seize a flimsy toe-hold in Korea and hang on to it until help arrived.

By September the North Korean army had met its Marne on the banks of the Naktong. The war of movement — from the North Korean perspective — had come to an end. Naval aviation in the bitter Pusan fighting had been crucial in acquiring time for MacArthur's counterstroke. One lesson of Korean air warfare was apparent: short of using atomic weapons, air power could not on its own defeat North Korea. But while it might not be able to produce a UN victory, it could and did prevent the North from overrunning the South.

Though the Commonwealth forces, and in particular the navies, played a comparatively small part in the campaign, Inchon must not be forgotten by history. Not only was it militarily brilliant, but it upset and reversed so much of the tide of war and the Communist hopes for a smash-and-grab conquest of a small, ill-defended nation. The original war aim of the United Nations, the defensive one of forestalling total invasion, was achieved at Inchon when the NKPA was broken. It also re-established amphibious assault (and maritime strategy) as a modern technique of war — seen again more than a generation later in the Falklands.

Apart from strategic goals, Inchon had four sequential objectives: capture of Wolmi-do island, the small spit of land controlling the harbour approaches; a landing in the city itself; rapid seizure of Kimpo airfield; and the restoration of the

Rhee government to power.

Inchon must be considered a masterpiece and as an example of Napoleonic nerve and acceptance of calculated risk. Chromite could never have succeeded without General MacArthur's overpowering

Ship bombardment of Wolmi-do, 15 September 1950.   *(Wood)*

personality and his self-confidence, his un*waver*ing sense of the objective, his unrelenting pressure in gathering the necessary forces and in his insistence on speed of execution. It was characteristic of all MacArthur's Pacific strategy, it would hit the enemy where he least looked for a blow, would sever his supply lines and trap him between an anvil and a hammer. While others thought of a way to withdraw our forces safely, MacArthur planned for victory. Inchon could not have happened under any other commander.

For boldness in concept, for competence in professional planning, and for courage, dash and skill in execution, this operation ranks high in military annals. It remains an astonishing achievement precisely because it was a triumph not of military logic and science, but of imagination and intuition.

However, insufficient attention had been given to planning for a

Pre-assault bombardment of Inchon, 15 September 1950.   *(Forrest)*

stunning victory, which it was. Large numbers of the NKPA escaped to the north as organised units or to the south as guerrillas.

Inchon finished the North Korean army as a fighting force, it was a profound defeat on the troops of Kim Il Sung. It has been suggested since that Inchon was unnecessary, that air power alone broke the back of the North Korean army, and that the troops landed at Inchon could have accomplished more if they had been inserted in the Pusan pocket. Such critics should recall the dreadfully slow struggle up the Italian peninsula in the Second World War or the post 1950 ebb and flow along the 38th Parallel. Given the often fierce resistance at Inchon and slow start of General Walker's break-out from Pusan, the likely Allied casualties would have been immense if the NKPA had remained intact and confronted the Allies on a single front. By 1952 air power enthusiasts recognised that overwhelming Allied air power alone could not force a decision. It was reported 'The rifleman is the central figure in the Korean War; he has not been supplanted by air power' — the PBI.

If Inchon had failed, or if it had never been attempted, the question arises as to whether the Pusan Perimeter could have been held and then used as a base for the successful re-conquest of South Korea; and would the Chinese have entered the war?

CHAPTER 4

HMS THESEUS

807 and 810 Squadrons
29th September 1950 to 23rd April 1951

Review

*T*riumph had arrived in Hong Kong early on the morning of 29th September 1950 to see, awaiting in harbour, the welcome sight of HMS *Theseus* (Captain A.S. Bolt DSO, DSC). The day was spent in turning over to the 17th Carrier Air Group of 807 and 810 Squadrons; in the words of *Triumph's* 827 Squadron diarist 'The evening that followed need not be described'.

The most serious weakness in the administration of and support for the Far East Fleet was the lack of a depot ship in Japan. HMS *Ladybird* was now established in Sasebo as the Headquarters Ship, from which the activities of all Commonwealth ships were controlled. *Ladybird* was satisfactory for the operations staff, but the administrative and technical staffs had to be accommodated in a mess and offices provided by the USN. The staff was split when the Admiral was at sea, with the Chief Staff Officer and the staff and secretariat remaining in *Ladybird* to deal with the administration.

Admiral Scott-Moncrieff was to report later, in June 1951, that 'Under modern conditions there will never be room for a full staff in fighting ships, and therefore it must be borne in a ship of the Fleet Train. It is just as important for the Fleet to move around with its administrative and technical staffs as it is to move around with any of the commodities of the Fleet Train'.

Captain A.S. Bolt, DSO, DSC.   *(FAAM)*

A NAAFI canteen had been set up ashore in Sasebo, but it could not be on an adequate scale to cope with the large numbers even of junior ratings, and a Chief and Petty Officer's canteen was set up later. Attempts were made to provide games facilities, but they were in Japanese schools out of town and transport was not easy to organise. It was very difficult to arrange healthy recreation for ships returning from long periods at sea, and the only real antidote was a complete change from Sasebo itself with its predominantly American atmosphere, its hordes of Japanese ladies of the town, gift shops, 'pedi-cabs', cabarets and other examples of Japanese ingenuity at relieving the sailors of their pay. The main means of giving ship's companies a change was to send the ship away from Sasebo either to Kure in the British Commonwealth zone of occupation, or to Yokosuka, within easy reach of Tokyo.

Ships had been brought up to full war complement by October 1950 by suspending discharges and calling up reservists. However, most ships could not accommodate their full complements, the County class cruisers in particular kept to 40 or 50 ratings below.

Another problem was a shortage of detention quarters, the Australian army ones could be used but the discipline tended to be lax. Some cells had been built ashore at Sasebo and offenders from small ships could be accommodated in the cells in the cruisers and carriers.

The operating cycle for ships was based on nine or ten days in the operational area with the same, less passage time, at base. This was particularly so with the Carrier Element where the period in the operational area was determined by the need to rearm the British Light Fleet carriers. The British armament supply ship was unsuitable for replenishment at sea so the carrier had to return to Sasebo. When the US Navy Light Fleet carrier was on the west coast, this period gave an adequate break to aircrew and the carrier's technical teams and handling parties. This method of operating them largely contributed to the exceptionally high output of sorties continuously achieved.

The cruisers and small ships planned their employment on a 36 day cycle. Frigates and destroyers aimed to have five days alongside without steam after every 30 days. The cycle was:

18 days in the operating area	50%
6 days on passage	17%
Total at sea on operations	67%
5 days maintenance (minimum)	14%
7 days (alternate harbour periods) as spare at 4 hrs. notice	19%

(they seldom spent their full time in harbour)

Nearly 67% overall was achieved throughout for long periods.

Maintenance was satisfactory, mainly due to the availability of well equipped and hard working Japanese dockyards at Sasebo and Kure, which, with British supervision, did an enormous number of jobs in very quick time. Had these dockyards not been available a depot/repair ship would have been a *sine qua non*. The biggest factors in ensuring proper maintenance were:

a) Full technical complement in HM Ships,

b) Sufficient technical supervision and repair facilities at base,

c) Sufficient, planned, harbour periods to allow a) aided by b) to catch up with outstanding jobs,

d) Ready availability of technical stores and equipment in good condition. In 1952 maintenance and notice for steam had to be increased to cope with ageing ships — from 4 hours for full speed to 4 hours for half power on one unit, and 12 hours for full power; cruisers maintenance periods altered from 6 days each two months to 14 days; and for frigates and destroyers from 5 days each month to 7.

On 25th September Task Force 91 — the British and Commonwealth Blockading Force covering the Inchon landing — was dissolved and became Task Group 95.1 with the same general blockading duties as before. The chain of command under Vice Admiral Joy, COMNAVFE, was:

Commander Naval Forces Far East
(Vice Admiral Joy USN)
Task Force 95
United Nations Blockade and Escort Force
(Rear Admiral Smith USN)

TG95.1	TG95.2	TG95.5	TG95.6	TG95.7
Korean One	Korean two	Escorts	Minesweepers	RoK Navy
(Rear Admiral	(Rear Admiral	(Captain	(Captain	(Commander
Andrewes RN)	Hartman USN)	Unwin RN)	Spofford USN)	Luosey USN)

Admiral Andrewes' international force was responsible for the west coast and Admiral Hartman's American force for the east coast. The tasks were complicated by the enemy's mine warfare, noticed before the Inchon operation, that was being intensified. The enemy used mines in three ways:

a) moored defensive minefields,

b) moored mines laid by junks in special areas, designed to catch blockade patrols on their normal runs,

c) floating mines sent down on the ebb tide from Haeju and Chinnampo.

Large jelly fish up to four feet across and floating below the surface looked like mines — some must have been reported as sunk!

There had been 54 separate sightings in September, most in the Yellow Sea between Chinnampo and Inchon but the first casualties had been off the east coast. USS *Brush was* mined on 29th September and USS *Mansfield* on the 30th, both were severely damaged and with heavy casualties. Two RoK motor mine-sweepers were also badly damaged, No. *509* on 28th September and No. *504* (off Mokpo on the south-west coast) on 1st October. The US minesweeper *Magpie* was sunk by a mine 30 miles north of Pohang.

Early in September *Charity* had intercepted an enemy junk and had interviewed some of the party who had laid the Kunsan minefield in the south 49 mines, some magnetic, had been laid from junks during the night of 9th September to catch *Jamaica* should she return to repeat her bombardment of the 6th. At the time there were inadequate minesweeping facilities, but after September the Americans took energetic steps to rectify matters.

The blockade patrol was taken over by HMS *Kenya* (Captain P.W. Brock) with *Charity* and *Concord* in the north, mainly off Fankochi Point, and with *Cayuga*, *Athabaskan* and *Sioux* in the area south of Inchon. Movements were governed by the risk from mines. To minimise the risk, Captain Brock kept patrols during dark hours either well inshore under a lee or well out to sea. RoK patrol craft were close inshore probing inaccessible areas and gathering information.

On 22nd September *Kenya* and *Charity* bombarded trenches, gun emplacements and troops in the Fankochi Point area, destroying several guns, causing damage and inflicting casualties. On 28th September a bombardment was carried out by USS *Manchester* and four destroyers together with two heavy strikes by aircraft from the large US carriers of Task Force 77.

On 25th September the patrol was taken over by *Ceylon* and *Cockade* Captain Lloyd-Davies considered the best way of enforcing the blockade and preventing minelaying was to bring certain focal points under control and to maintain RoK patrols from them. These were:

a) the Techong group of islands, dominating the channel between them and the mainland,

b) the island of Kirin, dominating the approaches to Ongjin,

c) the island of Teyonpyong controlling the entrance to Haeju River. Mines were a continual anxiety.

Meanwhile, the armies had advanced, with General Walker's 8th Army breaking out from the Pusan perimeter, and had contacted 7th Infantry. Seoul was recaptured on 27th September.

By 1st October, the United Nations first objective had been achieved — 'to repel armed attack'. However, since the North Korean Army remained in being, the second objective was unfulfilled — 'to secure international peace and security in the area'. The United Nations armies were very nearly back to the 38th Parallel.

General MacArthur had stated in mid-July, to Generals Collins and Xtandellburg, that his war aim was not merely the repelling of Kim Il Sung's invasion, but the destruction of his army, for which the occupation of North Korea might be necessary. There were reservations by the State Department and by the Joint Chiefs of Staff, and President Truman had made no decision as to future moves by UN and US land forces. On 9th September, almost a week before Inchon, the US National Security Council had approved MacArthur's request to cross the 38th Parallel in order to pursue and destroy the NKPA. He was, however, specifically instructed that under no circumstances were his forces to cross Manchurian or USSR borders. He was also told that only RoK troops were to be used in the border areas of the north-east provinces bounding the Soviet Union and Manchuria.

The problem was debated by the General Assembly of the United Nations and on 7th October, after lengthy discussion, a resolution was passed authorising MacArthur to cross the 38th Parallel if he considered it necessary. At the same time the UN created the Interim Committee of the UN Commission for the Unification and Rehabilitation of Korea. On the 9th MacArthur issued an unconditional surrender demand and on the 12th the UN Committee advised MacArthur to take over the civilian government of North Korea.

On 9th October the first US and Commonwealth troops crossed the frontier.

In this triumphant phase of the Korean War, from a position of desperate weakness MacArthur, in the space of three weeks, had turned the tables completely-and snatched a spectacular victory. His amphibious landing at Inchon had succeeded, Seoul had been taken, the NKPA had been cut off and pressure on the Pusan Perimeter released. Defeated and broken, the NKPA had withdrawn, losing thousands of prisoners and suffering many casualties. RoK units had swept across the 38th parallel and UN formations had followed although they had generally halted along the line of Pyongyang and Wonsan.

This success had hinged on the Inchon landing, and it was only when it was examined in retrospect that it was realised what a hair-raising gamble it had been. Military logic, science and calculation had all been against it. The narrow margin between victory and failure frightened the Pentagon planners and the risks taken sobered even the most enthusiastic. To quote two examples — a fault in the Communist intelligence network and a delayed minelaying programme were advantages that played luckily and unexpectedly into UN hands. Had there been no such fault — or delay — the outcome might have been very different. The assembly of an armada of ships and some 7,000 men took time and could not be completely concealed. Communist agents were aware of the operation, its objective, and even a few days before it took place, its date, but for some reason this intelligence was not passed back in time to Kim Il Sung at his Supreme Headquarters. Had he known of the pending assault he could have reinforced Inchon and organised effective defences. Again, the landing forestalled by a few hours the minelaying in the Inchon harbour approaches, which had been unexpectedly delayed. If it had been carried out as planned, it might have wrecked the entire operation.

MacArthur's strategy was guided by two principal considerations. He wanted forces moving fast north-eastwards up North Korea to cut off Communist forces retreating towards Manchuria. The Taebaek mountain range running up the spine of North Korea made east-west movement across the country very difficult. The major road and rail routes are determined by the north-south river valleys. MacArthur was one of the great twentieth century exponents of amphibious operations. The flexibility of seapower at Inchon had cut short what would have been a long drawn out land campaign across difficult terrain. He now proposed to do the same again. General Almond's X Corps would be withdrawn from South Korea through Inchon, loaded aboard its shipping, and would be transported direct to North Korea's major east coast port of Wonsan, from whence the US Marines and the army's 7th Division could strike north towards the Manchurian border.

He immediately initiated a northerly advance with RoK troops attacking in the centre and moving up the east coast aiming to capture the port of Wonsan. This advance received strong naval and air support.

In the west American, British, Australian and Philippine troops relieved US X Corps in the Inchon/Seoul area so that they could prepare for the amphibious operation against Wonsan. The object of capturing Wonsan quickly was to secure the iron and steel mills, the power plants and the port installations before they were sabotaged or badly damaged.

This plan aroused immediate opposition. General Walker considered it absurd to subject X Corps to the immense upheaval of withdrawal from Seoul, and sea movement to Wonsan, when the RoK army was already driving up the east coast in the face of negligible opposition.

Admiral Andrewes did not wish all the British and Commonwealth naval forces to be confined to a purely holding role on the west coast, so, at his request, *Ceylon*, *Cockade*, *Athabaskan*, and *Warramunga* joined the Gunfire Support Group (TG 95.2) under Rear Admiral Hartman USN; *Mounts Bay*, *Pukaki*, *Tutira*, and *La Grandière* became part of the Minesweeping Group (TG 95.6) under Captain Spofford USN.

TG 95.2 consisting of USSs *Missouri*, *Helena*, *Rochester*, *Toledo*, *Worcester* and those above bombarded Changjin, 60 miles from the Soviet/Korean border on 12th

October. Next day the forces split, *Ceylon, Athabaskan* and *Worcester* destroyed one road bridge and damaged three railway bridges at Songjin.

Initially, the Soviet mining effort in North Korea was to keep UN ships out of North Korean harbours and to limit UN naval offensive capabilities. Korea provided the opportunity for the Soviets to test the US Navy's ability to cope with mines. At the same time, Russia could help her North Korean satellite to delay the advance of UN ground forces.

The Korean peninsula was ideally suited for an experiment in defensive mine warfare. The landings at Pohang and Inchon were eloquent testimony of the United States' amphibious warfare skills. Both Hungnam and Wonsan on the east coast had good harbours, each with a large shelf of shallow water that was eminently mineable; on the west coast, however, the water was nowhere more than 10 fathoms deep and, with a tidal range of 21 feet, it was not ideal, but it was mineable. Minefields were laid off every suitable beach, and offshore moored minefields were laid to make coastal bombardments hazardous.

The greatest problem facing the Navy as the North Koreans fell back was the mining of Wonsan, Hungnam and Chinnampo. Intended to thwart Allied invasion plans, mines now hindered the usefulness of the ports for logistical supply. Conventional sweeping proved tedious and dangerous so COMNAVFE gave TF 77 a crack at it. Hydrostatically fused bombs were useless; helicopters were useful as minespotters; patrol aircraft with 0.5 inch guns were useful but the work was tedious and frustrating.

On 10th October Wonsan was occupied from landward by the RoK troops moving up the east coast, supported by aircraft from *Leyte*.

The 1st Marine Division left Inchon on 17th October via the Flying Fish Channel and arrived off Wonsan on the 19th, whence they were due to land on the 20th. The Marines were unable to get ashore until the influence mines had been cleared along the swept channels on the 25th, on which day they made an unopposed landing.

Minesweeping, that had been estimated to take five days, took fifteen. Six minesweepers, then nine, plus a helicopter from Worcester, swept a 3000 yard channel between the 100 and 30 fathom lines. Countermining with 1,000 lb. bombs delivered by aircraft from *Philippine Sea* and *Leyte* was not successful. One RoK and two fleet minesweepers were mined and sunk, with heavy loss of life. Magnetic mines had been laid close inshore; all mines that were swept were found to be of Soviet manufacture. The UN had temporarily lost command of the sea; the invasion fleet had been kept at sea for five days. As Admiral Sherman said 'If you can't go where you want to when you want to, you have not got command of the sea.'

Admiral Joy made the comment that 'The main lesson of Wonsan is that no so-called subsidiary branch of the naval service, such as mine warfare, should ever be neglected or relegated to a minor role in the future. Wonsan also taught us that we can be denied freedom of movement to an enemy objective through an intelligent use of mines by an alert force'.

Captain Unwin's five frigates, *Mount Bay, Morecambe Bay, Pukaki, Tutira* and *La Grandière*, were kept busy with the convoys, escorting transports, transferring mails and orders for their groups, and occasionally searching for missing American aircraft and aircrew; the weather was poor with high winds and fairly heavy swell. He reported

> 'Thus ended a period for the frigates of 46 days operational duty away from their base, under US command, of which no ship except *Morecambe Bay*, who joined up towards the end, spent more than 6 days at anchor; each ship steamed some 9000 miles during this time. Relations with the US authorities and ships were, as ever, excellent and all were extremely co-operative and successful...These operations have completed the welding of the frigates into a united family...an excellent team-spirit prevails throughout all the ships of the escort group...This was an arduous period for all, though of course as with most frigate work there were few highlights. No ship ever broke down or failed to do what I asked of her...
>
> 'The companies of all the ships are very young...given adequate leadership the modern sailor responds with great cheerfulness, keenness and enthusiasm, and can always be relied upon to play his part to the full. The standard of entry into the Royal Navy is as high as ever it was.'

The North Korean capital of Pyongyang was occupied by 8th Army on 19th October; RoK forces had taken Wonsan on 10th prior to the US Marines staging their amphibious landing there on the 25th (even Bob Hope had got there before them); 7th Division, after delays and counter-orders, landed at Iwon on the 29th; and by the end of the month UN forces were at the Manchurian border in the vicinity of Chosan on the River Yalu.

The retreat of the North Korean forces brought to the fore the plight of the islands off the west and south-west coasts. Most of them had at some time been held by the Communists — some still were — and many of the South Korean inhabitants were near to starvation. Three Canadian destroyers under Captain J.V. Brock RCN, together with some RoK vessels, were sent to eject the Communists and rehabilitate the islanders. By 5th October the RoK had taken over and the Canadian destroyers were freed for other duties.

The approach of winter, and the poor condition of the much-bombed road and rail communications leading north from South Korea, made the job of opening the port of Chinnampo a top military priority. The minefield problem at Chinnampo was different from that at Wonsan due to the wholly different hydrographic conditions on the two coasts. The direct seaward approach to Chinnampo was blocked by islands and delta-like areas of heavy silt brought down by the swift-currented Taedong River. The minimum tidal range was 12 feet with a maximum current of 5 knots. The south channel was 15 feet deep at maximum high water and the north channel 30 feet. Both were mineable, sweeping would have to start 69 miles from China and the delta was 33 miles from the docks. However, by the end of November 200 miles of channel had been swept and more than 80 mines destroyed.

During *Theseus'* passage out from the United Kingdom from 18th August, flying practice concentrated on achieving steady and consistent operation on and off the deck which is the fundamental requirement for high intensity flying operations. It was unreasonable to expect the maintenance personnel to cope with accident damage to aircraft at the same time as maintaining them and their equipment at the high state of efficiency required for war. Battle damage had to be expected and reserve aircraft at Singapore were a long way from the zone of operations. The Air Department had pursued a policy of giving overriding priority to the elimination of deck landing and taxying accidents. If there was any doubt about an approach, the pilot was Waved-off, and gradually a consistency was developed which proved so valuable later. Similarly great attention was given to catapult drill, as every operational sortie required to be either catapulted or 'ratogged'. This was to return average figures of 42 seconds each for ten Sea Furies.

Theseus sailed from Hong Kong at 1130 on Monday 2nd October. The Air Group had flown ashore to Kai Tak on 24th September where they stayed during the ship's hand-over from *Triumph*; all aircraft landed-on successfully during the afternoon of the 2nd. By 1800 that evening winds had reached gale force and there was a warning of a typhoon in the area, the aircraft were double lashed and hourly hangar and flight deck rounds were carried out. For a time speed was reduced to eight knots to avoid weather damage to the attendant destroyer. By Wednesday the typhoon had passed and on Thursday afternoon *Theseus* arrived in Sasebo where she anchored adjacent to *Warrior*. During the next two days 807 Squadron received two replacement aircraft from *Warrior* and the painting of British black and white stripes was completed on all aircraft. Arrangements were being made to establish a pool of reserve aircraft, together with the necessary maintenance staff, at Iwakuni.

Rear Admiral Andrewes by this time had under his operational control ships from Australian, British, Canadian, Dutch, French, Japanese, South Korean and United States navies, and a Commander from the Thai Navy was in Sasebo discussing a contribution to the force of three Thai frigates. Admiral Andrewes commented 'What we want now is the gift of tongues so graphically described in the second chapter of the Acts of the Apostles, a chapter which has proved the downfall of many an unwary lay-reader before now. Luckily we have no signs yet of any recruits from Phrygia or Pamphilia'.

On 7th October Admiral Andrewes, CTF 95.1, had reorganised his Group, TG 95.1, into:

TE 95.10 CTF 95.1 representative ashore at Sasebo (CSO)

TE 95.11 Air patrol and blockade element: *Theseus* and attached destroyers

TE 95.12 Surface patrol and blockade element: cruisers and attached destroyers

TE 95.13 Screen element: *Cayuga* (command), *Sioux*, HMAS *Bataan*, *Constance*, *Concord*, *Charity*

TE 95.14 Minesweeping element: *Whitesand Bay* and 5 Japanese minesweepers

TE 95.15 Inshore element: RoKN vessels

TE 95.16 Reconnaissance element: USS *Gardiners Bay* and 4 Mariner flying boats.

The tasks laid down for them were: (a) to continue blockade in the Yellow Sea, (b) to conduct air strikes and surface bombardments of selected military targets in the Chinnampo to Haeju area, in order to simulate preparations for landing operations, and (c) to keep the enemy off balance and to prevent his reorganisation.

In order to implement these instructions, approximately half *Theseus'* aircraft were to be used for continuous A/S and minespotting patrols over the carrier force and a CAP over the inshore force of mine-sweepers and supporting cruisers, the remaining aircraft to carry out attacks over the defined area — the south-west corner of North Korea including Haeju, Chinnampo and Sariwon. The targets for these air attacks — coast defences and communications — were chosen to create the impression of imminent UN landings. Anxiety was felt that *Theseus'* new aircraft, the Sea Furies, might give rise to unfortunate incidents; all concerned had been informed and no incidents did occur. A daily requirement was a reconnaissance flight as early as practicable of the west coast to check in particular on any shipping movements and to detect any enemy mining activities. In this connection special fishing sanctuaries by day and night were established for RoK sampans and junks. Bombardment spotting aircraft were to be provided for units of the Group as required, using Anglo-American combined procedures; surveillance of certain enemy airfields which might provide a threat to west coast forces was needed; and aircraft were to be provided in indirect or close air support of the land forces. In the later stages the CAP was dispensed with in order to increase the offensive efforts.

Minesweeping was continued, but only in the Haeju area because of the shortage of minesweepers; *Gardiners Bay's* Mariners kept up anti-mine patrols over the west coast of North Korea and the Gulf of Inchon.

It was known that the North Koreans had been presented with two submarines, and although the threat of submarine attack was regarded as slight, the precaution was taken of maintaining an A/S patrol of one Firefly. The substitution of 55 gallon nacelle tanks for radar sets on all Fireflies detracted little from their efficiency as A/S aircraft in daytime and it was regarded as worthwhile putting them up on A/S patrols. In any event the A/S patrol aircraft was always extremely useful for investigating any surface contacts.

A CAP was maintained during daylight hours and this represented a standing commitment on the ship's flying output. The ship normally operated in the Yellow Sea not far from the Shantung Peninsula and although air warning radar gave very good results, it was decided that standing fighter patrols were necessary. Considerable attention was given to the possible requirement to augment the CAP at short notice if required and this was not always easy with a single carrier. On no occasion did any of *Theseus'* aircraft have the good fortune to engage in air combat with enemy aircraft, though considerable experience was gained in intercepting aircraft subsequently identified as friendly, B-29 bombers or a Sunderland or Neptune on patrol. At this time, going up the coast, were quantities of B-29s, usually flying from Okinawa to bomb the bridges of the Yalu River. It was good practice for the radar control and for the aircraft to intercept these aircraft. In about 3,000 interceptions there were no mistakes in recognition, and no accidents occurred. During the winter months the CAP was frequently used under ship radar control to make a reconnaissance for snowstorms, and the information obtained from this source, as well as the ship's radar on the plan position indicator on the compass platform, enabled the carriers to keep the decks free from snow by evading the storms. It also meant that, with no meteorological reports from the west on which to base weather forecasts, the aircraft were always successfully recalled before the weather closed in. Only on one occasion was it necessary to divert them to a shore base.

Operational sorties were classified into three principal types, namely:

Armed Reconnaissance — AR. Air reconnaissance mission which had the additional task of searching for and attacking targets of opportunity within a specified area.

Close Air Support — CAS. In the military lexicon - air action against hostile surface targets which are so close to friendly forces as to require detailed integration of each mission with the fire and movement of those forces.

In layman's language - use of armament of an aeroplane in behalf of, or
near to, the soldier on the ground.

Interdiction — To prevent or hinder, by any means, enemy use of an area
or route.

AR, air strikes and CAS were co-ordinated through the Joint Operations Centre
(JOC) which was initially located at Seoul, but which in January moved back to
Taegu. This centre provided a connecting link between Eighth US Army HQ
(EUSAK) and 5th Air Force in Korea — it was an Air Force organization, not a
combined HQ. At the JOC were three USN and one RN liaison officers, the RN
officer being an observer seconded from *Theseus*.

At the start of each patrol the carriers sent a courier to collect Intelligence
material and target assessments from the JOC; during operations information such
as the position of the bomb line, targets being attacked by B-29 and B-26 bombers,
and flak positions, were passed by signal. For the purpose of assigning AR sorties,
special overlay maps were provided by the JOC, dividing the enemy-held territory
into a series of lettered areas and designating the main roads by colours and
numbers. Daylight AR by UN aircraft completely brought to a halt all enemy traffic
movements. Only by night was the enemy able to move; by day all road traffic was
very cleverly camouflaged and only by experience, and after getting to know the
country, were aircrew able to spot them. Flying at very low height for close
inspection of the countryside was not an economical proposition, it courted trouble
from rifle and burp-gun fire. Fifteen hundred feet was regarded as a normal good
reconnaissance height, but over towns and other heavily defended areas a height of
5,000 feet or more was regarded as prudent.

Bombing strikes were mainly directed against bridges. Close study of
photographs was needed in the selection of bridge targets. After the thaw, when road
transport could no longer traverse rivers on ice, some bridges became of vital
importance to the enemy while others could be bypassed by fords. A lot of fords
were constructed, the river beds being built up to a few feet from the surface and no
bombing attacks could be effective against them. Wheel tracks showing up on
photographs clearly disclosed where these fords existed. Thus bridge attacks were
concentrated on those which did not have adjoining fords. The selection of rail bridge
targets was dictated largely by the existence of any continuous stretch of undamaged
railway line. The enemy was very adept at effecting repairs, particularly if only a
span of a bridge and not a support had been knocked down and constant visits to the
same bridge became necessary Korea is a type of country for which road and rail
communications require a very large number of bridges. There was thus a very large
number of bridge targets. To discourage the repair gangs, 6 to 8 hour delay fuses
were often placed in a proportion of bombs used for the last strike of the day.

For CAS of ground forces, tactical air control parties and forward controllers were set up to correspond with the British type of forward control party and air contact teams. In addition, considerable use was made of Harvard aircraft for directing air attacks. The actual method employed made full use of the undisputed air superiority enjoyed by the UN forces. For the most part controlled attacks were made on ridges held by the enemy. It was usually impossible to see the enemy from a fast flying operational aircraft because they remained too well hidden amongst trees and in their foxholes. Spraying the area blindly with bombs, rockets and bullets may not always have been very effective, and the Americans' napalm, with its wider effective lethal area, was a more efficient weapon than those carried by RN aircraft, but even so, hundreds of casualties were caused by the Furies and Fireflies.

Since so much of Korea is mountainous country, with peaks of 5,000 to 6,000 feet, air operations required a high degree of flying skill when cloud covered the ground. It says a lot for the formation and instrument flying of the pilots that *Theseus* sustained no losses on this score, particularly on CAS missions when attacks were made on ridges which were very close to a cloud base.

In the Yellow Sea, the usual datum position, point Oboe, was some miles west of Clifford Island and the carriers usually remained close to that position. Shallow water and avoidance of radar echoes from land necessitated remaining out at some distance. This involved a 70- to 80-mile flight over the sea when proceeding to and from the target area. Initially, during very cold weather, a search and rescue destroyer, known as 'Bird dog', was stationed about half-way between point Oboe and Inchon. Later, when the enemy was evicted from Inchon, the Bird-dog duties were taken over by a Harbour Entrance Control Vessel.

Later, during the two year stalemate from April 1951 to the end of the war, Oboe moved further north so that it was about 50 miles from Paengyong-do and about 60 miles in a southerly direction from the most southerly and westerly point of enemy held territory on the west coast. The ship was seldom more than 15 miles from Oboe whilst flying operations were in progress, and before take off aircrew were briefed with courses and times from four friendly positions Able, Baker, Charlie and X-ray to enable them to return to Oboe.

Theseus carried 23 Sea Furies, 12 Fireflies and one Sea Otter or helicopter; two-and-a-half-hour sorties were planned, 45-gallon drop tanks were carried by Furies and 55-gallon nacelle tanks by Fireflies. Wind speed requirements for aircraft so fitted, and carrying armament stores, necessitated the catapult being used for all launches, and when the catapult failed for a short period, RATOG had to be used. Sea Furies with 2 x 500 lb. bombs and drop tanks needed 28 knots of wind down the deck for catapulting. Because 22_ knots was the maximum for *Theseus* (needing her bottom scraped), and because more often than not winds were liable to die down almost to nothing, it was decided to fit rockets to the Furies and leave bombing to the Fireflies, for which full load required only 21 knots of wind down the deck when being catapulted. With practice, catapulting intervals were cut down to a satisfactory extent and it was noticeable that when working in company with USS *Bataan* in April 1951 that *Theseus* kept pace with her launching from two catapults, while on no occasion did *Bataan* beat her deck landing intervals.

It was found that 50 sorties per day was a desirable flying target for five two-and-a-half- or three-hour details, although when an extra effort was required, it was possible to increase this, and on one day 66 sorties were flown. This high rate was achieved only by good drill. Every man learned what was required of him; servicing, re-arming, and aircraft handling were always conducted at a satisfactory speed even when temperatures were below freezing point on the flight deck.

Two-and-a-half-hour details allowed adequate time for refuelling and rearming, but there were frequent occasions when an aircraft requiring an emergency landing necessitated the range of aircraft prepared for the next event to be spotted forward. Since the wings of Furies and Fireflies were not folded with bombs and rockets on the bomb carriers and rocket launchers, these landings were liable to throve the planned programme out of gear. For some bombing strikes 2 x 1,000 lb. bombs were carried by each Firefly instead of 2 x 500 lb. bombs. The Furies carried rocket projectiles, and with their 20 mm cannons in addition, were very effective ground attack aircraft.

First Patrol

On Sunday 8th October Admiral Andrewes transferred his flag from *Ladybird* to *Theseus* who sailed from Sasebo at 1000, with *Kenya, Constance, Sioux* and *Cayuga* in company, for her first operational patrol in the Yellow Sea off the west coast of Korea. Vice Admiral H.T.W. Grant, CB, DSC, RCN, Chief of Canadian Naval Staff was on board *Cayuga was* detached later in the day to go to Inchon.

Flying started at 1530 with eight Sea Furies on CAP and practice interceptions on four Fireflies which had carried out a photographic reconnaissance. During the land-on Mr. Bailey in a Firefly floated over both barriers and landed in the deck park hitting two other Fireflies. The aircraft had actually caught the first barrier with its wheels, which were torn off, carried on through the second barrier that parted on impact and had then swung and struck the tails of both the other two aircraft. The offending aircraft was ditched over the side and the other two were reduced to spares and produce, giving urgently needed spare power plants. Though not a very good start to their first operational patrol, this was to be the last serious deck landing accident in the operational area. 810 Squadron's strength was reduced by about 25%. At the end of the patrol Admiral Andrewes remarked 'The regularity with which all nine Fireflies appeared each day went far to mitigate the loss of the other three'.

On the 9th, as a precautionary measure, Commander E.S. Carver, Fleet Aviation Officer, visited the local Tactical Air Control Centre ashore at Kimpo to make sure that they knew Admiral Andrewes' general plan and the types of aircraft that would be operating. It was as well he did so, for he found that 5th US Air Force had failed to inform the Control Centre of any British carrier operations in the area. He also brought back information of a helicopter rescue flight based at Kimpo and the means of contacting them.

During the first phase of the patrol, from the 9th to the 11th, air attacks were directed against enemy defences and communications in the defined area.

Flying operations were carried out from dawn to dusk with Furies on CAP and Fireflies on A/S and mine-spotting patrols. The first strike was launched at 0815 led by the Air Group Commander, Lieutenant Commander F.S. Stovin-Bradford DSC, consisting of six Furies armed with 8 x 60 lb. HE rockets and four Fireflies with 2 x 500 lb. bombs. An aerodrome and hangars were rocketed in addition to coaling wharves at a small port. The Fireflies bombed gun emplacements on Paengyong-do Island, but reported that little damage had probably been done since the bombing was fairly inaccurate, while the escorting Furies strafed various small targets. The aircraft landed on at 1015. The afternoon strike was made against harbour installations at Chinnampo; the four Fireflies bombed buildings and wharves with better results than during the morning while the five Furies rocketed and strafed buildings, wharves and railway trucks. There were no signs of North Korean troops and the buildings were

well camouflaged. Very little anti-aircraft fire was encountered but there was occasional small-arms fire. 'It would appear, flying over the area,' recorded 810 Squadron's diarist, 'that on the surface there is very little activity — it would also appear that the Americans — and *Triumph* — have been round the area before us!!'

Bombing Chinnampo, October 1950.   *(Stock)*

Next day, 10th October, CAP, A/S and anti-mine patrols were flown from dawn to dusk during one of which Lieutenant Hook and his Observer, Aircrewman Beeton, reported a minefield to the north of *Theseus'* operating area; strikes were flown in the forenoon and afternoon. Two Furies escorted four Fireflies to bomb a railway bridge south-east of Chang-yon; two spans were destroyed, Lieutenants Cook and Birch doing most of the damage, after which miscellaneous targets were strafed; P3 Grant, having flown too low after dropping his bombs, had his windscreen struck by shrapnel from the bomb bursts of the aircraft ahead. The Furies rocketed trucks in a railway station and strafed trucks and coaches at several places. The other four Furies, led by Lieutenant Commander Stovin-Bradford, strafed several camouflaged huts and transport and fired their rockets at a barracks and store depot. During this last attack Lieutenant Leonard's aircraft was hit during the rocket explosion or by small-arms fire from the North Korean troops. He managed to force-land almost immediately about five miles from the target in a paddy field in the valley and his aircraft broke up. Constant watch and patrol were kept by two Furies until relieved by Lieutenant Ford. Meanwhile the AGC had signalled the ship who called for a rescue helicopter from Kimpo. Ford in turn was relieved by a US Tigercat aircraft. About an hour after the crash the helicopter arrived with a doctor who, with the pilot's help, dragged Leonard from the cockpit under small-arms fire from a nearby farmhouse. The pilot gave covering fire from a machine-gun as Leonard was dragged to the helicopter which then safely took off. The Fury was later destroyed by cannon fire from the Tigercat. Leonard, who had suffered severe injuries, was given a blood transfusion in the air and on arrival at Kimpo beach was transferred to a US hospital ship. The rescue by the American helicopter team was extremely courageous, the pilot, Lieutenant Colonel John C. Schumate, USAF, was later awarded a British MC.

Strikes were again flown during the afternoon. Four Fireflies attacked a road bridge but none of the bombs hit the bridge though the road was severely damaged at one end. Six Furies operating in pairs carried out AR attacking various small targets including suspected flak positions, transports and railway targets.

Next day the weather deteriorated and flying was cancelled at noon. An early strike of six Furies was launched at 0615 in order to catch the North Koreans before their night movements had been completed. All their work was being done in the dark and generally no sign of life could be seen during the day. The aircraft split up into three pairs again; a small amount of movement was seen, but it quickly vanished as the aircraft flew overhead. Opportunity targets were attacked, while two of the CAP carried out a short reconnaissance of the coast near Haeju. A second strike of four Fireflies supported by two Furies was launched against an island off the west coast suspected of being the base for mine-laying operations. Nothing was observed so an attack was made on a road bridge south-east of Chang-yon, alongside the rail bridge attacked the previous day, but with negative results.

Theseus and her screen sailed for Inchon to replenish the destroyers, arriving there at 1600.

During the next phase of operations from 12th to 16th October *Theseus* resumed her attacks in the same area. A maximum effort strike was flown in the afternoon of the 12th, trenches were strafed and an ammunition dump was exploded by cannon fire, and rockets were fired at gun emplacements by the Furies. The Fireflies bombed a road bridge south of Chang-yong but no hits were made on the bridge though the embankment leading up to it was severely mauled. The target was obscured by low cumulus cloud so a low dive was made instead of the normal 50° high dive. Cloud affected the photographic mosaic carried out by another Firefly.

On 10th October the minespotting patrol had reported several mines in the Fankochi Point to Tegongpyong area and a considerable number of mines about four feet below the surface had also been observed, though subsequent experience suggested that they were probably jelly fish. However about 30 contact mines had been laid and 21 were accounted for. A channel had been swept by 31st October and the Japanese minesweepers returned to the Americans.

By 13th October it was clear that the majority of the enemy had evacuated the Haeju to Ongjin area. Admiral Andrewes decided to continue sweeping the approaches to Haeju since it would be a useful minor supply port, to continue harassing attacks on Chinnampo, and to interdict communications in the general area north and west of a line Changyang to Sariwon to Hwangju.

The Fireflies continued A/S and mine spotting patrols in the area around *Theseus* and also in the area from which *Kenya* was to carry out a bombardment. On the 13th the Furies, on their way back to the ship from escorting the Firefly strike against the dockside buildings at Chinnampo, strafed possible mine-laying motor junks. Because the wind was negligible in the forenoon the rockets had to be removed from the Furies. In the afternoon the Furies rocketed small ships in the Chinnampo estuary and strafed any small suspicious vessels, whilst the Firefly photo reconnaissance showed fires still burning in the Chinnampo area from the morning strike.

On the 14th, low fog over the Sariwon area prevented the Fireflies from bombing their principal target, a bridge to the west of

Chinnampo docks – 807 squadron.   *(FAAM)*

Aerial view of Chinnampo during raid by
810 Squadron Fireflies.   *(IWM)*

Sariwon, so they attacked their alternative target of installations at Chinnampo when many buildings were destroyed. The Furies rocketed dockside buildings at Chinnampo in the forenoon obtaining some first class results. Both squadrons encountered light flak. After leaving Chinnampo the Furies strafed two minelayers and North Korean troops in trenches on coastal defence positions. The minelayers were converted junks with three sets of laying rails built on to the stern. Each minelayer carried a cargo of 15 mines on deck under primitive camouflage. On the afternoon's strike the minelayers were rocketed by Furies which then went on to attack military huts near Chinnampo and to strafe gun positions on the coast; the Fireflies again destroying buildings and harbour installations at Chinnampo. On both the 13th and the 14th the Firefly dive-bombing was particularly accurate.

The weather closed in next day, preventing flying until 0900 when the Furies, attacking opportunity targets, rocketed some trucks north of Sariwon. One truck carrying inflammable material exploded. The Fireflies bombed a road bridge to the west of Sariwon but failed to destroy it — excuses put forward for the lack of success being lack of practice on high dives, lack of a good sight, or just 'ham' flying. When returning from the strike P3 Grant had engine trouble in his Firefly which was nearly a case of ditching, but he managed to reach the ship and made a good landing. On investigation, a connecting rod was found to be protruding through the crankcase. The AGC also had engine trouble with his Fury and returned to the ship early with his number 2 after rocketing a bridge and strafing hill gun positions on his way back. Many people in the fields were seen waving white flags. At 1330 the weather became very bad very quickly and great difficulty was experienced in landing on the CAP in visibility of about 600 to 700 yards. They were brought in to the ship one at a time by radar and the deck-landings were rather shaky.

By working overnight to change the engine, Grant's aircraft was ready for a run-up first thing on the morning of the 16th to bring 810 Squadron's serviceability to 100%. Bad weather delayed take-off until 1130 and the only event of the day was by Furies strafing three mine-laying junks, which were hit by all pilots whose shooting was excellent, and then blowing up warehouses with rockets at Chinnampo. Flying ceased at 1330 and- the force proceeded to Inchon for fuelling from *Wave Premier* and *Green Ranger* next day.

The standard of maintenance in both squadrons had been very high indeed, frequently 19 out of 20 Sea Furies and 11 or 12 out of 12 Fireflies to meet the flying programme. Holes due to small-arms fire and shrapnel were patched, and mainplanes were changed overnight.

The third phase of the current operations was from 18th to 21st October. *Theseus* sailed from Inchon at 0600 on the 18th and the first detail was launched at 0830; A/S and mine patrols by the Fireflies, CAP by Furies, and both Squadrons reduced to AR against such targets as 'likely' shipping, moving trains and vehicles. The advances made by UN troops had been too rapid for an accurate bomb-line to be kept up. The first strikes jettisoned their bombs and rockets leaving themselves with only 20 mm cannon. The Fireflies took the opportunity to 'show the flag' over the advancing troops and reported that they had not seen anything like it before — so different from the usual signs over their quiet zone. The Furies stayed further south, carrying out reconnaissance's of the Chinnampo, Pyongyang and coastal areas. Accurate, light AA fire was experienced over Pyongyang. Lieutenant Bevans had to make a successful emergency glide landing back on *Theseus* — having expected to have to ditch — when his Fury engine started cutting, necessitating the rapid re-spotting forward of all aircraft.

On the 20th and the 21st *Theseus* was operating in the far north-west corner of Korea, in the area Sinanju/Chongju/Sonchon. The Furies rocketed warehouses and engine sheds, setting them on fire; the Fireflies attacked storage buildings east of the town of Chongju, reporting that there seemed little of importance left in the town itself to attack due to the previous heavy raids by B-29s of the USAF. On the last day of the patrol, targets were attacked in the Chonju area including firing rockets into each end of a short railway tunnel in which it was thought there was an engine. Because there were so few targets available for the Fireflies they had to be satisfied with attacking one small road bridge.

During *Theseus'* first operational period a considerable advance was made by the United Nations forces to a line north of Pyongyang to Wonsan. Targets were attacked in the Hwanghae Province and as far north as Pakchon and Chonju. Everywhere the North Koreans were in retreat. Much attention had been paid to Chinnampo which it was hoped to open up as a supply port.

The first operational period was the time when the aircrew learned the terrain and it was fortunate that during this period the flak was neither intense nor particularly effective. The North Koreans had become somewhat demoralised and the UN forces were advancing.

Theseus, *Constance*, and *Sioux* returned to Sasebo; *Whitesand Bay* and the sweepers completed the clearance of Haeju; leaving *Kenya* and HMAS *Bataan* on patrol.

Theseus' air plan had aimed at sustained rather than intensive air operations since their required duration was unknown. At no time was she fully extended, and if an important target had suddenly offered there was a reserve of effort to deal with it. There was, of course, no air opposition, so that full war conditions were not reproduced.

The increased range and endurance of the Sea Furies and Firefly 5s as compared with *Triumph's* Seafires and Firefly 1s was a most welcome advantage, as was the

ability to launch Fireflies with bombs regardless of natural wind. The Furies demonstrated their accuracy with rockets, but in the later stages tier stowage had to be abandoned owing to damage to rocket posts and main planes on firing.

Firefly 5 with 2 x 1000lb bombs.   *(Cane)*

Another drawback to the Furies was their inability to take photographs; vertical photography was unsuccessful due to the rapid oiling up of the camera lenses, and none of them was equipped for oblique photography.

As regards *Theseus* herself, the authorised stowage capacity of rockets, and to a lesser extent bombs, was quite inadequate. Nearly three times the normal outfit of 60 lb. HE rocket-heads were fired, but foresight and improvisation prevented any question of running short. During the operations, *Theseus* had to catapult every operational sortie owing to aircraft loading, RATOG restrictions and the deck park. On her return to harbour, the reeving was found to be so stranded as to render the catapult unusable.

Second Patrol

The day before sailing from Sasebo a helicopter flew on board *Theseus* from USS *Worcester* and was to remain with the ship for mine-spotting duties working in conjunction with the mine-sweepers off the approaches to Chinnampo. As the land forces were so far advanced to the north they needed a nearer port for supplies than Pusan so *Theseus'* task for her next patrol was to cover and supply air support for the task of clearing Chinnampo and its approaches of mines.

Next morning, 27th October, prior to sailing at noon, three Furies were lightered ashore for repair in *Unicorn*, two for engine changes and the third for repair following P3 Lines barrier.

The lack of the catapult was serious, and during the whole of this second patrol she had to operate her aircraft without rockets, bombs or drop tanks, which could only be done at the expense of flying off six Fireflies to Iwakuni with their maintenance crews in order to reduce the deck park. Thus 810 Squadron, with only half its complement of aircraft, was reduced to A/S and minespotting patrols whose only excitement was to report jelly fish, porpoises and 'gash'. Those Squadron officers not on the flying programme were employed as Assistant Officer of the Watch on the bridge. Meanwhile 807 Squadron were flying more offensive, AR, sorties from Chinnampo along the coast to Chongju and Sonchon searching for shipping and following the progress of the UN ground forces. On 29th October, with *Theseus* operating between 50 and 100 miles off shore from the Chinnampo estuary, the helicopter started its job of mine spotting in conjunction with the US minesweepers in the estuary.

Next day it was necessary to use RATOG and the first three Furies took off without incident, but the fourth, piloted by P3 Johnson, banked hard to starboard as he became airborne and he only just prevented his aircraft from turning upside down into the sea. It was then decided that no more RATOGs would be carried out until all pilots had practised ashore.

An uneventful and dull patrol, limited mainly to providing CAP over the ship and over the minesweeping force, came to an end.

On passage to Sasebo the six Fireflies were landed-on from Iwakuni where the pilots had kept in flying practice with local flying. Whilst at Sasebo three new Fireflies were received from *Unicorn*. *Theseus* sailed from Sasebo on 8th November for Hong Kong, in company with *Sioux*, in deteriorating weather caused by typhoon Clare in the vicinity. Early in the morning of the 10th *Sioux* broached-to three times and had the port side of her upper deck swept clear of boats, dayits, carley floats and ladders. During the three days passage to Hong Kong the

Sea Otter, flown by Lieut. P. Crane, being retrieved after landing, October 1950.

(Stock)

ship's Engineering Department renewed both the acceleration and retardation ropes of the catapult, so that dead load trials could be carried out by the dockyard. So far as was known this was the first time any carrier had fitted new reevings without dockyard assistance, and took rather a long time on this first occasion as the wires had to be rat-tailed first; later on the job was reduced to about 48 hours.

Theseus anchored in Hong Kong at noon on Saturday 11th November. Next day Sunday Divisions, followed by a Remembrance Service, were held in the hangar. This was the first occasion on which Divisions had been held on board since leaving the United Kingdom in May.

In the afternoon of 13th November *Theseus* put to sea for catapult trials. These were successfully carried out by Fireflies at various all-up weights, led by the AGC. Land-on was completed at 1715 except for Lieutenant Birch who landed his Firefly at Kai Tak after he had experienced port wing heavy when in the landing circuit, found to be asymmetric flap incidence that took several days to correct.

For a couple of days, local flying was carried out from *Theseus*, Mr Bailey in a Firefly catching number 10 wire and finishing in the barrier, shockloading the engine and causing an engine change. Both Lieutenant Commander Smith and Lieutenant Keighley-Peach also had 10th-wire barriers in their Furies. On the 16th nine Furies and six Fireflies flew to Kai Tak for a week's flying whilst the ship remained in harbour. Lieutenant Debney had the unpleasant experience of having the starboard wing of his Fury fold during take-off, the starboard undercarriage collapsed and the aircraft skidding off the runway into the sea.

Some aircraft returned on board on the 26th, but due to a Fury accident on the deck that detail had to return to Kai Tak, in time to prevent the next detail taking off. By the end of the day all aircraft were recovered, Lieutenant Tobey in a Firefly coming in too low over the round-down, breaking the hook and finishing in the barrier. The remainder embarked on the 30th in conditions described by the AGC 'as the worst he had known since being in the ship'.

To Admiral Andrewes arriving in Sasebo on 22nd October it seemed the end of the war was in sight and that before long naval forces in Korea could be considerably reduced. He proposed to form a task group of one cruiser, five destroyers, three frigates and a corvette under an officer of Captain's rank, to remain in Korean and Japanese waters. He and his staff would return to Hong Kong.

Meanwhile the usual patrols were maintained, and mine-sweeping at Haeju and Chinnampo had been completed on 20th October.

On shore the UN northward advance was out-running its supplies. RoK forces had reached the Yalu on 25th October but had then suffered severe losses when they were attacked by Chinese soldiers, the first in action in Korea and thought then to be few in number. It seemed from reports of seeing small groups of Chinese and thousands of

RoK gunboat L.1503 apprehends a junk.   *(Nicholls)*

footprints in the snow, that the Marines in the eastern central sector were being encircled. Chinese attacks became so fierce that UN forces had to fall back to the Chongchon River in the west where the front was stabilised. UN air effort was stepped up, with aircraft from three US heavy carriers, two light carriers and powerful land-based squadrons pounding the enemy in what was thought to be the final assault.

There was some concern at this time that the US might use the atomic bomb to produce a decisive result. Mr Attlee visited Mr. Truman in Washington early in December where agreement was reached to avoid general war and a determination to remain in Korea.

General MacArthur had to extricate his army as best he could, and once again he based his plans on sea power.

At the end of November Admiral Joy warned Rear Admiral Doyle that his amphibious force (TF 90) would be needed to lift troops from North Korea for redeployment in the south.

Off the west coast was Captain Brock in *Cayuga* with *Athabaskan, Sioux, Warramunga, Tutira* and *Morecambe Bay*. The destroyers were patrolling off Shimnato (39°35'N, 124°55'E); *Tutira* was stationed off the entrance to Chinnampo and *Morecambe Bay was* in charge of the Japanese minesweepers at Haeju. Captain Lloyd-Davies was called to a conference with Rear Admiral Smith (CTF 95) on 30th November so sailed with his group for Sasebo. Admiral Joy also requested Rear Admiral Andrewes to return with *Theseus* and any other HM ships. Vice Admiral Andrewes, promoted that day, sailed in *Theseus* accompanied by *Constance*, from Hong Kong on 1st December and reached Sasebo on the 4th, having been delayed by north-easterly gales.

It was intended to withdraw Xth US Marine Corps from Hungnam by sea to Pusan. Evacuation of some units was already proceeding from Wonsan. The 8th Army was retreating southwards, Pyongyang was about to fall to the enemy, and plans were being made to evacuate troops through Chinnampo.

TG 95.1 had been given responsibility for all west coast areas, excluding the evacuation ports themselves; units of the task group would be lent to amphibious commanders at these ports as necessary, *Theseus* providing air support.

Third Patrol

Admiral Andrewes resumed the duties of CTG 95.1 when he sailed from Sasebo in *Theseus* during the afternoon of 4th December with *Concord*, *Cossack* and *Eversten*.

Theseus' efforts were amply rewarded by the results achieved, both Furies and Fireflies causing great destruction on bridges, rolling stock, M/T dumps, troops, and all the rest of the gear of an advancing army. The Air Force ashore at this time was handicapped by having to pull out of the forward air-fields, and a carrier, without the anxiety of having to watch its lines of communications, was able to put its whole effort into attacking the enemy — an ability of carriers which it is well to remember.

Flying started again on 5th December with the Furies providing a CAP of two over the ship and the transports moving out of Chinnampo. One strike of five Furies went to Chinnampo to give support to the naval vessels there which were evacuating casualties. They also covered the area to the north and attacked 20 railway wagons south of Sunan with rockets, destroying three and damaging three. The first Firefly A/S detail was cancelled due to poor visibility and snow showers and the second was recalled for the same reasons. A/S patrols were flown all day, but the strike was cancelled due to insufficient knowledge of the front line.

CAP and A/S patrols were flown from dawn to dusk on the 6th but once again the weather was very poor. Two Furies were sent on AR while three others escorted a Firefly strike to attack a crossroads and a village harbouring troops. To reach the target area, which was north of Chinnampo, the flight had to fly round the coast through snow showers and conditions of poor visibility. Due to bad weather the Fury strike never got inland but they rocketed Ian-ni on the coast. Troops were considered to be in the village which was left on fire. In the evening *Theseus* left the operational area for Inchon to re-pack one of the stern glands.

Theseus left Inchon at 0530 next morning and CAP and A/S patrols were mounted all day from first light. Four Fury strikes were launched into the area Chinnampo to Pyongyang. Troops, transport, warehouses, dumps, junks and other small craft were rocketed and strafed with good results. During the day Fireflies in pairs carried out general reconnaissance over the western area, particularly along the coast where many junks carrying refugees were seen. In the morning Lieutenant Winterton carried out a precautionary mine-spotting sortie round Inchon.

Next day, the 8th, 807's Furies mounted strikes in the same areas as the previous day; targets and results were similar and good. 810's Fireflies in threes carried out

AR sorties to the west and as far north as Pyongyang. Bombs were dropped on three bridges causing some damage but none was destroyed. Stores in Chinnampo were also attacked. Little real activity was seen except for the first detail's attack on some enemy troops in a village square, many were seen to be hit. The weather was very much better and a total of 115 hours were flown, a record for the ship.

The weather deteriorated next day; the first CAP of four Furies had been launched and when flying out to the coast found snow storms being driven towards the ship. They were not able to land before the snow reached the ship and conditions were too bad even for a Carrier Controlled Approach so they were sent to Kimpo. Heavy snow fell for another two hours and further flying was cancelled. A sea swell that developed during the forenoon caused the cancellation of the planned re-fuelling.

On the 10th the weather improved enough for the four Furies to return from Kimpo, but was not good enough for CAP and A/S to take off, they were kept at stand-by. The scheduled re-fuelling had to take place in the sheltered area of Inchon that evening. Five pilots were transferred to *Athabaskan* to go to *Unicorn* to collect four replacement Furies and one Firefly.

Theseus left Inchon early next day and flying started at 0930. Three Fury strikes were launched into the Chinnampo/Pyongyang area, one of which obtained eight rocket hits on a moving train leaving it a shambles. The Fireflies dive-bombed two rail bridges in the Pyongyang area and a tunnel north-west of the town, causing damage to the bridges and blocking the tunnel; shipping and stores were also strafed at Chinnampo. The replacement aircraft were flown in during the afternoon.

Road and rail bridges and a dam were bombed next day in the Pyongyang area by the Fireflies while the Furies rocketed buildings and dumps left by the retreating UN forces in the Chinnampo/Pyongyang area, and strafed trucks and boats.

Haeju and Chinnampo were the targets for 807's Furies on the 13th. Warehouses, buildings, a floating crane and troops were rocketed and four MFVs and a staff car were strafed. The Fireflies' targets were bridges, docks and stores at Chinnampo. The western area was thoroughly combed during the day to try to find Allied troops left in the area. Many parties of South Koreans were seen, and what was thought to be a small party of Americans. A message was dropped to the latter informing them of details of the American's LST and helicopter operating round the coast evacuating parties of troops and civilians. This party was found to be South Koreans when they were picked up.

On the 14th the Furies flew a CAP of two aircraft for the helicopter which picked up a number of stragglers from the previous day's operations and brought them back to the LST from which it was operating. At one CAP change-over the helicopter was attacked by MiG 15s which caused some minor damage. The AGC saw ahead of him during a CAP sortie in the afternoon another MiG which was lost behind a 'puff of black smoke' as it opened up and flew away. The Fireflies devoted their efforts to AR along the lines of communication. Bridges were attacked in the Changyon and Namchonjom areas. A rail tunnel was attacked but although hit on the top no penetration was achieved. Bridges were also attacked between Changyon and Sinchon. At the end of flying it was announced that *Theseus* was to go to Sasebo for 24 hours, but at 2045 it was reported that a US Mariner aircraft had sighted 20 Chinese merchant ships to the west and it was thought that they might have been the Chinese 3rd Army. *Theseus* turned about and headed north prepared for a search next day. It was a false alarm, the fleet was fishing junks, and course was set for Sasebo which was reached at 1530 next day.

Sea Fury on a catapult about to launch.   *(Stock)*

In the seven and a half flying days since 4th December the CAG had achieved the following:

Hours	838
D.Ls	342
Sorties	338
Average serviceability	
Firefly	95.5%
Sea Fury	93.5%

Theseus received a signal from the First Sea Lord, Admiral of the Fleet Lord Fraser of North Cape,: 'I was very interested to read in recent dispatches an account of your work and congratulate you on all you are doing'.

Fourth Patrol

The stay in Sasebo was all too short, just long enough for refuelling, storing and ammunitioning, but there was a large amount of very welcome mail for the ship's company for collection.

Theseus, with *Cossack, Consort* and *Constance*, left early next morning, 16th December, but the weather during the next two days was too bad for any flying during the passage north, with gale force winds from dead ahead, frequent showers of rain, sleet and snow; winds of 55 knots, gusting to 60, on the flight deck, and the ship only able to make good 10 knots through the water. On the 18th, the first details were delayed for an hour because the aircraft were iced up and there was snow all over the flight deck. However the first Firefly A/S patrol, a CAP of three Furies and a strike of two were launched. Korea was snow bound and the strike aircraft saw much evidence of enemy movement on the roads. They strafed trucks which had been trying to cross the River Chongchon over the ice and had got stuck. The strike and CAP were landed-on early due to bad weather and it was not until 1300 that the next CAP was flown off, followed by a strike of two Furies at 1400 which found much more evidence of the enemy, including two tanks which they destroyed. The Fireflies flew three A/S patrols during the day, before flying ceased at 1600 due to bad weather; their AR sorties had been cancelled due to the catapult hold-back going unserviceable.

The 19th was a successful day for the Furies. At least 17 trucks and 3 tanks were destroyed or damaged in the Hwangju/Sariwon area in four strikes. After midday a low cloud base and poor visibility over the target area made rocketing difficult. During the forenoon Lieutenant Leece chalked up the 2,000th deck landing since leaving the UK in May. The Fireflies also had a good day; three AR details being flown. By climbing above the weather and finding the odd 'large hole', bombing attacks were made along the Pyongyang/Sariwon and Sariwon/Sinmak roads damaging one bridge.

The weather was again poor over the target area next day, but the Furies strafed buildings in Chinnampo and Sariwon, damaged a road bridge, strafed a bulldozer and damaged two oil dumps and a couple of lorries. Lieutenant Noble had engine trouble and had to return early, causing a certain amount of confusion, but the Flight Deck team got the next detail off on time. The Fireflies were fitted for the carriage of rockets (60 lb. HE for shore attacks and 25 lb. A/P for A/S aircraft) in place of bombs. They attacked bridges around Sariwon and put a pontoon bridge out of action. One aircraft went in to Suchon to carry out bombardment spotting with *Ceylon*.

Weather around the ship — being cold and with frequent snow showers — affected the flying on the 21st, causing the last detail to be cancelled. The Furies found targets from the battle line to Pyongyang; three bridges, five box-cars and a barracks with a red flag over it were rocketed and destroyed or damaged, and nine lorries were strafed. Lieutenant Pinsent had to make an emergency landing after take-off, due to low oil pressure, but landed without any trouble.

Friday 22nd was a rest day for aircrew, while *Theseus* refuelled from *Brown Ranger* in Inchon.

The Fireflies found no target of any real value when flying restarted next day, indeed some aircraft jettisoned their rockets when returning. The Furies were a little more successful. It had been announced that 18 Chinese Divisions were in the area to the east of Pyongyang so their efforts were concentrated there. Troops, trucks and buildings were rocketed and strafed with good results. Pilots reported however that there was nothing like the activity that would have been expected from 18 Divisions in the area.

On Christmas Eve the Fireflies again saw nothing outstanding during their three details of AR. The Furies were more fortunate. It was estimated that over 200 casualties were inflicted on a column of troops marching south, around Sariwon, for the big offensive that was expected to start on Christmas Day. Also attacked were two trucks, a tractor, a railway engine and several buildings that were rocketed in Sariwon. One of the best targets was the old Power Station at Sariwon, that had already been ruined by bombing, but it was being used to house trucks and at least eight of them were destroyed inside. Lieutenant Kelly had engine failure just after take off and ditched four miles ahead of *Theseus* and was picked up unhurt by *Sioux* after 13 minutes in icy water.

Christmas Day. Two Fury strikes were launched before all aircraft were grounded to check their fuel filters for water. During a routine Starred DI (Daily Inspection) water had been found in the filter of a Firefly. Some Furies were found to be in the same state when checks were carried out on all other aircraft. Flying was then reduced to CAP and A/S. The strikes rocketed two large warehouses, and strafed four trucks, two stores and troops, all with good results. As the big push by the enemy started that day, the early morning strike also had a look at the enemy airfields at Chinnampo, Ongjin and Haeju for signs of air activity; none was seen.

The last day of the patrol was another successful one for 807 Squadron, less so for 810, two of whose Fireflies still had water in their fuel systems; the last detail had to return after 30 minutes due to one of their number having engine trouble. The Furies' efforts were concentrated nearer the front line and included rocket attacks on large buildings and rail targets at Kaesong and Kumchon. Also attacked were troops, two stores-carrying camels and a mule. On completion of the day's flying, course was set for Sasebo in company with *Cossack*, *Charity*, *Consort* and *Constance*.

The ship's and CAG's statistics for the three weeks

5th – 26th December were:

steamed	5054 miles
carried out	630 sorties
flown	1630 hours
fired	38,000 rounds 20 mm
fired	1412 R/Ps

Theseus anchored in Sasebo during the next afternoon, where three new pilots, Lieutenants Shirras, Beavan and Curry joined, and she then left early next morning for Kure. During the forenoon twelve Furies and four Fireflies took off for gunnery and flight drill exercises and a fly-past over Sasebo. Four Furies were then used for deck landing practice for the three new arrivals and for Lieutenant (E) Checketts who had been doing AEO's duties for the past month and was out of flying practice. All landed on at noon and flying finished for the Christmas break.

December 1950.   *(Cane)*

Having anchored in the Inland Sea a few miles from Kure for the night, *Theseus* secured alongside the floating pontoon in Kure dockyard the following morning where *Unicorn was* already secured the other side. Two Furies and two Fireflies were disembarked to *Unicorn* and three replacement Furies and one Firefly received. Those who went ashore into Kure for the first time reported it as 'much quieter than Sasebo — but nevertheless equally unattractive!!'

Sunday 31st December was *Theseus'* big day, the one chosen for Christmas celebrations and the announcement of half-yearly promotions. Commanders Larkin and Hopkins were both promoted to Captain, and Lieutenant Commanders White, Compston, Thompson and Stovin-Bradford all promoted to Commander. The Commander in Chief, Admiral Sir E.J. Patrick Brind, gave a short talk to the ship's company at Divisions, congratulating the ship on their efforts and saying his farewells.

As a result of the promotions, Lieutenant Commander Pattisson became Lieutenant Commander (Flying), Lieutenant Commander Smith became AGC, Lieutenant Commander Coy became CO 810 Squadron, and Lieutenant Bevans (promoted to Lieutenant Commander) became CO 807 Squadron.

Theseus had been carrying out intensive flying during practically the whole of December; her aircrew needed a rest, and there was an accumulation of maintenance items on the aircraft that could not be carried out at sea. For some time Admiral Andrewes had been making strenuous efforts to get a relief carrier or carriers from US 7th Fleet to take her place. By 24th December X Corps evacuation had been completed from Hungnam, and on the 26th USS *Badoeng Strait*, wearing the flag of Rear Admiral Ruble, and the escort carrier *Sicily* arrived off Inchon for duty in the Yellow Sea.

> Admiral Andrewes reported: 'Since arriving in the operational area on 5th December HMS *Theseus'* aircraft had flown 630 accident-free sorties in 18 flying days. This averaged more than one sortie per flying day for each pilot and each aircraft, a fine and enviable achievement, brought about by a combination of skill and stamina on the part of the aircrews and of hard work and keenness on the part of the air group's maintenance personnel.' The Boyd Trophy for 1950 was later awarded to 17th Carrier Air Group.

The table below shows an interesting comparison between the operations carried out by the aircraft carriers of the British Pacific Fleet (Task Force 57) in 1945, and those carried out by *Theseus*. The two sets of figures are not strictly comparable — there were great differences in the types of operations, in casualties and so on — but it does indicate the pressure at which the single light fleet carrier had been operating.

	TF 57 March April 1945	*Theseus* October November 1950	TF 57 May 1945	*Theseus* December 1950
Total sorties	2343	670	2249	632
Sorties per carrier	585	670	562	632
Average number of aircraft per carrier	about 54	28	54	33
Days operating	12	22	11	18
Period from first operational day — days	26	29	21	22

Theseus was spending longer at sea than her successors were to do, but she tended to fly fewer sorties per day. In December, for example, she spent 23 days at sea, in which periods of 10, 4, and 4 days flying were broken by 3 days and 1 day non-flying before she returned to Sasebo. The later carriers were to operate a more 'routine' war.

Lieutenant Commander P.H. London DSC, who was to command 802 Squadron in *Ocean* in 1952, had flown Corsairs as Senior Pilot of 1842 Squadron in *Formidable* in the BPF. He says:

'…operations against Japan were "our" war. There were thousands of prisoners to be liberated. We did not know that the atom bomb was being developed. We expected a long hard slog to invade and conquer Japan. The chances of survival were slim. My average sortie in Korea in Sea Furies was about two hours..[whereas]..in Corsairs against Japan and the islands it was more like three hours. The flak was heavier. The targets more specific, such as airfields, dockyards and so on. We spent longer at sea. We flew larger strikes, 16 aircraft at a time. We had individual maintenance and divisional duties for the pilots. I came away from all that with a much greater sense of achievement than I came away from Korea.

'Another main difference between the operations in the BPF and those in Korea was the carrier operating efficiency. In the BPF the Task Force consisted of four fleet carriers, two battleships, and a massive escort of cruisers and destroyers. When operating aircraft, the whole lot had to turn into wind. The USN had mastered group carrier technique and we were trying to prove we were as good as they were. I think we

Three replacement Sea Furies on a lighter.   *(Motley)*

succeeded. In Korea, however, we were operating a single carrier with
a single escort, so that the ship could turn into wind at the drop of a hat
as it were. This led to much greater flexibility in our operations and we
got deck-landing and take-off intervals down to record low levels.'

41st Independent R.M. Commando, under the command of Lieutenant Colonel
D.B. Drysdale MBE, had arrived in Tokyo on 10th September, just too late to be
able to take part in the Inchon operation. Their training had included four successful
raids in conjunction with US naval forces on enemy communications on the east
coast of Korea at the beginning of October. In mid-November they were ordered to
join the US Marines in the Chosin area. The Commando had no arctic clothing, no
transport and no tentage, but after getting hold of some equipment it moved off, in
borrowed transport, to join the US 7th Regimental Combat Team at Yudam-ni to act
as reconnaissance on the left flank of the regiment in its north-westerly advance.

Elements of the US 7th Division had reached Hyesanjin on the Manchurian
border — the deepest penetration that UN forces were to make into north Korea
during the war — on 21st November, whilst two RoK divisions ranged far up the
east coast. The leading units of 1st Marine Division had reached Yudam-ni, at the
north-west corner of Chosin reservoir, on 25th November, intending to attack the
road and rail junction of Kang-yi next day. They were thwarted by a Chinese
attack in strength, coinciding with the Chinese offensive against 8th Army in the
west, not only on their leading elements but for thirty miles down their only
supply route to the coast at Hungnam 78 miles away. There was no doubt that a
general withdrawal of UN forces was necessary.

There followed a fighting retreat by the Marine division for which it would be hard to find a parallel. Under constant attack by very superior numbers, the column slowly fought its way down the narrow, tortuous, ice-covered, mountain road toward the sea. The weather was execrable, with frequent blinding snow storms and temperatures about 25 degrees below zero, from which friend and foe alike suffered severely. There were two factors in favour of the Marines which were exploited to the full and more than counterbalanced the numerical superiority of the enemy — the UN command of the sea and air. Heavily laden US Air Force C-119s dropped cargoes of ammunition, medical supplies, water, food and petrol as required — on one occasion eight 2500 lb. spans to replace a bridge blown by the enemy; helicopters picked up the seriously wounded who, together with the sick and frost-bite cases were later evacuated from temporary air-strips at Hagaru-ri and Koto-ri lower down the Changjin River. Close support by aircraft from *Leyte*, *Philippine Sea* and *Badoeng Strait*, and Marine flights from Yonpo airfield was provided on an unprecedented scale, more than 200 aircraft being employed daily. On 4th December, for example, there were 239 sorties, 128 from the fleet carriers, 34 from the escort carrier and 77 from Yonpo.

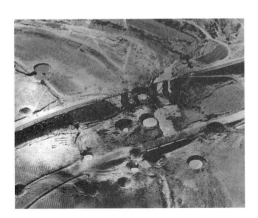

Bridge targets destroyed by HMS *Theseus*.   *(Cane)*

It was in these operations that Colonel Drysdale's Commando first saw serious fighting. It reached Koto-ri on 28th November, the day after the enemy had launched the offensive that had cut the road in several places between there and Hagaru-ri and between Hagaru-ri and Yudam-ni.

At first light on 29th November 41st Commando and the US Marine company moved out up the road to Hagaru-ri. They were joined by fourteen tanks which led the attack till they were a mile south of Pusong-ni. They were held up until shortly before dark by Chinese machine gun and mortar fire in what became known as Hellfire Valley. They were considering withdrawing to Koto-ri when a liaison officer brought a message saying it was imperative they reached Hagaru-ri at all costs. Led by the tanks, the column fought their way through three ambushes and arrived in Hagaru-ri that night. 41st Commando lost most of its equipment and transport, and suffered 70 casualties out of nearly 200 men, including Colonel Drysdale, who was severely wounded in the arm, but continued to direct and command his force throughout their difficult operation.

On 6th December the withdrawal from Hagaru-ri started, fighting a fierce battle that night as the rear-guard, and being cut off next day from the rest of the column until one troop could destroy enemy machine-gunners and snipers who were harassing them. They reached Koto-ri that night.

The following morning the break-out from there started. The 41st Commando reconnoitred enemy-held hills, climbing through two feet of snow in a blinding snow storm; the night was spent in the open in 47 degrees of frost. It was so cold the sweat on the Marines' feet froze inside their boots.

The column made slow and tortuous progress down the pass along a road mined in several places, under constant machine gun and sniper fire. They had close air support from the American carriers offshore — indeed the support was sometimes so close that some Marines later claimed that they owed their survival to the heat from the napalm dropped on nearby Chinese.

At last, after more than four days and 23 miles of almost constant fighting and marching over the mountains on empty stomachs and no sleep they reached Majondong and were taken in lorries and open cattle trucks to a tented camp at Hungnam. During this period the unit had suffered 98 casualties — 13 killed, 39 wounded, 27 missing and 19 from frost-bite, exposure and pneumonia.

'As Commanding General of the 1st Marine Division', wrote General Oliver P. Smith to Colonel Drysdale,

> 'I desire to take this opportunity to acknowledge the high qualities of leadership, heroism, devotion to duty and self-sacrifice displayed by the officers and men of the 41st Commando of the Royal Marines, while serving with this division in Korea. This history records many outstanding feats of heroism, devotion to duty, and self-sacrifice by

units and individuals alike. The performance of the 41st Commando during their drive from Hagaru-ri to the south will, in the perspective of history, take equal rank with the best exploits of the Royal Marines. I can give you no higher compliment than to state that your conduct and that of the officers and men under your command was worthy of the highest traditions of the Marines.'

In 1957 the Commando was awarded a US Presidential Citation for its services with the US Marine Corps seven years earlier. It was handed to the CO of the re-born unit in 1960 by the Commandant General, the Commando having been disbanded in 1952.

The Presidential Unit Citation is awarded by the President of the United States to the Navy. The Citation was awarded in May 1953 to the 'First Marine Division, Reinforced'. The 41st Independent Commando, Royal Marines, was not then listed among the reinforcing units owing to regulations excluding the award to foreign units. But by Executive Order 10694 of 10th January 1957 this restriction was abolished and 41st Commando was added to the Citation under the new heading 'Attached Foreign Units'.

Citation:

> For extraordinary heroism and outstanding performance of duty in action against enemy aggressor forces in the Chosin Reservoir and Koto-ri area of Korea from 27th November to 11th December 1950. When the full fury of the enemy counter attack struck both the Eighth Army and the Tenth Corps on 27th and 28th November 1950, the First Marine Division, Reinforced, operating as the left flank division of the Tenth Corps, launched a daring assault westwards from Yudam-ni in an effort to cut the road and rail communications of hostile forces attacking the Eighth Army and, at the same time, continued its mission of protecting a vital main supply route consisting of a tortuous mountain road running southward to Chinhung-ni, approximately thirty-five miles distant. Ordered to withdraw to Hamhung in company with attached army and other friendly units in the face of tremendous pressure in the Chosin Reservoir area, the Division began an epic battle against the bulk of the enemy Third Route Army and, while small intermediate garrisons at Hagaru-ri and Toko-ri held firmly against repeated and determined attacks by hostile forces, gallantly fought its way successively to Hagaru-ri, Koto-ri, Chinhung-ni and Hamhung over twisting, icy and mountainous roads in sub-zero temperatures. Battling desperately night and day in the face of almost insurmountable odds throughout a period of two weeks of intense and sustained combat, the First Marine Division, Reinforced, emerged from its ordeal as a fighting unit with its

wounded, with its guns and equipment and with its prisoners, decisively defeating seven enemy divisions, together with elements of three others, and inflicting major losses which seriously impaired the military effectiveness of the hostile forces for a considerable period of time. The valiant fighting spirit, relentless perseverance and heroic fortitude of the officers and men of the First Marine Division, Reinforced, in battle against vastly outnumbering enemy, were in keeping with the highest traditions of the United States Naval Service.

From 3rd to 7th December UN forces and material were withdrawn through Wonsan. Covering fire by the 8-inch-gun cruiser *St Paul* and two destroyers held the North Korean forces in the neighbourhood at such a distance from the UN perimeter that the troops were never seriously threatened.

General Almond's main forces were evacuated from Hungnam between 10th and 24th December. Rear Admiral Doyle (CTF 90) with his Amphibious Force assumed command of all naval activities and of all air activity within 35 miles of Hungnam. During the operation the Hungnam area was covered from the enemy by seven carriers. Rear Admiral Ewen's TF 77 — the fast carriers *Philippine Sea, Leyte, Valley Forge* and *Princeton* — flew close air support and air cover for forces inside the embarkation area during daylight hours. Outside the area, they attacked enemy supply lines, supported friendly ground operations, and provided air cover for the escort carriers and shipping to and from the embarkation area. They also contributed to 'heckling' missions by night in co-operation with the 5th US Air Force. Rear Admiral Ruble's escort carriers, *Sicily, Badoeng Strait* and USS *Bataan*, gave additional cover to the ground forces and shipping in the Hungnam port area.

Gun-fire support was provided by the battleship *Missouri*, two cruisers *St Paul* and *Rochester*, seven destroyers and three LSMRs. 'Deep' support could be given at ranges of up to ten miles. For the final day of the withdrawal, 24th December, a concentrated naval gun-fire barrage was maintained in a strip approximately 2500 yards wide and 3000 yards from the beaches and harbour.

There was no attempt by the enemy at any time to interfere with the Hungnam evacuation from the air or from the sea. Fearful of Chinese air attack, a radar picket destroyer was maintained off the coast and a US Navy and Marine Corps umbrella was maintained over Hungnam, the 22 shipboard squadrons (4 Panther, 14 Corsair, 4 Skyraider) continuously harassing the enemy.

It was an orderly, tough and bitter, fighting withdrawal — described by General O.P. Smith as 'an attack in another direction'. Without air power smashing Chinese concentrations, the fall back from Chosin would have degenerated into a disaster. Throughout the withdrawal to Hungnam Chinese troops were never able effectively to counter the Navy/Marine system of CAS. The Communists best defensive weapons were rifles and light machine-guns.

The US Navy had organised an Inchon in reverse, withdrawing personnel and whatever equipment and supplies they could, while destroying what had to be left behind. Between 11th and 24th December 105,000 military personnel, 91,000 refugees, 350,000 tons of cargo and 17,500 vehicles were methodically loaded and shipped to Pusan.

That the evacuation was a brilliantly executed operation there can be no doubt. The time was short and the planning extremely complicated. It was the first occasion on which a US amphibious force was called on to handle a large-scale evacuation, as opposed to an assault landing. But it must be remembered that there was no opposition by aircraft, submarines, or ground forces equipped with artillery; had there been, there would probably have been losses. Admiral Joy summed up the operation as follows:

> 'The Hungnam evacuation showed that a well-trained and well-led amphibious force can carry out an amphibious operation in reverse as effectively as the conventional type. It again emphasises the importance of having adequate forces in being and in a state of full combat readiness.'

By the end of December the UN forces were holding a line from Munsan-ni in the west, south of the Imjin River and roughly along the 38th Parallel to north of Yangyang on the east coast.

An important change had occurred in the UN Command on shore. General Walton Walker, the commander of the 8th Army had been killed in a road accident on 23rd December and he was succeeded by Lieutenant General Matthew B. Ridgway. At the same time X Corps was placed under the command of General Ridgway, thus ending the peculiar set-up under which the eastern and western sectors were independent commands in the field, though both were under the overall direction of General MacArthur in Tokyo.

The lull was shattered during the afternoon of 31st December. Fighting flared up along the whole front. The 8th Army carried out an orderly, but extremely rapid, withdrawal south of the River Han; Seoul was abandoned on 3rd January, and President Syngman Rhee and his Government retired once again to Pusan. By 14th January 1951 the line was stabilised from Pyongtaek in the west to Wonju to Chumunchin on the east coast.

On 15th January, a reconnaissance in force by US troops in the Pyongtaek area initiated a movement which brought the UN forces once more across the 38th Parallel by the end of March, a position approximately maintained for the remainder of the war.

Fifth Patrol

When the Chinese offensive started on 31st December, Admiral Andrewes was at Sasebo, *Theseus*, *Cossack* and *Constance were* at Kure, *Badoeng Strait* and *Sicily* were in the Yellow Sea, and the usual blockade and gunfire support patrols were being carried out.

During the first few days, the main naval interest at Inchon was covering the evacuation of UN forces to Taechon and Pusan. Rear Admiral L.A. Thackerey USN, who was in overall command of the evacuation and withdrawal from both east and west coasts of Korea, handed all ships in Inchon back to Admiral Andrewes' command on 7th January.

Theseus left Kure on 5th January to go to Sasebo whence she sailed for the west coast wearing Admiral Andrewes' flag.

Operational flying started on 7th January with the main task to maintain a coastal reconnaissance from the front line to Chinnampo, and to prevent troop movements or supplies from reaching the enemy by sea. Information had been received that North Korean and Chinese Communist forces might commence laying minefields and start moving troop convoys by night under their protection. Pilots had been warned to keep a good look-out for minelayers or large junks fitted with mine-laving gear. All vessels south of the 38th Parallel were to be reported and those ships north of the parallel were for the first three or four days to be given warning bursts of fire ahead. This was intended to give them warning that later they would be sunk, and thus to avoid the slaughter of refugees. The enemy showed little activity along the coast, many inlets and harbours being frozen up, and since the air effort required to maintain this daily surveillance was not so great, Admiral Andrewes offered up to 20 sorties per day to the 5th US Air Force in support of land operations. Co-ordination was effected through the Joint Operations Centre at Taegu, and by the afternoon of 8th January *Theseus'* aircraft were working in close support of US 25th Division on the left flank of the line southward of Osan. This was the first time close support had been given by Fleet Air Arm aircraft during the war; the control was mainly by airborne controllers using Harvard trainer type aircraft, known as Mosquitoes, which worked well in spite of some congestion on the voice circuit in use.

Apart from these activities, regular coastal patrols covered the enemy-held coast at least once a day, and also kept an eye on the still-unused airfields at Haeju, Ongjin and near Chinnampo. Attacks on shore targets were limited to the Chinnampo area, since friendly irregulars were operating south of the Taedong estuary, and refugees were leaving Chodo and other islands.

The distance aircraft had to cover between the operating area and their target area inland was considerable, and Admiral Andrewes stationed a 'bird-dog' south of the Inchon Gulf while flying was in progress. This was initiated by Coelsort on

14th January and withdrawn on 15th February when Suwon and Kimpo airfields and the port of Inchon were again in Allied hands, and with a harbour entrance control vessel in the approaches.

Ongjin airfield – 807 Squadron.   *(FAAM)*

The weather, showers and gusting winds, on 7th January caused the first details to be cancelled; CAP and A/S patrols were flown from 1000 to dusk. The Fireflies carried out AR of Haeju, dropping bombs on buildings reported by RoK troops as North Korean hide-outs, and photo reconnaissance over the various emergency airfields, the alternatives to Kimpo which was then in enemy hands. The Furies of 807 Squadron flew three strikes each of two aircraft armed with four R/P and cannon:

1) Kaesong — Seoul — Kimpo area,
2) Choppeki Point, along the coast to Chinnampo,
3) Choppeki to Inchon.

Large tin roofed buildings north of Haeju airfield, reported to house troops, were strafed and hit with eight R/Ps, and other buildings were destroyed and set on fire. Kimpo airfield was visited and a large store building, hit by three R/Ps, caught fire with black smoke rising to 3000 feet. Other huts and oil drums, as well as a Shooting Star and a Corsair — not totally destroyed by retreating Americans — were all strafed. The positions of junks and other minor vessels in the patrol areas were reported. Suwon airfield was reported destroyed and tracks were observed at ferry points over the frozen river Imjin. Thousands of refugees were seen streaming south along the Suwon to Osan road.

A full days flying was carried out next day with both Squadrons on AR in the forenoon and close support in the afternoon. 200 miles of coastline were searched for possible enemy forces or mine-layers, and airfields were inspected. All junks and RoK vessels were reported; no activity of any sort was observed at the airfields at Haeju and Onjong-ni; three warehouses were rocketed in the Haeju dock area. 100 miles of road were searched, three cars and a truck were beaten up, two oil dumps at Suwon were strafed of which one caught fire and two storage sheds near Haeju were destroyed by rockets.

Unusually, small groups of troops in parties of four to six men were observed on the Kumchon/Sariwon road. The Communist forces usually travelled overland by mountain trails and, being very clever at camouflage, were rarely seen by pilots.

The CAS details contacted the US 25th Division (which contained the British 29th Brigade) and were given an Air Controller, airborne in a Piper Cub or Harvard — 'Cobalt Mosquito' and 'Pickle Barrel'. As the targets were assigned by the Air Co-ordinator the aircraft event in and attacked, working on the front just ahead of the 25th Division. They were directed onto targets in Osan and to buildings containing an enemy command post and troops near Osan, obtaining direct hits. The pilots reported that the American controller seemed quite surprised at the accuracy of the attacks and confirmed that the correct targets had been hit and destroyed. The aircrews complained that he put a lot of heavy traffic on the air by thanking them 42 times in 2 minutes! The other detail were directed to attack a camouflaged radio hut, small concentrations of troops, and huts containing troops. 810 Squadron's diary commented:

> 'Generally speaking, all the aircrews felt as though they had, today, done
> a little more than their usual effort in helping the men in the front line.'

Bad weather, with the cloud base between 500 and 1000 feet and visibility reduced to less than one mile, restricted flying to the forenoon only on the 9th. The Furies completed an AR from Haeju to Chinnampo, seeing the usual fishing junk traffic and observing no unusual activity in the coastal area or in the Taedong estuary. Factories and railway storage sheds were attacked and set on fire in the Chinnampo area. One detail of Fireflies carried rockets instead of bombs which were dropped on targets round Haeju; the other detail carrying bombs jettisoned them because the cloud base was too low over the target for dive bombing.

Bad weather again held up the start of flying next day until 1015, and then prevented the planned army co-operation sorties in the forenoon. Both details had to attack alternative targets in the north, the Furies strafed groups of junks in the Han Can River and off the island of Kanghwa. The Fireflies attacked buildings, lorries and junks in Haeju and the island of Yongmae-do, the latter being a 'cry for aid' by RoK forces who had reported its being occupied by North Korean and Chinese forces. The Furies had more success with their close support missions during the afternoon. In spite of a low cloud base, snow showers and poor visibility, four aircraft contacted a ground observation point, 'Diplomat 14', situated near Osan. The target given was a village full of troublesome enemy troops which was rocketed, knocking down several houses, and on the second and third runs troops were strafed with cannon. The pilots noticed that the Allied troops were using red and yellow marker strips on the ground to mark their positions. The Furies carried out a final strike on the town of Oryu-Dong, attacking buildings which were left burning.

On the 11th snow storms, low cloud and restricted visibility again limited flying to two Furies on armed coastal reconnaissance who flew through snow storms to attack the village of Chang-ni containing Communist troops. One large and three smaller huts were destroyed in the centre of the village. One detail of Fireflies got to the front line where they found good weather for attacks. They were directed onto Chinese troops in front of 29th

Paengyong-do island with the village and beach used as an emergency airstrip.
(Emery)

Brigade who were bombed and strafed resulting in 200 casualties.

The 12th was replenishment day from *Wave Laird*. Weather conditions were by no means perfect, with snow showers and a cold wind, and rough seas causing connections to break and refuelling having soon to be discontinued.

No flying was possible next day due to heavy snow storms covering the flight deck and deck park. The day was spent clearing the snow and chipping ice.

On the 14th the weather improved enough for a full days flying, but another problem appeared. The catapult main reeving, which had been showing signs of stranding after only about 880 shots, became unusable during the afternoon. With a number of aircraft already airborne, the Furies had an adequate free take off run, but were stripped of long-range tanks and carried cannon armament only. The Fireflies, carrying normal armament and petrol loads, had to use RATOG, generally the first time for most pilots. No trouble was experienced in becoming airborne, but trouble did occur in jettisoning the equipment which left holes and indentations along the fuselage.

Weather round the target area gradually closed in as the day progressed, the cloud base dropping from 3,000 to 800 feet, while round the Yellow Sea the weather improved with sunshine for most of the afternoon.

The Furies started the day with an AR along the coast to Chinnampo, where it was observed that the railway line between Chinnampo and Pyongyang seemed to be extensively in use; engine sheds were rocketed and trucks strafed in the sidings. The Fireflies carried out AR in the Suwon airfield area, attacking stores. The Furies flew three and the Fireflies one close support missions for the 25th Division under the direction of American co-ordinators 'Cobalt 2' and 'Diplomat 14'. A factory south-west of Suwon was attacked, five huts were left burning in a village and a tunnel mouth was rocketed where motor transport tracks were seen to enter. Troops in groups of 10-12 were noticed in villages and on the roads in this area. Two Furies rendezvoused with the 'Cobalt' Mosquito at Suwon and were instructed to attack parties of troops. He then informed the Furies that he had to return to base because of fuel shortage, and that anything was fair game north of Osan. working in hazy conditions, with a 600 feet cloud base of 8/8 stratus and in mountainous valleys various targets were attacked — large store dumps on Suwon airfield were strafed, and a lorry and buildings hit with rockets. Six Furies armed only with cannon were directed by a ground controller 'Diplomat 14' to carry out a reconnaissance of the road from Suwon to Inchon. Parties of troops were seen moving along this road, at intervals interspersed with civilian refugees — or troops dressed as refugees — or troops mixed with refugees. Obvious parties of troops were strafed by aircraft. Fireflies were also part of the close support in the Osan area dropping 500 lb. bombs and causing 150 casualties in villages holding Chinese forces.

Two Furies carried out a road reconnaissance of Black 9, the name given to the Seoul to Kaesong road. The main roads leading from enemy held territory to their front line had been given code names by the Army who could then ask for certain sections of roads to be patrolled. Black 9 seemed to be well used, small parties of troops were seen on it and strafed. A number of makeshift bridges had been constructed along this route and tracks were seen leading to tunnels and villages near the road. Tracks were noticed leading into a haystack and none leading away — it was duly strafed and caught fire.

On 15th it was doubtful if flying could be started with a full deck park, but using RATOG for the Fireflies, and by ingenious parking, the Furies were launched in spite of a low natural wind speed. A full day's flying ensued with a total of 58 sorties being flown, the highest number so far, this to a certain extent being due to the fact that sortie lengths had to be reduced to two hours duration due to the reduction in fuel carried by the Furies, and having about twelve aircraft airborne to keep an uncluttered deck for Fury take-offs. By this time UN land forces had started their reconnaissance in force through Osan and Suwon; as a result a considerable number of enemy troops were on the move and the Fireflies and Furies made the most of their opportunities, inflicting about 350 casualties on them. During the day Lieutenant Highett carried out the 1000th accident free deck landing.

The first detail of Furies were directed by 'Cobalt' Mosquito to targets east of Suwon. Freshly dug gun emplacements were strafed and troops were seen leaving the dug outs. Various parties of troops and carts laden with stores were strafed on the roads. Light flak was experienced from one village. The Fireflies provided top cover for an army spearhead on a road leading north to Osan; the infantry was seen deploring and about 24 tanks marked with orange and yellow strips were seen advancing. The next detail was directed by 'Hazard' Mosquito to concentrations of troops north-east of Suwon. Many groups of troops moving south and east in parties of sizes varying from 10 to 50 were strafed. 'Cobalt' Mosquito sent another detail to the Suwon area to attack two small villages. A village hall of one was set on fire and troops running out were strafed. Most of the bridges were seen to be down on the

Seoul to Suwon road, but they had been by-passed and the road appeared to have been well used. A pair of Furies were sent on an AR to an area west of Haeju in support of a cut-off RoK unit who were reported in contact with enemy forces and who needed help. The aircraft carried out a detailed search but nothing unusual was sighted. The aircraft reported to *Kenya* who was in contact with an RoK vessel and was sending a boat across to obtain further information. All roads in the area were patrolled, and no unusual activity was seen on the airfield at Haeju or in the docks.

The 16th was a record day of 60 sorties. It was noted in 807's diary that a signal had been received from the Joint Operations Centre, Korea, stating that the carrier Air Group had flown more sorties the previous day than the entire 5th US Air Force. Apart from two reconnaissance details by the Furies, one along the coast from Chinnampo to Haeju and the other in the Seoul/Inchon area, both Squadrons were engaged in CAS to 25th Division. The reconnaissance missions produced the destruction of two cars and one oil tank; apart from these, large numbers of refugees were seen round Seoul and being embarked into sampans from the shore to an RoK vessel in the Chodo channel.

Mosquitoes 'Cobalt' and 'Hazard' directed the CAS flights onto enemy troops in dugouts and huts in the Osan and Suwon areas causing a number of casualties. During the afternoon Mosquito 'Hazard', a Harvard whose wing tips had been painted red as a recognition feature, seemed to be systematically working on the villages in a river valley five miles east of Suwon, on the right flank of the advancing UN column. The Furies orbited until four Corsairs had finished dive-bombing three villages and they were then given the next two. All the villages were alleged to contain enemy troops. The Fireflies bombed Suwon to assist the army patrol advancing on the town from Osan. The Fireflies that had bombed factories west of Suwon experienced intense light flak. On completion of the day's flying course was set for Sasebo which was reached the following day during the dog watches. Admiral Andrewes hauled down his flag and he and his staff disembarked for *Ladybird*.

Summary of the CAG's activities for the ten days from 7th to 17th January:

Miles steamed	3870
Sorties flown	301

Ammunition expended

20mm	47,770
60lb. rockets	236
500lb. bombs	144

Destroyed	136 buildings	13 oil dumps/tanks
	5 warehouses	1 railway station
	7 factories	26 junks
	5 trucks	3 power stations
	5 command posts 2 locomotive sheds	
	3 railway wagons 1 gun emplacement	
	1 railway tunnel 1 jetty	
	2 power sub-stations 1 mortar position	
	3 staff cars	

In addition 1000 troops were probably killed or wounded. A large amount of damage was caused under the direction of army control teams to villages around Osan, Suwon and Seoul areas.

Obviously it was beyond the capacity of a single carrier to operate permanently without periodical spells in harbour for rest and maintenance, and for some time Admiral Andrewes had been pressing for additional air support on the west coast. Early in January Admiral Struble felt able to detail the light carrier USS *Bataan* with screening destroyers to alternate with *Theseus* as TE 95.11. *Bataan*, carrying a US Marine Corps air group with 30 Corsairs arrived in Sasebo on 10th January and relieved *Theseus* as CTE 95.11 on the 16th. This welcome addition to Admiral Andrewes force enabled him to work the carriers normally on an eighteen day cycle, though naturally occasions occurred when the exigencies of war necessitated other arrangements. This cycle consisted of eight or nine days flying and one replenishing at sea; one additional day each way on passage, leaving six or seven days in harbour for maintenance and rest.

During the Army withdrawal, Admiral Andrewes had suggested holding a small number of islands off the coast with RoK Marine garrisons of 50-100 men. They would be useful as anti-mining and as advance patrol bases for RoK patrol craft. The islands chosen were Chodo in the approaches to the River Taedong, where there was the greatest mining menace, Paengyong-do and Taechong-do which, together with Chodo, controlled the only inshore route with reasonable deep water where large ships could get within gun range, and Tok Chok-do controlling the approaches to Inchon. The inshore route covered the Hwanghae promontory and allowed the

UN to pose a continuous threat of amphibious operations in the enemy's rear. There were similar garrisons on the east coast in the approaches to Wonsan.

On the east coast naval aircraft of TF 77 were employed on the interdiction of road and rail communications. Though these were a considerable embarrassment to the Communists in the next two-and-a-half years, they failed in their objective of isolating enemy forces in the battle area from their supplies. In addition to interdiction, CAS sorties were flown for ground troops; for naval gun-fire spotting; and for AR. Gunfire was provided by cruisers, destroyers and sometimes by the battleship *Missouri*. Enemy minelaying continued from junks and sampans, and the augmented US minesweeping flotilla was kept busy.

The furthest point the Chinese advance reached was on 24th January when the line was stabilised from Pyongtaek in the west to Wonju in the centre to a point on the east coast some ten miles north of Samchok. During the next three months, to the middle of April, the UN forces advanced to a line roughly along the River Imjin to Chorwon then eastwards to Hwachon, thence to the east coast near Taepo-ri. On 14th March Seoul was reoccupied by the UN for the second time.

The Communist Spring Offensive started on 22nd April with attacks on the left and centre-left, resulting in another UN withdrawal to the Han River but retaining Seoul. It was at the start of this offensive that the 1st Battalion the Gloucestershire Regiment fought their gallant rear-guard action at Solma-ri on the Imjin River, partly covering the difficult withdrawal of the Royal Northumberland Fusiliers and the Royal Ulster Rifles, during the three days and nights from 22nd to 25th April. When the battle was over only 169 of 850 Gloucesters mustered for roll-call, over half the remainder were in enemy hands.

That the UN forces did not retreat further, and that their counter offensive was launched so promptly and effectively, was due to the dedicated and inspired leadership of General Matthew B. Ridgway who successfully motivated his beaten and battered forces to make important gains, and decisively to demonstrate their ability to turn the tables on the Chinese. 'We now had a tested, tough, and highly confident army,' wrote Ridgway, 'experienced in this sort of fighting, inured to the vicissitudes of the weather and possessed of firepower far exceeding anything we had been able to use on the enemy heretofore. The only development that could possibly cause us to withdraw from the peninsula was, I felt sure, massive intervention by the Soviets.' In the spring of 1951, such intervention was not altogether an impossibility.

On 11th April General Douglas MacArthur was replaced as Supreme Commander of the United Nations Forces in Korea by General Ridgway. General James A. Van Fleet was appointed as Commander Eighth Army.

In mid-May the Communists launched another offensive forcing the right of the UN armies back to a line some miles south of the 38th Parallel. Towards the end of May the UN counter-attacked and forced the Communists to retreat to what was to become the Main Line of Resistance for the remainder of the war, apart from some continuous, small, exchanges of real estate between the opposing forces. There was to be many a bloody battle during the next two years, with such evocative names as the Iron Triangle, the Punchbowl, Pork Chop, Heartbreak Ridge, Old Baldy, Luke the Gook's Castle.

On 18th January, during the rest and maintenance period in Sasebo, the following signal awarding the Boyd Trophy for 1950 to the 17th Carrier Air Group, for operations in Korea, was received in *Theseus*. The trophy is a silver model of a Fairey Swordfish, presented in 1946 by the Fairey Aviation Company Limited, in commemoration of the work for Naval aviation of Admiral Sir Dennis Boyd, KCB, CBE, DSC. It is awarded annually to the Naval pilot(s) or aircrew(s) who, in the opinion of the Flag Officer (Air) Home, (now FONA), have achieved the finest feat of aviation during the previous year.

> TO: THESEUS   FROM: ADMIRALTY
> PERSONAL FROM FIFTH SEA LORD
> HEARTIEST CONGRATULATIONS TO THESEUS AND HER
> AIR GROUP UPON CROWNING A FINE RUN OF
> SUCCESSES AND RECORDS BY GAINING THE BOYD
> TROPHY, AND ACHIEVING THE OUTSTANDING FEAT OF
> 1000 CONSECUTIVE ACCIDENT FREE DECK LANDINGS.
> /JAN 51

Sixth Patrol

Before leaving for the next patrol a helicopter on loan from the USN was embarked in place of the Sea Otter which was sent ashore for *Unicorn* to fit a new engine. On January 25th *Theseus* sailed for Korean waters, carrying out DLPs for the new pilots whilst on passage.

The naval forces on the west coast, in addition to maintaining the blockade gave considerable assistance to the left flank of the UN army. On 23rd January *St Paul*, wearing the flag of Rear Admiral R.H. Hillenkoetter USN, with US destroyers *Hank* and *Borrie* arrived off Inchon (after the approaches had been scanned for mines by aircraft from USS *Bataan*) and carried out interdiction and harassing fire. They were reinforced at intervals by *Ceylon, Cayuga* and *Nootka*. This was to be an exciting first patrol for *Nootka*: she and another destroyer had a brush with a battery on Wolmi-do, she sank a floating mine in the approaches to Inchon, and she picked up a pilot who had ditched from *Theseus*.

Bataan was relieved by *Theseus* on 25th January with *Cossack, Constance,*

Comus and *Consort* in company. With fine weather at the start, in eight days flying 408 sorties were flown, of which 307 were offensive.

Throughout the 26th the Fireflies, operating with a heavier armament load of four 60 lb. HE rockets and two 500 lb. bombs, carried out CAS missions guided by Mosquito controllers. Their targets in the area north-west of Suwon, all successfully attacked, were villages suspected of harbouring Chinese forces, gun emplacements and road blocks. The Furies first detail was CAS in Suwon area, strafing and rocketing troops and houses. Routine reconnaissance was carried out round the coast from Chinnampo to Haeju but no activity was observed, though it was noted that Ongjin airfield had been recently bombed. Reconnaissance of roads in the Kaesong to Yonan area led to buildings in Yonan being rocketed, and several junks were strafed in the entrance to the Han River. Factories west of Kangwha were attacked with some success, troops and a few small boats were strafed. Lieutenant Commander Bevans' aircraft, operating over Sariwon, was hit by 40 mm flak on the top of the rudder making a hole approximately one foot square. He returned to the ship and made a successful landing although he experienced considerable lack of rudder control. Two spotting details were carried out with *St Paul*; a lack of suitable bombardment targets in the first resulting in the aircraft attacking troops in trenches, and in the second *St Paul* scored three hits on the target north-east of Inchon after 45 minutes shooting. In the afternoon an AR of the Seoul to Kaesong and Han River areas was largely uneventful except for setting a large junk on fire with rockets and strafing smaller ones. During a forenoon CAP detail the aircraft piloted by Lieutenant A.C. Beavan was seen to flick during a tight turn and seemingly spin, the spin continuing until the aircraft hit the sea about ten miles east of the fleet. HMS *Comus* was at the point of impact within 15 minutes and found various pieces of wreckage but unfortunately no sign of the pilot.

The Fireflies had another day of CAS on 27th with the general area of attacks being north-west of Suwon. Anyang-ni was bombed and a factory on its outskirts was rocketed. Other aircraft, under Mosquito control, dropped their bombs and rockets on villages and troop entrenchments which were ahead of our advancing forces. Mr. Young on his first solo A/S patrol, seeing a suspect submarine promptly dealt it a blow with his depth charges — and found a whale quietly floundering along afterwards! (Activity on an A/S patrol for a change). The Furies had one successful air spot for *St Paul*. Their AR details of the coast to Chinnampo, from Haeju to Seoul, and of roads to the north of Seoul, resulted in buildings being rocketed and railway trucks and groups of people being strafed. The early CAS detail rocketed and straffed a village under the control of the airborne 'Cobalt Mosquito Special' and a ground controller 'Desert 14'. The AGC, whilst flying between Inchon and Seoul, received a hit from small-arms or 25 mm fire somewhere in the engine of his aircraft and was obliged to ditch near *Nootka* who was 'Bird dog' patrol. He was picked up and on board within five minutes, uninjured by the ditching but suffering from the effects of the icy waters — suitable 'beverages' supplied by *Nootka* soon put this to rights. On completion of flying he was returned by jack-stay transfer. When *Nootka* came alongside to transfer him, she made the signal 'Your bird, Sir. My tail is wagging'.

The Fireflies again devoted their main efforts to CAS next day, bombing and strafing troop positions and villages to the west and north-west of Suwon. The diary commented 'Although results of these attacks are noticeable when against villages, the others against troop positions and entrenchments are very hard to observe fully, very often no enemy movements seen before the attack, let alone afterwards.' The Furies, in addition to reconnoitring the coasts and roads, spotted for shoots by *Ceylon* and *Hank*, some successful, others not.

During the reconnaissance of roads north and north-east of Seoul Lieutenant Keighley-Peach's aircraft was hit by A/A fire and he was obliged to crash land in a narrow valley near Tongduchon-ni. As he jettisoned the cockpit hood it temporarily stunned him and smoke filled the cockpit. The aircraft slid along for about 200 yards before coming to rest in a small copse, the tail breaking off. Keighley-Peach extricated himself from the wreckage and hid in a ditch until he was picked up by an American helicopter some 90 minutes later. A CAP was maintained by the remaining aircraft of his flight, relieved by another section, until the arrival of the helicopter. The wrecked aircraft resisted the efforts of the later Furies to set it on fire by strafing.

On the 29th Furies spotted for *St Paul* to direct her fire onto the Nippon Vehicle factory at Inchon, thirty 8 inch shells landing in the target area, causing fires and destroying several buildings. Other aircraft reconnoitred as far north as Ongjin where they rocketed a hangar on the airfield. Three aircraft were given targets in the Suwon area by 'Cobalt Three' Mosquito where they carried out a successful attack on a village at Faewango, causing a number of casualties, and strafing a camouflaged gun emplacement and trenches. The Firefly details concentrated on Mosquito directed CAS on villages in the Suwon area, where troop positions, a road block and an observation post were attacked with good results.

The Fireflies again devoted their efforts to Mosquito directed CAS details on the 30th, their one AR flight having to be changed due to poor weather in the north. They found it was difficult to observe the results of their attacks on troop emplacements due to the type of emplacement and their dispositions. The Furies spotted twice for bombardments by *Cayuga* in and round Inchon, targets being gun emplacements and an island, both with fair results Four aircraft gave support to the army north-east of Suwon, 'Lunchbox 14' (the controller), being very pleased with the results. Lieutenant Keighley-Peach was brought back to the ship in a Firefly, piloted by Lieutenant Davis, from Taegu — he was received with a big welcome and a band (of sorts!). He had suffered only shock and superficial injuries from his ordeal.

The 31st was a non-flying day, being devoted to replenishment and maintenance. The weather on the 1st February affected flying, low cloud over the front preventing support for the army until the afternoon; the early details attacked factories, bridges and tunnels in the clear area north of Haeju. The afternoon details bombed villages and factories north of Suwon, and, under Mosquito control, bombed, rocketed and strafed mortar positions on a hillside in the woods — good results were reported by the controller. The poor early morning weather also prevented the Furies from carrying out their assigned air-spots for bombardments by *Ceylon*, instead they event north and attacked dock installations in the Haeju area. During one CAS mission no Mosquito controller was available so large buildings at Anyang were rocketed and strafed. After this attack a ground controller, 'Rake-Off', called for assistance, and ridges near Kumnojong were strafed under his direction. Though the weather improved sufficiently during the afternoon to enable a shoot to go ahead, no suitable targets were found and the aircraft joined up with a CAS flight to attack ridges and mortar positions under the control of 'Desert 14' and 'Mosquito 5', with good results.

During the 2nd, the series of 1463 accident-free deck landings was broken when a Fury heavy-landed on a pitching deck in gusty weather, bursting a tyre, and straining the fuselage at the undercarriage attachment points. A morning detail of Furies carried out a successful shoot with *Ceylon* south west of Inchon, hitting stores, houses, railway lines and trenches, the aircraft then rocketing and strafing the same targets. Later in the afternoon the aircraft detailed to spot for *Ceylon* found she had forsaken them and was working with the Army, so they proceeded to contact 'Cobalt' Mosquito who directed them to attack the village of Mungham-ni believed to be containing numerous troops; a successful rocket attack was made on two large buildings in the centre of the village. The same controller sent another group of four aircraft to attack targets in the hills south of Inchon. A large fire was started after a strafing run on an oil container, and gun positions and troops were rocketed and strafed, causing numerous casualties. Earlier, three aircraft on a CAS detail were asked to act as CAP over a Mosquito aircraft shot down by flak. This they did until the crew had been picked up by helicopter. Due to early morning mist and cloud, the first Firefly detail was sent to attack Kimpo airfield and a village north-west of Seoul. For the rest of the day they flew CAS details in the Suwon area, attacking villages, troop positions, and gun pits and emplacements, all with good results.

On the last day of this patrol, 3rd February, 17th CAG achieved a record of 66 sorties, specially creditable to 807 Squadron who had lost four Furies. Apart from A/S, all the Firefly details were CAS attacking villages and foxholes north-west of Suwon, and gun positions around Anyang-ni. Other details pounded troop positions in the hills. Two Furies carried out the routine coastal reconnaissance to the Ongjin airfields, destroying a lorry in Haeju and blowing the roofs off two warehouses at Wonum with rockets. An early detail spotted for *Ceylon* bombarding anti-aircraft gun positions. Two other bombardments were spotted, both in the Inchon area: one with *St Paul* on gun positions; and the second with *Hank*, where three armoured fighting vehicles were the target of which one was destroyed and the other two damaged. During this sortie Lieutenant Pinsent's aircraft was hit by small-arms fire and he was forced to ditch alongside *St Paul* whose helicopter picked him out of the water within a very few minutes of the ditching. Unfortunately the hoist parted and Pinsent fell back into the icy water of the Han estuary. The second attempt at rescue was successful and he was soon aboard *St Paul* suffering from little worse than cold. On completion of the day's flying, Th*eseus, Cossack* and *Constance*, set course for Kure, *Theseus* being relieved by USS *Bataan*. Pinsent was transferred to *Cayuga* and returned to Kure with her.

The next day was spent on passage, anchoring outside the Inland Sea at 2300, so that *Theseus* could enter the Shimonoseki Straits and pass the islands to Kure in daylight on 5th February.

Unicorn was also in Kure with replacement aircraft. Lieutenant Birch rejoined 810 Squadron and Lieutenants Young and Fane joined 807, relief's for Lieutenants Highett and Pinsent. Leave was granted to aircrew officers for 48 hours if they wished; rating aircrew received the hospitality of the Royal Australian Army Service Corps, spending four days in the Sergeant's mess; and a full sports programme was enjoyed in off-duty hours. Full divisions were held on Sunday 11th, and on the 12th *Theseus* left Kure by the southern exit from the Inland Sea.

On 7th February UN forces had captured Angyang and the enemy had been forced to withdraw back across the Han River and surrender the Inchon peninsula.

Admiral Joy had been asked by General Ridgway to stage a feint landing at Inchon to draw off some enemy troops from the limited UN offensive, and Admiral Andrewes was to co-ordinate these feints. On 24th January transports had sailed from Pusan and Yokosuka for Inchon. A threat of a landing would only be effective while amphibious forces were known to be in the offing.

The plan was:

8th February (D-2) — Softening up bombardment of likely beaches; air strikes from USS *Bataan*; amphibious forces were to anchor in sight of the enemy during the afternoon.

9th (D-1) — Further softening up and air attacks; attacks on Wolmido by 5th US Air Force.

10th (D-day) — Final assembly of the amphibious force; further softening up during the forenoon; air attacks and bombardments from 1630-1830 (H-hour). Assault craft actions were to simulate night landings.

The planned actions were carried out on 8th and 9th but those for 10th were cancelled, the UN advance had been so successful that the feint was not needed, only bombardments being carried out. By the afternoon of the 10th, Inchon had been entered and Kimpo airfield reached.

The thaw was setting in and with it the possibility of renewed mine-laying by the enemy. Admiral Andrewes directed the Commanding Officers of the carrier groups to include mine assembly launching and laying areas in their daily reconnaissance's.

On the 19th February Admiral Andrewes was appointed in command of all UN Blockade and Escort Forces (TF 95). He had the overall direction of operations on both coasts and was responsible for policy. Rear Admiral Smith USN, who had been CTF 95, was, in effect, Admiral Andrewes deputy as regards US and RoK forces and was in immediate operational control of all Task Groups except TG 95.1 on the west coast. Close co-operation was maintained between both staffs, the Chief of Staff and senior officers from each attended the other's daily staff meetings. Admiral Andrewes' communications organization was put under a considerable strain: in the first 14 days 3,050 signals were distributed from the Cryptographic Office and 2,030 from the Main Signal Office.

Throughout the war, there were always problems with clandestine and guerrilla groups, whose existence was denied by Tokyo when Admiral Andrewes asked for information on their activities. They operated mainly on the west coast from friendly islands, and some of them were so secret that they were unknown to anyone else, and frequently to one another. Admiral Andrewes directed his CTE's to seek out and try to operate directly with groups operating in their areas. US Army officers controlled a healthy guerrilla organisation based on Paengyong-do that operated across to the Hwanghae promontory, and the RoK Navy ran a raiding organisation of its own; these two eventually working together.

On the east coast carrier operations remained the responsibility TF 77, part of Admiral Struble's 7th Fleet. The blockade of Wonsan — the siege — continued for the rest of the war. Wonsan was the best port on the east coast but it was too far north for the UN forces to occupy, the enemy had therefore to be denied its use. This was achieved by occupying islands overlooking the approaches to the port, by keeping a large area of these approaches continuously swept of mines, by maintaining a threat of a landing on the coast and by regular and frequent bombardments by a force of two cruisers and 18 destroyers or frigates. These bombardments threw a heavy strain on the ammunition supply lines. In April, 250 men of 41st Independent Commando RM, who had been in Tokyo since the retreat from Chosin in December, were landed from the LSD Fort Marion on the coast 8 miles south of Songjin where they demolished a section of main coastal railway. No serious resistance was encountered and no casualties were sustained.

Seventh Patrol

Theseus flew a short session of DLP for the new pilots on 13th February, on passage to the operational zone, in company with *Comus, Cayuga, Athabaskan* and *Nootka*. Next day, the first of the patrol, the 5th US Air Force was grounded due to low cloud over their bases. The Fireflies divided their effort into two CAS missions and to two strikes north-west of Seoul. Troops on ridges and in dug-outs were bombed, rocketed and strafed with good results reported by the controllers. The Furies carried out two reconnaissance details of the area from Seoul to Pyongyang, and from Sariwon to Haeju and Ongjin airfield. Little activity was reported, but there was some meagre and inaccurate heavy AA fire in the vicinity of Pyongyang with shells bursting around 9,000 ft. Pyongyang railway station and other buildings were rocketed and strafed, and other targets attacked with good results. CAS details, controlled by 'Picklebarrel' in the Seoul area and by 'Drummer 14' and 'Mastiff X-ray' in the Wonju areas, caused many casualties. In one attack, troops, whose positions had been marked with smoke by the artillery, were strafed on a ridge within 500 yards of our own forces. Lieutenant Curry hit the batsman's screen when landing, and Lieutenant Commander Pattisson's aircraft was hit in the centre section causing damage which could not be repaired on board. Three Fireflies had guns which fired on landing. From one of these Petty Officer Airman J.F. Wigley, an aircraft handler working in the forward deck park, was hit by a 22 mm shell and fatally wounded. He was buried at sea with full naval honours next day.

On the 15th the Furies, carrying out the northern coastal reconnaissance as far as Ongju, noted that the ice round the Chinnammpo estuary and in the northern area was beginning to melt which might permit enemy mine-laying operations to recommence. Their CAS details were with 'Townsend 14' and 'Spirit Mosquito 2' in the Inchon area, in support of 9th Brigade, strafing troops on ridges. Villages around Wonju were attacked, as were huts, railway trucks and buildings at Chowon. On the first Firefly detail Lieutenant Davis had to land at Suwon with a rough running engine. Petty Officer Algar was later flown in with spares,

HMS *Theseus* of the west coast.   *(Stock)*

and after changing the plugs the aircraft returned on board with the engine still slightly rough — the crew not wishing to spend a cold and dreary night ashore under canvas. The remaining aircraft of the first detail attacked bridges ten miles north-Northwest of Inchon. A later detail attacked a railway bridge twelve miles north-west of Seoul, failing to obtain any hits but damaging the tracks. Buildings and trucks in nearby sidings were hit with rockets. The Fireflies were also directed to store dumps in a village north-east of Inchon, where their attacks caused explosions.

The weather next day was poor, causing flying to be abandoned at 1230. Two details were flown as the wind increased until it was gusting at 45 knots, and the sea swell rose causing more than the usual number of *Wave*-offs. The Fireflies attacked road and rail bridges north-west of Seoul and an AA machine-gun was silenced by strafing. The Furies attacked some barrack buildings directed by 'Gosport 14', and later, directed by 'Destiny 14', eliminated a road block to the east of Seoul. Two aircraft from the second detail reconnoitred as far as the Ongjin airfields, attacking a field gun and vehicles in Chinnampo, where AA fire was encountered. Two Firefly accidents were caused by the weather: Mr. Bailey, when landing on the pitching deck, damaged the rear wedge beyond the capacity of the ship's maintenance teams to repair; and the second also suffered damage to the tail when being moved on the rolling deck with the tail wheel at right angles to the direction of roll.

On the 17th the weather was good, with little wind, a great contrast to the previous day. The Fireflies devoted nearly all their efforts to CAS to the north-west of Inchon, bombing and rocketing road and rail bridges and rail tunnels, but with somewhat limited success, obtaining no direct hits on any bridges or tunnel entrances. Troops and stores were strafed and rocket attacks were made on villages. The early Fury detail reconnoitred the coast from Tungansat to Kwanghwa-do, seeing no minelaying vessels, but attacking bridges and gun emplacements; and another pair took the northern route as far as the Ongjin airfields, observing no unusual activity in Haeju or Chinnampo, but attacking rail yards at Yasan. CAS missions for I Corps successfully attacked troops on ridges outside Suwon. Later in the day, working with a British controller, 'Newmarket', a flight of Furies carried out an accurate and effective attack by strafing and rocketing a hill where enemy troops were dug-in down one side with our own forces holding the rest.

High seas and winds again reduced flying to two details only during the forenoon. Low cloud over the front line prevented the first Firefly detail from carrying out its briefed CAS mission, so attacks were made on the secondary target, a village near Kaesong. Lieutenant Lavender had the misfortune to allow his Fury to tip up on its nose whilst running up in the range, the other three aircraft of his flight carried out a reconnaissance of the coastal areas to Chinnampo. Little activity was noted except that the roads and railway between Hwangju and Sariwon were well used. In poor weather conditions, three Furies of the second detail were working with a controller whose directions nearly resulted in an attack on our own troops. The target area was then moved to the bank of the Han River where troops and a machine-gun position were attacked.

Next day was replenishment of AVGAS and FFO, out of the area, with mail being delivered by *Hart*. As a result of the accidents to the two Fireflies reducing 810's effective strength to ten aircraft, A/S patrols were done by the Furies of 807 Squadron for the second half of this patrol.

On the 20th the Furies carried out reconnaissance sorties of the Ongjin airfields, of the Han River estuary as far north as Chaeryong and of the road from Sariwon to Pyongyang. Two small gauge railway engines were hit and bridges attacked at Kyomipo; junks, lorries and a village were attacked in the Han. Heavy flak was encountered round Pyongyang. Ridges close to the army in the Chuchon area were strafed under the direction of 'Granite Control'. The aircraft due to give support to the army in the Inchon area found no targets available so they attacked the village of Pupyong-ni. The Fireflies struck railway bridges west of Hwangju, badly damaging the track, and silencing an AA machine-gun. A briefed CAS mission had to attack their secondary target, the village of Paju-ri north-west of Seoul, because there were no controllers available.

Heavy rain and high seas prevented any flying after 1200 on the 21st. The Furies carried out one reconnaissance to Chinnampo where little activity was seen but buildings were attacked with good results. Mosquitoes 'Granite 1' and 'Granite 4' gave targets of troops in a valley and on a ridge at Songyueni where good results were obtained. Three other Furies destroyed buildings and caused casualties in the village of Yanyong. Lieutenant Keighley-Peach had to land at Suwon with engine trouble. The Fireflies struck railway bridges near Sariwon, causing damage to the tracks. Stores were strafed, starting small fires. A CAS mission attacking a ridge with bombs and rockets followed by strafing runs brought the comment 'Good work' from the Mosquito controller.

The full day's flying on the 22nd was hampered by 10/10ths cloud over land, with the base at 900 feet. For much of the day the Mosquito aircraft were grounded, the Furies flew reconnaissance sorties to Haeju and Chinnampo. Two small locomotives were strafed at Kyomipo and other opportunity targets were attacked. Lieutenant Shirras' aircraft was hit in the ailerons by small-arms fire. A Firefly strike on bridges north of Hwangju, escorted by Furies, resulted in one bridge being partially destroyed. The weather cleared sufficiently in the afternoon for a Mosquito to direct a Fury attack on ridges containing troops in the Wonju area. The Fireflies attacked opportunity targets south of Kaesong, strafing troops and starting fires. Lieutenant Nunn carried out a taxi service to Suwon with a Fury maintenance rating and returned with Lieutenant Keighley-Peach.

On the last day of the patrol, the Furies carried out one detail of reconnaissance to Chinnampo where railway installations were attacked, one shed blowing up with a brilliant blue flash. For the rest of the day they supported IX Corps in the Wonju area, attacking woods and ridges. The Fireflies were also involved with CAS. The first detail required them to attack a rail tunnel at both ends. Nearly all the bombs being 'right on the mark'. Troops in fox-holes near the tunnel were also strafed. On completion the ground controllers reported 'A very fine attack'. Ridges and stores were bombed, rocketed and strafed, and, although results were difficult to see, the ground controller reported 'Excellent'. Mr. Bailey's Firefly was hit in four places by small-arms fire. Lieutenant Winterton took Lieutenant Checketts to Suwon and later Lieutenant Stanley took a load of spares and personal gear — the Fury would be remaining behind until it was repaired and would then be flown to Japan. At the end of the day's flying *Theseus* set course for Sasebo, arriving the following evening at 1900. Four Furies and two Fireflies were exchanged from *Unicorn*, and *Warrior* arrived and stayed for a couple of days unloading stores.

USS *Bataan* took over from *Theseus* on 23rd February, and her patrol saw increased activity in the Chinnampo area. Minesweeping was carried out by *Cormick* and *Alacrity* with RoK motor minesweepers on the route to Chinnampo. On 2nd March likely landing beaches were bombarded while *Bataan* supplied a low CAP. The Amphibious Element entered the swept channel and remained there until dark, when they withdrew. This feint caused the North Koreans to move one division into the area. A continued landing threat was kept up in the Chinnampo to Choppeki area. *Kenya* returned to the west coast from Hong Kong after a three week self-refit period, to relieve *Belfast*.

Eighth Patrol

Theseus, in company with *Comus, Cayuga, Nootka* and *Athabaskan*, left Sasebo on 4th March for the west coast. The Fury that had been left at Suwon on 23rd February had been repaired and flown to Japan, and was landed-on during the forenoon.

A full day's flying was carried out on the 5th. The Furies reconnoitred the airfields of Ongjin and Haeju, and spotted for shoots by *Kenya, Consort* and *Alacrity. Kenya* and her escorts were patrolling and bombarding the coast from Chinnampo to Kuhsa-sung to maintain the impression of an imminent amphibious landing. The Fireflies concentrated on reconnaissance and bombing of bridges. Two spans of a road bridge at Chaeryong were demolished, and another span collapsed from a bridge north of Haeju; and sheds and rolling stock were strafed. Two Furies, one of which had to return with engine trouble, escorted three Fireflies on their last detail. The Fireflies were carrying 1,000 lb. bombs, with short-delay fuses, for the first time; and because of weight limitations, carried no 20 mm ammunition. The

Fury carried out a photo reconnaissance while his flock were bombing the entrance to a railway tunnel near Haeju and the ridge above it, resulting in a partial collapse of the embankment which blocked the entrance.

On the 6th weather conditions over the land prevented the Fireflies from carrying out any strike or CAS missions until the afternoon. The Furies, with limited success, carried out some reconnaissance of roads in the area west of the line from Haeju to Chinnampo. The weather improved in the afternoon; the Fireflies attacking a building reported by RoK intelligence as being an ammunition dump, (but without bringing about the explosions normally associated with such a target), damaging a railway bridge, and one minespotting sortie in the Haeju area. The Furies reconnoitred roads and railways from Haeju to Chungwon and the coasts and coastal roads from Chinnampo to Haeju, noting the state of railways, and that the previous day's damage by Fireflies to the rail tunnel had been practically cleared up. During one of the forenoon details the AGC was hit by a small-arms bullet which lodged in the wing between two rounds of 20 mm ammunition. P3 Johnson carried out a successful forced landing on the ship with an engine sputtering and banging, the trouble was later found to be cracks in the mouldings of the magneto distributor.

During the whole of the next day the Furies spotted and directed bombardments carried out by *Kenya* and other ships in the coastal area from Kuhsa-sung to the Chinnampo estuary. The targets were bridges and road junctions, results were variable depending on the efficiency of communications between the aircraft and the ships. Reconnaissance sorties were flown along the Seoul to Sariwon, and Sariwon to Haeju roads and railways, targets seen being rocketed and strafed, including a working party on Haeju airfield. The Fireflies carried out two details of CAS with Mosquito controllers. An enemy occupied hill was attacked with bombs, rockets and cannon. Though no results were observed, 'Good hitting' was the cry from the controlling aircraft. The second detail, operating west of Seoul because thick snow showers prevented operations further east, bombed a culvert suspected of harbouring a tank — two direct hits were obtained causing the culvert to cave in. Following this a double tunnel was attacked nearer to Seoul of which two of the four entrances were hit causing damage. Slight damage was done to Lieutenant Commander Coy's aircraft by small-arms fire.

The Fireflies had an unfortunate series of accidents. Mr. Young came in low from an A/S sortie, breaking his hook on the round-down, and entering the barrier with his depth charges still on their bomb-carriers; the midshipman in the rear cockpit, up for a pleasure trip, had more 'pleasure' than he had bargained for. During the final land-on of the day, Lieutenants Nunn and Tobey both caught late wires and gently entered the first barrier, though sufficiently fast to have shock-loaded the engines and causing engine changes. It was thought that these two accidents were caused by the hooks bouncing on the deck and missing the earlier wires. Hook-bounce had been a problem with Fireflies for some time. It was finally cured with a simple modification whose details are given in Appendix F.

On the 8th the Furies started with a reconnaissance of the Seoul to Kaesong to Sinmak area. Railway installations were attacked, newly dug gun positions strafed and the road bridge at Pangyong-ni rocketed. CAS details were flown for the 1st Cavalry Division, attacking ridges in the Chunchon and Yafu areas. Troops on ridges north-east of Taju and a mortar position were attacked. Because of the shortage of Fireflies, the Furies performed the last three A/S details. During the second Firefly detail, Mr. William Courtney, the correspondent for the Sunday Times and Graphic, flew with Lieutenant Commander Pattisson to take movie film of the attack by four Fireflies on two rail bridges west of Hwangju with 1,000 lb. bombs. A warehouse at Haeju was hit with rockets on the return trip. Other Firefly details attacked bridges and strafed railway engines and trucks. Lieutenant Stanley in a Firefly had a full barrier — losing his wheels on the first and being prevented by the second from going into the forward deck park. 9th March was replenishment; and with low mist and fog there was no flying on the 10th.

The Furies flew reconnaissance details during the next day. Railway lines and bridges were attacked and buildings were strafed. Two Fireflies took stores and equipment to Suwon airfield, and Lieutenant Winterton then carried on to Taegu with Mr. Courtney. Artillery and machine-gun positions were attacked under ground control. Workshops and other buildings were rocketed and strafed at Chinnampo. Two Furies escorted a Firefly strike with 1,000 lb. bombs (of which four had four- to six-hour delay fuses fitted) on a railway bridge north-west of Sariwon; bombs fell round the northern end of the bridge causing damage to the tracking. Reconnaissance next day confirmed that the bridge was still unserviceable after the delayed action bombs had exploded causing further damage to the track.

On 12th March the Furies encountered heavy, accurate and intense flak south of Hwangju during their photo-reconnaissance of Ongjin and Changyon areas. Hangars at Ongjin airfield were rocketed; fires started in supply dumps and a floating crane was strafed at Kyomipo. The railway track was severed at Paengo to the west of Sariwon and a bridge attack north of Sariwon tore up the track in several places but did not succeed in destroying the bridge, the prime target. Later in the day, during a photo-reconnaissance detail in the Sariwon area, the diary records the laconic statement 'A moving jeep strafed, crashed and caught fire. Damage to occupants not observed but thought to be sufficient'. The Firefly CAS details attacked foxholes and trenches on ridges held by the enemy south-west of Hongchon with 'excellent coverage' reported by the Mosquito controllers. A double railway bridge was knocked out with 1,000 lb. bombs in a position south-east of Sariwon, and another similar bridge was also dealt with near Hungsa-ri. On this detail Lieutenant James was hit by AA fire at 4,500 feet, damage being caused to the port wing of his aircraft above the aileron; this affected the flying characteristics somewhat so he decided to divert to Suwon, accompanied by his section leader Lieutenant Johnson. As the time did not permit his return on board before dusk, four weary aircrew spent a cold and dreary night there.

On the last day of the patrol the Furies carried out AR sorties in the Kangsan-sa to Chinnampo region, attacking workshops and leaving a junk burning, encountering flak near Changyong; Haeju railway station was also left burning. The Fireflies, under Mosquito control, attacked the enemy in foxholes and in gun pits on ridges south-west of Hongchon; and later the town of Hongchon itself, said to contain a battalion of troops, was attacked with bombs, rockets and cannon. Two strike details were flown, the first on bridges near Hungsu-ri and the second with 1,000 lb. bombs on a rail bridge east of Haeju. This was the most successful strike to date of the tour, the bridge being destroyed. During this detail, Lieutenant G.H. Cooles and Flight Lieutenant D.W. Guy RAF, on their return to the ship, crashed a few miles away from the bridge near Sariwon, the cause of the crash being due either to having been hit by AA fire or to damage due to their own bomb bursts. The Furies maintained a CAP over the wreckage of the aircraft, but finding no sign of the pilot or observer reported that the crew had perished in the crash. Vice Admiral Sir Guy Russell, CinCFES, transferred his flag from *Cockade* to *Theseus* during the afternoon to watch the flying operations and to attend the final de-briefing. On completion of flying, *Theseus* set course for Sasebo, arriving there during the following evening.

On this day, 14th March, Seoul was reoccupied by United Nations forces for the second time.

During the patrol, 339 sorties had been flown, 226 offensive and 113 defensive. The usual maintenance load had accrued, to be cleared during the harbour period, including some engine changes and the reception of six replacement aircraft from *Unicorn* and Iwakuni. On Sunday 18th March Divisions were inspected by Vice Admiral Sir William Andrewes followed by his farewell speech to the ship's company. A memorial service was held on board afterwards for Lieutenant Cooles and Flight Lieutenant Guy.

Ninth Patrol

Theseus, in company with *Consort, Nootka, Athabaskan* and *Huron* (successor to *Cayuga* who had returned to Canada) left Sasebo at 0700 on 22nd March for the west coast. During the passage the aircrew were given a lecture by Captain Murray, CBGLO, on bombardment spotting, in particular the differences between the British and American methods. Both he and the AGC lectured on the latest Escape, Evasion and Survival philosophy promulgated in the bulletins, and the techniques to be adopted should it be necessary.

On the first day in the operational area, the Furies carried out the normal reconnaissance of the area to report on the latest state of the railways, and a second detail attacked and damaged buildings in Kaesong and strafed installations at Sinmak airfield. Other Fury details spotted two shoots with *Kenya* on troops in trenches at Surin-ni and on gun pits at Sonyong-ni. CAS details were carried out by one flight of Furies, under the direction of 'Rake- Off', on troops moving north in front of I Corps. The Fireflies, on CAS, attacked troops in foxholes and gun pits on ridges near Kaesong. A second CAS detail failed to establish communication with the controller, radio interference due to too many people cluttering up the channel being the cause; they attacked the alternative target, a village 15 miles south-west of Kumhwa, with bombs and rockets, starting a number of fires. Two Furies escorted a strike of four Fireflies with 2 x 1,000 lb. bombs on a bridge at Kingyong-ni, 30 miles north of Seoul; one direct hit broke the bridge and other bombs fell on the road junction at the other end. Lieutenant Winterton was the victim of hook-bounce again, engaging the ninth wire and entering the barrier, fortunately not shock-loading the engine.

On the 24th the Furies found several concentrations of camouflaged vehicles in the Chosan-ni and Nanchonjon areas, several of which blew up and caught fire when attacked. During the briefed reconnaissance detail of the Haeju to Nanchonjon area Lieutenant Commander Gordon-Smith's aircraft was hit by a 0.5 inch armour-piercing bullet, snipping the corner off the main fuel tank which then failed to self-seal. He was nearly overcome by petrol fumes, but diverted and landed safely at Suwon; the aircraft was a write-off due to additional severe damage to the main bulkhead. The remaining aircraft of the flight made attacks along the Haeju to Kaesong road. The AGC was returned to the ship by 810 Squadron's taxi service. Other attacks were made on railway installations in Kaesong by the flight who could not give close support to the army due to a lack of targets. The Fireflies were given three details of Mosquito-directed CAS, during one of which they had to wait nearly 60 minutes before they could attack buildings in the target village 15 miles east of Kaesong just ahead of an advancing UN tank column. The second detail resulted in reported 'Very wonderful bombing' on troop positions on ridges 15 miles north-east of Seoul, only 200 yards ahead of advancing UN troops. Due to haze over the area, the third detail had to be cancelled; buildings were set on fire and damaged in the secondary objective, a village near Kumhwa. Intense flak was encountered near Sariwon by the Furies, Lieutenant Commander Coy's aircraft was hit by a 40 mm explosive shell and Mr. Bailey's aircraft was hit by flak or bomb shrapnel, both returned to the ship and landed on safely. Lieutenant Stanley's vision was affected, when in the 'break-up' circuit, by too much sun glare so he diverted to Suwon, landing with next to no petrol. He returned to the ship later.

Heavy rain and poor visibility prevented any flying next day. On the 26th the Furies flew three reconnaissance details, one of the coastal area from Ongjin to

Chinnampo, attacking buildings at Haeju; the others in the areas of Namchonjon and Kumchon, attacking vehicles in a village and railway installations. One aircraft had to land at Suwon with engine trouble. Two CAS missions were flown in support of I Corps under the direction of 'Rake Off 2' and 'Rake Off 4', villages being attacked, causing casualties and fires. Firefly effort was reduced due to the unserviceabilities arising two days earlier. The strike on a double railway bridge south-east of Sariwon failed to secure any hits, but villages near Haeju, reported by RoK Intelligence as containing troops were strafed and rocketed. Three aircraft with 2 x 1,000 lb. bombs, escorted by two Furies, attacked a railway bridge 25-30 miles east of Kaesong causing slight damage by near misses, and ripping up 100 yards of track with one bomb. A pump house was destroyed by the rockets from the Furies.

Next day the weather overland was cloudy, and at sea it closed in with rain and poor visibility so that flying ceased in mid-afternoon. The Fireflies flew one detail of CAS under Mosquito control causing two large explosions and a fire in a village 5 miles north of Chonchon. The other detail, having failed to make contact with any controllers, attacked the secondary target, a ridge 15 miles north of Yonan, destroying and damaging many buildings with bombs, rockets and cannon. The Furies concentrated on four details of reconnaissance: one along the coast from Haeju to Chinnampo, destroying buildings at Haeju and photographing airfields; the second along the Sariwon to Hungsu-ri road, obtaining much information on the state of Sariwon airfield and attacking a railway tunnel, during which small-arms fire was experienced; the third on the Yonan and Amnyang areas, where little of military interest was seen, but a bus was strafed and the roof blown off a building at Haeju; the fourth found a large concentration of well camouflaged vehicles in the hills north-west of the town of Namchonjon, three were left burning and several others were damaged. Two aircraft spotted for *Comus* bombarding gun positions on the south side of the Chinnampo estuary, destroying two.

After replenishment on the 28th, flying resumed next day with the Furies again devoting the day to reconnaissance. In the Haeju to Pyongyang area, attacks were made on a village reported to contain troops at Chongdang, leaving houses burning and causing casualties. AA fire was encountered during an attack on revetments near Hwangu. Two details searched the area round Namchonjon for vehicles, but none was found; nearby villages and camouflaged revetments were attacked. Four aircraft bombed a large wood containing camouflaged stores dumps at Kuwon-ni, north of Pyongyang, but no startling results were observed. Three bombing strikes were launched by the Fireflies. Both the first and third attacked barracks three miles south east of Chaeryong, the latter strike carrying 1,000 lb. bombs, some with delay fuses, was escorted by two Furies; most of the buildings were destroyed, the remainder were left uninhabitable. The second strike, with three direct hits, succeeded in causing the collapse of one span of a double railway bridge south-east of Sariwon, and sidings in the area were rocketed.

No unusual activity was seen by the Furies on the morning coastal reconnaissance from Haeju to Ongjong next day. Accurate and intense AA fire was encountered from a village near Sariwon which was rocketed, causing some damage. CAS details for IX Corps north-east of Chunchon, controlled by 'Pennyweight 14' and 'Pineapple 4' resulted in ridges and bunkers being strafed with good results. Eight camouflaged lorries were attacked and damaged during a reconnaissance east of Namchonjon. The Fireflies attacked bridges and a rail tunnel, damaging the entrance to the tunnel and the bridges. The strike with 1,000 lb. bombs on the barracks to the east of Sariwon, escorted by Furies, completely destroyed eight and damaged twelve buildings, the escort strafing troops and lorries. One Fury had to land at Suwon airfield with a rough running engine.

The following morning, six large boats in Haeju harbour were attacked by the Furies and rendered useless, many vehicles were destroyed and left burning near Namchunjon. A village and nearby ridge were attacked at Unsan-ni, with good results being reported by 'Cobalt Mosquito 2', the CAS controller. Furies again escorted Fireflies carrying 1000 lb. bombs to attack a bridge near Sariwon, near misses causing some damage only. An earlier strike on barracks to the east of Sariwon destroyed many buildings and damaged others. Lieutenant Commander Coy's aircraft was hit by AA fire in the port wing near the aileron hinge, causing quite a mess.

Low cloud on 1st April, the last day of the patrol, prevented coastal reconnaissance, but the Furies made attacks on hangars at Haeju airfield. Several vehicles were found and attacked near Namchonjon, damaging some and destroying two. The area appeared to have been vacated by the majority as many camouflaged revetments were found empty. 'Cobalt Mosquito 2' controlled a CAS detail to IX Corps north of Chunchon; a village containing a road block was attacked with good results. A second CAS detail, also in the Chunchon area, strafed and rocketed a village containing vehicles of which four were destroyed and four more damaged. The Fireflies flew one CAS detail, attacking, and reportedly knocking out, a company of troops on a ridge 30 miles north of Seoul. Strikes were made on four bridges, the destruction of two spans of a rail bridge near Sariwon being the only success. Lieutenant Nunn had to land at Suwon after his A/S patrol due to a break in the constant-speed-unit control. *Unicorn* had a maintenance party at Suwon changing a Firefly mainplane, so they robbed this aircraft to repair Nunn's, who then returned to *Theseus*. Mr. MacKenzie was flown ashore in the Sea Otter with spares, and waited at Suwon until *Unicorn's* party had completed their work and then flew the aircraft to Iwakuni. As a bank of fog rolled in from the west, the last detail was cancelled and *Theseus* with her screen set course for Sasebo, entering harbour and securing at 1500 next day.

During the harbour period, some time-expired Furies and a Firefly which had been suffering from excessively high oil pressure were exchanged for serviceable aircraft from *Unicorn's* pool.

Helicopters had proved their worth over and over again in the Korean War, and for search and rescue, they played an invaluable part. No fewer than four of *Theseus'* pilots were rescued from behind enemy lines, and four aircrew were picked up from the sea by helicopter. Arrangements had been made by Commander 7th Fleet for *Philippine Sea* to lend one to *Theseus*. A USN Sikorsky helicopter (similar to the British S.51 Dragonfly) and crew were transferred to *Theseus* on 3rd April for the last operational period, and operated as plane guard. It was fitted with an anti-coning device which permitted its operation from the flight deck in wind speeds up to 35 and 40 knots instead of about 22 knots. No difficulty was thus presented in flying it off and landing it on before and after each range of aircraft was launched and recovered. One of the disadvantages of these helicopters was that they were too small. When two aircrew were to be rescued the aircraft had to return to the ship with the first one and then go back to the scene of the rescue for the second. However, gift horses do not have their mouths looked into, and it was an enormous improvement on the Sea Otter.

US Sikorsky S51 over HMS *Theseus* with USS *Bataan* ahead.   *(FAAM)*

A number of changes took place in the Command structure during April. Rear Admiral A.E. Smith USN resumed command of TF 95 on the 4th. Admiral Sir William Andrewes hauled down his flag in Hong Kong on the 10th to be succeeded by Rear Admiral A.K. Scott-Moncrieff who sailed for Sasebo in *Belfast* on the 11th. Vice Admiral H.M. Martin USN had succeeded Admiral Struble as Commander 7th Fleet.

Since the meeting at Wake Island in October 1950 between President Truman and General MacArthur, there had been increasing divergence's of opinion between the US Home authorities and the Supreme Commander as to the strategy to be pursued in the Far East. Nor did he hide his views from the public in the United States. Eventually he put himself in such a position vis-à-vis the Government that, under the United States Constitution, President Truman had no alternative but to relieve him; and on 11th April 1951 he was succeeded by Lieutenant General Mathew B. Ridgway as Supreme Commander, who in turn was succeeded by General James A. Van Fleet as Commander 8th Army.

It had been becoming apparent for some weeks that the Communists were preparing for another offensive. Reconnaissance aircraft had reported heavy southbound traffic in the enemy rear areas. New enemy units were identified in increasing numbers within supporting distance of the front.

The blow fell a week after General Van Fleet had taken up his new command.

During the three weeks from mid-March HMNZSs *Tutira* and *Hawaea* had been supervising minesweeping in the waters around Paengyong-do. Considerable difficulties had to be overcome owing to conflicting and unpredictable currents. Lieutenant Commander P J.H. Hoare, Captain of *Tutira*, was struck by the zeal and enthusiasm of the RoK minesweepers, in spite of being long overdue for maintenance and being very short of foodstuffs — 'They proved competent seamen and pleasant companions'.

Also during this period, arrangements were made for improving naval co-operation with guerrilla forces in the Chinnampo to Haeju area. Captain Sir Aubrey St. Clair-Ford established contact, ripening into cordial relations with the three US officers concerned with these operations, Colonel McGee, Colonel Thompson and Major Burke, which was to prove of mutual benefit to the blockade forces and the Americans.

On 10th April a MiG 15 was reported shot down over Sinmi-do at the north end of the Yalu Gulf (39°53'N, 24°52'E). 5th US Air Force was anxious to recover it, so Captain P.W. Brock in *Kenya* was ordered by Rear Admiral Smith to form a temporary task element (TE 95.15) from ships on the west coast and to take charge of search operations. *Kenya* left Sasebo at 0200 on the 11th, ordering Captain O.H. Becher in *Warramunga* to start the RoK ships moving north.

Sinmi-do is surrounded by mudbanks, and at low water is joined to the mainland; to the east is a narrow channel about a mile wide and only seven or eight fathoms deep; it is only 40 miles from enemy air bases at Antung.

5th US Air Force provided air cover and search planes; a helicopter with LST 822 to act as its base were also provided, and a salvage tug USS Bolster added as a final precaution.

Kenya arrived off Sinmi-do at 1015 on the 12th. A day of much activity was enlivened by a heavy bombardment of the Yalu bridges by American B-29s, of which two were lost. Search by *Nootka, Warramunga* and *Amethyst* resulted in the recovery of only one body by *Amethyst*.

The MiG was not found, and the operation was called off on 16th April.

Tenth Patrol

On 14th April Admiral Scott-Moncrieff arrived in Sasebo to take over as CTG 95.1. The situation was unusual; the heavy carriers of TF 77 were operating off Formosa as a result of indications that Red China might contemplate an assault there, and since 8th April *Theseus* and USS *Bataan* had replaced them in the Sea of Japan. The west coast was thus deprived of carrier based air operations, but by flying across Korea a daily reconnaissance of the Choppeki area could be maintained. *Constance* and *Alacrity* were engaged on interdiction bombardments at Wonsan, and *Rotoiti* was employed as tanker escort on either coast as required.

This was the first occasion on which the British carrier had worked with another deck since *Theseus* left 7th Fleet the previous August. The teaming up into one unit of these two highly efficient and friendly rivals resulted in highly effective air operations. The competition between the two carriers produced a general speeding up of flying operations. *Theseus* with one catapult was usually able to launch quicker than *Bataan* with two and catapulting intervals for Furies dropped to 40-42 seconds. The US Marines Reserve Air Group could not quite compete with the landing rate of the more experienced pilots of the 17th CAG, but they much improved by the end of the week. It was also the first occasion on which a joint Commonwealth/US destroyer screen operated together.

Preliminary conferences were held at Sasebo to discuss the working of the two carriers in company, and liaison officers were exchanged to assist in operational and tactical problems. The great disparity in their speeds (*Bataan* 32 knots, *Theseus* 23) was of less importance than might have been expected, as both ships were operating aircraft of approximately similar characteristics. It was agreed that all sorties would be by catapult, ships turning into wind together. In the event no difficulties were experienced in operating in company. Both carriers took turns as guide of the fleet, and once *Bataan* accustomed to the slow acceleration of *Theseus*, station-keeping was found to be quite easy.

The two carriers with their screen *Consort*, HMAS *Bataan, Athabaskan, Huron* and USSs *English* and *Sperry*, left Sasebo in the morning of 8th April; they retained the designation TE 95.11 with Captain Edgar Neale USN being element commander. Flying operations were carried out from the 9th to the 15th, including the daily reconnaissance across Korea of the Choppeki area and, on the east coast, strikes on road and rail bridges, marshalling yards, rolling stock, supply dumps and warehouses at various places, AR as required and bombardment spotting in Wonsan and Songjin areas. Only very few sorties could be flown on the 11th owing to bad weather; apart from this, flying took place every day. *Theseus* replenished on the 13th, but flew 29 sorties that afternoon; *Bataan* replenished next day. In all *Theseus* flew 276 sorties and *Bataan* 244.

There were no deck-landing accidents in *Theseus*, Captain Bolt remarking that this was much to the credit of the pilots, as on four days there was a heavy north-easterly swell; swell is not experienced on the west coast, and they were unused to it. Aircraft casualties were the highest experienced, five Furies and one Firefly were lost or badly damaged.

The light carrier's flying operations on the east coast were a conspicuous success. Considerable damage was inflicted on the enemy by their combined efforts, and the operation of the two ships in company had gone very smoothly. But Captain Bolt struck a warning note in his report:

'There were many times when I wondered what would have happened if a few well-handled U-boats had been in the vicinity. Three destroyers on a closed concentric circular screen, screening two carriers steaming on a steady course at 12 knots was the situation on more than one occasion when replenishment was being carried out by members of the screen.'

It was announced on 8th April that there was to be a duty carrier system, the duty carrier providing the CAP and beacon guard, but *Theseus'* Fireflies to provide the daily A/S patrols. It was also decided that the spare aircraft would be manned before launch, so that in the event of unserviceability on the deck, each detail got the required number of aircraft into the air.

On the 9th the Fireflies carried out strikes on rail sidings, described as 'marshalling yards', and on warehouses and buildings in the Wonsan area; an attack on a possible minelaying base resulted in a large fire. The Furies carried out two west coast reconnaissance's but observed no activity; they rocketed buildings at Wallong-ni and encountered some flak, junks at Chinnampo were attacked and a floating crane damaged. Reconnaissance in the Wonsan and east coast areas resulted in junks and sampans being strafed and buildings and stores being rocketed.

The next day was a black day for 807 Squadron. Two Furies, piloted by Lieutenants Leece and Lavender, were carrying out a reconnaissance of the area south of Wonsan when they observed two Corsairs coming in on a menacing looking approach, and before the Furies realised that their intentions were hostile they opened fire. Lieutenant Leece's combat report, filed after the flight, makes interesting reading:

'Whilst flying No 2 to Lieutenant Lavender we were investigating enemy activity in a valley, map reference CU6002, when I saw two Corsair fighters which I reported to my No 1. We were turning to starboard at 4,000 feet and saw the two Corsairs dive into the valley and drop one bomb each.

'On recovering from the dive they must have sighted us because they started to climb in our direction. We continued a gentle Rate One turn to starboard until the Corsairs were astern and closing, when my leader ordered "Break". I opened the throttle fully and commenced a steep starboard climbing turn, but almost immediately there was a loud bang from the engine, so I throttled back and eased the turn as I did not realise I was being fired at.

'By this time the leading Corsair, which still had one bomb under his starboard wing, was dead astern of me and he opened fire. I saw many tracers flashing over my port wing and I turned violently to starboard breaking down. The Corsairs did not attempt to follow and, as the aircraft was vibrating and the starboard wing tank was on fire, I left the area and returned to the ship.

'I believe the Corsairs thought they had shot me down as they subsequently claimed "one La-9 destroyed". When they saw me break down, on fire, they concentrated on Charlie Lavender who kept going round in a very tight turn with the Corsairs firing at him. Charlie was obviously worried about me, plus his own, difficult, situation, but he eventually managed to out-turn his attackers and escaped to chase after me.

'For my part, as I started for home, my first thought was to bale out, as I could see the starboard wing was bright red and smoke was pouring out of the back end. However, the fire suddenly went out (I learned later that the bottom of the wing tank had burned through and the remaining fuel had just dropped out), and as the engine continued to give power and the aircraft was flyable I continued back to *Theseus*. Charlie eventually caught up as I was flying slowly, and after a visual inspection and a slow flying check I made a normal landing. There were 21 bullet holes in the aircraft and no right wing tank (internal, not drop). The bullets had severed some of the flying controls. There was no trim but the rest worked'.

Lieutenant Lavender's aircraft was hit in the wing by one 0.5 inch bullet.

Two other Furies were carrying out a reconnaissance of the Kowon area and had made several attacks on railway wagons and dumps when they heard the call for help from the two aircraft being attacked by Corsairs. On the way to assist them P3 H. Johnson's aircraft was hit by 37 mm flak and he crashed in a valley when trying to make a forced landing. He was presumed killed but was later known to have been taken prisoner. Lieutenant (E) Julian, in a detail searching for Johnson's aircraft, was hit by flak which severed the port aileron control rod and also left him without flaps. Julian managed to fly to Kangnung where he was obliged to land so fast, with the wheels locked down, that he overran the runway and went over on his back. He just managed to escape before the aircraft settled in the ooze. He was visited by Lieutenant Commander Gordon-Smith, the Air Group Commander, with his No 2 during the afternoon who found him suffering from minor injuries and shock. He was picked up two days later by a Firefly from 810 Squadron.

The Fireflies carried out strikes on rail targets, rocketing and strafing trucks and store dumps, and bombing bridges of which one was destroyed and another had one span knocked down.

With a cloud base of 200 feet and visibility only two miles, flying was called off on the 11th after only one abortive first detail.

Bridges in the Hungnam area were the targets for the Fireflies next day, knocking out two spans of one and damaging another, with barracks and store dumps being rocketed and strafed. During a strike on one of the bridges near Songjin Mr. Bailey's aircraft was hit by small-arms fire. Loss of oil pressure caused the engine to pack up, and he ditched 40 miles from the carriers, about 10 miles north-east of Hungnam. Helicopters from USS *Bataan* and *Theseus* escorted by Furies picked up Mr. Bailey and Aircrewman Loveys after they had spent about 40 cold minutes in their dinghies. The Furies attacked tanks, some of which were camouflaged, during their reconnaissance details; they spotted for *Manchester* and, directed by a Mustang 'Dona Dog', dealt Smith troops in dugouts near the bomb-line. Targets in the coastal areas of Wonsan and Sang-ni were bombarded by *St Paul* and *Hank* spotted by a section of Furies.

Much of the forenoon of the 13th was spent refuelling from *Wave Chief*, during which time some fuel lines parted and some radio aerials on the starboard side were written off. Flying re-commenced at 1140, in a considerable swell. During an inland reconnaissance to Hamhung, Lieutenant Humphries' aircraft was hit by flak and he was obliged to crash land. He landed in a small paddy field but skidded into a dried up river bed which provided some protection from small-arms fire. The remaining aircraft acted as a RESCAP while two other Furies in the area escorted a helicopter from *Manchester* at Wonsan, about 40 miles away. After 38 minutes he was picked up, and it was found, when in the expert care of the doctors in *Manchester*, that he was severely injured with head injuries and a badly broken ankle. A fortnight earlier, Mr Mackenzie had gone to Suwon to wait whilst his aircraft was being repaired and then to fly it to Iwakuni. He had arrived at Iwakuni on 7th April, but was unable to rejoin *Theseus* before she sailed. He finally caught up with his ship, via HMAS *Bataan* and a jackstay, during the afternoon, after replenishment. During the afternoon the Fireflies carried out strikes on three bridges, knocking out two spans. The Furies demolished some warehouses at Sontang-ni under the direction of 'Dona Dog', and attacked a village north of Wonsan where buildings were damaged and troops strafed.

Sea Fury heavy landing – starboard and wheel oleo collapsed.   *(Winton)*

The Furies carried out the west coast reconnaissance across the country on the 14th, while the Fireflies attacked various bridges in the Hungnam area, but with no spectacular results. Visibility was poor, but the Furies attacked the marshalling yards at Chinnampo where a large number of wagons were hit, and several small craft along the coast were left burning. Later details attacked tanks in the Hamhung area, and small craft around Wonsan. Intense flak of all types in this area made things unhealthy for these aircraft. Lieutenant Bowman's aircraft was hit by flak when to the south-west of Hungnam. He made a successful forced landing and, being in radio contact with the aircraft overhead, asked for transport to return him to his ship. All available aircraft in the area flew RESCAP over him until he was rescued by *Manchester's* helicopter. The helicopter was overloaded so the camera and stores were jettisoned. Intense small-arms fire made this rescue extremely hazardous, but no hits were made on the rescuing aircraft — Bowman thanked God that the North Koreans were such bad shots. His story continues:

'We got on the cruiser just at dusk, another half-hour and I would have been a guest of the North Koreans. After landing I was taken to the Captain and told my story. He asked me if I had tried to destroy the aircraft, which I thought was a fair question, but had never occurred to me. After dinner, which was enormous, I was taken to a cabin and told not to worry about getting up early, as they would call me at a respectable time. There were some magazines in the cabin by the bed and I read for a while and became sleepy and dozed off, but not for long. I remember hearing a bell and there was a hell of an explosion, the lights went dim, some of the ducting came down, the ship shook, I waited for something over the loud speaker system, nothing came but the bell. It rang again and there was another boom, and I realised I was under the ship's main turret and they were firing which they continued to do every five minutes for the next two hours.' *Manchester's* signal tells her side of the tale:

UNCLASSIFIED   PRIORITY
FROM: MANCHESTER CL83   ACTN: COMNAVFE
NAVY PRESS: USS MANCHESTER 14 APRIL…THE NORTH
COMMUNISTS ARE TODAY RICHER BY 23 CARTONS OF
CIGARETTES, 5 BOXES OF CANDY, ONE AERIAL CAMERA,
AND MANY BARS OF SOAP, AS THE CRUISER
MANCHESTER'S HELICOPTER MADE ANOTHER HEROIC
RESCUE OF A BRITISH FIGHTER PILOT, SHOT DOWN DEEP
IN ENEMY TERRITORY.
SHORTLY BEFORE DUSK TONIGHT, THE MANCHESTER
HELICOPTER TOOK OFF FROM THE CRUISER, ANCHORED ON

THE FIRING LINE IN WONSAN HARBOUR, LOADED DOWN
with CIGARETTES, CANDY AND BARS OF SOAP FOR
ANOTHER HELICOPTER CREW ABOARD THE LIST 0007.
BEFORE THE SUPPLIES COULD BE DELIVERED HOWEVER,
THE MANCHESTER RECEIVED AN EMERGENCY MESSAGE
FROM THE FLIGHT LEADER OF A GROUP OF SEA FURIES OFF
THE BRITISH AIRCRAFT CARRIER THESEUS, THAT ONE OF
HIS PLANES HAD BEEN SHOT DOWN AND REQUESTED A
HELICOPTER BE SENT TO ATTEMPT THE RESCUE OF THE
PILOT.
THE HELICOPTER PILOT LT. ROGER GILL OF NORTH
SEATTLE, WASHINGTON, AND CREWMAN THOMAS ROCHE
OF BRONX, NEW YORK, HAD JUST LANDED ABOARD THE
LST WHEN THE MANCHESTER ALERTED THEM OVER THE
AIRCRAFT'S RADIO. SECONDS LATER THE MANCHESTER
HELICOPTER "CLEMENTINE" WAS IN THE AIR AND HEADED
NORTH UP THE COAST, ESCORTED BY TWO SEA FURIES.
AS THE MANCHESTER WINDMILL APPROACHED THE
OUTSKIRTS OF HAMHUNG, PILOT GILL RELATED 'THE
FLIGHT LEADER OF THE BRITISH PLANE CAME UP OVER
THE RADIO CIRCUIT with "QUICK, GET DOWN LOW,
THEY'RE FIRING AT YOU". ABOUT THAT TIME A LINE OF
AIRBURSTS SUDDENLY APPEARED JUST IN FRONT OF THE
PLANE. I KICKED THE HELICOPTER DOWN TOWARDS THE
GROUND IN A 360 DEGREE TURN TO KEEP FROM RUNNING
INTO THE FLAK BURSTS, AND AS I TURNED I SPOTTED THE
WRECKED PLANE ON THE GROUND. FOR A MINUTE I
THOUGHT IT WAS THE SAME ONE THAT OUR OTHER PILOT,
HENRY CARDOZA, HAD RESCUED AN AIRMAN FROM
YESTERDAY, BUT AS WE HEADED FOR THE GROUND I
COULD SEE SOMEONE RUNNING AROUND THE TAIL OF THE
PLANE. I WAS STILL GOING ABOUT 100 KNOTS AND I
PASSED RIGHT OVER THE PLANE THE FIRST TIME. THE
PILOT RAN BACK AROUND THE PLANE AND AS SOON AS I
COULD GET DOWN ON THE GROUND HE CLIMBED ABOARD
AND I STARTED TO TAKE OFF. I WAS TOO NOSE HEAVY
THOUGH, AND WITH AN EMBANKMENT JUST IN FRONT OF
THE PLANE I WAS AFRAID I WOULD CRACK THE PLANE UP
AND EVERYBODY ELSE WITH IT. I HOLLERED AT MY
CREWMAN TO JETTISON SOME OF THE STUFF IN THE

PLANE TO MAKE IT LIGHTER, AND HE STARTED THROWING
OUT ALL THE CANDY, CIGARETTES AND BARS OF SOAP WE
HAD BROUGHT FOR THE LST. THE PLANE STILL WASN'T
LIGHT ENOUGH SO FINALLY HE HEAVED OUT THE BIG
AERIAL CAMERA AND WE TOOK OFF. THE LAST THING I
REMEMBER THINKING ABOUT AS WE HEADED OUT OF THE
AREA WAS "WITH ALL THOSE CIGARETTES, CANDY AND
SOAP SCATTERED AROUND THE GROUND THE GOOKS WILL
LIVE LIKE KINGS FOR A WHILE". JUST AS WE WERE
AIRBORNE THERE was ANOTHER LARGE SHELL BURST
NEAR THE PLANE AS THE NORTH KOREANS BEGAN TO GET
OUR RANGE. IT SEEMED LIKE A LONG TIME BEFORE WE
WERE OVER WATER AGAIN AND HEADED BACK DOWN THE
COAST OF WONSAN HARBOUR, BUT IT WAS A FAST TRIP
AND OLE CLEMENTINE REALLY HIGHBALLED IT HOME.'
THE PILOT OF THE DOWNED PLANE, LT. IRWIN L. BOWMAN,
OF CALGARY, ALBERTA, CANADA, STATED 'WE WERE
ROCKETTING A FUEL DUMP AND TRENCHES COVERED
WITH STRAW IN THE SIDE OF A HILL. WE BELIEVED THE
COMMUNISTS WERE HIDING THEIR TRUCKS THERE DURING
THE DAY. WE HAD BEEN RECEIVING QUITE A BIT OF ANTI-
AIRCRAFT FIRE AND ON ONE OF MY PASSES, JUST AS I
PULLED UP, I HEARD A LOUD "WHANG" AND MY ENGINE
CONKED OUT. I IMMEDIATELY LOOKED AROUND FOR A
FLAT PLACE TO LAND, AWAY FROM ALL THE SMALL
VILLAGES. I FINALLY LANDED NEAR THE RAILROAD
TRACKS THAT RAN RIGHT INTO HAMHUNG. THE PLANE
WASN'T DAMAGED VERY BADLY AND I WASN'T HURT AT
ALL IN THE CRASH. IN FACT, THE WHEELS UP LANDING WAS
ONE OF THE SMOOTHEST I EVER MADE. WHILE I WAS
WAITING FOR THE HELICOPTER TO ARRIVE I COULD HEAR
MACHINE GUNS AND LARGER ANTI-AIRCRAFT BATTERIES
FIRING AT MY WINGMATES CIRCLING THE AREA. THEY
SEEMED VERY CLOSE, JUST OVER A SMALL RIDGE A SHORT
DISTANCE AWAY. IT WASN'T LONG BEFORE I COULD SEE
THE HELICOPTER APPROACHING, AND I ALSO SAW THE
FLAK BURSTING AROUND IT. I DON'T KNOW HOW IT EVER
MISSED BEING HIT. THE WAY IT HEADED FOR THE GROUND I
THOUGHT IT HAD BEEN HIT AT FIRST. I CLIMBED ABOARD
AND THE NEXT THING I KNEW THE CREWMAN WAS

THROWING EVERYTHING OUT OF THE PLANE TO MAKE IT
LIGHTER.
THERE WAS STILL QUITE A LOAD ON THE PLANE BUT AN
EVEN BIGGER LOAD OFF MY MIND AS THE PILOT GOT IT
OFF THE GROUND AND HEADED FOR THE MANCHESTER.'
141342Z/APRIL

Lieutenant Roger Gill was awarded a DSC for this rescue and was presented with it by the British Consul in Seattle.

Operations on the 15th were reduced to three details by fog. The Furies attacked small targets along the coast from Wonsan, including the remains of Lieutenant Bowman's aircraft which was left burning. The village of Chungyang-ni containing motor transport and troops was attacked twice, starting several fires. The Fireflies had a more successful bridge-busting day, knocking out two spans of one bridge 15 miles north-west of Wonsan and leaving a second unfit for vehicular traffic. Lieutenant Bowman returned on board late in the afternoon, having been transferred to *Huron* in Wonsan where she had gone to refuel. He gave a very chatty account of his forced landing and subsequent rescue to the ship's company over the ship's broadcasting system.

TE 95.11's operations on the east coast came to an end at 1630 on 15th April, when USS *Bataan* with *English* and HMAS *Bataan* proceeded to Sasebo leaving *Theseus* as CTE 95.11, who with *Consort, Huron* and *Athabaskan* set course for her old haunts on the west coast. Admiral Scott-Moncrieff embarked in HMAS *Bataan* at Sasebo, and next afternoon he transferred by jackstay to *Theseus*, in which he spent the next few days.

Flying operations started as soon as *Theseus* was within effective range of targets on the 17th. The Furies reconnoitred the Haeju/Chaeryong/Sariwon area. It was noted that most of the bridges had been repaired; Sariwon airfield was attacked and left completely unserviceable, warehouses and stores dumps were attacked near Chaeryong where light flak was encountered; boat yards at Chinnampo and railway installations at Sariwon were also rocketed and strafed. The Fireflies bombed road and rail bridges in the Haeju and Chaeryong areas, knocking out the centre span of one and leaving the others damaged. Lieutenant Winterton's aircraft was hit by flak, one bullet hitting the HF aerial mast above the observer's cockpit.

Next day the Fireflies again bombed bridges with 1,000 lb. and 500 lb. bombs, knocking a span from one, collapsing the support of a second and obtaining a direct hit on the support of a third but the bomb failed to explode. The Furies attacked junks and stores in the dock area of Chinnampo. Mine-laying junks in the Chinnampo estuary were attacked and damaged. During the afternoon one flight attacked and wrecked stonecrushing machinery and vehicles in a quarry near Yonan. On return from this sortie, a Fury, piloted by Lieutenant Hamilton, landed in the sea about 60 miles from *Theseus*. He failed to retrieve his dinghy as he left the aircraft, before it sank, and was rescued practically unconscious after 55 minutes in water of about 42°F by the helicopter, but he made a good recovery in 24 hours. This was the fifth rescue affected by the helicopter since the ship had sailed on 8th April. Apart from the practical value of these aircraft, their effect on the morale of aircrews was outstanding.

This was the last day's flying carried out by *Theseus* before leaving the station, and that evening *Consort* was detached to meet *Glory*, then on her way to relieve her, in the Formosa Channel. The weather on the 19th — low cloud, short visibility, heavy rain and a pessimistic forecast — prevented flying over the land, and TE 95.11 withdrew to Sasebo. On arrival Admiral Scott-Moncrieff transferred to *Ladybird*.

On the 20th, coming into Sasebo for the last time, all aircraft were ranged on deck, and all available men were formed into the word THESEUS at the forward end of the flight deck; the helicopter, with a photographer, making numerous runs to record the event.

Unserviceable aircraft and surplus stores were transferred to *Unicorn*. Reports were received in *Theseus* that two US Marine aircraft from USS *Bataan* had shot down three Yaks and damaged another during her patrol on the west coast.

Glory entered Sasebo on 23rd April, watched by most of *Theseus'* ship's company from on deck. *Theseus'* officers had given a farewell party the previous day for other ships in harbour, and on 24th, after a full day's handing-over, another party was held on board for *Glory's* officers.

On Wednesday 25th April, at 0900, *Theseus* sailed for Hong Kong, first doing a tour of the harbour before passing through the boom. *Unicorn* and *Glory* both manned the side and cheered, *Theseus* returning the compliment. *Warramunga* remained in company until 1900.

Since her arrival in the theatre of war seven months before, *Theseus* had flown 3,446 operational sorties in 86 operational flying days. No operations had taken place in November 1950, the North Koreans had been defeated and the Chinese had not then come in. The main credit for this fine record was ascribed by Captain Bolt to the pilots for their high and consistent standard of flying, and to the Deck Landing Control Officers for their excellent work. Great attention was paid to the avoidance of deck-landing, taxiing and handling accidents; at the end of the last operational period the sequence of accident-free landings stood at 939, approaching four figures for the second time in six months.

Admiral Scott-Moncrieff wrote 'I was particularly pleased to be able to watch the last two days flying in this very efficient carrier…It is fair to say that the operations of HMS *Theseus* have been an inspiration to the

US carriers out here, and it is notable that for the first few days after the return of the TF 77 carriers to their own parish that they were provoked into flying over 200 sorties per day for the first time…a considerable increase on their normal operational outputs…There is no doubt that great credit is due to Captain Bolt and his officers and ship's company for a fine effort ably performed'.

He added, as a matter of interest, that during a recent period the two CVLs, alternating in 9-day cycles and operating from Sasebo (one day's steaming from the operational area) produced nearly 507 more sorties per pilot per plane than the *Essex* class carriers in TF 77, with a 20-day-out and 10-day-in cycle operating from Yokosuka (Two day's steaming from the operational area).

Theseus sailed from Sasebo for the UK on 25th April 1951. The US Navy was generous in its recognition of her achievements, her departure being marked by the congratulatory signals below from CinC US Pacific Fleet (Admiral Radford), Commander Naval Forces Far East (Vice Admiral Joy), Commander 7th Fleet (Vice Admiral Martin) and one from CTF 77 (Rear Admiral Smith), all of whom paid high tribute to her performance in the theatre of war. 'There is little doubt,' wrote Admiral Scott-Moncrieff, 'that the efficiency and skill of our "Naval Air" has been an eye-opener to the US Navy'; and the CinC Vice Admiral Sir Guy Russell, considered that *Theseus* had 'set an exceptionally high standard of operational flying…in Korean waters'.

TO THESEUS (R) CinCFES. COMNAVFE. CTG95. COM7thFLT
FROM CinC PACFLT
U/C
I WELL REMEMBER THAT BRITISH AND AMERICAN
CARRIER TASK FORCES OPERATED TOGETHER WITH GREAT
PROFIT TO OURSELVES AND GREAT LOSS TO OUR ENEMIES
IN THE CLOSING CAMPAIGNS OF WORLD WAR TWO IN THE
PACIFIC. THAT THIS FINE ASSOCIATION HAS BEEN
RENEWED IN KOREA HAS BEEN A SOURCE OF GREAT PRIDE
AND PLEASURE TO ME AND TO UNITS OF THE UNITED
STATES PACIFIC FLEET. THE WORK OF THE "THESEUS" IN
OUR JOINT EFFORTS HAS BEEN OUTSTANDING AND A FINE
EXAMPLE TO ALL. MAY YOU HAVE A GOOD TRIP HOME AND
MANY HAPPY LANDINGS. SIGNED A.W. RADFORD,
ADMIRAL, US NAVY, COMMANDER IN CHIEF US PACIFIC
FLEET.
260131Z APRIL

TO THESEUS   FROM COMNAVFE

U/C

THESEUS AND EMBARKED AIRMEN HAVE SET HIGH
STANDARDS FOR ALL AIRCRAFT CARRIERS DURING THEIR
MOST EFFECTIVE TOUR OF DUTY WITH THE UNITED
NATIONS FORCES. WE HAVE ADMIRED YOUR QUIET AND
CONFIDENT WAY OF ALWAYS DOING MORE THAN THE
SCHEDULE CALLED FOR. IT HAS BEEN A PRIVILEGE TO
HAVE SUCH A FINE UNIT SHARE THIS CAMPAIGN WITH US.
WELL DONE. GOOD LUCK. GOD SPEED ON YOUR
HOMEWARD VOYAGE.

SIGNED C.T. JOY VICE-ADMIRAL USN.

TO THESEUS   FROM COM7THFLT

U/C

YOUR FINE PERFORMANCE IN THIS KOREAN SHOW HAS
ADDED NEW LUSTRE TO THE BRILLIANT TRADITIONS OF
THE BRITISH NAVY. IT HAS BEEN A PRIVILEGE TO HAVE
YOU IN THE SEVENTH FLEET. GOOD LUCK AND MAY WE BE
SHIPMATES AGAIN. SIGNED VICE-ADMIRAL MARTIN USN.

CHAPTER 5

THE AIR WAR

Interdiction and Attrition

Triumph was the Far East carrier at the start of the war, operating obsolete aircraft with HMS *Simbang*, the Air Station at Sembawang in Singapore, and *Unicorn*, the repair and ferry carrier, as back-up support. She had covered the retreat into the Pusan Perimeter and had done noble work at Inchon — she could have achieved so much more with a full complement of Sea Furies and later marks of Firefly.

Theseus followed, covering the mobile war from post-Inchon to the start of the long stalemate period of the armistice talks.

Glory, Sydney and *Ocean*, for the next two years, had the unenviable task of fighting a 'routine', static, war, almost entirely off the west coast, on an 18 day patrol cycle of nine days in the area and nine out. From January 1951 a US Navy carrier (CVE or CVL) alternated with the Commonwealth carrier on the west coast, both being under the command of FO2FE as CTG 95.1.

Let us pause and look at the other air activity, waged by the US Navy, 5th USAF, RAAF and RAF.

For many months the airmen had been urging the Chiefs of Staff in Washington — as airmen so often urged commanders throughout the 20th century — that they could pursue the Allies' strategic objectives at far lower cost in lives by a sustained bombing campaign. But, nevertheless, it was clear that if pressure was to be put on the Communists, air power was the best way to do it.

From the very outset of the conflict until its ambiguous conclusion UN aircraft went after the enemy's communications network and his logistics support system for his armies at the front. It was expensive works for it risked a highly trained pilot and a costly aeroplane to bomb a culvert or strafe a truck; it was dangerous, flying at high speed and low altitude into possible anti-aircraft traps. And it was repetitive, for the same rail line or road bridge might well be destroyed today and repaired by tomorrow and destroyed again next day. But it was a vital part of halting the Communists' drives while they were on the offensive, of preventing build-up of resources when they were quiescent, or simply of making the whole effort so difficult that the Communists would eventually choose to give it up.

This was work for the fighter-bomber types, the US Air Force's Mustangs, Shooting Stars, and Thunderjets, the US Marine's Corsairs, the US Navy's

Skyraiders and Panthers, the Royal Navy's Fireflies and Sea Furies, and the RAAF's Meteors. In many ways this was the worst kind of flying, for overall it was the day-after-day kind of operation that could become almost routine — and then suddenly turn dangerous and kill people.

The interdiction work began in June 1950, and was among the earliest UN responses to the crisis. It gained increasingly in effectiveness, and was particularly useful in taking the impetus out of the Communist attacks. The Communists could bring sufficient supplies forward to mount an offensive, but once they were committed to one, UN airpower was inevitably able to prevent their sustaining it. After ten days or two weeks they would have used up their accumulation, and they would then have to pause and go through the build-up once again. Ironically, the more successful the Communists were in advancing south, the more vulnerable they were to wide-ranging fighter-bomber attacks. In that sense, they were up against a law of diminishing returns. Below the 38th parallel a relatively small advance cost them an inordinate amount of effort.

The United States Air Force contributed materially to the progressive retardation and eventual collapse of the armoured thrust made towards Pusan by the North Korean People's Army through the summer of 1950. Yet it achieved far less against the great offensive sustained in the last few weeks of that year by a People's Liberation Army (PLA) which had crossed the Yalu river border from its native China and which drove General MacArthur's multi-national, United Nations, army back into South Korea once more. This, because the PLA incursion was carried out very largely by foot soldiers, advancing well dispersed and well shielded by winter weather.

Most disturbing was the appearance of MiG 15 (Mikoyan and Gurevich) jet fighters. Design of the MiG had started in 1946, using the German swept wing concept plus a Rolls-Royce Nenes derivative engine, the Russians having bought Nenes after the Second World War. The appearance of the MiGs posed a problem for the bomber and attack crews near the Manchuria border.

The MiG outclassed all aircraft in Korea: it was 100 mph faster than the F80 Shooting Star and the US Navy's F-9F Panther, and, more seriously from the combat point of view, could out-climb, out-turn and out-dive them. Because of the Chinese pilot's lack of experience, US pilots had a good chance of survival. MiG pilots rarely made more than two firing passes before breaking off an attack. Piston engined types, if trapped, had to keep turning as tightly as possible and wait for an opportunity to dive away and head southwards at top speed on the deck.

On 8th November 1950 a B-29 formation en route to Sinuiju, preceded by Shooting Star fighters, was attacked by MiG-15s from Antung. Five turned away, but the sixth was shot down by Lieutenant Russet J. Brown — the first jet versus jet fight in history.

A facet of the Korean saga that merits some comment is an insistent USAF claim that, in many battles high above the southern approaches of the Yalu, its F-86 Sabres destroyed no fewer than 818 MiG-15s while losing but 58 of their own number. Doubts arise about this and about the related view that overall Chinese losses in fighter aircraft (a good 80% of which would have been MiG-15s) exceeded 2,000, this thanks to a combination of shootings down and training accidents.

Over-counting occurs all too readily in air war, the Battle of Britain affording famous instances. Besides by no means all the operative factors would have militated against the Chinese. Often they enjoyed a threefold superiority in numbers in action which would have enabled them to benefit greatly from F.W. Lanchester's square law, propounded in 1916 as: 'the fighting strength of a force may be broadly defined as proportional to the square of its numerical strength, multiplied by the fighting value of its individual units'. In other words, a marginal increase in numbers is liable to be more consequential than a marginal gain in quality. Also, their MiGs could be directed from ground stations securely located just beyond the Yalu, and the aircraft themselves were superior in some aerodynamic respects. Finally if Chinese losses had been all that mortifying, the fighter aircraft inventory could hardly have risen in the course of the Korean campaign from some 400 to 3,000. Nor could the resolve of its pilots have held up as well as it did.

On the other hand, certain considerations do point the other way. Grave deficiencies in advanced training and in-squadron experience obliged the Chinese to rely far too much on close formation mass attack. Furthermore, the F-86 had the potentially great advantage of a radar-directed gunsight, although the type then fitted was unreliable and hard to service, which meant that most kills still had to made without recourse to it. All in all, a good balance may have been struck by a revisionist assessment which puts the MiG loss rate at 1.7 per 1,000 sorties as against 1.3 for the Sabre.

Early in November 1950 General MacArthur had ordered the destruction by air attack of the bridges over the Yalu. General Stratemeyer had called on COMNAVFE for assistance in this bridge busting on the river, a unique and unfamiliar role for the Fleet carriers of TF 77, *Valley Forge, Philippine Sea* and *Leyte*. The fact that Manchurian air space was not to be violated imposed severe operational constraints. Traditional tactical practice called for aircraft attacking bridges to follow the road across the bridge, releasing their bombs so they would 'walk' across, inflicting the maximum damage. Under the best of circumstances bridges are difficult targets, the flooring can be easily replaced and the vulnerable points — trusses, supports and abutments — are difficult to damage. With Manchuria inviolable, aircraft had to attack the Yalu bridges from the side. The rules of engagement prevented flak suppression aircraft from attacking anti-aircraft installations on the Manchurian side of the river; TARCAP fighters were prohibited from engaging the enemy over the Manchurian border or 'hot pursuit' over the river.

The enemy's known capability for quickly effecting temporary repairs to damaged portions of these routes could be seriously impaired by the deliberate, methodical and total destruction of all piers, spans, approaches and embankments of each vital bridge in each critical area. The enemy could not accomplish makeshift repairs when nothing remained upon which to make them. Naval air and naval gunfire — where the bridges were within range — were good weapons with which to accomplish that job.

On 9th November TF 77 tried its luck, 5th USAF having failed on the 8th. Operating in the Sea of Japan, the strikes launched from *Valley Forge* and *Philippine Sea* had a 225 mile trip to Sinuiju. Skyraiders were armed with 1,000 or 2,000 lb. bombs, rockets and 20 mm cannon, the Panther TARCAP with cannon only. A typical strike consisted of 8 Skyraiders, 16 flak suppression Corsairs and 8 to 16 Panther TARCAP. The jet escort was launched 50 minutes after the propeller aircraft; they could give 8-10 minutes cover on the run-in to the target and 30 minutes coverage in the target area. There was a second jet launch 15 minutes after the first Panthers who would act as return escort. A MiG was shot down by Commander W.T. Amen USN of *Philippine Sea* on the 9th, and two more were destroyed during the week.

The attacks by 5th USAF and TF 77 were reasonably successful, three spans on the Sinuiju highway bridge, and two bridges at Hyesanjin were damaged. The Sinuiju railway bridge was left standing.

By the end of November the river was frozen, and for the rest of the winter the Chinese could cross it anywhere over the thick ice.

The UN also faced the almost impossible task of isolating the battlefield by air.

The emphasis from winter 1950 to mid 1952 shifted from battlefield support to interdiction. Admiral Struble failed to convince General Ridgway that CAS was better than interdiction, the Navy wished to stick to battlefield support as the key to victory. Control of interdiction effort was with 5th USAF.

The geography of Korea forced road and rail transport to the narrow east and broad west coast plains. The mountains in the east were steep and convoluted; the eastern plain was within easy reach of naval gunfire as well as air strikes, but risks to the aviators were high.

All roads were gravel or dirt, none were surfaced, and they paralleled the single track railways. The road network was estimated to have a capacity of less than 1,500 tons nightly. Tunnels were difficult to damage or destroy, and bridges were usually over shallot creeks and rivers which could be bridged quickly and easily by timbers if they were destroyed. It generally seemed to take 60 rounds of 16 inch naval guns or 12 to 16 Skyraider sorties (24 to 32 x 2,000 lb. bombs) to destroy a bridge. Repair crews, never in short supply, quickly restored the road surfaces, removed the rubble, replaced the track, filled craters and constructed bypasses that made interdiction prolonged and frustrating.

Communist logistics helped this frustration. The North Koreans, at 10 lbs per soldier per day, needed half the supplies of the RoK and less than 20% of that deemed necessary to support a US soldier at the front. The very primitiveness of the highway system was an advantage to the enemy and presented unprofitable targets to air assault. The North Koreans could make do with a large number of peasants moving supplies south. Horses, mules, camels and unlimited coolie-power were available to carry equipment to the front line using trails and paths instead of highways and rail lines. Using the A-frame they could move, albeit slowly, a prodigious amount of mortar rounds, artillery shells, ammunition, food, small arms and infantry weapons; it was a more reliable system than road or rail, and, because of peasants, the effect of disruption to road and rail was less decisive. The ubiquitous A-frame on the back of a sturdy Oriental peasant was one logistic system modern air power could not effectively counter.

It was a cat and mouse game of repairing and rebuilding damaged bridges by the North Koreans which were then attacked again by the Air Forces and Navies. General Van Fleet said 'We won the battle to knock out the bridges; but we lost the objective, which was to knock out the traffic.' It was a frustrating sequence, the aircraft bombed the bridges, bombed the efforts to repair the bridges, and finally confronted the problem of clever bypasses. The bridges became great flak traps.

The Chinese needed only 3,000 tons of supplies per day at the front to be transported by rail from Manchuria. The rail system was divided into two separate halves by the mountains running from north to south down the peninsula. On the west three lines run from Sinuiju to Pyongyang, which, after damage to tunnels, bridges, the roadbed and track, was carrying between 500 and 1,500 tons per day. On the east the railway ran close to the coast on a narrow plain to seaward of the mountains. This line was vulnerable to naval gunfire, particularly where the width of the plain was less than the range of the guns. After naval interdiction it was carrying about 500 tons per day. Despite an all out UN air effort the Communists were getting half their needs by rail alone.

Sea routes for the transport of supplies were securely closed by the blockade efforts of TF 95.

By June 1951 it was apparent that the battlefield was not being interdicted. A

Bomb craters reveal efforts to destroy a pair of road and rail bridges. The road bridge was by-passed and rebuilt, rail loop rebuilt but not yet cut. *(FAAM)*

great part of the troops, supplies and equipment had been choked off along the east coast, but much had been transferred to the west coast where the rail network was larger and more widely spread than on the east. On the west they were more dependent on truck transport with practically everything travelling at night. Skilful and highly organised over-night repair efforts could equal the rate of destruction of roads and railways.

With the stabilisation of the front across the waist of the peninsula, at the end of May 1951 FEAF initiated Operation 'Strangle', an attempt to paralyse the North Korean road network in the band 38°15'N to 39°15'N. This interdiction campaign, featuring intensive air attacks by Air Force, Navy, and Marine aircraft, was undertaken primarily to limit the fighting power of the Communist forward troops and hence to influence the armistice talks getting under way in Panmunjom. 'Strangle areas' were nominated: roads in defiles and constricted passes where detours would be difficult to construct; bridges and junctions; the rail network where the rails were easily seen, and there were accessible choke points, bridges, culverts, shunting yards, and roundhouses — but it took a direct hit with a 500 lb. bomb to cut a line, achieved by only one sortie in four. 5th USAF were responsible for the west and 1st Marine Air Wing for the east: dawn and dusk heckling raids were initiated; night strikes under flares; daytime interdiction and AR to 'seed' roads with delay fused bombs and anti-personnel 'butterfly' bombs. The North Koreans and Chinese accepted casualties in order to keep the roads Open.

It worked well while the advance was going on, preventing supplies moving southward and material being evacuated northward. Under static conditions the enemy had sufficient flexibility to avoid the worst damages the air forces could inflict.

But it was soon apparent that the strategy had failed. Breaks were repaired in twenty-four hours; portable bridges were hidden during the day and then moved into place and used at night; and other bridges were laid below water level. Nor was it a paying proposition to risk — and lose — highly trained pilots and expensive aircraft just to blow up a culvert and interrupt traffic for a couple of hours. By early 1952, when it was clear that its original hopes had not been fulfilled, Strangle was allowed to run down.

Strangle's name became an increasing source of embarrassment, though it lingered on and became attached to 5th USAF rail interdiction in 1951-52, becoming 'Saturate' in February 1952. Pre-war rail traffic was reduced to 4-5%, but was still enough, with human transport and trucks, to maintain Communist capabilities. Saturate was no more successful than Strangle, and, in May 1952, it too was allowed to run down.

Many targets were within gun range of TF 77. 'Package' targets were hit from the air, marked with radar reflectors, and could then be attacked by surface vessels at any time of day and in any weather; 'Derail' was limited to surface forces only, attacks being primarily by naval bombardment though sometimes by commando or other raiding parties. Package and Derail had some notable successes, pressure on Kowon resulted in the suspension of both north/south and east/west rail traffic into Wonsan for over a month between February and March 1952. However the inability of surface vessels to stay on station long enough to ensure full-time all-weather interdiction limited the usefulness of both programmes.

At the same time as Package and Derail, TF 77 launched 'Moonlight Sonata' to take advantage of the improved visibility of the Korean landscape in moonlit winter where rail lines and the surrounding terrain stood out in sharp relief in the bright sky. Each mission would be of ten aircraft, five pairs of Skyraiders or Corsairs patrolling a 50 mile stretch having been launched pre-dawn at 0300. It was not a complete success, depending as it did too much on the right combination of visibility, weather and target.

As the snows cleared, 'Insomnia' was more successful, missions being two strikes of six aircraft launched at 0100 and 0200. Insomnia began in May 1952 and concentrated on trapping locomotives by cutting the line to the front and rear so that daylight strike groups could attack the engines and rolling stock. Moonlight Sonata accounted for two locomotives, Insomnia for nine. The High Command, from the Commander 7th Fleet upwards, believed night attacks such as Insomnia were of little value unless a designated night carrier was stationed off Korea.

In April 1951 No. 77 Squadron RAAF returned to Iwakuni with its Mustangs to re-equip with 15 Gloster Meteor 8s and two Mark 7 trainers that had been ferried from the UK in HMS *Warrior* in February, to be followed by 20 more in April. The Australians had hoped for Sabres, some believing the Meteor to be hopelessly outclassed, others were reluctant to give up their Mustangs. A mock combat with a Sabre seemed to indicate that it would be able to hold its own against a MiG. The Sabre was better in a steep dive or in a long straight and level run, but the Meteor was superior in turning, zooming and in a sustained climb. The Australians then looked forward to taking them into action for the first time.

The Meteor 8 had not been tried out in combat although an earlier Mark had been operated against the V1 flying bomb in the closing stages of World War II. The Australian pilots knew its limitations, particularly a blind spot on a 30 degree arc on either side astern, but were confident that they could outmanoeuvre any aircraft they were likely to meet.

The first clash took place on 29th August 1951. Eight Meteors were on a fighter sweep 35,000 feet above Chongju when they saw six MiGs above them at 40,000 feet. The MiGs scored hits on two Meteors; a third, piloted by Warrant Officer R.D. Guthrie, was also hit. The aircraft's controls failed to respond and Guthrie abandoned the aircraft by the ejection seat at about 38,000 feet. The seat and the oxygen worked perfectly, and as soon as the seat had settled down under its parachute, Guthrie separated from it and opened his own parachute. He took about 23 minutes to reach the ground where he was surrounded by North Koreans and led into captivity.

A week later the Meteors again tangled with MiGs and came off second best. Six Meteors were providing fighter cover for two Shooting Stars on a photographic mission near the Manchurian border. Six MiGs approached from 9 o'clock to 6 o'clock high in three pairs, the two Meteors that were attacked breaking to starboard. A shell had hit one Meteor in the tail-plane and had exploded behind the port engine damaging the port flap, port wing and main fuel tank and putting holes in the fuselage and engine nacelle. Another shell had carried away part of the starboard aileron.

A few days after this encounter, Flight Lieutenant R.L. Dawson scored 77 Squadron's first effective hit against a MiG. Twelve Meteors were on a fighter sweep near Anju when they were jumped by fifteen MiGs. One Meteor was damaged by cannon fire, but Dawson scored a long burst from his 20 mm cannon. Liquid streamed from the damaged MiG's port wing but nobody saw the enemy aircraft crash.

On 1st December 1951 twelve Meteors were on a fighter sweep north of Pyongyang in clear cold weather at 19,000 feet when forty or fifty MiGs swept down on them out of the sun. It was all over very quickly. Once they had lost their initial advantage the MiGs turned for the Manchurian sanctuary but not before they had torn holes in the Australian squadron, three of the twelve Meteor pilots were missing, of which two landed safely but were taken prisoner.

During the dog fight Flight Lieutenant B. Gogerly found himself amongst a group of MiGs that had attacked the other flight. Gogerly turned inside the tight turn the MiGs had made to get at him and fired a five-second burst. He saw his cannon shells exploding on the fuselage and starboard wing root of one MiG. Other pilots said they saw this MiG explode in mid-air.

Another MiG was seen streaming to earth and several pilots shared credit for this kill. The battle had lasted for ten minutes and it was now clear that the Meteor was no match for the MiG. In three encounters the Australians had lost four pilots and had two aircraft badly damaged. The Meteors were rugged, and could take terrible punishment, but they were not nearly fast enough and they could not climb high enough to engage the MiGs on even terms and, with their blind spots astern, they were sitting ducks for the swept-wing enemy fighters. Nobody was surprised when 77 Squadron was taken off fighter interception duties early in 1952.

The Meteor proved to be a highly efficient aircraft for CAS and ground attack duties armed with cannon and rockets. Although lacking the range of piston engined aircraft, the jet planes provided easier maintenance problems and showed a remarkable capacity to absorb punishment and fly home. Air Marshal Sir Donald Hardman, then Chief of the Australian Air Staff, said:

'Although some criticism of the Meteor has been made in Australia, in Korea the men who fly and maintain it say it is a first class aircraft, that it gives no maintenance trouble at all. The life of the Derwent engines is being extended. They don't seem able to wear them out. The Meteor 8 is particularly good for its rocket attack role because, apart from anything else, it has two jet engines and can get back home even with one of them shot away.'

The MiGs became bolder in 1952, bigger enemy patrols flew over the Yalu and extended further south than hitherto. This gave the Meteors another opportunity to do some fighter sweeps, but at a lower level. On 4th May patrolling south-west of Pyongyang, Pilot Officer J.L. Surman attacked and probably destroyed a MiG and four days later Pilot Officer W.H. Simmonds shot down another. On 27th March 1953 the squadron had another successful tangle with MiGs over Sinmak, probably destroying one and damaging another without loss.

In June 1951 No. 1913 Light Liaison Flight had been formed at RAF Middle Wallop in Auster AOP 6s. The aircraft were shipped in crates to Iwakuni where they were assembled and delivered to units in Korean airstrips in No 1 Commonwealth Division's area. No. 1903 Independent Air OP Unit arrived in Korea in October 1951. Although RAF units — the only ones to fly from Korean soil — they were manned almost exclusively by Army personnel.

Based at Iwakuni was the Far East Flying Boat Wing, consisting of Nos. 88 and 209 Squadrons RAF with Short Sunderlands, whose task was reconnaissance cover and a ferry service between Iwakuni and the Korean coast. On one occasion in September a Sunderland had reconnoitred for mines and submarines as far north as the approaches to Vladivostock. No.2 'Cheetah' Squadron, South African Air Force, who had been fighting in Korea since November 1950 flying Mustangs, converted to Sabres in January 1953.

It was reported by guerrillas that a meeting was to be held at Kapsan of high level Communist party members of the Chinese and North Korean forces at 0900 on 29th October 1951. A raid was organised similar to the RAF Mosquito raids on

Gestapo headquarters in 1944 and 1945. The target was a compound east of Kapsan, containing a security police headquarters, a barracks and the record section of all Chinese and North Korean party members. Eight Skyraiders were detailed to attack it. They were armed with 2 x 1,000 lb. bombs, one with a proximity fuse and the other a contact, one napalm and 8 x 250 lb. general purpose bombs, and finally the 20 mm cannon belts made up with half incendiary and half high explosive rounds. All bombs but one fell within the boundary of the target, and only one wall was left standing, the remainder 'a smoking mass of rubble'. The guerrillas reported that 509 high level Communist party members had been killed and all the party records destroyed.

Overall, the interdiction campaign was only a partial success. The destruction achieved did not succeed in restricting the enemy's supplies to the front line or in 'isolating the battlefield'. The Communists showed considerable tenacity, determination and ingenuity in keeping roads and railways in operation and in their methods and organisation. Flak traps were plentiful. An open parachute hung on a tree would be visibly exposed to lure an unwary pilot; dummy trains, trucks, tanks and even troops (of cardboard and strafed were exposed at key points to welcome an attack. Tracks suggesting heavy traffic were made leading into an important looking but empty building. Steel cables were sometimes stretched across narrow valleys into which US aircraft would sometimes fly. Each flak trap was ringed with well placed and well-concealed guns.

The most effective deception was in keeping rail bridges and tracks unserviceable during the day but in use over night. At the end of the night's work, a crane would lift out a portable span and deposit it nearby in a tunnel until next night. Where bridges were over a river, one section would be floated clear, moored downstream and camouflaged during daylight. At such bridges piles of construction materials were kept, as though repair work was in progress. As far as rails were concerned, sections of track would be hand carried into the nearest tunnel and concealed there during daylight, leaving gaps in the lines which gave pilots the appearance of an unrepaired break.

It was only possible to attack the rolling stock that carried the supplies — locomotives, boxcars, vehicles and carts — and the routes themselves, not the sources of supplies in Manchuria. The routes could be cut, bridges demolished, tunnels blocked, twisting mountain roads and rail lines made impassable; but the limited number of aircraft available could not demolish, and keep out of action, 956 bridges and 231 tunnels. The patterns of attack that were adopted were to cut key bridges and to keep them cut; to select a belt across Korea and to destroy every route and target within it; and to inflict (and maintain) widespread damage on roads and rail lines.

General Mark Clark later wrote: 'The Air Force and the Navy carriers may have kept us from losing the war, but were denied the opportunity of influencing the outcome decisively in our favour. They gained complete mastery of the skies, gave magnificent support to the infantry and took costly toll of enemy personnel and supplies ... our air power could not keep a steady stream of enemy supplies and reinforcements from reaching the battle line. Air could not isolate the front.'

From early 1951 to the end of 1952, almost 100% of the offensive effort of the carriers, 60% of USMC aircraft, 70% of 5th USAF and 70% of the blockading effort of ships along the east coast were devoted to interdiction. The enemy forces at the front were supported by long supply lines confined to a closely blockaded peninsula, under constant, and largely unopposed, attack by considerable air strength. The UN supply line was never under attack.

> Several reasons can be advanced for the failure of interdiction in Korea:
>
> i) the ability of the Communists to absorb heavy punishment and, with unlimited manpower, to keep roads and rail lines operating,
>
> ii) UN forces could not attack the sources and fountain heads of the supply lines,
>
> iii) the inability of the UN to find and destroy at night and in bad weather, small targets that they were able to destroy in daylight,
>
> iv) a stalemated war, with static, dug-in lines, meant that the Communists were being fought on their own terms; there was no fluidity and the UN could not make use of their superior weapons and the advantage of mobility,
>
> v) the primitive nature of the enemy's exposed supply network.

The interdiction campaigns also suffered from a number of other drawbacks that might have been avoided with more careful planning. Foremost among these was the lack of co-operation between 5th USAF, US Bomber Command and the US Navy; although each had been assigned their own set of targets at the outset, attacks had generally been uncoordinated. The whole programme might have worked a lot better had all operations been under one control.

To a great extent it had been a victim of circumstances. Had it been carried out in conjunction with a major Allied offensive, it would probably have paralysed the enemy's ability to hold the battle line within a very short time. But the armistice talks dragged on at and it had already been decided that Allied politics and persuasion, and not Allied offensives, would be the principal factors in the bid to decide the outcome of the war. So interdiction remained in essence a defensive weapon, designed to maintain the status quo in Korea — and time remained firmly on the side of the Communists.

By the end of September 1952, strategic targets were few and far between, having been frequently hit; the transportation network provided unproductive targets; standard CAS missions were disappointing along the stagnant battleline; strafing attacks and the delivery of light bombs and rockets had little effect.

Much effort had been expended by the Communists getting supplies and ammunition down the peninsula from Manchuria, in avoiding interdiction strikes and in repairing the damage caused by them. Stores dumps were exposed near the front line but were out of range of artillery — they made excellent targets for concentrated surprise and pinpoint attacks by Naval aircraft.

Thus was born the idea of Cherokee strikes. The first one was on 9th October on a supply area 20 miles north of the Punchbowl, and by mid October 50% of TF 77's attack potential was devoted to Cherokee.

To the foot soldier, a large number of aircraft demolishing targets with heavy bombs was an exhilarating tonic, however they were being controlled and whatever title may have been given to the operation. CAS was a Mosquito controlling eight aircraft at a time loitering in the target area, whereas Cherokee was a pre-briefed in-and-out mission; CAS was between the Main Line of Resistance and the bomb line, whereas Cherokee was from the bomb line to about twenty miles further back. The ground commander could move the bomb line closer to the front for naval aircraft to strike, sometimes as close as 300 yards from friendly troops — a rare tribute to the accuracy of naval airmen.

Cherokee peaked in November and December when it was absorbing more than 50% of offensive effort, but they dwindled in the bad weather, especially by 5th USAF, though they continued successfully to the end of the war.

The general army opinion of the Cherokee strikes was excellent. The strikes, they said, usually demolished the targets. While the results were not always visible or measurable, the programme was undoubtedly hurting the enemy and reducing his attack potential. In fact several of the Cherokee missions had blunted and even prevented enemy attacks.

In June 1952 General Mark W. Clark, who had succeeded General Ridgway as CinC UN Forces in May, obtained approval for a plan to bomb North Korean power stations. It was a joint US Navy/Air Force plan to put out of action the sources of power to the industries of both North Korea and Manchuria over the border. In order to prevent the enemy defences from reacting fully, the operation had to be completed in about 48 hours. Ten plants were attacked, four each at Chosin and Fusen and one at each of Suiho and Kyosen. When the attacks ended, nine-tenths of

North Korea's hydro-electric system had been laid waste. The Allies lost only two aircraft both to ground fire, and in each case the pilot was rescued.

During the next three months the cement plant at Sungho-ri was put out of action, as was the lead and zinc mill at Sindok, the light metals plant at Sinuiju, the tungsten mine at Kiju and the chemical plant at In-hung-ni. On 1st September the biggest naval air strike of the war was launched by Banshees, Panthers and Corsairs from the carriers of TF 77, *Essex, Princeton* and *Boxer*, on the synthetic oil refinery at Aoji, destroying it completely. On 15th September aircraft from *Bonne Homme Richard* and *Princeton* struck supply depots and barracks in the town of Hoeryong on the Soviet border.

These attacks on Communist industrial targets continued well into the next year.

At the end of April 1953 the truce talks seemed to be breaking down again. Far East Air Force proposed knocking out 20 irrigation dams which would destroy the rice crop for the whole of North Korea and would severely damage roads and rail lines by flooding. The country's industrial capacity had long been destroyed, now it's very means of subsistence was attacked. It was decided to destroy them gradually so that the civilian population could blame the Communists for prolonging the war. On 13th May the first attack was made on Toksan dam on Potong River to the north of Pyongyang; five square miles of rice crops were swept away and 700 buildings destroyed, Sunan airfield was under water, five miles of railway line and a two mile stretch of road was destroyed or damaged. In this one raid more damage was done than in several weeks of interdiction work. Chosan dam was destroyed and that at Kuwonga severely damaged, depriving the rice fields of their water and causing severe suffering to the crop.

It has been claimed that these devastating strikes must have been what induced the Chinese and North Koreans to abandon, some time between 7th May and 4th June, a precept they had previously been adamant about: namely, the repatriation of PoWs regardless of their individual wishes. This economic pressure is best seen as complementary to a grim warning concurrently conveyed through various covert channels. This was that unless the negotiating deadlock were soon broken by the requisite Communist concession, the USA would widen the war's horizons and perhaps resort to nuclear release as well. The dambusting signified a degree of ruthlessness requisite for such escalation, a ruthlessness born of 2 years of military and diplomatic deadlock.

There is no doubt that air power was a major instrument of police in getting the Communists finally to sign a truce. But it was far from the sudden, catastrophic blow that theorists of air power had prophesied. The UN forces controlled the skies over Korea; they destroyed much of its industry, transport, communications, armed forces, even its agricultural base. But as long as there were numerous other variables, they could not by that alone end the war.

CHAPTER 6

HMS GLORY

804 and 812 Squadrons
23rd April 1951 to 30th September 1951

On 23rd April HMS *Glory* (Captain K.S. Colquhoun DSO) with No.14 CAG under Lieutenant Commander S.J. Hall, consisting of 804 Squadron of 22 Sea Fury 11 (Lieutenant Commander J.S. Bailey) and 812 Squadron of 12 Firefly 5 (Lieutenant Commander F.A. Swanton) and a helicopter, had arrived in Sasebo to relieve *Theseus*.

Like *Theseus*, *Glory* had carried out intensive flying training on her way out, and was ready to embark on operational duties without delay. As it happened, her arrival coincided with the start of the Chinese Spring offensive.

Interrogations of prisoners, documents, aerial reconnaissance and various other intelligence sources had all been pointing to the imminence of a Chinese offensive. They intended to drive the Americans from Korea, or at the worst, hoped to gain some ground to use as a bargaining counter should truce negotiations follow General MacArthur's dismissal.

On the night of 22nd/23rd April 1951 the Chinese attacked against 8th Army, along a line south of Kaesong to Chorwon to Kumhwa. 8th US Army started an organised movement to the rear. The enemy was employing new troops from Manchuria, making an all out effort to drive UN forces out of Korea.

A penetration near Kapyong was contained by US 1st Cavalry Division and 27th British Infantry Brigade. A heavy attack was launched from the direction of Kaesong in the west, which had gained a bridgehead across the Imjin River, in the area of the junction between 1st RoK Division and 29th British Infantry Brigade. The penetration was not allowed to become decisive, thanks to a gallant stand made by the 1st Battalion The Gloucestershire Regiment at Solma-ri, who held their positions for three days in the face of overwhelming attacks and until their fighting strength was reduced to barely a hundred men. The battalion was cut off and surrounded — efforts to relieve it failed. By this gallant stand, the enemy penetration was held up for three days; and he was prevented from making a rapid breakthrough.

Lieutenant Philip Curtis won a posthumous VC for leading a counterattack to

Captain K.S. Colquhoun, DSO.   *(FAAM)*

recover A Company's Castle Hill position, and Lieutenant Colonel J.P. Carne, who led the remnants of the battalion into captivity and was responsible for maintaining the morale of the prisoners for the next two years, was also awarded the VC. For a further three days the enemy continued to attack strongly in the west, and by 30th April the 8th Army was forced to fall back on a defensive line from the Kimpo peninsula, north of Seoul and from there to an area just north of Kosong on the east coast.

Seoul was again in danger of falling to the enemy, but it was held by a series of well-executed counter attacks. The penetration around Kapyong was also held, as were efforts to exploit the initial gains in the Imjin bridgehead.

By 3rd May the intensity of the attacks was abating. Although the Chinese had forced 8th US Army to withdraw, they had not gained a decisive victory — the line was intact and morale was high. The enemy halted, having outrun his supplies, and withdrew out of range of the massive UN artillery resources; many enemy divisions were uncommitted, so a second phase of attacks was expected. After a ten day lull, another general offensive started in an attempt to defeat 8th Army. Battle raged for three days during which the Communists suffered enormous casualties, and on the 21st the enemy's offensive capability was exhausted and he was forced to call a halt to the attack. 8th Army immediately passed to the offensive with strong counter-attacks which caught the enemy completely off balance. Within a week he was driven back across the 38th Parallel having suffered his worst defeat, bordering upon disaster. By the end of May it was estimated that he had lost 100,000 casualties and 12,000 prisoners as well as vast quantities of stores and equipment captured or destroyed — the UN forces were nearly back to their original April positions. By 15th June 8th Army had reached nearly all its objectives, it had established a line north and east from Munsan-ni to Chorwon, then east to Kumhwa and finally to the coast south of Kosong. UN forces were 15-20 miles north of the 38th Parallel in the west and central regions, and 35 miles in the east. The enemy had been driven out of South Korea, except for a small area west of the Imjin River.

The principal effect of the Chinese offensive on naval operations was that TF 77 temporarily discontinued interdiction attacks on enemy supplies and lines of communication, and concentrated on giving close air support to the Army.

On the west coast the Gunfire Support Element, TE 95.14, was reconstituted at Inchon under Rear Admiral Scott-Moncrieff. Gunfire was not required until 28th April when *Toledo* assisted by *Concord* silenced an enemy battery.

Rotoiti was engaged with RoK minesweepers in sweeping the previously cleared channel off Techong-do, where they cut two mines which were detonated by gunfire.

It had been expected that the Chinese offensive would be accompanied by air intervention on a massive scale. The only air activity of naval interest occurred on 22nd April when four Yaks attacked two Corsairs from USS *Bataan* at the entrance to Chinnampo estuary, where they were covering the rescue of a fellow pilot. Three Yaks were shot down and the fourth heavily damaged (it was thought that it crashed before reaching its base and was the one recovered, some days later, by an RoK ML on the north side of the Taedong estuary); the Corsairs returned safely, as did the rescued pilot. In expectation of air attack, Admiral Scott-Moncrieff had given instructions that the cruisers, when away from Inchon, should keep under the screen and CAP of the carriers; if blockading operations rendered this impossible, a special CAP was to be flown for the cruiser.

On 27th April *Belfast* joined *Glory*, who had arrived that morning to take over duties of CTF 95.11 on her first patrol. The start of her war service was inauspicious; low cloud and foggy weather prevented all flying until the afternoon of the 28th when 15 sorties were got off. Then the weather clamped down and a Fury on CAP disappeared into thick cloud and was never seen again. Thereafter her flying operations followed the usual lines, subject to the weather that varied from thick fog to perfect flying conditions. No enemy aircraft were encountered, but there was a steady increase in light flak. On 2nd May a Fury force-landed in a stream north of the bomb line. The pilot was promptly rescued by helicopter and his aircraft strafed and set on fire by the RESCAP.

Admiral Smith, CTF 95, proposed that USS *Bataan* should reinforce *Glory* for a few days to give CAS to the army. They started operating together on 2nd May with Captain Neale USN in tactical command. Operations were marred by bad weather, flying being possible on two days only, when about 90 sorties were flown. The enemy offensive was blunted and CAS was no longer urgent. On 6th May *Glory* went to Sasebo for a quick replenishment whence she returned to the west coast on 11th May to relieve *Bataan*.

The patrol of the River Yalu was intensified and a new patrol off the mouth of the River Hanchon was instituted. *Kenya* fired 81 x 6 inch rounds from north-east of Paengyong-do at gun positions where fires were started and many hits were obtained on the target area. On 5th May an RoK minesweeper hit a mine to the east of Sok-to, off Chinnampo, and sank.

Naval air effort shifted from CAS to participation in Operation 'Strangle', the interdiction of the enemy's build-up and supply lines further north.

Admiral Scott-Moncrieff met Admiral Martin, Commander 7th Fleet, in *Philippine Sea*, having returned to Sasebo in *Belfast* on the 27th. It was decided that the USN would step up anti-submarine training, as both Captain Bolt and Admiral Scott-Moncrieff had felt that the US had underestimated the submarine threat. It was also decided, in view of the possible development of air attack, that major units should operate by day under a CAP whenever possible.

At this time a change was made in the command structure on the west coast. Admiral Martin wanted a single officer with whom he could deal in emergencies in the absence of Admiral Scott-Moncrieff; the senior captain on the

HMS *Glory,* Sea Fury and Firefly range.   *(Binney)*

coast was appointed 'Officer in Tactical Command'. Normally this would be the captain of the carrier force (CTE 95.11); the commander of TE 95.12 was still responsible for normal blockade and escort duties.

It was agreed between Admiral Scott-Moncrieff and Admiral Martin that each would provide two destroyers continuously as screen for the west coast carrier force. Apart from this being an adequate anti-submarine screen, it had the advantage of exercising destroyers of various nationalities in working together. All replenishment ships to and from the operating areas were to have A/S escorts. Admiral Scott-Moncrieff welcomed this recognition of the submarine threat, but if a real threat had developed, he would have to drop some of TE 95's commitments to meet it and perhaps set up convoys.

Owing to the overall static nature of the war by this time it was possible to plan operations on a programme basis, and 50-60 sorties per day could be flown with out undue strain on the ship's handling and servicing capabilities. Event 'A' would be flown off, followed, one-and-a-half to two hours later, by Event 'B' and the landing-on of Event 'A'. This carried on throughout the day with the ship operating within the bounds of a circle 15 miles in diameter.

The ship's zone of responsibility was further sub-divided into smaller areas, and the aim was to cover each area at least once every day and work it over in detail. Flak from 88 mm downwards was encountered, and a good deal of massed rifle fire. The enemy technique was to hold fire until the aircraft started to pull away. There was also much use of flak traps and camouflaged dummies: 'Pilots soon learnt that there was AA fire about — and did not dally low down, making one attack only, and this probably a converging one from different angles'.

First Patrol
Glory left Sasebo on Thursday 26th April. Continuous rain, low cloud and poor visibility prevented flying on the 27th. Operations started next day with a permanent CAP of two Furies and an A/S patrol of one Firefly armed with two depth charges and markers. Although the weather was bad on the 28th, the Furies carried out AR of the Haeju area where they attacked factories with rockets, strafed vehicles and rocketed some craft on the mud east of Haeju. During the two aircraft CAP, Lieutenant E.P.L. Stephenson became detached from his leader in bad visibility, disappeared into thick cloud at 900 feet and apparently crashed into the sea. A search by other aircraft failed to find any sign of him. This sad loss made a gloomy start to operations. Of the four Fireflies on CAS, two had to return due to fuel transfer trouble while the remaining pair, being unable to contact UN ground forces, went on to Ongjin airfield and bombed the runway.

Better weather next day enabled a full day's flying to take place. The Fury early morning 'milk run' AR detail flew up the coast where they strafed and rocketed junks and attacked rail installations. A CAS detail to the north-east of Seoul attacked troop positions that had been marked with smoke by Mosquito Harvards. A later detail attacked the villages of Yanju and Chidong-ni with rockets and cannon. The Fireflies were briefed for CAS missions, but owing to the number of aircraft awaiting direction onto targets, only the last detail were able to be directed; the others flew north of the bomb-line and unloaded their armaments on dumps and unused airfields. One Firefly had to turn back with radio trouble, but joined up with the A/S aircraft, while another landed at Suwon with fuel shortage. He topped up and returned to the ship later.

Though the weather was hazy on the 30th the milk run attacked junks and rocketed a Bofors type gun emplacement. CAS details attacked troops and the Mosquito in the Uijongbu area reported good shooting and many casualties. Of the three CAS Firefly missions, the Mosquito allocated targets to the first and third, respectively a valley and a ridge containing troops; the second flight with no targets allocated, went north and bombed Kaesong.

At the end of the month, 804 Squadron organisation was:

99 Flt Lt.Cdr. Hall (AGC)
    Lt. Fane

12 Flt Lt.Cdr. Bailey (CO)	14 Flt	Lt. Campbell
Mr. Hefford		Mr. McKerral
Mr. Richards		Mr. Mason
Mr. Sparke		Mr. Darlington
15Flt Lt. Birrell (SP)	16 Fit	Lt. Young
Lt.(E) Barlow		Lt. Whitaker
Lt. Kilburn		Mr. Fieldhouse
Lt. Hart		P3 Collingwood

17 Fit Lt. Trelawney
    Lt. Winterbotham
    Lt. McNaughton

812 Squadron's record for April was:

	April	**Total Operational**
Flying hours	193-55	99-35
Sorties	99	46
Deck landings	95	43

May 1st was replenishment day with no flying, and *Glory* was joined by USS

Bataan next day so that the two offensive efforts could be combined. Both squadrons flew AR details of the coast and of railways inland, attacking junks and box-cars, the Fireflies bombing a large building in Haeju. On the last detail, the Leopard guerrilla organization had given a large tin-roofed building as the target which was rocketed by Furies. After this attack, Lieutenant Barlow had to ditch his aircraft in enemy territory, in a river, after engine trouble. He was rescued by an American helicopter and taken back to Seoul, none the worse for wear.

On the 3rd May, the Furies carried out a bombardment spot for *Kenya* and both squadrons reconnoitred the area attacking junks, gun positions and stores. Flak was found to be above average in intensity, especially around Pyongyang.

The weather next day was useless for flying with low cloud and fog over land. No sorties were flown, though *Bataan* made one attempt in rain. The weather continued until late in the afternoon of the following day when one detail was got off at 1630. The Furies attacked warehouses and severely damaged a gun position with rockets. Mr. McKerral had to land at Seoul owing to damage caused to his wing by one of his 20 mm cannon exploding. The Firefly detail bombed a railway bridge near Haeju, and rocketed and strafed Haeju city.

The chief Fury targets on the 6th were junks on the west coast which were rocketed and strafed. Since most of the sampans and junks were on the mud anything less than a direct hit merely covered them with mud. The Mosquito directing the CAS detail to a target of troop positions on the side of a hill reported good coverage and accurate shooting. This flight, of which Lieutenant Barlow was a member, went on to 'Bonkers Hill' and retaliated for some interference caused by guns on the hill while he was swimming near there four days earlier. During a CAS detail, one Firefly had to go to Suwon after the engine had suffered from over-speeding in a bombing dive. AR details in the Haeju area bombed railway bridges and rocketed and strafed troop concentrations. The last detail returned to the ship via Seoul and Suwon where they had to collect passengers. On completion of flying course was set for Sasebo.

The harbour period was shorter than usual — only two days — and, from the comment in 804's diary, 'the air group had a chance to sample what little Sasebo has in the way of rest and recreation.'

Second Patrol

Glory was back on patrol on 11th May. The Furies on AR details attacked fishing sampans and junks on the coast, then went inland and concentrated on roads and valleys to the north of Haeju seeking trucks and stores on their way to the front. In spite of the Fireflies having serviceability problems, they damaged two bridges and carried out some photo-reconnaissance.

Next day the Fireflies attacked bridges at Wontan and Yonan, and villages reported as containing troops. A comment in 804 Squadron's diary gives a nice indication of the innocence of fresh pilots to the problems of Korean operations: 'The first four Furies on bridge reconnaissance reported that most of the bridges in their area were working again. A tribute to the Chinese bridge repair gangs which are apparently conscripted villagers who work all through the night'. The old stagers knew the drill, that bridges were rebuilt overnight — a fact of life. Other Fury details concentrated on sampan and junk traffic in the Chinnampo estuary.

The diary entry for the 13th May makes the first reference to ox-carts being used for the transportation of ammunition, and therefore as being legitimate targets. The Furies, by means of a shallow dive, started firing rockets into the mouths at either end of tunnels to destroy stores or rolling stock taking refuge in the tunnel; while the Fireflies, using 30 second delay fusing on the 500 lb. bombs and dropping from 200 feet, attacked bridges, damaging two.

Since the 14th was replenishment day, there was no flying except the helicopter which picked up a stoker who had fallen overboard during refuelling. Stoker McPherson caught his leg in a bight of rope and was pitched into the Yellow Sea wearing oilskins and heavy sea-boots. Fortunately, the helicopter with Petty Officer Airman (Phot) E.J. King was airborne near the ship taking newsreel shots. The pilot saw everyone on *Glory* running aft, and King noticed the line of life-buoys stretching out from the carrier until he saw McPherson struggling in the water. The helicopter swooped over him, and to make room for him in the aircraft King volunteered to jump into the sea wearing his Mae West. There he supported the half-drowned man and slipped a sling around McPherson's body. He was hauled up, but was so exhausted that he could not be got into the cabin. With his head poking inside the aircraft and the rest of his body dangling down, and with the crew holding onto him for dear life, the helicopter flew back to the carrier. McPherson was well again after a spell in Sick Bay, and King returned to *Glory* as soon as the emergency flight was finished.

Nootka caused some consternation w hen she requested a CAP at dawn that morning because she was very far north catching junks when daylight arrived. However, she managed to complete her task and steam south at high speed.

In order to attempt to relieve some of the Communist pressure from the front, a simulated assault from the sea was launched in the area of Cho-do Island. The diversionary force consisted of *Kenya* and *Ceylon* with a minesweeping flotilla, destroyers and attendant craft. *Glory's* Furies provided the CAP for this force and over Cigarette route (the channel from Choppeki Point to Cho-do), while both Furies and Fireflies spotted for the cruisers.

Low cloud and drizzle persisted until well into the afternoon of the 15th, restricting flying to only one detail. The CAP was increased to four aircraft due to the likelihood of enemy air activity in the area. The Furies flew three sections of

AR, one along the coast, one in the area north of Pyongyang where considerable light and heavy flak was encountered, and the third to Chinnampo. Lieutenant Winterbotham's aircraft was hit by flak and he had to ditch it. The actual ditching, with flaps set at take-off, was most successful and he had plenty of time to get out. After swimming to a nearby sampan which took him to a friendly island, he was picked up by a helicopter from an American LSD and taken back there for the night. He returned next day in good shape. A flight of Fireflies bombed a bridge in the Sariwon area but failed to obtain any hits on it.

Variable weather had its effect on flying, but 155 sorties were flown by *Glory's* aircraft in the last three days of the patrol. The Fireflies bombed and rocketed villages and bridges, strafed ox-carts and spotted for both *Kenya* and *Ceylon*. On the 18th a Firefly piloted by Lieutenant Williams was hit by rifle fire and ditched in about three feet of water 70 miles north of *Glory*. The crew was promptly assisted by two South Koreans in a fishing sampan. They were subsequently picked up by *Glory's* helicopter; Lieutenant Williams was unhurt but his observer, Aircrewman Sims, was wounded in the arm. The Furies also spotted for the cruisers in addition to their AR of the Chinnampo area and further north. Buildings, junks and ox-carts were rocketed and strafed as well as junks and a large vessel on a slipway. Alongside the village of Kumsan-ni they saw a large sign saying 'Welcome UN army'.

The 19th May was *Glory's* last day in the operational area, being relieved by USS *Bataan* on the 20th. *Glory* could make only 19 knots on passage to Sasebo due to a defective stern gland.

Landings by two platoons of Royal Marines plus a demolition and medical party from *Ceylon* took place on two beaches at Naenjong and Sidong at 1630 on 20th May after completion of the minesweeping programme. The Marines embarked from USS *Comstock* (where they had been regaled with a glamorous film, large steaks and ice-cream) into three LCVPs, accompanied by nine more to make it appear that the landing was in force. The beaches had been mined, but Korean guides from Cho-do island led them ashore through gaps. There was no opposition, and after two and a half hours the Marines re-embarked without incident, having penetrated a mile and a half inland and fired two deserted villages. Air cover and support was provided by USMC Corsairs from USS *Bataan*, who was relieved by *Sicily* on 3rd June.

Glory arrived in Sasebo in the evening of 20th May. Much speculation was caused by reports in the latest newspapers from UK (9 days old) that *Glory* was to be relieved by HMAS *Sydney* in October for three months rest and recuperation. It seemed that 'Home by Christmas' could be forgotten, to be replaced by considerations as to whether the refit would take place in Sydney or Singapore. On the 22nd *Glory* moved into dry dock for a couple of days so that work could go ahead on the stern gland, and to have her bottom scraped. She left dock on the 25th and moved to her usual buoy in the stream. The harbour period vitas extended to 3rd June in order to rectify a number of machinery defects that had become apparent.

Aircrew were given a few day's leave to visit Kuratsu, and there were some changes in personnel. Lieutenant Fane and Mr. McKerral left for UK, and Lieutenant (E) Watson, Lieutenant Davis and Sub Lieutenant Howard joined 804 Squadron. They were straight away packed off to *Unicorn* for deck landing practice. Lieutenant Davis could hardly wait to join the select band of ditchers — he landed in the sea with engine trouble on his first circuit. He was picked up in what was record time — three minutes after his engine stopped he was back on board.

The statistics for 812 Squadron for May were:

	May	**Total Operational**
Hours	508-45	608-20
Sorties	211	257
Deck landings	202	245

Whilst still in harbour and replenishing, two comments must be recorded. During replenishment of *Black Swan* by the US ammunition ship *Titania*, the following classic exchange was overheard between an enlisted man in *Titania* and a forecastle leading hand of *Black Swan*:

Enlisted man: 'How's the second largest navy in the world?'
Leading hand: 'Not so bad. How's the second best?'

The other, a *cri de coeur* from 804 Squadron's diarist:

Left Sasebo at last. A fortnight in Sasebo is much too long and I for one will be glad to get back to some flying.'

By the end of May, the Chinese offensive had been definitely defeated; more than 10,000 Chinese surrendered as prisoners of war during the last week of that month, and the UN Army was pressing on to the north-east towards the enemy's vital supply area. The naval forces on both coasts settled down again to their normal routine activities, and Admiral Scott-Moncrieff, who had remained at Sasebo since his return from Inchon, felt able to pay some visits.

He hoisted his flag in *Unicorn* and went to Pusan for a memorial service at the UN cemetery on 30th May. Whilst in Pusan he met President Syngman Rhee, Admiral Sohn, CinC of the RoK Navy, and Commander Luosey USN its operational commander. He returned to Sasebo to meet Vice Admiral Joy and Admiral Radford, CinC Pacific Fleet, who was visiting the war zone. On 6th June he sailed from Sasebo in *Unicorn* to Yokosuka. There he met Vice Admiral Kiland USN and Rear

Admiral McManus USN. The latter gave an interesting dinner party, which included among other guests, Mr. Yoshida, Prime Minister of Japan, six US and four very senior Japanese Admirals, including Admiral Nomura, the Japanese Foreign Minister during the 1930s and who had been a special envoy to the USA in 1941. All the Japanese Admirals deplored their nation's part in the Second World War; each in turn made a point of telling Admiral Scott-Moncrieff how happy the Japanese Navy had been in the old days, when such a close bond existed between it and the RN. He discussed the possibility of using 41st Royal Marine Commando in raids on the east coast under the direction of CTF 95.

On 20th June Rear Admiral George C. Dyer succeeded Rear Admiral A.E. Smith as CTF 95.

By mid-June, General Van Fleet considered the war could have been won by amphibious landings leap-frogging up the east coast, but political considerations imposed a check on military operations. From the entry of Communist China into the war, the policy of the UN had been to limit hostilities to the confines of Korea and, subject to restoration of the Republic of Korea with its northern boundary approximately the same as before the North Korean aggression, they were ready to enter into armistice negotiations at any time.

Third Patrol

Glory sailed from Sasebo on 3rd June to relieve USS *Bataan*. Flying started on 4th, with the Furies attacking junks at Hanchon and Kumsan-ni, areas suspected as being off-loading ports for stores for the front line. Two details of CAS were flown, but due to bad weather they were unable to operate near the front; instead they went to Kaesong where they strafed troops and rocketed box-cars on the railway lines. When returning from the last trip of the day, an attack on a camouflaged store dump, Lieutenant Watson's engine stopped and he made a successful ditching near *Black Swan* who picked him up unharmed. The diary comment is interesting: 'Any suggestions that a Fury is a bad ditcher seems to have been disproved pretty conclusively since we have been out here, although all ditchings have been made in ideal conditions.' *Theseus'* pilots had also had to ditch a number of Furies, and in no instance had a pilot been lost as a result of an intentional ditching. The Fireflies, on AR details, bombed bridges, a headquarters building and a ridge containing troops. Lorries and ox-carts were strafed, as well as villages reported by intelligence to be containing troops.

Next day was somewhat uneventful for the Furies. Very little junk traffic was seen, and what there was attacked; ox-carts and their unfortunate means of locomotion, were destroyed. The Fireflies destroyed a railway bridge at Yonan and attacked the villages of Kamsan-ni, Sungtam-ni and Sunyang-dong, where buildings were seen to explode. Pilot 3 S.W.E. Ford's Firefly had received some damage during his sortie. On his final approach, after taking a *Wave*-off, his engine failed and he was forced to ditch. He was alone in the aircraft, with the wheels down and the flaps in their landing position (for maximum drag). The aircraft pitched forward and sank almost immediately, and, although the cockpit canopy was open, the pilot did not have time to escape from the aircraft and was unfortunately lost. The Fury ditched by Watson the day before would have had the wheels up and the flaps probably set at take-off to give additional lift and less drag.

A lot of aircraft were returning from sorties with holes in the skin, mostly caused by small-arms fire, but sometimes with pieces of earth and parts of their own rockets embedded in them; changes had to be made to attack rules. It was beginning to appear that many pilots were becoming increasingly heedless of the light flak. Repair of this minor damage imposed a heavy load on the maintenance crews, and reduced the number of aircraft available to meet the flying programme. On the 6th all the Fury details were AR, during which both a barge and a building in the Chinnampo area blew up with large explosions indicating that they had been full of ammunition on its way to the front. The Fireflies bombed targets in the Chinnampo estuary including the village of Songhya-dong and damaged a bridge at Hwasan-ni.

The Furies had a quieter day on the 7th, there were few signs of activity ashore and a dearth of active targets. The early morning detail caught a twin 20 mm gun firing at them and successfully destroyed it. An ox-cart, a jetty and two junks were also attacked. Some bombardment spotting was done for *Ceylon* and *Cossack* who destroyed stores dumps in villages. One Firefly was hit by flak in a nacelle tank. Lieutenant Wilson, the pilot, reached the coast and ditched alongside the island of Paengyong-do; both he and his observer Sub-Lieutenant Shepley were rescued by shore-based helicopter, the first of them after only four minutes in the water. They were later collected by *Glory's* helicopter and returned to the ship.

Ox-carts and troops in villages were the targets for the Fireflies on the 8th. The Furies blew up more ammunition supplies in railway trucks and in a stores dump near a factory. Low cloud over the target area made finding and hitting targets difficult for the later details who had to be content with oxcarts and railway trucks.

There was no flying on the 9th for replenishment. During this evolution it was discovered that the AVGAS from *Wave Premier* was contaminated, caused by corrosion in a supply pipe from tanks to the forward supply position, one that had not been used for many years. There was no truth in the rumours of sabotage which appeared in the press.

Operations restarted on the 10th with a combined strike by Furies and Fireflies on the village of Osan-ni. The entire load of 6 x 500 lb. bombs and 32 rockets hit the centre of the village which burned fiercely. Owing to the presence of flak the aircraft did not wait to find out exactly what damage had been done. The second detail of Furies knocked down some camouflaged buildings on the Chinnampo waterfront, after which they destroyed nine ox-carts, four of which blew up taking a number of soldiers with them. They then went on to Paengyong-do, where they were greeted with heavy flak, which was replied to from a respectable height of 7,000 feet. After dealing with some box-cars, their last gesture was to strafe and sink a loaded junk. All this must have caused a certain amount of thought by the enemy, as there was a shortage of moving targets for the rest of the day; three stationary junks were destroyed, two moving sampans damaged and the odd solitary ox-cart strafed. The Fireflies set fire to targets in Honsan-ni and buildings were destroyed in Chaeryong; the railway bridge at Sariwon was bombed but missed, no damage being caused. By evening it was clear that the contaminated petrol could not be dealt with and that the next day would be the last of the patrol.

On this last operational day, another successful combined strike was made by both Squadrons on the village of Osan-ni, used for billeting troops. The Fireflies made two attacks on the Sariwon rail bridge, causing damage with near misses. When landing-on after this detail, Lieutenant Blake's approach was too low and he hit the round-down, causing irreparable damage which wrote-off the aircraft. A new target for the Furies was transformers, three being attacked and damaged. Other Fury targets consisted of more buildings on the Chinnampo waterfront (which blew up), ox-carts, troops and junks.

Next day, on passage to Sasebo, the contaminated fuel was transferred to *Green Ranger.* 25,000 gallons of fresh fuel were embarked in Sasebo on the 13th, the tanks were flushed out, and the fuel then discharged overboard whilst on passage southabout to the Inland Sea on the 13th and 14th, arriving in Kure for the first time on the 15th.

On 12th June *Glory* was relieved by *Sicily* who had just succeeded USS *Bataan* as the US west coast carrier. For *Sicily* it was not a happy first patrol. She had a number of defective and old aircraft, and bad weather curtailed flying for the first few days. She had also failed to meet *Bataan* for briefing and handover, due to arrangements ordered and counter-ordered by US commanders in the chain of command (without reference to Admiral Scott-Moncrieff).

Although Commander E.S. Carver, Fleet Aviation Officer, boarded her before she sailed, on this patrol the air group never managed to get into its stride. By her second patrol (2nd - 11th July) a few new aircraft had arrived, and her output and performance improved daily, in spite of the loss of six aircraft. With eighteen left, she achieved 45 sorties in one day and over 36 on several others.

Glory secured alongside the pontoon jetty at Kure opposite *Unicorn,* whose wardroom was about to give a cocktail party to celebrate their departure for Singapore to collect much needed replacement aircraft. On the following day, *Glory* exchanged her wrecks for just about the last of *Unicorn's* serviceable

HMS *Glory* and HMS *Unicorn* at Kure. Firefly transfer using dockside crane.
(Binney)

replacements. The ship's company found Kure a cut above Sasebo. Currency was in sterling and prices were lower which made their cash go a long way further. For those who liked sport, the facilities were far and away better, especially the tennis courts of which there were any amount of first class clay ones. There was a very pleasant officer's club run by the Australians which, in sharp contrast to its jazzy American equivalent at Sasebo, was quiet and secluded. Similarly, the sailors much preferred the Australian run canteens and clubs to the American equivalents in Sasebo.

On two days parties of air group officers went to visit the 8th Hussars, who were based just outside Kure, to see and drive the new Centurion tank. They were very hospitably received during their short stay.

Before starting the next patrol, 804 Squadron reorganised the Flight List:

99 Flt	Lt.Cdr. Hall (AGC)		
	P3 Potts		
	Lt. Whitaker		
12 Flt	Lt. Cdr. Bailey (CO)	14 Flt	Lt. Kilburn
	Mr. Hefford		Lt. Hart
	Mr. Richards		Mr. Mason
	Mr. Sparke		Mr. Darlington

15 Flt	Lt.Cdr. Birrell (SP)	16 Flt	Lt. Bricker
	Lt.(E) Barlow		Sub-Lt. Howard
	Lt. Winterbotham		Mr. Fieldhouse
	Lt.(E) Watson		P3 Collingwood
17 Flt	Lt. Trelawney		
	Lt. Davis		
	Lt. McNaughton		
	Lt. Hubbard		

Fourth Patrol

Glory sailed from Kure on 21st June in company with *Cockade*, and next day Admiral Scott-Moncrieff embarked from *Cardigan Bay* and hoisted his flag in *Glory* for a few days. Throughout this patrol the helicopter was out of action and sorely missed, particularly as regards the effect on the screen of having one destroyer plane-guard most of the day, and in the daily distribution of flying programmes and operational summaries, without which the escorts could not be kept in the picture. The helicopter could accomplish in a few minutes what a destroyer could not perform in under an hour, during which time both the mobility of the force and the effectiveness of the screen were impaired. In order to be as near as possible to a shore based helicopter Captain Colquhoun shifted the area of his operations 30 miles north of the usual position (within a radius of 15 miles of 37°15'N 124°15'E).

Flying started on the 23rd with the Furies on CAS missions, sent by JOC, Taegu, to the east end of the line over country with which they were unfamiliar, whilst those from TF 77 in the Sea of Japan were sent to the west end. This uneconomic practice was to continue for the whole patrol, in spite of protests to Admiral Martin from Admiral Scott-Moncrieff. On this first day, one Fury detail failed to contact the Mosquito aircraft and had to abandon their mission. However, the other two details made contact and gave good coverage of enemy positions in support. The reconnaissance trips took them to the airfields in the western area. An ancient biplane had been dropping bombs on Suwon and was thought to be operating from these airfields, though nothing seen. Fireflies bombed Chaeryong, a bridge north of Sariwon, stores near Chinnampo and, with 1,000 lb. bombs, a rail bridge at Wonto hitting the track but missing the bridge.

The Furies carried out successful CAS missions again next day, attacking gun positions and houses. During a reconnaissance trip of roads and railways from Haeju to Chinnampo, Lieutenant Commander Birrell made a low run past more than 15 box cars and observed that none of them had wheels; judging by the reception it appeared that they were a flak trap. His aircraft was hit by a 20 mm shell that exploded in his ammunition box which was fortunately empty. The Fireflies bombed factory buildings south of Pyongyang which were left damaged and smoking. Buildings on an island in the Chinnampo estuary were bombed and strafed. Three aircraft with 1,000 lb. bombs bombed the railway bridge at Hwasan-ni, cutting the line and damaging the embankment. Admiral Scott-Moncrieff disembarked to *Alacrity* during the afternoon.

The CAS details for the Furies on the 25th were again most unsuccessful as they could not contact the Mosquito controllers via JOC. Reconnaissance sorties were made to Hanchon looking for junks and junk-pens, and around the local airfields looking for the 'Suwon Bomber'. On one of these details, Lieutenant Kilburn's flight was attacked by four US F-80 Shooting Stars. Their gunnery was not good, and luckily they did not stay long so no one was hit, but it was difficult to understand how to mistake a Fury with its distinctive black and white stripes. The Fireflies destroyed a hangar at Ongjin airfield during an AR detail. They bombed and strafed a ridge containing machine-gun nests on a CAS mission. On their last detail, escorted by two Furies because they were themselves unarmed but carrying 1,000 lb. bombs, two of which were fitted with delay fuses, attacked a bridge at Hwason-ni.

As a change from CAS, the Furies had two sessions of bombardment spotting next day. The first was for *Morecambe Bay* and the second for *Cardigan Bay*. Villages were quickly hit and set on fire. Each member of the flights took one shoot each and good practice and experience was obtained by everyone. A reconnaissance to the island of Ka-do in the far north resulted in a coaster being sunk. The other main item of interest was the discovery of five tanks alongside a road which were repeatedly attacked with rockets. The Fireflies bombed railway sidings and sheds at Toktong-ni, and headquarters buildings at Anak, where heavy flak was seen. Other attacks were made on a factory at Pyongyang and on a railway bridge east of Sariwon.

On replenishment day, the 27th, the CO of the Leopard guerrilla group visited *Glory* and said he thought the previous day's tanks were dummies, though he did not know why they were there. There had been no evidence of their being a flak-trap.

Both squadrons spotted for bombardments on the 28th, Furies for *Cardigan Bay* and *Morecambe Bay*, Fireflies for *Constance*. During an attack on a barrack building to the south of Pyongyang, Lieutenant J.H. Sharp's aircraft was shot down and crashed in flames. Both the pilot and his observer Aircrewman 1 G.B. Wells were killed. On the last detail Lieutenant Binney's aircraft was hit by flak on a strafing run after bombing the rail bridge west of Allyong Reservoir, and he landed at Suwon for repairs. Fury attacks on junks and oxcarts proved that they were not merely filled with fish and hay — one junk blew up and an ox-cart exploded with an orange flame.

Next day, the Furies made their usual attacks on junks and buildings with good results. Ongjin-ni airfield was inspected closely and it was observed that more concrete floors had been laid in some of the blast pens. Most of the numerous bomb holes had been filled in and the airfield looked as though it was capable of operating aircraft again. There had been constant reports that the enemy was building up his air strength. The Fireflies made two bombing attacks on the road bridge over the river north of Kyomipo, the northern span being knocked down after an accurate dive by Mr. Purnell.

Rumours were reaching the fleet of the peace proposals that had been put forward.

The first detail on the 30th was a combined strike by Furies and Fireflies on villages around Ongjin-ni airfield. The damage could

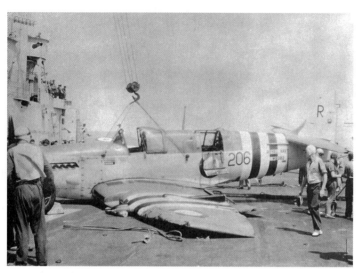

Firefly WB382/206R accident being lifted by Jumbo mobile crane.   *(Binney)*

not be assessed as the area was covered by smoke and dust. While Sub-Lieutenant Howard was taking off on the afternoon detail, the strop came off the catapult trolley and the aircraft trickled over the bows. After a considerable time under water, Howard broke surface and was picked up by *Constance*. He returned to *Glory* in a very short time, none the worse for his very unpleasant experience. The trolley, being freed of its load, struck the stops too hard and put the catapult out of action for the rest of the patrol. The remaining launches were made using RATOG. The other Firefly strike was made on the village of Tajung-ni where large fires were started with smoke to 4,000ft.

All launches on 1st July were made with RATOG, 29 Fury and 18 Firefly, an achievement thought to be a record and which reflected great credit on electricians, ordnance ratings and maintenance crews. By working ceaselessly in the two hours available between details, all commitments were met, and the only sortie lost was one when the aircraft had to return to the ship with unserviceable instruments. The Furies gave CAS to the eastern flank of the front, and though some communication difficulties were experienced, excellent results were reported by Mosquito. The Fireflies spotted for bombardments by *Cardigan Bay* and *Constance*. Sangwha was bombed and gun emplacements were attacked to the west of Chinnampo. The Firefly that had been repaired at Suwon returned during the afternoon. At the end of the day's flying, course was set for Sasebo.

Statistics for June were:

	804 Squadron	**812 Squadron**	
	June	Operational	Total
Flying Hours	1177-25	668-00	1276-20
Sorties	435	276	533
Deck landings	424	256	501

On 29th of June, the Furies had sunk a junk, which was subsequently found to be friendly, causing five fatal casualties two of which were highly trained intelligence agents belonging to an organisation known as 'Salamander', of which Captain Colquhoun had not heard. The junk had made no recognition signals in spite of a warning burst of fire ahead. The pilots were in no way to blame for this unfortunate occurrence; indeed so long as the various secret organisations insisted on working unknown to the task element commanders, such incidents were bound to occur from time to time.

The passage to Sasebo was wet and windy due to typhoon 'Kate', which was fortunately too far to the north to give any trouble.

Five days leave was given to aircrew on arrival in Sasebo on 3rd July. The journey to Asokanko took 12 hours, many of which were spent waiting for connections. The party arrived at noon on the 4th and celebrated Independence Day with the American contingent. The hotel was a building 3,000 feet high on the edge of a volcanic crater. It was set in a National Park and had been designed to house winter sports competitors for the 1940 Olympic Games which should have been held in Japan. In 1951 it was run by the American Army for officers leave. Sports facilities included tennis courts, an open air swimming pool and sulphur baths.

Meanwhile in Sasebo the aircraft were maintained, the catapult repaired and the ship fuelled, stored and ammunitioned.

From June˙ to August the surface craft of the Blockade Element carried out their usual activities. Anti-junk measures continued vigorously, several craft and prisoners were sent in to South Korean ports. Useful intelligence was obtained from some of the prisoners. At the request of the RoK Government, some fishing areas were extended to banks where fish were more abundant in order to feed the people on the islands.

A number of small raids on the mainland were made by the Leopard organization. It was intended that these would culminate with a large scale raid on the shore opposite Sok-to off the entrance to Chinnampo, but, due to difficulties with the guerrillas, this was abandoned. Various RoK organisations laid on raids in the vicinity of Haeju and Ongjin, without consultation with the Blockade Commander, though he did hear of two by chance. Steps were taken to put an end to these 'private' activities. The Leopard guerrillas were all anti-Communist North Koreans. Though ready to fight the Communists, they and the RoK forces disliked each other almost as much, and would not co-operate. The most that could be hoped was that they would not actually fight each other.

The increase in bombardment during the last week in June, of which many shoots had been spotted by *Glory's* aircraft, was of targets reported by Leopard. It fitted well with the policy of exerting maximum pressure on the enemy in order to start armistice negotiations from strength.

On 9th July Rear Admiral Dyer USN hoisted his flag in *Ceylon* and proceeded in her up the Cigarette route, between the mainland and Chodo, for a conference with Leopard representatives.

On the east coast, the destroyer USS *Walke* struck a mine off Hungnam suffering severe damage and with the loss of 26 members of her crew.

Armistice talks started on 11th July 1951 with the first meeting between delegates being held at Kaesong. General Ridgway was represented by Vice Admiral C. Turner Joy and Rear Admiral Arleigh Burke, the Communists by three North Koreans and two Chinese. At the beginning of October the negotiations moved six miles east of Kaesong to.

The battle ashore became static, with a buffer zone line agreed on 27th November.

In August, 5th US Air Force began a co-ordinated plan for interdiction of all road and rail communications and neutralisation of airfields in North Korea, (an extension of Operation 'Strangle'), at the expense of support of ground troops. The MiG-15 was being assembled in large numbers on the Manchurian border. The attrition rate of 5th USAF was becoming high, and day raiding by bombers was no longer a paying proposition.

At sea on both coasts, operations followed the underlying pattern of the past six months, but at a higher intensity.

On the west coast, the carrier element continued to operate in the southern part of the Yellow Sea, while the blockade element of a cruiser and four or five destroyers or frigates patrolled between the Han and Taedong estuaries. Night patrols, and sometimes day patrols, would go as far north as the Yalu Gulf in support of the islands there, from some of which intelligence and airsea rescue organisations were working. In the middle of July a MiG had been shot down and was lying in shallow water about 100 miles behind enemy lines; the Americans were keen to have it recovered.

On 9th July reports had been received by JOC of a MiG-15 in position 39°26'N

125°22'E, its position was in very shallow water and there was no prospect of one of HM ships being able to reach it. Captain Thring in *Ceylon* (CTE 95.12) requested *Sicily* to search for it during the daily reconnaissance. On the 11th aircraft from *Glory* sighted the tail unit 13 miles to the south and west of the reported position, and on the 13th the remainder of the aircraft was sighted nearby. The wreckage was just awash at low water, 40 miles north of Chodo, along a narrow channel flanked by sand bars and blocked at the southern end by a minefield. Admiral Joy directed that every effort be made to recover as much of the wreckage as possible.

The forces involved were *Glory* and four destroyers (TE 95.11) and TE 95.12 consisting of *Cardigan Bay* (Captain W.L.M. Brown) with *Hawea*. Admiral Scott-Moncrieff arrived in *Kenya* and transferred his flag to *Glory*, keeping *Kenya* in company by day, and by night reinforcing Captain Brown's force.

Captain Brown had evolved a salvage plan using the tidal range of 17 feet at springs and 8 feet at neaps. He proposed that two shallow draught junks be towed in at next springs, lashed to the MiG at low water and towed clear at high water. He had heard of the existence at Inchon of a special LCM fitted with a crane, and he decided to substitute this for the junks. His plan was that *Glory's* helicopter, led by aircraft, would buoy the position of the MiG on 18th July; an RoK JML, supposed (erroneously) to have local knowledge, would lead the LCM there after dark; *Cardigan Bay* would proceed to the area of operations on the 19th to provide counter-battery fire and AA support; and aircraft from *Glory* to provide LOW level CAP and 5th USAF jet aircraft high level CAP.

Admiral Scott-Moncrieff went to Inchon in Kewlyn to arrange the LCM himself. There was no such craft, but an LSU with crane was provided instead. This was shipped in LSD Whetstone, and arrived in Chodo on the 19th July escorted by *Kenya*, which then proceeded to sea to the north-west to provide early radar warning of aircraft approaching from Manchuria during the salvage operations.

Cardigan Bay sailed from Chodo at 1230 on the 19th, avoiding the minefield, successfully crossing the outer bar at high water and anchoring in the inner channel for the night. LSU 960 and JML 302 were to have joined her that evening, but owing to the former's running aground and the latter's inability to navigate in the dark, they did not do so until 0830 next morning. The ships arrived in the vicinity of the MiG at 1235 and waited till low water at 1730. The weather was fine with good visibility and no sign of the enemy movement or interest in their presence was detected by the ships.

At 1600, with the tide nearly out and sandbanks exposed to view, *Glory's* helicopter dropped two buoys with great accuracy to mark the tail section and fuselage of the MiG. *Cardigan Bay's* motor boat, with Lieutenant M. Ross in charge, led the LSU up the channel. The position of the sandbanks bore little resemblance to the chart of the area, and the water was yellow with disturbed mud; however the CAP Furies could make out the passage and indicated it by flying along it at low altitude — an ingenious and effective navigational aid. When about three-quarters of a mile from the main part of the aircraft, the LSU grounded on a still falling tide. Boats closed the aircraft and found, in addition to four large portions, which would require the crane to lift them, a very large number of small pieces scattered over an area of about 400 yards radius, mostly on sandbanks which dried at low water. All visible small parts were recovered and loaded into the LSU's shallot draught boat, while the remainder of the party attached slings to, and buoyed, the main sections. At 1930 the water had risen sufficiently for the LSU to get inshore; by 2115 all except the cockpit and wing section, which broke away from its slings and slipped back into the water, had been recovered. The strong current and a rising tide frustrated diving operations to recover the wing section, so the party returned to *Cardigan Bay* which anchored for the night, less hazardous than remaining under way in confined and swift-flowing waters. Early next morning boats were sent in at low water to prepare the wing section for lifting. The tide was extreme low water springs, three feet lower than the previous day, and other small pieces of the wreck were found and collected. At 0730 the LSU arrived on the scene and the lift of the wing section was completed in 10 minutes. The salvage party returned to seaward.

Throughout the operation, no interference was attempted by the enemy. Some sporadic AA fire at the low CAP revealed the position of a heavy battery, and after the salvage party had finally withdrawn from the beach, *Cardigan Bay* fired 72 rounds high explosive delayed action rounds at it with good results.

The withdrawal passed off without incident. Visibility shortened as they neared the end of the channel and Captain Brown decided to lead the other ships to Chodo accepting the risk of crossing the minefield at high water. This was successfully negotiated and the force arrived off Chodo at 1700 on the 21st July. Next day LSD *Epping Forest* arrived and, escorted by *Rotoiti*, returned the LSU to Inchon where the MiG was handed over to 5th USAF.

> 'Your highly successful operation,' signalled Commander 7th Fleet, 'is deserving of our number one well done.'

Fifth Patrol

Glory sailed from Sasebo on 10th July, and during the afternoon the new pilots carried out some DLP which also tested the catapult after the work that had been done on it during the harbour period.

Foggy and cloudy conditions made targets difficult to find on the 11th, but the Chinnampo area was clear and buildings and junks were hit by the Furies with good results. When clouds allowed, photos were taken and a thorough search was made of an area west of Chinnampo where coastal batteries were suspected, that had been firing on friendly islands. Nothing was seen but camouflaged pits. 804's diary records:

'During the early morning detail the tailplane of a jet fighter was seen [by Lieutenant Hart] in mud near Hanchon. From intelligence at debriefing it must have been a MiG which had been shot down by Americans about four days earlier'. Throughout this patrol there are references to the MiG whose recovery has been described above. The Fireflies bombed Changyon and barracks buildings at Kumsan-ni.

The first CAS detail next day, to the front north of Seoul, failed to raise the Mosquito, apparently JOC had got the timing wrong. The attempt in the afternoon was successful, and good results were obtained. Quite a lot of flak was met, one Fury was hit but returned to the ship, another had to land at Seoul. The Fireflies successfully bombed Kumsan-ni and dropped delayed action bombs on Hwasan-ni.

On the 13th the Furies attacked the usual targets of railway trucks, junks and barracks; a moveable haystack was encountered and set on fire. The crashed MiG was photographed, part of the fuselage being visible for the first time. Light flak was in evidence from a junk in the vicinity firing a 45 mm gun. Support was given to the front line: in one instance the target was a battalion of troops resisting the UN forces who were within 1,000 yards of them, and more light flak was met. The Fireflies damaged one railway bridge north of Sariwon, and destroyed another to the west of Chaeryon. One detail spotted for bombardments by *Mounts Bay* and *Ceylon*. The last detail of six aircraft, each with 2 x 1,000 lb. bombs, made short work of two railway tunnels in the Chongyan area.

The Furies next day went to take photos of Yondang Dong airfield, to the north, which was, according to the flak map, practically undefended. On arrival the aircraft were met by plenty of light and heavy flak up to 6,000 feet and higher. Results showed that although the airfield was damaged it was still in use. The 'Welcome UN Army' sign at Kumsan-ni was strafed and set on fire. The Fireflies bombed Ullul and Kumsan-ni, and when attacking a railway tunnel on the Haeju to Sariwon line, two bombs supposedly fitted with delay fuses exploded instantaneously, luckily not damaging the aircraft. Direct hits were seen in the mouth of the tunnel; one aircraft was hit by flak.

The 15th was replenishment day; in the afternoon a deck hockey competition was held, resulting in an all air group final which the aircrew narrowly won.

Flying started again on the 16th in low cloud which ruled out CAS details and generally restricted activities. The Furies took another look at the MiG, and channels and mud flats were noted to see if small craft could get in to it. Three aircraft were damaged by flak. A Firefly carrying out a bombing attack to the north of Sariwon was hit by flak, crashed behind enemy lines, and was burnt out. Lieutenant R. Williams and Sub-Lieutenant L.R. Shepley were both killed.

An increase in enemy activity was noted by the Fury AR details on the 17th. In the Chinnampo area a large group of troops was found and the area was rocketed and strafed. Lieutenant Hart had to ditch his aircraft near some friendly islands south of Choppeki Point with engine trouble, probably due to flak, but was quickly rescued by an RoK frigate PF 61, and via, *Cardigan Bay* and *Constance*, was returned on board by helicopter the same day. Camouflaged vehicles were attacked at Ongjin. Increased activity was also noted in the Yonan area, a few miles west of the peace talk area at Kaesong.

The first Fury flight went up the west coast on the 18th, photographed Yondang Dong airfield from 15,000 feet, then attacked buildings and railway sidings near Osan-ni. While searching this area, two aircraft were hit. Lieutenant Young having a shell explode in the cockpit behind him and Lieutenant Davis being forced to ditch further south. Young arrived back safely, but Davis had considerable trouble with his Mae West and dinghy, and was rescued, after one-and-a-half hours difficult time in the water, by *Glory's* helicopter. From the next detail, while attacking a gun position Commissioned Pilot T. Sparke's aircraft was hit by flak and he reported it on fire. A short while later the aircraft dived into the ground and exploded, with no chance of survival for the pilot.

Glory moved 70 miles north to an area centred on 38°15'N, 124°00'E to give constant air cover to Captain Brown's force recovering the MiG.

Next day was scheduled as the big day for MiG removal and an attempt to break the record of 72 sorties set up by *Theseus*. Bad weather prevented any movement toward the MiG and at noon flying finished. The base for recovery operations was to be Chodo island; two Furies were to be permanently over the island as CAP for the frigates and the lifting ships.

The weather in the forenoon of the 20th was not suitable for the helicopter to fly, but it cleared in the afternoon. Two Furies provided cover for the ships already assembled near the MiG and two others escorted Lieutenant O'Mara USN in *Glory's* helicopter from Chodo to the scene of operations. At dead low water the body of the MiG was sighted and the helicopter marked it with a buoy. A short while later the tail could be seen and this was marked with a life jacket and fluorescent dye. As soon as this was done the helicopter was escorted back to Chodo and landed with its fuel tanks nearly empty. The two Furies then went back to the MiG and watched the boats arriving and the activities on the mud. After three-and-a-half hours the Furies were recovered, having been relieved by four Corsairs from *Sicily*. Markers were also dropped by Lieutenant Commander Swanton from his Firefly. During the land-on, Lieutenant Johnson hit the round-down during his first approach, then on the over-shoot one wheel hit a Fury in the deck park (much to the alarm of the pilot in the cockpit!), and when he did land-on, he had to do a wheels-up landing. On completion of the day's flying, *Glory* set course for Kure.

> Next day on passage a signal was received saying '...the success of the MiG operation was entirely due to the work of *Glory's* aircraft and helicopter, for which we are very grateful'.

Glory arrived in Kure on the 22nd in brilliant weather. On the 24th, much to everyone's surprise, the ship was ordered to reinforce *Sicily*.

The emergency that had arisen was a new commitment on the west coast, expected to last a few days but which actually continued for four months.

Peace talks were hanging fire, but there was a prospect of agreeing an agenda, of which the first item was the military demarcation line. It was considered important to emphasise that the area south of the 38th Parallel in the Ongjin and Yonan vicinity, though actually held at the time by the Communists, was controlled by the UN. On the 24th Admiral Joy, acting in his capacity as the senior delegate at the armistice conference, addressed a personal message to Admiral Dyer (CTF 95), requesting a show of strength in the Han estuary as close as possible to the neutral area around Kaesong.

Admiral Dyer at once ordered all activities on the west coast to be subordinated to the requirements of this demonstration. *Sicily* and *Glory* concentrated their air operations on this area, to the exclusion of coastal reconnaissance. All available frigates and RoK vessels on the west coast were ordered to the Han estuary.

Captain Brown as CTE 95.12, with *Cardigan Bay, Murchison, Rotoiti, Hawea*, RoK PF 62 and the usual patrol craft were at Inchon. They sailed at 0530 on 25th July, met *Sicily* to arrange with Captain Thach USN for CAP, spotting and other air assistance and proceeded to the rendezvous off the Han estuary where the rest of the Blockade Element had assembled. Because of the limited gun power of the New Zealand frigates, *Rotoiti* was left in the Cigarette area and Haroea in the outer approaches to the Han estuary as radar picket and crypto link, and with the secret publications of the other frigates on board, who retained only their dangerous-waters sets during the operation.

The approaches to the Han River are shallow and include many islands surrounded by shifting mud-flats which dry at low water. No navigation marks existed, and tidal streams run at from 4 to 8 knots. Aerial photographs were of little help, and even at low water it was difficult to gauge the best channels.

Admiral Dyer (together with JOC and the Leopard organisation) had indicated targets, mostly of minor importance, but had not mentioned the underlying, political, object of the operation. It was difficult to assess the importance of targets in relation to the navigational hazards of shifting sand and mud-banks and fast tidal streams.

On 27th July, after the force had with difficulty reached the 'Fork', bombardment of the north shore started, moving inland when aircraft spotting was available. The 'Fork' was the frigate's bombardment position off the north-east point of the island of Kyodong-do. Nearly all military targets were within range of the frigates' guns, including those adjacent to the 5 mile safety zone around Kaesong. Apart from sporadic small-arms fire there was no enemy reaction.

To Captain Brown it seemed the object of the operation had been satisfactorily completed; but not to Admiral Dyer, the ships were ordered to try to get further into the estuary. Admiral Scott-Moncrieff was doubtful of the military value of the operation, and, conscious of the hazards his ships were running, feared the development of a 'prestige' commitment similar to Wonsan. Admiral Dyer was determined to continue and was unwilling to submit alternative suggestions to higher authority, or to reduce the number of frigates in the area.

Three episodes occurred during these operations emphasising the importance of full inter-service co-operation. On the 4th August, a bomb fell near *Mounts Bay* from an aircraft which momentarily appeared through a 300 feet cloud base, and on the 7th, frigates engaged a jet aircraft that made two passes out of low cloud. There was a similar incident on the 9th. It transpired that they were aircraft of 5th US Air Force, unaware of the frigate operations in the Han estuary; the frigates were equally unaware that one of the fixed air routes to Kimpo airfield crossed the area in which they were operating. Admiral Scott-Moncrieff remarked that these incidents 'could but reflect on the [American] inter-service co-ordination and briefing'. As the threat of enemy air attack in this sector was negligible at this time, he ordered the ships not to open fire unless an aircraft was positively identified as hostile, while the matter was being straightened out.

From August to November two or three frigates were continuously in the estuary. Much ammunition was expended at targets of dubious value, without provoking the enemy into making any reply until seven weeks had elapsed from the start of the operations. On the 18th September the enemy fired on JML*302* on a surveying mission; she was hit by a 40 mm shell which did no serious damage, and the gun position was fired on by *Amethyst* and *Murchison*. After this display of temper, the enemy resorted to his normal passivity.

On 30th September, *Murchison* came under heavy fire; she was holed in several places, without serious damage, and suffered three casualties, one severely wounded.

Admiral Scott-Moncrieff had not seen eye-to-eye with Admiral Dyer as to the value or method of execution of these frigate operations; he reported

> '...the aim of the operations was "to demonstrate naval control of the
> north Han estuary approaches". The frigates were doing no such thing,
> they were only there by kind permission of the Communists; the effect of
> this type of demonstration on oriental negotiators is of doubtful value.'

Operation 'Retribution' started on 3rd October with the objective of razing villages and destroying all cover on the coast west of the River Yesong. For two days *Black Swan* and *Rotoiti* bombarded the area with air spotting from *Rendova* who also carried out co-ordinated air strikes with napalm, bombs, rockets and cannon.

On 7th October CinC FES, Vice Admiral the Hon. Sir Guy Russell, paid a visit to the estuary with Rear Admiral Scott-Moncrieff in *St Brides Bay*.

Bombardments, with air spotting and strikes, continued for 'demonstration' twice daily, including one at 1015 when the truce delegation met, if in session.

Negotiations over the cease-fire line were making progress, and Admiral Dyer sanctioned a reduction of the force to one frigate and one JML on 10th November. On 30th November, demarcation of the cease-fire line having been settled, the operations were brought to a close.

Admiral Scott-Moncrieff wrote

'Whatever the value of these operations to the peace talks, there is no doubt that they have maintained the prestige of the Commonwealth Navies, and the determination and resolution with which they were carried through, especially by Commanding Officers and Navigating Officers, often under unpleasant, and always under trying conditions, has been in accordance with the best traditions of the Service'.

Sixth Patrol

Though at 24 hours notice, *Glory* sailed at 0700 on 25th July, only 9 hours after receiving her sailing orders, to join *Sicily* on the west coast on the 26th. Owing to the hurried departure from Kure, several aircrew were left ashore, some test flying replacement aircraft at Iwakuni, others on leave. It was not possible to embark the replacements, so the Air Group was short of six aircraft for this patrol. The pilots from Iwakuni joined by helicopter on the way out, the leave stragglers arrived some days later by destroyer.

Bad weather with 8/8ths cloud restricted flying on the 27th to CAP only until 1500, after which the Furies attacked three villages in the coastal area from Yonan to Haeju where 2,500 troops had been reported. On one village two drop tanks which would not transfer were jettisoned and strafed in their own form of napalm attack; only small parts burned. The Fireflies throughout the patrol had a varied collection of jobs, including bombardment spotting and photographing the Han River channels to assist the frigates' navigation.

The weather next day was much the same, preventing any strikes until mid-afternoon, which even then were forced by the weather to find targets further to the north. Buildings and railway sidings were attacked by the Furies in the Chinnampo area where light flak was experienced. Because of a crash on *Sicily*'s deck, a Corsair with hydraulic trouble landed on *Glory* after one of their own batsmen had been flown over by helicopter. The ship went to action stations in the evening when one of the destroyers got an Asdic contact and depth charged it. Oil slicks were seen to come to the surface, but nothing more definite was seen.

On the 29th the weather improved to allow the Furies to fly AR sorties in the Yonan area all day. Over 4,000 troops had been reported in the area, but they were not very conspicuous. Many people seen in the fields may or may not have been peasants. Targets attacked included buildings, villages, railway trucks and a tunnel. P3 Cockburn had a stroke of bad luck when landing his Firefly — the arrestor hook snapped up, and, through no fault of his own, he entered the barrier. *Sicily* left for Sasebo on completion of the day's flying.

On 30th July rough seas, high winds and low cloud put a stop to flying in the afternoon. Most Fury details were bombardment spotting with *Ceylon* and *Morecambe Bay*. Villages and gun positions were engaged by the ship's guns with variable results. On one occasion details of channels through the mud were passed to the frigates for navigation. Two aircraft with rockets were permanently acting as CAP for the frigates who were well up the Han River and in restricted waters.

Bad weather prevented any flying on 31st July. The Squadrons' statistics for July were:

	804 Squadron	**812 Squadron**	
	July	July	Operational
Hours	989-00	542-55	1151-15
Sorties	392	234	491
Deck landings	384	226	471

With 8/8ths low cloud and bad weather around the Han River in the forenoon, it was decided to replenish with AVGAS and FFO on 1st August. Although cloud conditions were still bad for spotting at midday, a full half-day's missions were flown in the afternoon and evening. Most were for *Morecambe Bay, Mounts Bay and Murchison* when villages were fired on but bad visibility prevented the Furies from seeing much of the fall of shot. One flight carried out a bombardment with *Ceylon* and one flight had to jettison its rockets over the sea because of the weather. All spotting aircraft carried rockets and, with the exception of the latter, good targets were found in enemy occupied villages.

On the 2nd the Furies carried out AR sorties to Kumsan-ni where rafts and boats had been reported under construction. Two junks were destroyed and numerous others damaged; many buildings were damaged and one blew up; one aircraft was hit by light flak but returned safely to the ship. Spotting was carried out for *Ceylon* and three frigates. *Ceylon's* shooting was very good, but the frigates', with the exception of *Murchison*, was rather wild and spreads were capable of straddling a large village continuously without hitting it.

Low cloud next day prevented any large amount of bombardment spotting; villages were engaged with indifferent results by ships in the Han River, but weather again restricted activities and reduced their accuracy. 60 enemy troops were found in the open and were strafed and rocketed by Furies with good results.

On the 4th bad weather again restricted flying and from 1330 onwards no attacks were possible on land. The Furies found quite a lot of enemy soldiers in khaki in the south coast area who were hit with rockets and cannon. It was a rare and welcome sight to catch troops in the open in that area, but that group probably thought they were safe with the very low cloud base. An unidentified twin engined jet aircraft dropped a bomb on the frigates and disappeared into the murk, causing no damage.

Glory was relieved by *Sicily* on 4th August and sailed for Sasebo, arriving there late on the 5th.

During the frigate operations in the Han estuary, the carriers of TE 95.11 concentrated their offensive efforts also in the Han estuary, and in the Taedong and Hwanghae areas, while the other blockade and patrol activities continued with depleted forces.

On 29th July *Ceylon* relieved *Los Angeles* as CTE 95.12. Four American minesweepers were ordered to sweep as far up the main channel to Haeju as they could get. They were under the command of Captain R.C. Williams USN in LSD *Colonial*; 'As usual,' remarked Admiral Dyer, 'the enthusiasm and teamwork of these minesweepers was admirable'. By 4th August channels were swept to positions from which Haeju city and railway line could be brought under gunfire. This was *Warramunga's* last visit to the operational area — she delivered '… some admirable bombardments, highly reported on by air spotters'. She left the area on August 15th, sent on her way with Admiral Scott-Moncrieff's comment 'She has been a tower of strength and done an incredible amount of steaming with no trouble at all. I cannot speak too highly of Captain D.H. Becher and his men'. Her place was taken by *Anzac* (Commander J. Plunkett-Cole RAN).

Earlier there had been indications of enemy actions against Sok-to in the south approach to Chinnampo. Troop concentrations and two 120 mm guns were seen and became targets for the Cigarette patrol of *Van Galen, Warramunga, Cayuga* and *Consort. Kenya* bombarded guns on the Amgak peninsula on 12th August, knocking out one emplacement.

From 16th to 24th August typhoon Marge interrupted naval operations. Warning of its approach had been promulgated by CTF 77, and all commanders were authorised to remove ships from confined waters in the war area.

Admiral Scott-Moncrieff left Sasebo and transferred his flag to *Glory* on 17th August north of Makau Islands. She moved to the latitude of Quelpart Island to get more sea room, cruising whilst waiting to see what the typhoon would do. Reports of its progress were contradictory, it was clear it had slowed up and for the next 30 hours the weather in the Yellow Sea was perfect. 'I had visions,' said Admiral Scott-Moncrieff, 'of the enemy seizing his opportunity, laying mines in the Cigarette route and the Han estuary; of a landing on Sok-to; and a number of possibilities.' He felt it was essential to keep sea room, especially as *Glory's* deck park of aircraft was an anxiety.

By the forenoon of the 19th the escorts were low on fuel; *Cardigan Bay, Morecambe Bay, Murchison* and *Cayuga* were sent to shelter in the Inchon area; *Glory, Ceylon Kenya, Charity* and *Concord* moved to the south. That evening the weather deteriorated and next day winds had reached force 10 with a heavy, confused, sea and a 30 foot swell. The ships stood up to it well; the aircraft on *Glory's* flight deck were unharmed, and the only damage was done to the cruisers' whalers, each losing the starboard seaboat turned in at the dayits. The force went into Buckner Bay, Okinawa, on 21st August. Typhoon 'Marge' was menacing the Chinese coast in the vicinity of Saddle Island. Conditions on the 22nd had not improved, the typhoon turned north across the Shantung promontory, and later turned further east; it eventually passed south of Inchon and across Korea on the 23rd.

By the evening of the 22nd it was clear there could be no more operations before the 24th, the day *Sicily* was due to relieve *Glory*, therefore *Glory* went direct to Kure escorted by *Charity* and *Concord*. Admiral Scott-Moncrieff transferred his flag to *Kenya* and sailed for Sasebo. While on passage, *Concord* lost a man overboard; despite rough weathers she recovered him in 9 minutes using a whaler — a fine feat of seamanship on the part of her Commanding Officer, Lieutenant Commander I.D. MacLaughlan.

HMS *Kenya*.   *(Author)*

Seventh Patrol

Glory had arrived in Sasebo on 5th August. Warrior arrived from UK on the 7th with spares and replacements for *Glory*; and ammunition for the army and navy. On the 10th *Glory* left Sasebo for Kure with a stop at Iw-akuni to pick up replacement aircraft. Eleven aircraft arrived on board in very quick time and by midday the ship was on her way again to Kure, where she stayed for another day, leaving at 0830 on 13th August.

On the 15th the Furies carried out AR searches from Hanchon to Chinnampo;

three junks were destroyed and many damaged; a steam tug was damaged and two 45 gallon drop tanks were dropped on a village which burned well. Spot CAPs were carried out for the frigates, *Murchison's* shooting at Yonan being particularly accurate. One aircraft was hit by flak, Mr. Newton had to land at Kimpo with engine trouble and Lieutenant Hubbard landed at Paengyong-do because of falling oil pressure. The Firefly strikes concentrated on the Yonan area. Sub-Lieutenant Tait had joined 812 Squadron at Kure five days earlier. He had an unlucky start: in the morning he got the cut when he was well over to starboard and did not appreciate the fact until too late, when the aircraft hit the crane; in the afternoon he had a 'prop-peck'.

Next day the Furies destroyed two junks in the Chinnampo area, of which one blew up with an orange flash, and others were severely damaged; ox-cart activity was seen and at least four were destroyed. A gun position with four 20 mm guns was found with troops in jungle green in attendance — both were well hit by rockets and cannon. Lieutenant MacNaughton's aircraft was hit by flak near Chinnampo and he was forced to land on the beach at Chodo Island which he accomplished successfully. Mr. Newton burst a tyre and ended up in a ditch ashore at Kimpo after a test flight on the aircraft he had landed there the day before. He returned to the ship the same day — not so MacNaughton who was stranded on Chodo for some time. In the evening *Glory* moved south as the typhoon Marge was heading their way.

For the next two days *Glory* waited off the south-west tip of Korea to see which way Marge would go. It was reputed that winds were in excess of 100 knots at the centre with the pressure only 900 Mb. On the 19th it was decided to try to get round to the west of the forecast track and then down south along the China coast. The nearest *Glory* got to Marge was about 150 miles and for two days and nights the ship rolled heavily. Winds were recorded up to 60 knots but no damage was done to any aircraft apart from covering the deck park with salt. *Glory* arrived in Okinawa on the 21st and sailed next day for Kure. Though intending a day's flying, the swell prevented it, and she arrived alongside on 25th August.

All the aircraft that were on the deck during the typhoon were found to have salt everywhere and in some cases the finish was beginning to flake off. They did not have to last much longer as they would be collecting a new set at Singapore on their way to Australia. P3s Collingwood and Potts of 804 Squadron were promoted to Commissioned Pilot at the end of August; the new Flight List was:

99 Flt	Lt.Cdr. Hall (AGC)	12 Flt	Lt.Cdr. Bailey (CO)
	Mr. Potts		Mr. Hefford
	Lt. Whitaker		Mr. Richards
	Mr. Newton		Sub-Lt. Howard

14 Flt Lt. Kilburn   15 Flt Lt.Cdr. Birrell (SP)
        Lt. Hart   Lt.(E) Barlow
        Mr. Mason   Lt. Fraser
        Mr. Darlington   Lt.(E) Watson
16 Flt Lt. Bricker   17 Flt Lt. Trelawney
        Lt. Winterbotham   Lt. Davis
        Mr. Fieldhouse   Lt. McNaughton
        Mr. Collingwood   Lt. Hubbard

Statistics for August were:

	804 Squadron	812 Squadron	
		Aug.	Operational Total
Hours	444-20	185-09	1340-20
Sorties	206	105	596
Deck landings	189	88	559

On 25th August *Kenya* left to refit and recommission in Singapore. She was one of the veterans of the war; she had steamed over 63,000 miles, had fired 3.386 x 6 inch and 1,000 x 4 inch shells, and had rescued 10 airmen from the sea.

Amgak peninsula and Wolsa-ri were bombarded by *Ceylon* and *Charity* on 25th August. Much intelligence of enemy intentions and troop concentrations was unreliable, so a small scale raid was organised to get prisoners for corroboration. A party was landed at Sogon-ni, covered by *Charity*. One Able Seaman was killed but no prisoners were captured.

Charity went north to patrol off the Yalu on the 27th and *Ceylon* looked in at Haeju, bombarding an enemy position in the Chongyong Myon peninsula. *Ceylon* then went to meet Lieutenant Colonel Ergott USA who had relieved Colonel Burke in command of the Leopard guerrilla organisation.

RoK minesweepers under the direction of *Rotoiti* operated in the vicinity of Taedong, Chodo and Sok-to, extending to Chinnampo and further north as time went on.

An unfortunate raid was carried out on 30th August. The object was to round up enemy troops reported by Leopard to be in Chonidong, near Mongumpo. No serious opposition was expected, but heavy flanking fire was met, 15 casualties were caused, one serious, and the party withdrew. Next day *Sicily* attacked canvas covered positions and supply dumps ashore with good results. There could be no doubt that information of the intended raid had leaked out, and Admiral Scott-Moncrieff ordered such activities to be discontinued unless CTF 95.12 could be certain he was not being double-crossed.

Ceylon, with the casualties, went south to turn over the duties to *Belfast* who had just returned from a long refit. Captain Sir Aubrey St. Clair Ford then visited Inchon, Paengyong-do, Chodo and the Han estuary to bring himself up to date and to get back into the picture.

Eighth Patrol

Glory relieved *Sicily* on 31st August. In spite of the scarcity of targets it was still required to put the main effort in to the Han area, but strikes were laid on in the Amgak region and spotting aircraft provided whenever requested.

Glory returned to the operational area on 2nd September. It was a routine day's flying with both squadrons attacking junks, railway trucks and villages. Sub-Lieutenant Howard's Fury was damaged by flak and he made a forced landing on Paengyong-do beach where the aircraft overturned in soft sand, the pilot managing to burrow his way out watched by a crowd of admiring South Koreans. He returned on board that evening in the ship's helicopter. A second Fury was also damaged when making an emergency landing on Paengyong-do; the aircraft were left stranded on the island but were salvaged some weeks later.

On the 3rd the Furies attacked targets from Taedong Gang in the north to Yonan in the south. Many junks were seen, and buildings rocketed which had been reported by Leopard as containing troops. These Leopard targets were usually a few days out of date by the time the aircraft attacked them, when the troops might have flown, but on many occasions good results were reported.

Next day a group of eight Furies was briefed to deal with the collection of junks seen the day before, but unfortunately bad weather interfered and the aircraft could not reach them. Another motor junk was sunk, and troops and vehicles strafed and rocketed.

On the 5th warehouses and houses were damaged in Taedong Gang, and other flights carried out photo reconnaissance for the recently formed British Commonwealth Division, as well as spotting for the frigates in the Han estuary where one large brick building was seen to explode. An unwelcome increase in the amount of flak was reported.

After replenishment next day, it was intended to fly in the afternoon, but after two shaky catapult launches further flying ceased. The two aircraft airborne landed at Kimpo.

The catapult continued to give trouble for most of the 7th and all launches but the last two details were by RATOG, creating a lot of additional work for the ordnance ratings. Most of the trips were CAS at the west end of the line, making a welcome change from AR. Mosquito aircraft reported more than 100 troops killed.

The catapult still gave some trouble early next day, but it was soon cured and

RATOG was discarded. Two junks were sunk and six damaged in the north, in addition to attacks on Leopard targets. In one of these attacks on a headquarters building, 60 casualties were later reported, but it was doubtful how reliable these reports were.

On the 9th, the last day of the patrol, a record number of 84 sorties (66 offensive, 18 defensive) was achieved by the two squadrons, beating *Theseus'* 66. 100% serviceability was maintained throughout the day, a fine example of first class maintenance. When the last event of 19 aircraft was launched, every aircraft carried was airborne. Several pilots flew three sorties during the day. Junks in the north were attacked on the first detail, and Furies escorted Fireflies to Suichon and attacked flak positions while the Fireflies bombed a headquarters building. Camouflaged vehicles were attacked on Mosquito-directed CAS missions which were met by intense light flak. On the last detail, Lieutenant Morris and his observer Lieutenant Legge landed on a mud flat in enemy territory near Haeju. The helicopter went to pick them up, but with a faulty fuel gauge and without a full load of fuel, it had to make a precautionary landing on a small island, while *Glory* remained in the area overnight. Petrol was sent in cans by destroyer, and the helicopter and the Firefly crew were recovered next morning, after which *Glory* sailed for Kure.

When *Glory* had sailed into Sasebo to relieve *Theseus* in April the Royal Marine band on the flight deck had the temerity to be playing 'Anything you can do we can do better'. As she entered Kure on 11th September the band was playing the same tune. A signal was received from Admiral Scott-Moncrieff:

> 'Your magnificent performance yesterday [9th] makes an all time high.
> Tune played on your arrival now completely vindicated. My heartiest
> congratulations to you all.'

On the east coast, operations continued their usual pattern with aircraft of TF 77 almost entirely confined to attempts to cut enemy communications from the north. Admiral Dyer's destroyers and frigates of TF 95 had the defensive role of keeping Songjin and Wonsan open for the use of UN forces.

The policy of keeping one or two Commonwealth ships on the east coast continued, except when increased demands on the west coast rendered it impossible. *Morecambe Bay* carried out a patrol from 8th to 23rd July. The coastal rail route had been reopened as aircraft had been diverted to targets further inland, and *Morecambe Bay* picked off a number of trains in the Songjin area, for which she received a congratulatory signal from the Commander 7th Fleet for her prowess.

Admiral Scott-Moncrieff visited Wonsan in *Kenya* from 24th to 26th July. The enemy had much to gain, as bargaining points at the armistice talks, if he could drive the ships out of the Wonsan area and recapture some of the islands. He took advantage of the breathing space on shore to reinforce the troops and defences there. By mid July there were 40 gun positions and 20,000 troops in Hodo Pando peninsula alone. Two LSMRs had been at Wonsan for three weeks, and whenever the shore batteries opened fire, Operation War Dance was carried out, 10,000 rockets having been fired at them in twenty days; an operation described by Admiral Scott-Moncrieff as being stimulating to the enemy and like 'stirring up a wasp's nest with a stick from a safe distance, and then waiting till it settles down before prodding it again'.

Kenya returned to Sasebo and *Ceylon* took her place. She did not stay long at Wonsan, she was needed to relieve *Los Angeles* at Haeju on 29th July. *Ceylon's* bombarding was reported by a US spotter as the best he had ever seen which led the Chief of Naval Operations at Washington to ask for details of her fire control equipment.

From 10th to 25th August Admiral Dyer visited the west coast, flying his flag in Toledo and escorted by *Van Galen*. *Van Galen* got in a number of bombardments at various places, and earned high praise for her efficiency particularly in her anticipation of requirements when manoeuvring —

> 'I know that this is fully deserved,' wrote Admiral Scott-Moncrieff,
> 'and I cannot but feel that it is the result of British training, but this
> matter of initiative by junior officers never fails to surprise the US
> Navy'.

On 17th August, *Consort* joined the Wonsan element, to be relieved by *Cossack* on the 24th. *Cossack* supervised the establishment of an RoK Marine garrison on the island of Yang-do, 15 miles north of Songjin, whence some covert activities were conducted.

During *Charity's* patrol from 3rd September, the enemy made a sudden determined effort to use the railway with a shuttle service between Tanchon and Songjin. For many weeks this line had been believed dead, but soon after her arrival it was apparent that it was being used, thanks to the technique of erecting temporary buildings by night and removing them by day (it had been frequently reported, but this is the first occasion seen). *Charity* carried out successful bombardments with support and spotting from the air.

Reports were coming in from US airmen that the enemy was building up large defences in the town of Wonsan and close to the harbour. TG 95.9 was organised, with Admiral Dyer in command, consisting of *Toledo* (flag) and *John R. Craig, Glory*, three Commonwealth destroyers, three US destroyers and three LSMRs. They arrived off Wonsan on 18th September, *Glory* with *Sioux, Cayuga* and *Concord* operating to seaward, the destroyers and LSMRs entering the harbour.

Impressed by *Glory's* fine performance of 84 sorties on 9th September, Admiral Dyer had hoped for 84 each day of the Wonsan attack. When it was explained to him that she could not keep this up for two days in succession, he then accepted a target of 66 per day — two per aircraft per day. On 18th September, *Glory* flew 68 sorties, three strikes of 16 aircraft plus bombardment spotting and CAP, US Mariners flew A/S patrols for the Carrier Element. In spite of low cloud over the target, good results were obtained, though it was necessary to clear the area for bombardment immediately after attacking, and assessment of damage was difficult.

On 19th September flying operations were hampered firstly by bad weather and secondly by a catapult defect so only 21 sorties were laid on before TG 95.9 was dissolved that evening, *Glory* returning to the west coast after first calling at Sasebo. From what had been seen it appeared doubtful that the reported activities at Wonsan were actually taking place; the whole city seemed dead and very little flak had been encountered.

Anzac took over from *Charity* as CTE 95.22 on 13th September and remained in the Songjin area until the 26th. She had an interesting spell of duty including patrols to Changjin, support of the garrison at Yong-do, landing intelligence teams and some 'train-hunting'. On the 19th she recovered Lieutenant P.M. Fant USN, a pilot belonging to *Boxer,* echo had come down in the sea off Chongjin. He turned out to be an old acquaintance of one of *Anzac's* officers, Lieutenant Commander Buchanan, whose radio operator he had been eight years before during the Second World War at Fort Lauderdale, Florida.

Belfast spent five days on the east coast from 26th to 30th September as Admiral Dyer, visiting the west coast in Toledo, asked for a cruiser to take her place. She carried out bombardments of Wonsan, Tanchon and Songjin, and on the night of 28th September she covered a small raid by a troop of 41st RM Commando.

41st Royal Marine Commando wanted to be used, as suggested by Admiral Scott-Moncrieff, for raids all along the east coast, between the bomb-line and Changjin, to force the enemy to garrison all 350 miles of the coast. This was not approved by the US authorities. They were used instead to increase the garrison of the islands off Wonsan on Yodo and Modo.

By the end of September the Commando had carried out some operations outside Wonsan. A small, partially successful raid had been made on the railway near Chaho, 50 miles south-west of Songjin. On the night of 4th/5th October a similar raid was launched in the same area, but the enemy spotted the canoeists before they landed and the raid was called off. In October and November activities were limited to the Wonsan area; two raids were carried out from *Horace Bass* on 2nd and 3rd December, after which the Commando handed over to RoK Marines, and they left the area.

Admiral Scott-Moncrieff reported: 'Although not employed tactically as effectively as they should have been most of the time…there is little doubt that the presence of these troops and their employment on raiding activities was well known to the enemy from almost before they arrived in the Wonsan area. Shortly after this, the vigilance and defence all up and down the east coast improved. It can thus be said that their employment in containing the enemy in increasing numbers was profitable, and once again showed the value of raiding and potential raiding to contain troops out of all proportion to the raiding troops involved, provided they are properly trained and efficient, transportation is available, and their operations are co-ordinated with the main operational plans, both naval and military'.

On arrival at Sasebo on Christmas Eve, signals warmly expressing high appreciation of their achievements were received by Lieutenant Colonel F.N. Grant (who had succeeded Lieutenant Colonel D.B. Drysdale MBE in October) from Admirals Joy, Martin and Dyer.

Ninth Patrol

Sicily took over from *Glory* on 10th September, on what was her last patrol before relief by *Rendova*, and continued carrying out similar operations until the 16th.

Glory's time was drawing to a close, HMAS *Sydney* being on her way to take her place. From 16th to 20th September she was operating on the east coast and back to the west on the 21st. Air operations concentrated on the Taedong area and on providing useful support for a guerrilla raid on the Amgak peninsula. *Belfast*, wearing Admiral Scott-Moncrieff's flag, joined TE 95.11 on the 22nd and the Admiral embarked in *Glory* to witness, as he reported, 'the flying operations by this most efficient carrier'.

Glory left Kure on 16th September in company with Toledo for operations on the east coast. Shortly after sailing, Jumbo, the flight deck mobile crane, was being used to lower a whaler into its crutches when it tipped up, dropped the whaler into the sea and fell half way over the side itself. No one was hurt, but the whaler was lost and Jumbo was rendered unserviceable. *Glory* returned to Kure to

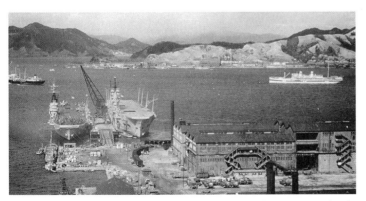

exchange her Jumbo for *Unicorn's*; being a Sunday afternoon it took a long time to get a floating crane to effect the exchange and *Glory* did not sail until 1600.

Operations started on the 18th with Fury and Firefly strikes on Wonsan and with

HMS *Glory* and HMS *Unicorn* alongside in Kure. HMHS *Maine* at anchor in stream.   *(Kellaway)*

aircraft spotting for Toledo and other US destroyers. Toledo gave airburst fire over flak positions just before the strikes went in, and throughout the day no flak was seen.

On the 19th strong winds and a heavy swell delayed the start of flying, and when the ship was in the lee of the land and all set to go, the catapult broke down. This was a bitter and most disappointing anti-climax as it was their first and last visit to the east coast, and the previous day had been well up to *Glory* standard with a total of 68 sorties. All aircraft had to be launched with RATOG, the Furies rocketing groups of buildings and then spotting for the destroyers. The ship was getting very short of RATOG equipment, so left the area for Sasebo where she arrived during the afternoon of the 20th to embark RATO gear and fuel, sailing for the west coast that evening. Several Fireflies were transferred to *Unicorn* for *Sydney*, leaving seven on board so no more A/S patrols were flown.

One detail was flown in the late afternoon of the 21st, and a full, but reduced, day's flying was carried out on the 22nd with all aircraft still being RATOG launched. During one launch, Mr. J.P. Hack's RATOG failed to fire and his Firefly went straight into the sea ahead of the ship. Mr. Hack was rescued by the helicopter but his observer, Sub-Lieutenant R.G.A. Davey, was not seen again — a sad loss on the last patrol. No one liked RATOG, and work proceeded with a degree of urgency on the catapult which was tested and pronounced cured in the late afternoon — a source of great relief to everyone. The Fury pilots reported that while *Glory* had been away the Chinnampo junk traffic appeared to have increased, showing this to be a well used supply route, and that there were more wagons on the railways. Junks were the main targets, while a large group of soldiers at Hanchon were rocketed, causing many casualties. Buildings and villages containing troops were also attacked, as were Leopard targets, though results on these were difficult to assess.

Next day 804 Squadron reached 1,000 accident free deck landings. During the day they strafed and rocketed many loaded junks, one of which blew up.

On the 24th the Furies contacted *Comus* and searched for a reported gun position. They failed to find it, but attacked villages with good results. While attacking junks in the Chinnampo area, the AGC, Lieutenant Commander S.J. Hall, started having engine trouble, the flight made for Chodo and then turned south until he was forced to ditch some miles south of the island off the coast. He made a good ditching, and after about an hour in the water, which at this time was becoming quite cold, *Glory's* helicopter won the race to pick him up. A flying boat was taxying out from the shore at the same time, but the open sea was too rough for it to land. He returned to the ship cold, but otherwise unhurt.

The 25th September was *Glory's* last day of operations for this tour. The Furies destroyed seven junks and damaged many more in the Chinnampo area; during a Leopard strike they damaged a rarely sighted tracked vehicle that was apparently not a dummy. Lieutenant P.G. Young, transferred from *Theseus*, flew his 100th sortie on his last mission. Lieutenant Commander Swanton flew off in his Firefly with the last strike and then went on to Kimpo. He was delayed in-shore and returned an hour or so after the strike had returned. The ship's band and half the ship's company turned out to see him land on — the last of the operational tour — after which *Glory* set course for Kure.

During the 26th, on passage, the day was spent servicing the aircraft, and in particular getting all the Fireflies into good and clean order for transfer to *Sydney*. On the 27th *Glory* arrived in Kure, to find *Sydney* berthed on the other side of the pontoon; the hitchers union' bade farewell to the very efficient and popular Lieutenant O'Mara USN and his helicopter crew before they too transferred to *Sydney*. During the next four days, all the Fireflies and most of the air stores were transferred to *Sydney*.

FO2FES, Rear Admiral Scott-Moncrieff, visited the ship, as did Rear Admiral Creery RCN. CinCFES, Vice Admiral Sir Guy Russell, inspected divisions on Sunday 30th September. He congratulated Captain Colquhoun, his officers and ship's company, on her fine war record, and wished the ship a happy time in Australia. The record achieved by the 14th CAG since her arrival in April are shown below. Throughout most of her operating period, the servicing and maintenance units under Lieutenant Commander (E) I.F. Pearson maintained a 90% serviceability record which rose to 100% before the end.

Accompanied by *Anzac*, and to the strains of the Royal Marine Band playing 'A birds-eye view of Sydney', *Glory* sailed from Kure for Hong Kong at 1630 that afternoon.

Kimpo airfield.   *(FAAM)*

Results achieved by 14th CAG
22nd April to 30th September 1951

Miles steamed 37,159   Days at sea   107

Sorties	Offensive	Defensive	Other	Total
Firefly	768	254	33	1055
Sea Fury	1132	684	4	1820
				2875

Deck Landings		Accidents	
Firefly	1053	6	
Sea Fury	1818	3	

Flying Days	59
Catapult launches	2762
Total hours flown	7231
RATOG launches	113
Weapons expended	
20 mm	538000
R/P	9242
500lb. bombs	1450
1,000lb. bombs	94
Confirmed damage	
Junks	679
Buildings	1261
Ox-carts	794
Rail trucks	236
Vehicles	25
Gun positions	60
Tunnels	7
Bridges	40
Store dumps	81
Rail cuts	31
Villages	264
Observed casualties	1273

CHAPTER 7

HMAS SYDNEY

805, 808 and 817 Squadrons
30th September 1951 to 27th January 1952

In the second half of 1951 three more RAN warships arrived in Korean waters. The aircraft carrier *Sydney* (Captain David H. Harries RAN with Commander V.A.T. Smith RAN as second in command), *Anzac* (Commander John Plunkett-Cole) and *Tobruk* (Commander Richard I. Peake).

The commitment of *Sydney* was a substantial increase in Australia's contribution to the Korean War and a significant development in Australian history. It arose from a request from the First Sea Lord, Admiral of the Fleet Lord Fraser, to Vice Admiral Sir John Collins, Chief of Australian Naval Staff, for *Sydney* to relieve *Glory* for 'Two or three months operational flying if the Korean business is still going'. This would allow *Glory* to give her crew a rest after months of intensive operations. The Australian Government agreed on 11th May, at the same time indicating that a radical change in the international situation would mean that further consideration would need to be given as to the 'field of *Sydney's* employment'. At the same time the Government decided not to agree to a request for an additional army contribution.

HMAS *Sydney*, HMAS *Warramunga* and HMS *Unicorn* at Hong Kong.   *(ANAM)*

USS *Rendova* sailed from Sasebo for her first patrol on the west coast on 25th September, escorted by *Athabaskan* and *Sioux* in which Rear Admiral W.B. Creery CBE, CD, RCN, CANFLAGPAC, was embarked who was visiting Canadian ships in the war area. *Rendova* carried a new air group with new aircraft and did not experience the difficulties that beset *Sicily* on her first patrol. She at once put up a high rate of performance, averaging a steady 38 sorties a day. Admiral Creery transferred to *Athabaskan* on the 26th, joining TE 95.12 to see something of its work before proceeding to Kure in *Charity*.

Operations of the surface blockade continued without a pause, the ships being worked very hard. In addition to bombardments and blockade patrols, escorts for fleet auxiliaries and important shipping had to be fitted in, and screening destroyers to be provided for the carriers of TE 95.11, a commitment aggravated by the not infrequently sudden withdrawal of one or both of the American destroyers by Admiral Dyer for other duties; and the River Han demonstration was a constant drain on the frigates.

From 15th to 24th September Admiral Scott-Moncrieff visited various areas of the west coast in *Belfast*. He went to the Yalu and Chongchon areas where patrol activity had increased, partly owing to reports of increased coastal traffic, partly to support various clandestine organisations based on several islands in the neighbourhood. *Belfast* carried out a night bombardment of the main railway line in the vicinity of Kwaksan, while *Cossack* bombarded a gun position on Chorusan peninsula. This was the first time the enemy had been attacked by ship's guns so far north on the west coast. *Belfast* then went to Inchon via a bombardment of Haeju. Admiral Scott-Moncrieff went to the Han estuary in *Murchison* on 21st September, while *Belfast* went north to Sinmi-do where she bombarded railway installations at Kwaksan, after which she rejoined *Glory* and returned to Sasebo on the 24th.

On 24th September *Comus* supported a raid by Leopard's guerrillas on the Amgak peninsula. They landed after midnight and returned at 0600 with nine prisoners including a North Korean colonel accompanied by his concubine. The former expressed himself as 'fed up with the war'. The Communist troops had been alerted by the raid, and *Comus'* gunfire and strikes by aircraft from *Glory* were effectively brought into play.

Another guerrilla raid was made in the Pungchon area, south-east of Chodo, on 29th September, supported by *Comus* and USS *Taussig*; the latter was Admiral Dyer's escort during his visit and was lent for the purpose.

That evening Captain Norfolk received an urgent call from Leopard for support against enemy forces threatening the islands of Yuk-to and Mahapto in Taedong Bay. These islands are only 10 miles from Paengyong-do, the headquarters of the Leopard organisation, about whose security alarm had been felt for some time. *Black Swan* and *Comus* bombarded troop concentrations and stayed in the area for two days.

First Patrol

Early on Thursday 27th September 1951 *Sydney* was joined in Kure by *Glory* who secured to the opposite side of the pontoon. All the Fireflies from 812 Squadron were transferred to 817, together with a large quantity of the air stores. On the same day, CinC Far East Station, Vice Admiral the Hon. Sir Guy Russell arrived in Kure in HMS *Alert* where he was met by Rear Admiral Scott-Moncrieff flying his flag in *Unicorn*. Besides her, there were *Glory*, about to depart for Australia, *Sydney* and nine other craft — *Cossack. Concord, Amethyst, Charity, Cayuga, Anzac, Tobruk, Brown Ranger* and HM Hospital Ship *Maine*.

Embarked in *Sydney* was No. 21 and part of No. 20 CAG under the command of Lieutenant Commander M.F. Fell RN, 805 Squadron of Sea Furies commanded by Lieutenant Commander W.G. Bowles RAN, 808 Squadron of Sea Furies commanded by Lieutenant Commander J.L. Appleby RN and 817 Squadron of Fireflies commanded by Lieutenant Commander R.B. Lunberg RN. The USN helicopter with Lieutenant O'Mara and its crew were transferred, on loan, from *Glory*. Although the Carrier Air Groups had been disbanded on 30th June 1951, the CAG organization was retained and operated as such throughout *Sydney's* Korean tour.

The CinC proceeded to Sasebo where he visited ships in harbour and 41 Commando R.M. and called on Admiral Dyer. He then embarked in *Belfast*, wearing the flag of Admiral Scott-Moncrieff, on 5th October to go to Inchon to meet US Officers and Major General A.J.H. Cassels, Commander of the Commonwealth Division, at Divisional Headquarters.

For the previous five days there had been a limited offensive on the UN I Corps front, of which the Commonwealth Division had been the spearhead, and all objectives had been achieved. The two Admirals took the opportunity to visit the front line, where they were shot at by enemy tanks and had to take shelter under a Centurion tank.

On 10th and 11th October, Admiral Dyer had ordered a co-ordinated strike on Kojo on the east coast using *Belfast*, *Sydney* and destroyers. *Sydney* was carrying out her first patrol, as also was another RAN newcomer, *Tobruk*, who had taken the place of *Anzac* on the screen. The first operational sortie, five days earlier on 5th October, led by Lieutenant Commander Fell, conferred on *Sydney* the distinction of being the first Dominion carrier to send her aircraft into action. She flew 47 sorties on the usual missions on each of the first two days and 29 on 7th October up to 1400. She refuelled from *Wave Premier* and then shaped course to the south to join *Belfast* for passage to the east coast. *Sydney* had not previously operated a helicopter:

'The quiet and efficient way in which Lieutenant O'Mara and his crew go about their SAR duties and perform their many invaluable miscellaneous missions has been fully appreciated,' wrote Captain Harries.

Admiral Scott-Moncrieff had received no previous intimation of this operation, nor did the signal indicate its object or scale. Later he gathered that the opportunity had been taken to combine the business of striking the enemy with the pleasure of providing Sir Guy Russell with a spectacle of action on the more exciting east coast — 'a courtly gesture of modern hospitality', commented Admiral Scott-Moncrieff. Further intelligence signalled during the passage round included a target list of 35 guns of 120 mm and above in the immediate vicinity of Kojo.

The two Task Elements arrived off Kojo at 0630 on 10th October, TE 95.91 consisting of *Belfast*, *Concord* and USS *Colohan* and TE 95.92 of *Sydney*, *Comus*, *Cayuga* and USS *Shields*. For the next 36 hours combined strikes and bombardments were carried out, with spotting from *Sydney's* aircraft. Six events had been scheduled, but a heavy swell from the north-east had got up in the afternoon and the last event was cancelled owing to the difficulty of landing aircraft.

At noon Admiral Scott-Moncrieff was informed by *Colohan* that the operations were interfering with the activities of the guerrilla organization Kirkman. The Admiral was, not unnaturally, surprised that Kirkman had not been informed of the intended operation. Later, Major Coke USA, CO of the organisation arrived on board *Belfast* with the news that the targets were out of date; he detailed the fresh ones which were immediately dealt with. Coke remained on board and got into direct contact with his agents by radio that he had brought with him. The agents indicated the targets and passed spotting corrections, and *Belfast* carried out two successful shoots against troops, causing many casualties.

Cayuga was patrolling as a precaution against minelaying sampans. On 7th October *Small* had struck a mine off Hungnam and suffered serious damage. She made her way to Kure but her bow fell off on the way. *Cayuga* carried out a night area bombardment with 5th US Air Force spotting for her.

On 11th October *Sydney's* aircraft spotted for shoots by *New Jersey*, wearing the flag of Vice Admiral H.M. Martin, and for *Belfast*, the shooting being reported as being very accurate; in return, Admiral Martin and *New Jersey* commended the air spotting of *Sydney's* aircraft.

The niceties of naval etiquette were observed. Admiral Martin, Commander 7th Fleet, called on the CinC in *Belfast* by helicopter in the forenoon; Admiral Russell accompanied him back in the helicopter to return the call, and with Admiral Scott-Moncrieff stayed to lunch in *New Jersey*. The Admirals received an unexpected salute when, at the request of the oncoming air strike, *Belfast* opened fire on three flak positions simultaneously, just as their helicopter was taking off from her.

Operations ended at 1700 on 11th October, and as the ships left an ammunition dump ashore exploded. Ordnance expended during these two days was: 184 x 16 inch, 529 x 6 inch, 284 x 5 inch, 309 x 4.5 inch shells from the ships and 88 x 500 lb. bombs, 648 x 60 lb. rockets and 23,335 x 20 mm Hispano rounds by the aircraft.

Once in the operational area, war routine in *Sydney* was carried out with the ship's company exercising dawn action stations and the ship darkened at night.

Operational flying started on 5th October with three Firefly strikes, and Furies on AR to the Sojong-ni area where buildings, box cars and junks were damaged, a stores dump was strafed and six ox-carts were destroyed. Lieutenant Beange's aircraft was hit b Z flak.

Lieutenant Commander F.T. Lane RAN, (a Sub-Lieutenant in 805 Squadron in 1951) describes armed reconnaissance:

> About half a junior officer's flying time in Korea was spent on AR, starting with full 20 mm and twelve rockets for a one-and-threequarters to two hour sortie. Our chief operational area was 'Wales', a west coast area, north of the Han River to the Chinnampo estuary and inland 60 miles or so to the Sariwon Waterways. We did take an interest in the area north of Chinnampo from time to time, but we avoided Pyongyang and the radar-predicted 88 mm

Fireflies being armed with 60lb rockets.
(IWM)

> and 105 mm guns that studded the coast up near the Chinese border. We also flew on the east coast two or three times for special events. The primary aim was to stop all enemy stores movement by land and water.
>
> Soldiers, ox-carts, junks and sampans were the most frequent targets, but they were always difficult to find. Any group of twenty or more people were deemed to be soldiers, according to the advice of 'Leopard'. Our major opposition was well-camouflaged light AA and small-arms.

AR gave us a pretty good licence to roam almost at will sometimes.

Next day the Furies carried out the usual 'milk run' along the coast north to Hangchon. Five villages were attacked in the Yonan area and a bombardment spot was carried out with *Cossack* along the Hwang-po coast. 808 Squadron's diary comments on the apparent cruelty of destroying oxcarts and oxen, but since they exploded when they were hit they were being used to carry fuel and ammunition when motor transport dared not show itself in the daytime. The Fireflies attacked a road bridge west of Chinnampo and another bridge at Ayang-ni. Both Lieutenant Commanders Lunberg and Wotherspoon had hook trouble when landing-on and entered the barrier. Lieutenant Campbell burst a tyre of his Fury, damaging the propeller which had to be changed.

On the 7th only one event was flown due to poor weather. The Furies attacked the ferry area in the Taedong Gang, the Fireflies a bridge and a large building south of Sinchon. *Sydney* refuelled from *Wave Premier* during the afternoon.

During the next two days Sydney was on passage to the east coast to the target area of Kojo, where, on the 10th the Fireflies spotted for *Belfast* and *Colohan*, and launched strikes on gun positions. Sub-Lieutenant Macmillan's Firefly lifted its tail on landing and the propeller caught a bow spring supporting an arrestor wire.

On the 11th *Sydney* in company with *New Jersey, Belfast, Concord* and *Hanson*, took part in the biggest sea bombardment of 1951. The Fireflies attacked troops and the town of Tongchon. All three squadrons spotted for *New Jersey's* 16 inch and *Belfast's* 6 inch guns which carried out a ceaseless bombardment all day. On this, only her fifth day of operations, *Sydney* equalled *Glory's* record of 89 sorties, finishing with an attack by 16 Furies on at least 2,000 enemy troops caught digging in on hills covering the beaches; at a conservative estimate, 200 were killed and three aircraft suffered minor flak damage. Seven Events were flown from first launch at 0626 to last recovery at 1649. A few days later she received the following signals:

FOR COMMANDING OFFICER   FROM CHIEF OF NAVAL
                                                          STAFF
I WOULD ADD MY CONGRATULATIONS TO A PERSONAL
MESSAGE I HAVE RECEIVED FROM FIRST SEA LORD
CONVEYING HIS CONGRATULATIONS ON HMAS SYDNEY'S
OUTSTANDING PERFORMANCE ON HER FIRST
OPERATIONAL PATROL.

                                                    171047Z/OCT

TO SYDNEY   FROM FO2FES
YOUR AIR EFFORT IN THE LAST TWO DAYS HAS BEEN
UNPRECEDENTED IN QUANTITY AND HIGH IN QUALITY. IT
HAS BEEN A MAGNIFICENT ACHIEVEMENT ON WHICH I
WARMLY CONGRATULATE YOU. EIGHTY-NINE SORTIES IN
ONE DAY IS GRAND BATTING BY ANY STANDARD,
ESPECIALLY IN THE OPENING MATCH.

TO SYDNEY   FROM [HMAS] BATAAN
MANY CONGRATULATIONS ON YOUR NINETY NOT OUT-X (2)
WE HAVE RESERVED YOU A GAME WITH THE WEST
INDIANS IN ANTICIPATION OF YOUR CENTURY-X

                                                    150020Z/OCT

On the west coast the usual air and blockade activities continued. On 9th October *Rendova* achieved a record for US escort carriers of 50 sorties, the usual daily average was 45.

Sydney spent the 12th and 13th refuelling and re-arming in Sasebo.

Sydney had been in Sasebo about 24 hours when they were informed of a tropical revolving storm — a typhoon called Ruth — which was heading towards Sasebo; Admiral Scott-Moncrieff ordered the Commonwealth ships to sea from Sasebo on 14th October where they remained hove-to until the storm passed. *Sydney* was told to be at immediate notice for steam by 0900 on the 14th. At 0700 typhoon condition 2 (the second highest typhoon warning) was set, and at 1030 the ship slipped and proceeded to sea. On clearing Sasebo swept channel, some six hours later, course was altered to the west at a speed of 14 knots; the wind at that time was from the north-east at force 8. *Sydney* began to roll heavily, torrential rain beat down on the crew working on the flight deck, with the sea turning brown. By late in the afternoon the typhoon was getting worse, at 1527 a maximum roll of 22° was recorded. To prevent damage speed was reduced to two knots, hove-to by heading up to the sea using the main engines just enough to hold her in position where it was hoped she would ride more safely. Visibility was down to not much more than the length of the ship, the air was filled with spray and foam and the sea was almost completely white, looking like steep hills or houses covered with soap suds.

Typhoon Ruth, 14 October 1952   *(Corkhill)*

At about 1700 the Skimmer, a 16 foot motor dinghy, stowed just below the flight deck level, 36 feet above the waterline, was washed over the side by a wave close to 45 feet in height. This was followed ten minutes later by a large fork lift truck going over the side from the flight deck. An hour later the starboard 36 foot motor cutter stowed in-board on the weather deck was smashed to bits by a huge wave. The remainder of the ship's boats were damaged to some extent.

Below decks the whole ship shook each time the angry sea hit her. The Chief and Petty Officer's galley had been put out of action, and the only meal served from the ship's company galley was a sausage between two pieces of bread, and that had to be eaten standing up, as the forward cafeteria had sea water in it, which turned into a wave as the ship rolled, smashing everything from one side of the cafeteria to the other. Down below in the machinery spaces the stokers were working in up to one foot of seawater.

Long range fuel tanks were ruptured and soon the ship's ventilation system seemed to be full of AVGAS fumes. No smoking was allowed and the pipe 'FIRE-FIRE-FIRE' was frequently heard as there were a number of small fires during the night caused by sea water getting into electrical equipment. It was undoubtedly very fortunate that there was not a major explosion and fire.

Of *Sydney's* 37 aircraft, only 24 could be lashed in the hangars, the remainder were lashed on deck from the island aft. The rear ones in particular felt the effects of the whip in the stern in the big seas and the under-carriages of some aircraft collapsed. As the huge seas covered the flight deck with many hundreds of tons of water and the ship pitched and rolled, lashings got pulled out or broke and aircraft began sliding on their bellies across the flight deck into the gun sponsons — six aircraft were complete write-offs. Lieutenant Guy Beange's Fury 135 made several determined attempts to go over the side, but on every occasion it was frustrated by the deck hook engaging a bow-spring with a shower of sparks, as the aircraft had somehow become live. In the hangar, the pairs of chocks at each aircraft main-wheel were held with wooden battens nailed fore-and-aft to the chocks, whereas those on the flight deck were secured only with their normal rope lashings. Battened chocks would permit no movement at the wheels, whereas the rope lashings could ease, the aircraft would start to move and pull the main lashings.

Up on the flight deck, the aircraft handlers, secured to lifelines, worked on each aircraft checking and securing the wire lashings. When they were relieved they went down below looking like drowned rats and collapsed from physical exhaustion. In the hangar a two ton power plant almost broke loose, and Naval Airmen risked their lives lashing it to the bulkhead. Some sailors were walking through the ship with life jackets on. Anyone not on duty turned into their hammocks, but sleep was almost impossible.

At 2100 the typhoon was at its worst, with the barometer reading its lowest at 820 Mb. The wind recorder went off the board and broke, and it was estimated that the typhoon was between force 12 and force 13 with winds in excess of 70 knots, that the wave height was from 40 to 45 feet, and with very high precipitation's and confused seas. At about 2200 a Firefly was washed overboard and disappeared into the boiling seas in a matter of seconds.

Van Galen was screening *Sydney*; every now and then a destroyer shape appeared in the gloom astern. *Sydney* sent her a signal that she need not keep station; back came the reply by flickering hand held Aldis lamp to say that she had all boilers flooded except one, her boats and rafts were stove in or washed overboard, she was using emergency steering, she had no electricity, she had three major fires, and please may she stay in company.

Not far from *Sydney* a US Navy leased troop transport *Kongo Mare*, nicknamed the 'Red Ball Express', with 500 American troops aboard, sailing from Sasebo to Pusan ended up aground on an island 35 miles from Sasebo, its holds filling with water and with waves pouring over its superstructure. There were 12 other wrecks as a result of Ruth. Shortly after midnight, as the centre of the typhoon moved north, conditions improved sufficiently for *Sydney* to alter course to the north-east at a speed of eight knots. By 0800 the sea, although still rough, was not a limiting factor in the ship's movement and she returned to Sasebo at about 1200 on 15th October securing to No. 18 buoy near *Unicorn* and sent over by lighter aircraft written off in the typhoon, receiving replacement aircraft in exchange.

Most ships suffered some superficial damage from the typhoon that struck Sasebo that night. *Ladybird*, being of shallow draught, yawed violently and was threatened by USSs *Bryce, Canyon and Gloucester*, both of which parted their bridles, and by a gigantic floating crane which broke adrift. Altogether three ships broke adrift and five parted their bridles; thanks to fine work by tugs there was no major disaster.

Second Patrol

Sydney's next patrol was from 18th to 28th October. Weather impeded flying on two days, and on replenishment day, the 22nd, there was also no flying. A total of 474 sorties were flown, the Fireflies concentrated on railway bridges and tunnels with considerable success, and the Furies attacked coastal shipping and troop concentrations reported by Leopard. Two strikes per day were laid on in the Han River area with a large amount of bombardment spotting. The most popular task was close air support for the Commonwealth Division, particularly for the Royal Australian Regiment, though on this duty the heaviest flak was encountered. In the course of the patrol, three of *Sydney's* 5 aircraft were shot down and 28 were damaged by flak, but fortunately there were no casualties to personnel.

The first Fury detail on 18th October attacked a target recommended by 5th USAF of 1,600 troops and gun positions at the northern tip of the peninsula near Pungsan. No movement was seen and the defences appeared deserted. A village was strafed and rocketed. The milk-run to Hanchon produced nothing of interest though some medium intense flak was experienced. Thirty box cars were rocketed at Chinnampo, of which two were destroyed. The Fireflies attacked underground locomotive and railway shops east of Haeju and a rail bridge north of the town. Buildings, barracks and box cars were struck at Sinchon. Two Fireflies damaged their propellers in deck-pecks when landing-on.

The Furies rocketed a camouflaged gunboat on a slipway at Chinnampo next day, together with junks and buildings along the waterfront. A factory at Kyomipo was strafed and damaged. Three aircraft were damaged by flak. The Fireflies bombed a large building at Ullyul and struck targets at Sinchon and Ongjin. On return from his sortie Lieutenant Dunlop caught number 10 wire and entered the barrier.

Poor visibility over the whole of the target area on the 20th resulted in flying ceasing at 1330. Before that, the Furies destroyed a large building at Yonan. In the

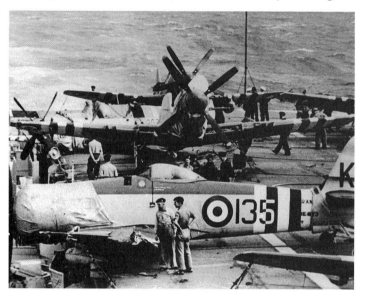

area just to the north of the Han River, villages and woods that had been reported as containing troops were thoroughly strafed, and houses rocketed nearby, destroying two and damaging one. Some 40 mm AA fire was seen but no damage was done to any aircraft.

On Trafalgar Day, 21st October, a very successful attack was made on junks

Typhoon Ruth aftermath.   *(Beange)*

in the Yalu Gulf, in response to urgent calls from Leopard who reported a junk-borne invasion of Tae Wha-do. Heavy damage was inflicted on the junks drawn up on the mainland coast and six were sunk whilst under way. Unfortunately, despite prior assurances to the contrary by Leopard that no friendly junks were in the area, two of the latter belonged to one of the clandestine organisations. As Admiral Scott-Moncrieff frequently pointed out, with loose control exercised over such friendly craft, the chances of such occurrences were high, but the organisations concerned considered this acceptable, whatever might be thought by the actual victims.

On the same day the Furies carried out their first CAS missions, in good weather. They had been briefed to report to I Corps, where initially communications were bad. Eventually 'Conrad' control, the British Commonwealth Division, asked for a village about 15 miles north-east of Munsan to be attacked. It was very close to the bomb line and since there was no Mosquito or smoke available, the flight leader decided not to attack. They went instead to two villages further behind the bomb line though still near the British Commonwealth Division's area. Intense light flak was experienced, but no damage was done to any aircraft. A second detail also had some communications difficulties, but eventually got on to the target, entrenched troops, who were rocketed and strafed. The Fireflies attacked and damaged a bridge at Chinnampo. A camp north of Undong-ni, a railway station at Yongwon and rolling stock were all strafed and damaged.

The 22nd October was replenishment day, during which Captain Harries reported

'...I performed a notable service in the cause of the Church in transferring by helicopter the RC Chaplain from *Athabaskan* to *Murchison* for subsequent transfer to *Black Swan* for onward passage to Kure so that he could meet a party of visiting Canadian RC bishops. Formal recognition of the performance of this pious duty is daily awaited from His Holiness, although *Athabaskan* intimated by signal that the Chaplain, during this aeronautical experience, had achieved his nearest to Heaven'.

The Furies on the first detail on the 23rd went to the far north of the Yellow Sea searching for enemy shipping. Though poor visibility restricted flying, several large sampans and junks were attacked and damaged. A village south of Chongju was attacked, destroying two troop shelters. The railway line from Changyong to Chaeryong was reconnoitred and seen to be intact, with two tunnels containing rolling stock. Five houses were destroyed in attacks on four villages in the Imjin area. Fireflies bombed railway bridges near Haeju and Changyon. Other attacks were made on a tunnel between Haeju and Ongjin, and on targets near Sokjong-ni. 5th US Air Force had had a bad day — four B-29 Fortresses were shot down in a strike against northern airfields, and two ditched north of Chodo. Thirteen Fury sorties during the day helped in the search for survivors, some of whom were picked up by a USAF amphibian and some by *Murchison*. Four Furies escorted a Firefly with a 'G' Dropper which was dropped to a US airman who had baled out from one of the B-29s. He was seen to climb into the dinghy and was later taken aboard *Murchison*.

Bad weather next day restricted flying to only two serials. Furies attacked targets in the Han River area and the Fireflies a railway tunnel. Sub-Lieutenant Roland had a number 10-wire barrier.

The weather improved on the 25th for the Fury milk-run to Hanchon where no shipping was sighted. On the return a Leopard target of a supply centre was rocketed and strafed. Troops were sighted firing at the aircraft and, whilst strafing these, Lieutenant Wheatley's aircraft was hit twice. He made a successful ditching 22 miles west of Chinnampo and was recovered unhurt by an American amphibian, Dumbo Dog, and he subsequently reached Kimpo. This was *Sydney's* first operational loss. Six Furies, briefed to report to I Corps, were allotted to Mosquito Conrad over the British Commonwealth Division. They were directed to a village near Taegwang-ni containing troops and supplies. With the target indicated by the Mosquito's smoke rockets, rocket and strafing attacks were carried out covering

80% of the target. Accurate, intense automatic AA fire was encountered. Lieutenant Commander Appleby's aircraft was badly hit in the port wing and he made a precautionary landing at Kimpo. The Fireflies attacked tunnels near Changyon and Haeju and strafed box cars.

Next day the Furies concentrated their efforts in the Han River area. Sub-Lieutenant Knapstein's aircraft was hit by flak and he made a successful forced landing on a mudflat from which he was speedily rescued by boat from *Amethyst* which also salvaged remnants of the aircraft. Another detail rocketed an enemy headquarters in the Haeju area that was left burning and carried out a spot for an accurate bombardment by *Ceylon* on a mainland village close to Sok-to. The last Fury detail rocketed and strafed supply dumps on a railway line to the west of Kaesong and then flew a RESCAP over the Firefly crew on the same event, who had forced landed. This was a combined RAN, RAAF and USAF operation, culminating with a classic 'double-cross' ground fire suppression manoeuvre during the opposed helicopter pick-up. The Fireflies had earlier destroyed a bridge and, on this last event, closed both ends of a railway tunnel north-east of Chaeryong. It was during this tunnel attack, 10 miles south of Sariwon, that five Fireflies ran into intense flak, one of which was shot down. The pilot, Sub-Lieutenant N.D. MacMillan, made a skilful crash landing in a field three miles west of the target in enemy territory. Neither he nor Observer 1st Class J. Hancox, was injured but their situation was far from pleasant. It gave rise to a remarkable rescue operation.

It was extremely doubtful if *Sydney's* helicopter could reach them and get clear of enemy territory before nightfall; but Captain Harries decided to make the attempt — a decision 'received with enthusiasm' by the American crew, Aviation Device Chief A.K. Babbit USN and Aviation Technician's Mate C.C. Gooding USN. This welcome news was convened to MacMillan by Lieutenant Commander Fell, who in flying low over him to tell him that the helicopter was on its way, was hit by flak, but succeeded in reaching Kimpo airfield. Furies gave cover over the scene of the crash, and were joined by Meteors of Number 77 Squadron RAAF. On the ground, the two airmen helped them to keep the

Sea Fury being armed with 1000lb bombs.   *(IWM)*

encircling enemy at a distance with bursts from their Owen sub-machine guns. At 1715 the Meteors had to leave; the Furies, too, had been ordered to leave, being at the limit of their endurance, but the pilots, Lieutenants Cavanagh and Salthouse, decided to hold on a few minutes longer. Ten minutes later the helicopter, which had been making a good 20 knots more than its accepted maximum, touched down. As it landed, Gooding jumped out and shot two of the enemy who had crept up to within 15 yards. An hour later, the helicopter, with an escort of Furies, landed with the last of the daylight, at Kimpo airfield, an achievement beyond anyone's expectation. Captain Harries reported:

> 'Apart from the fine performance of the helicopter's crew, the whole rescue organisation worked with copybook exactitude, and it was felt that the ship's guardian angel had had a very hard-working and successful day.'

Captain Harries had evidently gone into the question of rescue very carefully, and was responsible for the introduction of a novel rescue aid. This consisted of fluorescent panels carried by all aircrew. They speedily proved their value; already on two occasions where aircraft had crashed in enemy territory the rescuing aircraft had seen the panels long before they sighted the crews. Admiral Scott-Moncrieff lost no time in recommending the general adoption of this device to the Commander 7th Fleet and to Admiral Dyer and gave great credit to *Sydney* for the introduction of the idea.

At the end of flying on the 26th *Sydney* set course for Kure where she arrived on the 28th and where MacMillan and Hancox rejoined their ship.

REPORT OF FORCED LANDING AND RESCUE
by Sub-Lieutenant (P) N.D. MacMillan RAN

At 1500 on Friday 26th October 1951, 26 Flight, consisting of 5 Fireflies was catapulted off HMAS *Sydney* to attack a railway tunnel north-east of Chaeryong. On approaching the target the flight split into two sections, 26 Leader and No. 2 were going to attack from the south, while 26-3 and I, as No. 4, were to attack from the north. The first section went in, made their attack and pulled away. At this time my section leader and I commenced a steep diving turn to port, preparatory to running in on the target. We were to carry out a low level run, endeavouring to place our bombs, fused for a 25 second delay into the mouth of the tunnel.

On the run-in I was positioned about 300 yards astern, and just below, my section leader, who was strafing the tunnel entrance as an anti-flak precaution. It was prior to releasing my bombs that I saw what I thought to be ammunition links from my leader's aircraft passing over my canopy. This was later ascertained to have been tracer from a flak position situated near the entrance to the tunnel. At no time during this period had I felt any hits on my aircraft.

After releasing my bombs I pulled away and at the same time my observer, Observer 1 Hancox, informed me that we had been hit. The port nacelle tank was streaming fuel, while the starboard wing had two six-inch holes in it, one through the gun-bay, the other through the rounded I immediately informed my section leader of the damage and asked him to come and check my aircraft for any further signs of hits. As I did this I smelt burning in the cockpit and on checking the engine instruments found the oil pressure to be reading zero.

At this time my altitude was 1,000 feet, so I immediately switched off the engine and fuel and told my leader that I was carrying out a forced landing, there being quite a few paddy-fields in the area. I had to abandon the field I had first chosen due to high tension lines across my approach path. I chose another and my observer jettisoned our canopies. I failed to jettison my nacelle tanks. The approach and landing was quite satisfactory, the aircraft coming to rest at the intersection of two large ditches in the western corner of the field. The time of landing was 1555. The nacelle tanks remained on the aircraft and the radio was still working. However, not knowing what enemy concentrations were in the area, my observer and I cleared the aircraft at once. (It was later pointed out at FEAF HQ that enemy troops have been ordered to shoot at the cockpits of forced-down aircraft for the very purpose of preventing the survivors from using the radio).

We moved about 50 yards along the ditch running east-west. I carried my parachute while Observer Hancox brought the Owen submachine-gun and his navigation bag and maps. On settling into the ditch we placed out our yellow fluorescent panels to signal to the remainder of the flight, now acting as a RESCAP, that we were both uninjured.

Having done this we took stock of what we had and where we

were. Between us we had:

1 .38 pistol and 50 rounds

1 .45 automatic and 40 rounds

1 Owen sub machine gun and 2 magazines each of 28 rounds

3 emergency rations (tins)

4 special rations (tins)

1 pair binoculars

50 cigarettes

2 "X" packs

We were both warmly clothed and wearing heavy boots.

As for our position: Approximately 200 yards to the north-west was a small group of houses. Two of the inhabitants, wearing white robes, were peering at the aircraft through a picket fence. Assuming them to be civilian we did not worry about them. To the west was a knoll about 200 feet high, about a mile distant, from which concentrated automatic fire was engaging the RESCAP all the time we were down.

About five minutes after landing one of the aircraft from 26 flight fired a green Very cartridge, letting us know that help was on its way. This cheered us up no end. By this time the Fireflies had been joined by four Sea Furies and a flight of Meteors from 77 Squadron [RAAF].

We then noticed several men situated on the knoll to the west, looking in the direction of the aircraft. Through the binoculars we identified them as enemy troops. However, they disappeared over the side of the hill and we did not see them again.

45 minutes after landing, the Air Group Commander flew low over our position and dropped a message in a container, which landed about 25 feet from the edge of the ditch. The Air Group Commander's aircraft was hit during this run and subsequently returned to a friendly air-field. The message was a welcome one, stating that the ETA of the rescue helicopter was 1730.

From that time, until about 1720, Hancox and I kept a look-out for signs of enemy activity and awaited the arrival of the helicopter. At 1720 we heard two bursts of machine-gun fire nearby. Looking over the edge of the ditch we saw a Chinese soldier about 100 yards away, who immediately started waving his arms about and shouting — no doubt calling on us to surrender. At that moment Observer Hancox saw the helicopter coming in, so I opened fire on the soldier with the Owen gun. He very smartly dived into the ditch running at right angles to ours. I then placed the red panel alongside the yellow, pointing to the enemy. (This is the Air Group's signal meaning that we were being fired on from the direction indicated). At once two Furies dived and strafed the area.

By this time the helicopter was on its way down, while the aircrewman in it was firing his sub-machine-gun at the enemy troops. The helicopter landed some 20 feet from our position, alongside the ditch. I fired several rounds at the enemy position as Hancox climbed aboard, and then I followed him - at the rush. As we were taking off one of the enemy stood up to fire at the helicopter, whereupon he was shot by Aircrewman Gooding.

The trip to Kimpo was uneventful except that the last 30 minutes were flown in darkness.

I should like, here, to praise the helicopter crew for their devotion to duty in travelling 120 miles to effect the rescue, knowing full well that they could not return to a friendly base before nightfall.

Surface patrols in October were carried out in the Hwanghae and Yalu Gulf areas.
Cossack bombarded Chodo and patrolled the Haeju/Hwanghoe/Inchon areas. *Amethyst* was recalled from the east coast to support the withdrawal of guerrillas who had got themselves encircled in the Pungchon area. On 9th October *Ceylon* bombarded Haeju.

Sea Fury flight.   *(ANAM)*

Most of the islands in the Yalu Gulf were in friendly hands, except Sinmi-do which was held by the Communists with what was believed to be a small garrison. It was decided to attempt to capture this island by guerrillas and their attack was launched on 9th October. The island is 8 miles long and 4 miles wide with a ridge of hills 900 feet high down the centre and with most of the villages on the west side. 800 guerrillas, covered by *Cossack*, landed on the east side with the object of capturing the high ground so that they could attack the town of Nae Dong from landward. The party secured the beachhead and advanced to the hills, where they met stiff opposition, but gunfire support from *Cossack* proved invaluable. *Cossack* remained until daylight on the 12th when she left for Sasebo and her place was taken by *Cockade*. *Cossack* had spent longer in the operational area than any other destroyer in the flotilla; she sailed from Sasebo for Hong Kong to refit and re-commission on the 17th. The enemy had landed reinforcements over the mudflats at low tide during the night of the 11/12th. *Ceylon* arrived on the evening of the 12th and found the guerrillas withdrawing; she covered this withdrawal successfully during the night of the 12/13th and carried out a heavy bombardment of rail communications at Sonchon on the mainland.

The decision to withdraw was a relief to Admiral Scott-Moncrieff. The feasibility of reinforcement over the mudflats had always been appreciated, and any attempt to hold the islands permanently became more of a liability than an advantage. A successful raid had been carried out, and enemy troops had been killed and disabled, but it was nevertheless a disappointment for the guerrillas. Admiral Scott-Moncrieff decided that the risk of mining by sampans in the narrow channels round Sinmi-do was no longer acceptable and ships were forbidden to enter these waters. There was also a resurgence of activity by MiGs from Antung at this time so cruisers were restricted to daylight operations south of Chodo.

Belfast patrolled in the Chorusan area during the night of the 19th where junks had been reported; these were subsequently attacked by *Sydney's* aircraft on the 21st. *Ceylon* and *Belfast* patrolled the islands of the Yalu estuary nightly. On the night of the 25th, enemy single-engined aircraft bombed Tae Wha-do inflicting casualties who were embarked by *Cayuga* and taken to Paengyong-do.

On the 28th *Cayuga* carried out bombardments in the Chang San Got area during the day. Two days later, when sending a boat to the assistance of a friendly junk near Sok-to, she was fired on from the Amgak peninsula and had to slip her cable and make a rapid stern-board to get clear. These Amgak batteries were bombarded by *Ceylon* and attacked from the air, but they were not destroyed, they continued to fire on Sok-to and passing junks when no ships or aircraft were present.

No Commonwealth ships were present on the east coast during October, they were too heavily committed elsewhere. Mine clearance off Hungnam was completed, and check sweeps were carried out along the whole coast. Aircraft of TF 77 flew interdiction missions across North Korea.

Truce talks resumed at Panmunjon during October and by the end of November agreement had been reached on a cease-fire line and buffer zone.

The Communists had been building up their forces, and could launch a general offensive with about 40 infantry, 3 armoured and 1 mechanised divisions and with support from an airborne force of 1 regiment. The duration of any such offensive would be limited to between five to ten days on account of their supply difficulties, and the United Nations Command was confident of its ability to check it.

On 4th November the enemy launched a heavy attack, in divisional strength with 22 tanks, on the 1st Commonwealth Division in the sector held by Kings Own Scottish Borderers; they withdrew 1000 yards and had stabilised the situation by 12th November.

By the end of November the frigates had been withdrawn from the Han River estuary. Because of the tendency to infiltrate Chinese Communist troops into the Hwanghoe area and the north islands in the Yalu Gulf, occupied by RoK guerrillas, the defence of these islands grew to a heavy commitment. *Rendova* and *Sydney* alternated as CTE 95.11. Both carriers achieved a high output of sorties and had considerable success in keeping railroads cut. Close Air Support to the Commonwealth Division continued.

On 3rd November Admiral Scott-Moncrieff left Sasebo in *Belfast* and embarked in *Rendova* on 4th. Captain E. Fickling USN and his officers gave the Admiral a most cordial welcome and a thoroughly enjoyable day. Though only 18 aircraft were available, 60 sorties were flown, including air spot for a bombardment by *Murchison*, destruction of supply craft in inland waterways, CAS for I Corps and strikes in the Han estuary. Admiral Scott-Moncrieff addressed the pilots, and was left in no doubt that 212 Squadron US Marine Corps was a fine unit. Their unofficial name was Devilcats, and the Admiral was presented with a leather jacket emblazoned with Devilcat insignia as an Honorary Devilcat.

Third Patrol

Sydney left Kure on 4th November to relieve *Rendova* next day when Admiral Scott-Moncrieff hoisted his flag in her for a couple of days on board — leaving in *Comus* for Sasebo on the 7th. She started operational flying on the 5th, in poor weather, with the Furies on Mosquito controlled CAS for US 1st Cavalry Division. Houses were destroyed and fires started. Other Fury missions strafed box cars in the Sindok area and carried out a reconnaissance in the Han River area attacking troop positions and loaded box cars in sidings. *Sydney* suffered her first casualty when Lieutenant K.E. Clarkson, senior pilot of 805 Squadron, was killed, when his aircraft failed to pull out of a dive, probably shot down in a flak trap, while attacking enemy transport in the Han River area. Another aircraft picked up a couple of 20 mm holes while orbiting the position 3,000 feet up some ten minutes later, one bullet nearly severing the rudder control. The Fireflies bombed three bridges, at Wonto, Yongnamni and to the north of Haeju, and carried out a shoot with *Murchison*.

The weather was poor with low cloud on the 6th, but a full day's flying programme was carried out, including two special operations. At dawn four Furies joined *Belfast* and *Athabaskan* in a decoy operation in the hope of drawing the fire, (and thus revealing themselves), of the guns of Amgak, a peninsula to the south of the Taedong Gang, opposite the friendly island of Sok-to. *Athabaskan* stopped within range, *Belfast* remained hidden behind Sok-to (with a shore fire control party ready on its crest) and the air strike orbited 15 to 20 miles away. The flight established satisfactory communications with *Belfast* and went to the pre-arranged rendezvous south of Chodo. *Belfast* informed the flight that if the enemy did not open fire on *Athabaskan* the aircraft were to strike the pre-briefed gun position. The shore battery did not open fire and disclose their positions — the Communists obviously smelt a rat! — so the aircraft struck the area in general. No guns were observed which may have been due to excellent camouflage and siting.

Later in the day eight Furies carried out a successful attack against junks and small craft round the Chorusan peninsula and along the north side of the island of Ka-do, one of the islands in the Yalu Gulf, which had just been occupied by the enemy. The Communists retaliated that afternoon with an attack by eleven 2-engined bombers on Tae Wha-do to the south of Ka-do; following this Leopard reported that the island was being invaded. Captain Sir Aubrey St Clair Ford ordered *Athabaskan* to support the guerrillas on Tae Wha-do and followed himself in *Belfast*. It was ascertained during the night that it was Tan-do that had been occupied by the enemy, a few miles north-east of the reported Tae Wha-do. *Belfast* and *Athabaskan* evacuated air raid casualties to Paengyong-do. At the request of 8th Army, increased attention was paid to Tae Whae-do, but its security could not be guaranteed by naval forces alone.

Other Fury details strafed and rocketed serviceable box cars intermixed with unserviceable ones at Sugyo-ri. Reconnaissance details along the coast to Hanchon and Chinnampo produced few notable targets, just a building and some box cars. Lieutenant Johns completed 100 accident-free deck landings. The Fireflies again, as for all this patrol, attacked bridges — road at Mungjon-ni, Chiwiya-ri and Haeju, and rail near Haeju.

On the 7th Furies rocketed and strafed troops and destroyed seven ox-carts in the area of the village of Unbong-dong, and dealt with troop concentrations in the Han River area. The Fireflies' bridges were at Sinchon, Yonan and the southern end of the Allyong reservoir.

In addition to ox-carts and rail trucks next day, the Furies carried out a CAS detail for the Royal Australian Regiment being directed by a Mosquito controller onto 40 enemy troops in trenches and bunkers on a ridge. The trenches were thoroughly rocketed and strafed; 90% coverage was obtained and it was estimated that 25 troops had been killed. The Han River reconnaissance struck at two villages reported as containing troops. The Fireflies visited bridges at Haeju, Wonto and to the west of Samchon-ni.

After replenishing on the 9th, the Furies attacked targets in the Han River area on the 10th, reported by *Whitesand Bay*. 300 NKPA troops were rocketed in a village where six houses were destroyed and fires started. Of the groups of ox-carts on the Yonan/Haeju/Ongjin road, nine were destroyed and six damaged. In good weather of 4/8ths cloud at 4,500 feet over the Ayang-ni target area, three huts in a barracks complex were rocketed and damaged, and rail trucks loaded with bridge repair material were hit with rockets, but it was not possible to assess what damage had been caused. CAS was given to 25th Canadian Army Brigade, and spotting was carried out with *Belfast* and *Murchison*. The Firefly targets were rail bridges at Sariwon, Wonto and one north of Chinnampo, all of which were attacked.

The Furies gave CAS to the 28th Infantry Brigade on US I Corps front next day, being directed by a Mosquito onto enemy troops in bunkers which were rocketed and strafed, 90% coverage was reported as having been obtained but the enemy trenches were too deep to allow an assessment of the success of the attack. Radio communication had been good throughout and the target had been indicated with white smoke. Small-arms and 12 mm AA fire was intense, damaging two aircraft. In the Hanchon area a sail boat was destroyed and others were damaged, troop concentrations were rocketed and strafed, eleven houses were destroyed and six damaged, a railway line was cut at a tunnel mouth and four ox-carts were destroyed. After bombing a rail bridge near Chaeryong and both a road and a rail bridge near Ongjin, 817 Squadron diary claimed 'It can now be stated that ALL RAILROADS in our area are at present unserviceable'.

Only one event was flown on the 12th because of poor weather, the Furies attacked three troop concentrations in the Han River area. Several houses and large buildings were destroyed by low level rocketing and strafing, and four ox-carts were destroyed. One flight of Fireflies bombed a rail bridge at Yongwon. On return from his A/S patrol, Sub-Lieutenant Roland completed the 1,000th operational sortie from *Sydney* in 18$^{1}/_{2}$ days flying since arriving in Korean waters.

On 13th November *New Jersey* wearing the flag of Vice Admiral Martin, accompanied by Admiral Scott-Moncrieff, was visiting the west coast for the first time and joined TE 95.11. During the forenoon, the two Admirals boarded *Sydney* by helicopter to watch flying operations. *New Jersey* and her escort Shields bombarded a village reported occupied by enemy troops in the Changyon area, air spotted by two of *Sydney's* Furies. During this bombardment *New Jersey* fired her 3,000th 16 inch round in the Korean War.

The weather had improved the following day, permitting a full day's flying. The Furies had a successful milk-run to Hanchon, destroying a junk and eight sampans. Rolling stock was rocketed and strafed at Wonam-ni where two box-cars were

Replenishment in the Yellow Sea. HMAS *Sydney*, RFA *Wave Premier*, USS *Hannah* and
HMS *Alert*.   *(FAAM)*

destroyed. At an AA gun emplacement the gun and crew were destroyed, the first confirmed AA gun. Six ox-carts were destroyed and nine damaged. The CAS detail for the Australian Infantry Battalion rocketed and strafed troops on the enemy front line. The target had been indicated by artillery smoke; 80% coverage was reported, but it was not possible to assess what damage had been caused. During a reconnaissance of the waterways, one junk was sunk and two damaged, five sampans were sunk and another four damaged. The Fireflies bombed bridges at Allyong reservoir and Wonto; one flight bombed the village of Chihyon-ni causing two secondary explosions. Captain Harries was to report at the end of the patrol

> '...on 13th November no railway line was serviceable in the area covered by my aircraft, each one having at least one bridge down or one line cut.'

At the end of this third patrol Lieutenant Commander Lunberg, CO of 817 Squadron, reported 'It is of interest that over 400 Air Group sorties were flown during the last patrol, which reflects credit on everyone who helped to make such an achievement possible'. It was also noted that as the aircrew gained in experience the percentage of aircraft hit by flak showed a considerable drop.

Sydney secured to the buoy in Sasebo next day, 14th November, after relief by *Rendova*.

Winter had set in, the weather was cold, snow had appeared and strong gales restricted flying on most days.

On 16th November 5th US Air Force requested the west coast carrier to assume responsibility for harassing the route Sariwon/Sinmak/Kumchon, to be undertaken so far as normal blockade tasks permitted.

Blockading interest was concentrated on the islands in the Yalu Gulf and at the north end of Cigarette route — the channel from Choppeki Point to Chodo — by *Comus, Whitesand Bay, Athabaskan, Cayuga* and *USS Edmonds*; *Ceylon* supported a raid on Haeju; and *Hawea* supported guerrillas in the Chodo area. New batteries threatening Chodo were reported at Wolsa-ri (four 76 mm guns) and at Mongumpo; the former were bombarded by *Comus* on the 23rd, raided by guerrillas covered by *Cayuga* on the 24th and both batteries were bombarded by *Ceylon* on the 27th.

Fourth Patrol

After four days in Sasebo *Sydney*, in company with *Belfast, Sioux, Constance* and USS *Hyman* sailed on 18th November for the east coast to take part in Operation Athenaeum.

This operation, a co-ordinated air and surface strike against Hungnam on the east coast, was carried out on 20th and 21st November by Admiral Scott-Moncrieff's forces. The shore batteries at Hungnam had been markedly aggressive, at considerable ranges, against minesweepers and destroyer patrols so opposition to this operation was expected.

The force, designated TG 95.8 under Admiral Scott-Moncrieff flying his flag  in *Belfast*, consisted of three elements: TE 95.81 *Tobruk* and *Van Galen*; TE 95.82 *Sydney, Constance, Sioux* and *Hyman*; TE 95.83 LSMRs 401,403 and 404.

All elements arrived on station at 0745 on the 20th. The weather was clear, with a slight haze inland and a calm sea. Five air events had been

HMS *Ocean* and HMS *Belfast* prior to the transfer of Rear-Admiral Scott-Moncrieff.   *(IWM)*

planned for each day, with co-ordinated flak suppression shoots before each strike and with spotting aircraft remaining behind to observe the ship's gunfire on pre-arranged targets.

Meagre and inaccurate flak was experienced, and to Admiral Scott-Moncrieff's surprise, no enemy batteries opened fire on the ships. He surmised that the enemy was expecting an invasion and was reserving his fire until landing craft appeared. This supposition was strengthened when the beaches were floodlit and occasional star shell were fired throughout the night. After the last event at 1600, the ships withdrew and the LSMRs moved into firing positions and rocketed the town for 35 minutes. *Tobruk* remained inshore overnight to prevent minelaying.

A similar programme was carried out next day, but without the LSMR rocket attack. *Sydney* flew 113 sorties in two days (78 Sea Fury and 35 Firefly) of which 78 were strike and 38 CAP over the carrier and bombarding elements. Air spot for bombardments was provided by two aircraft after they had completed their strikes. Shipping vessels and junks were destroyed and damaged, 11 buildings were destroyed and 31 damaged and at least three ox-carts destroyed. Communications throughout were very good; there was no case of any strike leader, CAP or air spot aircraft failing to establish good communication with CTG 95.8. The only damage to aircraft was from two deck accidents — Lieutenant Oakley caught number 10 wire and ended up in the barrier, and Lieutenant Simpson pecked the deck with his propeller. Lieutenant Wheatley completed 100 accident free deck landings. On both days A/S patrols were provided by US Mariner aircraft.

Admiral Scott-Moncrieff remarked that material damage caused by 200 tons of rockets, bombs and shells seemed very slight, only a few fires and secondary explosions were started, but numerous smokeless factory chimneys and gutted buildings testified that the city was of little use to the enemy. On completion, *Sioux and Hyman* went south to CTG 95.2 at Wonsan; *Sydney*, *Constance* and *Van Galen* went to the west coast; *Belfast* to Yokosuka and *Tobruk* to Kure.

During *Belfast's* stay in Yokosuka, Captain A.C.A.C. Duckworth succeeded Captain Sir Aubrey St. Clair Ford; Senator Alben Barkley, Vice President of the USA, honoured *Belfast* with a call and was received with full military honours. Admiral Scott-Moncrieff visited Admiral Martin to give him an account of Operation Athenaeum, stressing the need to conserve the effort with HM Ships, especially destroyers and frigates, in order to meet their present commitments. Admiral Scott-Moncrieff also met Lieutenant General W. Bridgeford, the new CinC of the British Commonwealth Occupation Forces.

The 22nd was spent on passage to the west coast in deteriorating weather of rough seas, strong winds and snow showers. On rounding the south-west tip of Korea in the evening, the force encountered heavy head seas, reducing speed to 11 knots, and, all the next day, north winds up to force 8. The remainder of this patrol was notable for the appalling weather, it virtually put a stop to flying except for the last two days.

The same poor weather prevented any flying next day. Although the wind had eased to force 5 by daylight on the 24th, sleet, snow and low visibility made flying impossible until 1000, after which 31 sorties were flown. Towering cumulus cloud to 13,000 feet made it difficult to get through to the briefed targets so attacks were made on targets of opportunity, rail trucks, box cars, buildings and ox-carts in the Chinnampo area; two spans of a bridge to the west of Haeju were destroyed, and one CAS mission was flown for 3rd Battalion Royal Australian Regiment.

Next day strong westerly winds, with a rising sea and swell, seriously interfered with refuelling from *Wave Chief*; by evening the wind had risen to force 10, gusting to force 12, from the north-west. *Sydney* and her screen hove-to 20 miles north of Makau.

On the 26th flying was restricted to only one event of seven sorties that was launched during a temporary lull in the bad weather. Reconnaissance showed that all the railway lines and bridges that had been destroyed on the previous patrol had been repaired.

The weather at last improved on the 27th to allow a full day's flying. The Furies destroyed four houses in the Han estuary and damaged several others. Four loaded box cars were caught out and heavily strafed in the Sariwon area. Lieutenant Goldrick had to land at Kimpo due to trouble with his throttle. The Fireflies attacked the village of Orijong containing Communist troops, and four bridges: one between Changyon and Sinchon, one to the east of Changyon, one at Wonto and one between Haeju and Yonan. Lieutenant Commander Wotherspoon made a spectacular return from his sortie by entering the barrier via the gun sponson aft of the bridge.

The weather allowed another full day's flying for the last day of the patrol. Troop concentrations to the west of Pyongyang were attacked; an uneventful CAS mission for Anaconda control was carried out; and bridges north and south of Allong reservoir, as well as the one at Wonto, were all attacked. 110 sorties were flown in these two days, only two aircraft were damaged by flak and there were no injuries to aircrew.

Sydney berthed at Kure from 30th November to 5th December.

Lieutenant Dennis Lankford RNVR had served in RN ships in the Pacific during the Second World War, and had loved it. He had been fascinated by the places and the people; so, in an attempt to recapture those, perhaps the happiest, days of his youth, he had decided to leave civilian life and to return for a spell to the Royal Navy by volunteering for service in Korean Waters.

He was sent to Sasebo where he became Fleet Naval Information Officer with the task of securing newsreel and press pictures for distribution about the world. After an exciting and exhilarating spell in *Glory*, followed by attachment to *Rotoiti*, he joined *Murchison*.

On the evening of 28th November he was put ashore with a rating, Naval Airman Penman, on Tae Wha-do. His mission was to discover a vantage point on high ground from which he could take pictures of a forthcoming naval bombardment of the mainland, less than ten miles away. Chinese forces invaded the island the next day and they were both taken prisoner on the 30th. He was the first Royal Navy officer to be captured in Korea.

November 1951 closed with the emphasis shifting more and more to the defence of the UN occupied islands in the Yellow Sea.

November had seen action by cruisers, destroyers and frigates in support of the UN held islands off the west coast. They were largely garrisoned by guerrillas and RoK Marines, and with air-sea rescue parties and emergency landing strips on the beaches of Paengyong-do and Chodo. Apart from this support for the carriers, it was important to retain control of Chodo, the Techong islands and Paengyong-do to guard against enemy minelaying activities.

During the summer of 1951, guerrillas and other clandestine forces had occupied islands in the Yalu estuary. They were a sort of no-mans land; neither side permanently occupied them, but the Chinese knew they were used by the UN from time to time — a thorn in their flesh. The small island of Tae Wha-do had been occupied from September to the end of November when it was evacuated.

On 2nd December Rear Admiral Dyer received directions that the islands of Sok-to, Chodo, Techong, Yong Pyong-do (south of Haeju) and Tok Chok (in the outer approaches to Inchon) were to be given the highest priority in defence, even over blockade and escort. Admirals Martin, Dyer and Scott-Moncrieff agreed that their defence as a naval commitment could not be guaranteed.

Sydney could not provide air support for the defence of these islands owing to having been sent as escort to troop convoys in the south Yellow Sea, her tasks in her usual area being taken over by 5th US Air Force. 5th USAF had no knowledge of the spotting procedures used with ships on the west coast.

Throughout operations around Chodo and Sok-to, anxiety had been caused by considerable night air activity that could only be caused by friendly aircraft.

HMS *Belfast* approaching for the transfer of Rear-Admiral Scott-Monacrieff by jackstay.   *(Mather)*

A difficult situation had arisen as a result of lack of interservice co-operation. On one occasion bombs had been dropped, and on another an aircraft had given a wrong IFF signal. It took 24 hours to elicit a reply from Joint Operations Centre, Korea, that no friendly aircraft had been assigned to the area, but that 5th USAF night interdiction routes passed close by and it might have been one of them. CTF 95.12 had ascertained that friendly aircraft had actually dropped medical supplies, before receiving a reply from JOC.

Rear Admiral Scott-Moncrieff was outspoken in his criticism of certain aspects of the US system of command:

'The operations of the past three weeks bring out all the weaknesses of the American command system...The lack of any joint Service planning; the lack of a combined headquarters in Korea; the inability to work direct with other organisations and commands, except right up and down through the chain of command; the rigid command and lack of confidence in the man on the spot; the need to "go on record" resulting in long and sometimes confusing directions; the insistence on being told every detail immediately anything happens; the appallingly overcrowded signal communications causing further delays, and aggravated in the present case by the unwieldy chain of command and the objection to any signal on any policy matter being made "for info" up and down the chain.

'A further weakness is the lack of intelligence available to me under present conditions when the local organisations who normally keep me supplied with operational intelligence...are bottled up [in the islands]. Although there has been an improvement recently in passing on, by CTF 95, of certain TOP SECRET information, the source or reliability is never stated, and, except in verbal discussions, no qualifying information is ever passed on, so I am in no position to assess the strength or reality of the threat at this moment...

'In the meantime ... some 16 (including RoK) ships of value well over £10,000,000 are tied up in yet another of these static tasks, in a vulnerable position, as a result of a threatened attack which may be launched by a few junks and a large number of small collapsible boats, and is only credible having regard to the characteristics of a resourceful and fanatical enemy. This loss of naval mobility, which has been such a feature of this war, is the price that has to be paid for the insufficiency of regular soldiers to carry out static garrison duties. More particularly, it is directly the result of failure to evaluate and agree the basis of military requirements on a joint service basis, less directly it is the result of the uncoordinated activities of the "funny parties" and the irregular forces... A study of recent naval operations in the light of the established "principles of war" is most revealing.'

Admiral Scott-Moncrieff was concerned when he heard from Admiral Dyer that Commander 7th Fleet would require an Admiral permanently on the west coast. He replied that he could not be permanently in the area, as he had other duties as Flag

Officer Second in Command of Far Eastern Fleet. He asked Admiral Dyer to ask Admiral Martin to dispense with 'Duty Admiral, Sok-to', the situation was well in hand and he had every confidence in his cruiser captains; and with this, to his relief, Admiral Martin concurred.

The usual patrol and carrier operations were carried out on the west coast throughout December, so far as the defence of the islands and other commitments permitted.

Rendova carried out her last patrol as CTE 95.11 up to 6th December when she was relieved by *Sydney*. Admiral Scott-Moncrieff remarked that during her two and a half months on the west coast she had put up a remarkably fine performance with her Devilcats, and he was glad that this fine squadron transferred to her successor USS *Badoeng Strait* (Captain R.L. Johnson USN). In the RN, Squadrons and Air Groups remained with their parent carriers throughout their tour in Korea; the aircraft were essentially the carrier's main armament, and not merely a lodger unit in the ship.

Sydney remained until 18th December. The main emphasis of the patrol lay in support of CTE 95.12 in anti-invasion operations in the Chodo/Sok-to area, including TARCAP in daylight over ships in this vicinity, in addition to the usual strikes against enemy communications and targets indicated by Leopard. For the first five days, there was fine clear weather at sea, though ground fog ashore occasionally hampered attacks; thereafter the weather on this patrol deteriorated.

Fifth Patrol

In mid-December replacement of the US 1st Cavalry Division by 45th Division commenced. Escorts for personnel convoys imposed an extra load on the destroyers and frigates in the Yellow Sea. TE 95.11 had the responsibility for providing air cover for these convoys.

Sydney sailed from Kure on 5th December and reached the operational area on the 7th. The first day's flying was one of very mixed fortunes. Four aircraft were hit and two Furies were shot down by gunfire, one piloted by Sub-Lieutenant Smith RN, who was unhurt, being forced to land on Paengyong-do, but Sub-Lieutenant R.P. Sinclair RAN was killed while attempting to bale out from his Fury. During a low level run over salt flats just north-west of Chinnampo, he called that he had been hit and could smell burning. On gaining about 1,500 feet his aircraft was seen to emit flame from the underside and commence a gentle dive which was increased to about 60° on impact. He bailed out at about 200 feet, using an Mel09 technique, to trim forward, unstrap, jettison the hood and kick the stick. He left the aircraft but struck the fin or the tailplane and failed to open his parachute. His body was recovered by the ship's helicopter and he was buried at sea with full Naval honours.

The Fireflies had one of their most successful days. They bombed a rail bridge at Wonto and another at Allyong then strafed stores dumps along the rail lines. Another flight bombed two rail bridges at Chong-dan and another west of Yonan. A third flight attacked rail lines east of Ongjin. The Fury details attacked junks and other targets on Chinnampo waterfront as well as TARCAP sorties in the Chodo and Sokto-ri areas.

On the 8th, invasion of the friendly islands of Chodo and Sok-to was expected and the Furies were almost continuously employed beating up anything and everything that looked as if it could be useful in an amphibious landing, including barges, sampans and straw covered 'objects' near the coast. Large piles of logs that appeared to be for raft construction were rocketed. The routine early morning shipping check in the Taedong Gang and Chaeryong-gang sighted junks and sampans which were rocketed and strafed, destroying two junks and damaging six others. Rolling stock in Sinwon-ri rail yards were attacked, destroying one box car and damaging three trucks. Leopard reported troop targets in villages that were rocketed and strafed, killing many troops and destroying and damaging houses. Two aircraft were damaged during the afternoon coastal reconnaissance during which a 30 foot junk in a shed on Chinnampo waterfront was destroyed. The Fireflies attacked bridges west of Chaeryong and west of Haeju, and barracks at Ongjin. Lieutenant Oakley had to make a wheels-up landing on a beach at Taechong-do island. He and his observer, Lieutenant Hickson, were uninjured and were entertained by the Leopard organiser at Bromide Baker (Paengyong-do) until being transferred to *Tobruk* together with Sub-Lieutenant Smith for return to *Sydney*.

Next day the Fireflies bombed a rail complex north of Chinnampo, an attack which resulted in all lines in the south of *Sydney's* area having been cut at least once in the three days of this patrol. The Fireflies also attacked barracks buildings and a large working zinc and lead mine to the north of Ongjin. The Furies destroyed 11 junks and 19 sampans during coastal sorties.

Leopard targets of troops and gun positions were rocketed and straffed causing damage to a village in the Ongjin peninsula and to freshly dug gun emplacements. Two aircraft were damaged by flak.

Targets for the Furies on the 10th were mainly troops in villages and in the city of Changyon. The pilots on the routine Hanchon milk-run were briefed to continue attacks on troop concentrations as well as the normal coastal shipping check. Three 45 foot junks and one small craft were all damaged. The Fireflies attacked bridges to the north of Allyong reservoir and north of Chinnampo as well as bombing targets on the Kaeryong-san peninsula.

On the 11th the Furies destroyed 35 small craft, including three junks. Troops were attacked in the village of Paeksu-dong where some houses were hit and damaged. A combined strike was launched by both Furies and Fireflies on the Chinese forces outside the city of Sinchon. Two aircraft were damaged by flak.

Normal mid-patrol replenishment from *Wave Premier* took place on the 12th, and on the 13th the Fireflies attacked a village on the Ongjin peninsula and rail bridges between Wonto and Allyong reservoir. On return from his sortie, Lieutenant Robertson was marshalled into the rescue helicopter 'Shine Angel', rendering it unserviceable for the rest of the patrol, but a helicopter from Paengyong-do (known as Pedro Fox) performed notable service in its place. The Furies started the day with the routine milk-run to Hanchon where they strafed a large number of small craft in the estuaries, damaging three junks and five sampans. During an attack on box cars north of Chinnampo Lieutenant Cooper had to bale out from his aircraft after it had been hit by AA fire. His flight flew RESCAP over him until he was picked up uninjured by Pedro Fox and taken to its base at Paengyong-do, refuelling at Chodo on the way. The next Fury event attacked the gun position that had shot Cooper down, results were difficult to assess, and in fact they failed to knock the guns out. Two events later, during the afternoon, Lieutenant Commander Bowles, CO of 805 Squadron, was hit by fire from these guns. He baled out safely into shallow water, was picked up by a friendly junk and taken to a friendly island whence he too was rescued by Pedro Fox. RESCAP was provided for him by the remainder of his flight and by Fireflies on completion of their mission. *Tobruk* collected both pilots during the night but the subsequent days were so inclement that they made an extended stay in that ship until the 16th.

Van Galen joined the screen for the remainder of the patrol to act as plane guard.

The weather then decided to make up for its earlier excellence and on the 14th and 15th gave continuous high winds and rough seas with frequent snow showers. Flying was restricted on the 14th to only one serial by 805 Squadron; no flying was possible on the 15th, and that evening *Sydney* proceeded to the vicinity of Makau Island to cover a troop convoy to Inchon. Although the seas continued high with considerable accompanying deck movement one detail of Furies from 808 Squadron provided top cover for the convoy on the 16th.

On the last day of the patrol one flight of Fireflies were loaded with 1,000 lb. bombs to dive bomb suspected gun positions on the Amgak peninsula, other flights hit buildings in Ullyul and attacked rail bridges and box cars in the Yangwon area. The Furies also made all out attacks on the Amgak guns. Several aircraft were hit by flak. After the last land-on the ship headed south.

383 sorties had been flown; 25 cases of flak damage resulted in the loss of five aircraft. Of the these 25, no fewer than 11 occurred in the area of the Amgak peninsula, a damage rate that was not surprising when numbers of aircraft were continually carrying out attacks in one small area. A similar trend was noted after the frequent attacks in the Han River area.

It was on this patrol that Leopard started to pass results of air strikes on targets given by him to the ship. The results were very good and when compared with the pilot's claims, indicated that in the Leopard targets that had been attacked previously a lot more damage had been done than had been claimed. Though it was realised that damage claims made by the Air Group were nearly always an underestimate, the strict rules that were then in force were adhered to as it was considered that underestimation was far preferable to overestimation.

Sydney turned over to *Badoeng Strait* on 18th December and proceeded to Kure where she berthed at 1130 on the 19th. 130 bags of mail greeted her arrival. Lieutenant Commander Wotherspoon left temporarily, his place as Senior Pilot of 817 Squadron being taken by Lieutenant Gledhill. On Christmas Eve a new helicopter arrived on loan from the USN with its crew of Lieutenant Barfield USN and Ensign Dixon USN. Most of the aircrew spent the harbour period in and around Kure, with Army establishments turning on parties and luncheons and being as hospitable as restrictions would allow. On the 27th, when the ship sailed for the west coast, 808 Squadron's diary recorded:

> 'It can be said without exaggeration that more than half the Squadron
> was relieved to be once again at sea and enjoy a little sobriety'.

On 23rd December, reports of a build up of enemy troops in the Haeju area drew attention to the island of Yong Pyong-do off the approaches to the town. HMNZS *Taupo* was sent to patrol on Christmas Eve, while *Belfast* bombarded the Amgak batteries, with the distinguished shore observation team of Admiral Scott-Moncrieff, the Fleet Gunnery Officer and the Fleet Communications Officer. Christmas was miserable, snowing and blowing hard. Ships remained on station or patrolling locally; most postponed Christmas celebrations until their next return to harbour. The more fortunate ships that were in harbour were *Sydney* and *Tobruk* in Kure, *Alacrity, Constance, Sioux, Hawea*, and *Van Galen* in Sasebo, *Ceylon, Cardigan Bay, Morecambe Bay, Amethyst, Cossack, Comus, Concord* and *Murchison* in Hong Kong.

Bombardments and harassing fire in daylight, with star shell at night, were carried out on the Amgak and Wolsa-ri battery positions. Admiral Scott-Moncrieff visited the islands and discussed problems

Rear-Admiral Scott-Moncrieff transferring his flag by jackstay from HMS Belfast.   *(Zammit)*

with the officers in command at Sok-to, Chodo, Paengyong-do and Yong Pyong-do.

At this time there was a revival of interest in the Han Estuary. There was no chance of a settlement to the agreement to a cease-fire line (at the armistice talks) by the deadline of 27th December, and there was also the possibility of a Communist attack in force. The Army, sensitive about its left flank, wanted ships stationed in the Han to cover it. The Naval authorities were averse to tying down ships permanently on this duty, but they agreed to occasional visits by ships on passage, *Mounts Bay* on the 18th and *Whitesand Bay* for 36 hours on 19th December.

On 23rd December the defence of the islands of Kyong-do and Kang Whado was given 'highest priority'; defence commanders were appointed, but no troops other than guerrillas were available, and those with very little ammunition. *St. Brides Bay* was sent to the Han for a few days on the 23rd, and since nothing abnormal had occurred by the 27th she was withdrawn on the 28th.

On the night of the 27th/28th an attempt was made by guerrillas from Sokto to recapture the island of Ung-do. After air strikes and a softening up bombardment they approached the island in three junks supported by *Cayuga* and an RoK gunboat JML 302. The attackers were greeted by heavy fire from 15 machine-guns and mortars. One junk was sunk, one retired and the third landed men on the neighbouring island of Chong Yang-do and had to withdraw in the early hours of the 28th having lost nine men killed or missing and twelve wounded. *Cayuga* fired 427 rounds in support during the night. It was clear the defence was alert and well dug in; such an operation was quite beyond the capacity of guerrillas in junks. It might have been better to have avoided preliminary bombardments and to have relied on achieving surprise, but softening up was always an essential preliminary in American doctrine.

Throughout 1952 armistice discussions dragged on without any appreciable progress. Attempts to resume them in December were turned down by the Communists, and no further progress was made until March 1953.

On 28th April the Japanese peace treaty with the USA and British Commonwealth was signed, finally ending the Second World War, but bringing legal and diplomatic problems in its train. The immediate result was that the RN lost its cruiser dock in Kure and became rent-free tenants of the USN in Sasebo. Japan and USA had concluded a defence pact between themselves giving only the USA any legal standing with regard to base facilities.

On shore, the war was static. In July the UN decided to hit the enemy harder. Bitter, stubborn fighting occurred in the Chorwon area, which, by the end of September had extended along the whole front; November and December saw some of the hardest fighting of the whole war. The enemy strengthened his whole line with trenches and tunnels. Increases in artillery and armour gave him a numerical superiority over the UN; casualties rose from 1:3 to 1:2, mainly RoK troops.

In the air, interdiction continued by 5th US Air Force on the western front and by 7th Fleet on the eastern. Great damage was inflicted on the enemy's roads, bridges, railway lines and rolling stock, but the effort did not succeed in its purpose, and with the advent of the static war the Communist armies never suffered from a shortage of ammunition or supplies.

Meanwhile the enemy was making steady attempts to recondition the airfields of North Korea, starting north of the Chongchon River, intending to move his air effort forward until he could support the main battle. An increased willingness by enemy pilots to engage UN fighter-bombers at lower altitudes than before was noticed, coupled with greater aggressiveness.

In June there was a change in UN air policy. Heavy attacks were made from 23rd June on the 13 most important hydro-electric power plants in North Korea. Attacks on these targets had been in abeyance since June 1950, partly from political and partly on humanitarian grounds, but eventually almost to Russian order. In October, after interdiction was clearly not being achieved, Vice Admiral J.J. Clark USN initiated a policy of bombing areas behind the enemy front lines by aircraft of TF 77 to destroy store dumps not sited underground. These were the Cherokee Strikes on front line store dumps that were beyond artillery range. They represented the result of costly, time consuming and dangerous road, rail, pack animal and human transportation down the Korean peninsula, and were therefore lucrative targets.

The West Coast Blockade and Escort Force, which should perhaps more properly have been called the Naval Defence Element, was almost exclusively concentrated on the Sok-to to Chodo area.

A 'Wolfpack' organisation, similar to Leopard, was operating in the Han estuary area, based on Kanghwa-do. It came under fire from the north bank of the Han, from an area adjacent to Kaesong and. Attacks on the area were prohibited except air strikes under ground or Mosquito control.

Gun positions were pinpointed and Admiral Scott-Moncrieff ordered immediate bombardments by *Mounts Bay* and *Hawea*. These were followed up with air strikes from *Sydney*, in which he spent the next day carefully briefing the pilots himself. These measures had the desired effect, there was no more enemy fire for some weeks. It was decided to keep a ship in the Han area more or less permanently, mainly as liaison with Wolfpack and US I Corps.

On 5th January the Amgak batteries opened fire on minesweepers in the Taedong Gang. *Alacrity and Van Galen* silenced them and they were attacked by aircraft with rockets and napalm.

Next day it was decided from Supreme Headquarters that full responsibility for the defence of all important islands off the coasts of Korea would be transferred to

HMS *Alacrity*   *(Author)*

the navy. This responsibility was developed through a chain of command from Admiral Dyer as CTF 95; so far as islands on the west coast were concerned, the responsibility was Admiral Scott-Moncrieff's, which included land defences and logistic support of the garrisons.

From the 13th to the 18th January bombardments were carried out on the Amgak batteries with specially briefed air spotting from *Badoeng Strait*. Success was problematical as they were well concealed and, unless they opened fire, there was little the aircraft could do.

Sixth Patrol

Throughout January the carrier force was mainly employed supporting the islands' defence forces. This task had to be discontinued periodically due to the carriers being too far south providing air cover to troop convoys in the Yellow Sea; on those occasions air support for the islands was provided by 5th US Air Force, but this was not altogether satisfactory owing to difficulties in communications. The problem was improved later by the appointment of a liaison officer to JOC, Lieutenant Commander P.R. House RN.

For the New Year 817 Squadron was reorganised as follows:

	Pilot	**Observer**
24 Flt	CO Lt. Cdr. Lunberg	Lt. O'Connell
	Lt. Dunlop	Obs.1 Kenerdine
	Lt. Bailey	Lt. Gordon
	Sub-Lt. Lee	Obs.2 Bunning
25 Flt	Lt. Gledhill	Lt. J.T.Williams
	Lt. Brown	Lt. Christley
	Lt. Robertson	Lt. J.S.Williams
	Sub-Lt. MacMillan	Obs.1 Hancox
26 Flt.	Lt. Oakley	Lt. Hickson
	Sub-Lt. Roland	Obs.1 Hughes
	Lt. Simpson	Obs.2 Chalmers
	Sub-Lt. Champ	Obs.2 Morris

On 28th December *Sydney* had relieved *Badoeng Strait* as CTF 95.11. Her primary task was the provision of TARCAP and strikes in support of island defence, especially against gun and mortar positions, and against suspected boat concentrations in the Sok-to/Chodo area. Clever camouflage and deceptive measures by the enemy rendered the detection of gun positions or invasion preparations extremely difficult. A small proportion of the air effort was put into interdiction of the main communications in the Hwanghae area and routine CAP and reconnaissance sorties were maintained.

A full day's flying was carried out on 29th December. The Furies damaged a locomotive water tower at Chongyon and destroyed a 30 foot junk. The Fireflies attacked bridges west of Haeju, including a very successful attack on a railway bridge, a diversionary target, and on other Leopard targets. Lieutenant Simpson's aircraft was hit in the tailplane by flak and he made an emergency landing at Seoul. Next day was spent escorting and providing CAP for a south-bound convoy from Inchon carrying troops of 24th Division, the first UN troops to go into action against the North Korean enemy.

On the 31st 54 operational sorties were flown, though the weather left much to be desired. The Furies destroyed a large building at Anak during the milk run detail and two houses at Songsan-ni. Two villages reported by Leopard as housing guns that had been firing on friendly islands were rocketed. The Fireflies attacked bridges near Allyong reservoir and at Wonto whilst a third flight attacked a village near Kumsu.

The New Year started off badly with the catapult breaking down for the first time since operations began. This combined with a hasty rearrangement of the flight deck caused by a damaged Firefly needing an emergency landing at exactly the most inconvenient moment, held up operations for nearly two hours. The assistance of 5th US Air Force was requested and they provided TARCAP until *Sydney* was able to start again. A strong effort in the afternoon was put in to make up for the delay in the morning and a total of 51 sorties were flown.

The chief success of the day was the assistance *Sydney* was able to provide for friendly troops on the island of Yongho-do, in the Sunito anchorage, 7 miles north of Fankochi Point in the approaches to Haeju, which was invaded and captured early in the morning by a small force of Leopard guerrillas after heavy fighting. Good targets were reported by Leopard and through using his radio station on Paengyong-do as a Tactical Air Co-ordinating Post for air-briefing the aircraft, air cover was provided. The Furies with rockets and 20 mm cannon, the Fireflies with 500 lb. bombs and cannon attacked the assault forces and enabled Leopard to withdraw a 90-man rearguard.

The Fury TARCAP resulted in a negative beach reconnaissance, but an active light AA position was rocketed where hits were observed and the gun silenced. Two caves with vehicle tracks leading into them were rocketed, the entrance to one of them being destroyed. Lieutenant Rickell missed all wires on return from his sortie and entered the barrier. Lieutenant Commander Lunberg's Firefly was hit in the main fuel tank but he managed to return safely to the ship.

Heavy snow and visibility down to a few hundred yards on the 2nd restricted flying. Some details were abandoned after take off, some before. The Furies destroyed houses and strafed troops in the Han river area. The milk run of the waterways destroyed one junk and two sampans and damaged two junks. While operating just on the edge of thick cloud and in very uncomfortable weather conditions, a Fury, piloted by Sub-Lieutenant R.J. Coleman RAN, got separated from his leader and was lost. An immediate air and surface search by Fireflies and USS *Hanson* was ordered and continued for the rest of the day, but visibility was short and though a wide area was covered, no trace of the pilot or wreckage was sighted. The Fireflies attacked a suspected Chinese transportation unit north of Yonan. Lieutenant Dunlop's throttle jammed, due to icing, and he was diverted ashore; on the way he was hit by flak but landed safely at Seoul. Lieutenant Robertson, on return from an A/S patrol had an engine bearing failure but was able to do a quick circuit for a 'just in time' landing. The last event, other than search, CAP and A/S, was cancelled.

Next day air and surface cover was required for a convoy of two LSTs making for Inchon; by sending the CAP further afield from the ship than was usual, a full day's flying was made possible, but offensive sorties were necessarily curtailed. The Fireflies destroyed a railway bridge near Yangwon, their 38th. Other bridges attacked were between Haeju and Sinwon-ni. The Furies destroyed three buildings during their TARCAP detail at Changyon. Their shoot with *Eversole* had to be abandoned because the target was crested. Sub-Lieutenant MacMillan carried out the 2000th deck landing since the start of *Sydney's* Korean operations.

Replenishment day on the 4th was fine and clear, and refuelling was carried through from *Brown Ranger* without difficulty, the only inconvenience being that with a *Ranger* class tanker the carrier had to refuel in two separate operations since it was not possible to pump oil fuel and AVGAS at the same time, as could be done by the waves. Refuelling of *Sydney* and her three destroyers was completed in ten hours.

HMS *Ocean* and HMCS *Nootka* refuelling from *Wave Sovereign*.   *(IWM)*

On the 5th Admiral Scott-Moncrieff embarked in *Sydney* from *Belfast*. He arranged strikes on two gun targets near the river Yesong on the north side of the Han River, and, because the targets were in a zone which *Sydney's* aircraft were not officially allowed to attack, being delicately close to Kaesong, the Admiral personally briefed the pilots. The first Fury detail attacked NKPA concentrations reported as an immediate threat to the friendly islands nearby; fires were started and five houses were destroyed.

The afternoon detail, briefed by the Admiral, obtained direct hits on dug-in tanks and mortar positions but they could not accurately assess the damage they had caused. One Firefly detail, with 1,000 lb. bombs, attacked the rail tunnel east of Ongjin. Other details bombed the rail bridge outside Sinwonni, strafed box-cars at Sugyo-ri and bombed a target on the outskirts of Yonan where 200 Chinese troops had been reported. Lieutenant Goldrick was wounded in the arm near the elbow by a 12 mm bullet but managed to return to the ship and land-on successfully. *Belfast* remained in company until 1530 when the Admiral returned to his flagship.

During the last two days of the patrol, bad weather was encountered with low cloud, snow squalls and short visibility, and little flying was possible, only 14 sorties being flown on the 6th and none on the 7th, during which the Fireflies bombed the village of Kuom-ni where 300 Chinese troops had been reported. Many of the Australian ship's company, coming as they did from a somewhat warmer climate, had never before seen snow in any quantity, but they made good use of it in a traditional snow-fight as the ship left the area for Kure on 7th January after relief by *Badoeng Strait*, berthing alongside at 1130 on the 9th. A total of 362 sorties were flown during the patrol, 50.3 per day (including the one on convoy protection), and 73,440 rounds of 20 mm cannon, 1,197 rockets, 144 x 500 lb. and 10 x 1,000 lb. bombs were expended on the enemy. Eleven aircraft were damaged in action.

Badoeng Strait, screened by *Charity*, *Van Galen* and *Hanson* remained on patrol until 16th January. Operations were mainly directed to support in the Chodo/Sok-to area and in attacks on a reported build-up against Yuk-to. *Badoeng Strait* made a speciality of cutting roads and tracks into Chinnampo from the north. There was considerable flak around the main target areas, and she lost three aircraft; in two cases the pilots were not recovered.

Seventh Patrol

Sydney, screened by *Sioux* and USS *Redford* took over from *Badoeng Strait* in the evening of 16th January. This was to be her last operational patrol before return to Australia. It was largely marred by bad weather and uncertainty as to convoy requirements, liaison between TF 90 and TF 95 in this respect being indifferent. So far as weather permitted, usual air operations were carried out. In response to a suggestion in a prisoner of war interrogation report, some effort was devoted to the destruction of railway water towers. It was thought that these would take about a month to restore, whereas it was known from experience that the enemy could make good a rail cut in 24 hours or so.

The Fury Squadrons organised all their flights into Battle (or Finger) formation, the usual attack procedure being to cross the enemy coast at about 5,000 or 6,000 feet, quickly to strike the pre-briefed target with rockets and cannon and then to proceed on reconnaissance or photographic runs as required, at an altitude between 500 and 3,000 feet.

817 Squadron re-arranged its crew list on the return of Lieutenant Commander Wotherspoon as Senior Pilot to:

	Pilot	**Observer**
24 Flt	CO. Lt. Cdr Lunberg	Lt. O'Connell
	Lt. Dunlop	Obs.1 Kenderdine
	Lt. Oakley	Lt. Hickson
	Sub-Lt. Roland	Obs.1 Hughes
25 Flt	Lt. Cdr. Wotherspoon	Lt. Cable
	Sub-Lt. Champ	Obs.2 Morris
	Lt. Bailey	Lt. Gordon
	Sub-Lt. Lee	Obs.2 Bunning
26 Flt	Lt. Gledhill	Lt. J.T.Williams
	Lt. Simpson	Obs.2 Chalmers
	Lt. Robertson	Lt. J.S.Williams
	Sub-Lt. MacMillan	Obs.1 Hancox
Spare	Lt. Brown	Lt. Christley

Flying operations began at 0750 on 17th January in fine clear weather. That morning Flag Officer Commanding Australian Fleet, Rear Admiral J.W. Eaton arrived in *Tobruk* and joined *Sydney* to watch flying for a few days, *Tobruk* joining the anti-submarine screen. The first Fury detail on AR of the Yonan/Chaeryong road, destroyed three ox-carts. Later Fury details on TARCAP missions destroyed houses in villages and rocketed a gun position. The Fireflies bombed rail bridges at Samchon-ni and strafed locomotive sheds at Ayang-ni. The weather deteriorated during the day and heavy snow compelled the cancellation of the last event.

The main effort on the 18th was a combined strike by Fireflies and Furies against troop concentrations at the end of the Kaeryong-san peninsula, reported to be preparing to invade the islands of Wollae-do and Yuk-to. Villages were bombed, rocketed and strafed, and though no troop movements were seen many houses were destroyed. Three aircraft were damaged by flak, two returning to the ship and Sub-Lieutenant Roland in the third making an emergency landing at Seoul, accompanied by his CO Lieutenant Commander Lunberg.

Next day 817 Squadron continued its successful bridge and rail interdiction with considerable success. It was not unusual for them to destroy two or three, and sometimes four, bridges per day. This day's bag included rail bridges at Munjong-ni, one north-west of Sinwon-ni and one west of Haeju, and a road bridge east of Changyon. The Furies devoted much of the day to attacking troops in villages with rockets and cannon, destroying several houses and catching small groups of troops. Sampans and ox-carts in the Han River area were destroyed by cannon, whilst the TARCAP in the Chodo/Sok-to area strafed 17 boats of up to 30 feet in length on the beaches at Changin-do.

On the 20th the weather was fine and clear at sea but targets were obscured by fog which prevented the first Fury detail from reaching its pre-briefed target of a concentration of troops, so the village of Maktong was struck instead, destroying two houses. The Furies also struck junks and troops reported by Leopard in the village of Yuk-to. The Fireflies attacked bridges to the east of Haeju, at Yeigyam and three round Allyong reservoir, once again putting all bridges in *Sydney's* area out of action. After a combined attack with Furies on Changin-do Lieutenant Simpson landed his Firefly on the beach at Paengyong-do out of fuel, refuelled, and returned to the ship. Admiral Eaton left the ship during the afternoon for a visit to the islands in *Tobruk*, whose place on the screen was taken by *Constance*; *Sydney* proceeded south to cover a convoy.

January 21st produced meteorological conditions such that it was difficult to maintain the flying programme. The day dawned fine and clear, but with a good deal of haze, which, as the front approached became very thick, markedly reducing visibility, particularly from the air. All aircraft were landed-on at 1130, and waited more or less patiently for the front to pass. When it did the visibility improved at once but the wind veered sharply and increased considerably. The next event was flown off, but this second attempt to provide cover for American troop ships heading for Inchon was thwarted when it had to be recalled, as the strong wind began to make conditions somewhat hazardous. Advantage was taken of the lull in flying to refuel *Sioux* from *Sydney*, and it was intended to refuel *Radford* as well, but the seas rose quickly with the wind so it was deferred until next day when the whole force refuelled from *Wave Premier*.

On the 23rd the Furies noticed troops with some stores in the villages of Changyon and Oru-dong which were strafed. Fireflies attacked bridges to the east of Ongjin and at Sugyo-ri. A combined strike with Furies was made on the town of Taetan where houses were destroyed and damaged. The Furies made strafing runs on boats around Changin-do. The CAP and A/S aircraft were employed during a part of the time to search for a possible B-29 wreck. Nothing was sighted other than a drop tank which was recovered by *Constance* and was subsequently proved to have been from a Sabre.

During the night of the 23rd/24th the temperature had dropped to 16°F on the flight deck, and at Flying Stations the hands were greeted with frozen undercarriages and sheets of ice over barriers and wires. The weather was not good and only two serials were flown before the second was landed on at 1130 as the front approached, once more just in time, for the weather closed in and remained unsuitable for the remainder of the day. The Furies succeeded in destroying a small mobile crane and damaging a locomotive; the Fireflies bombed troop concentrations in the city of Yonan. Admiral Eaton rejoined from *Tobruk* during the forenoon. The night was spent practically hove to, suffering a wind of force 9 and a very rough sea.

January 25th was to be the last operational day for the ship, and it was with some disappointment that the air group found flying postponed right from the start, with high winds and heavy seas. They remained at short notice throughout the day while the handling and maintenance ratings were kept busy de-icing the flight deck and thawing out aeroplanes which were frozen up after the rain and cold temperatures throughout the night. But it was of no avail as the weather remained consistently inclement, high winds and seas giving way to low cloud, heavy snow and poor visibility, and in spite of good weather reports and tempting targets being offered from up north, the flying programme was cancelled during the afternoon. There was not a little disappointment that the last day should have been rather an anticlimax, but also some relief that the flyers had not been given that last dashing opportunity in which to get themselves shot down.

When flying was cancelled, *Radford* was detached to carry the turnover notes to *Badoeng Strait*. After relief, *Sydney*, with *Tobruk* and *Sioux* in company, proceeded to Sasebo on the first stage of her homeward journey, arriving there at 1300 on the 26th.

During the patrol, which included one day on convoy escort and the greater part of two days in which weather prohibited flying, 293 sorties were flown, no aircraft were lost though ten suffered damage in action. Ammunition used during the patrol was 70,815 rounds of 20 mm cannon, 128 x 500 lb. bombs, and 1,065 RP.

HMCS *Sioux*.   *(Kellaway)*

Since her arrival on the station, *Sydney* had spent 64 days in the operational area, not including time spent on passage to and from Kure and Sasebo. Of those days nine were on replenishment or passage between the east and west coasts of Korea, 12 full flying days were lost through bad weather, leaving 43 full flying days during which 2366 sorties were flown, giving an average daily rate of 55.2. The cost in losses during the four months tour in Korean waters was three pilots, eight Sea Furies and nine Fireflies, including one during typhoon Ruth.

Admiral Scott-Moncrieff described the performance of *Sydney* and her Air Group as 'quite excellent'.

Sydney sailed from Sasebo accompanied by *Tobruk* on 27th January and arrived in Hong Kong on 30th, having rendezvoused with *Glory* to transfer six Fireflies by air.

On 9th February she sailed from Hong Kong for her home waters. There she was to form part of the royal escort for the projected visit of HRH Princess Elizabeth and the Duke of Edinburgh to Australia in February. But that was not to be.

For on 6th February 1952 the postponement of the Royal visit *sine die* was compelled by an event which shocked and saddened the Commonwealth and its friends throughout the world — the sudden death of His Majesty King George VI.

In the war zone the news was received with deep regret. The accession of Her Majesty Queen Elizabeth II was marked by the firing of 21 gun royal salutes by HM Ships *Ceylon* and *Charity* at her enemies in their respective areas, and by HMS *Belfast* who was at Kure.

King George VI had taken a keen interest in the doings of the Commonwealth forces in Korea, and six months previously, on 25th July 1951, had authorised the issue of a medal in recognition of their achievements. Memorial services for His late Majesty were held on Friday 15th February, the day of the funeral, in all HM Ships and minute guns were fired by HMS *Belfast* in Kure and by HMS *Unicorn* in Sasebo. A memorial service in the latter was attended by Rear Admiral Dyer and other senior US naval officers. Messages of sympathy were received by Rear Admiral Scott-Moncrieff from all our allies, including each of the RoK Navy ships on patrol, and also by voice radio from guerrillas in the islands behind the enemy lines.

There is no doubt,' wrote the Admiral, 'the event has made a profound impression.'

CHAPTER 8

HMS GLORY

804 and 812 Squadrons
6th February to 29th April 1952

West Coast Interlude

By the end of January 1952 it was clear that the defence of the islands was a permanent, high-priority commitment and Admiral Scott-Moncrieff issued new directives with the object of giving effect to the defence measures and at the same time breaking away from the static warfare they threatened to impose upon his ships. Each defensive Task Unit area was to be patrolled during the day.

Task Element 95.12 was organised into four Task Units:

TU 95.12.1 — Sok-to/Chodo unit. Patrol area, code name Cigarette, from Sok-to to Choppeki Point.

TU 95.12.2 — Paengyong-do unit. Patrol area, code name Worthington, from Choppeki Point to 125°15'E, to include Wollae-do, Yukdo and Kirin-do.

TU 95.12.3 — Han unit. Patrol area, code name Guinness, in the Han estuary.

TU 95.12.4 — Haeju unit. Patrol area, code name Brickwood, from Worthington to the east.

Ships were assigned by CTE 95.12, who himself, in a cruiser, was not assigned to any particular unit, but was available to reinforce anywhere that was necessary.

Areas were to be patrolled actively with the following aims:

a. to discourage offensive operations by the enemy by a display of activity in the widest possible area;

b. to support TE 95.15 and guerrilla activity;

c. to prevent enemy minelaying;

d. to prevent the movement of enemy junks in the areas not covered by anti-invasion stations;

e. to control movements of clandestine craft;

f. to control refugees and to capture unauthorised craft;

g. the Han unit to provide a link with Wolf-pack and to provide gunfire support if required RoK light craft were to patrol inshore in Cigarette when not required for check-sweeping.

Admiral Scott-Moncrieff followed up with new directives for bombardment policy and deployment of air effort in TE 95.11. As regards bombardment, all ships were to be prepared to engage opportunity targets with direct fire, including counter-battery fire against active gun positions.

Directions for obtaining air spotting from TE 95.11 and 5th US Air Force were laid down. Unobserved fire was to be used sparingly; ships were reminded that effective use could be made of ship's observers landed on suitable friendly islands, and that in certain circumstances guerrillas could be of use. Commanding Officers were authorised to use ammunition as necessary to achieve the object of any shoot.

Duties of the carrier element, TE 95.11, were defined as:

a. TARCAP of the Chodo/Sok-to area. To provide two aircraft for day TARCAP, relieving on station or with the minimum practicable interval.

Acting under the control ship, tasks in order of priority were:

(1) To strike enemy artillery active against our forces.

(2) To give cover against attack by enemy piston-engined aircraft.

(3) To keep the coastal area from Amgak to Sang-ri under regular surveillance.

b. Air spot for planned bombardment of pre-arranged targets

(1) One pair of aircraft daily as requested by CTU 95.12.1

(2) One pair daily if requested by CTE 95.12 or other CTU.

These two defensive requirements would absorb up to two thirds of the available effort. Other tasks in order of priority were:

a. strikes requested by CTE 95.12 or CTUs;

b. armed reconnaissance of the coastal area, including enemy held islands, from the Han to Chinnampo. The primary task was the detection and destruction of enemy personnel, artillery, craft and equipment threatening invasion of the friendly islands;

c. armed reconnaissance and interdiction of supply routes in the Chinnampo, Hwanghae and River Han area, and CAS;

d. strikes on other targets.

When a day CAP over troop convoys in the Yellow Sea was required, arrangements were to be made with 5th USAF to take over TARCAP in the Sok-to to Chodo area, and the remaining activities were to be modified or suspended as necessary. The OTC, West Coast, was authorised to revise this deployment at his discretion to meet changing situations.

Owing to these requirements for the defence of the islands and for screening of convoys to Inchon, there was an acute shortage of destroyers and frigates which was chiefly felt on the east coast.

About this time a regrettable incident occurred which was nevertheless to facilitate the exercise of blockade and patrol operations. A clandestine craft with US Army officers on board was engaged and sunk by a US destroyer on the east coast. As a result authority was given to prevent such 'accidents' on both coasts. Both Admiral Andrewes and Admiral Scott-Moncrieff had frequently urged that movements of these clandestine craft should be notified in time to promulgate them to ships operating in the area, and also a proper means of identification should be carried. Authority was given to enforce the co-operation of local authorities to notify their movements, and it became possible, in theory, to inform ships and aircraft on blockade and defence patrols of craft likely to be met in their areas and their means of identification, and so avoid a recurrence of unfortunate incidents of the past.

Another commitment on the west coast was the evacuation of evacuees from the mainland to the islands, and from northern islands to Mokpo in the south. Those who were averse to going as far as Mokpo were encouraged to move in their own junks to suitable islands not so far south.

Also, in the event of the, then imminent, armistice the landing craft that were being used for the refugees would be needed for returning prisoners of war and for the removal of heavy equipment from Paengyong-do, Yong Pyong-do and Chodo. As things turned out, eighteen months were to elapse before the situation arose.

Evacuation of civilians as a defence measure was practically completed by mid March. CinC UN Forces had ordered that mass evacuations were to cease at the end of February, but that any civilians who might be the subject of Communist reprisals could be moved. At this time there were 455 natives and one cow on Sok-to awaiting evacuation. A special case was made for them (approval took eleven days to come through, via the tortuous UN chain of command). In the meantime the local garrison of the island bought the cow, which promptly rewarded their enterprise by giving birth to a calf.

Early in February 1952 Admiral Dyer and Admiral Scott-Moncrieff agreed that the important islands were reasonably secure against any attempt at invasion. For the rest of the year, naval operations on the west coast continued along the lines laid down in Admiral Scott-Moncrieff's directives; the work was unspectacular but arduous in the extreme, particularly for the destroyers and frigates.

Belfast and *Ceylon* alternated as CTE 95.12, *Ceylon* leaving the area in July, being replaced by *Newcastle* (Captain W.H.F.C. Rutherford), and in September

Birmingham (Captain J.D. Luce) relieved *Belfast*.

During the first quarter of 1952, the Chodo/Sok-to area was the scene of the main activities. Enemy batteries opened fire whenever UN aircraft were not overhead, and ships in the area retaliated. It was noticeable that the enemy seldom opened fire until the TARCAP aircraft had departed before dark, or if for any reason they were not present. On 14th February HMAS *Bataan* was straddled and hit in the CO's cabin; some damage was done to his apparel, but there was little other harm done. On 17th February a special air strike from USS *Bairoko* was launched against the gun batteries of Wolsa-ri, supported by gunfire from *Ceylon* and *Cardigan Bay*. In spite of this action, the battery was able to fire 80 rounds at *Mounts Bay* and USS LSI(L) *1091* on 23rd February. Both ships were straddled and no damage was done, but as a result ships were forbidden to anchor in daylight within range of enemy guns.

Bombardment of Wolsa-ri by HMS *Cardigan Bay*.   *(Emery)*

Carrier operations became almost a matter of routine — TARCAP over the island defence forces, reconnaissance and interdiction in Hwanghae, strikes on request by commanders of task units of TE 95.12, and of course normal A/S and CAP. By the end of February the Rivers Taedong and Chaeryong were largely free of ice; junk and sampan traffic was starting again and provided additional targets. Coastal reconnaissance was extended to 39°15'N, to Hanchon.

Badoeng Strait's last patrol was from 25th January to 6th February, when she was relieved by *Glory*, newly returned from Australia. For this patrol, the Executive Officer, Commander R.L. Alexander, was in temporary command whilst Captain Colquhoun was in HMHS *Maine* recovering from a minor injury. Admiral Scott-Moncrieff reported:

'*Glory* immediately got into her operational stride and started off on her operations just as though she had never been away'.

Despite the absence of six Firefly pilots, disembarked before sailing for DLPs, an average of 50 sorties per flying day were maintained. She was fortunate in the weather, which, except for the last day, was uniformly good.

First Patrol

Glory completed taking over from *Sydney* in Hong Kong on 1st February and sailed for Sasebo next day, arriving on the 5th. Lectures were given on aircraft recognition and escape and evasion, and the aircrew were issued with new dinghy packs and Mae West's during the passage.

The Flight organisation for the two Squadrons was:

804 Squadron

12 Flt	Lt.Cdr. Bailey (CO)	14 Flt	Lt. Fraser
	Lt. Cordell RAN		Lt. Overton
	Mr. Hefford		Mr. Newton
	Sub-Lt. Swanson		Sub-Lt. Wyatt RAN
15 Flt	Lt.Cdr. Birrell (SP)	16 Flt	Lt. Whitaker
	Lt.(E) Watson		Mr. Potts
	Mr. Darlington		Lt.(E) Barlow
	Sub- Lt. Haines		Mr. Collingwood
17 Flt	Lt. McNaughton	18 Flt.	Mr. Fieldhouse
	Lt. Peniston-Bird		Sub-Lt. Powell RAN
	Lt. Davis		
	Sub-Lt. Howard.		

812 Squadron

99 Flt	Lt.Cdr Swanton (AGC)		Mr. Gibbs
	Mr. Griffith		Sub-Lt. Kendall
	Lt. Pope		Sub-Lt. Jenvey
	Sub-Lt. Wood		Acm. Leigh
21 Flt	Lt.Cdr. Culbertson (CO)		Lt. Hooper
	Sub-Lt. Cotgrove		Acm. Japp
	Lt. Reynolds		Acm. Edwards
	Sub-Lt. Tait		
22 Flt	Lt. Hone (SP)		Lt. Hubbard
	Mr. Purnell		Sub-Lt. Bates
	Lt. Jacob		Sub-Lt. Apps
	Mr. Sleight		
23 Flt	Lt. Meadowcroft		Lt. Fursey
	Mr. Clarke		
	Lt. Kinna		Acm. Stevens
	Sub-Lt. Cox		

Glory sailed for the west coast on the 6th. Commander Carver, SO (Air) on the staff of FO2FES, gave a talk to all aircrew on the new task of the defence of the friendly islands off the enemy coast, of which the two most important were Chodo and Paengyong-do (Bromide Baker). The Communists had been seeking to reoccupy them and had been successful further north. A standing TARCAP was to be mounted over the group at the mouth of the Chinnampo estuary, armed with rockets, and also a routine daily roving strike operation around the coast looking for hostile intentions. He also warned that the whole of the coastal area, including the entrance to Chinnampo, was heavily protected by coastal batteries that the enemy had erected during the winter.

Operations started on the 7th with area familiarisation, particularly for the new pilots and observers. The countryside was covered in snow which made map reading far from easy and aircrews had difficulty in selecting targets. It had been reported that the enemy had cleared the coastal area of civilians in an effort to counter the UN intelligence organization by making the entry of strangers much more difficult. It partially rebounded in that any signs of life observed on the ground must have been enemy troops and were then dealt with. The Furies rocketed and strafed villages and gun positions on TARCAP and AR missions. Logs and other potential raft material on the beaches was strafed to deter the enemy from attempting landings on the islands.

During a reconnaissance of the bridges on the Haeju to Wongol rail line next day, the Furies reported that most were down and that the line did not appear to be of much use to the enemy. One man was observed by Sub-Lieutenant Powell, whilst in the attacking dive, to be firing at the Fury flight with a rifle. It is thought unlikely that he survived this one-sided encounter! Lieutenant Whitaker's Fury was hit by enemy fire during a strafing attack on fresh earthworks showing signs of occupation, and he returned safely to the ship. The Fireflies, using a low-level skip-bombing attack with short fused 500 lb. bombs, attacked two rail tunnels to the east of Changyon, damaging the track and causing a small landslide. The detail led by Lieutenant Commander Swanton destroyed a bridge to the east of Haeju by dive bombing.

On the 9th the Fireflies bombed a rail tunnel to the north of Haeju, one bomb being seen to burst right in the entrance, blocking the mouth and cutting the line. The Furies spotted for *Porterfield* and *Ceylon*, destroying and damaging houses in villages. A large construction at Wongol, in the form of four 'blisters' surrounded by machine gun posts and trenches, was attacked with inconclusive results.

Next day the Furies again attacked the 'blister', but no hits were obtained. It was lightly camouflaged, with no earthworks over it, and inside could be seen a covered object. Targets reported by intelligence were attacked in the coastal area south of Changyon. Nothing of note was discovered, but houses in one area reported as being active were attacked. Two tin roofed stores buildings were set on fire. Three large junks were attacked at Chingyongpo, setting one on fire which burned fiercely indicating something more inflammable than North Korean wood. The Fireflies bombed and strafed troop concentrations and supplies. Many houses were seen to explode in a spectacular manner, indicating that they were being used as stores of a military nature. Strafing and destruction of ox-carts had averaged three per day.

The element refuelled on the 11th and flying restarted next day with the morning reconnaissance by the Furies of the Koho-ri to Yonan area which attacked buildings and reported a large number of hayricks, ideal for camouflaging stores. Whilst investigating intelligence reports of troops in the coastal area north of Paengyong-do, 50 were seen on the beaches, either drilling or foraging for sea food, who must have had the shock of their lives when four Furies hurtled out of nowhere at them with guns blazing. At least 20 casualties were claimed by the delighted pilots. More of the enemy were seen further along the coast doing their best to look inconspicuous, but without much success. On this detail the enemy registered his first success against *Glory's* air group on this tour — Lieutenant Knight's aircraft was hit by small-arms fire in the oil cooler. Making full speed for Paengyong-do with precious oil streaming out behind him, he had very nearly made the emergency landing strip when the engine packed up. Fortunately he had enough height and speed to reach the nearest mud-flat where he made a successful belly-landing. Later in the day he was picked up by the ship's helicopter and returned none the worse for his experience. Six houses were destroyed and seven damaged by *Ceylon* and the aircraft spotting for her in the Chodo area. The Fireflies bombed villages suspected of harbouring troops and stores in the Yonan area; several small fires were started, but smoke and bomb-burst prevented an accurate assessment of the damage caused.

Although it had been reported that the enemy was preparing to cross the mouth of the Han River on the 13th, the Fury reconnaissance found no signs of anything in the way of craft that would enable this operation to be carried out, in spite of the fact that the whole area seemed to be active. Another flight, searching the area of the Koho-ri peninsula south of Yonan for invasion material, attacked a warehouse with rockets. Four fell wide and chanced to fall on a wooden shack which at once exploded sending smoke up to 2,000 feet. During an attack on the village of Najimporo the Furies were subject to light flak, the first they had experienced during this tour. The excitement for the day was provided by a TARCAP mission. On the morning event, after pulling away from an attack on the 'blister' area south-west of Pungchon, Lieutenant Overton experienced complete engine failure. With about 4,000 feet in hand and sea just ahead, he was able to carry out a normal ditching south of Chodo. Leaving the aircraft wearing his parachute he became the Squadron's first ditchee to abstract a dinghy from the aircraft. Fortunately he did not have to use it for very long because he was picked up unharmed after only a few minutes in the water by an RoK AMS (US auxiliary motor minesweeper) 501, which got under way very promptly to go to his rescue. While the possibility of mechanical failure cannot be dismissed it is thought the aircraft was hit by one of several heavy machine-guns in the area then under attack. The Fireflies carried out a highly successful attack on a village south-east of Ongjin, scoring direct hits which started a large fire with smoke rising to 1,500 feet.

Due to rough seas, fog and poor visibility, the first detail on the 14th was not launched until 1100. On one of the rare visits to the Chinnampo estuary the Furies found the river still had a lot of ice in it, but it was generally free for navigation, and they strafed some small boats. They also attacked villages in the coastal area around Ongjin, damaging six houses, and strafing sampans to prevent their use against Paengyong-do. Several large boats were discovered hidden at various points along the coast; three drawn up on a beach close to a village were rocketed and set on fire. Lieutenant Overton returned to the ship, looking none the worse for his cold bath of the day before. Although he had been in the water for only a short time he was able to give some useful information on the cold water survival equipment. The highly rated Mark 6 immersion suit was found to leak through the crutch and boots; effective action was taken to rectify these faults. The Fireflies destroyed several houses and a large warehouse in the town of Punchon. On completion of the day's restricted flying, *Glory* proceeded to Sasebo, arriving there on the 15th.

While in Sasebo, *Unicorn* arrived on the 17th with two replacement Sea Furies. Ammunitioning ship was carried out under unpleasantly cold conditions. Three US officers lectured on Escape and Evasion. The opportunity was taken to show 50 RoK Cadets and 20 USAF aircrew and maintenance ratings round the ship.

USS *Bairoko*, having taken the place of *Badoeng Strait* on the west coast, relieved *Glory* on 16th February and continued on the same lines. It was during this, her first patrol, that one of her aircraft inadvertently bombed Leopard's headquarters on Paengyong-do at a most inopportune moment. Admiral Dyer had arrived on the west coast in *Rochester* for a short tour of the islands. On 22nd February he was at Leopard's headquarters when a bomb exploded close to the headquarters building, doing considerable damage but fortunately causing no casualties. One of *Bairoko's* aircraft, while dropping a message for Leopard had inadvertently released the bomb at the same time. Three Corsairs and one pilot were lost to enemy gunfire during the patrol, and an average of 40 sorties per day were flown.

Second Patrol
Glory relieved *Bairoko* on 24th February and started operations next day, with Captain Colquhoun once more in command. The weather was cold but good for flying except for a few periods when snow storms reduced visibility.

Flying started on the 25th with the Furies doing much damage with rockets to Sogang-ni, west of Chinnampo, the important staging post for Communist troops heading south. Sub-Lieutenant Wyatt's aircraft was hit by a machine gun bullet passing harmlessly through the wing when at 4,000 feet, the highest yet for small-arms fire. Three aircraft were also hit when pulling away from a strafing attack when on their TARCAP mission. Mr. Fieldhouse had the closest call when a .303 in bullet passed through the cockpit canopy. The Fireflies blew up buildings at Yonchodo-ri, and destroyed and damaged houses in the village of Chanyon. While the 1230 detail was away the weather closed down to 8/8ths cloud and the visibility deteriorated. For the first time in eleven months the aircraft were recovered by carrier controlled approach (CCA); all the pilots made good approaches, which was particularly laudable as many of them had had very little experience in this form of homing and considering that the visibility was such that the destroyer screen, less than half a mile away, was invisible.

The early morning detail of Furies next day surprised seventeen ox-carts in the Koho-ri area, destroying eight with 20 mm cannon fire. The Fireflies on the same event bombed a rail tunnel and bridge at Charyon, damaging the bridge and blocking the tunnel. Later, Furies on a bombardment spotting mission had some difficulty in initially contacting the US destroyer *Gurke*, and when the bombardment did start, the shooting was poor and the aircraft found it impossible to get the ship onto target in the time available and had to return to base.

The early morning 'milk-run' coastal reconnaissance to Hanchon on the 27th reported the coast still being iced up and no junk traffic possible. They flew on to the Chinnampo estuary to reconnoitre bridges around the town, finally rocketing installations in Pungchon and starting fires. Fireflies bombed road and rail bridges at Chaeryong in the morning. During the afternoon, six, armed with 1,000 lb. bombs and escorted by Furies, attacked three gun positions to the north of Pungchon but succeeded only in near missing them. The escort rocketed a bridge near Haeju, knocking out one span. The Fury TARCAP strafed white-clad personnel on the beach which, when attacked, immediately became airborne. The CO was later heard to claim four large birds destroyed! While landing-on, Sub-Lieutenant Powell knocked off the tail wheel of his aircraft, damaging the fuselage, and causing a complete rear-wedge change; the first accident in 425 deck landings.

The 28th was a very routine day for both Squadrons: troops and buildings were strafed and rocketed, rail trucks were strafed, Ongjin and the village of Yachon were bombed. The TARCAP made a successful attack on a village setting several houses on fire.

The last day of the month was devoted to refuelling. Both Squadrons reported very favourably on the new, small Mae West and on the 'L' type dinghy pack; the former made it impossible to float face down, and because the latter was attached to the back-side of the Mae West, the pilot did not have to reach into the cockpit to retrieve it on ditching.

Statistics for February for the two squadrons were:

	804 Squadron	**812 Squadron**	
	February	February	Operational
Hours	737-10	239-55	2138
Sorties	382	184	1036
Deck landings	380	197	993

On 1st March low cloud over the land delayed the start of flying, the first event not being launched until 1045 when the Furies carried out a road and rail reconnaissance of the Haeju to Sariwon, and Sariwon to Changyon routes, rocketing Songchon-ni with good results; and the Fireflies bombed Changyon and strafed villages, gun positions and warehouses, damaging houses and causing casualties to the gun crews. Other details rocketed rail cars, strafed gun positions and a lighthouse in the Chinnampo estuary. A rail line was cut by Firefly bombs near Changyon.

Lieutenant Commander Bailey tried out the new Sea Fury drop-tank cameras with success, where a 45 gallon drop-tank was modified to carry both a forward facing and a rear facing camera. This gave a far better picture of attack results than the normal vertical camera, since photographs could be taken in the attack and in the pull out. Admiral Scott-Moncrieff subsequently remarked that the oblique photographs taken with cameras mounted thus considerably helped in the difficult problem of accurately locating well camouflaged targets, such as guns in the Amgak and Wolsa-ri areas which had been menacing the ships of TE 95.12. The advantage over the standard fuselage mounting was that aiming was much easier since the gyro gun sight could be used, and close-up pictures were possible. The technique was to make a low dive on the target taking pictures as low as possible, and then pulling up sharply and taking another shot while going away.

Returning from an early TARCAP mission, the engine of Lieutenant Fraser's Fury cut out due to loss of oil pressure as he was about to pass down the starboard side and he was forced to ditch close astern of the ship. The USN helicopter, airborne just above the flight deck, picked him up unharmed in the record time of only one-and-a-half minutes from ditching to deck! The aircraft had never been a good one, so whether it was as a result of enemy action or mechanical failure could not be known.

The Fireflies on the 2nd had one of their less successful days: the first detail attacked a tunnel to the north-east of Changyon, cutting the road with four bombs; the second detail near-missed a rail bridge at Sugyo-ri; while the third near-missed gun positions north of Pungchon. They did, however, strafe villages and sampans, destroying and damaging buildings, stores and ox-carts. During a rocket attack on stores on the beach at Yongho-do by Furies one aircraft was damaged. Furies escorted the Firefly mission to the gun positions in the Chodo area in cloudy, overcast weather, and continued to Chinnampo where they attacked a North Korean naval headquarters with rockets, eight direct hits were observed and sixteen probables; junks and sampans along the waterfront were strafed on the way home. A special flight by Furies was laid on in the evening to check reports of an invasion of the friendly island of Sunmi-do, south of Ongjin. No sign of activity was seen and no serviceable junks were observed in the area. A house reported to contain 70 troops was rocketed and damaged; another village reportedly containing 200 troops was rocketed, damaging houses, and a further hideout of 150 troops was strafed.

Next day two details of Fireflies attacked a rail tunnel north-east of Changyon. Both ends were partially closed by four bombs exploding inside the mouths. The Furies attacked marshalling yards at Sinchon and locomotive sheds at Haeju, causing considerable damage to both. Buildings in villages in the Yonan area were also set on fire. The TARCAP spotted a shoot for *Cossack* on targets north of Pungchon.

On the 4th, leaking pipes rendered the catapult unserviceable and shortage of RATOG equipped aircraft reduced the first event to only two aircraft on CAP and another two on TARCAP — all other details were catapulted normally. In a Firefly attack on a rail tunnel north-east of Ongjin smoke was seen to pour from each end; another attack on the village of Sugyo-ri destroyed or damaged ten houses and started fires. *Glory* turned over to *Bairoko* on the evening of 4th March and proceeded to Kure.

During the patrol, the 5,000th deck landing of the commission was recorded, and by the end of the patrol eight pilots celebrated the completion of 100 operational sorties in the Korean theatre — Lieutenant Commander Bailey, Lieutenants MacNaughton and Whitaker, Lieutenant (E) Barlow, Mr. Fieldhouse, Mr. Collingwood, Mr. Hefford and Mr. Darlington. Despite the catapult unserviceability and the absence of five pilots (one at Iwakuni and four in *Unicorn* for Exercise Vortex), a daily average of 50 sorties was achieved; 168 x 500 lb., 24 x 1,000 lb. bombs and 1,440 rockets were expended on the enemy.

During the six days alongside the jetty at Kure, one over-speeded Firefly was lightered to Iwakuni, one replacement and one spare Firefly, and one replacement Fury, were received. Divisions were held on the jetty on Sunday 9th March, and all the usual storing, ammunitioning and maintenance took place.

Third Patrol

Twelve Army officers embarked in *Glory* for sea experience before she sailed on 12th March, and on her way to the operational area she met *Concord* with Admiral Scott-Moncrieff on board who transferred his flag to *Glory* to witness flying for a few days.

Operations followed the usual lines, but strikes against enemy troops, transport and store concentrations met with greater success than during the previous two patrols, owing to greater activity on the part of the enemy and good targets reported by Leopard.

Weather was fine to fair, with good visibility on 14th March and 50 sorties were flown. The first Fury detail of four aircraft was launched at 0645 on a new, early, enlarged TARCAP mission, with the object of catching the enemy napping in the

HMS *Concord.*   *(IWM)*

outer

regions of the area. With four aircraft available, two remained in defence in the vicinity of the patrolling ships, while the other pair could wander further afield without having to worry about enemy intentions over Chodo. This new policy was quick to pay off, the first deep thrust in the area west of Anak produced a startling number of targets. While the old area was as quiet as ever, the backwoods were literally alive with enemy. Three ox-carts out of a train of ten on the Chinnampo to Anak road were destroyed and several groups of troops in the hills were strafed. A photo-reconnaissance was made of proposed rescue points for which aircrew should make if they were shot down and were compelled to remain in enemy territory overnight. Many enemy were seen in the town of Sinchon where the rail yard was attacked with rockets, damaging several warehouses. More personnel were observed in Chodo-ri on the south side of the Chinnampo ferry. The Fireflies carried out two spotting missions for *Belfast* who was bombarding villages. A bridge near Taetan and a headquarters were bombed.

Next day broke fine, but low clouds and restricted visibility compelled the abandonment of flying during the afternoon after 42 sorties. The early morning Fury TARCAP damaged a number of very well camouflaged junks on the beach opposite Chodo, after they had reconnoitred dams in the area and had damaged various installations and stores. The Furies had to be content with opportunity targets in the coastal belt, while the Fireflies attacked villages and a bridge on the Ongjin peninsula. The afternoon Firefly TARCAP could not go north to Pungchon but a coastal reconnaissance resulted in the large village of Kumchon being bombed. Lieutenant R.J. Overton was shot down and killed while covering his section leader during a low photographic and strafing run over the Amgak peninsula on the south side of the Chinnampo estuary. His Fury was hit by a battery of five guns, either 0.5 inch or 20 mm, the aircraft turned on its back and crashed into the hillside catching fire at once.

The following day was fine with good visibility and 62 sorties were launched, including a continuous air patrol west of Chodo to cover aircraft searching for an American aircrew who had been shot down; wreckage was sighted but no sign of survivors. The Fireflies took over TARCAP duties from the Furies after the first event of the day, bombing villages in the coastal area. Gun positions and trench works were rocketed by Furies where many hits caused considerable damage. A large personnel building at Yultong-ni was attacked.

Monday 17th March was *Glory's* big day, visibility being extreme with light winds from the north. An extra effort was required because of a report of an impending attack on Sok-to, and a full offensive was launched. The record for the greatest number of sorties in one day was recovered, this time with the excellent total of 105 of normal duration, (one-and-a-half to two-and-a-half hours) — 65 by 804 Squadron and 40 by 812; 68 x 500 lb. bombs and 408 rockets were expended on good targets. Actually 106 aircraft were launched and landed-on, but one Firefly had a rough running engine and was obliged to jettison the bombs and return early. The previous best had been 89 by *Sydney* in reply to *Glory's* 84 on 9th September the previous year. When the last detail had been launched every aircraft in the ship, with the exception of one damaged earlier in the day in an accident, was in the air. The day's flying reflected the utmost credit on all concerned. Special praise must go to the maintenance personnel who produced 100% serviceability throughout the day and kept the aircraft flying. All pilots flew three sorties, and some four.

'A truly remarkable achievement,' wrote Admiral Scott-Moncrieff, 'which brought forth congratulatory signals from high quarters — both US and British.'

The first Fury detail of the day attacked and badly damaged two buildings at the edge of salt flats near Koho-ri, thought to be pumping stations of salt evaporating plant. The next TARCAP detail made the first of a series of attacks that were mounted throughout the day on stores-dump targets in an attempt to strangle the enemy's build-up. Other Fury targets included rail trucks at Chinnampo, ox-carts and sampans, a village reported to contain 200 troops, and gun positions. All the bridges along the Haeju to Chaeryong rail line appeared serviceable. In many cases craters had been bridged with light trestle work instead of being filled in, which gave the impression that the line was still unserviceable. Lieutenant Barlow and Mr. Newton both had barrier accidents, one aircraft was repaired on board but the other had to be returned to *Unicorn*. The Fireflies bombed villages causing extensive damage. From the village of Kasong-dong heavy explosions were felt by aircraft at 3,000 feet, sheets of orange flame were seen, and debris and some white objects were thrown hundreds of feet into the air. On the last detail of the day Lieutenant Meadowcroft had to return due to engine trouble, reducing the number of effective operational sorties to 105.

The following signals were received:

FROM FO21/CFES (AFLOAT)   TO GLORY

INFO CINCFES, FO21/CFES (ASHORE)
I AM VERY HONOURED TO HAVE BEEN FLYING MY FLAG IN
GLORY WHEN SHE ACHIEVED THE REMARKABLE DAILY
TOTAL OF 106 SORTIES. WELL DONE ALL ON BOARD ON
THIS RESULT AND PARTICULARLY THE 14TH CAG. I HAVE
WITNESSED SOME FIRST CLASS AIRMANSHIP AND
TEAMSHIP TODAY AND I CONGRATULATE YOU ALL.

DTG 171509Z
(1723091TEM)

FROM CTF 95   TO GLORY INFO CTG 95.1
THE UNPRECEDENTED RECORD OF 105 SORTIES IN ONE DAY
SETS A MARK AT WHICH ALL FUTURE CVLS ARE WELCOME
TO SHOOT. IT IS UNEXCELLED AS AN EARNEST OF OUR
PRESENT INTENTIONS TOWARDS THE COMMUNIST FOE. IT
REFLECTS THE SUPERIOR STANDARDS SET BY YOU AND
MAINTAINED BY THE FINE OFFICERS AND MEN OF YOUR
SHIP AND YOUR AIR GROUP. WELL DONE. REAR ADMIRAL
GEORGE C. DYER.
                                                            DTG 180709Z

FROM COMNAVFE   TO GLORY
INFO CINC PAC FLEET, COM 7TH FLEET, CTF 95, CTE 95.1, CTE
95.10, COMNAVFE CONVEYS HIGHLY MERITED WELL DONE
TO THE GLORY. THE DESTRUCTION INFLICTED ON THE
ENEMY BY THE 105 SORTIES FLOWN 17TH MARCH IS A
SPLENDID ACCOMPLISHMENT BY COURAGEOUS PILOTS
SUPPORTED BY EFFICIENT HARD WORKING SHIPBOARD
PERSONNEL. VICE ADMIRAL C.T. JOY SENDS.
                                                            DTG 210742Z

FROM ADMIRALTY   TO GLORY INFO CINC FES, FO2FES (A
                                                                & A)
PERSONAL FROM FIFTH SEA LORD. CONGRATULATIONS ON
YOUR FINE CENTURY.
                                                            DTG 211812Z

Note - Addressee FO2FES (A&A) is Afloat and Ashore, i.e. *Glory* and *Ladybird*, the Fifth Sea Lord was Vice Admiral E.W. Anstice.

After the excitement of the previous day, the 18th was replenishment, when the carrier forces proceeded to Paengyong-do and spent the rest of the day fuelling. Early that morning *Glory* had rendezvoused with *Belfast*, when the Admiral transferred his flag to her for a round of visits to various areas including Inchon, returning to Sasebo on 24th March.

The weather was steadily deteriorating, and on *Glory's* return to the operational area next day, a northerly gale with low visibility and heavy seas prevented all flying. On the 20th flying was again hampered by bad weather, with visibility down to 5 or 6 miles, allowing only 53 sorties to be flown. The Furies attacked warehouses and camouflaged bunkers in the rear areas and strafed sampans on a beach near Chodo. The town of Kangso was found to be busy with activity, and was attacked with rockets and 20 mm cannon fire; light, inaccurate flak was encountered. Four villages in the Yonan area containing troops were rocketed and strafed. The Fireflies bombed the rail bridge at Sugyo-ri, hitting the rails at one end. The TARCAP detail had been briefed to bomb a coastal battery, but were unable to do so due to low cloud and poor visibility. They carried out a successful attack during the afternoon on a rail tunnel north-east of Haeju: four bombs were placed in the tunnel entrance and the remainder fell on top or short of the tunnel, extensive damage was claimed by the aircrew on return to the ship.

The weather was again poor on the 21st, but the Furies supported a landing by RoK Marines across the mouth of the River Han at the village of Ponghwa-ri. Two villages in the area were attacked with rockets, where buildings in both burst into flame. The landing craft opened fire on the objective, whilst the aircraft rocketed and strafed mortar positions as well as the village. Three junks moved inshore to land the troops on the beach. Meanwhile the aircraft carried out a low patrol at 200 feet to keep the enemy heads down. They strafed an enemy command post on a hilltop and a group of houses from which fire was holding up the advance of the Marines. By 1000 the troops were in full possession of the village and were in the process of setting it on fire when the second Fury detail arrived overhead. No enemy opposition was seen, nor any movement noticed; villages in the area were attacked, in which two large buildings were destroyed including a headquarters. Due to bad weather over the mainland the midday detail was cancelled, but during the afternoon reconnaissance rail sheds and yards were severely damaged in Chinnampo. It was noted that in the Hanchon area the coast was free of ice. The early morning Firefly strike could not attack its briefed target due to bad weather, so Lieutenant Commander Swanton selected a village south-east of Chanyon where considerable activity had been reported. It was bombed through a gap in the overcast, eight bombs falling on the village. Of the eight Fireflies launched on the last detail of the day, two had to return unserviceable before they reached the target. The remaining six attacked the rail bridge at Sugyo-ri with 1,000 lb. bombs, obtaining one direct hit and several near misses; two spans were destroyed.

Next day, the last of the patrol, the weather was worse than ever, raining with short visibility and winds gusting to 50 knots. No flying was possible and in the evening *Glory* left the area, her place being taken by *Bairoko*. *Glory* set course for Sasebo arriving at 1700 on the 23rd, to stay until the 31st.

The Sea Furies were modified to carry 500 lb. bombs, so 804 Squadron pilots went to Iwakuni for bombing practice with the new technique. This was a 45° dive from 4000 feet, releasing at 2,000 feet, using the gyro-gunsight set on 'gunsight' and 275 feet on the range scale, sighting the target at the bottom of the six o'clock diamond. Greater accuracy could be obtained if the range setting was moved to the 'S' position and the bombs were released at 1,500 feet.

After Lieutenant (E) P.A.L. Watson left for UK, the 804 Squadron flight organisation was:

12 Flt	Lt.Cdr. Bailey CO		14 Flt	Lt. Fraser SP
	Lt(E). Normand			Lt. Peniston-Bird
	Mr. Hefford			Mr. Newton
	Sub.Lt Swanson			Sub.Lt. Wyatt RAN
15 Flt	Mr. Fieldhouse		16 Flt	Lt. Whitaker
	Sub.Lt. Powell RAN			Mr. Potts
	Mr. Darlington			Lt(E). Barlow
	Sub. Lt. Haines			Mr. Collingwood
17 Flt	Lt. MacNaughton			
	Lt. Cordell RAN			
	Lt. Davis			
	Sub.Lt. Howard			

Squadron statistics for March were:

	804 Squadron	**812 Squadron**	
	March	March	Operational
Hours	737-10	316-55	2 454-55
sorties	382	199	1235
deck landings	380	193	1186

Fourth Patrol

Glory again took over as CTE 95.11 on 31st March after a stormy passage from Sasebo during which speed had to be reduced on account of the destroyers. For some time past it had been found that the 60 lb. rockets carried by the Sea Furies lacked sufficient hitting power for many of the available targets, and on this patrol they were fitted to carry 2 x 500 lb. bombs instead. The experiment was a great success; the Fury proved to be an excellent dive bomber, and at once achieved a measure of success against well dug-in gun positions. Bombs were fused for 30 seconds delay; this enabled the pilot to deliver his attack from a lower altitude with a corresponding increase in accuracy.

Flying started early on 1st April from a position 50 miles south of the normal flying-off area, so the early details had over 100 miles to cover to the coast. Both squadrons were now armed with 500 lb. bombs and cannon on AR and strike details. The Furies bombed warehouses at Simpo and Kyomipo. Many sampans were seen in the flooded area of the creeks and waterways of the Taedong River where a loaded junk was strafed. The TARCAP details covered minesweeping operations in the Chinnampo estuary and spotted for *Ceylon* and *Chevalier* bombarding gun positions on the Amgak peninsula. 804's diarist made the laconic comment 'Bombing unimpressive, due to lack of experience.' Lieutenant Hone led a strike of Fireflies to the villages of Soho-ri and Sahyo-dong where all bombs fell in the target area, starting several large fires and damaging many houses. A later strike bombed and breached a road bridge near Sochon with eight 500 lb. bombs.

On the 2nd the Fireflies attacked bridges near Yonan and Haeju. Catapult unserviceability during the afternoon caused the cancellation of a strike and reduced a TARCAP detail to patrolling the Chodo area armed only with 20 mm cannon. The Furies bombed a group of road and rail bridges in the northern outskirts of Chinnampo, knocking one out. The minesweeping operations in the Chinnampo estuary were again covered and gun positions were bombed.

Next day the Furies started by bombing a village harbouring workers from Sariwon airfield, all bombs falling in the target area. Four direct hits were obtained on a factory in Chinnampo on a reconnaissance detail, during which three trucks were destroyed in the rail sidings at Chinji-ri. A later detail paid these sidings a second visit destroying three trucks and damaging the lines. In an effort to clear up the coastal guns which hampered the efforts of the ships in the Chodo area, the TARCAP details made an all out effort against their positions. By means of very effective photo-coverage, three positions were wiped out with direct hits. The positions were so well constructed that only direct hits would knock them out. During the first Firefly detail led by Lieutenant Commander Culbertson, one aircraft experienced rough running, jettisoned its bombs and made a wheels-up landing at Paengyong-do. Mr Griffith and Aircrewman Japp returned to the ship later by helicopter in time for lunch. The remainder of the detail successfully bombed a road bridge at Taetan. A later detail knocked out one span of a rail bridge to the west of Sinchon.

On the 4th the Furies carried out the first CAS mission of this operational tour. Using smoke rockets, a Mosquito marked the target of an enemy held ridge to the north of the Imjin River in front of the 1st Commonwealth Division. Bombing and strafing attacks were made under fire from enemy small-arms and light AA guns. The ridge was bombed with a reported 80% coverage. On a later detail enemy barracks in Chinnampo were attacked, three direct hits were scored, destroying six living-blocks and damaging the remainder. One aircraft had one bomb hang-up so had to jettison the carriers. Fireflies bombed the villages of Yuchon-ni and Changyon, starting several fires and destroying some houses. Next day was replenishment day.

By the 6th, 804 Squadron's bombing was getting very much more accurate, one detail knocked out a rail bridge north of Chinnampo, another was damaged to the south-east of Sariwon and a road bridge was cut near Yonan. One TARCAP detail discovered several new gun positions firing on ships off the coast. One near

Chingangpo was knocked out and others near-missed. 812 Squadron was also successfully interdicting the enemy's supply lines: a six-aircraft strike on a rail tunnel to the south-west of Haeju totally blocked the north end and cut the line in two places at the other end; other attacks by the Fireflies during the day were on the village of Tuktong near Chaeryong, and on another rail tunnel the other side of Haeju where, unfortunately, damage could not be assessed due to smoke and dust.

The Furies on the 7th flew another CAS mission for 1st British Commonwealth Division. The ridge target was passed to the aircraft from the Tactical Command Post and marked with smoke by artillery. Bombing and strafing attacks were carried out, under scattered light flak and small arms fire, obtaining hits on enemy trenches and dug-outs. The TARCAP aircraft continued pounding gun positions, achieving one direct hit which was followed by a secondary explosion. During the forenoon Sub-Lieutenant Swanson made a wheels-up landing on Paengyong-do after experiencing engine trouble on CAP; examination later revealed that the supercharger impeller had disintegrated. The Fireflies attacked a village north-east of Haeju with good results, two houses burst into flames immediately and many were damaged.

A thick belt of sea fog caused all flying to be cancelled next day; Sub-Lieutenant Swanson returned to *Glory* via *Warramunga* who had picked him up from the island the previous evening.

On the 9th the Fury CAS detail for 1 US Marine Corps bombed and strafed an enemy held ridge, indicated by red smoke. In spite of the attack being opposed by intense light AA fire, the controlling Mosquito reported 90% coverage. The TARCAP aircraft carried out several bombardment spots for *Belfast* in the Chodo area whose shooting was, as usual, excellent. The Firefly attack on a road bridge to the east of Haeju failed to destroy it, but damaged it sufficiently to put it temporarily out of use. In a spectacular attack on a village in the Ongjin area, all bombs fell within the target area causing an exceptionally large secondary explosion with flames and debris being thrown hundreds of feet into the air. On completion of the day's flying, *Glory* left the operational area.

In the seven flying days an average of over 58 sorties had been maintained and 568 bombs dropped on the enemy. No aircraft had been lost through enemy action, but in both cases of the aircraft force-landing at Paengyong-do, full salvage was not worth while owing to immersion in the sea, though the important equipment had been saved. The CAS missions were not essential for the prosecution of the land battle, but they served as good training for the pilots, and were also of excellent value for the morale of the troops.

Bairoko relieved *Glory* on 9th April and remained on patrol until the 18th. This was her last patrol before departure from the west coast. A fine effort on her last day produced a figure of 80 sorties.

'This for an aircraft complement of 20', wrote Admiral Scott-Moncrieff, 'is highly creditable and compares with *Glory's* 105.'

Glory secured alongside the jetty at Kure during the afternoon of Friday 11th, to find *Unicorn* already secured the other side to supply stores and replacement aircraft during the next two days. After an enjoyable party given by her Wardroom on the Saturday evening, an excellent boxing match was staged which was won by *Unicorn* six bouts to four. She sailed for Singapore on the 14th.

Divisions were held in *Glory* on Sunday at which Captain Colquhoun made a farewell speech to the ship's company. Throughout this period in harbour many opportunities were taken to enjoy soccer, cricket, hockey, tennis and other sporting activities. 812 Squadron challenged 804 to a hard fought hockey match which they won 3-1, and a ship's cricket team beat an army 11 which had been unbeaten for the past eleven months. Lieutenant Scott joined 804 Squadron for one patrol before joining HMS *Ocean* in May. This last period in a Japanese harbour came to an end at 0700 on the 17th when *Glory* slipped and proceeded to the west coast for the last time.

Fifth Patrol

Glory started her final patrol on 18th April. The weather during the first four days was overcast, fog reducing the number of sorties to 22 on two of them. On 21st April 55 were flown, and 56 on the following day.

Low cloud and poor visibility prevented any flying on the 19th until the afternoon, and even then visibility over the target area was poor; the Fireflies bombed a road bridge near Haeju. The Furies found three new junks in Hanchon harbour, but light flak prevented an attack from being made. Rail trucks and stores at Wonum-ni, to the west of Chinnampo, were attacked with bombs and cannon fire. Many trucks, stores and three sheds were destroyed or damaged Villages containing troops on the north bank of the Han River were strafed and set on fire. The two TARCAP details spotted for *Morecambe Bay*'s shoots in the Chodo area.

An early morning overcast and fog next day delayed the start of flying until 0800 when a Firefly detail struck a village near Haeju, starting some small fires. The catapult broke down before the next detail could be launched. There was no more flying for the Fireflies; but from 1200 the Furies, launched by RATOG, struck at Wonum-ni again where they destroyed ten rail trucks and a storage shed in the rail yard, cut the lines and damaged more trucks. The TARCAP obtained two possible direct hits on two gun positions.

The catapult was repaired by 1000 on the 21st when the first details were launched. The Furies were briefed to attack a suspected petrol dump and nearby village in the Chaeryong area; one bomb fell on the suspected dump but no fires or explosions were seen, so they concentrated on the village. During a reconnaissance of the rail line from Sariwon to Sinwon-ni a group of machine guns opened fire from a bridge near Chaeryong. In the afternoon Lieutenant Barlow had some engine trouble but made a successful wheelsdown landing on the beach at Paengyong-do. The TARCAP details spotted for *Morecambe Bay* bombarding mortar and machine gun positions near Pungchon, and for *Cossack* bombarding the town of Pungchon: *Cossack's* shooting was reported as being excellent. The section then went on and obtained two direct bomb hits on a gun position in the area near Chodo, observing an explosion followed by a large sheet of orange flame with brown and white smoke. Twelve Firefly sorties attacked various villages during the day, destroying and damaging houses and stores, and in one village destroying eight tractors under a line of trees. Two villages in the Haeju area were nearly completely destroyed by *Ceylon's* 6 inch guns during a bombardment spotted by two Fireflies.

On the 22nd a Firefly detail destroyed the centre of the village of Singsongdong. Near misses were scored at both ends of a rail tunnel to the east of Chwiya-ri but the line was cut. The Furies attacked and destroyed a factory on the river south of Pyongyang. A large explosion followed the bombing with ammunition or pyrotechnics exploding afterwards. On following up intelligence reports, a group of four T-34 tanks were discovered skilfully concealed to the north of Chinnampo. Strafing attacks were inconclusive though hits were scored on two. Two men setting up a machine-gun on a nearby factory were eliminated. On the afternoon detail, briefed to attack the tanks, Lieutenant Normand forced landed, wheels down, on Paengyong-do before reaching the target; the remainder of the flight bombed the tanks amidst intense light flak but with disappointing results, no hits being claimed and one aircraft bombing the wrong target. Some difficulty was experienced in locating the tanks because they were very well concealed and energetically defended. Three spotting details were carried out — two with *Morecambe Bay* on gun positions, and one with the US destroyer Brush on the town of Pungchon. Lieutenants Barlow and Normand flew their aircraft back to the ship, after they had been serviced by a maintenance team under CPO Turner, sent in by destroyer.

The US Navy operated Avengers in the Carrier On-Board Delivery Service (CODS), a most efficient organization which proved its usefulness throughout the war. During the 22nd Captain T.A.K. Maunsell arrived on board *Glory* in one of these Avengers and assumed command next day in succession to Captain Colquhoun.

Glory replenished from *Green Ranger* during the 23rd, and at 1800 lower deck was cleared to say good-bye to Captain Colquhoun as he left the ship. Admiral Scott-Moncrieff gave great credit to Captain Colquhoun for his work in the war: 'By his leadership and drive he has worked up his ship's company and air group to the highest peak of efficiency'.

For two days all went well; then the weather broke and fog, rain and low cloud restricted flying for the next three days.

The element returned to the operating area on 24th April after completing with fuel. The Furies attacked a group of camouflaged buildings in a wood near Kangso with good results, destroying two. A later detail was sent to attack a pre-briefed target of trucks in a rail siding to the south of Sariwon, but when they arrived they found a large number of the trucks had vanished. The attack was pressed home, and although the trucks escaped major damage a rail cut was achieved. The early morning TARCAP spotted for *Cossack* bombarding the enemy villages of Hwado and Kumsa-ri, destroying nine houses. The sharp shooting was good enough to get special praise from the pilots, Lieutenant Davis and Mr. Griggs, who later showed their own merits by destroying two gun emplacements and a blister type bunker with direct hits. Lieutenant Fraser and Lieutenant Scott obtained direct hits on a camouflaged shelter which must have contained stores for it burned after the attack with dense white smoke. The Fireflies attacked a reported Communist ammunition factory north of Haeju. Four small buildings were found near the map reference answering the description given, and were attacked and damaged. A rail tunnel north-west of Changyon was bombed, partially blocking the northern entrance with rubble and concrete. A successful attack was made on an enemy gun emplacement on the British Commonwealth Division's front, under Mosquito control and working with artillery fire.

On the 25th the Furies made two attacks on villages in the Kangso area north of Chinnampo, destroying three large buildings and a shelter in the hillside harbouring vehicles. The AR flight of the rail line south-west from Chaeryong to Sonchon-ni had been briefed to search for a large tile-roofed building, reported to contain prisoners of war. Only one building of this nature was seen in the town of Segori, it was presumed to be the one and was photographed. The TARCAP main targets were gun positions, vehicle shelters and camouflaged bunkers; two other attacks were made on Changyon tunnel, cutting the rail line in one place. One section was asked by the controlling ship to investigate a group of men reported to be laying mines on the beach opposite Sokto. The first Firefly detail were briefed to attack the tunnel north-east of Changyon, but due to bad weather over the target they selected their alternative target and made a successful attack on the road bridge at Taetan. All the bombs fell in the target area and the bridge was demolished.

Only two events were flown on the 26th, all the afternoon details being cancelled due to low cloud and poor visibility. Four Fireflies attacked the village of Hwanson under difficult conditions, damaging some houses. Furies attacked camouflaged shelters in the Kangso area, five bombs landing in the target area of which two were possible hits. The early TARCAP spotted for *Bush* and engaged targets in Pungchon, in the village of Wolgwon-dong and a suspected flak position.

Weather, with low cloud and poor visibility, again restricted flying next day until 1000. The Furies knocked down one span of the rail bridge south of Sariwon, one of the most strongly constructed bridges in Glory's operational area. The CAS detail, under Mosquito control, destroyed a gun and mortar position opposite the 1st British Commonwealth Division's position north of the Imjin River. Large fires were started, and a large secondary explosion was set off (throwing flames and debris high in the air), from one of several villages in the Haeju area attacked by the Fireflies.

For the fourth day, on the 28th, there was no flying until the afternoon due to low cloud and poor visibility. The Fury TARCAP met solid cloud over the Chodo area but the weather was clear inland in the Sinchon area. There was considerable enemy traffic on the roads — taking advantage of the weather — which was strafed, burning two lorries. During a strafing attack on two villages in the Pungchon area, Sub-Lieutenant Swanson began to have trouble with his engine which eventually cut out as he reached the coast. He ditched south of Chodo and was picked up unharmed from his dinghy after about 15 minutes by a US helicopter which took him to the island. Over Sinchon light flak from small arms fire was encountered which resulted in an extraordinary incident when a bullet hit one aircraft in the wing and operated the drop tank release, jettisoning the long range tank. The only Firefly detail of the day carried out a low level bombing attack on a tunnel to the north of Changyon: four bombs hit the target, blocking part of the tunnel and cutting the line.

Tuesday 29th April was the last day of Glory's last patrol, and was not a very nice day to finish. Although the weather was fine with good visibility at sea, there was thick haze all day over the whole of the target area, with visibility down to three miles and an overcast sky. In the forenoon low cloud covered most of the land, and for the early details the Haeju area had the only clear gap for attacks. Because of a surplus of bombs some Fury CAPs were able to carry out some offensive sorties, much to their delight. Six Fireflies on the first detail attacked their alternative target, Chegung tunnel south-west of Ongjin, blocking the entrance and cutting the line with seven bombs.

> From 812 Squadron's diary: 'Amid a certain amount of tension, the last detail of the day and tour took off at 1500. Four Fireflies led by Lieutenant Commander Swanton attacked the south end of Chegung tunnel; on the return journey villages and ox-carts were sprayed with cannon fire. Lieutenant Commander Culbertson and Sub-Lieutenant Cotgrove visited the TARCAP area, bombs were dropped on a village in the area damaging many houses. Sub-Lieutenant Cotgrove made the last land-on and thus completed Glory's second tour in the operational area. To celebrate the occasion a bottle of beer was presented to Sub-Lieutenant Cotgrove by Commander (Air) S. Keane. Needless to say the bottle was emptied by a "very" appreciative audience.'

Fifty two sorties were flown during the day, and that evening Glory left the operational area for Sasebo, where she arrived the following afternoon to de-ammunition.

Glory sailed for Hong Kong next day, 1st May, arriving on the 3rd to turn over to *Ocean* who was already there. Aircraft, stores and pilots were ferried over during the course of the next few days; on Sunday 4th *Glory's* officers were 'At Home' to *Ocean's*, and on Monday *Ocean's* to *Glory's*. The Commander in Chief, Admiral Sir Guy Russell, walked round the ship and visited the wardroom on the 5th; lower deck was cleared at 0640 on 6th when Admiral Scott-Moncrieff addressed the ship's company before she sailed at 0700 for Singapore.

During her two spells in Korean waters she had flown 4,835 sorties for the loss of 27 aircraft and 9 aircrew. Aircraft serviceability throughout had been excellent.

Admiral Scott-Moncrieff reported after she left:

> 'I consider HMS *Glory* and her Air Groups have made an outstanding contribution to the prestige of British naval aviation during her two spells in the Korean theatre, and she will certainly be missed, not least by the Communists…I was always very happy to fly my flag in HMS *Glory*, whose atmosphere of efficiency and cheerfulness combined with very hard work by all hands was a tonic, and most refreshing.'

Throughout the tours of all the carriers during the static war period of nearly two years, from November 1951 to July 1953, ox-carts were a permanent opportunity-target. They were a prime transport vehicle for the Communist troops, for although each one could only carry a comparatively small load of supplies or ammunition, they were so numerous that large quantities of stores could be moved in nearly all weather conditions and along roads and tracks impassable to motor transport.

From the diaries of 804 and 812 Squadrons during this second tour of five patrols, an analysis of carts seen and/or destroyed produced the following figures. On some days no actual number is given, merely 'many' or 'several'; in one instance 12 were seen and 8 destroyed. In 39 flying days, on only 8 were no carts seen, due to the briefings and targets given to the aircrew rather than to an absence of carts. 804 Squadron accounted for 143 carts, 812 for 47, making a total disruption to the Communists of 189 carts, an average of nearly 5 per flying day. The diaries do not necessarily cover every sortie or flight, nor do they mention every cart observed, they tend to highlight the day's activities and operations.

It has been suggested that sending front line aircraft against archaic cart transport was an expensive use of resources. This is not so, in no case was the sole target attacked on any sortie an ox-cart; they were always additional to the briefed targets, and normally were strafed by the flights on their return journey to their ships, in order to use up any 20 mm ammunition left in the aircraft's tanks. Nor were any aircraft lost when attacking ox-carts.

Flying statistics for the Squadrons for April, and the operational totals were:

	804 Squadron		**812 Squadron**	
	April	Operational	April	Operational
Hours	1057-20	7167-45	544-25	2999-20
Sorties	529	3115*	306	1541
Deck landings	517	3118	290	1476

*100 launched by RATOG

Statistics for *Glory* and the 14th CAG during the two Korean tours were:

Miles steamed (north of Hong Kong) 59,730

Ammunition expended:

20 mm cannon	886330	500lb bombs	3114
60 Lb. rockets	13098	1,000lb bombs	126

Approximate figures for targets hit:

junks	796	buildings	2364
ox-carts	1031	rail trucks	308
vehicles	43	gun positions	158
tunnels	21	bridges	66
rail cuts	61	store dumps	111

observed casualties   1572

CHAPTER 9

HMS OCEAN

802 and 825 Squadrons
5th May to 8th November 1952

From mid-April 1952 to the end of August there was much activity by RoK guerrillas and surface ships in the Haeju area. An enemy attempt to cross the mud-flats to Yong Mae-do (10 miles north-east of Yong Pyong-do) had been foiled in March. In May and June raids were made by both sides; those by UN forces being supported by *Whitesand Bay*.

During this period two searches were carried out for aircraft that had come down in the Haeju area. One, an American F-94 fitted with special equipment, was not found; the other, a Firefly from *Ocean*, was floated across from mud-flats in the northern part of Haeju Bay to Taesuap by guerrillas, using motor junks, sampans, and oil drums. The Firefly was found to be too badly damaged to be repaired so it was abandoned after all valuable equipment had been removed.

On 19th May 400 guerrillas from junks landed on the west side of Haeju Bay. Air support was provided by aircraft from *Ocean*, and gunfire support by HMAS *Bataan*, air-spotted by *Ocean*, destroyed a complete command post. A similar raid was launched on 25th May, when the guerrillas remained ashore for about five hours. Destruction and casualties caused by naval gunfire and aircraft seemed to be very effective.

These guerrilla raids had Admiral Scott-Moncrieff's full support: they were good for the morale of UN forces and they kept the enemy on tenterhooks. An unconfirmed report was received that guerrillas had shot 50 prisoners in cold blood. Admiral Scott-Moncrieff referred the matter to Admiral Dyer to take up with the South Korean Government and with US Army authorities, since such uncivilised behaviour would give the UN a bad name and invite reprisals.

In May and June there were changes in the high command. Rear Admiral J.E. Ginrich USN succeeded Admiral Dyer as CTF 95 on 31st May. He agreed with Admiral Scott-Moncrieff's appreciation of the situation of the previous December, and instructions were given to ships not to waste ammunition as expenditure was getting high, and to commanding officers to ensure maximum value for every shot fired — preferably to be observed.

May saw two new carriers operating on the west coast. USS *Bataan* took USS *Bairoko's* place, and had embarked her Air Group, (VMA 312), so her pilots were familiar with the terrain. HMS *Ocean*, (Captain C.L.G. Evans DSO, DSC), with 802 and 825 Squadrons, all fresh to the area and operations, had succeeded *Glory*. In the RN, the Carrier Air Group philosophy had been discarded, and Carrier Air Groups had been disbanded, in February 1952, in favour of the original policy of independent, largely self-contained, Squadrons whose Commanding Officer was responsible directly to the Commander (Air) of his parent carrier or air station, making for administrative simplicity and operational flexibility. The Australian and Canadian navies continued with the Air Group concept until 1954.

During their work-up period and before arriving in Korea, 802 Squadron had had a lot of fuel trouble. The engines would intermittently cut and continue running for about five minutes before finally cutting out, giving enough time as a rule to make an emergency or forced landing if near the ship or over land. The cause was pinned down to deterioration of the self-sealing compound in the fuel tanks that was cured after new tanks were installed.

During the hand-over period in Hong Kong, several aircrew transferred to *Ocean* from *Glory* having flown a few patrols to gain operational experience to pass on to their shipmates. They were: Lieutenant Peniston-Bird, Lieutenant (E) Normand, Sub-Lieutenants Haines and Swanson to 802 Squadron; Lieutenants Reynolds, Kinna, Hubbard, Fursey, and Aircrewman Edwards to 825 Squadron. *Glory* also flew over her two Westland Sikorsky S.51 Dragonfly helicopters to *Ocean*. After reciprocal RPCs in both Wardrooms, *Ocean* sailed from Hong Kong for Sasebo at 0845 on Tuesday 6th May 1952, arriving at 0800 on the 9th, after flying off two Fireflies for Iwakuni.

Rear-Admiral C.L.G. Evans, DSO, DSC.

(FAAM)

Whilst in Sasebo Lieutenant Commander Swan USN and three USAF pilots gave a lecture to all aircrew on Escape and Evasion, relating their experiences of having been shot down; a lecture considered to have been the best yet on the topic, after which most of the assembled company felt easier about things. Escape kits and flying clothing were decided upon.

The escape kit consisted of a 0.38 inch revolver with 24 rounds, a Sten gun stowed in the cockpit forward of the seat, cloth escape maps, ground recognition panels, a commando knife, 2-star-red flares, a barter kit of a blood chit, watch, fountain pen and compass, emergency rations, a fishing kit, mosquito net, medical kit, marching compass, spare socks and various oddments prompted by personal taste.

On their feet they decided to wear jungle boots as issued to the Army. String vests had also been issued, but a certain amount of scepticism amongst the majority caused the garments to find their way back into bottom drawers. Knee pads had to be altered; the existing systems had to be modified to contain the important daily codes, ciphers, challenges and recognition signals. Added to those items, each individual had to be prepared to carry two or three maps — one of the general area, one large scale map of the proposed target and occasionally a second large scale one of a secondary, 'dump', target.

The main operations were bombing bridges, trains, etc. and supporting army landings. As time went on the pilots became careless about risks. One tactic with two aircraft was that one would fly low to attract AA gunfire while the other one stayed high to spot the gun flashes and then attack their positions. The pilots usually returned from these missions with machine-gun or rifle bullet holes in their aircraft. On one occasion the vertical camera saved the elevator control wires from being shot away in Lieutenant Commander Shotton's aircraft — the camera went instead.

First Patrol

Ocean sailed from Sasebo on 10th May for the west coast; the weather was too bad to permit replacement aircraft to be flown on board from Iwakuni. This first patrol was remarkable for the high average sortie rate, on the first day 87 sorties were flown, and in seven-and-a-half flying days 569 — an average of 76 per day.

On the 11th the squadrons' flight deck teams were needed at 0315 for a 0515 take off, and the aircrew were given a call for their breakfast at 0330. 802 Squadron diary gives a good impression of the anticipation, tinged with not a little apprehension, of the first day's operational flying for the majority of the pilots.

> 'In the UK, this Sunday undoubtedly passed uneventfully, but here, on board HMS *Ocean*, over 1,000 men tensed and found their blood run a little faster as we began our private war against the Chinese and Korean Communists off the west coast of Korea. It certainly was a thrilling and spectacular day — a day few of us will ever forget. The first wave of aircraft got off at 0500 — two Furies remained overhead as CAP — two went to the coast area south of Chinnampo as TARCAP (a regular feature of our task), four other Furies went inland to strike a railway bridge. This combination continued throughout the day and though no spectacular results were claimed much value was

HMS *Ocean* on passage from Sasebo to west coast of Korea.
(IWM)

gained by merely flying over the terrain.

'I regret to record that our first day was costly in aircraft, fortunately not in life. Lieutenant Scott had to ditch whilst on CAP owing to a mysterious fire that occurred in the cockpit of his Fury. He was picked up by USS *Lowry*. His hands were burnt and it was necessary to confine him to Sick Bay. It appears that he will have to go to hospital for a period after our first patrol. The second aircraft was lost when Lieutenant McEnery did a wheels-up landing at Paengyong-do — an emergency landing beach on a friendly island — nickname is Bromide Baker. Lieutenant McEnery was forced down by fuel shortage and his aircraft was unfortunately damaged by sea water before any attempt at moving it above high water mark was possible. As a point of interest it is possible to force-land at Bromide Baker wheels-down providing the tide is low. Besides being a safety factor the island also acts as a Shepherd because it checks all our aircraft in and out of Korea over the R/T.

'Later on in the day two more Furies were damaged in a taxying accident on the Flight Deck.

'A truly memorable day blessed by beautiful weather and in the ship one sensed that the standard of morale was very high.'

825 Squadron flew 28 sorties of AR in the Ongjin and Han River areas, destroying and damaging two railway warehouses, six rail coaches, one sampan, huts and buildings. Three replacement aircraft were flown in from Iwakuni by

Lieutenants Reynolds, Kinna and Jacobs. During a rocket attack in the Haeju area, Lieutenant Gandey's aircraft had a complete power failure due to unexplained causes. Gandey pointed his aircraft well away from the enemy coast and carried out a normal ditching about 15 miles south-southeast of Haeju and 6 miles away from the target area. After spending 65 minutes in the sea he and his observer Sub-Lieutenant Bishop were picked up by a US rescue amphibian, a Grumman Albatross 'Dumbo', provided by JOC Korea, and taken to Kimpo airfield, very cold, blue and suffering from shock.

An explanation of the TARCAP task is given by 802's diarist in the entry for next day.

> 'In the coastal area south west of Chinnampo the Communists have established elaborate shore defences and have built up large coastal gun positions. These defences are obviously present to prevent an Allied landing in the Taedong Estuary. This Communist fear is heightened by the presence of UN warships that patrol off the friendly islands of Sok-to and Chodo. In consequence the situation is that our ships (cruisers, destroyers and frigates) are fired upon by these shore guns. It was found that the coastal guns did not fire when aircraft were in the vicinity — thus a requirement arose and is now fulfilled by Furies from *Ocean*.'

In addition to the TARCAP details, the Furies attacked rail bridges in the Sinchon and Haeju areas, and road targets and buildings to the west of Chinnampo. The Firefly AR flights attacked a variety of targets including gun pits, camps, buildings, tank hide-outs and transport positions in the Han River, Ongjin, Haeju, Changyon and Hwanghei Reservoir areas. Lieutenant Gandey and Sub-Lieutenant Bishop were flown back from Kimpo.

On the 13th Fury strikes were launched against targets in the Chungsan district and Ongjin area, while the Fireflies attacked villages and huts in the Haeju, Han River and Hwanghei Reservoir areas destroying eleven huts and leaving many others burning and damaged. Flying ceased after 1230 because water contamination was discovered in the fuel systems of some aircraft.

Next day Lieutenant (E) K. McDonald was shot down and killed whilst on TARCAP. Just before attacking a gun position on the Amgak peninsula he reported that he had been hit and went into a spin from 4,500 feet. His aircraft did not recover and exploded on hitting the ground. A later TARCAP detail spotted for bombardment shoots with patrolling ships, heavily shelling the gun pit suspected of having shot down McDonald's Sea Fury. The guns were in caves on the hillside and could not be hit from the air. Later, during a party with the Command Staff in Sasebo, a promise of support was given. US destroyers with flat trajectory guns were sent to the area and their shooting was spotted by *Ocean's* aircraft in order to place their shells directly into the cave. The Firefly AR details destroyed and damaged buildings and huts in the Ongjin, Chanyong, Sinmak, Haeju and Han River areas.

Thursday 15th was replenishment day with no flying. 825 Squadron diary commented:

> '... tension has eased considerably since last Sunday. None of the Firefly pilots have reported seeing any heavy flak as yet but we are taking no chances with small-arms fire that cost *Glory* so much.'

Next day the Furies' bombing strikes were mounted against rail targets; one bridge just south of Sariwon was definitely claimed by Lieutenant Davis and numerous rail cuts were made by near misses. The Fireflies, in addition to AR flights, carried out a CAS mission on a target marked by a Mosquito. A successful attack was made with 48 rockets and cannon, 95% coverage of the target being reported. Five bunkers and a length of trenches were destroyed, and an ammunition dump may have exploded because excessive blast effect had been noted by the Mosquito. Lieutenant Commander Roberts and Lieutenant Cooper were shot down south of Changyon and, being fortunately close to the sea, were able to make a text

book ditching. The aircraft floated for 15-20 seconds and enabled them to take their time to get clear of the aircraft. They were picked up very quickly by the US 'Dumbo' and taken to Kimpo. They returned during the afternoon dressed in borrowed American sneakers and denims. A very sharp lesson had been learnt — that of not making a second attack on any target. The CO had made a second photographic run over the same target and was set on fire by small arms fire.

HMS *Ocean.*   *FAAM)*

On the 17th the Air Department hands turned to at 0430, the ship was going all out to break the existing sortie record of 106 in one day set by *Glory*. Weather was fine with little wind, calling for speeds of 22 knots from the engine room staffs when launching and recovering aircraft — no fun for them as the temperature in the machinery spaces would soar at those speeds, particularly after the land-on, when the ship's speed and the machinery space fans' speed are reduced, the very hot machinery radiating a considerable amount of heat that could not be adequately dissipated. A new daily record for Light Fleet Carriers of 123 sorties was flown, 76 by 802 Squadron and 47 by 825, with everything working like clockwork and serviceability being excellent — after the last detail was launched, 28 of the total complement of 31 aircraft were still serviceable. The Furies dropped 90 bombs on enemy territory — targets ranging from railway bridges to radio stations and every imaginable type of target was strafed. The Fireflies blew up ammunition dumps and oil supplies as well as strafing ox-carts and blasting and destroying troop concentrations.

All the aircrew flew four sorties, some five, still maintaining landing intervals at the end of the day of around 25 seconds. Lieutenant Commander Shotton's flight would regularly land-on at a 15 second interval, and the average for 802 Squadron was 20 seconds — there were occasions when the barrier was not always up in time for the next touch-down.

802 had no incidents, but 825 were unfortunate in that on the last land-on, the port undercarriage leg of Lieutenant Terry's aircraft collapsed after a normal landing. The high sortie rate made armament replenishment necessary during the patrol, and it was carried out, in complete darkness, that night at anchor off Paengyong-do, from an LST loaded with rocket projectiles, brought out from Sasebo.

Next day operations resumed at a more normal pace. The Fireflies carried out strike and reconnaissance details in the Sinmak, Haeju, Injon and Changyon areas, causing extensive damage to troop emplacements, buildings and supply dumps. Lieutenant Fraser destroyed a bridge using a 45° dive bombing technique. This form of attack had been almost completely adopted by 802 Squadron. It had the attractive advantages of being adaptable to flight co-ordinated attacks, the start of the dive was swift, no excess speed was experienced and the target was always in sight. Besides those technical advantages, it was basically easier and more effective. In the afternoon a frantic call was received from Sub-Lieutenant Swanson that his section leader Lieutenant Peniston-Bird had baled out over the sea in the TARCAP area. After a low strafing attack on a village Swanson noticed that Peniston-Bird's port wing was blazing. After flying over the coast, he baled out by sitting on the port cockpit coaming and flying the aircraft until he was in a position to drop clear without getting burnt. He was rapidly picked up by the 'Dumbo' and eventually returned to the ship completely unhurt.

On the 19th both squadrons gave air support to a small invasion landing on the coast south of Ongjin, with bombardment provided by HMAS *Bataan*. The operation was a complete success, the invading forces losing only one man. The Furies had a lot of success with 1,000 lb. bombs causing extensive damage to troop emplacements and living quarters. This was the first occasion on which 802 Squadron had used these bombs — a new weapon! Armed with two, and sometimes with empty drop tanks, they had to use RATOG, the object being to pack the deck and use a short take off run instead of the catapult. An interested audience watched the first detail get airborne led by Lieutenant Commander Shotton, armed with 2 x 1,000 lb. bombs plus overload fuel tanks. Everybody was astounded to see his aircraft trundle down the flight deck, over the bows and sink towards the sea without the rockets firing. Having gained a couple of knots in sinking from the level of the flight deck, he was riding the ground effect over the water until he had burned off enough fuel to accelerate and climb away. For ten agonising seconds he hugged the surface, dragging the tail wheel in the water, and achieving what Messrs. Hawkers would undoubtedly call the impossible until finally getting airborne. He was faced with two problems: he could have jettisoned his bombs to make the aircraft lighter and so climb away, but that would have aborted the mission; his other concern was to reassure all those waiting to go that there were no faults with the rockets. On returning to the ship he admitted he had forgotten to make the master switch! A third course might have been possible — to have made the master switch and then to have fired the RATOG, accelerating away from the surface of the sea, with the undercarriage retracted. Other Fury details using 1,000 lb. bombs caused enormous explosions on gun positions near Punchon and on bridges near Sinchon and Chaeryong, whilst Fireflies launched strikes in the Haeju and Changyon areas, causing extensive damage to warehouses and troop concentrations.

To mar this final day of the first patrol, two fatal incidents occurred. In the first, the RATOG master switch was inadvertently made whilst a Fury was still in the range, and the port side of the rocket battery fired. It should not have done so until the firing button on the throttle was pressed, igniting the rockets on both sides. The aircraft over-rode the chocks and the blast blew the port chockman, Naval Airman Herbert, over the round-down. The plane-guard destroyer Marsh promptly lowered a boat, but he sank before it could reach him, and subsequent search failed to find his body. In the other incident, Lieutenant Commander T.J.C. Williamson Napier, Senior Pilot of 825 Squadron, and his observer Aircrewman L.M.E. Edwards, were both killed when, on a CAS mission over the Commonwealth Division, their aircraft was shot down by AA fire as they made a second pass at a selected target in the Front Line. The aircraft was seen to hit the ground and explode on impact.

At the end of the patrol, during which six aircrew had been rescued from the sea by the US ASR service, Captain Evans remarked on 'the gratification shown by aircrew when they first saw the highly efficient American rescue service in operation…The direct result of an efficient rescue service on aircrew morale cannot be overstressed'.

Ocean left the area on 19th May on relief by USS *Bataan* and arrived in Sasebo at 1730 next day. During this harbour period, Lieutenant Hunter became Senior Pilot of 825 Squadron and Sub-Lieutenant Carter joined 802 Squadron. unicorn provided replacement aircraft — which at that time were getting scarce in the Far East — and stores; and Divisions were held on the Sunday. Ammunition was in short supply for two main reasons: demands were different and exceeded those of previous carriers, and also there was only one ammunition supply vessel, RFA *Fort Sandusky*, to provide for the needs of the whole effort of the RN in Korea. *Ocean* sailed for the west coast at 0930 on 28th May.

Second Patrol

Ocean's second patrol was from 29th May to 6th June. The weather was generally favourable, though for the first few days there were periods of low cloud and fog over the coast. The supply of bombs and rockets was limited so it was decided to restrict the number of sorties to 68 per day. Should the weather on any particular day reduce this number, the sorties the following day would be correspondingly increased. This number provided the basis for an easy and comfortable programme — 544 sorties were flown in 8 days. It was noticeable that as the pilots became more familiar with the area, their accuracy in finding and destroying targets improved considerably; but the ingenious camouflage used by the enemy still proved very effective.

Fog over the operational area on the 29th restricted the accuracy of attacks by the early details. Generally, the first day of each patrol was mainly spent on a general reconnaissance of the area, finding suitable targets, and information to provide targets for the remaining days. The general impression was that military activity was on the increase around Hanchon. When the fog lifted in the afternoon, a combined strike of Furies and Fireflies was launched on rail yards between Pyongyang and Chinnampo. Twelve trucks were reported as being destroyed and at least six damaged in addition to causing considerable disturbance to the tracking. Furies on TARCAP attacked gun positions in the Punchon area. A Fury piloted by Sub-Lieutenant Mallace entered the barrier when his hook bounced over the wires due to unserviceability of the damper.

The weather improved next day over much of the area. The Furies reconnoitred the railways to bring the 'bridge state' up to date, reporting most of them as serviceable. Lieutenant Fraser and his section were unable to carry out their briefed CAS mission for the Commonwealth Division on the front line north of Seoul due to bad weather. Lieutenant Commander Dick (he had been promoted that day) and his flight attacked a rail yard at Chinnampo destroying several trucks. Lieutenant

Commander Shotton and Lieutenant Jenne knocked out a coastal gun emplacement in the TARCAP area. The CAP flight on one detail escorted a Firefly to Paengyong-do and Sub-Lieutenant Ellis' Fury to Seoul with flap trouble. The Fireflies attacked troop shelters, troops and villages reported as housing troops in the Han River, Hanchon, Haeju, Changyong, Chaeryong and Ongjin areas, and rail yards at Hanchon, although low cloud over some of their targets was a nuisance and tended to make map reading virtually impossible.

On the 31st two details of Furies on reconnaissance flights were armed with 20 mm cannon only, due to the shortage of bombs, which, if nothing else, increased the score of ox-carts destroyed. On two most successful missions Lieutenant Fisher's flight destroyed two bridges on the Pyongyang to Chinnampo rail route, using the 45° dive bombing technique. Leopard targets were attacked by the Fireflies, destroying and damaging several huts, but due to the inadvisability of returning to a target after an attack, few results were observed although all rockets fell in the target areas. Several aircraft had trouble with wing fuel tanks not transferring.

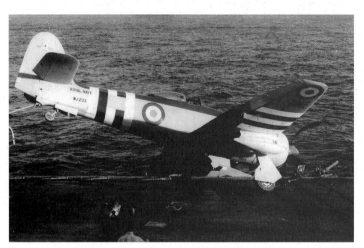

Lieutenant Watkinson had to land his Firefly at Paengyong-do due to a connecting rod failure. In the previous three months 825 Squadron had suffered three such failures, and a further three aircraft had ditched in circumstances which

Sea Fury WJ233 over the edge of the flight deck.   *(FAAM)* pointed strongly to the same cause.

> 'It is indeed unfortunate,' reported Captain Evans, 'that aircrew should have to fly over enemy territory in aircraft powered by such unreliable engines'.

Both squadrons were involved on 1st June with Operation 'Billhook' in support of South Korean guerrillas landing in the Ponghwai area of the Han River from junks. This type of landing was a fairly frequent occurrence in *Ocean's* area and was designed to harass the North Korean army, to gain enemy information, and to support the Leopard organisation that provided so many targets. Because the wind failed the sailing junks, and enemy ground opposition was stronger than expected, the result from the army point of view was not a great success. The aircraft were engaged in CAS of the landings and in neutralising the enemy ashore. Selected villages, troop bunkers and trench systems were attacked just inland from the landing beaches, and once the friendlies were ashore, *Amethyst*, the controlling ship, conned the aircraft on to targets of opportunity in even closer support of the troops. The withdrawal of the guerrillas was covered during the afternoon.

Other attacks during the day were made on the rail yards at Chinnampo where the Fireflies destroyed at least five trucks. Lieutenant Commander Dick's flight of Furies destroyed a bridge north of Chinnampo. Another flight had their attack upset when they saw two aircraft on their tails which turned out to be friendly! Sub-Lieutenant Haines' Fury, in taxying forward after landing-on, hit Lieutenant Carmichael's aircraft and chopped off the rear of the fuselage, writing off the aircraft. Three other Furies, piloted by Lieutenants Normand and Crosse and Sub-Lieutenant Mallace, had to divert to Seoul with either hook or throttle trouble. At the end of the day's flying two Furies had to remain at Seoul. They flew back next day after replenishment.

Weather restricted flying on the 3rd to the morning only. The Furies piloted by Lieutenant Commander Shotton, Lieutenants Hallam, Normand and Jenne, achieved some useful rail cuts in the Chinnampo to Ongjin railway, while Lieutenant Commander Dick and Lieutenant Crosse attacked gun positions and brought down the cliff face on the entrance. Lieutenant Peniston-Bird had to divert to Seoul because of trouble with his aircraft's hook. The first Firefly detail, being of shorter duration than normal, struck at Chinnampo with a full load of 16 rockets per aircraft instead of the usual full wing fuel tanks and 12 rockets. Two further details also attacked Chinnampo destroying two rail trucks; other results could not be observed due to the target area being completely obscured by low cloud and smoke. The last detail returned to the ship in extremely bad weather with visibility reduced to 400 yards and a ceiling of 200 feet. Flying was cancelled after these three details.

The next day started with poor weather delaying the start of flying for 40 minutes, the first detail not getting airborne until 0530. The Fireflies found low cloud over all targets but managed to attack troop concentrations, rail yards, and supply and ammunition dumps, starting several fires in villages reported as containing troops. One rail truck was destroyed and two damaged; a junk containing troops was strafed and set ablaze.

For the Furies it was not such a good day, most of the bombs that were dropped missed their targets (which ranged from gun pits to buildings), two aircraft were lost and one written off. At about 1130 Lieutenant Hallam called the ship from the TARCAP area and reported his wing-man Sub-Lieutenant (Oggie) Swanson had been shot down. After attacking a gun position his aircraft was seen to be blazing from stem to stern; it was seen to level off at 1,500 feet and then suddenly the tail-plane fell off and the aircraft spun into the sea. Shortly before it hit the water Swanson's parachute was seen to open and he landed in the water near the small enemy-held island of Chongyang-do. Lieutenant Hallam, aided by four USMC Corsairs, acted as a RESCAP until Swanson, suffering from burns, was picked up under fire by helicopter from Chodo and taken to USS *John A. Bowle*. The next TARCAP detail conducted a shoot against the position suspected of shooting Swanson down. Shortly afterwards, Lieutenant McEnery's engine started to run rough and he requested an emergency landing. As he approached the ship, his engine failed and he ditched, wheels and flaps down. He was recovered by the ship's helicopter — the second remarkable escape of the day. Two new replacement pilots joined 802 Squadron, Lieutenant Jones and Sub-Lieutenant Randall; Jones, in landing-on, put his port wheel over the edge of the flight deck resulting in the aircraft having to be written off.

On the 5th the Fireflies obtained good results from a CAS mission in support of guerrilla forces in the Hwangchon area; considerable flak was seen with tracer climbing to well over 4,500 feet. The reconnaissance flights in the Ongjin and Pungchon areas attacked troop positions, airfields and dumps. Few results could be observed due to the targets being obscured by smoke, though twelve rockets did hit one hangar. Lieutenant Kinna suffered from a rough running engine but got rid of his rockets on a hill position before returning to the ship. Unusually, serviceability, at 60%, was bad all day, causing many alterations to the flying programme. Lieutenant Fraser's Fury flight obtained the best CAS result to date, a reported 75% effectiveness on troop bunkers on the reverse slopes of enemy held hill positions. Lieutenant Hallam destroyed a bridge to the north of Chinnampo. The most amazing event of the day was when Lieutenant Commander Dick attacked a bridge from low level. His bomb went into a field, bounced and followed the rail line for half a mile and eventually disappeared into a tunnel. A lot of damage was done by this freakish piece of luck, which developed into the chancy ploy of skipping low level bombs into train tunnels and then having to pull up smartly to miss the mountain. Some pilots were hit by the debris from their own bombs in skip-bomb attacks.

On the last day of the patrol, the Furies destroyed the spans of a bridge north of Chinnampo, while Lieutenants Treloar and Punchon spotted for a shoot with *Athabaskan* that put a gun position out of action. The unfortunate Lieutenant McEnery again had an engine rough running — the third in two days. He force-landed at Paengyong-do, and subsequent inspection revealed a large quantity of metal in the oil filters. A working party was sent ashore to repair the aircraft and make it serviceable for the next patrol. Both replacement pilots had barrier accidents and went to Iwakuni during the harbour period for a session of ADDLs; and Sub-Lieutenant Swanson returned to the ship with his burns heavily bandaged. The

Fireflies attacked a series of targets in the Pungchon, Hanchon and Haeju areas —
ammunition dumps, troop concentrations, and a Brigade headquarters — starting
fires and destroying huts; a telephone exchange went up with a large blue flash and
burnt fiercely for some time afterwards; and junks and sampans were strafed.
Lieutenant Commander Roberts had to land at Seoul with hook trouble. At the end
of this patrol, 802 Squadron had destroyed nine bridges.

Sub-Lieutenant Randall had recently joined *Ocean* and during this patrol had
had an early introduction to the hazards of operational flying:

> 'I went off the catapult with 2 x 500 lb. bombs on. As the wheels left
> the deck my Fury went into a hard roll to the left which I just managed
> to hold with both hands and one knee.

> 'Climbing away I told the ship of my problem and they asked
> whether I wanted to land-on again or ditch. I knew that a deck-
> landing would be impossible and I wanted to delay thoughts of
> ditching for as long as possible. Probably foolishly, I elected to
> continue with the sortie and we continued to our target which was a
> stores dump. When it was my turn to make the 65° dive attack I
> started down and, naturally, the stick forces increased with increasing
> speed and then, suddenly, the aircraft gave a wiggle of the wings and
> the out-of-balance aileron force disappeared.

> 'When we returned to *Ocean* they wanted to know my intentions and
> I elected to land-on.

> 'In the subsequent investigation it was found that the torsion-bar
> connection to the aileron spring tab had a worn spline end. The rest is
> conjecture, but it was thought that whilst arming-up one of the bigger
> and stronger armourers had bent-under the spring tab and displaced it
> several notches of the spline. When I went off the catapult the tab was
> demanding a roll to the left, regardless of stick position. It was surmised
> that in the dive-bombing attack at 500+ knots the tab had blown back to
> the neutral position and then the ailerons were normal again.'

Ocean left the operational area for Kure on 6th June after relief by USS *Bataan*
where she arrived at 0930 on the 8th to secure alongside the pontoon. During the
week, replacement aircraft were received from Iwakuni, normal servicing and
maintenance was carried out, and there was the usual embarkation of stores,
ammunition and fuel. On the 10th the Squadron officers challenged the Wardroom
to a cricket match and thoroughly trounced them.

Shortly after leaving, the cricket enthusiasts noticed a column of smoke rising
from the direction of the ship. Some wag made a remark to the effect that 'there she
goes'. Unfortunately and unwittingly he was partially right. Whilst AVGAS was
being embarked some petrol had been spilled; a Japanese dockyard welder dropped
a hot welding rod into the water alongside, setting fire to the pool of floating fuel.

The three-second flash ignited the paint on the port side from aft of the gangway space to the stern. Three Fireflies were damaged, one had to be sent to Iwakuni for renewal of the after section, the other two needed their rudders replacing, and the Quarter Deck and some officers' cabins received superficial damage. The fire was quickly brought under control, preventing what would otherwise have been a very serious incident.

825 Squadron was one year old on 12th, but unfortunately there was nowhere ashore where the whole squadron could get together, so a compromise was reached — birthday cakes for the rating's messes and an RPC to the ship's and 802 Squadron's officers in the wardroom.

On 15th June Field Marshal Lord Alexander of Tunis, Minister of Defence, accompanied by Mr. Selwyn Lloyd, Minister of State, and General Van Fleet paid a visit to the Fleet. In perfect weather, *Belfast*, wearing the flag of Admiral Scott-Moncrieff, together with *Ocean*, *Ceylon*, *Consort* and *Amethyst* assembled in the anchorage at Inchon. Lord Alexander visited each cruiser and *Ocean* and addressed very representative gatherings from all ships. His speech was not particularly popular with the ship's companies being entirely confined to praise of our front line troops and of General Van Fleet.

Between the 24th and 28th June 'reliable information' of Communist assaults on some of the islands came to nothing. Two UN guerrilla raids were carried out on the night of 26th/27th June when 200 guerrillas were landed on the mainland opposite Chodo and returned in daylight, without Captain Coleridge (*Cardigan Bay*) (CTU 95.12.1) knowing anything about it.

Investigation failed to disclose the 'higher authority' who had ordered the raid.

Another raid was made in the Haeju area on 29th June when Wolf-packs made a dash across the mud-flats from Yong Mae-do to find out the enemy strength and to deal him a blow. The raid was made in a gale of wind and heavy rain, and some groups had a narrow escape from

Smoke rising from the enemy shore batteries after bombardment by HMS *Whitesand Bay*.   *(IWM)*

drowning since the wind caused the tide to rise more quickly than had been expected.

On the east coast, operations followed their accustomed pattern. TF 77 concentrated its efforts on the interdiction programme while the destroyers and frigates of TF 95 maintained the beige' of Wonsan; and patrolled off the bomb-line, and off Hungnam and Songjin as far north as Changjin. Many Commonwealth ships were concerned with the patrols in the Changjin area, where the work was of a routine nature which included frequent bombardment, anti-minelaying patrols and support of the RoK Marine garrison in the island of Yangdo (north of Songjin); though these patrols were strenuous, very little of special interest occurred. The ships involved were: *Charity, Taupo, Athabaskan, Alacrity, Warramunga, Morecambe Bay, Cossack, Concord, Amethyst, Nootka, Constance, Whitesand Bay* and HMAS *Bataan*.

Third Patrol

Before she sailed from Kure at 1630 on 13th June a contingent of Army officers joined *Ocean* to spend a few days at sea to see how the Navy operated and to witness flying from *Ocean*. She anchored overnight in the approaches to the Shimonoseki Straits in order to make the passage in daylight the following morning.

All the next day was spent at sea bound for Inchon where she arrived early on the 15th. Divisions were held for Lord Alexander who addressed the ship's company. On completion of the ceremonies, *Ocean* proceeded to the operational area. Admiral Scott-Moncrieff remained on board for the next three days.

Operations started on the 16th with a general reconnaissance by the Furies of the roads, railways, rivers and military installations in the area. In an early morning shoot, Lieutenant Davis directed *Athabaskan's* gunners on to a village containing troops with exceptionally good results, at least 20 houses were destroyed. On returning to the ship, Sub-Lieutenant Ellis had to ditch alongside, having lost his engine oil pressure, and he was quickly picked up by the ship's helicopter. The Fireflies attacked a vehicle repair and oil storage area in the Chaeryong district, and reconnoitred airfields where some activity was seen at Ongjin, but Haeju was deserted.

Low stratus cloud and fog next day made operations south of Chinnampo impossible. The Furies spent the day attacking targets in the Hanchon and TARCAP areas. Lieutenants Treloar and Brown knocked out an AA pit near Wonsan; Lieutenant McKeown and Sub-Lieutenant Cook shared the credit for destroying a gun emplacement menacing Sok-to; and Lieutenant Carmichael with Sub-Lieutenants Haines and Ellis destroyed two gun positions on the north bank of the Taedong Gang estuary. Sub-Lieutenant Mallace went to Paengyong-do in the helicopter to ferry back the aircraft landed there by Lieutenant McEnery on 6th June and since repaired. Weather and unserviceability frustrated several

Firefly missions; three aircraft returned early, two rough running and the third with a fuel gauge problem. Troops in bunkers and huts were attacked in the Hanchon area, and rail trucks were destroyed and damaged at Haeju. They did, however, bring back some interesting information about Sillyong Myon, a peninsula to the west of Chinnampo — an area of about 3 x 2l/2 miles that showed signs of considerable military activity in the way of fresh trench works, gun pits and many troop shelters with new camouflage.

On the 18th fog from before sunrise remained around the ship until mid-afternoon. Lieutenant Commander Shotton and Lieutenant Jenne obtained direct hits on a coastal gun and saw ammunition exploding for more than five minutes after the attack. At the request of Leopard, a combined strike and photo-reconnaissance mission by four Furies armed with 2 x 1,000 lb. bombs and four Fireflies with twelve rockets attacked and heavily damaged the two villages of Paeyon-ni and Haejong-dong.

Again next day fog prevented any flying until the afternoon, when the ship was in the north of the Yellow Sea between Chodo and the Yalu where she found a clear patch and launched the first Fury strike to the Hanchon area where Lieutenant Commander Dick's flight destroyed a bridge at Kyang-ni, north of Chinnampo. Lieutenant Commander Roberts led a strike on a supply dump in the Chanyon area where eight huts were destroyed or severely damaged. The CO had to make an emergency landing on return with a rough running engine, due to a broken connecting-rod. Sub-Lieutenant Hanson's aircraft was hit and damaged by a 20 mm shell case. Lieutenant Hunter's flight attacked a group of 14 rail trucks near Chinnampo. Admiral Scott-Moncrieff returned to *Belfast* during the afternoon.

A full day's flying in good weather achieved 80 sorties on the 20th. Four Fireflies attacked a Leopard target in the Chanyong area. A rice mill was heavily damaged and 15 North Korean soldiers were seen to be running into a building which was promptly set alight by 20 mm cannon fire. The Furies attacked junks and sampans, of which 12 were sunk or left sinking; several burst into flames on being attacked. Flak was encountered in the Haeju area but no aircraft was hit. The last event of the day was probably the most successful of the patrol when Fireflies and Furies struck a covered gulley and motor transport shelters. The strike of four Fireflies each with 16 rockets, and four Furies with 2 x 500 lb. bombs was led by Lieutenant Commander Roberts, who, with his No. 2, marked the target for the Fury bombing run followed by the Fireflies. Much smoke and dust was created, and a large bright red flame and thick black smoke suggested that a fuel dump in the gulley had been hit. The Fireflies reported the discovery of a number of transformer stations, but with no authority to attack them, they had to be left untouched, as were reservoirs and dams.

Next day was replenishment, when fuel oil, AVGAS, fresh water and some stores were all embarked from *Wave Sovereign*. One Firefly needed an engine change, and another a mainplane change due to a rocket fin going through the main spar. Both evolution's were carried out on the flight deck, where the repair crews had plenty of room to manoeuvre the Jumbo crane and space to handle engines and mainplanes.

On the 22nd, in brilliant weather, on the 0900 detail, Lieutenant Carmichael on Fury TARCAP, reported a concentration of 400 troops in a wood. He and his flight strafed them and at the same time he called up the ship and requested a strike against them. His call was received as the next event was being briefed, and the Firefly target in the Han River area was rapidly switched to these troops. Lieutenant Hunter's flight fired 42 rockets into the wood, followed by a strafing run, and troops were seen running in all directions. On the last event of the day a flight of Fireflies went to a nearby village where the survivors of the morning raid had concentrated, setting two houses on fire and damaging a number of others. Other Firefly details attacked rail trucks near Haeju and left a floating crane 'fully useless'. Lieutenant McEnery and Sub-Lieutenant Mallace, in Furies armed with 500 lb. air-burst bombs, destroyed a village reported to be harbouring troops. Lieutenant Treloar, on TARCAP, conducted a shoot with Sitting Duck (the air control ship) and knocked out an AA pit.

The main effort next day was a combined strike in the afternoon by six Furies and four Fireflies led by Lieutenant Commander Roberts. Four guns and a predictor had been identified by photographic intelligence in the Pungchon area of the Sillyong Myong peninsula. Two Furies, Lieutenant McEnery and Sub-Lieutenant Mallace, strafed the target from high level, followed by Sub-Lieutenant Ellis who marked the target with two 500 lb. airburst bombs. He was followed by the remaining three Furies dropping 500 lb. bombs with 0.025 second delay fuses and finally the Fireflies with 16 rockets each. Three bombs and all the rockets fell in the target area, knocking out all the guns. It was noted that because the Fireflies built up speed in their dives so quickly and tended to overtake the Furies, in future combined attacks they would lead and clear the target before the Furies started their dives. Quite a lot of flak — probably 37 or 40 mm — at 4,000 feet followed the strike, but no aircraft was hit. The whole area was reported as being well defended by heavy and automatic weapons.

June saw a change in the policy with regard to aircraft targets in North Korea, and on 18th June all restrictions on attacks on electrical power installations were lifted.

One effect of this change of policy was that enemy reprisals might be expected so *Ocean's* CAP was changed from two aircraft at 5,000 feet to two at 10,000 and two at 20,000 feet all day — not a popular move with the pilots.

On the 24th, *Ocean's* aircraft joined the attacks on enemy electrical plant. The Fireflies attacked seven transformer stations in the Changyon and Haeju districts. The most successful Fury pilots were Lieutenants Crosse and McKeown who scored direct hits on transformers causing blue flashes and heavy smoke. On the last of the day's sorties, Lieutenant Commander Dick reported his engine to be running rough and he intended dropping his bombs in the sea and landing, but as he neared the ship he decided to go for a bridge in the coastal province of Haeju. Accompanied by one of the CAP he did so and destroyed the bridge. On completion of flying, *Ocean* set course for Sasebo, arriving at 1815 on 25th and immediately embarked AVGAS.

During the period in harbour the ship was secured to a buoy just off the old seaplane base which entailed a 20 minute boat trip to go ashore. *Bonne Homme Richard*, a 27,000 ton *Essex* class carrier with Panthers, Skyraiders and Corsairs embarked, secured to a nearby buoy. Many aircrew struck up friendships with their opposite numbers and much time was spent entertaining and being entertained. On the 29th *Unicorn* arrived from Singapore with replacement aircraft and stores. Three Firefly's with modified connecting rods fitted were exchanged for un-modified aircraft. 825 Squadron then had eight aircraft with modified engines and four with recent new Rolls Royce engines; all twelve aircraft were fitted with the hook damper modification. During ammunitioning, 100 extra 500 lb. bombs were embarked but no extra rockets.

Commander A.F. Black DSC (Commander (Air)) was promoted to Captain and Lieutenant Commander O.N. Bailey (Lieutenant Commander (Flying)) was promoted to Commander on 30th June. Lieutenant Graham joined 802 Squadron before *Ocean* sailed on 3rd July.

The last year of the war saw a more flexible use of the carriers (particularly TF 77). Interdiction continued, but with less emphasis, and a more flexible employment was made of carrier aircraft; the enemy was kept guessing, he could not be so sure of when or where attacks would come.

In mid-1952, US Navy and US Air Force jets were fully integrated, and there was a fundamental shift in the pattern of air operations against North Korea. Operation Strangle was discredited, Operation Saturate was more effective but did not bring about the abrupt reduction in North Korean capabilities that the interdiction proponents had hoped for. June saw the beginning of strikes at electrical networks and remaining industry after an enemy General had said during interrogation that electric power was a great comfort to the North Koreans — for radar, for aircraft control, and for heat and power.

The power generation strikes involved attacks on four major hydro-electric generating facilities, three supplying the east coast grid and one the west. The three east coast ones were at Chosin, Fusen and Kyosen reservoirs supplying the area from the Soviet frontier as far south as Wonsan and nearly right across the peninsula. The west coast depended on the huge Suiho hydro-electric plant, the fourth largest in the world (400,000 kw). It was on the north side of the Yalu River only 35 miles from the Antung complex of 250 MiGs. An attack on this plant would be the first attack in MiG Alley since the attack on the Yalu bridges in the autumn of 1950. Destroying all these plants would pull the plug on North Korea's power supply — and much of Manchuria's as well.

Until the summer of 1952, political constraints dictated that the North Korean hydro-electric system be left alone. During the opening phase of the war, the planners had hoped that, after the liberation of North Korea, the grids would be in place for friendly use. It was thought that China's dependency on Korean supplied power might cause China to think twice about intervention, lest the Allies destroy the network. These ideas did not work. Once China had entered the war, there was little reason not to attack the network. In retrospect, the hydro-electric strikes could have taken place at least a year earlier, and probably with greater effect.

Carriers from TF 77 on the east coast and TF 95 from the west coast were chosen, partly for the element of surprise that would not have been possible with B-29 Superfortresses, but primarily for the requirement for pinpoint accuracy from the bombing to avoid bombs falling on Manchuria.

H-hour was scheduled for 0930 on 23rd June, but due to weather the attack had to be re-scheduled for 1600.

The full task force of four carriers was used, the biggest of the Korean War. Thirty five Skyraiders were launched from *Boxer*, *Princeton*, *Bonne Homme Richard* and *Philippine Sea*, of which thirty one were armed with 2 x 2,000 lb. and 1 x 1,000 lb. bombs; and four with 2 x 2,000 lb. bombs and a survival pack. Also from the same four carriers, thirty five F-9F Panther jets accompanied the strike aircraft for flak suppression. Eighty four F-86 Sabres reported from MiG Alley that 200 MiGs were grounded.

Complete surprise was achieved. In 180 seconds, 90 tons of bombs were dropped, all of which fell in the target areas. Stiff aerial opposition had been expected but it never arrived, the only defence was from AA guns.

During the day twelve other power complexes were also attacked. Pyongyang had no power, factories on both sides of the Yalu were paralysed and there were no lights in North Korea or Manchuria.

The attacks re-kindled the enthusiasm of the (US) naval aviators after the monotonous routine of interdiction. The Navy's flexibility and its ability to surprise and accurately hit heavily defended targets was demonstrated once again.

In two days the USN flew 546 sorties and the USMC 139 for the loss of only two aircraft whose crews were saved.

On 25th June 1952 the war had entered its third year; in another two weeks the armistice negotiations would enter their second; the front lines were static; and naval operations on both coasts assumed a form that was to remain unchanged for the remainder of the war.

Early in July Admiral the Hon. Sir Guy Russell, CinCFES, visited the war area. He flew to Tokyo where he called on General Mark Clark and Admiral Briscoe. He then flew to Iwakuni, from where he took passage in *Cardigan Bay* to Kure and transferred to *Belfast* in which Rear Admiral Scott-Moncrieff was awaiting him. The two admirals flew from Iwakuni to visit Vice Admiral Clark in USS *Iowa* off the east coast. Having watched a shoot on the bomb-line, they transferred to *Boxer* for the night. Unfortunately the weather was so bad next day that they were unable to witness any flying from the imposing task force of fleet carriers consisting of *Boxer*, *Enterprise* and *Bon Homme Richard*. *Belfast* had gone to Inchon where they joined her on the afternoon of 3rd July. In the evening Major General Cassels and officers of the Commonwealth Division dined in *Belfast*. During the next few days, Admiral Russell went on to visit Chodo and Paengyong-do and spent a couple of hours in *Ocean* watching flying, and on 6th he went to *Unicorn*, who was carrying out deck-landing practice in the area, and took passage in her to Sasebo.

On 9th July a combined gun and air strike was carried out by *Belfast*, *Warramunga*, *Kimberley* and *Ocean's* aircraft against positions on the north side of the Taedong estuary. Each strike was preceded by flak suppression and bombardment.

Fourth Patrol

Ocean and *Unicorn* sailed in company with five destroyers from Sasebo at 0600 on 3rd July for operations to start on the 4th, with *Unicorn*, 10 cables from *Ocean*, acting as spare deck, and conducting DLP for the three pilots who had recently joined 802 Squadron.

Lieutenant Commander Shotton's flight of Furies started the day by sinking three junks and destroying a coastal gun when on TARCAP. Lieutenants Treloar and Brown destroyed a second coastal gun whilst Lieutenant McEnery and Sub-Lieutenant Mallace collapsed a railway tunnel on the system just north of Ongjin peninsula. Lieutenant Carmichael's flight, finding the weather unsuitable over their briefed CAS target, journeyed north to the railway north of Chinnampo where they achieved a remarkable success — eight bombs completely destroyed two bridges. On returning to the ship they learnt that MiG's had been in their area at the same time and had shot down four US Corsairs off Chodo. It was thought that this aerial activity was in some way connected with a big Sabre strike against an officer's school on the Yalu River. The first Firefly detail, led by Lieutenant Commander Roberts, discharged half their rockets at ten stores dumps at Changyon that had been revealed by photographic intelligence, whilst the other half were fired at camp fires observed along a ridge — the fires were extinguished promptly between the time the aircrew saw them and the time the attack was delivered. Lieutenant Hunter's division attacked a Leopard target of a village housing troops and equipment in the

Hanchon district to the west of the Ongjin peninsula. A transformer station near Chanyon was completely destroyed by Lieutenant Hawkesworth's division.

The successful day's flying was marred by the death of Lieutenant R.C. Hunter, Senior Pilot of 825 Squadron. During the afternoon he took off from the ship with his observer, Lieutenant J.R.A. Taylor, on a test flight. Shortly after take off the engine failed, forcing him to ditch the aircraft near the ship, both he and Taylor managing to get clear of the aircraft before it sank. The helicopter arrived on the scene almost immediately and picked up Taylor, but unfortunately during the four minutes that it took the helicopter to drop him and return, Lieutenant Hunter had disappeared. An extensive search by the ships in the force and all the aircraft airborne at the time proved to be fruitless. The most likely explanation put forward was that his Mae West burst as it was being inflated and he could not remain afloat.

On the 5th both squadrons gave CAS to a guerrilla raid on the southern tip of the Haeju peninsula, the object of which was to obtain prisoners and loot. *Comus* provided gunfire support and acted as aircraft direction ship. Two serials were flown, each consisting of a division of four Furies armed with 2 x 500 lb. bombs and another of four Fireflies with 12 rockets, that remained over the area throughout the action from 0530-0830. After the first division of Furies had attacked their pre-briefed target, the aircraft's duties consisted of reconnaissance of the area to prevent the enemy from bringing up reserves, and in attacking particular targets requested by the guerrillas through *Comus*. Damage claimed was one village destroyed, two houses destroyed and several damaged, and an enemy troop concentration of approximately one company being neutralised. Low fog over the actual fighting area prevented the aircraft being of much use over it, but further north it was clear enabling them to deter movement of reinforcements along the roads. The Firefly divisions were led by Lieutenants Hawkesworth and Williams.

Of the more routine events of the day, the Furies achieved several rail cuts and Lieutenant Hallam destroyed a bridge west of Chinnampo. Lieutenant Carmichael's division attacked another bridge, near Sariwon, which was severely damaged and distorted but, being constructed of steel, was not destroyed. Lieutenant McKeown and Sub-Lieutenant Cook destroyed a coastal gun position near Sillyong Myon. The three new pilots completed their DLP in *Unicorn* and flew CAP from *Unicorn* for the rest of the day. They later transferred to *Ocean* by way of one of the screen. One minor accident occurred in *Unicorn* when the port wheel of a Fury piloted by Lieutenant Graham, during an emergency landing, hit an arrestor wire spool and the aircraft nosed-up and the propeller pecked the deck. The Fireflies attacked rail targets, Lieutenant Commander Roberts' flight damaging a turntable in the middle of Changyon, Lieutenant Hawkesworth's destroying and damaging trucks north of Sinwon and Lieutenant Williams' some box-cars at Chinnampo.

Next day *Unicorn* detached from the Element and returned to Japan during the afternoon. Lieutenant Hallam's Fury division destroyed another railway bridge to the south-west of Pyongyang and obtained a direct hit on a gunpit near Punchon, while Lieutenant McEnery and his wingman destroyed a camouflaged enemy bunker near Ullyul. The Fireflies concentrated on a variety of troop targets: Lieutenant Kinna led a flight to attack a troop concentration at Sin-ni; Lieutenant Hawkesworth attacked a village and a hill well covered with trenches and bunkers; Lieutenant Watkinson found 150-200 troops in a narrow valley that were attacked with rockets and 20 mm. A Fury flight achieved a new landing interval record of 18.6 seconds, and the squadron's average daily landing interval was seldom greater than 24 or 25 seconds, a reflection on the skill of the pilots and batsman, and of the efficiency of the deck handling and arrestor and barrier crews.

On the 7th the Fireflies took over TARCAP from the Furies. 'Sitting Duck', the controlling ship off the coast in the Pungchon area, between Chodo and Sok-to, had no targets for any of the events, so the pre-briefed targets were attacked, in spite of cloud at times. Patchy cloud throughout the day affected the accuracy of attacks on transformers and on troop and vehicle concentrations by the Fireflies. In one event, flights from both squadrons, led by Lieutenant Commander Dick, combined in giving CAS to a guerrilla landing off Haeju, causing a large number of casualties. Two bridges were attacked on the Chinnampo to Pyongyang rail line, one by Lieutenant Commander Shotton's flight being destroyed and the other being damaged by Lieutenant Treloar's. Bombardment spots were carried out for *Comus* on trenches and troops in woods by Lieutenant Commander Shotton and Lieutenant Jenne off Haeju, and for *Belfast* against Amgak by Lieutenant Hallam.

Next day was replenishment with AVGAS, FFO and fresh water from *Wave Sovereign*. The squadron maintenance personnel were fully occupied with starred DIs and supplementary inspections.

On the 9th the Fireflies again took over the majority of the TARCAP missions releasing the maximum number of Furies to combine with Fireflies on two large combined strikes on the Sillyong-Myon peninsula — Operation Boodles. The enemy had been left alone for some while to build up and to ensure good targets for the day's strikes in the area at the entrance to and on the north side of the Chinnampo waterway, which would then be bristling with flak and troop positions. *Belfast* and her two screen destroyers were to provide flak suppression during the attacks and bombardment afterwards. At 0906 the first strike of six Fireflies and twelve Furies, led by Lieutenant Commander Roberts, was airborne; at 1002 they were in the target area, at 1003 Roberts called for flak suppression fire under Lieutenant Commander Shotton's direction, and two minutes later the aircraft attacked. No flak suppression fire was seen — and fortunately no flak either. A village hit by Sub-Lieutenant Mallace with 2 x 500 lb. air-burst bombs appeared to blow-up. After the strike, about one third of each village that had been hit had been destroyed. The aircraft left the area at 1009. The afternoon strike, again led by Lieutenant Commander Roberts, attacked the same villages with the squadrons swapping targets. Flak suppression fire this time arrived on time and at the right place. Smoke obscured the target area so damage assessment was not possible. On completion of the aircraft strike, a Firefly spotted for a bombardment shoot by USS *Kimberley*, one of *Belfast's* screen. Operation Boodles was considered to have been entirely successful.

In other operations, Lieutenants Treloar and Brown destroyed a road bridge near Chinnampo, and two other bridges were severely damaged in the same area; Lieutenant Hawkesworth's flight of Fireflies destroyed a transformer station.

The Fireflies again carried out the TARCAP duties next day, setting the village of Kowang-ni on fire, destroying two stores dumps and a workshop building and damaging a coastal gun position. Lieutenant Davis and Sub-Lieutenant Ellis, during an early Fury detail, destroyed a gun position and then unearthed a number of 'beautifully camouflaged shelters' in the TARCAP area, providing the Fireflies with a good target later in the day. In other Firefly strikes, Lieutenant Hawkesworth's division destroyed a group of huts said to contain troops in the Han River area; Lieutenant Reynolds blew the roof and ends off a pumping station with all 12 of his rockets. On the last event of the day, intended as a road and rail reconnaissance, Lieutenant Hawkesworth's division, before starting up, were hastily diverted to a target of opportunity reported by a previous flight in the south Chinnampo district. The target was a convoy of about 20 ox-carts moving along a road. Damage claimed was more than eight oxen killed, six carts destroyed and two left in flames, and one ox and cart forced into a nearby dyke. The convoy was continuously strafed until all 20 mm ammunition had been expended; the flight literally went into a left hand circuit, going downwind along the road for strafing. Lieutenant Watkinson's aircraft was hit by a rifle bullet in the starboard wing, whilst some piece of the road damaged one of his radiators. The Furies destroyed a rail bridge near Kyang-ni and damaged a road bridge in the same area. Lieutenant Commander Dick returned to it later in the day, and with his flight destroyed it with 1,000 lb. bombs. Dick later flew an abortive CAS mission when the Mosquito directing aircraft seemed to be in some doubt as to the target, an unfortunate state of affairs that had been becoming all to frequent.

On 10th and 11th July, Admirals Clark and Ginrich visited the west coast in *Iowa*. Admiral Scott-Moncrieff met them at Inchon where they lunched with General Van Fleet, General Kembell (Commander I Corps) and General Selden (Commander US 1st Marine Division). Admirals Clark and Ginrich then embarked in *Belfast* to go to Sok-to to visit Lieutenant Colonel Wilbur USMC, Commander West Coast Island Defence Element, and then to Chodo.

11th July was undoubtedly a red letter day in *Ocean's* Korean life. For some days past there had been rumours of a large raid on a secret target — it was mounted on the 11th against Pyongyang, capital of North Korea, which had always been considered the *bête-noir* of North Korean targets because of its strongly deterrent flak. The raid — Operation Pressure Pump — was carried out by aircraft of 5th USAF, TF 77, 1st US Marine Wing, 77 Squadron RAAF and *Ocean*, co-ordinated by 5th USAF, and lasted throughout the day except for a two hour break at lunch time. A total of 1,254 offensive sorties were flown attacking military concentrations in and around Pyong-yang of which *Ocean* contributed 39 — 24 by 802 Squadron and 15 by 825. These 1,254 sorties were up to then a record, but on 29th August 1,403 sorties were flown with equal success in the same area and thereafter Pyongyang lost all military value for the rest of the war.

Ocean's effort was divided into two combined strikes. In each one the target, Target No. 29, remained the same, railway marshalling yards which were piled high with large wooden crates thought to contain aircraft parts, possibly crated MiG-15s. In each strike the Furies were to bomb the north end of the target containing the largest number of crates and the Fireflies were to rocket the other half where the crates were more dispersed.

The first strike took off at 0900 to be over the target at 1004: seven Fireflies led by Lieutenant Commander Roberts were followed by twelve Furies, the flights of Lieutenant Commander Dick, and Lieutenants Carmichael and Treloar. On the way to the lead-in point, the aircraft climbed to 12,000 feet and from there to the target the Fireflies went in a shallow dive to gain speed, the actual attack dive starting at about 6,000 feet. Damage assessment was impossible at the time due to smoke from secondary explosions and fires that were started. A dense brown layer of dust and smoke hung over the whole of the city at about 4,000 feet but no difficulty was experienced in picking out the conspicuous target. There was considerable flak in and around the target area: on the run-in heavy flak was seen at 9,000 feet during the attack and during the subsequent get-away some 37 mm was seen extending from 2,000 to 4,000 feet. One Firefly was hit during the attack dive by a piece of shrapnel in the starboard nacelle tank causing little damage and failing to pierce the tank; no Furies were hit. Photographic coverage by 5th USAF had shown the town to be defended by 84 heavy AA guns of 88 mm calibre and upwards, and at least 40 radars had been predicted.

The second strike in the afternoon followed similar lines. Eight Fireflies and twelve Furies, again led by Lieutenant Commander Roberts, were over the target at 1605. All the aircraft's weapons hit the target area causing secondary explosions and fires. Results of both strikes were excellent and all aircraft returned safely in spite of heavy AA fire, though it was thought the Americans lost three aircraft and several others were forced to land at Chodo. Corsairs, Skyraiders, Mustangs, F-84s and F-86s were seen over and near the city.

During the afternoon Admiral Scott-Moncrieff, accompanied by the two American admirals, transferred to *Ocean* and watched the return of the second strike.

'I was very pleased', wrote Admiral Scott-Moncrieff, 'that Admiral Clark, an experienced airman, should see *Ocean* operating; she did very well, and our guests were suitably impressed'.

'Routine' operations were flown as well as the two strikes. The Fireflies flew six TARCAP missions attacking stores dumps and transformers. *Iowa*, spotted by Lieutenant Hawkesworth and Mr. Brand, carried out a 16 inch shoot against guns on the Amgak peninsula, destroying an AA gun and damaging a coastal defence battery. During an attack in the Popchon San area, Lieutenant Commander Shotton had his Fury hit by AA fire that made a few small holes and caused the loss of the vertical camera. In the same attack, Lieutenant Jenne's aircraft received heavy flak damage when an explosive shell burst under his wing, damage that was beyond the ship's facilities to repair.

Fog delayed the start of operations on the 12th before two combined strikes were launched at a large power and transformer station north of Chinnampo. Lieutenant Commander Roberts led the first strike consisting of four Fireflies with Lieutenant Commander Shotton's flight of four Furies. The attack was successful, a large column of black smoke rose from the target, many small fires were started and a large secondary explosion was seen. The second strike was led by Lieutenant Hawkesworth with Lieutenant Carmichael's Furies. Fewer rockets hit their targets than in the earlier attack, but the Furies obtained a number of direct hits on crates, rails and box-cars in the area of the power station. Another unsuccessful CAS mission was flown by Lieutenant Carmichael's flight when not only did six bombs out of eight fail to explode, but it was thought that they were directed onto the wrong target by the Mosquito controller. There were strong feelings in 802 Squadron that the whole CAS system needed an overhaul. A friendly minesweeper was testing her guns when Lieutenant Treloar flew over her and was accidentally fired on — without being hit. The Furies rounded off the day with a big junk-hunt in which a large number of vessels were hit and destroyed. Four Fireflies led by Lieutenant Williams took passengers to Seoul in the afternoon where unfortunately on landing Lieutenant Gandey's aircraft caught the slipstream of the aircraft landing ahead of him. On hitting the ground, the undercarriage collapsed and after sliding along the runway for about 50 yards the nacelle tanks caught fire and the aircraft was destroyed. Both Gandey and his passenger Lieutenant Kinna escaped without injury.

Next day was spent on passage to Sasebo, arriving in the evening, having recovered Lieutenant Williams' division during the forenoon — they had spent the night at Seoul due to delays caused by the accident.

During the harbour period, USS *Yancey* of the Fleet Train secured alongside and supplied FFO and AVGAS. Lieutenant Commander Shotton, Lieutenant Fraser and

Sub-Lieutenant Swanson were all dined out before leaving for UK in the troopship *Devonshire*; an RPC was held for officers of the ships in the screen during the previous patrol; divisions were held on the Flight Deck on the Sunday, much to the interest of the crew of *Yancey* who was still alongside. Two new Fireflies were embarked from *Unicorn* and one unserviceable one sent away.

Mid-July saw a recrudescence of enemy activity in all areas of the west coast. It started in the Paengyong-do area, usually the quietest, when batteries to the south of Choppeki Point started firing on friendly small craft and on the island of Yuk-to (not to be confused with the island of Yuk-to in Haeju Bay). On 13th July *Belfast*, *Amethyst*, LST 883 and aircraft from USS *Bataan* supported a successful guerrilla raid which put an enemy gun out of action in this region. Early on the 16th the enemy occupied Changmi-do. Captain Duckworth grasped an opportunity: *Belfast*, *Amethyst* and RoK PC 702 surrounded the island, attacked it with *Bataan's* aircraft, and recaptured it with guerrilla forces on the 17th. Of 156 North Koreans who had landed, 80 were killed, 30 were drowned and 38 captured. Enemy activity then died down in the area. On the 23rd the Amgak batteries in the Chodo area opened fire on LSMR 536. *Newcastle*, carrying out her first patrol as CTE 95.12, and *Mounts Bay* returned the fire. USS Strong was fired on by the Amgak guns on 28th July and 1st August; *Belfast* on 29th July was hit forward by a 76 mm round from a new position on Wolsa-ri, being holed in the side and having one Chinese rating killed and four others wounded.

In the Haeju area there was more activity. On 22nd July the enemy was observed to be digging trenches and building gun pits on the west side of the gulf and several

engagements with *Nootka* and RoK PC 701 took place. On 28th July intelligence reports were received that the enemy was determined to stop our ships operating in the Haeju Gulf. Constant air cover for the next week was provided for ships in the area;

HMS *Newcastle* in arctic weather conditions off the west coast of Korea.   *(IWM)*   there was no serious attack though Mu-do was fired on.

At the end of July, USS *Bataan* was required to operate troop-carrying helicopters in assault exercises conducted by the US Marine Corps. The Corsair squadrons disembarked to K.6, the airfield at Pyongtaek 30 miles south of Seoul, and acted from there as TE 95.11 on a reduced scale.

Fifth Patrol

For the next three patrols 825 Squadron Division Line-up was:

31 Div.	Lt. Cdr. Roberts	Lt. Cooper
	Mr. Wigg	Mr. Beynon
	Lt. Gandey	Sub-Lt. Bishop
	Lt. Kinna	Lt. Taylor
32 Div.	Lt. Hawkesworth	Lt. Clancy
	Mr. Brand	Acm. Dunmore
	Lt. Watkinson	Lt. Fursey
	Sub-Lt. Arbuthnot	Acm. Potter
33 Div.	Lt. Williams	Lt. Hubbard
	Sub-Lt. Hanson	Acm. McCullagh
	Lt. Reynolds	Acm. Vaughan
	Lt. Jacob	Acm. Hearnshaw

Ocean sailed from Sasebo at 0600 on 21st July, screened by *Concord, Iroquois, Craig* and (later) *Hubbard*. The weather for much of the patrol was largely unfavourable, and for the first time the average daily sortie rate fell below 68. Whilst on passage the ship's gunners were exercised against a radio controlled target. This small aircraft was piloted by an American ship astern of *Ocean*. On the fifth run one of the port Bofors crews hit its tail unit, a parachute popped out and the aircraft floated down. Its parachute became entangled in a port-side gun sponson and after a struggle to haul the trophy aboard, the aircraft fell into the sea to be retrieved by its parent ship.

Operations started next morning with the flight deck pitching in a 25 knot wind. This movement was partially the cause of Sub-Lieutenant Randall's 10th wire barrier, which for some reason was not counted as a 'spoiler' of the accident-free record. Lieutenant Carmichael's Fury division went to Chinnampo for an early morning transformer strike. They had the unusual experience of seeing a belt of fog about 25-50 feet thick obscuring the base of their target. The bombs fell on the target and in addition to causing extensive damage, each bomb created a shock wave which rippled through the fog layer in much the same way as a stone thrown into a pond sets up a concentric series of waves. After marvelling at this, Carmichael proceeded on the usual first day rail reconnaissance. Lieutenants Peniston-Bird and McEnery successfully attacked and collapsed a tunnel just north of Haeju. Lieutenant Commander Dick with Lieutenants Crosse and Brown knocked out three gun positions in the TARCAP area. Fog, mist and low cloud prevented the Firefly pilots from accurately identifying their targets in all areas except around Chinnampo where Lieutenant Commander Roberts division attacked a number of supply bunkers. An engine shelter on the line north-east of Chinnampo was attacked and demolished by Lieutenant Williams' division. During this attack Sub-Lieutenant Hanson's aircraft was damaged by a rocket motor exploding on being fired, ripping open the port nacelle tank and making seven holes in the port wing. It was noted that agricultural activity had increased — in practically every field Koreans could be seen tending their crops unconcerned about the presence of enemy aircraft overhead.

Two transformer stations were destroyed on the 23rd, one near Chaeryong in a combined strike of four Fireflies led by Lieutenant Commander Roberts, and four Furies led by Lieutenant McEnery, and the second in the Chinnampo area. Lieutenants Hallam and Jones destroyed a road bridge in the TARCAP area and damaged a large rail bridge near Chaeryong. Lieutenant Carmichael had the pleasure of seeing two jeeps and a lorry together, and the intense disappointment of having his guns jam. To the west of Chinnampo, Lieutenant Commander Dick and his flight severely damaged a considerable length of causeway and demolished the large road bridge at its end. Vehicle shelters and a gun position were attacked and damaged by the TARCAP Fireflies at the request of Sitting Duck. Choppy sea conditions, giving rise to a certain amount of movement of the flight deck, resulted in heavy landings by three Furies that strained their main spars beyond acceptable limits and beyond the capability of the ship's maintenance crews to repair.

On the 24th Lieutenant Commander R.A. Dick DSC, who had recently succeeded Lieutenant Commander Shotton as CO of 802 Squadron, was killed when he failed to recover from a low strafing dive on a sampan, his aircraft crashing into the Taedong Gang just north of Kyomipo. Shortly before making the attack he reported that he had been hit but decided to continue. It is thought the aircraft had been hit in a control cable which would account for his failure to recover from the dive if the cable had fractured during the pull-out. Apart from an oil streak, no sign of the aircraft or pilot was seen by searches of the area.

'The loss of this very gifted pilot, inspiring leader, and in all respects most able officer, by flak was a sad blow to the ship and to the Service', wrote Captain Evans.

The Furies had a successful day against the bridges. Earlier in the day, before his sampan attack, Lieutenant Commander Dick's flight had knocked down two: Lieutenant Davis and Sub-Lieutenant Ellis demolished a span of a road bridge in the TARCAP area; and Lieutenant McEnery damaged a rail bridge near

Chinnampo. Three Fireflies led by Lieutenant Gandey attacked shelters near the Amgak peninsula. After the attack Gandey reported his aircraft was losing coolant, and he finally ditched about three-quarters of a mile off Chodo beach landing strip, and both he and his observer Sub-Lieutenant Bishop were rescued without injury by a helicopter from the island. Lieutenant Williams' division attacked a gun position, causing a small secondary explosion, and a village in the Hanchon area reported to be containing troops.

Poor weather hampered the early details next day with a big layer of strata-cumulus cloud extending from 2-4,000 feet up to 6-7,000 feet. An early morning detail of eight Furies and four Fireflies were briefed to give CAS to a planned guerrilla landing in the area near Haeju. As the aircraft approached they were forced below 200 feet by a layer of treacherous stratus cloud which made any support operation impossible. The landing was called off and the aircraft attacked road and rail bridges in the clearer area to the north of Chinnampo. Lieutenant McKeown and Sub-Lieutenant Cook broke two bridges on this event and a third later in the day. The weather improved during the afternoon so that Lieutenant Hawkesworth's Firefly division successfully attacked railway trucks near Pyongyang, destroying three and damaging several others. A USMC squadron, operating from K.6 (Pyongtaek) airfield, took over TARCAP duties from the west coast carrier. In the afternoon two CODS Avengers took Lieutenant Davis, Sub-Lieutenants Haines and Ellis, Mr. Wigg and Mr. Beynon to Iwakuni to collect badly needed replacement aircraft.

The 26th was replenishment day with AVGAS, FFO, fresh water and some stores being supplied from *Wave Chief*. During the dog watches three Furies and one Firefly were flown on board from Iwakuni via K.16 (Seoul).

For the remainder of the patrol the weather was bad; most of the mainland was blanketed in low cloud, fog and drizzle, rendering the airfields in South Korea unusable.

HMS *Ocean's* SAR Dragonfly.   (Mather)

Captain Evans shifted *Ocean* 70 miles north of her usual operating area where he found entirely suitable conditions, the northern part of North Korea being clear. This well illustrated one of the inherent advantages of a carrier over an airfield as an operating base.

Weather delayed the start of flying on the 27th until 1000, and when it did a new twist was introduced into the war, best described in the words of 825 Squadron's diarist:

> 'Today for the first time since the Korean War started Russian built Mig-15 jet fighters attacked British naval aircraft. Lieutenant Hawkesworth's division was the one that was bounced. This attack was due primarily to the weather conditions prevailing in the operational area. A cold front lay east/west across Korea just south of the Chinnampo estuary. To the north the weather was good, 3/8ths cumulus with a base at 4,000 feet and good visibility; while to the south of the front conditions were such as to ground all 5th USAF.
>
> *Ocean's* aircraft were the only ones operating throughout the day on the west coast.
>
> 'In Event Baker four Furies reported seeing three MiGs in the Chinnampo area, but these did not attack the Furies. Also in Event Baker the CO [Lieutenant Commander Roberts] led his division to attack a warehouse, one of a group of three in the Hanchon area. The attack was successful and the warehouse completely gutted. On return to the ship the CO reported that the area had been thoroughly alerted and that his division had encountered more flak in the area than had been seen previously and that most of it was accurate. The majority of

MiG 15 in Russian markings.   *(Taylor)*

the flak was thought to be 37 mm type — bursts being seen up to 7,000 feet. This division saw no enemy aircraft.

'There were no Fireflies on Event Charlie. But on Event Dog Lieutenant Hawkesworth's division was briefed to attack a target in Kyomipo. Unfortunately during the briefing no mention was made of the MiG report from Event Baker. On arrival over the target area it was found that 8/8ths cloud, base about 2,500 feet, covered the whole area of Kyomipo. An alternative target in the shape of a large warehouse was found on the western outskirts of the town of Kangso to the north of Kyomipo. While pulling out of the attack, which severely damaged the building, the No. 3 Lieutenants Watkinson and Fursey were hit by flak and began to lose coolant. The division then set course for the coast escorting the No. 3. In a position some 10 miles north of Chinnampo at a height of 4,500 feet three MiGs, there was possibly a fourth but it was not seen in the ensuing action, made a stern attack on the division coming from above cloud and out of the sun. It was rather a half-hearted attack except on the part of the MiG which had singled out the No. 4 Sub-Lieutenant Arbuthnot and Aircrewman Potter. This MiG fired one long burst closing the range while firing to approximately 100 yards, before breaking away over the No. 4 and in front of Lieutenant Hawkesworth. Another MiG made a firing pass at No. 2 who received a bullet through his starboard wing tip. This aircraft was flown by Mr. Brand with Aircrewman Dunmore as observer. The third MiG just flew through the division without firing. In spite of the surprise, the No. 3 was able to fire a burst at the MiG which attacked the No. 2; whilst Lieutenant Hawkesworth was able to fire a burst at the MiG which had attacked the No. 4. Unfortunately it is thought that the enemy was not damaged by these bursts. As a result of the MiG's attack on No. 4, No. 4's starboard tailplane, which received a direct hit by what was thought to be a 23 mm cannon shell, was severely damaged and the starboard after part of the fuselage was holed in seven places. The starboard wing was also hit in three places, one uncovering part of the wheel. After the attack was over, the MiGs did not attempt to renew the engagement although they remained overhead until all our aircraft had crossed the coast. On nearing the coast the Fireflies were joined by a division of Furies led by Lieutenant Hallam who unfortunately had no ammunition left. They had all seen the attack developing but had been unable to warn Lieutenant Hawkesworth in time. It appears that they saw 12 MiGs in all above the Fireflies in three flights of four, of which one flight only took part in the attack.

'On reaching the coast No. 3 of the Fireflies [Watkinson and Fursey] was forced to ditch off the west coast of Chodo and both the crew were rescued safely almost immediately. No. 2, after the ditching, was escorted back to the ship by a Fury as his starboard wing tip showed signs of falling off; whilst Lieutenant Hawkesworth and his observer Lieutenant Clancy, together with Lieutenant Hallam in a Fury, escorted No. 4 to the emergency beach at Paengyong-do where he made a safe landing, wheels and flaps up.

'In the following event, Event Easy, Lieutenant Williams' division attacked a coastal gun position in the Pungchon area. Three lots of RP fell in the target area, one batch fell in the sea. A small fire was started. Rail reconnaissance. No flak.

'Two further strikes each of three Fireflies were launched. Lieutenant Hawkesworth at 1625 attacked a Leopard target with Mr. Brand and Lieutenant Reynolds. The target, a village containing troops in the Ongjin area, was set on fire in one place. The aircraft continued to K.16 [Seoul]. In the last event Lieutenants Williams and Jacob with Sub-Lieutenant Hanson attacked a large municipal building in Haeju, severely damaging the east end of it. Cloud made reconnaissance of the area difficult.

'*Ocean's* aircraft had one further brush with MiG-15s after Event Dog. In Event Easy four Furies led by Lieutenant Peniston-Bird were attacked by two MiGs at 4,500 feet one mile south of Chinnampo. The MiGs opened fire at extreme range. Two Furies retaliated, also at extreme range, and the MiGs made off.'

Sub-Lieutenant Arbuthnot's log book entry reads: 'Division bounced by 2 plus MiG 15s. My aircraft hit by 37 mm cannon fire in starboard tailplane…'

The accident signal added more detail: 'Tail plane was severely damaged and fuselage and one mainplane received minor damage…. Subsequently when flaps were lowered to cruising position aircraft went into dive from which recovery could only be made after flaps had been retracted.'

Also in Event Dog, Lieutenant Hallam's flight had demolished a bridge and had used up all their ammunition; it was on their return from this attack that they were involved with the MiGs — a flight of four attacking his division and damaging his aircraft. Lieutenant Peniston-Bird's division out manoeuvred the MiGs and is credited with damaging the enemy flight leader before the action was broken off when the Furies entered cloud. And on the first event of the day, before all the MiG excitement, Lieutenants McKeown, Crosse and Graham had destroyed three rail bridges on the Chinnampo to Pyongyang line.

Next day adverse weather again affected flying. On practically every mission there was 6/8ths to 8/8ths layered cloud from 500 feet to 25,000 feet. On Event Able at 0525, three Fireflies dumped their rockets on an old Leopard target near the coast south of Haeju because the

Sub-Lieut. Arbuthnot and Acmn. Potter's Firefly on the beach at Paengyong-do – wheels and flaps up.   *(Arbuthnot)*

weather prevented them from approaching either their primary or secondary targets. On the next event Lieutenant Williams' division could not reach their briefed target, but they found what appeared to be a stores dump and obtained direct hits on three houses. In two sorties, Lieutenant Commander Roberts first found and photographed a gun position near Haeju that had been firing at *Nootka*, and then on a later event attacked it, all rockets from the division landing in the target area. The Furies had an equally frustrating day. Their only good result was the complete destruction of a transformer station 15 miles north of Chaeryong by the division led by Lieutenant Carmichael — acting CO of 802 Squadron. Lieutenant Peniston-Bird, in a 'creeping beneath the weather' sweep, surprised a 5-ton truck driver and destroyed the truck. It was not a good day, but then Korea is notorious for the murkiness of its weather when influenced by the south-west monsoon.

On the 29th the weather was so bad that the Fireflies only flew one detail, led by Lieutenant Williams, to a village in the Ongjin/Haeju area. After 0800 the Furies flew 'weather test' CAP details only, on return from one of which Lieutenant Jenne entered the barrier. During the day an unfortunate accident

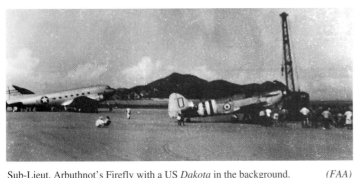

Sub-Lieut. Arbuthnot's Firefly with a US *Dakota* in the background.   *(FAA)*

occurred when PO/REM Jordan of 802 Squadron walked into the rotating propeller of a Fury whilst changing its radio set and received injuries from which he later died.

On the last day there was no break in the weather until 1630 when two strikes got off. The first one, a combined strike by Furies and Fireflies on a transformer station near Chaeryong led by Lieutenant Commander Roberts, caused explosions and sheets of orange flame. The second strike, and last event of the day at 1830, of four Fireflies was led by Lieutenant Hawkesworth on their secondary target of a village south of Chinnampo, causing primary and secondary explosions. *Ocean* left the area that evening, her place being taken by USS *Bataan*.

The 31st was spent on passage to Kure where *Ocean* arrived at 1000 on 1st August. That evening a concert was given in the after lift well by Bill Johnson from 'Annie Get Your Gun', and by a comedian and a pianist. On the Wednesday make and mend a ship's sports meeting was held at the main recreation field. The event was well supported and was won by the Royal Marines with the combined Chief Petty Officer's messes coming second. RPCs were held for the military establishments in and around Kure and for *Crusader*, *Iroquois* and HMAS *Bataan*.

Three RNVR pilots, Lieutenants Adkin, Buxton and Clark from 1832 Squadron at RNAS Culham, joined 802 Squadron and spent the period at Iwakuni on familiarisation and ADDLs. They arrived in a blaze of publicity as the first RNVR pilots in Korea, but they had been preceded by Sub-Lieutenants Randall and Cook early in June who had already established the image of the RNVRs as perfectly normal squadron pilots.

Two replacement Fireflies were received from Iwakuni. Due to a shortage of rockets, 825 Squadron had to be rationed to 1,000 RPs for the next patrol. The inboard rocket launchers were removed from the Fireflies and their place taken by 1,000 lb. bomb carriers. The armament load was then either 2 x 1,000 lb. bombs or eight RP and 2 x 500 lb. bombs, but both bombs and rockets were never carried on the same sortie.

On the night of 12/13th August, the enemy massed in strength on the mainland opposite the island of Cho-do in the Haeju estuary, about eight miles north of Yonpyon-do. *Concord* broke up the attacks before they could be launched at the island, directed by a shore fire-control party on the island. *Concord* and USS *Strong* neutralised two guns, one each side of Haeju Gulf, on 21st August. Heavy air attacks in the area caused casualties estimated at 400-500.

On 14th/15th August, in the Paengyong-do area, a 'model' guerrilla raid was launched on Ongjin, near Kirin-do. Supported by *Rotoiti* and *Crusader*, 120 men under Lieutenant MacBride USN landed in junks and penetrated 4 miles inland, inflicted 80 casualties on the enemy, destroyed one gun and returned unscathed with four PoWs after spending five hours ashore.

Sixth Patrol

Ocean, with *Charity*, *Kimberley*, *Yarnall* and *Strong* sailed from Kure at 1700 on 8th August. The weather was uniformly good, 600 sorties were flown — the highest number then reached for a single patrol — at a daily rate of 75. The opening days were enlivened by the attention of Mig-15s operating mainly over the Hanchon/Chinnampo/Pyongyang triangle, strategically the most important area to the enemy in the whole of North Korea. As targets were attacked by *Ocean's* aircraft at least twice per day, it was not long before air encounters occurred.

Flying operations started on the 9th, the early events well described by 802 Squadron's diary:

'Lieutenant Carmichael, Lieutenant Davis and Sub-Lieutenants Haines and Ellis started the ball rolling this morning by flying the first AR of the patrol. By 0600 they had entered the area and had commenced their Hanchon and Pyongyang to Chinnampo rail search. By 0630 they had reconnoitred as far south as Chinji-ri, a small village about 15 miles north of Chinnampo. As they meandered down the line, checking the bridge state as they went, they suddenly saw eight jet bogies to the north. Almost immediately the bogies were identified as MiGs — and they were closing. By this time drop tanks were fluttering earthwards and the flight had assumed proper battle formation and No. 4 — Sub-Lieutenant Ellis — had noticed a shower of red tracer streaming past both sides of his fuselage. He cried "Break" over the R/T and the flight commenced a "Scissors". It was soon apparent that four MiGs were after each section of two Furies but by continuing their break turns our aircraft presented practically impossible targets to the enemy who made no attempt to bracket.

'On one occasion a MiG came head-on to Lieutenant Carmichael and Sub-Lieutenant Haines — they both fired — it broke away and proceeded to go head-on to Lieutenant Davies and Sub-Lieutenant Ellis — they both fired and registered hits. On another occasion a MiG pulled up in front of Ellis with its air brakes out and he was amused to find the range closing. He gave a long burst and noticed hits on the enemy's wings. The aircraft then proceeded northwards at a reduced speed with two other MiGs in company. Meanwhile the flight, still in its battle formation, managed a dozen or so more firing passes at MiGs head-on. The dog fight lasted 4-5 minutes and then the MiGs disappeared as quickly as they had arrived — as they departed an aircraft was seen to crash into a hillside and blow up. At first Lieutenant Carmichael thought it was one of his flight and ordered a tell-off. However when No. 4 came up "loud and clear" it was realised that the Royal Navy had shot down its first Communist aircraft. Lieutenant Carmichael as flight leader is being credited with its destruction officially but the rest of the flight are claiming their quarter as well.

'As a result of that five minutes fight one Mig-15 was destroyed and two others badly damaged — a remarkable feat achieved without a scratch to any of our machines.

'The ship was still humming with excitement about this when at 0800 a report came through that Lieutenant Clark, who was on a "Cook's tour" of the coast had been hit by MiGs in his starboard wing. His wing caught fire — but by side-slipping and releasing his drop tanks he put it out and brought his aircraft back to the ship. With him was Lieutenant McEnery who scored hits on the tail of one of the three attacking MiGs.

'By the time Lieutenant Clark had landed-on the ether was buzzing again with MiG reports. This time Lieutenant Jones reported that his leader, Bob Hallam, was bounced after attacking a rail bridge north of Chinnampo. By some trick Lieutenant Hallam was leading a weaving procession of one Fury, two MiGs and one Fury down the Taedong Gang towards Chodo. Eventually his aircraft was hit when he broke towards the enemy and the MiGs veered off. Bob Hallam was obliged to make a wheels-up landing on Chodo. On inspecting his aircraft afterwards, he found a large hole just behind the cockpit where a 37 mm had found its mark.

'This indeed was a fabulous start to our sixth patrol. On restricted sorties (nobody went north of Chinnampo) throughout the rest of the day, Lieutenant Carmichael and Sub-Lieutenant Haines destroyed a road bridge east of Haeju. Lieutenant Peniston-Bird obtained a 50% coverage on CAS with his flight, Lieutenant Jenne got a road bridge near Changyon and McEnery and Treloar got two more near Haeju. Lieutenant McKeown destroyed a transformer station north-east of Haeju with his flight and then got hit himself when flying over Chinnampo Waterways.

'In the forenoon Lieutenants Adkin and Buxton carried out DLP.

'What a day — Whew!'

Although the diary suggests that all four members of the flight claimed a share of the MiG, from a confused situation Carmichael as flight leader got the credit for its destruction; and Captain Evans had no hesitation in accepting Lieutenant Commander London's, the CO's, recommendation for the award of his DSC.

Indeed, what a day; a historic day for the Fleet Air Arm. To Lieutenant (now Commander) Peter 'Hoagy' Carmichael has fallen the unique distinction of being the pilot of the only piston-engined aircraft to shoot down a jet-engined aircraft, a formidable testimony to the Sea Fury's ruggedness and its excellent dog-fighting characteristics. In his own words:

> 'We, as usual, were flying at about 4,000 feet, and we always flew with gyro and fixed ring on the gunsight. Suddenly a MiG came down behind me: I turned towards him and as he flew past me I noticed he had his air brakes out. He made the fatal mistake of trying to dog-fight with us. I put my gyro sight on him and started to fire. At this point he realised he was in trouble and put his dive brakes in and started to accelerate like mad. I then switched to fixed ring and held him quite easily and my bullets started to hammer him. He started to roll over on his back and crashed into the ground with no attempt at baling out.'

And what a rugged debut in Korean operations for Lieutenant Clark RNVR, normally a week-end aviator!

Lieutenant Hawkesworth's Firefly division were briefed to attack a village 20 miles south of Chinnampo with 500 lb. air-burst bombs. One aircraft went unserviceable on the deck and Mr. Brand jettisoned his bombs and returned with a rough running engine shortly after take-off. Hawkesworth, with Sub-Lieutenant Arbuthnot, pressed on for the target. When just east of Chodo they saw a MiG which turned out to be one of those engaged with Lieutenant Hallam's Furies. The Fireflies were not attacked and continued to their target. Of the four bombs dropped, two burst among some houses and the other two failed to explode. In a later event Lieutenant Hawkesworth's division attacked a factory of six buildings with rockets, causing fires and destroying two buildings. Due to unserviceability, they had to land at Seoul; Lieutenants Hawkesworth and Watkinson returned to the ship later, but the other two stayed overnight. Other Firefly flights attacked a gun position south of Haeju and a factory on the outskirts of Sinchon.

In an early morning Fury strike on the 10th, Lieutenant McKeown and Sub-Lieutenant Cook knocked down a railway bridge north of Chinnampo, Cook receiving a hit in his tailplane after a strafing run on the Chinnampo wharves. At 1100 Lieutenant Carmichael, Sub-Lieutenant Carter, Lieutenant Davis and Sub-Lieutenant Ellis arrived over Chaeryong and destroyed one rail bridge and badly damaged another. At 1130 the flight was intent upon some photography in this 'peaceful' southern area when Carter saw two jet bogies and then six more. Drop tanks fluttered earthwards and for the second time in two days Carmichael started dog-fighting. This time the MiGs showed far more skill than previously. Nevertheless after ten minutes desperate fighting the four Furies made cloud and one MiG was seen heading northwards with black smoke pouring from it. Lieutenant Davis and Sub-Lieutenant Ellis were responsible for this aircraft's condition. When the flight returned to the ship they met Lieutenant Colonels Taylor and Lynch and Major Collins of 5th USAF who had gone out to *Ocean* to consult with Captain Evans and his Officers in order to find a way of removing this MiG threat. Finally, in an afternoon strike Lieutenant Normand and Sub-Lieutenant Carter destroyed a rail bridge. Carter, on landing from this trip, caught an arrestor wire that was still re-setting which tore out his hook and he plunged into both barriers. The Fireflies bombed and damaged two bridges, and, in two separate strikes, both bombed and rocketed a group of buildings between Haeju and Ongjin. At Leopard's request, Lieutenant Hawkesworth and his division rocketed a village in the Changyon area, starting three fires.

The result of these encounters was on balance favourable to the Furies, but it was realised that this was largely due to the stupidity of the MiGs in sacrificing height and remaining at low altitude to 'mix it' with the Furies. If they were to learn to adopt the proper tactics of diving to the attack and then using their vastly superior performance to climb away for the next attack, Captain Evans had no doubt that the balance would immediately shift in favour of the MiGs. He asked 5th USAF to provide US jet cover, preferably Sabres, for our aircraft when they were operating north of the River Taedong, but owing to other commitments it could not be arranged. Captain Evans was convinced that any diminution in the scale of interdiction in this important area would be of great advantage to the enemy, so decided to time the strikes to coincide with a scheduled Sabre sweep and that in these circumstances Fireflies would accompany the Furies. Sometimes if there was only one Sabre sweep in a day, another strike would still be carried out, but that by Furies only, and never with fewer than eight aircraft. The pilots generally were under the impression that Sabres stayed over the Yalu from dawn to sunset and it came as a surprise to learn they only conducted sweeps over North Korea once, or at most twice, each day.

After the experiences of the past two days everyone was very bogey conscious. Early the next morning the ADR detected an echo orbiting the ship which was intercepted by the CAP and found to be a B-29 with American markings. The Fortress showed no IFF or visual recognition and was 'escorted' for nearly three hours before JOC at Seoul reported it to be friendly. In a three division co-ordinated strike, the first timed to coincide with a Sabre sweep, Lieutenants Treloar, Peniston-Bird and McKeown led their flights against the Chinnampo to Pyongyang road and rail sections, claiming four bridges destroyed or badly damaged. Lieutenant Hallam and Sub-Lieutenant Randall added another bridge to the score when they collapsed one in the TARCAP area. Lieutenant Carmichael seriously damaged a transformer station in the Han River area. The Fireflies bombed a road bridge east of Ongjin, cutting the road and destroying five houses. Lieutenant Commander Roberts' division rocketed hangars at Ongjin airfield, reporting that a number of craters in the runway had recently been filled in. Lieutenant Hawkesworth's division rocketed warehouses in a village in the Changyon area causing damage and secondary explosions. After some communications difficulties with Sitting Duck's transmitter, the division was given a target of troops digging a gun position which was strafed, but no troops were seen. During the last event of the day, Lieutenant Williams' division suspended their operations when two jet aircraft were seen to commence a dive on them. During evasive action the attackers never came within gun range and they were quickly lost. An American flight was heard to give a 'Tally-Ho' at the time on the R/T. There was no further MiG activity after the 11th.

On the 12th Lieutenants Carmichael's and Treloar's divisions went north with Sabre cover and destroyed two more bridges up there, on their return trip strafing three sampans and five ox-carts. Lieutenants McKeown and Brown with Sub-Lieutenant Mallace destroyed three road bridges in the eastern end of the TARCAP area. During the day two emergency landings and one barrier accident caused delays that were irritating to the pilots airborne waiting to land-on, and caused considerable unscheduled work for the flight deck crews who had to unravel the barrier and to move aircraft up and down the deck for the emergencies. Lieutenant Williams' Firefly division gutted a small factory in the Haeju area, and Lieutenant Hawkesworth's damaged another south of Taetan. On the last event of the day, Lieutenant Hawkesworth's division destroyed both ends of a road bridge which he had been attacking with little success for the previous two days. Lieutenants Peniston-Bird, Oldham and Sub-Lieutenant Carter were air-lifted to Iwakuni to collect three replacement Furies.

Next day was replenishment of FFO, AVGAS, fresh water and stores from *Wave Chief*. During the day the bomb carriers were removed from the Fireflies, leaving them with RP rails for eight rockets. At 1800 the three replacement aircraft were landed-on.

Early on the morning of the 14th Lieutenant McKeown's division gave CAS to a guerrilla landing on the Ongjin peninsula. They were called in to bomb two villages and strafe a mortar position. The village responded explosively to air-burst bombing, and according to the guerrillas the mortars stopped immediately after the strafing run. The rest of the Fury effort was devoted to bridge-busting. Near Haeju, Sub-Lieutenant Mallace destroyed one and later in the day Lieutenants Oldham, Graham and McKeown added three more to the score. North of Chinnampo Lieutenant Carmichael severely damaged two large road bridges. Lieutenant Commander P.H. London DSC, the new CO, and Lieutenant M.C. Crosley DSC, both for 802 Squadron, joined. They had been collected from Seoul by two Fireflies of 825 diverted at the end of an early strike. Lieutenant Commander Roberts' division rocketed a gun position in the Haeju area and later in the day successfully attacked a gun position and huts in trees near Ongjin. Lieutenant Jenne had to do a wheels-up landing at Paengyong-do after his hydraulic lines had been shot up by flak. A serious accident occurred during RATOG launches. Sub-Lieutenant Clark piloting a Fury had allowed the rockets to give him height rather than forward speed, and when the rockets ceased firing the aircraft immediately stalled, flipped on its back and dived, inverted, into the sea. It took him 80-90 seconds to get out of the aircraft as it sank and he surfaced about half a mile astern of the ship where he was picked up by the helicopter with bumps on his head and a few cuts and bruises. He was probably saved because of his unusual habit of always having his oxygen turned on, not normally done until flying above 10,000 feet.

Next morning Lieutenant Carmichael led his division to the Haeju and TARCAP areas where they destroyed two bridges and damaged a third. Lieutenant Hallam knocked down two road bridges and Lieutenants Treloar and Normand knocked out a span of a road bridge south of Pyongyang. A large combined strike, timed to coincide with a Sabre sweep over the Yalu River, of eight Furies in two divisions led by Lieutenants Peniston-Bird and Carmichael, with one flight of Fireflies led by Lieutenant Commander Roberts, attacked camouflaged huts, other installations and vehicle shelters in a village east of Hanchon. Although it could not be assessed at the time, considerable damage was done.

The Furies had a comparatively quiet day on the 16th. A large strike against a bridge south-west of Pyongyang was unsuccessful, the bridge remained intact, but flak suppression by Lieutenant Carmichael's division kept the active 88 mm guns from firing. Lieutenant McKeown and Sub-Lieutenant Carter both knocked down road bridges north of Chinnampo. A transformer in the Haeju harbour area was damaged by Lieutenant Williams' Firefly division. Three TARCAP details were given targets by Sitting Duck of troops and a gun pit, but when they reached the positions there were no signs of troops or the gun.

On the last day of the patrol, the weather deteriorated due to typhoon Karen approaching Korea, flying being cancelled after 1500. The first Firefly strike, led by Lieutenant Williams, destroyed a command post for three coast defence guns in the Pungchon area and went on to strafe a village harbouring troops, a target reported by Leopard. During the land-on after this event Lieutenant Reynolds floated straight into the barrier without touching the deck. This was the first serious deck landing accident for 825 Squadron in 847 landings. During the same land-on the tail oleo of Lieutenant Jacob's aircraft collapsed, damaging the tail wedge of the aircraft, and a Fury also entered the barrier. There were a number of other minor incidents during land-ons as a result of the swell ahead of Karen. A transformer station near Sinwon-ni was attacked by Lieutenant Hawkesworth's division, who strafed and sank a ferry boat half way across the river near Haeju. Lieutenants Crosley and Peniston-Bird led bridge-busting Fury divisions to coincide again with a Sabre sweep.

Apart from the heavy swell, *Ocean* was not affected by Karen, having had time to clear the typhoon's path on passage to Kure where she arrived at 1745 on 19th August. *Unicorn* arrived from Singapore on the 21st and berthed the other side of the jetty from *Ocean*. Damaged aircraft were transferred to *Unicorn* and two replacement Fireflies received to bring 825's complement back to 12 aircraft. Lieutenant Carmichael left 802 Squadron to return to the UK, Lieutenant Heaton joined 825 and Lieutenant Illingworth, as Air Weapons Officer, with Lieutenant Scott RAN joined 802. They all went to Iwakuni for ADDLs and Scott for flying practice after a long absence in hospital. 825 Squadron re-fitted their 1,000 lb. bomb carriers, and both squadrons eliminated the black and white identification stripes on wings and fuselages of all the aircraft, an Admiralty instruction that had been issued so that enemy MiGs would have more difficulty seeing them.

Ocean carried two Midshipmen (S) under training who were required to keep a daily journal of the ship's activities and of their own doings. The following is an extract from the journal of Commander D.C.V Isard:

'On Tuesday 12th August, Mumford [the other Midshipman (S)] and myself went across to the Canadian destroyer *Crusader* which was doing the Worthington patrol that night and the following night, while *Ocean* retired southwards on the 13th to replenish.

'The object of the Worthington patrol is to safeguard the islands which are held by us on the west coast of Korea. The islands are continually being attacked by the Communists, as they represent a line of festering sores because the troops and guerrillas on the islands are continually making raids on the enemy mainland.

'We proceeded along the coast at 28 knots and arrived at Taechong Do at about 1900 coming alongside the oiler *Brown Ranger* to oil. By the time our oiling was completed darkness had fallen and with it a thick mist which spread around and about the islands like a shroud.

'The ship proceeded north on patrol, navigation being made reasonably easy by using the Sperry Radar set … Another very sound piece of equipment is an infra-red searchlight which enables *Crusader* to signal to another ship similarly equipped, without being seen. They informed me that it was most useful for spotting enemy junks without letting the junks know that they had been picked up.

'Nothing much happened during the night but two star shells were fired at about one o'clock but they failed to break open the blanket, thus in the early hours of the morning the ship anchored.

'The ship sailed at 8 o'clock and proceeded south down the coast towards Haeju steering a course which was just outside the range of the Communists 76 mm shore batteries.

'We continued on a steady course all the forenoon …

'At about 2 o'clock the ship came across a junk and a boarding party was sent away. The junk when we first saw it was flying a South Korean flag which had probably been put up as soon as they saw us. The junk was brought alongside and it was seen to contain three men. The three men were brought on board and thoroughly searched and told by armed-to-the-teeth Canadian sailors to "put them up and keep them up". The number one man was brought to the bridge and cross examined by the Captain with the aid of an interpreter. A large amount of nearly worthless Won was found in the junk together with an American rifle and some ammunition. Subsequent reports announced that *Crusader* had captured an armed junk!

'Upon receipt of instructions from guerrilla headquarters on one of the islands, the junk and its crew was set free and *Crusader* steamed towards Haeju through a glassy sea. Just after tea a report came through from the guerrilla headquarters informing *Crusader* that the junk was to be picked up as it was suspicious after all.

'We therefore proceeded back at high speed, but our haste was hardly necessary. The junk, in the almost negligible wind, had moved approximately two miles in two hours. The Koreans expressed no surprise at seeing us again and the Captain neatly came alongside and took the junk in tow. The Koreans, now deemed prisoners, were locked in the laundry....

'We proceeded to return to one of the guerrilla held islands (Tinfoil) — the junk, not a very large one by any means, bobbing about in our wake.

'A motor junk came out from a cove in Tinfoil and took over our prisoners and their junk. We proceeded to Taechong-do to refuel with oil and to top up with water. Before we arrived, however, a report was received that a mine had been seen floating on the surface so we rushed off to search for it. Dusk soon fell, however, and as visibility became worse the search was called off and we commenced our night's patrol.

'I was awakened at 5 o'clock in the morning by the alarm rattlers, blearily put on my clothes and rushed up to the bridge to find the ship anchored just off the coast.

'A raid was in progress controlled by HMNZS *Rotoiti*. A party of guerrillas was attacking the enemy and signs of the attack were the clouds of smoke arising from places along the coast. The raid was successful and the guerrillas retired losing no-one and gaining four prisoners.

'Then we saw a very pleasurable sight, silhouetted against the rosiness of a dawn sky four Sea Furies came down to strafe the enemy. They made a great picture as they came into the attack pulling out very low and then hurtling up into the sky again leaving behind them the palls of smoke to indicate where their bombs had fallen.

'Ultimately it was *Crusader's* turn. She fired 78 rounds with her 4.5 inch guns, 16 broadsides in all. The deafening racket up on the bridge made it necessary to stuff ones ears. The ship's broadsides straddled the target...

'We sailed back to Taechong-do to refuel and eat a belated breakfast.

'After we had finished refuelling *Crusader* sailed back to the screen.'

Seventh Patrol

Ocean's next patrol from 26th August to 4th September was with *Comus, Nootka, Charity, Piet Hein* and USS *Marsh*. Weather was poor on the fifth, replenishment, day, but excellent for the first six flying days when 80 or more sorties were flown per day. One Firefly was lost and only superficial damage was done to other aircraft from flak, no enemy fighters were encountered. *Unicorn* joined on 1st September, and for the next two days the force ran into rough weather. On the 4th the weather was perfect; 97 sorties were flown, bringing the total for seven days to 583.

On 30th August two guerrilla raids were launched simultaneously in the area of Paengyong-do, each being supported by *Ocean's* aircraft. The first, 5 miles east of Choppeki Point, had as its objective 400 North Korean troops; gun fire support was provided by *Newcastle*. The guerrillas inflicted 50 casualties on the enemy without loss to themselves and returned with some equipment. The other raid, supported by *Taupo* and *Piet Hein*, was directed on a command post on the peninsula north of Sunmi-do, but the enemy was on the alert and met the landing party with mortar fire — not much was accomplished. A useful raid was carried out in the Haeju area on 10th September. Guerrillas, supported by *Belfast* and *Iroquois*, with aircraft from *Sicily*, landed on the Changdong peninsula north of the island of Yong Mae Do. The enemy was caught off

Choppeki Point bombardment – inside the gun turret.   *(Kellaway)*

balance and lost 30 casualties; a considerable quantity of intelligence was obtained about an impending attack on Yong Mae Do.

Ocean left Kure on 25th August with 450 x 500 lb. and 52 x 1,000 lb. bombs, and 1,900 RP of which she was only supposed to use 1,000. In the pre-patrol briefings, aircrew were informed of a 'new' American bombardment spotting procedure. They learned some interesting facts about UHF and radar coverage (or as some thought lack of it) from the islands of Paengyong-do and Chodo, codenamed Tinfoil and Postcard, which went some way towards explaining the occasionally poor communications with these islands. It was also learnt that the USAF Sabres were running very short of engine hours which might curtail their anti-MiG operations.

Choppeki Point bombardment – from the flight deck.   *(Kellaway)*

Operations started on the 27th. Lieutenants Treloar and McEnery and Sub-Lieutenant Mallace knocked down or damaged three road bridges; three rail bridges were destroyed and one damaged by Lieutenants Brown, Jones and Davis and Sub-Lieutenants Haines and Ellis. On the last strike of the day, Lieutenants Peniston-Bird and Crosley destroyed a dozen box-cars, Peniston-Bird having to make an emergency landing on return to the ship. On the second event Lieutenant Williams' Firefly division on TARCAP attacked a radar station with rockets where they encountered intense and accurate small-arms fire. The radar station was extraordinarily well hidden and the division attacked the wrong part of the hill. During the attack, Lieutenant Jacob and Aircrewman Hearnshaw had their aircraft hit in one of the radiators and were forced to ditch off Chodo. Lieutenant Commander Robert's division, on another TARCAP detail, found no signs of two groups of troops at the positions where they had been reported, so went on to attack a transformer station, hitting the main building — an attack that would have been more successful if, of the four aircraft involved, two of them had not had a total of eleven rockets hang up.

The Furies had more successes in their bridge-busting campaign next day, five being destroyed by bombing — Lieutenant Adkin a road bridge near Haeju; Lieutenant McKeown, rail at Chaeryong; Lieutenant Jenne and Sub-Lieutenant Randall, rail on the Chinnampo to Pyongyang line; and Sub-Lieutenants Carter and Haines a road bridge each. Lieutenant Commander London and Lieutenants Treloar and Hallam, on separate details, strafed concentrations of 400 to 500 troops in the Ullyul area, causing many casualties. Sub-Lieutenant Mallace, as a result of a probable supercharger failure, had to make a wheels-up landing at Paengyong-do. Lieutenant Hawkesworth's Fireflies carried out another attack on the previous day's radar station, encountering some small arms fire. Lieutenant Commander Roberts' division, armed with 500 lb. bombs with 0.025 second delay fuses, were diverted from their pre-briefed target in Haeju to attack a small wood in which a number of enemy troops were sheltering from Fury strafing runs. Four bombs were dropped in the wood and four on the outskirts; many bodies were seen lying on the ground after the attack.

As part of the interdiction campaign to destroy the Communist lines of supply, the Furies destroyed three more bridges on the 29th — Sub-Lieutenant Haines knocked down a road bridge to the north of Chinnampo, Lieutenant Oldham one south-west of Pyongyang and Lieutenant Carter an obviously important one in the TARCAP area because it was being repaired two hours after he had destroyed it. Lieutenant Davis spotted for a bombardment by HMAS *Bataan* of coastal guns south of Haeju. The Fireflies attacked six villages at the request of Leopard. Lieutenant Commander Roberts' division bombed a suspected radar and W/T station, but they were of the opinion, when they returned to the ship, that it was a North Korean graveyard, what appeared on the briefing photographs as aerials actually being white painted headstones. A small dam and adjacent sluice were damaged causing a large area of paddy fields to be prematurely drained. On their next mission, Lieutenant Commander Roberts' division destroyed two of three gun emplacements in the TARCAP area.

Next day both squadrons combined to give cover and support to two guerrilla landings on the Ongjin peninsula. Lieutenant Crosley, controlled by the New Zealand frigate *Taupo*, led a division of Furies armed with 500 lb. air-burst bombs to attack command posts, mortar positions, trench works and villages. Invariably from the air these positions had the accustomed ambience of Korean dereliction, and many pilots felt that the effort of bombing them was largely wasted. However, eye-witness reports and profuse thanks from the guerrillas indicated that the desired results were achieved. An American major from the Leopard organization had stated that 50% of the raids would have ended in disaster if it had not been for the support provided by the carriers. Lieutenant Commander London led a second detail, again under control from *Taupo*, to strafe gun positions, huts and AA pits in the south of the Ongjin area. His aircraft was hit by small arms fire but suffered no serious damage. *Newcastle* controlled the Fireflies; Lieutenant Hawkesworth's division was the first, reporting in at 0615, and successfully attacked a command post, the leader demolishing the hut with his rockets and the others strafing large numbers of men seen to be running in the vicinity. Hawkesworth handed over to Lieutenant Commander Roberts at 0720 who, at the request of *Newcastle*, rocketed and strafed a hill where the guerrillas had been held up. The attacks were concentrated on the north and west slopes of the hill where normal gunfire was ineffective, driving off about 150 of the enemy. The raids ended before mid-day with aircraft covering the withdrawal of the guerrillas.

The Furies continued their attacks on bridges, Lieutenants Normand, Crosse and Jenne knocked down three, one rail and two road. The combined flights of Lieutenants Davis and Hallam gave support to HMAS *Bataan* by dive-bombing 76 mm gun positions in the west of the Yonan peninsula. Lieutenant Davis went on to strafe villages in the same area, attacks made on the strength of Wolfpack reports that North Korean guerrillas lived in huts in the villages, and judging by the number of people that ran out of the huts, the reports must have been correct. The Fireflies also attacked villages where troops and guns had been reported, but none were seen though several houses and huts were destroyed and damaged.

On replenishment day, the 31st, *Wave Chief* supplied FFO and AVGAS, while routine maintenance was carried out on the aircraft, including the removal of drop tanks from the Furies to enable 2 x 1,000 lb. bombs to be carried.

On 1st September the Furies started by destroying two road bridges, Lieutenant Treloar one to the north of Chinnampo and Lieutenant Clark one in the mountainous Sinmak district close to one destroyed by Lieutenant Oldham. By mid-day low cloud was across the target area north of the Taedong Gang and many of the best bridges were obscured. Sabres were tangling with MiGs above the Yalu and Chongchon Rivers which prevented the MiGs from interfering with *Ocean's* operations. In an oblique photograph taken earlier in the day, Lieutenant Rolton, the ship's photographic interpreter, discovered a dispersal of motor transport and store dumps consisting of several shelters and two farmhouses spread out along a road. Treating it as a priority target, Lieutenant Davis' Fury flight and Lieutenant Hawkesworth's Fireflies were sent to attack huts and shelters housing the vehicles. One building, obviously a petrol store, went up in an enormous sheet of flame, two shelters were hit and many soldiers were killed as they ran from buildings to ditches. Earlier in the day Lieutenant Commander Roberts' flight on TARCAP had obtained a direct hit with a salvo of four rockets into the mouth of one gun position and a plume of white smoke was seen from a second. *Unicorn*, who had joined the force after replenishment, was responsible for the operation of CAP, the pilots being transferred by helicopter just before take-off.

Lieutenant Brown and Sub-Lieutenant Haines destroyed a bridge in the Sinmak area early next morning, and later Lieutenant Treloar's flight must have established something of a record when they destroyed three bridges between Sinmak and Haeju in one mission. Lieutenant Commander London made an odd discovery during the forenoon whilst on TARCAP. He called up Sitting Duck and after a few minutes without reply he gave up. Suddenly an American voice came up and said he was Sitting Duck. The fact that he was an American made the Duck shoot suspicious because the air control ship was known to be an English frigate. On receiving no reply to an authentication challenge, the CO realised that a phoney, Chinese or North Korean, Sitting Duck was in operation. He responded again, later in the day, when Lieutenant Commander Roberts' division was on a TARCAP detail. Lieutenant McKeown had to divert to Seoul with a bomb hang-up. There had been a lot of trouble with bomb release gear during this patrol, and consequently there was beginning to be a shortage of bomb carriers. Sub-Lieutenant Haines, on his last — 125th — operational trip had to make an emergency landing on *Unicorn* with a rough running engine due to a connecting rod failure. Lieutenant Hawkesworth's Fireflies obtained a possible direct hit on a gun pit to the north-east of Pungchon during a TARCAP detail. Two Fireflies led by Lieutenant Watkinson carried out an airspot for *Iroquois* in the Haeju area while two others carried out a normal TARCAP in the Pungchon area. It transpired that, though Lieutenant Watkinson's section had spotted for one of the four shoots made, they had only been required to protect *Iroquois*' ground spotters ashore on the peninsula north of Mu-do. On the last event of the day, Lieutenant Commander Roberts' division carried out a strike on an active gun position and its associated supply and personnel shelters in the Ongjin area. Two attacks were made, each pilot selecting his own target from the group, and using half his rockets on each run. Two shelters were destroyed and the gun pit damaged.

There was no flying on the 4th as typhoon Mary moved through the area. *Ocean* took avoiding action by moving north and by evening the Shantung province of China was in sight. Quite heavy seas had been experienced together with heavy rain, but no damage was done to the ship or the aircraft, the latter was a tribute to the lashings and the people responsible for their security. By evening the worst had passed on into Korea, and the ship headed south to the operational area during the night. *Unicorn* was forced to heave-to during the forenoon and early afternoon.

The 5th was the last day of the patrol. Lieutenant Commander London's flight obtained a 50% coverage on a CAS detail for the Commonwealth Division; and on another mission they destroyed a transformer with a 37 mm gun for its defence. Lieutenant McEnery and his flight destroyed two road bridges between Chinnampo and Pyongyang. Jets were seen making their way to and from the Yalu. Lieutenant Davis, accompanied by Lieutenants Brown and Scott and Sub-Lieutenant Ellis, destroyed a large road bridge north of Chinnampo and sank three or four junks progressing down the swollen Taedong Gang. Lieutenants Hallam, Jenne, Jones and Sub-Lieutenant Randall knocked out 6 spans of a 21 span road bridge near Chaeryong. Whilst these strikes were in progress, a number of MiGs flew into the area (Postcard went to air raid warning red). Fortunately the MiGs did not locate the Furies. MiG and Sabre activity was very strong during the afternoon when the Sabres claimed to have shot down 14 MiGs — an all time daily record. A Sabre pilot baled out near Paengyong-do and landed safely in the water. At one time this gentleman had 10 Furies and 4 Fireflies over him as RESCAP — he was picked up by Dumbo, the amphibian. Overall this patrol had been one of the most successful for 802 Squadron. Over 32 bridges had been destroyed, set against very little damage done to the aircraft by ground fire.

Of the Firefly missions, Lieutenant Hawkesworth's division damaged a transformer station and strafed a village, supposedly containing troops, in the Ongjin area. South of Sariwon, Lieutenant Commander Roberts' division attacked a large mound with camouflaged holes and entrenchments, all rockets successfully finding the target. Lieutenant Gandey rocketed two villages of troops and strafed a gun position to the south of Haeju. The standard of rocketry by 825 Squadron on this patrol was of a high order, though they considered that their standard of dive bombing, on the few occasions when bombs were allocated, was poor.

That evening *Sicily*, which had replaced USS *Bataan*, took over from *Ocean* and the two British carriers retired to Sasebo, arriving at 1700 on 5th September. During the harbour period Captain A.F. Black left for the UK on relief as Commander (Air) by Commander O.N. Bailey; Lieutenant Peniston-Bird and Sub-Lieutenant Haines from 802 and Lieutenants Jacob, Kinna, Reynolds and Hubbard from 825 Squadrons left for the UK. Sub-Lieutenant Wailes joined 825 Squadron.

Between 29th September and 4th October the enemy tried to capture the island of Tok Som in the Haeju estuary, attempts easily frustrated by *Condamine*.

During September Admiral Scott-Moncrieff had fallen ill and had hauled down his flag. Captain W.F.H.C. Rutherford in *Newcastle* assumed duty as CTG 95.1, and Captain J.H. Meares, Chief Staff Officer, ran the administration and

Arming a Firefly with a 20mm cannon.   *(FAAM)*

routine operations from *Ladybird*. Admiral Scott-Moncrieff's time was anyway coming to an end and his successor, Rear Admiral E.G.A. Clifford, was already on his way to the Far East. He hoisted his flag in *Newcastle* on 23rd September and in *Ladybird* on the 26th. *Newcastle* had relieved *Belfast* as CTE 95.12 who was returning to the UK. Since July 1950, *Belfast* had steamed more than 80,000 miles, had spent 404 days at sea and had fired more than 8,000 rounds of 6 inch shells.

Eighth Patrol

The weather was excellent throughout *Ocean's* next patrol; 749 sorties were flown in 9 days, an average of 83 per day. No aircraft were lost to enemy action, though several were damaged by flak. MiGs were seen on most days of the patrol but they did not interfere with *Ocean's* aircraft. On 16th September all the rail bridges on the line from Pyongyang to Chinnampo had been destroyed.

Because many of the rail bridges were out of action there were indications that the enemy was using road transport at night, overcoming the lack of road bridges by fording the rivers which were mostly dry at this season. Captain Evans decided to fly some night reconnaissance flights. A number of lorries with head lights burning were detected and immobilised, and first light revealed a number of laden ox-carts on the roads. Thereafter, further attention was paid to this traffic on subsequent patrols.

Ocean sailed from Sasebo at 0645 on 13th September and whilst on passage heard that *Sicily*, her American opposite number, had accounted for a Mig-15 in TARCAP country. Since the danger of enemy air interference was still present, pilots were once again obliged to restrict their activities north of Taedong Gang to periods when USAF Sabres could give them high cover. At the same time TARCAP details were increased to four aircraft from two. Chodo had received a new air raid warning radar set and it was expected that some measure of protection would be afforded to *Ocean's* aircraft from that direction.

For this patrol, 825 Squadron reorganised their Division line up:

31 Div.	Lt. Cdr. Roberts	Lt. Cooper
	Mr. Wigg	Mr. Beynon
	Lt. Gandey	Sub-Lt. Bishop
	Lt. Terry	
32 Div.	Lt. Hawkesworth	Lt. Clancy
	Mr. Brand	Acm. Dunmore
	Lt. Watkinson	Lt. Fursey
	Sub-Lt. Arbuthnot	Acm. Potter
33 Div.	Lt. Williams	Lt. Taylor
	Lt. Heaton	
	Sub-Lt. Hanson	Acm. McCullagh
	Sub-Lt. Wailes	

Operations started on the 14th, and for the Furies, like so many first days of patrol, it was unexciting but gave much information and targets that would receive their attention during the following few days. Lieutenant Commander London led the first detail on a reconnaissance of the rail section between Pyongyang and Chinnampo so that the operations people could shape the programme to account for the road and rail bridges that were still standing. His division in the afternoon destroyed a bridge to the north of Chinnampo. Lieutenant Treloar's flight demolished two bridges during the day in two events — a rail bridge half way up the main line and a road bridge in the same district. Lieutenant McEnery's aircraft was hit by flak while attacking a rail bridge on the Chinnampo to Pyongyang line, a heavy machine-gun bullet going through the starboard inter-spar fuel tank, but because the tank was full it did not catch fire; the damage put the aircraft beyond the ship's facilities to repair. Lieutenant Commander Roberts' Firefly division started the day by damaging three coastal gun positions in the Haeju area, and caused some damage to a 120 mm gun position, a Leopard target, during their afternoon detail. Lieutenant Hawkesworth did a photo-reconnaissance of three water control dams in the Haeju/Han River area. He had long agitated for an attack on these dams which appeared to control the irrigation of three large areas of paddy fields. Lieutenant Williams' division damaged four box-cars in the yards at Chinnampo and later in the day returned to the CO's guns damaged in the first event. Throughout the day Chodo reported considerable MiG activity over the area and returning pilots expressed a high degree of confidence in the new radar set.

Next day Lieutenant Commander London found a large concentration of people at Munhwa, but they were not attacked as they might have been refugees from local towns. Lieutenant Davies' flight sank a sea-going junk after receiving permission from Sitting Duck, and Lieutenant McEnery's sank four sampans in Taedong Gang. Lieutenant Hallam's Fury flight destroyed two rail bridges on the main line. Lieutenant Jenne's aircraft was hit in the wing tank by flak from the same position as Lieutenant McEnery the day before, and returned safely to the ship. Lieutenant Davis' flight destroyed a road bridge in the TARCAP area.

When Lieutenant Commander Roberts was attacking a 120 mm gun in the Taetan area, one of his rocket motors disintegrated some 100 feet ahead of his aircraft, debris and broken parts narrowly missing the aircraft. Lieutenant Hawkesworth's division rocketed vehicle shelters in the area of Ullyul, destroying four. During the following reconnaissance they found the remains of what they took to be a Sabre near Pungsan and alerted Chodo (Postcard) and the ship. Postcard knew nothing of the wreckage and the ship ordered the aircraft to remain in the area, but no sign of life was seen. After some delay it was found that the aircraft had crashed there early in July. Whilst in the area, the division saw two US pilots bale out of unidentified jets over Chodo. Lieutenant Watkinson and Sub-Lieutenant

Arbuthnot circled one of them in his dinghy until Dumbo landed and rescued him. The other was picked up by a helicopter that was waiting for him to land.

Of 56 Fury sorties on the 16th the accent was on search — 30 photo-reconnaissance missions were flown. The CBGLOs were running out of bridge targets and the Communists did not seem to be coping with repairs to them as efficiently as they had in the past. However, two rail bridges on the Chinnampo line were knocked down by Lieutenant Commander London's and Lieutenant Davis' flights. Lieutenant Crosse's aircraft was hit by flak on one of the attacks. Lieutenant Davis, on a TARCAP mission, spotted a shoot for USS *Bradford* against Amgak after the friendly island of Sangchwira-do had been fired on. Lieutenant Williams' Fireflies attacked eight open rail trucks in the Chinnampo yards, causing three secondary explosions and leaving six trucks on fire. Lieutenant Hawkesworth damaged huts and a gun position in the TARCAP area, and on a later event, four barges and a tug in the docks area. This was Lieutenant Fursey's 125th and last Korean sortie.

Photographic reconnaissance on previous patrols had revealed the existence of sluice-gates in three positions at the mouths of rivers in the Haeju and Yonan areas. There were extensive rice fields in the vicinity which was also very near to the enemy's front line. It seemed that the rice might be intended to play an important role in the enemy's menu. It was not known whether the function of the sluice-gates was to retain fresh water to irrigate the fields, or to exclude salt water at high tide, or both, but whatever the object, it would be defeated if the gates were destroyed.

The Fury effort on the 17th was almost entirely devoted to attacking these sluice gates at the period of spring tides. Lieutenants Hawkesworth and Illingworth, the Air Weapons Officer, evolved a scheme whereby the Furies would breach the sluice gates with 30 second delay, 1,000 lb. and 500 lb. bombs. The planned method of attack was to do a 20° dive along the line of the sluice gates, plant the bombs alongside and trust that the hydrodynamic force of the bombs exploding would breach the wall. When this was put into practice about 50% of the bombs skipped and a further 20% hit the wall and broke up. However two of the three dams were breached in the initial attacks and lessons learned from the morning missions were to be put into practice during the afternoon. Lieutenant Commander London and Lieutenant Hallam led two successful attacks during the morning and it was observed that fresh water was flowing into the sea. In the afternoon Lieutenant Davis led his flight against the unbreached sluice gates in normal dive bombing attacks, breaching the gates. Lieutenants Crosley and McEnery led their flights to plant 12 hour delay bombs around the dams to discourage any attempts to repair them at low water. *St. Brides Bay* was in the vicinity when one bomb exploded within 6 minutes of the delay set on the fuse. In this operation 802 Squadron was entirely successful, though doubts were expressed as to the exact damage that had been done to the rice crops as in all cases water appeared to be flowing seawards. The Fireflies followed up the Fury attacks with photo-reconnaissance sorties.

Sub-Lieutenant Brian Randall gives a good description of the attack on the sluice gates by Lieutenant Hallam's flight. He was flying No. 4, to Lieutenant Jenne No. 3 leading the second section, Lieutenant Jones was Hallam's No. 2:

> 'Since the attack required a low, straight-and-level pass it was decided to minimise the risk by attacking in pairs. This meant that each section leader would position the attack, the wingmen would formate on them, and the section leader would count down for the release.
>
> 'I formated on Chris Jenne. He counted "5-4-3-2-1-now" and I released my [500 lb.] bomb.
>
> 'We passed over the dam, and to my horror I saw my bomb spinning slowly as it bounced into the air, came up over my wing and fell down behind (the 30 second fuse ticking away all the time).
>
> 'Chris had positioned himself perfectly to get his bomb as close as possible, but I was on the dam side from him so my bomb hit the top of the dam and came up again. When it exploded it cut the road at the side of the dam so it was not a total waste, but I was distinctly horrified at the thought of how nearly I did myself down with my own bomb. A shorter delay would have been disastrous.'

During the day three Firefly details were warned from Postcard of approaching MiGs in their areas. Lieutenant Commander Roberts' division had been investigating a gun position north of Chodo and left at low level; and Lieutenant Hawkesworth's had rocketed a transformer station and were already well south of Chodo on their way back to the ship when the enemy aircraft were reported north of Pyongyang. Lieutenant Williams' division had attacked a gun position that had been firing at Chodo and had damaged the gun pit. Postcard gave a warning that bandits were 40 miles north-north-east of Chodo; the

Arming a Sea Fury with a 20mm cannon.   *(Kellaway)*

bandits closed to 20 miles and the division dropped to sea level; three silver jet bandits were seen over Chodo, and as the AA guns opened fire the division departed south to the ship. Lieutenant Mather joined 802 Squadron from Iwakuni.

Next day Lieutenant Davis' Furies destroyed two bridges near Changyon whilst on a TARCAP mission; Lieutenant Crosley and his flight damaged one at Hanchon. During this mission Lieutenants Adkin and Clark were hit by AA fire. Lieutenant McEnery's flight on a CAS detail dropped their bombs in an area known to contain Chinese troops and stores, obtaining 759 coverage. Lieutenant Hawkesworth's division carried out further photo-reconnaissance of the previous day's sluice gates. The attacks had been very successful, many fields that were normally covered in water were seen to be drained at low tide. Other attacks were made on a Leopard target of bunkers; on a small factory south of Sinmak; and on a 150 mm coastal gun position. 825 Squadron set a record for both squadrons during their time in *Ocean* in achieving an average deck landing interval of 22.7 seconds.

The 19th was replenishment of FFO and AVGAS from *Wave Chief*. Sub-Lieutenant Simmonds joined 802 Squadron from Iwakuni by CODS Avenger. During the forenoon the aircrew heard a lecture from Colonel Descent, an Intelligence Officer from EUSAK, on Escape and Evasion.

MiGs were much in evidence next day and the reported tracks from Chodo kept several sorties away from their targets. Sampans and box-cars at Chinnampo were attacked and damaged by Furies; road bridges at Sinmak and Sinwon-ni were destroyed; and trucks, ox-carts and sampans in the environs of Chinnampo were strafed, provoking a splendid array of flak which did no damage to any aircraft. On returning from Chinnampo, Lieutenant Crosley was surprised, when over Chodo, to see flak bursting near him. On complaining to the radio station he was informed that the flak was a form of air raid warning for the outlying ships and posts. Lieutenant Commander Roberts' Firefly division was briefed to give CAS to a guerrilla landing in the area east of Haeju. He reported at 0615 to Abuse-4 *(St. Bride's Bay)*, who was controlling the landing, and was told the beaches were clear of friendlies. They investigated two suspected gun positions, during which the CO was fired on by an automatic AA weapon, and the division rocketed a gun emplacement, scoring a number of direct hits. On the next event Lieutenant Hawkesworth's division reported in to Abuse-4, and were told there was no further need for aircraft since the withdrawal of the guerrilla forces had been completed before the CO's division had arrived. The ship asked them to investigate another gun position which was attacked with 16 rockets. Two gun positions in the TARCAP area were attacked by Lieutenant Williams' division, eight direct hits were observed on the first but no results were seen on the second.

On the 21st Lieutenant Hallam's Fury division broke two spans of a main road bridge in the Han River area. Lieutenant Treloar got a bridge in Sinmak and the rest of the flight attacked and severely damaged a road bridge. A lot of flak was seen, most in the area of Sinmak where pointed flak followed Lieutenant Treloar for some distance at 4,000-5,000 feet. Further bursts of 40 mm were encountered over Hanchon, a well known black spot, and Lieutenant McEnery's aircraft was damaged whilst strafing ox-carts to the west of Chinnampo. Lieutenant Commander Roberts' Fireflies struck a transformer station in the Sinwon area, making two attacks with most of the rockets falling in the target area. A low run after the strike showed that the target appeared to have been completely derelict before the attack. Lieutenant Hawkesworth also attacked a transformer station at Chinnampo. A gun position in the southern Haeju area was attacked for the third time and was considered destroyed. 825 Squadron broke its deck landing interval record, set up only three days earlier, by reducing it to 21.6 seconds. Lieutenant Hawkesworth's division reduced the division interval from 20.7 to 20 seconds. The Furies best day's average interval was 23.8 seconds and their best division interval 18.6 seconds.

The 22nd was a bad day for 802's maintenance teams. Lieutenant McEnery severely damaged a Fury when he had a full-toss barrier. Lieutenant Graham brought his aircraft back with sufficient flak damage to warrant a write-off, and Lieutenant Commander London did the same thing after an encounter with a battery of 20 mm machine-guns defending the rail yards north-west of the Sillyong-myon peninsula. More flak was encountered between Kyomipo and the main supply route to the east when Lieutenant Treloar's division destroyed one of many small and tricky bridges on the main road. Three road bridges were knocked down in the southern part of the TARCAP area and one near Haeju. The Fireflies attacked a Leopard gun position in a tunnel entrance on the mainland opposite Chodo. A village and stores were attacked in the Changyon area. The last event of the day was a full squadron attack on the tunnel entrance and troop positions seen earlier in the day. As there was no wind the second attack had to fire their rockets into smoke left from the first marking run. The damage could not be assessed and the aircraft had to return to the ship before the smoke had dispersed.

On the last day of the patrol Lieutenant Commander London inaugurated a new 'service' when his flight was launched at 0515, 45 minutes before first light. On reaching the enemy coast the flight split into two sections. One ranged over the area north of Taedong Gang while the other concentrated on the southern part of the province. Near Pyongyang a truck with headlights on was seen, was strafed and set burning; two further vehicles were seen and successfully attacked. In the south one lorry was destroyed in Sinchon and a large number of ox-carts were seen in ones and twos but were not attacked as Lieutenant McKeown wanted to preserve his ammunition in case he saw better targets. Although results were not as good as had been hoped, the operation was a success and provided invaluable information and data for planning similar sorties in the future. The squadron continued its successes against bridges. Lieutenant Hallam and his flight destroyed two east of Kyomipo; and on the same event Lieutenant Davis and his flight finally destroyed a much-attacked one in Hanchon and provoked considerable flak in doing so. Lieutenant Treloar destroyed an unusual underwater bridge near Haeju. Most of the Firefly events were TARCAP, with limited results. One difficulty occurred as a result of local call signs (except Sitting Duck) having been changed — the division failed to contact Dutchboy that had been Postcard (Chodo). A division was sent to strike a village where 250 North Korean anti-guerrilla troops had been reported. When they got there they found no signs of troops and the village had been recently bombed and napalmed. Sitting Duck asked another division to investigate two gun positions, they were then told to 'skip it' and were given a fresh target of a command post which received half the division's rockets. After the attack Sitting Duck told the aircraft to leave the area, no reason being given. Lieutenant Hawkesworth's division had more success when they were briefed for a strike on a transformer station east of Haeju. Low cloud hampered the first attack, but after a suitable interval a second attack was made when eight rockets hit the main building.

At the end of the day's flying *Ocean*, with *Piet Hein* in company, set course for Kure, arriving at 0800 on 25th. *Ocean* secured to a buoy until 1600 while fuelling from *Green Ranger*, after which she secured alongside the usual jetty. Aircraft were exchanged with *Unicorn* and five pilots joined 825 Squadron, four of them were from 821 Squadron who were joining for experience in the operational area before re-joining *Glory* in Hong Kong in November — Lieutenants Skinner and Sherlock, Sub-Lieutenant Millet and Mr. Kent — and Lieutenant Robbins who joined from UK.

There had been a recurrence of mining in the Cigarette route where HMCS *Nootka*, (Commander Richard M. Steele RCN), had the signal honour of capturing a North Korean minelayer, the only enemy ship captured at sea during the war, in the act of laying mines in the north part of the channel. On 28th September *Nootka* was south-east of Chodo island on patrol 'Blackburn', when at 0223, radar detected an unidentified vessel on a northerly course inshore near Chingangpo. When off the headland to the north of this, the vessel turned and set course for the south-east tip of Chodo.

When the unidentified vessel reached the swept channel, it changed its heading towards the customary anchorage for 'Blackburn' patrol destroyers. Commander Steele decided to close the suspicious craft, and turned *Nootka* to give chase, when the blip on the screen immediately showed a new course, toward the mainland. Direct chase would take *Nootka* over the area recently traversed and possibly mined by this craft, and as this seemed unwise to Steele, he set *Nootka* on a course to pass to the south and round up to intercept, while the enemy vessel reached the protection of waters too shallow for the destroyer.

After three-quarters of an hour, *Nootka* established contact a second time well up the Namchon River, whereupon Steele moved her quietly and slowly round the end of the suspect area and closed the coast to seek any deeper darkness that the loom of land might offer, and thus prevent, as long as possible, the enemy vessel's seeing her. When the enemy vessel was well out in the route 'Cigarette' in a position Steele thought was the furthest she would venture, *Nootka* closed at over 30 knots and succeeded in cutting off a good-sized vessel which was frantically attempting to reach the land. The crew took to the boats when *Nootka* was half a cable away and jettisoned what looked like floating mines, so *Nootka* put several Bofors shells into the waterline. The boarding party reported the vessel to be deserted. She was secured with lines and towed to the west, clear of the mined area, for examination in daylight.

The crew of two Lieutenants and three Chief Petty Officers of the North Korean Navy was picked up at daylight. They were expecting to be tortured, but after being given hot baths, coffee and hot food they became very talkative and stated that four mines had been laid in the south part on 19th/20th September. Altogether, the minelayer yielded a considerable amount of information about this and other minefields.

Cigarette was then declared dangerous until the mines had been swept.

On 9th October the First Sea Lord, Admiral Sir Rhoderic McGrigor, accompanied by Admiral Sir Guy Russell, arrived in Japan for a 10-day visit. He called on General Mark Clark, Vice Admiral Briscoe and Mr. Yoshida, Prime Minister of Japan. He flew to Iwakuni where he met Admiral Clifford and then took passage to Kure in *Cossack*, where he stayed with Lieutenant General W. Bridgeford, Australian Army, CinC British Commonwealth Forces in Korea, while he visited all ships and naval and military establishments in the Kure area on the 11th. On the 12th he flew with Admiral Clifford from Iwakuni to Seoul in a Dakota kindly put at his disposal by Admiral Briscoe. At Seoul he met Major General Alston-Roberts-West and visited the British Commonwealth Division area, and had discussions with General Van Fleet and General Barcus, commanding 5th US Air Force. In the evening he joined *Birmingham* at Inchon and proceeded to sea to rendezvous with the carrier force next morning, the 13th, when Admiral McGrigor and Admiral Clifford transferred to *Ocean* and watched flying for three hours, before returning to *Birmingham*. In the afternoon she anchored off Paengyong-do, whence the First Sea Lord visited *Newcastle* and *Hawea*, and met the Island Defence Element Commander, Colonel Wilbur USMC, before returning to Inchon.

On 14th October Admiral McGrigor flew from Kimpo to *Bonne Homme Richard* off the east coast where he lunched with Rear Admiral Hickey USN,

Commander Carrier Division, and Vice Admiral Clark, Commander 7th Fleet, and witnessed air operations. Admiral McGrigor rejoined *Birmingham* at Inchon that evening and sailed for Chodo, where she arrived next morning. At anchor were *Newcastle*, *Mounts Bay*, *Charity*, *Constance*, *Piet Hein*, and USSs *Yarnall* and *Mataco*. Visits to all these ships had been planned, but had to be abandoned owing to very rough weather. In the afternoon all the ships bombarded known enemy positions, watched by the First Sea Lord. *Birmingham* sailed for the Haeju area, anchoring off Yong Pyong-do in the morning of the 16th. Admiral McGrigor visited *St. Bride's Bay*, *Morecambe Bay*, USS *Competent* and three RoK patrol vessels operating under the orders of *St. Bride's Bay*, and he met the island commander and some guerrilla leaders. *Birmingham* arrived in Sasebo at 0900 on 17th October where Admiral McGrigor met Rear Admiral Ginrich and Rear Admiral Biggs, Commander Service Squadron 3, and later visited British Commonwealth ships in harbour and naval establishments in the Sasebo area.

Birmingham relieved *Newcastle* as CTE 95.12 on 21st October and Admiral Clifford left Sasebo in *Newcastle* for Yokosuka. He visited Tokyo where he met HBM Ambassador, Sir Ester Denning, General Mark Clark, Admiral Briscoe and Commonwealth representatives in Japan.

Throughout the last quarter of 1952, though there was heavy and bitter fighting on shore along the whole front with little change of position, there was little enemy activity on the west coast. Chodo was bombed by three or four single engined enemy aircraft on the night of 12th/13th October. Fifteen small bombs fell near the radar station, which was undamaged, but four Koreans were killed and three Americans wounded.

Ninth Patrol

Ocean, *Nootka*, *Anzac* and USS *Vammen* were on patrol from 3rd to 13th October. The weather was good but strong winds delayed the start of flying on the 11th. No aircraft were lost to enemy action though a number were damaged by flak. MiGs were in the area but no attempt was made to interfere with *Ocean's* operations. The total number of sorties flown was 746, a daily average of 85.

The Unit sailed from Kure on 2nd October at 1330. 825 Squadron reorganised their division line-up to absorb the new pilots:

31 Div.	Lt. Cdr. Roberts	Lt. Cooper
	Mr. Wigg	
	Lt. Gandey	Sub-Lt. Bishop
	Sub-Lt. Millett	
32 Div.	Lt. Hawkesworth	Lt. Clancy
	Lt. Skinner	
	Mr. Brand	Acmn. Dunmore
	Mr. Kent	
33 Div.	Lt. Williams	Lt. Taylor
	Lt. Heaton	
	Sub-Lt. Hanson	Acmn. McCullagh
	Sub-Lt. Wailes	
34 Div.	Lt. Watkinson	Mr. Beynon
	Sub-Lt. Arbuthnot	Acmn. Potter
	Lt. Terry	
	Lt. Sherlock	
Spare Pilot Lt. Robbins		

After their first reconnaissance mission over the area on the 4th, Lieutenant Commander London's flight reported that two rail bridges had been repaired and that there was evidence that the Hanchon to Chinnampo road, parallel to the coast, was being used. So far as targets were concerned, it was going to be a difficult patrol for the CBGLOs, few major bridges were intact and there was going to have to be a switch to other targets such as small road crossings and factories, and CAS over the front line. Lieutenant McEnery's Furies destroyed a road bridge near Ullyul and Lieutenants Crosley and Brown with Sub-Lieutenant Mallace attacked rail bridges in the vicinity of Chinnampo, collapsing one and distorting one. MiGs were reported on three occasions in the Pyongyang and Chodo areas by the Fireflies. Lieutenant Watkinson, with his new division, attacked two gun positions in the TARCAP area, obtaining direct hits on both. Lieutenant Williams' division carried out a photo-reconnaissance of the Haeju area, checking on bridges, dams and transformer states.

Lieutenant McEnery and his Fury flight damaged a road bridge on an early TARCAP detail next morning; Lieutenant Treloar's flight damaged a bridge near Chaeryong; Lieutenant Commander London severely damaged factory buildings near Hanchon and Lieutenant Crosley hit stores, trucks and rails in the railyard at Ongjong-ni. The first, early morning, Firefly TARCAP detail led by Lieutenant Hawkesworth carried out a reconnaissance of the roads from Pungchon to

Changyon but nothing was seen due to mist in the valleys and long shadows. Lieutenant Williams spotted a bombardment for *Condamine* (Abuse-4) in the Haeju area. After some time spent correcting the fall of shot, four houses were damaged and the road was cut in a village south of Ongjin. On his first TARCAP detail, Lieutenant Hawkesworth had a hydraulic leak in his aircraft that he at first thought to be coolant, so he detached to the coast while the remainder of the division attacked two gun positions near Sariwon, but with no spectacular results. On a later event they struck at the village of Songju-dong to the south of Changyon, destroying four out of six houses.

On the 6th Lieutenant McKeown led a pre-dawn reconnaissance. They found a lorry and an ox-cart in the south of the area and then, going north, they stopped and badly damaged a train near Pyongyang by accurate strafing. Sub-Lieutenant Cook's aircraft was hit in the wing and fuselage by machine gun fire. Four bridges and a viaduct were damaged during the day's operations, and a CAS mission damaged a group of 75 mm guns facing the Commonwealth troops. Whilst returning from Sinmak Lieutenant Treloar saw a frantic battle between MiGs and Sabres over Haeju — surprisingly far south for such an encounter.

During the day, due to damage and other unserviceability, 825 Squadron ran short of aircraft but they managed to fulfil nearly all their tasks. On one photo-reconnaissance detail by Lieutenant Watkinson's division, Lieutenant Sherlock failed to take off and Lieutenant Terry was forced to return with a rough running engine. Whilst making a photographic run at 4,000 feet, Watkinson's aircraft was hit by a 20 mm shell that entered through the starboard wheel-bay and smashed the flap operating jack before emerging through the starboard wing fillet. The two aircraft had encountered an unusual amount of small arms fire, but Sub-Lieutenant Arbuthnot returned to the ship while Watkinson diverted to Seoul. Lieutenant Hawkesworth's division carried out a strike in the Han River area on a hill with trenches and light gun positions round the top, causing some damage, and they then went to Seoul to pick up two passengers. Mr Brand's aircraft had an oil and hydraulic leak, and Lieutenant Skinner was unfortunate in that he damaged the tail oleo on landing. By late afternoon there were then three unserviceable aircraft at Seoul. On the next event Lieutenant Heaton's aircraft received a hole in the leading edge from a rocket during an attack on wharves at Chinnampo. He retired to Chodo with Sub-Lieutenant Wailes to wait while Lieutenant Williams and Sub-Lieutenant Hanson made a further search for troops in the TARCAP area, all four aircraft then returning to the ship. One of the unserviceable aircraft that had spent much of the day at Seoul returned to the ship with the last land-on.

Fog in the low lying areas of Anak and Chinnampo, which later lifted to low stratus cloud, hampered the early morning strike and reconnaissance details on the 7th. Lieutenant Crosley obtained 50% coverage on two gun positions during a CAS mission. Lieutenant Brown's flight attacked a bridge south of Sinwon-ni which was destroyed by Lieutenant Mather. They met intense, but luckily inaccurate, medium flak east of Chaeryong. Lieutenant Commander London's flight knocked down two road bridges on the Ongjin peninsula, and Lieutenant Treloar's two rail bridges in the Sinmak area. Lieutenant Williams' Firefly division on TARCAP attacked a Leopard target, a village said to contain troops, hitting and seriously damaging ten houses. Dutch-Boy (Chodo) reported three unidentified jets high over the island; the division saw three swept-wing aircraft at 30,000 feet and retired south. On the next event, Lieutenant Watkinson's division, reduced to three as a result of Lieutenant Sherlock's aircraft pouring petrol on starting, attacked the village of Sochon-ri, near Yonan, reported as the home of 350 Chinese troops. Two houses were destroyed and three damaged, but a lack of movement in the village indicated that the troops were not at home. Lieutenant Commander Roberts' division launched a strike in the south of the TARCAP area on five newly camouflaged buildings set into the side of a culvert. In five separate attacks, to make sure that as many buildings as possible were destroyed, three were completely demolished and one was set on fire. On the next TARCAP detail, Lieutenant Hawkesworth was asked by Sitting Duck to investigate some twenty troops in a position that could not be reached by the ship's guns. The aircraft found troops cowering in water just off the beach who appeared to be trying to out-flank some friendly troops further down the beach. The division claimed to have killed or wounded all the enemy.

Strong winds next day, and targets selected from a series of very small bridges, resulted in an unsuccessful day's bridge-busting. Lieutenant Treloar's flight, however, did hit a road bridge at Sinwon, breaking the centre span and killing four bridge builders carrying planks; and Lieutenant Hallam's flight knocked down another bridge at Sinmak. Sitting Duck asked Lieutenant Commander Roberts to investigate a gun position opposite Sokto and three rectangular slits covered with canvas opposite Chodo. Both sites were rocketed, but damage was difficult to assess. 600 Chinese troops were reported by Wolfpack to be living in bomb shelters in bushes near Ongjin. No shelters were seen but rockets were put into a bush-covered area and into bunkers by Lieutenant Williams' division. Lieutenant Commander Roberts' division demolished the last two of the five camouflaged buildings he had attacked the previous day.

After replenishment of FFO and AVGAS on the 9th from *Wave Sovereign*, Lieutenant Commander London led an early pre-dawn Fury detail next morning, but it was too dark at first over the target area to see anything. However, when the light improved, three lorries were attacked near Chinnampo, one blew up and another was forced off the road. On the next detail, Lieutenant McEnery set it on fire after his flight had bombed a mine storage area south of Taedong Gang, opposite Chinnampo. Lieutenant Davis' flight, armed with 1,000 lb. bombs, was RATOGed off to attack one of the sluice gates breached on the previous patrol but which was now in a reasonable state of repair. Using a 45° dive, 50 to 100 feet of gate crumbled and water gushed seawards. This day with light winds was almost a record for the number of bridge kills. Lieutenant Hallam's flight put a bridge north-east of Ullyul out of action; Lieutenant Davis' hit and destroyed a rail bridge south of Sinmak; Lieutenant Crosley's destroyed a road bridge, in the face of much flak, east of Chaeryong; Lieutenant Commander London claimed two road bridges near Changyon, and Davis returned to Chaeryong to collapse two more. Lieutenant McEnery, in his anti-truck war, destroyed another three and sank four sampans in the Chinnampo waterways. Sub-Lieutenant Simmonds had to divert to Seoul with a rough running engine, and Sub-Lieutenant Carter damaged two aircraft in a taxying accident on the flight deck. Lieutenant Hawkesworth's Firefly TARCAP detail hit six houses in a village south of Changyon. Lieutenant Williams' division encountered an unusual amount of flak from AA guns, bursting up to 3,500 feet, and from machine-guns during their strike on a camouflaged, covered-in position in a trenched area to the north of Chaeryong. All rockets fell in the target area and black smoke poured out from the target. During the afternoon, Lieutenant Hawkesworth photographed the sluice gates attacked by Davis in the forenoon.

Rough seas and low cloud prevented flying until 1030 next morning, and for the rest of the day deck-landing conditions were not good due to turbulence and high winds, but there were no accidents. Lieutenant Treloar broke a bridge near Anak and killed a number of people working nearby, while Lieutenant McEnery destroyed a bridge west of Pyongyang. Lieutenant Brown had a bullet through the hydraulic system and made a wheels-up, hook-down landing at Suwon. Sub-Lieutenant Ellis had earlier landed at Suwon with a bomb hang-up and could not restart his engine. Both pilots remained ashore overnight. Sub-Lieutenant Simmonds returned from Seoul during the day. A Firefly TARCAP division, led by Sub-Lieutenant Hanson, attacked and severely damaged a house surrounded by trenches, believed to be a communications centre. Lieutenant Watkinson's division attacked a transformer station on the Chinnampo waterfront.

On the 12th another pre-dawn strike of eight Furies led by Lieutenants Hallam and Treloar roamed the area, attacking 11 trucks of which two blew up. Lieutenant McEnery later in the day found another two outside Sinchon that also blew up and six to the west of Pyongyang of which three caught fire. Lieutenant Commander London found two more and destroyed them, as well as destroying a bridge near Ongjin. On a later event Lieutenant Hallam knocked down a road bridge to the south-east of Ullyul. Lieutenant Watkinson's Firefly division attacked a motor transport depot at Chinnampo, destroying one building in a large red explosion with black and brown smoke. Lieutenant Hawkesworth attacked and destroyed a communication centre reported by Leopard. On a later detail, he was armed with four 4.5 inch reconnaissance flares on a light series bomb carrier. They were dropped from a low height onto a village, another Leopard target, and it proved to be a most effective attack, one house was completely gutted and a haystack was left burning.

During the forenoon of the last day of the patrol, the First Sea Lord Admiral Sir Rhoderick McGrigor with Rear Admiral Clifford, visited *Ocean*. The two Admirals transferred by jackstay from *Birmingham* at 0845 and left by helicopter at 1145. Whilst on board, they witnessed two launches and recoveries, and visited the Operations Room, the ADR and other compartments. The Furies attacked three road bridges during the day: Lieutenant Treloar's flight one east of Haeju; Lieutenant Davis' one at Sinwon-ni and Lieutenant Commander London's one west of Chaeryong, where he was accompanied by Lieutenant Crosley's for flak suppression. Other targets attacked were sampans, lorries, buildings, stores and a small transformer sub-station. Lieutenant Jenne made a wheels-down landing at Paengyong-do after engine trouble, and recovered the gunsight, the bomb carriers, the instrument panel and the compass from the stricken aircraft. Lieutenant Williams' Firefly division investigated troop concentrations to the south of Ongjin reported by Leopard to be threatening the friendly island of Sunmi-do. After a strafing attack a large number of people ran out into a nearby paddy field, and the aircraft then fired 16 rockets into a village near the reported position, destroying four houses and damaging three. The remaining 16 rockets were fired into a nearby village, destroying another three houses. Lieutenant Commander Roberts' division on a TARCAP detail were warned by Sitting Duck of bandits over the mouth of the Chongchon River. Shortly afterwards they were reported to be heading for Chodo, after which they retired to the north. The Fireflies then attacked two caves in the cliff face on the mainland between Chodo and Sok-to, reported to contain coastal guns. After the attack the results were photographed with a hand held K.20 camera and it was noticed that one cave no longer appeared to exist while the entrance to the other had been reduced in size.

During this patrol enemy air activity had increased. MiGs from airfields just over the Manchurian border were ground controlled and it seemed they were scrambled as soon as any of *Ocean's* aircraft crossed the line of the Taedong Gang, reaching the area in 15-20 minutes. It was a common occurrence for the MiGs to sweep down to Haeju and around the coast back to the Yalu. More and more often they appeared to harry the Sabres of 5th USAF all the way back to Seoul after the Sabres had been on fighter sweeps up to or past the Chongchon River.

Ocean, *Anzac* and *Piet Hein* left the operational area for Sasebo, arriving at 1730 on the 14th and straightway embarking AVGS from *Green Ranger*. During the week an RPC was given to the masters and officers of the RFAs *Wave Sovereign*, *Fort Langley* and *Green Ranger*.

On the 13th CinCFES, Vice Admiral Sir Guy Russell visited *Ocean*; Admiral

McGrigor, accompanied by Rear Admiral Clifford, inspected divisions on the Flight Deck on the 15th; and on 21st Rear Admiral J.E. Ginrich USN, CTE 95, also inspected divisions.

The arrival of the USN CVLs *Badoeng Strait* and *Sicily* on the 18th gave rise to an attractive social exchange of visits and farewells, culminating in a first class cocktail party given for 802 and 825 Squadrons by the USMC Squadron VMA 312 in the Navy Officers' Club in the dockyard on the final evening in harbour, 22nd October.

Tenth Patrol

Ocean sailed from Sasebo for her tenth patrol in company with *Charity*, *Iroquois* and USS *Swenson* at 0700 on 23rd October. The weather was not so good, but 493 sorties were flown in six flying days, a daily average of 82.

During *Ocean's* absence there had been no US carrier operating in the area, so there had been only a small amount of air activity by day over land. The first four bridge reconnaissance details on the 24th were led by Lieutenant Commander London and by Lieutenants Treloar, Crosley and Davis who all returned with the same reports, that most of the bridges had been rebuilt and were protected by flak. For some reason — supposedly because of harvest activity — the enemy had started to repair his roads and bridges in a manner that had hitherto been confined to certain selected, indispensable lines of communications. Bridges that had been down for the previous twelve months had been repaired, and there was evidence that they were in use — impressions that had been gained from all the Squadron's favourite areas: TARCAP, Hanchon, Chaeryong and Sinmak. Flak was observed from Hanchon, from the 'Soho' (Chaeryong) bridges and from an innocent looking area in the heart of the Sinmak district. Lieutenant Commander London hit a road bridge near Ullyul and Lieutenant Davis claimed another spanning a steep gully in the Ongjin peninsula. Lieutenant McEnery attacked two 76 mm guns during a CAS detail, and on his way back to the ship he found two lorries (in the McEnery fashion of following wheel marks), setting them on fire. Lieutenant Jenne brought in a replacement aircraft from Iwakuni. Lieutenant Williams' Firefly division attacked piles of stores on the waterfront at Chinnampo. Although all the rockets fell in the target area, no fires or secondary explosions were caused, the stores were probably rice. Sitting Duck asked them to investigate an area near Pungsan for vehicles and sampans; two sampans were strafed but no vehicles were seen. Lieutenant Watkinson also sank two sampans loaded with stores and damaged five others that were beached.

The Fury pilots were hampered next morning by an opaque covering of salt and exhaust smoke on their screens caused by strong, cold, spray-carrying winds. Lieutenant Commander London's flight, together with Lieutenant Brown leading Lieutenant Davis', searched for lorries throughout the area; they found two, and also four ox-carts. Lieutenant McEnery continued his truck-hunting, destroying ten in two events. High winds during the day made bombing difficult, but two bridges were hit in the Sinmak area, one by Lieutenant Crosley's flight and the second being destroyed by Lieutenant Hallam's. Lieutenant Hawkesworth's Firefly division were asked by Sitting Duck to reconnoitre round Chodo as she was minesweeping in the area, but nothing was seen. Bandits, reported by Dutch Boy (Chodo) to be north-west of Pyongyang, approached to within 30 miles of Chodo before returning north. On a second detail later in the day the division blew up a factory in Chinnampo. Lieutenant Commander Roberts led a strike to the Haeju area on a small group of revetted huts in a culvert, of which one was destroyed, another damaged and a third set on fire. About 200 people had been seen running into pits from the huts as they were attacked, but none was claimed killed. The aircraft were fired on by 20 mm type guns from a village about half a mile from the target, Mr. Wigg's aircraft being hit in the port nacelle tank, but no serious damage was done. Lieutenant Watkinson's division returned to this group of huts later in the day and destroyed or damaged five of those remaining; no troops were seen but a group of five 20 mm guns fired on them from the village.

Next morning Lieutenant Crosley's flight of Furies found two large barges in a bend of the river near the town of Kyomipo which were strafed and brewed up; one sampan of a group of three was sunk further downstream. After a photo-reconnaissance flight of Chaeryong and the Han River, Lieutenant Davis' flight was heavily fired on, when over Sinmak, from open ground; since there were no known important targets in the vicinity it was thought to be an area where Chinese troops took occasional periods of rest. Lieutenant Treloar knocked down the spans of two road bridges over the Han River, Lieutenant McEnery knocked down two bridges in the TARCAP area, and Lieutenant Commander London knocked down a fifth near Haeju. Lieutenant Mather made a forced landing at Paengyong-do after engine trouble. Sitting Duck requested Lieutenant Commander Roberts' division to spot a shoot for Abuse (*Birmingham*) on two coastal villages to the south of Chodo. The range was 27,000 yards, and after only four corrections the spotter was able to call for 'Fire for effect'. When the smoke had cleared eight houses were seen to have been destroyed. The aircrew considered the shoot to have been excellent, the best they had seen since the start of operations in May. Lieutenant Hawkesworth's division attacked a transformer station near Haeju, causing heavy damage.

The 27th was a day of many surprises for 802 Squadron. On the first event of the morning, Lieutenants McEnery and Crosley were on a lorry hunt. Lieutenant Mather was following his section leader, Lieutenant Adkin, along the Hanchon 'coastal' road (6-10 miles inland) in an area where there were many enemy troops, when suddenly a stream of tracers shot past his aircraft and he reported being hit. In Mather's own words:

This trip was unfortunately cut short by rifle bullets in my main fuel line. I tried to glide out to sea to avoid the possibility of capture, but unfortunately I had insufficient height for this, and I made a good forced landing in some rice paddy fields. Due to inaccurate map references being reported on my position, I had to wait about an hour before I was picked up.

As briefed, I stayed by my aircraft as being the best place to be seen from the air; I had a strong RESCAP of Sea Furies [Lieutenant Davis and his flight], Fireflies [10 aircraft from *Ocean* and [2] USMC Corsairs which were very valuable as some guerrilla [enemy] troops were heading my way about a quarter of a mile off. Between them they had a splendid battle and I had a grandstand view. Finally two choppers and a Grumman Goose amphibian came. The chopper [piloted by Lieutenant Christy USN], a Whirlwind type, lowered it's rescue strop and I climbed in it well inside the regulation five seconds. I dangled in the strop till we got out to sea, and then I was hauled into the cabin and off we went to the island of Chodo, where I had a breakfast of scotch and cereal. (I might mention that the price normally paid for the rescue of one of our pilots was a half-crate of scotch to the rescuing aircrew).

The Fury was destroyed by Davis' flight in an approximate position 15 miles north of the Taedong Gang estuary. Very shortly after this incident Sub-Lieutenant Randall force-landed on the beach at Paengyong-do with a rough running engine. In the early afternoon, Lieutenants McEnery and Treloar attacked the 'Soho' rail and road bridges east of Chaeryong. These bridges were heavily flak-defended, and McEnery's aircraft was hit and sufficiently damaged to make it a write-off, but two bridges were knocked down in this strike. Lieutenant Commander London attacked and damaged the remaining bridge in this collection. Lieutenant Treloar later destroyed two road bridges near Anak. The first Firefly TARCAP was reconnoitring the railway from Chinnampo to Ongjin airfield when they turned north to join the RESCAP over Lieutenant Mather, but were ordered to remain on TARCAP. A division led by Mr. Wigg attacked a village containing motor transport shelters in the Haeju area, destroying three houses and six huts. Two TARCAP details led by Lieutenant Williams and Lieutenant Commander Roberts covered *Nootka*, a minesweeper and a tug sweeping mines near the enemy coast. The CO's division attacked one gun position on a ridge with half their rockets, doing little damage, and caused some damage to a second coastal gun with the remaining rockets.

After replenishment for the last time from *Wave Chief* on the 28th, the first two events next day were CAS for a Leopard attack on the mainland opposite Paengyong-do near Cheiang-ni to the west of Ongjin by both Fireflies and Furies. Lieutenant Williams' division of Fireflies was on station at 0700 and reported to

Jackstone (*Iroquois*), the controlling ship. He was told to carry out a reconnaissance 5 miles east of the bomb line, to look for enemy movement and possible reinforcements. At 0730 the aircraft were told to investigate some troops on a ridge; the troops were seen, Jackstone ordered the aircraft to attack them, but before the attack commenced the order was countermanded. The aircraft were then ordered to attack troops on the beach to the north of the friendly landing junks; at the last moment they were ordered to stop because the troops were friendly. The division was finally ordered to attack the village of Yongsu-dong, which it did with all its rockets landing in the village. At 0810 Lieutenant Hawkesworth's division reported to Jackstone and were told to orbit the ship. At 0820 the ship gave the division the position of troops on the beach, and told them not to attack south of that map reference because of the presence of friendly guerrillas. After three low runs over the beach only one man was seen; and at 0825 the division was ordered to orbit the ship which had withdrawn to 8,500 yards from the landing beach. At 0847 the division made a low reconnaissance over the beach. Jackstone then reported that all friendlies had withdrawn to a small island just offshore and that the aircraft could attack anything on the mainland. Two groups of troops were found that were rocketed and strafed.

In the afternoon Lieutenant Williams led an armed reconnaissance strike on railyards at Sinchon. The attack was made through a hole in the cloud layer at 25 box-cars in the sidings, but although all the rockets fell in the target area, due to the dispersion of the cars only six were hit. 'Dam Buster' flights of Furies led by Lieutenants Hallam and Davis were airborne again when they attacked the sluice gates in the Yonan peninsula with 1,000 lb. bombs creating new breaches. Lieutenant Williams had led a photo-reconnaissance mission four days earlier that showed they had recently been repaired. Lieutenant Crosley's flight hit a railway bridge on the Chinnampo to Pyongyang railway line, but it was too tough for 500 lb. bombs to break, it only twisted. Lieutenant Davis caught a train in a tunnel and strafed the entrance after which clouds of steam issued forth. Lieutenant McEnery found two more lorries in the Haeju district and destroyed them.

Thursday 30th October was the last day of Korean operations for *Ocean* and her Squadrons. 802's diary recorded that:

> 'Fog hampered the lorry hunters this morning and they all returned negative reports. Lieutenant Crosley at 0900 brought back news of the day's first success - he claimed one truck, two barges and five sampans. On our last fling at bridge-busting the CO [Lieutenant Commander London] damaged a bridge near Haeju, Lieutenant Hallam knocked down a rail bridge north of Chinnampo, and Lieutenant Brown and Sub-Lieutenant Mallace collapsed a neighbouring span on the same line.
>
> 'It was on the midday bridge-busting mission that 802's Korean

venture came to a rather inglorious full stop. To start with, Lieutenant (E) Jenne experienced engine failure [due to water in the fuel] shortly after take-off. He made a successful ditching and was returned on board by the helicopter. Within 20 minutes of this, Lieutenant Davis who was about 15 miles south of Pyongyang had excessive rough running and cutting [of his engine]. The full Mayday action was initiated but fortunately Davis made the coast, then the islands and eventually the ship by operating his cut-out! After he landed, his filters were dropped and the fuel was found to be heavily contaminated. All the Furies were grounded when a closer inspection revealed that all but two of our serviceable aircraft were in a similar condition.

'So ended our Korean operations - an odd, unexpected, finale that nearly became a disaster.'

The Fireflies carried out four TARCAP missions before they, too, were grounded for suspected contaminated fuel. They were clear, and flew two final details, the last one in the words of the diary:

'H - Last event by the original 31 Division that commenced Squadron operations out here. Consisted of CO [Lieutenant Commander Roberts] and Lieutenant Cooper; Mr. Wigg with Lieutenant (O) Edwards as a passenger; Lieutenant Hawkesworth and Lieutenant Clancy; and Mr. Brand and Aircrewman Dunmore. The aircraft reported to Sitting Duck at 1628, were not required for any particular task but were asked to call again after attacking their pre-briefed target. The CO pointed out that this target was on the way home. Sitting Duck then asked them to investigate a gun position in a cave, which was located and damaged with rockets. On the way back to the ship a large sampan was strafed and two ox-carts in the same area were damaged.

'After the last aircraft, flown by Mr. Wigg, had landed on, there was a short memorial service on the after end of the flight deck at which wreaths were dropped overboard for the eight shipmates who had lost their lives operating from *Ocean* during her Korean operations, serving their country and the United Nations.'

That evening *Ocean* left the operating area for Sasebo where she arrived at 1730 next day, embarking FFO throughout the night. At 1145 on 1st November FO2FES, Rear Admiral Clifford visited the ship and made a short speech to say good-bye to the ship's company on the flight deck. *Ocean* sailed from Sasebo for the last time at 1515 in the afternoon.

'*Ocean's* record in Korean waters', wrote Admiral Clifford, 'is outstanding and is an example of what can be achieved by bold leadership and good teamwork. The spirit, courage and skill of her

well-led squadrons have resulted in much damage to the enemy and
have been backed up by the consistently high standard of the conduct
and tempo of her maintenance and deck operations.'

The subsequent award of the Boyd Trophy for 1952 jointly to Numbers 802 and
825 Squadrons for their operations in the Korean War zone need cause no surprise.

She rendezvoused with *Glory* at 0445 on 4th November for Exercise Tai-Pan,
the air defence of Hong Kong. During the final land-on Sub-Lieutenant Randall
had a tenth wire barrier and Lieutenant Heaton set an all-time low for Firefly
landing intervals in *Ocean* of 13 seconds, after Sub-Lieutenant Wailes. On
completion of the exercise, both ships retired to Hong Kong, *Ocean* securing
alongside in the dockyard, *Glory* in the stream.

Lieutenants Buxton, Adkin, Mather and Sub-Lieutenant Simmonds left to join
801, and Lieutenants Skinner, Robbins, Heaton, Sherlock, Sub-Lieutenants Millett,
Wailes, and Commissioned Pilot Kent to join 821, both Squadrons in *Glory*.

Flying statistics for the ship and Squadrons for the first Korean tour are:

Ship

Record number of sorties in one patrol	767
Record number of sorties in one day	123
Average sortie rate per day	76.3
Maximum number accident-free deck landings	1613
Deck landing accident rate	1 per 398

Squadrons	**802**	**825**
Total flying hours	7097	3243
Total sorties	3964	1907
Total deck landings	3911	1984
Best average catapult launch interval	33.7 secs	36 secs
Best average landing interval	17 secs	19 secs
Number of RATOG launches	735	
1,000 lb. bombs	420	
500 lb bombs	3358	96
60 lb. rockets	378	16868
20 mm rounds fired	560000	264700
Aircraft lost to enemy action	9	7

CHAPTER 10

ARMISTICE NEGOTIATIONS

By 24th November 1950, United Nations forces had reached Sianju (75 miles south-east of Sinuiju on the River Yalu), and some elements of RoK units had reached the Yalu at Hyesanjin. On 26th November Chinese Communist forces launched an offensive against UN troops, forcing them to start withdrawing. By 25th December the Chinese had crossed the 38th Parallel. Their New Year offensive started on 1st January, driving UN troops south until the Chinese were held to the south of Wonju two weeks later. United Nations counter-attacks and offensives finally established, by early July 1951, what was to be known as the Main Line of Resistance, a line running from north of the Imjin River at Munsan-ni generally north-easterly to Yonchon, Chorwon, Kumwha and to the east coast about ten miles north of Kansong, a line substantially unchanged for the remainder of the war.

President Truman and his advisers had determined to resist the calls of the Allies for an immediate cease-fire, and to resist any such resolution in the UN. MacArthur's army must improve its military position and regain some lost ground, in order to be able to negotiate from reasonable strength. However, to appease world opinion, Washington felt obliged to take a desperate diplomatic gamble, supporting a UN resolution calling for an immediate cease-fire in Korea proposed by a three-man cease-fire group, established by the Political Committee of the General Assembly of the United Nations on 14th December 1950. The Americans, who wanted no such thing, counted on the Chinese rejecting it.

Fortunately for the Administration's hopes, on 23rd December, the Chinese dismissed the resolution, since it included no call for the removal of foreign troops, or for the withdrawal of the 7th Fleet from Taiwan, or for the recognition of Peking at the UN. Washington now forced through its own resolution, against the deepest misgivings of Britain and the other allies, branding China an aggressor. Even such a moderate man as General Omar Bradley believed that, if the United States suffered the humiliation of military expulsion from Korea, she should retaliate with air attacks upon the Chinese mainland.

At the suggestion of Britain the cease-fire group was asked to draw up a statement of principles for the next session of the Political Committee. The 'Five Principles' produced by the group on 11th January 1951 attempted to bridge the gap between the US and China while avoiding a breach with India which could prove fatal for both the Commonwealth and the UN. Under the terms of the Five Principles a Korean cease-fire would be the prelude to a general discussion of Far East problems, including the issue of Taiwan and Peking's claim to a UN seat. These questions would be considered by a body established by the General Assembly which would include British, Soviet, US and Chinese representatives. In Korea itself all foreign troops would be withdrawn by 'appropriate stages' and the future of the country be decided by the Koreans themselves under UN principles.

Mr. Dean G. Acheson, US Secretary of State, finally advised acceptance, but only on the belief that the terms would be rejected by the Chinese. As Acheson had predicted, China rejected the UN approach on 18th January and came up with counter proposals which were totally unacceptable to Washington.

On 20th January the US representative on the Political Committee tabled a draft resolution condemning China as an aggressor and calling for a special body to consider further measures against Peking. Washington made it plain that it expected the support of its allies.

India, supported by Britain and Canada, was reluctant to close the door on further negotiations. It refused to accept China's response as outright rejection of the Five Principles and sought further clarification of the Chinese position. This produced some moderation of Chinese terms on 22nd January. A cease-fire was the first item on the agenda of the proposed seven nation conference, the Taiwan question was to be settled and a definite affirmation of the legitimate status of Peking in the UN was to be ensured. These concessions were insufficient to deflect Washington, which pressed forward with its own proposals. Mr. Acheson was furious with these further contacts with China, accusing the Canadians and Indians of manoeuvring behind Washington's back. While Australia and Canada expressed their reluctant support for the US resolution in the last resort, they continued to express reservations about American insistence on further measures against China. The most troublesome ally was Britain. Not only did London urge moderation on Washington, but it also lobbied Commonwealth representatives in an attempt to modify the American position.

Britain was concerned lest condemnation of China not only foreclosed further negotiations but also led to extreme measures against Peking. London was apprehensive about the military situation, fearing that, by continuing to retreat, General MacArthur was 'creating facts' and forcing an evacuation of the peninsula which would compel retaliation against China. It had picked up disturbing rumours of pessimism at the Pentagon and growing sentiment there in favour of withdrawal. When asked by Mr. Attlee, President Truman affirmed US determination to hold a line in Korea and denied any intention of seeking a UN mandate for limited war with China.

The Attlee Government had to consider not only Indian opinion and its implications for Commonwealth unity, but also British opinion. The Cabinet noted on 18th January, 'There would be great difficulty in enlisting the support of public opinion in this country for any extreme action by the United States.'

Chinese intervention ended the popularity of the war. Disillusion with the UN cause was further encouraged by fresh evidence of RoK atrocities. There was growing public concern that Washington, under the influence of McCarthyism, was dragging Britain towards global conflict. There was widespread fear of an atomic war with Russia. The British people, exhausted by the continuing effects of the earlier struggle, were sick of war. Mr. Attlee was warned that the public questioned the need for further sacrifices in the cause of rearmament.

Until this point, Britain had been content to influence US policy from the inside, not by opposing or discouraging the government and people, but by avoiding an open breach in the Far East. On 25th January the Cabinet decided to vote against any condemnation of China which was coupled with a demand for sanctions.

Mr. Acheson again was furious, believing that the resolution would lose much of its force without British endorsement; he blamed the influence of Mr. Pandit Nehru, Prime Minister of India. The US had made it clear that military sanctions against China were not envisaged. Additional measures against China would be political and economic; London would not be expected to break relations with Peking.

A revised resolution was endorsed at the UN on 1st February, China was no longer charged with having 'rejected' the Five Principles but with 'not accepting' them.

UN forces approached the 38th parallel in early March. While the objective in Korea was to regain control of territory south of the parallel, it was not to constitute a barrier to military operations. The UN command would wage an aggressive defence, penetrating up to twenty miles inside North Korea. As UN forces approached the parallel, a new appeal would be made for a cease-fire. If this were rejected, a maximum attrition would be imposed upon the enemy without a general advance or military actions directly against mainland China.

On 19th March a draft announcement was prepared for Truman to issue as UN forces approached the parallel. This was intended as much to reassure allies such as Britain as to appeal to the Chinese. It was suspected in Washington that Chinese withdrawal behind the parallel was the prelude to a new offensive. In these circumstances a declaration was useful and necessary since it would prove that Peking and not Washington was responsible for continuing the war. The planned appeal kept within the bounds of the Five Principles which the US had accepted in January. It noted that with UN forces approaching the 38th parallel, the UN Command was prepared to enter into arrangements which would conclude the fighting and ensure against its resumption. A cease-fire would pave the way to a Korean settlement and consideration of other problems in the Far East. This represented an attempt to fulfil the demands of both international and domestic politics.

Early in December, President Truman had issued a presidential order to all US theatre commanders, warning them to exercise 'extreme caution' in their public pronouncements, and to clear all of these with the State or Defence Departments. In a press interview on 15th March, General MacArthur had given a broad interpretation of his war aims, arguing that his command should not be ordered to halt short of 'accomplishment of our mission … the unification of Korea'. This interview had breached the directive, but was a transgression ignored by his superiors.

Informed on 20th March of the President's planned statement MacArthur took a step which could not be overlooked. He sabotaged the cease-fire initiative, precipitating a crisis in his relations with Washington, alarm amongst the UN allies and a new political furore in the United States.

On 24th March MacArthur issued his own statement on Korea which cut across the presidential plan. He claimed that recent tactical successes had proved that Chinese manpower could not prevail against the technical resources available to the UN command. China was incapable of waging modern war. The enemy must be painfully aware that if prevailing restrictions were lifted, 'an expansion of our military operations to his coastal areas, and interior bases, would doom Red China to the risk of imminent military collapse.' The Korean problem could therefore be settled on its own merits, without being burdened by extraneous matters such as Taiwan or Peking's claim to a UN seat. MacArthur was ready to confer with the enemy commander in the field to find a means by which UN objectives in Korea could be realised. This statement amounted to a demand that Peking admit defeat. No attempt was made to save Chinese face by compromise. Instead China was being invited to renounce aggression or accept destruction. The effect was to torpedo Washington's planned initiative. Peking could not respond without appearing to defer to the threat of American power.

On 11th April President Truman had no alternative but to replace General MacArthur as Supreme Commander by General Matthew B. Ridgway.

A major Cabinet row in the United Kingdom Labour government ended in the resignation of Mr. Aneuran Bevan, Minister of Labour, ostensibly over the imposition of prescription charges in Mr. H. Gaitskell's Budget of April. A section of the Labour Party was unhappy about the pace of rearmament demanded by the Americans; it disliked German rearmament; it distrusted US policy towards China and moves to revive and rearm Japan. There was believed to be a real danger that American anti-Communist hysteria would drag the world into war.

In an effort to contain the split, the government pressed Washington to adopt a conciliatory line in the Far East. The British demanded a statement of UN war aims which would offer China a means of ending the fighting without loss of face. London believed that a Five Power Conference of Britain, France, the US, the USSR and India might provide the way forward. This group could request the President of the UN General Assembly to appoint a cease-fire committee representing the belligerents. With a cease-fire agreed, the conference could consider a peaceful settlement of the Korean problem, including the withdrawal of foreign troops, elections and unification. The British scheme, which was supported by Australia and Canada, represented an attempt to reconcile the Five Principles with the Chinese note of 22nd January. It was also a gesture to domestic opinion. The idea was anathema to Washington.

On 1st June, the UN Secretary-General Mr. Trygve Lie declared his conviction that if a cease-fire could be achieved roughly along the 38th Parallel, the resolutions of the Security Council would have been fulfilled. The next day, Mr. Dean Acheson made a speech in which he reaffirmed the objective of a free and independent Korea; but he spoke of the prospects of peace resting upon the defeat of Communist aggression, and the creation of suitable guarantees to prevent a repetition of that aggression. On 7th June, he told a US Senate committee that UN forces in Korea would accept an armistice on the 38th Parallel. The world was learning to live with an acknowledgement of changed military and political realities in Asia. On 23rd June Mr. J.A. Malik, Soviet Ambassador to the UN, made a radio broadcast in which he called for 'Discussions between the belligerents for a cease-fire and an armistice providing for mutual withdrawal from the 38th Parallel.'

Mr. A.A. Gromyko, Soviet Deputy Foreign Minister, confirmed that the statement represented the official Soviet view. It was an important breakthrough since it indicated that the Russians would not support Chinese demands for political preconditions on Taiwan and the UN seat. This olive branch was received with overwhelming relief in the Western world. The Peking People's Daily endorsed the Russian initiative. At last, the end seemed in sight. Some compromise could be agreed, and the armies could go home.

'I believe,' General Ridgway had concluded a report to the Joint Chiefs of Staff on 20th May, 'that for the next sixty days the United States government should be able to count with reasonable assurance upon a military situation offering optimum advantage in support of its diplomatic negotiations.'

Washington was determined to conduct negotiations through the commanders in the field. In this way it could guarantee control. At the UN there was always a risk that political questions would be raised and that the allies would speak with different voices, offering openings to Soviet diplomacy. Moreover, a strictly military approach allowed Washington to avoid dealing directly with Peking on an official basis. Chinese forces were technically 'volunteers', acting on their own responsibility. As Mr. Gromyko pointed out, however, their commander could speak for them. Washington experienced little difficulty with the UN allies over the field commander approach. It was welcomed as removing the political obstacles which had previously inhibited movement towards a cease-fire. The practical result was that the armistice talks were conducted by the UN Command under American instructions. Other Governments were kept informed of their progress, and sometimes even consulted, but the UN itself played no active role. This was an arrangement which Britain in particular was later to question. For the moment, however, relief at the sudden breakthrough obscured all other considerations.

In acting on the Soviet suggestion that the UN command approach the Chinese and North Koreans, Washington was anxious to avoid any impression that it was suing for peace. From the beginning the propaganda dimension of the issue was recognised. General Ridgway broadcast the following message to the CinC of the Communist forces in Korea:

'As Commander-in-Chief of the United Nations Command I have been instructed to communicate with you the following:

'I am informed that you may wish a meeting to discuss an armistice providing for the cessation of hostilities and all acts of armed force in Korea, with adequate guarantees for the maintenance of such armistice.

'Upon receipt of word from you that such a meeting is desired, I shall be prepared to name my representative....'

General Ridgway went on to suggest that the meetings should be on board the Danish hospital ship *Jutlandia*, which would be anchored in Wonsan harbour. The *Jutlandia* was rejected as a meeting place by the North Koreans, who insisted that they should take place at Kaesong on the 38th Parallel some 35 miles north of Inchon. To this the UN agreed on 3rd July. The message was phrased to put the idea across that it was the Communists that had asked for peace but without humiliating them, as had General MacArthur's of 24th March. On 2nd July Peking radio broadcast an acceptance signed by General Kim Il-Sung, the North Korean Prime Minister and CinC, and General Peng Teh Huai of the Chinese People's Volunteers. The message stated that they were 'authorised' to hold negotiations and suspend military operations.

From the purely military point of view it will be seen that such negotiations were entirely in favour of the Chinese. Operations on shore developed into static warfare in the region of the 38th parallel, where, with unlimited coolie labour at their disposal, they were able to construct formidable strong-points and entrenchments, and the disadvantages of their slow and primitive communications were to a large extent mitigated, while the UN, being denied a war of movement, were unable fully to exploit their superior logistics and above all the amphibious weapon, which hitherto had stood them in such good stead.

During the last week of June and first week of July, there was a considerable increase in the bombardment of military targets reported by the Leopard organization; some twenty targets were engaged within eight days up to 2nd July. This increased activity, though fortuitous, fitted in very well with the policy of exerting maximum pressure on the enemy in order to start the armistice negotiations from strength.

The Communists had won the first trick. Their propaganda would now be able to represent the United Nations as coming to them to sue for peace, a not unimportant consideration in view of the importance attached to 'face' throughout the Far East, and one which nothing was left undone to foster.

The American decision to halt the northward advance at the Kansas/Wyoming line, a defensive position just north of the 38th parallel, at the end of June and to wage an offensive defence has sometimes been criticised in that it let the Chinese off the hook, giving them time to rebuild their shattered armies. It also allowed the Communists to drag out the cease-fire talks. General Ridgway was not optimistic about a further advance. Although the Chinese had been badly hurt, he credited them with the ability to defend strongly in the north on terrain well adapted for the purpose. Moreover, the further the UN command moved north, the less effective air power became, as enemy lines of communication shortened. Lastly, in military terms the possibility of casualties had to be considered. An attack on an enemy fighting a defensive war from good positions was a different prospect from the flexible war General Ridgway had been fighting, of allowing the Chinese to attack and destroying them primarily with air power and artillery. In such a struggle, UN losses were likely to be heavy. On all counts, the risks of a further advance far outweighed any possible benefits.

In June 1951 the Korean War entered a new phase. While the fighting continued it was on a reduced scale, at least as far as the ground forces were concerned. There would be no further dramatic advances and retreats along the length of the peninsula. The fighting was now limited and directed to a narrow purpose, that of influencing negotiating positions at the cease-fire talks. It is unlikely that when this phase of negotiating while fighting began, any of the principals foresaw that it would outlast the earlier stages of the war. It soon became clear that far from producing a quick settlement, the military armistice talks merely accentuated the political and ideological differences between the two sides.

Despite the moves towards an armistice in July 1951, it proved difficult to end the fighting. The armistice rapidly became the subject of bitter debate. Since it was recognised that a political settlement was unlikely and that a cease-fire would define future developments on the peninsula, compromise was difficult. Both sides sought to end the war, but not at any price. It was recognised that if talks collapsed, the US administration would face public pressure to adopt General MacArthur's recipe for 'ending the war and getting the boys home'. As General Bradley remarked, it was better to make concessions than to risk all-out war with China. At the same time, there was concern lest the negotiations be unduly prolonged. In this case the American people might prefer clear-cut victory to an indefinite stalemate. The case for limited war depended for continued legitimacy on achievement of results at the conference table.

Washington did not expect a political settlement to follow an armistice. Nor did it believe that the Communists would abandon their designs on the south. A cease-fire was regarded as an interim measure against the renewal of aggression. The terms envisaged by the administration reflected a desire to avert a new surprise attack. The armies were to disengage and a twenty-mile demilitarised zone (DMZ) was to be established, based generally on the position of the opposing forces at the time the armistice arrangements were agreed upon. No ground, air or naval reinforcements were to be introduced, although individual and unit replacements would be permitted. PoWs would be exchanged on a one-for-one basis. The cease-fire would be policed by a military armistice commission, representing both sides. Observer teams would have free and unrestricted access to the whole of Korea.

By 4th July, a general lull in the fighting on shore had set in all along the front, and on the 6th a preliminary meeting of liaison officers took place, at which details were arranged for the first meeting of the delegates.

On 10th July, Communist and UN delegations met for the first time in the town of Kaesong to open cease-fire negotiations. The Communists contrived, by keeping the UN delegates waiting, and by excluding the UN press but including their own, that it appeared as the UN were representatives of a defeated enemy summoned to the conqueror's territory to accept dictated terms. It was fortunate for the peace of mind of the governments of the west that they had no inkling of the two years of struggle and bloodshed that still lay ahead. The Communists were about to teach the world yet another bitter lesson in Korea: that war can be waged as doggedly and painfully at a negotiating table as with arms upon the battlefield.

In retrospect, it may seem that the United Nations was premature in consenting to talks at this stage, but it must be remembered that the political leaders had to regard the world-wide situation, and, at the time, armed intervention in Korea by Soviet Russia was assessed as a real possibility. It now appears that Russia had no such intention, and indeed in 1951 was in no condition to become involved in a third world war. What the Russians undoubtedly aimed at, once the UN had committed themselves to military measures in Korea, was to keep as many UN forces as possible (especially American and British) tied down there as long as possible in order to impede the formation of forces to support the recently-born NATO. With the Chinese armies in Korea seriously compromised in June 1951 (and, if General Van Fleet's view is correct, in serious danger of expulsion from the peninsula) then protracted armistice negotiations would seem the best method of achieving this object. At the same time such negotiations would provide the Chinese Communists with a breathing space in which to retrieve their position and shaken prestige in North Korea.

During these negotiations crisis followed crisis. Past experience in other conferences with Communists had clearly shown that attempts to placate them and to take conciliatory measures were merely taken by them as a sign of weakness. Power and strength were terms the Communists understood, and they were not influenced by much else. Consequently, General Ridgway decided early that the only way to obtain equitable terms for an armistice was to choose a sound, vigorous course of action and state it forcibly; and while care was taken to ensure that UN demands were reasonable, it was on these lines that the delegates conducted negotiations.

General Ridgway urged the toughest possible posture upon his government towards the Communists in negotiations:

'To sit down with these men and deal with them as representatives of
an enlightened and civilised people is to deride one's own dignity and
to invite the disaster their treachery will bring upon us.'

Western correspondents provoked a near-riot in Seoul because of the UN Command's initial refusal to allow them to attend the truce meetings. Floyd Park, the Pentagon's Chief of Information, issued a defensive statement:

'Arranging for an armistice during the progress of actual fighting ...
must ... be conducted in strictest secrecy.... ultimate success must
depend ... upon the willingness of the public to await concrete
results, ... and to refrain from violent reaction to incomplete and
unfounded reports and rumours.'

Yet within weeks, all these sensible considerations would be buried without trace, as the peace talks began their rapid deterioration into a public circus.

The UN Command saw no special import in the Communists proposed choice of site for talks until they began on 10th July. General Ridgway rapidly came to regret his agreement to Kaesong. Although it was originally between the lines, the Communists moved up troops to surround the town before discussions began. Since Kaesong lay south of the parallel and was the ancient capital of Korea, it possessed considerable propaganda value. The Communists used their control of access to portray the UN as a defeated enemy, suing for peace. UN delegates were humiliated and harassed by Chinese guards; the Western press was excluded while Communist newsmen exposed reels of film. General Ridgway was represented by Vice Admiral C. Turner Joy and Rear Admiral Arleigh Burke. The Communist delegation consisted of three North Koreans, led by General Nam Il, and two Chinese. The significance of the fact that Kaesong was firmly in Communist hands quickly became apparent: the Chinese and North Koreans were not seeking the give-and-take of armistice negotiations. They had come to receive the UN's capitulation, or at least to score a major propaganda triumph. It had been agreed that the UN party should fly to the talks under a white flag which the Westerners regarded as an emblem of truce. They quickly discovered that the Communists were presenting this symbol to the world as a token of surrender. The American admirals were obliged to wait an hour for the Communist delegation, probably a deliberate slight, as North Korean time was an hour slow on that being kept by the United Nations. Joy's delegation was also seated in lower chairs than their Communist counterparts.

After General Ridgway had made it clear that the UN Command would not continue discussions under these conditions, it took five days to straighten out the problems — to establish the neutrality of the conference zone, to substitute military police for armed troops in the area, and to secure the admission of the UN press — and it was not till the 15th July that the first meeting to discuss the agenda took place.

Every exchange was delayed by interminable adjournments demanded by Nam Il's delegation. One of the most urgent UN demands, for the Red Cross to have access to prisoners in Communist hands, was unhesitatingly brushed aside. A low point was reached on 10th August when the two delegations stared across the table at each other in complete silence for two hours and eleven minutes, a Communist gesture intended to display their rejection of the preceding UN statement.

By 22nd August, the talks had got nowhere. The Communist delegation had wrung every conceivable propaganda advantage from the meetings, while talking for long enough to see that the UN delegation had not the slightest intention of yielding on acceptable terms. Nam Il therefore broke off the talks, claiming that UN forces had tried to murder his delegation by air attack. General Ridgway denied the charge, arguing that the enemy had fabricated the incident.

On 10th September the accidental strafing of Kaesong by an American aircraft offered an opportunity to build a bridge to the enemy. The UN Command accepted responsibility for the attack and apologised. On 20th September the Communists agreed to a meeting of liaison officers at the village of. The enemy pressed for a meeting of the full delegations but was unwilling to consider an alternate site, until on 7th October they proposed full delegation meetings at. The village lay between the lines where its neutrality could be guaranteed and the scope for incidents reduced.

Talks began once more on 25th October 1951, at Panmunjom Military pressure was then pushing the Communists back and eventually, after another long suspension of talks, the current battle-line was accepted on 27th November as the line of demarcation. On 12th November, General Van Fleet, 8th Army's Commander, was ordered to desist from major offensive action and restrict his forces to the defence of their existing front, the Main Line of Resistance. Local attacks were still permissible, but no operation in greater than battalion strength could be mounted without authorisation from General Ridgway. This was the prelude to a striking negotiating bid by the UN delegation: if the Communists signed an armistice within thirty days the existing front could be frozen into the final demarcation line between the two sides.

This was a move designed to show the Communists, and the world, that the UN had no interest in further territorial gains in Korea. The Communist negotiators hastened to ratify the proposal on 27th November. Then, for thirty days, they talked empty nothings at Panmunjom. And while they talked, immune from major UN military action, their armies dug in. For 155 miles from coast to coast across Korea, through December 1951, they created a front of defensive positions almost impregnable to artillery fire and assault, manned by 855,000 men.

By November the war had entered its longest and most frustrating period — of stalemate on the ground and sterile attrition at the negotiating table. The UN Command had renounced any military objective beyond the defence of the Main Line of Resistance, and spasmodic local operations, designed to sustain morale and demonstrate the army's continuing will to fight.

The close of 1951 saw some progress in the armistice talks, which had been resumed after long adjournments, the Communists had been strengthening their defence lines and building up their forces and supplies; by the end of the year it was thought that they could launch a general offensive. General Headquarters estimated that the duration of such an offensive would be limited to between five and ten days on account of supply difficulties, and the UN Command was confident of being able to check it.

On 4th November there was a heavy enemy attack on the 1st Commonwealth Division, in the sector held by the Kings Own Scottish Borderers. By 12th November the KOSBs and Leicesters had stabilised the position and the situation was fairly static.

On 18th December 1951, prisoner-of-war lists were exchanged by the delegates. Naturally, the UN was anxious to recover its prisoners, who were known to be abominably treated, and it was hoped that this matter could be settled reasonably quickly. But it proved the knottiest point of all to solve, and was under discussion practically right up to the signing of the armistice more than eighteen months later.

From the last months of 1951 until the end of 1952, while the negotiations at

Panmunjom dragged interminably on, the USAF waged a massive campaign to bring pressure upon the Communists by bombing. Yet by December 1952, the Communists had been able to increase and supply forces in Korea numbering 1,200,000.

While the talks continued, Washington sought the continued support of its allies. The most troublesome was South Korea. President Syngman Rhee was bitter about the negotiations which he realised meant a new partition of his country. Korean representation at the discussions was purely symbolic. Once more the future of the peninsula was being decided by the great powers. His nightmare was that Washington would abandon the South after the armistice and lay it open to a new invasion. Despite reassurances from President Truman he continued to snipe at the negotiations. From the US point of view, the most encouraging development was the modernisation of the Korean army. A new professional officer corps would later give Rhee considerable leverage over the truce talks — the greater the role of the RoK army, the larger Rhee's scope for sabotaging the armistice, a fact which became clear in 1953.

If the most troublesome ally was South Korea, the most important remained Britain. London was anxious to reach an honourable settlement in Korea which would allow the withdrawal of UN troops. Mr. Herbert Morrison, Foreign Secretary, expressed concern at Rhee's opposition to an armistice, an attitude shared by his Conservative successor, Mr. Anthony Eden. Nor did Britain have unreserved confidence in American policy. Containment was defined as a success and Morrison was to maintain the alignment with the US on which British security depended. At the same time there was the danger of pushing the Soviet Union into preventive war.

On 11th September Mr. Acheson and Mr. Morrison discussed the situation if armistice talks collapsed. Mr. Morrison emphasised the need to avoid all-out war with China and British inability to reinforce the Far East. Korea must be regarded as merely one example of Soviet 'trouble-making'. Britain was reluctantly prepared to agree to measures such as a ground advance to the waist and the bombing of the Yalu electric power plants. It had reservations about some of the political measures proposed by Mr. Acheson. Political and economic sanctions by the UN were also unwelcome.

In November 1951 the Labour government was replaced by a Conservative administration with Mr. W.S. Churchill as Prime Minister and Mr. Anthony Eden as Foreign Secretary. Churchill was anxious to restore the Anglo-American partnership of the Second World War. On his visit to Washington in January 1952 he was fulsome in his praise for the decision to intervene in Korea, arguing that it was a turning point in the cold war. He agreed with Mr. Acheson's view that the continuing impasse at was part of a Soviet scheme to transfer the Korean problem to the UN where political issues could be raised. The allies must stand firm against this manoeuvre and publicise the real source of frustration at the armistice table.

No aspect of the Korean War was more grotesque than the way in which the war was allowed to continue for another 16 months from February 1952, after the last substantial territorial obstacle to an armistice had been removed by negotiation. From then until the end of July 1953, at the combatants wrangled about one bitterly contentious issue — the post-armistice exchange of prisoners. The UN Command wished to gain the return to freedom of every man of their own held by the Communists, but the difficulty arose from the Communist insistence that all the prisoners in the hands of the UN should be returned, regardless of their personal desires. This was the last thing many of them wanted to happen to them, and the UN were equally determined, for reasons of common humanity, that none should be compelled to fall into the hands of the Communists again against their wishes.

Both Mr. Churchill and Mr. Eden had been party to the Yalta Agreement and recalled the fate of those repatriated to Russia in 1945. Neither President Truman nor Mr. Churchill wanted a similar situation to arise in Korea. In mid- January 1952 General Ridgway was authorised to agree to an all for all exchange of prisoners provided no forcible return of prisoners would be required; then early in February a solution was suggested which would avoid forcing the Communists to agree to voluntary repatriation. The idea was to screen the PoWs by interviewing the prisoners and segregating them into repatriates and non-repatriates. The non-repatriates would be removed from the PoW lists and the Communists offered an all-for-all exchange for the remainder. If the grounds for refusal were narrowly defined, a total might emerge which the Communists could accept without loss of face. It was recognised that any deal depended on a high number of repatriates. Only if a prisoner indicated a determination to resist exchange would he be removed from the PoW lists. The President approved the plan at the end of February. After an initial screening, it appeared that only about two thirds of prisoners demanded repatriation, a figure which, if offered, would be too low for Peking to accept.

The deadlock at continued. In May rioting broke out in the Koje PoW camps; General Dodd the camp commandant was kidnapped, and his replacement General Colson seemed to admit to charges of brutality by UN guards. General Ridgway was promoted to General Eisenhower's NATO post and was succeeded by General Mark Clark who took firm measures to restore order. Further to embarrass Washington, these riots coincided with the Communist germ warfare accusations that the UN were dropping insects infected with typhus, bubonic plague and other epidemic diseases on North Korea. The Chinese and North Koreans refused to allow either the International Red Cross or the World Health Organization to investigate the situation on the grounds that both organisations were biased towards the West. Their case rested on the confessions of captured airmen and on the findings of an international scientific commission sponsored by the World Peace Council, an organization backed by Moscow. In the West, the germ warfare charges were dismissed as propaganda, designed to compensate for the humiliation of the repatriation figures and to discredit the US in Asia.

In an attempt to resolve the impasse the air war was intensified and directed at economic targets, the most prominent ones being the power stations along the Yalu providing power to Manchuria as well as to northern Korea. The escalation of the air war drew protests from Australia, New Zealand, India and Britain.

In early May Mr. Chou En Lai, Chinese Premier, suggested to India that London should use its influence to secure an armistice. While a formula was still under discussion with Washington, Mr. K.M. Pannikar, Indian Ambassador to Peking, and Chou En Lai agreed on a suggestion that PoWs be re-screened by a neutral commission in a neutral zone. This initiative came to nothing.

There were those who argued that the stick should be coupled with the carrot in dealing with Peking. The State Department worked out a possible settlement during the summer. The repatriates would be exchanged and the problem of the non-repatriates left over for consideration by the political conference demanded by the armistice agreement. This linked in to a Mexican proposal that the non-repatriates be sent to neutral nations and allowed to work while their status was being decided.

General Clark and the Pentagon were opposed to any form of compromise with the Communists. He asked for, and was given, an increase in the RoK army after General Eisenhower had urged that 'Asians fight Asians'. Military and psychological pressure on the enemy would continue. On 8th October, the UN Command recessed the talks at as a symbol to Peking of American determination.

The general situation at the close of 1952 differed little from that at the beginning of the year. The front line, despite bitter fighting — especially in the latter part of the year - remained practically unchanged. The UN attempt at interdiction by air attack, though inflicting much damage and inconvenience on the enemy, had failed to achieve its purpose. The armistice talks had been hanging fire for months. On 1st December the UN approved a plan for their resumption based on a plan put forward by India.

Under this plan, the PoWs would be handed over at the armistice to a neutral commission; they would be available for persuasion for ninety days after the truce after which the problem of those that remained could be taken up by the political conference. In default of a solution after a further thirty days, the UN would assume responsibility for their 'ultimate disposition'. This clumsy procedure was necessary to reconcile the US and Chinese positions on the problem. All PoWs were to be made available for exchange, but the 'hard core' of non-repatriates would be offered an alternative. The ambiguous phrase 'ultimate disposition' covered American determination to turn these men over to the RoK and Taiwan. On 15th December,

Peking followed Moscow's lead and rejected these terms. The only hopeful sign was that the Chinese reply was 'not in either abusive or even excessively belligerent terms'. Mr. Nehru believed that Mr. Chou En-Lai had been overruled by the Russians. It has been argued, however, that at this stage both Moscow and Peking were prepared to wind down the war. Both powers were perhaps reluctant to deal with the outgoing Truman administration, representing a party which had been repudiated at the polls. There was little point in endorsing a compromise which might be rejected by the Republicans. A solution to the PoW problem, therefore, awaited the inauguration of General Eisenhower in January 1953.

On the 30th November General Eisenhower, President-elect of the United States since 4th November, arrived in Korea for a three-day visit to study the situation on the spot. On 14th December he stated that a satisfactory solution could be reached, but the UN resolution was rejected by Peking and Moscow on the 15th, and on the 18th by the North Koreans. It was, incidentally, equally unpopular in South Korea.

A development of much more direct impact upon the Korean peace negotiations was America's test detonation in January 1953 of the first nuclear device capable of adaptation for artillery — a tactical nuclear weapon. The Joint Chiefs of Staff in Washington recognised its relevance to the Korean stalemate in a study issued on 27th March:

'The efficacy of atomic weapons in achieving greater results at less cost of effort in furtherance of US objectives in connection with Korea points to the desirability of re-evaluating the policy which now restricts the use of atomic weapons in the Far East....

'In view of the extensive implications of developing an effective conventional capability in the Far East, the timely use of atomic weapons should be considered against military targets affecting operations in Korea, and operationally planned as an adjunct to any military course of action involving direct action against Communist China and Manchuria.'

Mr. John Foster Dulles, the Secretary of State, was visiting India. He told Mr. Nehru that a warning should be conveyed to Mr. Chou En Lai: if peace was not speedily attained at Panmunjom the United States would begin to bomb north of the Yalu. The Pentagon had recently carried out successful tests of atomic artillery shells. The implication was plain.

It will never be certain how close the United States came to employing nuclear weapons against China in the spring and summer of 1953, or how far the JCS study and the Dulles warning were intended as bluffs. If such they were, there is no doubt of their success. Through its agents in the US and Europe, Moscow was undoubtedly informed of American progress on tactical nuclear weapons, and Washington's change of policy towards active consideration of their use. General Eisenhower said after his return from Korea:

'We face an enemy whom we cannot hope to impress by words, however eloquent, but only by deeds — executed under circumstances of our own choosing.'

Early in February Mr. Dulles spoke of the need to make the idea of nuclear weapons more acceptable. President Eisenhower suggested the Kaesong area of North Korea as an appropriate demonstration ground for a tactical nuclear weapon. By March Eisenhower and Dulles were 'in complete agreement that somehow or other the taboo which surrounds the use of atomic weapons would have to be destroyed'.

Later in March Eisenhower said that although there were not many good tactical targets, he felt it would be worth the cost if a major victory could be gained in Korea.

Here is clear evidence that the President and his senior advisers talked with considerable open-mindedness about the possible use of nuclear weapons in Korea. Yet today, nearly 40 years later, it remains difficult to believe that, had the military situation remained unchanged, Eisenhower would have authorised their employment. It is entirely probable that he would have done so, had the Chinese offered some new and dangerous military provocation. But if America had detonated a nuclear weapon in cold blood, at a time of military stalemate on the battlefield, Eisenhower would have faced the certain, bitter, lasting anger and hostility of America's allies around the world. He was a cautious, humane man; it seems unlikely that he would have taken so drastic a step.

But in the spring of 1953, the Russians and Chinese almost certainly allowed themselves to be persuaded that the new Administration was willing to use nuclear weapons if the US was denied an honourable escape from Korea. After so many months of deadlock, the talks at suddenly began to move with remarkable speed.

For almost two years it had been apparent that the Korean War could not be settled on any terms that provided for the reunification of the country. During the interminable struggle during which each side laboured for face the fate of the prisoners held at the two extremities of the Korean peninsula remained the dominant issue.

In December 1952, when the Red Cross in Geneva urged the exchange of sick and wounded prisoners in Korea as a 'gesture for peace', General Mark Clark welcomed the proposal, but the Soviets and Chinese firmly rejected it. On 23rd March 1953 the heaviest fighting since the autumn flared up south-west of Chorwon. Whether the course of this battle, or the change of leadership in the Soviet Union following the death of Stalin on 6th March, affected the views of the Chinese Communists cannot be stated with certainty. But on 28th March, without warning, Kim Il Sung and Marshal Peng not only announced their acceptance of the swap, but also declared that this would pave the way to a settlement for all PoWs, and a cease-fire 'for which people throughout are longing'. Chou En Lai endorsed this commitment on 30th March. Although he restated Chinese rejection of an exchange that left any Chinese or North Korean prisoner in the UN hands, he proposed that any prisoner whose will was in doubt should be placed in the hands of a neutral state, for further investigation. On 1st April Mr. Molotov, the Soviet Foreign Minister, endorsed Chou's proposal and offered Moscow's support in seeing it carried out. On 8th April the North Koreans released the civilian internees who returned to the West via Moscow. Mr. Eden pressed for an early resumption of talks. President Eisenhower and Mr. Dulles felt that an exchange of sick and wounded must precede any broader negotiations.

Washington at first regarded the Chinese declaration with deep suspicion. Again and again over the past two years, an apparently straightforward proposal from Peking proved, on closer inspection, to be capable of such different interpretations as to be worthless. Yet on 11th April at Panmunjom the liaison officers at the conference table were astonished to reach rapid agreement with the Communists for 'Operation Little Switch', the exchange of sick and wounded. 700 Chinese and 5,100 Koreans were to be sent north, 450 Korean and 150 non-Korean soldiers were to come south. The exchange was completed at between 20th April and 3rd May.

A new wave of revulsion about the Communist conduct of war swept the West when the world beheld the condition of the UN prisoners who were released: in addition to wounds and disabilities that had effectively gone untreated for months, even years, many men were corroded by prolonged starvation, or psychologically crippled. Yet negotiations for the next exchange began at once, and the full UN and Communist delegations met at for the first time in six months. The main point at issue was the selection of a neutral 'quarantine nation' where prisoners refusing repatriation should be held. The UN opened by proposing Switzerland, with no man to be held in quarantine for more than two months. The Chinese rejected Switzerland, and demanded six months. Pressed for an alternative neutral site, they named Pakistan. Then the Communist delegates appeared to undergo a sudden change of heart. They no longer insisted that the prisoners' political screening should take place outside Korea, they cut the proposed period from six months to four, and they demanded the creation of a Neutral Nations Repatriation Commission made up of Poland, Switzerland, Czechoslovakia, Sweden and India.

The Americans were at last convinced that the Communists genuinely sought peace. Stalin was dead, and in the dark shadows of the Kremlin new forces, albeit no less hostile to the West, were setting policy. President Eisenhower was by now wholly committed to a Korean settlement.

Americans perceived they had the balance of strength at the negotiating table. It seemed that time was pressing the Communists more urgently than the UN. General Mark Clark requested, and received from Washington, permission to drive home the advantage. The bombing campaign of the Far East Air Force was intensified, with attacks on dams in North Korea deliberately intended to destroy crops and food supplies. The UN delegation at tabled a new and final proposal: a single neutral power would screen all reluctant PoW repatriates within ninety days inside Korea. If this proposal was rejected, all unwilling North Korean repatriates would be unilaterally freed inside Korea within a month. The UN air attack on North Korea would also be intensified.

Inside South Korea entirely different emotions reached boiling point. For President Syngman Rhee and his followers, the prospective armistice that offered peace to Seoul's foreign allies signalled the collapse of all their hopes. Rhee had always been stubborn, now he was bitter. He saw that President Eisenhower proposed to accept a cease-fire based on the permanent division of Korea, and the continuance of a Communist threat to the Seoul government. He declared again and again that he would never countenance a settlement that did not remove the Chinese from North Korea, and effectively demilitarise the North. Rhee, supported by opposition politicians, directly threatened Eisenhower: if a deal was made at which permitted the Chinese to remain in North Korea, the RoK army would continue the fight unaided, if need be, until the Communists were pushed north of the Yalu. However empty this simple threat in military terms, it caused the utmost alarm in diplomatic and political ones. Rhee's behaviour might shatter the whole fabric of the peace talks.

General Mark Clark did his best to assuage Rhee's fears. The expansion of the RoK army would go ahead whatever the outcome at ; he believed he had been successful in persuading Rhee of the futility of trying to sabotage the peace negotiations.

Encouraged by the success of Little Switch, the UN Command agreed to reopen the main truce talks, and on 26th April the 199-day recess of armistice negotiations came to an end for the time being. There was only one major obstacle to the truce: what to do with the 114,500 Chinese and 34,000 North Korean prisoners who refused to return to their homelands. The UN were determined that no prisoner who refused repatriation should be returned to Communist control against his will.

Nor were the Chinese finished. On 26th April their delegation at the peace conference entered a new proposal about the prisoners: three months after a cease-fire, those who refused repatriation should be moved for another six months to a neutral state, where representatives of their own government would have access to them. Those who still refused repatriation at the end of this process would remain in confinement while further negotiations were held to decide their fate. American counter-proposals were rejected. For four days the talks returned to the stultifying rhetoric that had characterised the earlier stages of the negotiations until they were finally adjourned.

The United States government determined to make the very concession it had refused for so long, that was certain to provoke an upheaval in relations with President Rhee: the UN delegation was to agree that Koreans, as well as Chinese, who refused repatriation should be handed over to the Indian neutral supervisory commission. Rhee's rage when this news was conveyed to him brought relations between Seoul and Washington to their lowest ebb since the war began. Rhee threatened to withdraw his army from UN command. The Americans undertook hasty preparations to implement Operation Ever-Ready, a politico-military operation to seize control of South Korea from Rhee's regime. If necessary the Korean President would be held in protective custody, incommunicado, unless he agreed to accept the terms reached at. Either Chang Taek Sang, the Prime Minister would be installed as head of government or a military regime would be established.

On 26th May the US ambassador in Moscow met Mr. Molotov and presented an outline of the UN offer. He emphasised that rejection would mean the end of talks and the creation of a situation the US would prefer to avoid — Washington was raising the spectre of a wider war. The allies were informed that if the terms were not accepted within a week General Clark would step up air and naval action and denounce the agreement neutralising Kaesong and. He would unilaterally release the Chinese and Korean non-repatriates, presenting the Communists with a fait accompli. These were more modest measures than were being suggested to the Communists at the time and displayed President Eisenhower's awareness of allied sensitivity on the atomic issue. While the allies welcomed these developments, they were universally reluctant to break off talks if the terms were rejected. The entire armistice would be sacrificed over a narrow gap between the sides on the PoW question. There were doubts as to whether President Rhee would fall easily into line, doubts which were to prove well-founded.

On 8th June agreement was at last reached on the terms of repatriation of prisoners and Mr. Dulles informed the President 'Barring unforeseen developments, it appears the PoW issue has been solved'. Those who wished to go home could be exchanged immediately. Those who did not wish to return to the blessings of their Communist homelands would be left in the hands of the Neutral Nations Repatriation Commission for ninety days, during which their governments would have free access to them. Their future would then be discussed for a further thirty days by a 'political conference'. After that period, those who remained would be considered civilians.

President Rhee condemned the terms as appeasement. The RoK would fight on alone, rather than accept an arrangement which left Chinese troops in the north. As for the NNRC, he repeated his pledge that 'no Indian soldier would be allowed to set foot in Korea'. His Foreign Minister, Mr. S. Pyun, argued that to allow Communists access to the prisoners for explanations was tantamount to forced repatriation. Rhee had no faith in President Eisenhower's reassurances. He suspected that once the war was over the US and UN would wash their hands of Korea.

General Clark believed that Rhee was exaggerating, but nevertheless he was prepared to go to the brink in his opposition to an armistice. The RoK delegation was withdrawn from the truce talks and demonstrations were engineered in Pusan. In these circumstances the threat to withdraw from the UN command had to be taken seriously. As Clark recalled,

'Since South Korean troops manned two-thirds of the front, a sudden decision to remove them from my command presented all sorts of nightmare possibilities'.

On 5th June, in an effort to buy Rhee off, President Eisenhower offered him a mutual security pact after the conclusion of the cease-fire. When Clark delivered this message he found the Korean leader at his worst. He continued to insist that he would fight on, but he promised to inform Clark before taking any steps to withdraw Korean forces from the UN command.

All that remained, then, before declaring a truce was the readjustment of the military demarcation line on which the armistice was to be based. As previously, whenever truce prospects had improved, the enemy increased his efforts to gain ground along the Main Line of Resistance. This was largely a question of 'face' so dear to the oriental mind; they wished to appear on the offensive when the armistice was signed, and to gain enough ground to give colour to the claim that the United Nations had signed in order to avoid military defeat. Early in June, many concentrations of Communist armies in the forward area were noticed; attacks along the line increased until the Chinese attacked in strength on 11th June. They succeeded in breaking through the eastern central sector of the main Allied line, but after some fierce fighting — in which aircraft from TF 77 bore an important part — the situation was restored.

Meanwhile, the truce talks at had continued satisfactorily, and a truce agreement was finalised on 16th June. All that remained was to translate the terms into the various languages, and it was expected to be signed in three or four days. At this juncture, President Rhee elected to throw a spanner into the works.

The details of this arrangement were still being concluded on the night of 18th June 1953, when to the astonishment and bewilderment of the handful of Americans at the huge Pusan PoW compound, they saw that the main gates were open, and a vast horde of North Koreans was streaming out into the countryside, watched with supine indifference by their South Korean guards. The same process was taking place at three other compounds around the country. Some 25,000 North Koreans who had expressed unwillingness to return to their homeland after the armistice disappeared into the darkness. President Rhee had acted. Seoul's police and soldiers gave them clothing, and directed them towards shelter, while US troops rushed to the compounds to take over guard duties. By 22nd June, only

9,000 North Koreans remained in captivity out of a total of 35,400. Only 1,000 of those who had gone were rounded up.

General Clark lacked the manpower to replace the RoK guards and was reluctant to risk a clash between the Korean army and other contingents of the UN command. The Korean leader obviously regarded his coup as revenge for the humiliation of 25th May. The Chinese compounds were not affected. The whole incident was an open gesture of defiance which publicly flouted Clark's authority and demonstrated that Rhee's wishes could not be ignored. It was a bombshell, since the articles of the armistice had been finalised.

Steps were taken to secure the remaining PoWs. US reinforcements were rushed from Japan, and the Korean non-repatriates' compounds were broken up into smaller cages guarded by American troops. The Chinese PoWs were more important to the armistice negotiations than the Korean: while Peking might accept the fait accompli which freed the Korean prisoners, it was likely to react strongly to any interference with Chinese prisoners. It was difficult for the Chinese non-repatriates to escape since they were confined on the island of Cheju-do.

On 22nd June the UK sent a note of protest to the South Korean Government, and on the 25th Mr. W. Robertson, President Eisenhower's representative, arrived in Korea with a secret message from Mr. Dulles, the Secretary of State. On 30th June President Rhee dismissed his Defence Minister, who was held responsible.

It caused consternation in Washington — the Communists might break off the negotiations. Peking deplored the episode but was willing to listen to American explanations provided at , which were accepted.

While protracted and critical discussions were taking place between General Clark, Mr. Robertson and President Rhee, the Chinese launched their heaviest offensive since 1951 against the RoK east-central front on 13th July. Attacking with some 40,000 men, they at first made some penetrations, but their troops were insufficiently prepared for a general offensive. The South Koreans withdrew in good order, and on the 15th — again powerfully supported by aircraft of TF 77 — counter-attacked with success. By the 19th the momentum of the enemy onslaught had expended itself. Further counter-attacks were gradually reducing the initial penetration, and on this day the Communists at agreed to begin preparations immediately for the actual signing of the armistice. On 9th July President Rhee finally accepted the agreement reached between the delegations at Panmunjom. He refused to sign the armistice, but would not obstruct it.

President Rhee's frolic with the prisoners had prolonged the war by five weeks, during which the UN sustained 46,000 casualties, mainly South Koreans, and the Communists an estimated 75,000.

Work began on 23rd July to draw up a final demarcation line as the basis for a demilitarised zone. The date for the signing of the complete armistice was arranged for 27th July. At the last moment the Communist commanders refused to come to Panmunjom They refused to sign an agreement with a representative of the RoK present. As a result, General Clark never met his adversaries face to face. Instead the truce documents were signed at by the armistice delegations and subsequently by the commanders at their respective headquarters.

At 10.00 a.m. local time (0200 BST) on 27th July, from opposite sides, the two delegations entered the building where the armistice was to be signed, two years and seventeen days since talks began, three years 33 days after the outbreak of hostilities. Lieutenant-General William K. Harrison led the UN contingent, General Nam Il the Communist. By 10.12 a.m. all nine blue-backed copies of the agreement had been signed, and the two men left by their respective exits.

Twelve hours later the guns fell silent. It had taken five days for the United States to become involved in a ground war on the Asian mainland. It had taken two years to conclude a satisfactory armistice. The war had cost the US 142,091 casualties and had ended in a draw. For the first time in its modern history, America had failed to leave the battlefield victorious.

CHAPTER 11

HMS GLORY

801 and 821 Squadrons
8th November 1952 to 19th May 1953

On the east coast operations had continued in their usual pattern, but in July there had been a change in American bombardment policy: indiscriminate bombardments were discontinued and firing was only carried out when proper observation of shot was available. Throughout the latter half of 1952 enemy firing technique had greatly improved, especially in the Songjin area and for about 70 miles south where a good many ships suffered damage and casualties. TARCAP and air spotting, though frequently asked for were seldom available because the US 7th Fleet directive laid the emphasis on the interdiction programme with no mention of support for small ships operating inshore.

Destroyers and frigates from the west coast, one at a time, continued to operate on the east coast, usually as part of TE 95.22 off Songjin and to the north. The ships were: *St. Bride's Bay*, *Mounts Bay*, *Condamine*, *Charity*, *Constance*, *Iroquois*, *Crusader*, *Haida*, *Anzac* and *Piet Hein*.

Enemy fire was increasingly effective. On 20th July USS *Orleck* was hit by 75 mm fire at a range of about five miles, sustaining some casualties. On 6th August USS *Pierce* received seven hits at a range of one mile, stopping her offshore. *St. Bride's Bay* went to her assistance, sending over her Medical Officer, *Pierce* not having one. *St. Bride's Bay* was relieved by *Mounts Bay* on 8th August who, two days later, was hit three times, killing one and seriously wounding four. Five American ships were hit during August, causing damage and casualties: *Pierce* with three killed and twelve wounded, *Barton* one killed and one wounded, *Thompson* three killed and ten wounded, *Porter* seven wounded and *Grapple* with no casualties.

Heavy weather due to a typhoon caused a large number of moored mines to break adrift in the Changjin and Hungnam areas where 30 were sighted and sunk. Admiral Scott-Moncrieff reported that it was better to keep under way at moderate speed, using minimum wheel, rather than remaining at anchor. The ship's wash helped to keep the floating mines clear of the ship's side. The US tug *Sarsi*, when lying off at Hungnam, bumped one and sank almost immediately with the loss of five lives. Attempts to salvage *Sarsi* were abandoned on 5th September after the ships so engaged had come under fire three times from shore batteries at 5,000 yards range.

TARCAP had to be provided for them, and this, plus air support generally, continued for all inshore ships, with enemy opposition becoming much reduced during September. On 2nd October *Iroquois*, while bombarding a railway line at Tanchon, south of Songjin, with USS *Marsh*, was hit at 5,000 yards, one officer and two ratings were killed and eight wounded. On 20th October USS *Lewis* was hit by a shell which entered one of her boilers, where escaping steam killed six and wounded two.

On 15th October a large scale diversion was set up north of Kojo, consisting of 112 ships: one battleship, six carriers, four cruisers, 36 destroyers, minesweepers, transports, supply ships and landing craft. The amphibious force, supported by US 7th Fleet and TF 77 went through the full landing organization until 3,000 yards from the shore, when they turned round and re-embarked. 2,500 rounds of 16 inch, 8 inch and 5 inch shells were fired at the enemy in the vicinity by the supporting forces; it was considered to have been a successful exercise.

'Train-busting' was a recognised sport on the east coast, with ships endeavouring to destroy a train travelling at full speed on the exposed lengths of line between cuttings and tunnels. North Korean engine drivers were highly proficient at stopping and reversing, and would keep going at full speed even when some trucks had been hit. Admiral Clifford remarked that it was always the biggest train that got away, but *Haida* and *Piet Hein* achieved the distinction of completely destroying some good-sized trains.

During the last several months of the war, the enemy flew Russian built YAK-18 and PO-2 aircraft, old training machines with a speed of about 100 knots and carrying one or two small bombs, from North Korean grass airfields over Seoul and the battlefield at night — the Bedcheck Charlies. (The Polikarpov biplanes looked like something that had strayed into the combat zone from an antique air show.) A few bombs were dropped and the damage they caused was trivial, but air raid alarms were sounded and the harassment and nuisance value to UN troops was far from insignificant. Flying as low as possible to avoid radar detection, they posed a difficult problem as neither 5th USAF nor 1st Marine Air Wing had night fighters that could slow down sufficiently to engage them, and they had to be careful to keep clear of ships in the area. It was not until Naval Corsairs landed from TF 77 at the end of June that their activities were checked.

South Korean gunboat *L.1503*.   *(Nicholls)*

On the west coast, on 16th November *Anzac* had been shelled when she was off Chodo, but otherwise the batteries remained quiet except for some sporadic firing on minesweepers working in the Cigarette route until 23rd December.

In the Paengyong-do area, two RoK motor-gunboats operated at intervals in November and December. Under the direction of *Hawea* they proved themselves useful in penetrating the shallower inlets and carrying out surprise attacks before dawn on troops and gun positions. There was an unusual calm in the Haeju area.

First Patrol

Glory returned to the Korean theatre for her third operational tour in November 1952 with the air complement consisting of two independent squadrons — 801 Squadron (21 Sea Furies) commanded by Lieutenant Commander P.B. Stuart and 821 Squadron (13 Fireflies) commanded by Lieutenant Commander J.R.N. Gardner — embarked in place of the 14th CAG.

She rendezvoused with *Ocean* on 4th November 100 miles south-east of Hong Kong for Exercise Taipan, the defence of Hong Kong. At the end of the exercise five Sea Furies, three Fireflies and two Dragonflies were flown on board from *Ocean*. During the two day hand-over in Hong Kong, Lieutenants Adkin and Buxton RNVR, on special leave of absence from their civilian jobs and normally in 1832 Squadron at Culham, together with Lieutenant Mather and Sub-Lieutenant Simmonds RNVR joined 801 Squadron from *Ocean*.

Lieutenant Skinner, Sub-Lieutenant Millett and Mr. Kent rejoined 821 Squadron after their two familiarisation patrols in *Ocean*, leaving Lieutenant Sherlock in HM Hospital Ship *Maine* suffering from appendicitis. Three other ex-825 pilots joined 821 — Lieutenants Robbins and Heaton and Sub-Lieutenant Wailes. 821 Squadron was then organised into four divisions led by the CO Lieutenant Commander Gardner, the Senior Pilot Lieutenant Cane, and Lieutenants Dallosso and Sample. The Fireflies were modified for operational work by having HF radio and ASH radar removed — a fuel tank was fitted in place of the radar nacelle on the starboard wing, and a map box fitted in place of the pilot's PPI mounting. A Sten gun was carried in the front cockpit in case of an emergency landing on enemy territory. An R/T press-to-transmit switch was fitted in the rear cockpit so that the observer could give a warning of hostile aircraft approaching whilst he was facing aft. The white spinners were painted grey.

Glory left Hong Kong on 6th November for Sasebo. While on passage Squadron Leader Leatherfield gave a lecture to aircrew on Escape and Evasion; and maps of Korea were issued, together with pistols and ammunition, and escape gear. The escape gear consisted of flying rations and a first aid kit; a knife, a heliograph, a burning glass, a map, a compass and socks for use when travelling; signal panels and cartridges; a cheap watch, a pen and a 'blood chit' in Korean and English to help in encouraging friendly Koreans to give assistance to downed aircrew. She arrived in Sasebo on the 9th, embarked FFO, AVGAS and stores and left next day for the operational area.

Accompanied by *Comus*, *Consort* and USS *Taylor*, *Glory* left Sasebo early on 10th November for the first patrol of her third tour of duty in the war area and took over as CTE 95.11 that evening. Rear Admiral Clifford hoisted his flag in *Glory* for the passage, transferring to *Comus* next day to join TE 95.12. Captain Maunsell had experienced a few days of operations on the west coast in April, but the squadrons were new to it, so as much reconnaissance as possible was planned for the first three days, in order to familiarise the aircrews with the area and to provide up-to-date target information.

During the early part of the patrol much bad weather was experienced; low cloud, rain and short visibility with strong winds from the north-east curtailed flying. The usual support was given to the island defence forces; systematic attacks were made on bridges, tunnels, road and rail transport, on transformer stations and on troop concentrations as opportunities were offered.

Because the truce talks were still proceeding, albeit in a desultory fashion, the operational area was carefully delineated. The northern and eastern line limiting *Glory's* area was from Hanchon on the west coast, south-east to Pyongyang, then following the rail line south and east to Chunghwa, Hwangju, Sariwon, Sohung, Kumchon and then along the river to the coast at Tosong-ni. The 'Not to be attacked' line then continued along the coast and up the estuaries of the Han and Imjin rivers to Yongjong-ni, thus ensuring that the area surrounding the Kaesong truce talks should be inviolate. On 8th November the Communists had rejected the UN final offer on the question of prisoners of war, and had announced an indefinite recession of the talks.

Five two-hour events were flown on each of the eight flying days on this first patrol: eight Furies and four Fireflies on two events, four Furies and four Fireflies on the other three and two Furies on CAP on each event. The Furies were armed with 2 x 500 lb. bombs and 20 mm cannon, the Fireflies with 8 x 60 lb. rockets and 20 mm cannon. Bombs, rockets and cannon shells were strictly rationed by the Admiralty, and in order not to exceed the quota of rockets, the Fireflies carried either 2 x 1,000 lb. or 2 x 500 lb. bombs on the last day of the patrol.

A new forming up procedure was used during this patrol: aircraft joining up at 500 feet on the starboard beam of the carrier instead of at 1,500 feet on the port bow, thus avoiding any interference with aircraft in the squadron circuit.

Flying got off to a slow start on the first day, low cloud with drizzle and poor visibility prevented any flying until after lunch on the 12th, but it was good for the succeeding days. The Fury's main targets were on lines of communication, road, rail and river bridges, ammunition dumps, entrenched troops, gun emplacements, and TARCAP. Maintenance was of a high standard, 100% serviceability was often obtained, and 18 out of the squadron complement of 21 aircraft airborne at any one time was not uncommon.

Firefly divisional missions were either strikes on selected targets or TARCAP over 'Sitting Duck', a destroyer or frigate operating close inshore in the Chodo to Sokto area observing enemy movements. Throughout the day a division of either Fireflies or Furies had to be in the area to attack any targets she may have observed, to silence coastal guns firing on her or to spot for her bombardments.

Divisions on an operational mission had to report to one of the UN radio and radar stations, and had to approach the coast over point Dog (Chodo), X-ray (Choppeki Point), Able (Taechong island) or Baker (Yonpyon island). Junks and sampans sighted en route had to be investigated: friendly vessels displayed recognition signals such as two straw hats.

Sea Fury at 'Cut'.   *(Cook)*

Over Korea aircraft gently weaved to confuse any enemy who might have been firing on them, and to facilitate observation of the ground. Enemy forces appeared to have few heavy AA guns, and those were concentrated around important targets. Flak experienced on this patrol was from light automatic and massed small-arms fire with the occasional 40 mm gun. Aircraft were seldom fired on when not actually committed to an attack.

The countryside in this area was razor-edged hills and rivers with paddy fields in the valleys. Towns were small and generally badly damaged; small villages, in which troops were billeted, abounded. There was an almost complete lack of movement during the day; the enemy had become past masters in the art of deception and camouflage, stores and vehicles were hidden in ruined buildings and in civilian houses, trains remained in tunnels, camouflaged trucks were parked in stream beds and woods, and the troops remained in hiding until a target near them was attacked. Civilian oxcarts were used to transport vital supplies and ammunition, and they too were difficult to spot from the air.

Should any enemy aircraft venture far south from the Yalu River area, the radar station on Chodo would detect them and broadcast warnings. There were two MiG scares during this patrol, but the aircraft were later identified as friendly.

The Fireflies carried out rocket attacks from 5,000 feet or cloud base, firing at 1,800 feet. Boost of +4 lbs and 2,400 rpm gave a release speed of 280-300 knots; the centre dot or 6 o'clock diamond of the gyro gun sight was used for tracking, depending on the angle of dive which varied from 30°-45°. Pilots making individual dives followed closely, from a slightly different direction, their next ahead. It was found best to make only one run at the target, heading, if possible, towards the coast. Withdrawal was best achieved by maintaining speed and weaving, climbing when away from the target area.

On the 13th a Firefly in the forward deck park became out of control as the deck rolled heavily in a rough sea. The tail wheel jumped the deck edge beading and the aircraft came to rest on the beading with the fuselage twisted.

There was a marked increase in flak on the 18th which caused the death of Lieutenant R. Nevill-Jones of 801 Squadron. His aircraft was hit by AA fire and he crashed into marshy ground whilst he was leading his division in a dive bombing attack on a rail bridge in the Chaeryong area south of Sariwon.

On the same day and in the same area Lieutenant Commander Gardner had the bullet-proof windscreen of his Firefly splintered by a bullet as he fired his rockets. Later that day while attacking a transformer station near Chaeryong, the aircraft piloted by Lieutenant Robbins was hit in the port radiator. The aircraft quickly began to lose coolant, Robbins maintaining 2,000 feet and making for the coast. Whilst still over land the engine cut and the aircraft ditched about two miles from the coast in Tatong Bay. The remainder of the division acted as CAP over the pilot, who was unable to inflate his dinghy, and called up the rescue organization at Paengyong-do. Within 25 minutes Robbins had been picked up by a helicopter and flown back to the rescue base.

Nine Furies and six Fireflies were damaged by enemy fire and one Firefly by a shell exploding in one of its guns. Commander Place picked up a bullet hole in the port wing tip of his Fury but returned to the ship safely, and Lieutenant Adkin's aircraft was hit whilst on CAS to the 1st British Commonwealth Division on the central front, resulting in an oil leak. He landed on the emergency airstrip on Paengyong-do with three gallons of oil left.

On the last day of the patrol a division of Fireflies and another of Furies took off an hour before dawn intending to reach the coast at first light when there might have been some movement of troops or transport. In this they were successful, the Firefly division destroying four railway trucks and two lorries.

Flying statistics for this patrol were:

	801 Squadron	821 Squadron
Hours	680.55	330.10
Operational sorties	282	141
Deck Landings	282	149

Damage inflicted on the enemy:

	Destroyed	Damaged
Transformers	1	1
Gun positions	2	5
Bridges	4	7
Motor transport	34	36
Rolling stock	4	22
Stores	1	2
Rail tunnels		6
Ox-carts	12	

After these figures 821 Squadron's diarist added the wry comment:

'All this contravening the Regulations for Naval Aviation, AFO 1/52, Article 113, para 2:

'The pilot of an aircraft is forbidden to fly or manoeuvre his aircraft in the air in a manner likely to cause accident or annoyance to any person or persons likely to be in the vicinity, or damage to livestock or property, or to the aircraft itself.'

During the harbour period in Sasebo from 20th to 27th November, *Unicorn* arrived from Singapore bringing the remainder of *Ocean's* aircraft, two Fireflies for *Glory*, the remainder going on to Iwakuni. Lieutenant Wemyss joined 801 Squadron and Lieutenants Adkin and Buxton left for return to the UK.

As part of the programme of liaison visits, Commander Place and Lieutenant Commander Stuart visited the 1st British Commonwealth Division in the front line; and Lieutenants McCandless and Wheatley visited *Badoeng Strait* during this period.

From 26th to 29th November Admiral Clifford visited Pusan in *Unicorn*, where he met the British Minister Mr. W.G.C. Graham, Vice Admiral Sohn, Chief of Naval Operations RoK Navy, and others. On 30th November he transferred his flag to

Newcastle at Kure and on 2nd December left for the operational area where he visited each island in turn and met the island commander Colonel Totman USMC.

With the concurrence of Admiral Ginrich, he flew his flag from 8th to 10th December in *Badoeng Strait* who was then CTE 95.11. Admiral Clifford was met with a cordial welcome, he visited all sections of the ship, attended briefings and witnessed flying operations.

Second Patrol

Glory left Sasebo on 28th November, passed *Badoeng Strait* during the night, and reached Point Oboe early the following morning. Captain Maunsell had to retire, sick, to Sasebo on 30th November in *Consort*; Commander D.E. Bromley-Martin was appointed in temporary command with the rank of Acting Captain.

It was learned that the enemy was preparing to invade the friendly islands of Sok-to and Sunmi-do. Sok-to was a stepping stone to Chodo with its landing strip and radar installations; Sunmi-do was a base for 1,000 or more friendly guerrillas. The policy this patrol was, in particular, to attack troop concentrations and to destroy stores areas opposite the islands; as well as general interdiction and disruption of communications by attacking road and rail bridges and tunnels, and by attacking gun positions and troops wherever they were found.

Unusually bad weather caused flying to be cancelled on three-and-a-half days. A persistent north-easterly airstream from Siberia brought a succession of snow storms, and on the other days snow had to be cleared from the flight deck and the aircraft before flying could commence. A sudden drop in temperature had a marked effect on serviceability, particularly the Fireflies. Aircraft had to remain parked on deck overnight, and the cold resulted in contraction of the coolant pipes causing a number of leaks. Oil dilution had to be used after the last two details landed-on. A small quantity of petrol was pumped into the lubricating oil as the engine was switched off in order to reduce the viscosity of the oil so that the engine would start next morning. The overnight temperatures on the flight deck were so low and the oil became so stiff, without this dilution, that the cartridge starters had difficulty in turning the engine over sufficiently fast for the engine to fire. The Fireflies emitted a thick cloud of black smoke from the starboard exhaust stubs when they started and became known as the Coal Burners! Another effect of the low temperatures on the oil caused over-speeding of the Griffon engines. The pilot set the engine speed at a certain number of revolutions per minute; the propeller pitch to maintain this speed was altered automatically (between fine and coarse) by oil pressure acting on one side or the other of a piston at the front of the propeller, inside the spinner. This piston and cylinder were in the cold airstream and the oil trapped at the front cooled and congealed when the aircraft was flying straight and level with few or no changes in speed during the return to the ship. During the final approach and land-on, when engine power might be being changed rapidly by the pilot, the thick oil in the front of the propeller could not move fast enough through the small-bore pipes to coarsen off the pitch, resulting in the engine overspeeding beyond allowable limits and having to be changed. In order to overcome this problem, the pilots would exercise the pitch control during the return flight to get hot oil of low viscosity into the system. Overspeeding was no longer a problem. A third problem brought about by the extreme cold was that the water/glycol coolant in the Griffon engines started to freeze overnight, getting mushy and treacly, imposing an unacceptable load on the coolant pump on first start-up in the morning. To overcome this, the proportion of glycol to water was increased from 30/70 to 40/60.

Because of the increasing efficiency of the flight deck crews in arming and refuelling the aircraft, the flying programme was altered to 6 events of 1 hour and 40 minutes to give 28 Fury and 24 Firefly offensive sorties per day. And due to the bad weather only one pre-dawn strike was flown, Lieutenant Commander Gardner's flight taking off one-and-a-half hours before sunrise and, surprising some road transport with headlights on, destroyed two vehicles and damaged several others.

On 6th December, after attacking troops south-west of Haeju, Lieutenant Marshall was returning to the ship when his aircraft developed a severe coolant leak, probably due to enemy flak. He ditched the aircraft 26 miles east of *Glory*, well away from the enemy coast. With no swell and very little wind he made such a smooth entry into the water that the aircraft remained afloat for 40-45 seconds. He was rescued unhurt from his dinghy by *Glory's* helicopter after 15 minutes.

Nine Furies and one Firefly were damaged by flak and there were four deck-landing accidents. Owing to the weather only 327 sorties were flown at a daily average of 47.

Statistics for the second patrol were:

	801 Squadron	821 Squadron
Hours	380.40	224.15
Operational sorties	203	120
Deck landings	203	124

Damage inflicted on the enemy:

	Destroyed	**Damaged**
Gun emplacements	1	6
Bridges	4	2
Rolling stock		31
Motor transport	4	47
Vessels	2	1
Rail tunnels		4
Rail lines		4
Store dumps		4
Radar stations		2

During the harbour period from 9th to 15th December, this time at Kure, Lieutenants Mitchell and Anson joined 801 Squadron, Lieutenant Sherlock re-joined, and Lieutenants Hamon and Fogden joined 821 Squadron from Iwakuni where they had been for ADDLs. *Glory* sailed for the operational area on 15th December.

After his two day visit to *Badoeng Strait*, Admiral Clifford returned to Sasebo in *Anzac*. On 22nd December he left for the west coast in *Cockade*. He visited *Glory* (CTE 95. 11) on the 24th, and then proceeded in *Birmingham* to the Chodo area which, the day before, had been the subject of unwanted activity when enemy guns, after weeks of quiescence, had fired 500 rounds at Chodo and Sok-to, causing no damage or casualties. *Cossack*, *Consort* and *Constance* as well as the recently installed two 90 mm guns on Chodo silenced the enemy.

Admiral Clifford had intended spending Christmas Day in the Chodo area and to visit all ships of TU 95.12.1, but during the evening of Christmas Eve trouble blew up in the Haeju area. Guerrillas on the island of Taesuap had mutinied and an invasion of the island seemed possible, and also the neighbouring island of Mudo had been shelled. *Birmingham* sailed for Haeju arriving early on Christmas morning when she carried out a successful bombardment of the guns opposite Mudo with air spot from *Glory*. The mutiny was quelled by 1000 and the position restored to normal, enabling Christmas lunch to be enjoyed. Admiral Clifford remarked that the generous gift by the Daily Mail of a bottle of beer, 20 cigarettes and a bar of chocolate to every man in the forward area was much appreciated.

Third Patrol
Captain E.D.G. Lewin assumed command of *Glory* at Kure on 14th December,

the day before she left for the west coast. The recently joined pilots carried out DLP while on passage on 16th, and in order to clear the flight deck of the deck park, 8 Furies and 8 Fireflies flew interceptions and a navigation exercise. During this practice, the ship suffered the loss of the SAR helicopter in gusty weather when the aircraft was caught in a crosswind and started to topple to starboard. Lieutenant A.P. Daniels and Aircrewman 1 E.R. Ripley lost their lives as it crashed into the sea.

Operations started on the 17th on a patrol extended to ten days so that *Badoeng Strait* could remain in harbour on Christmas Day. The operational plan for 801 Squadron was to continue the interdiction programme with the emphasis on railways. Tunnels, especially those known to be the daytime hiding places for locomotives, were high on the list of targets. Low level bombing with 500 lb. bombs fitted with 30 second delay fuses was the favourite form of attack, and the pilots soon became proficient at lobbing their bombs into the entrances and blocking the tunnels. Each day was to consist of six events of 1 hour 35 minutes duration, with two pre-dawn takeoffs on suitable days.

Captain E.D.G. Lewin, DSO, DSC & bar.   *(FAAM)*

The weather was better during this patrol, flying was restricted on only one day when three events had to be cancelled due to snow storms, otherwise sorties went according to the scheduled programme. The Fireflies continued to experience trouble with coolant leaks due to the low temperatures.

A major policy decision promulgated on 17th December was the abolition of TARCAP missions. Though possibly a deterrent to the enemy batteries, it was by no means fully effective and it was felt that the aircraft could be better employed in attacks on other targets. TARCAP was only to be provided for special operations such as minesweeping close to enemy coasts or unloading LSTs on beaches opposite the mainland. The enemy in the TARCAP area had recently been very inactive, and Sitting Duck had only very rarely been able to provide targets for the aircraft. During this patrol, however, enemy guns began to bombard Chodo and friendly ships at about 1645 when the aircraft were on their way back to *Glory*. A TARCAP of four Furies was re-introduced on the last event each day to cope with this.

During the first half of the patrol the Fireflies successfully attacked road and rail transport; they spotted shoots for *Opossum* and *Birmingham*, the latter in support of a coastal raid by friendly guerrilla forces.

In the first two patrols trouble had been experienced with 20 mm cannon ammunition. On the 18th the ammunition exploded in one of the guns of Lieutenant Leahy's Fury, blowing panels off, wrecking the gun and leaving a large hole gaping in the mainplane. He was fortunately able to bring the damaged aircraft over the coast and reach the emergency landing strip at Paengyong-do where he landed safely. Whilst attacking a junk in a bay south of Haeju on the 20th, an explosion was seen to occur in the wing of the Firefly piloted by Lieutenant P.G. Fogden. The aircraft crashed into the sea and sank at once, taking Lieutenant Fogden with it. The cause again was faulty 20 mm ammunition exploding in the cannon. The ammunition was of 1943 vintage, and prior to this regrettable accident, had caused countless stoppages and two minor explosions. It was decided, therefore, that until better ammunition could be obtained, cannon would be used only in self-defence. Firing trials from the flight deck were carried out on subsequent days to attempt to determine which lots, if any, of cannon shells on board were serviceable. Because of this restriction there were no pre-dawn strikes, and strafing of opportunity targets after completion of bombing and rocketing attacks was brought to a halt.

On 20th Lieutenant Marshall made 821 Squadron's 1,000th deck landing since formation in September 1951, and two days later Lieutenant Skinner completed *Glory's* 10,000th landing since she left the UK in May 1951.

On the same day a Fury piloted by Sub-Lieutenant Baynes landed at Paengyong-do with an oil leak; and on 21st Lieutenant Mitchell, on only his third sortie, had the engine of his Fury hit by flak when in the Haeju area. He put the aircraft down about a mile offshore, quickly abandoned it and sat in his dinghy. The remainder of the division formed a RESCAP over him until an SA-16 Grumman Goose amphibian of the USAF 3rd Rescue Group landed alongside and picked him up. He was in the dinghy for 59 minutes in water at a temperature of 35°F (2°C) but was none the worse for his adventure when picked up. His experience gave all aircrew confidence in the Mark 6 immersion suit.

On Christmas Eve, Lieutenant Sherlock, returning from a rocket attack on troops near Haeju, experienced severe vibration in the engine of his Firefly. He was unable to obtain 1,800 rpm without vibration and landed at Paengyong-do. The aircraft was found to be unfit for flight until the engine could be changed. As there were no spare Griffon 74s on board, the aircraft had to remain ashore until it could be salvaged and returned to Iwakuni.

For the last two days of the patrol, the Fireflies were engaged in dive bombing. Their efforts were concentrated on the railways between Haeju and Ongjin, and

Haeju and Chaeryong, with considerable success. Two tunnels were blocked, two bridges destroyed and one damaged, and lines were cut in 16 places. 1,000 lb. and 500 lb. bombs were used, with one long delay fused bomb in every eight designed to disturb the enemy during the hours of darkness when he would be repairing the damage. The standard form of attack was a 45° dive from 6,000 or 7,000 feet to 3,000 feet with slight 'pull-through' before release. During one of these attacks on Christmas Day on a railway bridge west of Haeju where, earlier in the day, flak had been reported, Lieutenant R.E. Barrett failed to recover from his dive. His aircraft was seen to be spinning at about 1,000 feet, and on impact with the ground, it exploded and burst into flames.

Casualties during this patrol had been heavy.

Having flown 566 sorties at a daily average of 61, *Glory* left the operational area on the evening of 26th December, being relieved by *Badoeng Strait*. She set course for Iwakuni where she arrived and anchored-off on 28th to embark three replacement Fireflies. Later, while on passage to Sasebo, a fourth was flown on board by Lieutenant Sherlock.

Flying statistics for the patrol were:

	801 Squadron	821 Squadron
Hours	643.40	346
Operational sorties	358	208
Deck landings	355	233
Ammunition expended was:		
1,000 bombs	32	
500 lb. bombs	508	
60lb RP	1148	
20 mm cannon shells	52500	

Damage inflicted on the enemy was:

	Destroyed	Damaged
Bridges	9	8
Rail lines		41
Rail tunnels		9
Rolling stock	9	68
Locomotive sheds		3
Motor transport	25	25
Stores dumps	14	19
Factories		2
Transformers	1	4

During the period in Sasebo from 28th December to 3rd January the usual storing and ammunitioning took place, this time including dis-embarking the suspect 20 mm ammunition, while a belated celebration of Christmas was held on New Year's Eve. Lieutenant Commander Joy, the Naval Liaison Officer at JOC Seoul had fallen sick and his duties were taken over by Lieutenant Hunter of 821 Squadron at K.16, a secondment expected to be for about six weeks.

1953 opened with little hope of a speedy end to hostilities. In January and February the fighting on shore consisted of harassing probes and limited objective offensives. On 14th January the biggest air battle since the 4th September 1952 was fought over north-west Korea when 40 Sabres and 38 MiGs were involved. On 29th January Lieutenant General Maxwell D. Taylor took over command of US 8th Army in succession to General Van Fleet. There was not much change in the situation until towards the end of March. Several attacks by the Chinese on front-line positions yielded no gains of ground.

On 20th January the Eisenhower Administration took over in the United States, and on 2nd February the President announced that the US 7th Fleet would no longer neutralise Formosa. On 6th March the death of Stalin was announced in the United Nations, and in mid-April Mr. Vyshinsky, the permanent USSR delegate to the UN, accepted the West's peace proposals.

On 23rd March the heaviest fighting since the autumn flared up south-west of Chorwon, on the base of the 'Iron Triangle'. On 28th March, the Chinese and North Korean commanders accepted the UN proposal for the exchange of sick and badly wounded prisoners, which took place on 20th April.

The final agreement on prisoners was signed at on 8th June 1953.

On 1st January a new nomenclature had been introduced for the forces on the west coast:

Old Name	Duty	New Name
CTE 95.11	Carrier Force	CTU 95.1.1
CTE 95.12	Inshore cruiser	CTU 95.1.2
CTE 95.12.1	Chodo (Naval)	CTU 95.1.4
CTE 95.12.2	Paengyong-do (Naval)	CTU 95.1.5
CTE 95.12.4	Haeju (Naval)	CTU 95.1.6
CTE 95.15	Island defence (shore)	CTU 95.1.3
CTE 95.15.1	Sok to defence	Sok to Garrison
CTE 95.15.2	Chodo defence	Chodo Garrison
CTE 95.15.3	Paengyong-do defence	Paengyong-do Garrison
CTE 95.15.4	Yong Pyong do defence	Yong Pyong do Garrison
CTE 95.15.5	Tok Chok to defence	Tok Chok to Garrison

The guerrillas were also re-organised and designated Partisan Command. Five Partisan Infantry Regiments were allocated to the west coast, the headquarters and one regiment at Paengyong-do, and one each at Kangwhado, Yodo, Yong Pyong do and Chodo, each with a strength of 7,500. There was also the 1st Partisan Airborne Infantry Regiment at Seoul.

In January and February the winter weather — snow showers and blizzards, bitter cold, and ice flows, especially in the Chodo area — hampered all operations. *Birmingham*, (Captain J.D. Luce DSO, OBE had succeeded Captain C.W. Greening on 12th January), and *Newcastle* alternated as CTU 95.1.2; on two occasions, to ease the load on the cruisers, this duty was carried out satisfactorily by the smaller ships *Crane*, (Captain R.L.H. Marsh), and *Anzac* (Captain G.G.O. Gatacre DSO, DSC, RAN).

Early in January Vice Admiral Clark, accompanied by Rear Admiral Ginrich, flying his flag in *Missouri* and escorted by *Tingey* paid another short visit to the west coast. Rear Admiral Clifford, flying his flag in *Birmingham*, met them at Inchon on 5th January. General Van Fleet and army and air force commanders lunched on board *Missouri* and exchanged views on the war situation. The three ships proceeded to Chodo under Admiral Clifford's operational command, and next day bombarded Amgak, Wolsa-ri and mainland batteries, Missouri firing 72 x 16 inch shells, air-spotted by aircraft from *Glory*. In the afternoon the three Admirals visited *Glory*, taking passage in *Missouri's* helicopter, to witness flying operations.

Admiral Clifford went to Hong Kong in *Birmingham* to meet the CinC, Admiral the Hon. Sir Guy Russell in *Alert* on 13th January. Admiral Russell left Hong Kong in *Birmingham* with Admiral Clifford on 19th January for a farewell visit to Japan and the war area. At Sasebo on the 23rd, Admiral Clifford transferred his flag to *Ladybird*, and the CinC, after visiting ships in harbour and meeting UN authorities ashore, went on to Kure in *Newcastle*.

Enemy activity had been negligible during January and February. Guns opened fire on *Pelican* when she was sweeping on 15th January and on Chodo for a few minutes on 24th January.

In the Paengyong-do area, apart from firing on Wollae-do and Yukto on the 6th, the enemy was quiescent. Ships of TU 95.1.5, assisted by *Newcastle* and *Birmingham*, bombarded a large number of targets. RoK PT boats operated in the area, with periodical spells in Chinhae for maintenance.

In contrast to other areas, the enemy was fairly active around Haeju, Mudo and Changjae-do being fired on several times. Ships of TU 95.1.6 returned the fire and carried out a number of harassing bombardments. On 15th January *Sparrow* was hit on the quarter-deck, suffering no casualties and only superficial damage.

The Han estuary was visited by *Opossum* between 10th and 12th January. She bombarded targets on the north bank, using her own fire control party to spot from an island.

Fourth Patrol

Glory sailed on 4th January 1953 for a patrol shortened to seven days instead of the normal nine. It was planned to fly for four days, take half a day for replenishment and then a further two and a half days flying, but bad weather on the fifth day prevented any flying. Twelve events were cancelled because of inclement weather, and on several days there were thick banks of cloud between *Glory* and the coast with heavy snow storms beneath. Low cloud over land frequently obscured the intended targets and opportunity targets had to be attacked.

The Fireflies were armed with rockets for the whole patrol. A high percentage of their targets were villages where partisans had reported enemy troops being billeted. Generally speaking the coastal areas had been cleared of civilians, even farming was being done by troops. A new railway disruption policy was tried. Previously railways had been attacked at tunnels and bridges which were considered to be the most vulnerable points. The enemy kept large stocks of repair materials close to these points and labour gangs could get the line back into working order in a short space of time. It was decided that attacks would be made on lines in remote and inaccessible places, far from human habitation and from main roads, aiming to make eight separate cuts in each mile of track. A total of 33 rail-cuts of this nature were made, and the policy proved effective in further disrupting rail communications.

Investigations into bad ammunition that had plagued the previous patrols continued, all high explosive shells were removed from the belts and ball substituted; the Fireflies were armed with SAP in the outer guns and ball in the inner. Restrictions were still imposed on the firing of guns, but it was permitted to strafe important targets provided it was something worthwhile, not just a single ox-cart!

Operations started at first light on the 5th in poor weather. During his first sortie of the patrol Sub-Lieutenant Foster had all the electric's of his Fury fail and his engine started to cut, but he made a successful wheels-up landing at Paengyong-do. A little later in the morning while operating in the Chaeryong area Lieutenant Mather's aircraft was hit by flak and caught fire. He successfully abandoned his aircraft and was seen to be parachuting down safely but the point at which he touched down was unfortunately not observed and it was not possible to determine the exact point to which to summon the SAR helicopter, although it was known that he was not hurt. The remainder of 51 Division formed a RESCAP over the area but nothing was seen of Mather's position. However, the rescue helicopter from Chodo was called in and was being escorted by Sub-Lieutenants Rayner and Keates. Regretfully Sub-Lieutenant B.E. Rayner lost his life while carrying out these escort duties in low ceiling conditions. It is not certain if he was hit by flak or if he hit high ground in the low cloud, but a large fire was seen by Keates on a nearby hillside and Sub-Lieutenant Rayner did not return to the carrier.

The helicopter had to return to Chodo because of the weather and it was later learned that Lieutenant Mather had been captured by the Communists.

The weather suspended flying for an hour or two after lunch, but later in the afternoon aircraft were flown off to continue strikes and to continue the search for Lieutenant Mather. Unfortunately a further fatal accident occurred, Sub-Lieutenant J.M. Simmonds being seen to go into a spin and crash in the Chaeryong area, having made no attempt to abandon his aircraft.

Whilst attacking road transport next day near Ongjin, Lieutenant Heaton's Firefly was hit by small arms fire, smoke entered the cockpit and the engine started to vibrate. Heaton headed out to sea towards Paengyong-do, but on the way the vibration became worse until five miles off the enemy coast, north of the friendly island of Kirin-do, he ditched the aircraft. Thirteen minutes later he was picked up from his dinghy by a US Army helicopter and returned to the ship, which gave rise to the following signal:

FROM: GLORY   TO: COMNAVFE, (R) F02FE, CINCFES,
                                                                                                ADMIRALTY.

PRESS RELEASE. IN GATHERING DARKNESS HELICOPTER
LANDED GLORY'S FLIGHT DECK. US AIR FORCE PILOT AND
DOWNED BRITISH AIRMAN LIEUTENANT WILFRED RUSSELL
HEATON, ROYAL NAVY, OF NOTTINGHAM, ENGLAND,
GREETED BY VICE ADMIRAL CLARK USN, COMMANDING
7TH FLEET, REAR ADMIRAL GINRICH USN, COMMANDING
KOREAN BLOCKADE AND ESCORT FORCES, BRITISH REAR
ADMIRAL E.G.A. CLIFFORD CB, COMMANDING KOREAN
WEST COAST NAVAL FORCES, ALL ON VISIT TO BRITISH
CARRIER.
GLORY'S CAPTAIN E.D.G. LEWIN DSO, DSC AND BAR, A
ROYAL NAVY PILOT, EXPRESSED GRATITUDE OF HIMSELF
AND SHIP'S COMPANY WITH A BOTTLE OF GENUINE
SCOTCH WHISKY.

On the 11th, the last day of the patrol, a division led by Lieutenant Sample took off at 0615, two hours before sunrise, forming up at 1,000 feet six miles off the port bow round two flame floats. No road or rail traffic was seen during an hour's reconnaissance of the Haeju and Ongjin areas, but a stores dump was attacked with success. During this raid, warning fires were lit on the ground; these appeared two or three miles ahead of the aircraft, and the aircrew, looking back, could see a long line of them stretching behind. Earlier, on the 5th, Lieutenant McGrail had made 821 Squadron's 1,000th deck landing since embarking in *Glory* four months earlier in the Mediterranean.

On the way to Kure, *Glory* anchored off Iwakuni to embark replacement aircraft and to disembark one Firefly for a full rigging check.

Flying statistics for the patrol were:

	801 Squadron	821 Squadron
Hours	354	218
Operational sorties	197	118
Deck landings	194	122

Damage inflicted:

	Destroyed	**Damaged**
Road and rail bridges	2	5
Rail lines	33	
Rolling stock	9	7
Tunnel	1	
Motor transport	4	12
Gun emplacements	2	2
Store dumps	10	9
Transformers	1	
Troop billets	150+	15

It had been intended to dock *Glory* during this harbour period in Kure from 13th to 18th January, but at a late moment it was discovered that the dock was no longer fit to take large ships.

Lieutenant P. Cane, Senior Pilot of 821 Squadron, left on the 15th for the UK after nine years continuous flying, which had included operating *Triumph's* and *Theseus'* Sea Otter SAR amphibian in Korean waters from June 1950 to April 1951. He was succeeded by Lieutenant Dallosso as Senior Pilot.

Lieutenants Pearce and Leahy visited the Commonwealth Division front line, and Sub-Lieutenant Keates went to *Essex* on the east coast to witness jet aircraft operations.

Fifth Patrol

Glory left Kure on 19th January to relieve *Badoeng Strait* on the 21st. Although there were still some gun stoppages, most of the problems with ammunition had been cleared, aircraft were armed with HE and SAP, and restrictions on the use of guns had been lifted. It was planned to fly for four days before and then three days after replenishment, the Fireflies with bombs for the first half and rockets for the second. Strong winds of 40-45 knots and an appreciable swell on the last day suspended all flying — this after a day of no wind and a flat calm! Lieutenants Robbins and Sherlock were left behind, ill, in Japan, and with other pilots sick with 'flu and minor ailments, three sorties per day for the remainder was not uncommon. On the 22nd Lieutenant Wemyss left for UK, and on 24th Lieutenant Heaton completed 100 operational sorties, 56 in *Ocean* in 825 Squadron and 44 in 821.

It was learned from *Badoeng Strait* that ice was forming in the sheltered waters between Chodo and the mainland, and in Haeju Bay. Ships of the blockading force had to act as ice breakers to prevent a solid sheet of ice forming as a possible path for invasion of the friendly islands. Ice reconnaissance sorties were flown on the first and last events each day, the progress of the ice being reported to the nearby ships.

Because of the increased invasion risk, *Glory's* effort was again concentrated on villages quartering troops, on known strong concentrations of Chinese and North Korean forces, and on guns in coastal areas. Roads to the coast were continuously searched for transport, with considerable success, much being damaged or destroyed. A number of guns, well hidden in cliffs on the south-east corner of Ongjin peninsula, which for some time had been harassing friendly shipping and the island of Mudo, with day and night bombardments, were attacked by the Fireflies and, at least for a while, were silenced.

On 22nd January, as he was returning to the ship, Mr. Kent discovered that he was unable to lower the hook of his Firefly and he was ordered to land on the beach at Paengyong-do. It was only two hours after high water and there was a strong off-shore cross wind of 25 knots. After touch-down, the aircraft slowly swung to starboard into about nine inches of water and tipped onto its nose. It was later transported by sea to Iwakuni for repair. Before the end of the patrol Mr. Kent had flown-in a replacement aircraft.

Patrol statistics were:

	801 Squadron	821 Squadron
Hours	435	273
Operational sorties	238	146
Deck landings	240	155

	Destroyed	Damaged
Railway bridges	1	
Rail lines cut		14
Rolling stock	9	12
Locomotives	1	2
Tunnels		5
Road transport	31	13
Troops and billets	200	large number
Command post	1	1
Gun positions	1	1
Transformers		2
Store dumps		9
Ox-carts	67	36

During the period in Sasebo Lieutenants Bawden and McGregor and Sub-Lieutenants Hayes and Pearson joined 801 Squadron from *Ocean*.

On 11th February Rear Admiral C.E. Olsen USN became Commander of the Blockade and Escort Force (TF 95) in succession to Rear Admiral Ginrich. Admiral Ginrich had always been most appreciative of, and co-operative with, the Commonwealth contingent, and Admiral Clifford remarked that 'it had been a pleasure and a privilege to serve under him.'

Towards the end of February, Vice Admiral E.R. Mainguy, Canadian Chief of Naval Staff, and Commodore L.G. Durlacher, Chief of Staff to Admiral Russell, paid visits to the operational area.

A more humanitarian activity than normally fell to the lot of those employed on the west coast arose at this time. HMHS *Maine* was refitting at Hong Kong and a medical unit of Surgeon Commanders D.W. Pratt and B.W. Watford with two Sick Berth ratings was established at Paengyong-do on 7th March. Their services to the garrisons and to the local inhabitants were much appreciated.

Ice remained in the Chodo area until mid-March, and on 14th March Sok-to could be visited for the first time for three months by CTU 95.1.4, *Cardigan Bay*.

Sixth Patrol

Glory's departure from Sasebo on 5th February was delayed until an escort of two destroyers could be arranged because of intelligence reports that submarines might be operating in the area. In view of these reports, Captain Lewin decided to fly an anti-submarine screen of one Firefly during daylight. It resulted in a number of contacts being reported, all of which eventually proved to be 'non-submarine', and in future patrols this precaution was discontinued when there were three or more destroyers in the screen.

The Task Unit, with *Anzac*, *Consort*, *Comus*, *Charity* and USSs *Collett* and *Hanna* joining *Glory*, was not so fortunate with the weather on this patrol: on some days there was a little high cloud or none at all with visibility to 50 miles; on others snow showers, low cloud and poor visibility; flying was restricted on the 10th and 11th, and was stopped on the 15th, 14 events had to be cancelled giving a total of 491 sorties. The main air effort again was on troops and stores. Particular attention was paid to villages south-south-west of Chinnampo, said to be housing about 1,400 troops for 'Partisan subjugation'; and to the Ongjin peninsula where troops were reported to be massing with rubber boats for attacks on friendly islands. About two strikes per day attacked the rail system.

It had been intended to have five flying days before replenishment, but officers of the tanker *Wave Knight* were all taken ill, and replenishment was delayed one day while officers from *Birmingham* brought the tanker out to the Task Unit. For

HMS *Glory.*   *(Neep)*

the first six-and-a-half days the Fireflies were armed with rockets, for the last two-and-a-half with bombs. Each day consisted of six one-and-three-quarter hour events. In addition to four strike aircraft per event, the Fireflies had to provide one additional aircraft for continuous A/S patrol around the Task Unit. This called for a minimum of ten aircraft serviceable throughout the day, which was achieved until the loss of two aircraft and accidents to two others caused the strike effort to be reduced by 25% — on alternate events two-aircraft strikes were flown.

Aircraft on ASPROs carried two 250 lb. depth charges set to explode at 32 feet. To keep within the maximum allowable weight for landing, the starboard nacelle tank was left empty. A perimeter patrol at 10 miles from the carrier, or less in bad visibility, was flown. Aircrew were ordered to report and track any submerged submarine sighted unless it was found to be within the lines of submerged approach of any ship or seen to commit a hostile act; it could then be attacked. Surfaced submarines were only to be attacked if they showed signs of attacking the Task Unit.

The screening vessels obtained several sonar contacts, but they all proved to be 'non-submarine'. The aircrew sighted nothing except many square miles of ocean. During the night of 9th February the frigate *Crane* obtained a sonar contact, classified as a submarine, 20 miles south of Point Able, the island of Kirin-do. Two other frigates, *Opossum* and *Hawea* joined *Crane*, and a Firefly patrolled over them during the forenoon and afternoon of the 10th. Several patterns of Squid were fired but no wreckage came to the surface. Contact was lost during the forenoon, after which the search was abandoned.

The primary task for the Fireflies was the defence of friendly islands, with the main strike effort devoted to coastal troop concentrations and stores dumps. Some interdiction missions were carried out: in particular the marshalling yards at Haeju were bombed on four occasions. Targets were obtained from 5th USAF as well as from partisans and the ship's own intelligence.

801 Squadron's first encounter with enemy aircraft occurred on the first day of the patrol. Whilst returning from a strike and reconnaissance in the Hanchon area 53 Division, Lieutenants Leahy, Wheatley, Fiddian-Green and Sub-Lieut. Baynes, was attacked by a section of MiG-15s. They came in from very high astern, diving very fast; no damage was inflicted on the Furies.

Two pre-dawn strikes of four Furies and four Fireflies were launched, on the 8th and the 14th. Take-off was at 0520 and the aircraft would be in the northern part of the area in the vicinity of Hanchon and Pyongyang at about 0545, giving over an hour of darkness in which to attack motor transport convoys. Several convoys, as well as single vehicles, all with headlights on, were seen and strafed. Damage was not assessable in the dark and with their lights switched off as soon as the attacks started, unless they caught fire. On the morning of the 8th the Fireflies had little success; but the Furies, led by Lieutenant Commander Stuart, attacked several vehicles. During this event, Sub-Lieutenant Belleville had engine trouble, the oil temperature was rising and the pressure falling. He entertained serious thoughts of baling out, having jettisoned his hood, but he was fortunately able to land safely on Paengyong-do. On the 14th the Fireflies led by Lieutenant Marshall made several successful strafing attacks on transport moving in the Hanchon, Pyongyang and Chinnampo areas.

On the 9th Sub-Lieutenant Hayes, having been with 801 Squadron a few days and only on his third sortie, had his Fury hit by flak, cutting the oil lines. An oil leak was apparent after having attacked the target near Chaeryong but by the time the Taedong-Gang estuary had been reached the oil pressure had dropped considerably and the temperature had risen until eventually the engine seized. The SAR organization on Chodo had been alerted and in only one or two minutes after actually ditching — fortunately in water clear of ice — a helicopter was over him and picking him up. He was transferred to *Anzac* on patrol in the vicinity of Chodo and transferred to *Glory* a couple of days later.

On the 11th Lieutenant C.A. MacPherson lost his life when his Fury was hit while carrying out a low-level strafing attack on a stores dump in the vicinity of Chaeryong. The aircraft crashed on a hillside, exploded and burst into flames.

Just prior to landing-on on the 14th, Sub-Lieutenant R.D. Bradley had an engine failure in his Fury and announced on the RT his intention of ditching. He jettisoned his hood and the aircraft struck the water nose down at an estimated 140-150 knots after which it broke up and sank within 10 seconds. No trace of the pilot was subsequently found after an immediate search by the destroyers of the screen.

Two deck landing accidents broke 821 Squadron's sequence. On 9th Sub-

Accident series – Wave off.   *(Author)*

– Stalled and sinking.   *(Author)*

– Waterbourne.   *(Author)*

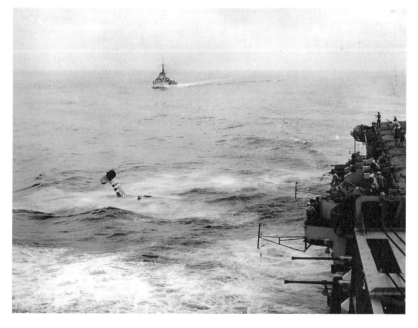

– Rescued by a destroyer.   *(Author)*

Lieutenant Millett was returning from an A/S patrol with Captain R. Bury RA, one of the CBGLOs, in the rear cockpit. After the 'Cut' the starboard wing dropped and the aircraft started to swing to starboard. The pilot applied power in an effort to keep straight, but the hook engaged number four wire and the aircraft swung over the side abreast number nine wire and into the water. Both aircrew escaped from their cockpits — Bury with some difficulty and assisted by Millett — and were soon rescued by *Comus*. On the 13th Lieutenant Bacon was fast on the 'Cut', he checked too soon and the aircraft engaged number 10 wire and entered the first barrier.

On the 10th, immediately after being launched, Lieutenant Dallosso experienced very rough running in his engine, possibly overheating as a result of loss of coolant. He jettisoned his two depth charges and endeavoured to make a circuit but the engine stopped and he ditched from 300 feet. Dallosso and Sub-Lieutenant Harrison were soon in their dinghies and were picked up by Hanna.

The weather on the 15th was unsuitable for flying, with excessive wind speed over the deck and the weather inshore was also considered to be unsuitable for operations. There was thus no flying and *Glory* set course for Kure where she arrived on the 17th. During the patrol two Fireflies and two Furies had been damaged by enemy fire.

During the patrol, Sub-Lieutenant Wailes completed 120 operational sorties, 74 in *Glory*, and Lieutenant Heaton 116; they both left for UK on the 21st during the harbour period.

Statistics for the patrol were:

	801 Squadron	821 Squadron
Hours	538	367
Operational sorties	281	148
A/S patrols		47
Decklandings	290	209

	Destroyed	Damaged
Rail bridges	1	
Rail lines	12	7
Rolling stock	12	43
Gun positions		11
Road transport	80	112
Transformers		2
Supply dumps	5	3
Billets and buildings	large numbers	

Occasionally some confirmation of the success of strikes was forthcoming from the North Korean partisans, for example after this patrol the 1st Partisan Infantry Regiment signalled reporting that in two of 801's strikes, Lieutenant Pearce and Sub-Lieutenants Pearson, Keates and Baynes had killed 11 and wounded 17 North Korean soldiers; and Lieutenant Commander Stuart, Lieutenant Anson, and Sub-Lieutenants Belleville and Smith had killed 11 and wounded 28 as well as destroying two ammunition dumps and one warehouse.

Operation Pinwheel was used to help *Glory* go alongside the jetty at Kure, an evolution carried out quickly and smoothly. Whilst in harbour, replacement aircraft were lightered aboard from Iwakuni, and the helicopter, that had been ashore for repair, was flown aboard. Lieutenant Hunter returned from JOC at Seoul.

Seventh Patrol

After long negotiations between the Admiralty and the Treasury, dollars had been made available for the purchase of 50 aircrew emergency radios from the USAF which were to be worn for the first time on this patrol. The battery and the transmitter/receiver were worn under the armpits in the pockets of a vest (waistcoat — in English). To keep them warm and dry they had to be worn under the immersion suit blouse which made dressing and undressing difficult, but the effort was worthwhile since it was known that many US aviators owed their lives to this equipment. The radio — Dodo — was crystallised on the distress frequency and could be voice or morse activated. In tests carried out between a Dodo on *Glory* and an aircraft, clearly audible signals were received at 20 miles range at 2,000 feet, and at 60 miles at 5,000 feet. They proved to be a not too uncomfortable addition to the already large amount of flying and survival kit worn, but the morale value far outweighed any discomfort. Typical flying kit for operations in below-freezing conditions consisted, besides a lot of warm clothing underneath, of the personal radio set waistcoat, an immersion suit, Mae West, survival backpack plus a holster and .38 inch revolver.

During this patrol from 25th February to 6th March, *Glory* with *Anzac*, *Athabaskan*, *Haida*, *Cockade*, USSs *McCord* and *Hanson* experienced the worst weather since her return to the station. Rain and snow, with extensive low cloud, and gales with steep seas and a heavy swell, were all encountered, added to which the foggy season had started. Radiation fog over land during the night was often brought out to sea by the south-east winds; an increase in wind speed during the day would then lift the fog to become a layer of stratus cloud that, over land, obscured targets. On other days high winds and rain storms affected flying, severely curtailing it on two days and making it impossible on one. 371 sorties were flown, a daily average of 53, but 23 events totalling 229 sorties were cancelled.

Operations started on the 26th, planned for five days flying before replenishment and three days after. As daylight hours were increasing, seven events of 1 hour 35 minutes were scheduled for each day with the first launch at 0700 and last recovery at 1805.

Firefly strike targets were mainly troop concentrations and stores, and road and rail transport; and as a result of a change in the anti-submarine policy, no ASPROs were flown unless there were fewer than three destroyers in the screen. Early in the morning of 2nd March *Hanson* reported a confirmed sonar contact. She was detached to hunt the submarine while the rest of the Task Unit turned away. At dawn two Fireflies were launched, in bad weather, one to assist in the hunt, the other to patrol around *Glory* and the remaining two escorts. Depth charges were dropped by one aircraft when *Hanson* fired a pattern but no wreckage or oil was seen. Late in the afternoon the contact was classified 'non-submarine' and the hunt was abandoned.

On the 27th, with sea fog covering the ship and valley fog over land, operations began at 1100 and were suspended at 1500; on the 28th there was no flying due to thick fog. On 1st March the first event was cancelled, after which a full programme was flown, though valley fog over Korea obscured a fair proportion of the ground. A signal was received later from the 1st Partisan Army reporting that 29 North Korean soldiers had been killed, 23 wounded and 12 houses had been destroyed; the Fury flight responsible was Lieutenants Leahy, Wheatley, Fiddian-Green and Mitchell.

Since *Glory* had returned to Korean waters, efforts had been made to build up a close liaison with the guerrillas — these efforts were now bearing fruit. Far more information was being received from the partisans, and the results of strikes left little doubt of its authenticity and value. A good piece of work which particularly pleased the partisans was carried out by Lieutenant Commander Stuart and Lieutenant Anson on 2nd March. The weather was so bad that only defensive sorties were being flown, and these two pilots were being briefed for a Fury CAP mission when an urgent request was received for an immediate air strike on an island north of Sunwido. To avoid delay while getting the strike ready, it was decided to send the CAP at once. Lieutenant Commander Stuart's section dealt so severely with all they could see that it was not necessary to follow up with a strike.

The second half of the 1st Partisan Army signal confirmed their action, reporting 34 North Korea soldiers killed. A signal of thanks and congratulations on the speed of response to the request for help was received from the American organisation CCRAK (Covert, Clandestine and Related Activities, Korea); and another congratulatory signal from CTF 95, Admiral Olsen USN — WELL DONE.

After replenishment on the 3rd, Operation Paperchase was planned for the 4th and 6th on the first four events of each day for both squadrons. It was part of a co-ordinated plan for the east and west coasts to cover a lot of the larger towns and villages in selected areas with leaflets. The '500 lb.' bombs were supplied by the US authorities; they were set to burst at about 2,000 feet and had to be dropped up-wind from 5-8,000 feet, depending on the wind strength, to scatter the leaflets over the towns and villages in *Glory's* area. The bombs required some adaptation before they could be dropped from British aircraft, and when this had been effected they were dropped without incident on the 4th and 6th, but on the second day the programme had to be curtailed due to a great increase in wind speed over the deck and to an increasing swell.

Preparations were made for a pre-dawn strike on the 5th. To assist spotting motor transport convoys after they had extinguished their lights, a fifth Firefly with eight parachute flares was to accompany the strike aircraft. Sunrise was at 0714 and at 0500 the aircraft and aircrews were all ready. Two Furies piloted by Lieutenant Pearce and Sub-Lieutenant Keates were launched and the ship then sailed into a thick bank of fog that persisted for about an hour. The Furies flew to the target area but had very limited success due to fog in the Hanchon and Pyongyang areas. The remainder of the launch was abandoned and the two Furies returned to the ship at 0700, now in the clear. After this false start, a full day's flying was achieved.

During this patrol confirmation was received from the Partisan Regiment operating in North Korea of Sub-Lieutenant Rayner's death. He was, as previously reported, missing from a sortie on 5th January, when, after his aircraft had been hit, he crashed near to the village of Chang Yang Dong 12 miles south of Chinnampo. His body was buried just north of the village by the Chinese.

After inviting the special attention of USS *Bataan* to an enemy radar station, damaged by a strike that morning, *Glory* left the area on 6th March, arriving in Sasebo on the 8th. No aircraft had been lost during the patrol, but three Furies and two Fireflies had been damaged by enemy fire.

Operation Paperchase 2-sided leaflet – 4 sketches black on white on red background:

If you do not want to lose your life do not participate in Military Operations.
Escape to the hillside. Keep away from main roads.

Help the Anti Communist Guerillas. Give help for free Korea now.
Co-operate with United Nations forces.

Statistics for the patrol were:

	801 Squadron	**821 Squadron**
Hours	347.40	246
Sorties	227	142
Deck Landings	227	144

Firefly serviceability, which had always been good, reached the very high level of 98.2% during this patrol.

	Destroyed	**Damaged**
Bridges	1	2
Rail line cuts	17	3
Tunnels		3
Rolling stock	1	24
Gun emplacements		6
Radar stations		1
Vessels	5	
Store dumps	1	8
Road transport	35	60

In many military billets, a large number of troops were killed and wounded in attacks on troop concentrations. Confirmation of casualties was reported by 1st Partisan Infantry Regiment.

During the period in harbour Lieutenant Crawford joined 801 Squadron and Lieutenant Banner joined 821 in place of Sub-Lieutenant Wailes.

Rear Admiral Clifford spent the latter part of March on the west coast. Leaving Kure on the 19th, having met Lieutenant General H. Wells, CinC British Forces in Korea, he went to Inchon flying his flag in *Newcastle*, relieving *Birmingham* as CTU 95.1.2 en route. He called on General Maxwell Taylor, the new commander 8th Army who was much interested in west coast operations and arranged to pay a visit there with the Admiral in April. On 21st March Admiral Clifford left Inchon, taking as his guest Major General Alston-Roberts-West to see what the Navy was doing. The General's trip was disappointing owing to weather; a full gale prevented landing at Chodo, and it was too bad for flying operations when he visited *Glory*, but he witnessed a bombardment by *Newcastle* of enemy troop and gun positions in the Paengyong-do area on 26th March.

Admiral Clifford, accompanied by Lieutenant Colonel Totman USMC, West

Coast Island Defence Commander, landed at Sok-to, Chodo and Yong Pyong-do where he met local commanders. The latter area had been unusually quiet, enemy activity during the previous month had been limited to a few bombardments of Mudo — one on 4th March replied to by *Whitesand Bay* and *McCord*, and again on the 16th and the 28th when *Anzac* silenced the enemy guns.

Eighth Patrol

Glory left Sasebo on 15th March with *Charity, Athabaskan, Cowell and Higbee*. Nine flying days, each of eight events of 1 hour 25 minutes, were planned, but bad weather interfered with flying on three days. Haze persisted almost the whole time. Mist and fog at sea, fog in valleys with low cloud over hills, and low overcast conditions with some rain, was general; and there were gales with winds gusting up to 45 knots and a heavy swell. Because at this time of the year the Yellow Sea suffers from sea fog, the first event each morning consisted of two Furies on CAP and weather reconnaissance, and the first Fury and Firefly strikes would be not launched until 0905. In addition to ensuring that aircrew were not overworked, and the allowance of bombs and rockets was not exceeded, the scheme had the advantage that the aircraft for these first strikes were armed in the morning instead of late the previous evening. Even so, three sorties per day for aircrew was not uncommon. In order to use the extra daylight more efficiently, clocks were advanced one hour so that King time, 10 hours ahead of GMT (Zulu), was being worked in the operational area instead of Item, 9 hours ahead.

The spring thaw was exploited as much as possible by attacks on road and rail bridges, tunnels, railways and transport. The thaw increased the flow of water in the rivers and the enemy found rebuilding these vital communication links was not as simple as it had been during the winter months, he was not able to construct water level by-pass bridges so quickly.

Most of the remainder of the air effort was devoted to troop concentrations reported by partisans, and stores. The Fireflies were armed with bombs for one-and-a-half days and rockets for the remainder.

On the 17th the Fury strike on a railway bridge known to be well defended — there was an accurate AA position on an adjacent hill — took with them a flak suppression section who dive-bombed the gun position at the same time as the main attack was being made on the bridge. The action was completely successful and no AA fire was encountered.

Drizzle and low overcast caused all flying to be cancelled on the 19th, nor was there any on the 20th, it being replenishment day. Fine weather on the next two days allowed complete programmes of operations to be flown. The whole area was continually covered by the Furies, particularly the northern section where on several occasions motor transport was seen moving along roads. Such lorry movement in broad daylight was most rare and successful strafing attacks were made, leaving lorries wrecked at the roadside or in flames.

During the morning of the 21st, Lieutenant Wheatley's aircraft developed a high oil temperature shortly after take-off. He made a successful precautionary landing on Paengyong-do and was brought back to the ship in a Firefly during the afternoon. A further flak suppression mission was flown on the 22nd in support of a division attacking a radio station near Sariwon. Photo reconnaissance had revealed three AA gun positions in the vicinity of the target. Complete success was achieved, no flak was encountered and the radio station was destroyed.

Operations were suspended early on the 23rd due to a large amount of cloud, and on the 24th low cloud and poor visibility allowed only one event of two aircraft to be flown at 0945 for CAP and weather reconnaissance. The pilots Lieutenant Commander L. Baker (Senior LSO) and Sub-Lieutenant Keates, remained airborne for two-and-a-quarter hours but the weather showed no sign of improvement. They landed-on under a 300 feet cloud base and in visibility of less than one mile. Flying was cancelled for the rest of the day. The 25th was overcast with approximately 45 knots wind over the deck and an appreciable swell. Flying was cancelled early and the ship proceeded to Kure.

455 sorties were flown, a daily average of 76; four Fireflies and two Furies were damaged by enemy fire. During the patrol, 821 Squadron flew its 1,000th operational sortie; and Lieutenant Skinner, Sub-Lieutenant Millett and Mr. Kent all completed 100 sorties. Lieutenant Dallosso returned to Sasebo in *Consort* to await passage to the UK and Lieutenant Sample became Senior Pilot.

Statistics for the patrol were:

	801 Squadron	**821 Squadron**
Hours	464	259
Operational sorties	288	159
Deck landings	287	175

	Destroyed	**Damaged**
Bridges	17	2
Tunnels		6
Rail lines cut	13	
Rolling stock	9	7
Road transport	36	39
Gun positions		1
Store dumps		8
Transformers	2	
Vessels		9
Radio and radar stations	3	1
Sluice gates		1

Unicorn, on the opposite side of the jetty to *Glory* at Kure, had brought up replacement aircraft from Sembawang, and exchanged two Fireflies with defective engines and a Fury. Visits were paid to the island of Miyajima, to the shrines on the islands that were visited by World War II Kamikaze pilots who trained at Iwakuni.

On Tuesday 1st April the ship's companies of both carriers combined to participate in a memorial service on the jetty to the late Dowager Queen Mary whose death had been announced on 25th March.

Admiral Clifford arrived back in Sasebo on 1st April where he transferred his flag to *Ladybird* for the last time. At last a depot ship, with a reduced complement, had arrived to take her place. HMS *Tyne*, (Captain A.J.F. Milne-Home), arrived in Sasebo on 7th April and took over from *Ladybird*, which in due course was returned to her owners in Hong Kong. Admiral Clifford wrote:

'During her time as headquarters ship of the British Commonwealth Naval forces, HMS *Ladybird*, though quite inadequate for the job, has done yeoman service to a degree far above that which could have been expected. The undoubted prestige of her name amongst all UN forces is a tribute to all who worked and served in her under trying and crowded conditions'.

The improved spring weather brought a sharp increase in coastal activity in early April. During the month both Chodo and Sok-to were fired at on a number of occasions, the heaviest bombardment was on 5th April when Chodo received 330 x 76 mm shells, causing only a few casualties and slight damage. *Cardigan Bay* and two 90 mm guns on the island returned the fire. Aircraft from 5th USAF and *Glory* attacked enemy gun positions. Just after the bombardment Admiral Clifford arrived in the area in *Birmingham* accompanied by General Taylor. The Admiral took the opportunity of pressing him to provide Sok-to with some artillery to retaliate on batteries which were frequently taking the island under fire. Two 90 mm guns from 8th Army headquarters were soon forthcoming. Enemy aircraft — the Bedcheck Charlies — started to carry out periodical light bombing raids in the Chodo area at night, which they later extended to Seoul.

Enemy activities in the Paengyong-do area were on the increase. Several partisan-held islands were shelled and mortared, *Whitesand Bay*, *Haida* and *Condamine* all came under fire at different times, but suffered no casualties or damage.

An extensive tour of the west coast was made by Rear Admiral Olsen USN under the guidance of Admiral Clifford in *Birmingham*. It was the first occasion on which Admiral Olsen had been able to visit the west coast since assuming command of TF 95 in February.

Ninth Patrol

Glory sailed from Kure on 3rd April to start operations on the 4th, accompanied by *Haida*, *Athabaskan*, *Herbert J. Thomas* and *Higbee*. It was planned to fly eight events per day from 0715 to 1930, again using King time, and to replenish on the fifth day. Towards the end of the patrol a strike of four Fireflies was included with the two CAP and weather Furies on the first event. 467 sorties were flown, a daily average of 67.

The main targets were again road and rail bridges, tunnels, railways and transport, troop concentrations and stores, with support being given to partisans when requested. The Fireflies were armed with bombs for-one-and-a-half days and rockets thereafter. Their bombing targets were road and rail bridges, but strong, variable, winds made aiming difficult and results were poor, only one bridge was destroyed and two damaged.

A new type of rocket projectile was used having a 60 lb. hollow charged head. The effect of the hollow was to concentrate the explosion ahead of the rocket. The projectile had greater penetrating power and could be used effectively against tanks and armoured vehicles. However, against targets then available in Korea it was not appreciable more efficient than the old type RP.

Weather again interfered with the flying programme, 130 sorties were cancelled.

Point Oboe, the datum point for carrier operations approximately 30 miles west of Paengyong-do, was moved south-east in an attempt to avoid the coastal fog which persists throughout the spring season in the Yellow Sea. In addition to this coastal fog, sea fog spreading rapidly from the south-west was also encountered on several occasions, flying being suspended whilst the ship steamed into an area free of fog with sufficient sea room to operate aircraft. The ship was sometimes sandwiched between two banks of fog and on one occasion strayed too close and the wing destroyers disappeared from view.

It had been calculated that theoretically a carrier equipped with 33 aircraft flying sorties of 1 hour 20 minutes duration, should be able to launch about twelve sorties for every daylight hour. After due deliberation by the meteorological experts Easter Sunday, April 5th, was chosen for an experiment to be carried out to test the validity of this estimate: 101 aircraft were launched in 8 hours, which afforded supporting evidence of its accuracy. A further 22 sorties were flown during the remaining five-and-a-half hours of daylight to equal — but not surpass — the record set up by *Ocean* the previous summer. As the result of this experiment and of his own experience, Captain Lewin recorded his considered opinion that an efficient light fleet carrier with 33 aircraft and 50 pilots ought to be able to fly 200 sorties in a 16 hour day as a set piece.

It proved to be a fine day, hazy but with only one sign of bad weather, a large shower cloud which drifted across the operational area during the afternoon.

A high rate of serviceability was required, with the flight deck and hangar crews having to work at top speed repairing minor defects and preparing aircraft for relaunching. 100% Firefly serviceability was kept up throughout the day, and when one Fury was damaged in a taxying accident early in the morning, necessitating a complete tail plane change, 19 of the remaining 20 aircraft had to be kept airworthy, a task achieved by the Squadron maintenance ratings. The aircraft with the new tail plane was serviceable during the afternoon and was included in the later events. In another case a complete sparking plug change was carried out in the one hour and twenty minutes between events, the aircraft remaining on deck and being re-armed and re-fuelled at the same time so that it could be included in the next event.

Maximum flying effort was maintained from before dawn until 1445 by which time 107 sorties had been flown. The effort was then reduced to the minimum required to achieve the target of 123 sorties. On the last three events, therefore, only CAP and TARCAP were airborne. It had been necessary to fly continuous TARCAP from 0930 as Sitting Duck and Chodo island were being shelled intermittently by enemy coastal guns. These guns were rocketed and strafed several times and temporarily silenced.

All pilots flew four sorties, some five; of the ship's officers, Commander J. Sleigh (Commander (Air)), Lieutenant Commander D. Berrill (Flight Deck Officer)

Sea Fury TARCAP over the ice, Winter 1952/3.   *(Fiddian-Green)*

and Lieutenant A. Lacayo (LSO) flew two sorties each and Lieutenant Commander L. Baker flew one. When flying was finished, 801 Squadron had flown 71 sorties and 821 had flown 52.

During a strafing run on the 11th, the ailerons of Lieutenant Handscombe's Fury jammed. He carried out a successful emergency landing in shallow water just off the beach at Paengyong-do, and it was later discovered that a link-chute had fouled the control rod linkage. Only two aircraft were damaged by enemy action during the patrol.

Glory sailed for Sasebo on completion of flying on the 11th, arriving on the 12th. A record number of visitors was entertained during the patrol, 33 officers (including General Maxwell Taylor USA, Admiral Olsen USN and Admiral Clifford) and 16 ratings.

Statistics for the patrol were:

	801 Squadron	821 Squadron
Hours	459	276
Operational sorties	288	177
Deck landings	287	179

	Destroyed	**Damaged**
Road and rail bridges	16	4
Tunnels		1
Rail lines	12	2
Rolling stock	2	4
Road transport	54	65
Vessels		6
Gun positions		4
Store dumps	2	9
Troop billets	61	38
Buildings	10	
Factory	1	
Transformers	1	1
Lock gates	1	

During the harbour period from 12th to 18th April, Mr. Kent left to return to UK, Sub-Lieutenant Millett was promoted Lieutenant, and Lieutenants Spelling, Bacon and Smith (three large gentlemen, collectively referred to as the Three Grocers), joined 821 Squadron. They had flown from London to Tokyo in a Comet jet aircraft of British Overseas Airways Corporation in under 48 hours, a flight which in 1953 was sufficiently quick to cause a comment in the diary. Mr. Lines joined 801 Squadron.

Record Day gave rise to the following signal:

FROM…GLORY   TO…ADMIRALTY FOR CNI

INFO…FO2FES (A&A), CINC FES, COMNAVFE, CINCMED

FOLLOWING FOR PRESS RELEASE

1. BRITISH NAVAL AIRCRAFT FROM LIGHT FLEET CARRIER GLORY HAVE TODAY SUNDAY COMPLETED 123 OPERATIONAL SORTIES OVER NORTH KOREA.

2. STARTING WITH ONLY DIM LIGHT OF WATERY MOON PILOTS OF 801 SEA FURY AND 821 FIREFLY SQUADRONS WHO HAVE BEEN FLYING THROUGHOUT KOREAN WINTER MAINTAINED CONTINUOUS EFFORT UNTIL MID AFTERNOON SO THAT RECORD FOR CARRIERS ON WEST COAST KOREA ESTABLISHED BY HMS OCEAN LAST YEAR SHOULD BE EXACTLY EQUALLED.

3. FULL LOADS OF BOMBS ROCKETS AND CANNON SHELLS CARRIED TO VITAL MILITARY TARGETS IN HEART OF ENEMY TERRITORY WHILST REINFORCED AMMUNITION SUPPLY PARTIES AND AIR ENGINEERS IN CARRIER WORKED AGAINST TIME TO PREPARE AIRCRAFT FOR RELAUNCHING.

4. EVERY AIRCRAFT IN SHIP LAUNCHED ALTERNATE FLIGHTS ALL PILOTS COMPLETING FOUR SORTIES TOTALLING MORE THAN SIX HOURS FLYING.

5. THROUGHOUT THIS EASTER DAY CHAPLAINS WERE TRANSFERRED BY GLORY'S HELICOPTER BETWEEN THE CARRIER AND HER UNITED STATES AND CANADIAN DESTROYER ESCORTS WHERE FULL SCHEDULE DIVINE SERVICES HELD.

6. GLORY NOW IN HER THIRD YEAR FOREIGN SERVICE COMMISSION HAS ALREADY STEAMED 147 THOUSAND MILES ALMOST ENTIRELY KOREAN SERVICE. HER AIRCRAFT HAVE COMPLETED OVER TWELVE THOUSAND FIVE HUNDRED FLIGHTS INCLUDING EIGHT THOUSAND FOUR HUNDRED IN KOREAN WAR.

DTG…050900Z

Note. Addressee FO2FES (A&A) is (Afloat and Ashore), i.e. *Birmingham* and *Ladybird*.

Damage inflicted on the enemy on Record Day:

	Destroyed	Damaged
Road and rail bridges	7	4
Tunnel		1
Rail cuts	4	
Gun positions		3
Houses	28	19
Ox carts	5	

FLYING PROGRAMME — RECORD BREAKER FOR SUNDAY 5th APRIL

Duty officers 801 Bawden 821 Lt. Agnew

Event	Off	On	A/C	Mission	C/S	Crews
	0645	0805	2Fu	C.A.P.	54	BLUE GREG
A			4Fu	Strike	52	PEAR PSON KETE BYES
			3Fu	Strike	53	LEAH FIDO MICH
			6Fi	Strike	77	SAMP BANN SKIN ROBB KENT SHER
	0805	0925	2 Fu	C.A.P.	88	BAKE BAWD
B			4Fu	Strike	51	C.O. BELL SMIT ANSN
			3Fu	Strike	55	HAND FOST CRAW
			6Fi	Strike	76	C.O./WEST MILL GARV HAMN MARS GRAI
	0425	1045	2Fu	C.A.P.	99	AIR KETE
C			4Fu	Strike	52	PEAR PSON BLUE HYES
			4Fu	Strike	53	LEAH GREG FIDO MICH
			6Fi	Strike	77	SAMP BERR SKIN ROBB KENT SHER
	1045	1205	2Fu	C.A.P.	88	LAYO BELL
D			3Fu	A.R.	51	C.O. SMIT ANSN
			4Fu	Strike	55	HAND BAWD FOST CRAW
			6Fi	Strike	76	CO/HARI MILL GARV HAMN MARS GRAI
	1205	1325	2Fu	C.A.P.	99	AIR PSON
E			4FLI	Strike	52	PEAR KETF BLUE HYES
			4Fu	Strike	53	LEAH GREG FIDO MICH
			4Fi	Strike	77	SAMP BANN SKIN ROBB
			2Fi	Tarcap	80	KENT SHER
	1325	1445	2Fu	C.A.P.	88	BAKE FOST
F			4Fu	Tarcap	51	C.O. BELL SMIT ANSN
			3Fu	A.R	55	HAND BAWD CRAW
			2Fi	Tarcap	76	C.O. MILL
			4Fi	Strike	79	GARV/COLE HAMN MARS GRAI
	1445	1605	2Fu	C.A.P.	52	PEAR MICH
G			3Fu	Strike	53	LEAH PSON FIDO
			4Fu	Strike	54	BLUE HYES KETE GREG
			4Fi	Strike	77	SA.MP BANN KENT BERR
			2Fi	Tarcap	76	SKIN ROBB
	1605	1705	2Fu	C.A.P.	88	LAYO ANSN
H			4Fi	Tarcap	76	C.O. MILL GARV HAMN
	1705	1815	2Fu	C.A.P.	53	LEAH HYES
J			4Fi	Tarcap	78	MARS/AGNE BANN GRAI SHER
	1845	1925	2Fu	C.A.P.	51	C.O. SMIT
K			2Fu	Tarcap	55	HAND FOST

Flying Stations:- 0545 Cat Required:- 0645 Briefing:- 20 mins before launch

ORDNANCE:- Fury 2 x 500 except on A.R. and C.A.P.
Firefly 8 x 60 lb. R/P throughout.
Bombs Required:- 104 x 500lb. R/P Required:- 384 x 60lb.

FUEL:- Fury full internal plus full drop tanks.
Firefly full internal plus half nacelles.

NOTES:-
1. No C.A.S. — Gun co-ordination or Courier.

	Moon Rise	0107
2. Helicopter required after event ABLE.	Nautical Twilight	0625
	Sunrise	0723

WHEELS UP:-

| Paengyong Do 0945 — 1245 | Sunset | 2009 |
| Chodo 0945 — 1545 | Nautical Twilight | 2106 |

(Sgd.) J.W.SLEIGH.
COMMANDER (AIR).

Vice Admiral Sir Charles Lambe had hoisted his flag as CinCFES in succession to Admiral Russell on 20th March, and between 19th and 27th April made a tour of the theatre of operations. He visited all the principal islands and ships in the west coast area, going on to Sasebo and other cities in Japan to meet senior officers of the UN and British Commonwealth forces, and to see ships and establishments in Japan.

HMS *Charity* showing line for a jackstay transfer.   *(Author)*

Tenth Patrol

Glory left Sasebo twelve hours earlier than usual on 19th April so that the four new pilots could have some deck-landing practice, while, to clear the deck, two Fireflies and eight Furies carried out a navigation exercise of the south Korean coast. Lieutenant Anson and Sub-Lieutenant Foster ferried replacement Furies to the ship from Iwakuni. *Glory* took over as CTU 95.1.1 on the evening of 19th April, with *Charity*, *Consort*, *Anzac* USSs *Southerland*, *Cowell* and *Herbert J.Thomas* all being part of her screen during the patrol.

On 20th April the exchange of sick and wounded prisoners of war started taking place at — Operation Little Switch. The UN prisoners were being transported from camps north of Pyongyang, along the main supply route to the 'Holy Land' around Kaesong. Because of this, and to safeguard these prisoners from attack by UN aircraft, USS *Bataan* had had her operations severely restricted while the movement of convoys carrying the returning prisoners was taking place.

Major Scott RM, senior CGBLO, was flown by Firefly to Seoul to get the latest information, and returned to say that it was permitted to attack targets south of the Taedong Gang and west of the line Chinnampo/Anak/Haeju, but before making an attack, the aircraft would have to be identified and have its position confirmed on the radar of the TADC (Tactical Aircraft Direction Centre) at Chodo, or by Mosquito. Attack on any form of road transport was not permitted.

As there were no Mosquitoes in the area, and it was difficult for technical reasons to obtain a TADC fix, *Glory* was unable to take full advantage of this concession. Obtaining clearance during the restricted period was a tiresome process for the pilots, it often meant climbing to 10,000 feet over a target to ensure identification on Chodo's radar. However, at the request of JOC, close air support for troops of the Commonwealth Division was provided by 24 Furies on 21st April, and next day the restriction was lifted. The daily programme was arranged so that a short strike by the Fireflies was followed by a longer Fury mission, extra time being required to cover the double journey of 130 miles to and from the Front Line. After the first few, confusing, trips, the pilots soon settled down and understood the patter from the American Mosquito pilots indicating targets. The usual bridges, troop concentrations and stores dumps were attacked, and CAS for the troops by 12 Furies continued for the rest of the patrol.

The UN Command had offered a large reward to any Communist pilot who would desert. Aircrew had been warned that these deserters would fly south to Paengyong-do then east to Kimpo, and were not to be attacked — but none was seen.

On the 23rd, 54 Division was attacked by MiG-15s while operating just south of Chinnampo. Lieutenants Bluett and McGregor were covering Lieutenant McCandless and Sub-Lieutenant Hayes who were commencing a photographing run and were approached by two MiGs from ahead and two from astern diving from

HMS *Charity* showing the hazardous conditions in which many transfers were carried out.   *(Author)*

about 8,000 feet. Lieutenant McGregor had time for one firing burst, but after 'Break' the MiGs climbed away to the north. Lieutenant McGregor's aircraft was hit in the outer mainplane by one cannon shell, but he returned to the ship safely.

In the evening of the 25th Lieutenant J.T. McGregor was taking part in a strike on the Soho bridge, six miles south of Sariwon. There was considerable flak in the area and on recovering from the attack both the Division leader and the Number 2 observed Lieutenant McGregor's aeroplane rolling and in a steep dive. He crashed in the vicinity of the target, and it was assumed that either he or his aircraft had been hit during the dive. An hour later the same evening Sub-Lieutenant W.J.B. Keates, flying the CAP, was ordered inland with his section leader to bomb some ammunition caves south-west of Changyon reported by the partisans. On pulling out of his dive Sub-Lieutenant Keates was seen to flick into a spin and to crash into the ground at a shallow angle.

Weather had been uniformly fine until the night of 26th April, when on the last day sea fog, which reduced visibility to less than one cable, followed by continuous rain and overcast, prevented any flying. 447 sorties were flown at a daily average of 74; 448 x 500 lb. bombs, 904 RP and 47,400 x 20 mm rounds were dropped and fired on the enemy. The Fireflies had been armed with rockets for four days and bombs for two; ox-carts had been more in evidence, 75 had been sighted and strafed.

On 20th April the CinC, Vice Admiral Sir Charles Lambe, visited *Glory*, and flew in a Firefly with the CO of 821 Squadron, Lieutenant Commander Gardner, over the enemy coast and watched dive bombing and rocket attacks by Furies and Fireflies.

On the same day Lieutenant Millett had gone to Paengyong-do to pick up a Fury pilot, and during take off with an off-shore cross wind, the aircraft developed a crabbing movement, ran into shallow water and nosed over. The engine was found to be shock-loaded and would have to be changed, and so the aircraft could not be flown back to the ship; the FIR aircraft took its place. Three Fireflies and another Fury were damaged by enemy fire during the patrol.

Two jackstay transfers were carried out in fog. The first was to return a rating for whom cell accommodation had been provided to *Consort*. Visibility was estimated at two cables (four hundred yards), and *Consort* was given positional data from *Glory's* pilotage radar (Type 974). *Consort* reported holding *Glory* visually at two-and-a-half cables, but she was not visible from *Glory's* bridge (60 feet above the water line) until she was less than two cables away.

The second transfer was with *Southerland* to send turn-over material to USS *Bataan* and twelve ratings on an exchange agreement between the two carriers. A similar procedure was followed, but as 'cables' are not used in the USN, ranges were passed in yards. *Southerland* reported visual contact at 300 yards. In addition to thick fog, this operation was accompanied by strong winds, an electrical storm and heavy rain. In spite of the conditions, the manoeuvre was satisfactorily executed.

Statistics for the patrol were:

	801 Squadron	821 Squadron
Hours	469	296
Operational sorties	264	177
Deck landings	262	208

	Destroyed	Damaged
Bridges	7	4
Rail lines		3
Rolling stock		2
Road transport	76	44
Gun positions	5	
Stores dumps	2	10
Transformers	1	1
Troop billets	94	33

During the passage to Kure, three Fireflies flew to Pusan airfield with three army officers who had been visiting *Glory*. The aircraft, whose engine hours were nearly expired, were flown on to Iwakuni for overhaul. Replacements for both squadrons were later received by lighter during the harbour period from 29th April to 4th May.

Eleventh Patrol

Glory's third tour in Korean waters was drawing to a close, and on 5th May she assumed duty as CTU 95.1.1, with *Cossack*, *Crusader*, *Southerland* and *Herbert J.Thomas* for her 25th and last patrol.

Because of recent losses of Corsairs by US Marine Squadron VMA 312 in USS *Bataan*, Commander 7th Fleet had ordered that no unnecessary risks were to be taken by naval aircraft operating off the Korean west coast. Specifically he forbade all low level attacks against heavily defended targets without flak suppression from shore-based jet aircraft. CTF 95, in command of the west coast blockading force, ordered these restrictions to be applied to *Glory's* aircraft.

Basic principles of ground attack were therefore again emphasised at aircrew briefing. Aircraft were to weave except when actually attacking. Only one attack was to be made on each target, an order that was much respected; it was generally considered that the initial attack woke up the 'gook' gunners, and a second attack, within about twenty minutes, found them awake and accurate — regrettably some members of the Air Group discovered this to their ultimate cost. Aircraft were to remain above 3,000 feet, the safety height for small-arms fire, as much as possible, since rifle bullets would not reach that far, and the gooks were so short of ammunition that they did not use the heavier 40 mm unless they were being attacked. Recovery from attacks was to be made by 1,500 feet, to avoid any danger of flying into their own shrapnel, or into pieces of ammunition dump in the event of a successful hit. This height also gave the gooks less aiming time at an aircraft in a steady dive. Lieutenant Sample reported a railway engine being hit by one of his rockets in Haeju marshalling yard, and its coming apart in exemplary fashion, bits going well up in the air. Road and rail targets were only to be attacked when several were sighted together. However, ox-carts seldom moved in convoy and they were used to carry ammunition and fuel, generally under cover of manure or some such; they occasionally blew up when strafed with 20 mm, the air then being full of flying cow-pats! A Nelsonian blind eye may have been turned to that instruction when ox-carts were encountered.

Keenness to ensure an accurate attack, with maximum damage to the target and a desire to keep the enemy off the roads and railways had often meant that these principles were temporarily forgotten. During this last patrol they were, in the main, remembered.

Targets were principally troops and stores. Some bridges were attacked, but the rivers were drying up and they were ceasing to be worth the effort. Attacks were also made on coastal guns, and a radar station reported by partisans was bombed.

Photographs showed it to have been destroyed, and also showed another station nearby which was similarly dealt with. The Fireflies were armed with rockets at the beginning of the patrol, and bombs for the latter half.

Flying intensity was slightly less than on the previous two patrols, 417 sorties were flown averaging 60 per day, but the armistice talks were progressing well at the time, and this level of effort was found quite adequate in the state of 'unnatural calm' which prevailed in the area.

Flying was restricted by weather that was very variable, ranging from cloudless days, through overcast and low cloud to thick fog. Operations were not possible until the late forenoon of the 6th, the first day, due to sea fog; there was low cloud and uncertain weather on the 7th, but on the 8th it was fine and a full programme was flown from dawn to dusk. A north-westerly airstream brought down masses of minute dust particles from the Gobi desert and caused extremely hazy conditions on many days. Even on the finest days, haze and short visibility made it impossible to do much photo-reconnaissance, resulting in a shortage of target information.

During the nights of the 7th and 9th partisans invaded a section of the Ongjin peninsula with the intention of taking prisoners. The guerrillas had requested early morning air support for their Operation Hammer on the 10th, which was laid on for 0615, 0715 and 0815. A TARCAP of four Fireflies and a division of Furies for close support was flown off before dawn to cover their withdrawal. Enemy troops in positions near the beaches were rocketed and strafed whilst the partisans headed out to sea in their junks towards the safety of the Yonpyon Islands. However, they had evacuated from the mainland earlier than had been planned so the 0715 and 0815 details attacked alternate targets. The weather deteriorated during the day, permitting no strikes after 1530 and the last CAP was landed-on at 1700.

Whilst strafing enemy troops on the Ongjin peninsula, Lieutenant Sherlock's aircraft developed a coolant leak, probably caused by small-arms fire that had been seen coming from near the target. He successfully ditched his aircraft near *St. Bride's Bay*, anchored off the Yonpyon Islands, and climbed into his dinghy from which he was soon rescued by a boat from the frigate. No other aircraft were damaged during the patrol.

'Target – troops in the village'.   *(FAAM)*

Replenishment on the 11th was cancelled due to bad weather, and there was no flying on the 12th due to sea fog and horizontal visibility of 50-100 yards. On the 13th there was severe haze with visibility seldom more than one mile, but operations were flown until 1700, when they were suspended, with CAP only thereafter.

May 14th, the last day of operational flying, was a day of good weather.

Targets considered 'safe' were selected for attack, but after these had been dealt with divisions made a general reconnaissance of the whole area, and many 'hot spots' were visited — from a safe height — for the last time. A near maximum effort was flown for six hours from 0645 until 1330 when operations were completed. Aircraft were armed and pilots stood by in the event that partisans might require air support. A call was received and Lieutenants Anson and Mitchell with Sub-Lieutenants Pearson and Hayes flew off. After their mission they flew to Seoul and on to Iwakuni.

The last strike was led by the Lieutenant Commander Gardner with his observer Lieutenant Hunter and his original division of Lieutenant Millett, Lieutenant Sample with his observer Lieutenant West, and Lieutenant Skinner. (Lieutenant Skinner, who had completed 124 operational sorties, had spent the first seven days of the patrol in the Canadian destroyer *Crusader* on the screen.) Three of the four aircraft (WB 410, VT 370 and VT 494) were the only survivors from the ten Fireflies Mark 5 received when the squadron re-equipped at Machrihanish (HMS *Landrail*) in May 1952. The final deck-landing was made by Lieutenant J.M. Bacon who was bringing Commander D.E. Bromley-Martin back from Seoul.

After holding memorial services at 1800 on the flight deck and in the chapel to commemorate those officers and men who had lost their lives during this term of operations in Korean waters, *Glory* left the operational area for the last time on the evening of 14th May. Since leaving the United Kingdom in May 1951, the ship had spent 530 days at sea and had steamed 157,000 miles. The period included 15 months of war service and 316 days in Korean waters. Of a total of 13,700 flights from her deck, 9,500 had been operational sorties over North Korea.

> 'Through the severe weather of her second winter "on the line"', wrote Admiral Clifford, '*Glory* has kept up a most creditable tempo of air operations and has inflicted much damage on the enemy. This ship has fully maintained the reputation built up by our carriers in this war.'

Statistics for the patrol were:

	801 Squadron	**821 Squadron**
Hours	389	268
Operational sorties	244	161
Deck landings	242	172

	Destroyed	**Damaged**
Bridges	8	1
Rail lines		3
Gun emplacements	2	4
Stores dumps	4	10
Radio and radar stations	3	1
Sluice gates		4
Buildings	12	12
Troop billets	57	23
Oxcarts	3	2

On the 15th, on passage, aircrew returned their escape and evasion kits and survival gear, and five Fireflies and three Furies were flown off to Iwakuni to be available as spares for *Ocean*. *Glory* anchored off Iwakuni that evening, and the following day aircraft needing some maintenance were lightered ashore, in exchange for others requiring major repair and overhaul to be taken to HMS *Simbang* at Singapore.

Glory arrived in Sasebo early in the morning of 17th May to see the welcome

HMS *Glory*, HMS *Cossack* and RFA oiler.   *(Neep)*

sight of *Ocean*, with 807 and 810 Squadrons, already there. Stores were transferred during the day; Lieutenants Banner, B.V. Bacon, Spelling and Smith left to join 810 Squadron, and Lieutenants Anson, Mitchell, Bawden and Crawford and Sub-Lieutenants Pearson and Hayes to join 807.

On Tuesday 19th May at 1000 FO2FES, Rear Admiral F.A.G. Clifford CBE, went on board to address the ship's company. At 1100 *Glory* slipped, made a stern board down *Ocean's* port side in order to cheer her, the Royal Marine band played 'Old Lang Syne', and *Ocean* returned the cheers. *Glory* had left Sasebo for the last time en route for the United Kingdom.

To speed her on her way, *Ocean* sent:

FROM: OCEAN   TO: GLORY
ECCLESIASTES CHAPTER NINE VERSE SEVEN.

When *Glory* referred the signal to her padre they found that the message was:
'Go thy way, eat thy bread with joy and drink thy wine with a merry heart, for God now accepteth thy works.'

Three congratulatory signals were received from UN commanders:

FROM: COM 7TH FLEET   TO: GLORY   INFO: COMNAVFE
COMMANDER 7TH FLEET SENDS. WELL DONE TO OFFICERS
AND MEN HMS GLORY ON COMPLETION OUTSTANDING
TOUR OF DUTY IN KOREAN WATERS. YOU HAVE BEEN A
VALUABLE MEMBER UNITED NATIONS TEAM.

V.ADM CLARK
130424Z/MAY

FROM: FO2FES   TO: GLORY
MY CONGRATULATIONS TO ALL OF YOU ON THE
SATISFACTORY COMPLETION OF YOUR STRENUOUS AND
VALUABLE TOURS OF OPERATIONS OFF THE WEST COAST
OF KOREA.

2   YOU MAY WELL LOOK BACK WITH GREAT PRIDE ON YOUR
    ACHIEVEMENTS IN THIS WAR TO WHICH YOU HAVE
    CONTRIBUTED SO MUCH TOWARDS DEFEATING ENEMY
    AGGRESSION AND UPHOLDING THE PRESTIGE OF THE
    ROYAL NAVY

3. I LOOK FORWARD TO COMING ON BOARD TO THANK YOU
    PERSONALLY AND SAY GOODBYE BEFORE YOU SAIL

161345Z/MAY

FROM: COMNAVFE   TO: GLORY

INFO: ADMIRALTY, CINCFES, CTG 95.1, CTF 95, CINCPACFLT,
                                                    COM7THFLT
THE PROFICIENCY, COURAGE AND ENERGY WITH WHICH
YOU HAVE EXECUTED YOUR ASSIGNMENTS HAVE BEEN A
SOURCE OF PRIDE TO ME AND A CREDIT TO THE ROYAL
NAVY.
WELL DONE. GOOD LUCK AND GOD SPEED
                                    VICE ADMIRAL R.P.BRISCOE
                                             190647Z/MAY

A press release was also sent:

FROM: FO2FES   TO: ADMIRALTY (FOR CNI)
           INFO: CINCFES, GLORY, FO(AIR)MED, ACNB, NZNB,
                        CINCMED, CANAVHED, COM HONG KONG
HMS GLORY HAS JUST COMPLETED LONGEST PERIOD
NAVAL AIR OPERATIONS BY ANY BRITISH
COMMONWEALTH CARRIER IN KOREAN CAMPAIGN.

2. SINCE LEAVING UK JANUARY 1951 SHIP HAS SPENT 530
   DAYS AT SEA AND STEAMED 157000 MILES. DURING THIS
   PERIOD GLORY HAS COMPLETED 15 MONTHS WAR SERVICE
   AND SPENT 316 DAYS AT SEA IN KOREAN WATERS. OF A
   TOTAL OF 13700 FLIGHTS FROM CARRIER DECK MORE THAN
   9500 HAVE BEEN OPERATIONAL SORTIES OVER NORTHERN
   KOREA. A CONSTANT TOLL OF ENEMY TROOPS,
   DISRUPTION AND DESTRUCTION OF ROAD AND RAIL
   COMMUNICATIONS AND WIDE RANGE OF MILITARY
   TARGETS HAVE CONTINUED DURING TWO KOREAN
   WINTERS ICE AND SNOW HAS BEEN REPEATEDLY HAD TO
   BE CLEARED FROM FLIGHT DECK AND AIRCRAFT BUT
   OPERATIONS HAVE BEEN SUSTAINED IN SOME OF THE
   WORST WEATHER EVER EXPERIENCED BY NAVAL AIRCREW

3 GLORY'S FIREFLY AND SEA FURY AIRCRAFT HAVE BEEN
   SURPRISING RAIL AND ROAD TRANSPORT BY NIGHT IN
   NORTHERN KOREA WHILST A NOTABLE FEATURE OF
   DAYLIGHT OPERATIONS HAS BEEN CLOSE AIR SUPPORT
   FOR THE BRITISH COMMONWEALTH DIVISION AT THE
   FRONT LINE.

4. EXTENT OF UNITED NATIONS ORGANISATION BORNE BY
   FACT THAT NEARLY 100 DESTROYERS OF ROYAL NAVY,

UNITED STATES, ROYAL AUSTRALIAN, CANADIAN, NEW
ZEALAND AND NETHERLANDS NAVIES HAVE OPERATED AS
ESCORTS TO THE BRITISH CARRIER.

5. ON HER LAST DAY IN KOREAN WATERS BEFORE
    RETURNING TO ENGLAND SHIP HAD A MEMORIAL
    SERVICE. DURING PAST 6 MONTHS 12 MEMBERS OF
    GLORY'S AIRCREW HAVE FLOWN ON MISSIONS FROM
    WHICH THEY HAVE NOT RETURNED

                                                              160943Z/MAY

And finally, a story that occurred during one of the last patrols of this tour:
    It was the policy in this Squadron (as in all Squadrons) to give each
    pilot his own aircraft to fly whenever possible.
    The first event of four aircraft on a strike mission took off at about
    0830 and landed-on at 1000. As was the normal practice the Chief
    Radio Artificer — a quiet, efficient young man, not given to
    histrionics — met each aircraft, jumped up onto the wing and asked
    the pilot if the radio was serviceable. 'No, Chief,' was the reply by one
    particular pilot to this innocent query.
    The third event, again strike, took off at 1145 and returned at 1315. It
    was the second sortie for this same pilot in the same aircraft, and his
    reply to the Chief REA's request was 'No, Chief, still u/s'.
    Being a normal, but busy, day of eight events, some pilots were
    programmed for three sorties. On this particular day the intrepid
    aviator, in this same aircraft, took off on his third sortie at 1815 and
    landed on at 1930, the last event of the day.
    'Radio OK, Sir?' from the Chief REA, on his return.
    'Bloody thing's still u/s, Chief.'
    'I think, sir, it is probably u/s between the headphones.'

Glory had completed three operational tours in the Korean War. The copy of the
memorandum on the next two pages collates the flying statistics from all three.

Air Office   H.M.S. GLORY   18.5.53

KOREAN ANALYSES

		1st Tour (9 patrols)	2nd tour (5 patrols)	Last tour (11 Patrols)
1. SORTIES	(a) Defensive)	–	726	950
	(b) Offensive)	2892	1336	3605
	(c) Others)	-	12	143
	Total	2892	2074	4698
				(+ 381 helicopter)

Notes:

(a) On last tour 6167 sorties were programmed in the 87 days available. This represented 71 sorties per day.

(b) Due to bad weather 21 days comprising 14 full days and 7 part days were lost. This represented 1469 sorties.

(c) Daily average achieved on the 73 days when flying was possible was 64 sorties per day. Overall average was 54 per day.

2. FLYING	(a) Fury	–	) 5198	
HOURS	(b) Firefly	–	) 5846	3113
3. DECK	(a) Furies	–	1300	2871
LANDINGS	(b) Firefly	–	780	1869
	(c) Other	–	–	30
	Total		2080	4770
4. DECK	(a) Fury Rate	638 for 1	–	261 for 1
LANDING	(b) Firefly Rate	158 for 1	–	467 for 1
ACCIDENTS	(c) Combined Rate	–	–	316 for 1
	(d) Best Sequence	1115	581	888

		Accident Free	Landings	Landings	Landings
5. ORDNANCE	(a) 1000 lb bombs	)	46	232	
EXPENDITURE	(b) 500 lb. bombs	) 1500	1072	4508	
	(c) Rockets	9000	6470	8768	
	(d) 20 mm	500000	420000	521000	
	(e) Depth Charges			20	

6. DAMAGE INFLICTED   3rd Tour

	Destroyed	**Damaged**
(a) Road Bridges	33	19
(b) Rail Bridges	37	18
(c) Rolling Stock	49	216
(d) Motor Vehicles	55	105
(e) Other vehicles	337	390
(f) Locomotives	1	3
(g) Boats	–	212
(h) Rail Cuts	162	
(i) Tunnels	–	33
(j) Stores Dumps	36	89
(k) Buildings	712	202
(l) Radar Stations	3	3
(m) Radio Stations	2	–
(n) Transformers	6	12

CHAPTER 12

HMS GLORY

Prisoner

The author is indebted to Captain D.G. Mather RN for permission to reproduce below the lecture 'Resistance to Interrogation' which he gave, when a Lieutenant Commander, to the School of Military Intelligence in 1965.

On the first day of the fourth patrol in *Glory* (5th January 1953) I found myself in the first detail for a bridge bombing mission. The weather was rather miserable as we were in good wintry conditions — snow storms, cloud and poor visibility. We pressed on and located our primary target, and the CO and his number 2 went in first and got the main bridge. I was his number 3 and section leader and held off and went away to do some armed reconnaissance to let the area quieten down a little. After 20 minutes or so we went back and I led in for an attack on the secondary target — another bridge — and as I was about to release my bomb I felt the aircraft hit by a 76 mm shell.

I pulled up immediately to gain height and called up my leader to tell him of my plight and then my aircraft blew up. I came to in a vertical spin with little or no engine or front cockpit left and I gathered later no tail either, and I just managed to undo my safety harness QRB and I left the aircraft. My wing-man, Lieutenant Anson, afterwards said I appeared over the side in a conventional ball, but this I do not remember at all. I again woke up on the way down free falling and I pulled the 'D' ring and floated down to the snow below. I still had a Remington 45 automatic and as I was being shot at, I replied in kind, but as I hit the snow I tossed the gun away and stood up to surrender to the Korean troops who were waiting for me. This was unwise as the odd bullets were still flying around and so I lay down and waited to be captured. This particular incident remains very vividly in my mind as, whilst on Christmas leave in Japan I had seen a film entitled *One Minute to Zero* starring Anne Blyth and Robert Mitchum in which the final scene showed an American Air Force pilot also floating down to earth in his parachute and being shot at by ground troops, his parachute burst into flames and he crashed to his death. I thought on the way down that this could well have happened to me.

The enemy troops searched me and then marched me off to the local Command Post where I was further searched and my 'translation' sheet and 'blood chit' were taken from me and also my watch. I tried to explain that conversation would be difficult without the language sheet but they apparently were indifferent to my conversational problems. I spent the night at this post and was marched away the following day. Fortunately my only wounds, if they could be called such, were a few flash burns on my face where the bare skin was exposed between my goggles and my oxygen mask, which I always wore. I also had a singed beard on one side. I asked for medical treatment and they put on some antiseptic liquid, and this was all the treatment I ever had. Because of the extreme cold, however, the wound healed fairly rapidly without getting septic.

I was marched northwards up a frozen river-bed and we were attacked by a friendly Firefly aircraft carrying out a rocket attack on a nearby bridge. I must admit that there is a considerable difference being at the receiving end of such weapons. To make marching more comfortable I pulled off the immersion suit ('goon-suit' to aircrew) wrist and neck seals and separated the boots from the trouser legs. This enabled my body to breathe without overheating. The immersion suit itself was not too bad an article of clothing for wintry conditions. It kept the wind out, the boots kept my feet dry and it was not liable to be filched by the Korean and Chinese captors, like most of the attractive American equipment. However unless you were moving and because you had cut the seals there was little or no insulation, so when you slept in sub-zero temperatures you got damned cold. To slake my thirst on the march I was able to lick the frozen breath off my beard and moustache — an illustration of the low temperatures we were experiencing.

My captors at this time were reasonable fellows and I attributed this mainly to their having been in action themselves. I found this all along, that those who had had front line experience had a degree of fellow feeling, whereas those who had come straight from China or North Korea were full of indoctrination, were rather beastly, and had most peculiar ideas about life and conditions in general.

This march was up to Sariwon and I think this was a journey of 10 or 20 miles. Sariwon was a headquarters town and from the air I had thought it to be pretty well deserted. However from the ground I realised the errors of my observations, and saw that the town was full of transport that was expertly camouflaged to fit into the background of snow and derelict buildings. I wished that I could have called up an armed reconnaissance patrol.

At Sariwon we spent part of the night in a dug-out house. The Korean families lived right in the rubble — suitably excavated and really apart from the lack of light and small size, no more uncomfortable than in their own homes, and possibly in the winter, warmer too being out of the cold winds. Once again the civilians were not particularly hostile even though there was little or nothing of their town remaining standing. In the middle of the night we joined a queue for transport and eventually got on top of a truck and started northwards.

I did not know at the time but our destination was Pyongyang, capital of North Korea. This was only about 50 or so miles northwards. The roads were poor, plenty of snow and ice, and the convoy did not move very fast, and I think it took two nights to do the journey. During the night we had an interesting system of air raid warnings, then, depending on the closeness of the enemy aircraft, the truck either switched off the headlights and stopped, or rolled off the road into any shelter it could find.

The enemy camouflage was very good, and by night we saw the extremely valuable use of human labour. Prefabricated bridge sections were stored in areas close by bridges, and repairs to these bridges were accomplished very swiftly overnight by hordes of peasant labourers. Some bridges were in fact little more than two railway lines crossing a gap — not very safe, but sufficient to last a week or so, the time they could count on before the bridge would be knocked down again. They had also built big shelters at the side of the roads like those in mountainous areas of America and Italy which prevent roads and railways being carried away by landslides or avalanches. These were to hide the railway trucks during the day. The last part of this journey was apparently through the middle of Pyongyang and for this I was transferred to a Jeep and was covered with a blanket to avoid any hostile action which could be expected in the capital. Throughout the journey I childishly thought I was en route to a German type PoW camp, and this thought somewhat cancelled out the low spirits due to my capture.

The first camp was a Korean Headquarters Interrogation Centre. There I met some USAF aircrew and Army ground crews who had, like me, been captured in recent days. We lived, about ten of us, in one room of a size so small that not all of us could lie down on the floor at the same time. We were fed a bowl of rice twice per day, at dawn and dusk, and that was it. We exchanged names just to make the maximum chance of getting the records straight should one of us get out and not return. We had some odd birds among us; one was a very strange case, he claimed he was a Captain in the US Army and commanded two or three tanks. He was coloured and had obviously had a lot of wounds which had all healed up white giving him rather a macabre appearance. One day we were asked to fill out a Red Cross form — name, address, next of kin etc. — and he could not even write his name! My thoughts of the US Army went downwards, and I found out months later that he was in fact a Private First Class, considerably shell shocked as his tank had been blown up with him inside it, and he was very lucky to have got away with his life. He did, however, have one very valuable attribute and that was a splendid voice much like Nat King Cole and he had a full repertoire of the latter's songs, this kept us going for quite a long time and kept our morale up.

Two of the other prisoners remained particularly in my mind. One, Sam Massemburg, a USAF Captain of a B-29, had already lost two fingers to frost bite and the third was going. He had been tied up so tightly that the circulation in his hands was almost nil and had then been left out all night outside a command post. The other chap had been captured after evading for two or three days after crashing with his aircraft, and when captured the Koreans had taken his shoes and flying boots away. When I met him his feet could just fit into his over snow boots, and they were beginning to smell rotten with frost bite and gangrene. He could not move or feed himself and we had to do everything for him, and he was given no treatment whatsoever for his condition. He certainly looked as though he was on his last legs, and I learned afterwards that he died a few days after I left this camp.

After a few days I was taken away for interrogation, and I decided I would try and limit myself to name and rank only. After a few days of this I was taken out to a solitary cell. This was a cold cell, that is, no fire just a hut — I was not allowed to go to sleep at all and every few days my interrogators would come back and ask me questions, seldom referring to previous visits. Sometimes I was asked specific military questions, sometimes questions on training, sometimes questions on background and private life. After a while this did not seem to have very much future, especially as I had had my immersion suit taken away and all I had was No. 8's working dress with 'Long Johns', pyjamas and socks. Each day I was also made to stand outside for an hour or so in the snow, where the temperature was below freezing. I therefore decided that I would give some form of story but would confine myself to non-essential information. In this hut I had found a pile of four to five months old air mail Daily Telegraph newspapers, which indicated to me that their lines of communication must have been pretty reasonable.

I decided that to lie completely would be of no advantage and I told them a superficial story. I stayed in my hut for some time further and I was eventually allowed to have a fire once per day, I was given back my boots and immersion suit and finally was sent back to the communal hut, to the other prisoners I had met before.

I had probably been in the cold solitary hut some three or four weeks all told. Once back in the main hut I met some other newer prisoners and similar actions took place with them from time to time, and you never knew whether you would see those next to you again once they had gone out for interrogation, as sometimes they never returned. Of course, all this time one was expecting to be told 'Right, off we go to a prisoner of war camp now', but this day never seemed to arrive. I occasionally asked about PoW camps, but the standard answer was 'You don't qualify, you are not a prisoner of war but an enemy of humanity, a war criminal; therefore you are not subject to the Geneva Convention; one day if you manage to atone for your sins you might go to a PoW camp,' which by one's guard was reported to be comparative heaven — lots of sport, good food, books, everything fine except you were a PoW. Still during this period of captivity we had nothing to read at all, in fact nothing to do, other than to wait to be called out again.

We were not allowed to wash or clean our teeth during any of this period and thus after a very short time we became literally lousy. This state of affairs continued for some nine weeks or so. I was very unpopular at one period, because as the Senior Officer I reckoned that the lack of exercise and general conditions were having a bad effect on our health. I therefore kept requesting exercise, until at last we were given some — digging slit trenches with the ground frozen to a depth of three feet, and the temperature outside well down to the zero mark. My fellow prisoners felt this was a bit too much; however, it gave them something to get their teeth into, and to stop them thinking about themselves, which was all for the good. Finally, after about nine weeks we were all marched off for a hot bath, and believe me it felt really good. It did not get rid of the lice, which were very itchy, but I suppose by that time we had got used to them, and were not so worried about them.

Eventually after about the tenth week of capture, I was one day called out and to my surprise instead of the usual interrogation I was put on a truck, and off I went again. This journey was about 50 or 60 miles to the south-east, to an old gold mine called Bean Camp, a Chinese controlled transit camp at Suan, about 45 miles south-east of Pyongyang, where beans were the main diet. There was one change, however — it was a Chinese truck and Chinese guard and the mining camp was a Chinese Interrogation Centre. Again my hopes of a PoW camp were dashed to the ground.

At this camp all my clothes were taken away, and I was issued with Chinese cotton uniforms, a padded overcoat and a pair of hockey type boots. Soap, a toothbrush, a tin of DDT and tobacco were also given us. I had in my previous ten weeks occasionally been given some tobacco with which to roll cigarettes in old Chinese newspapers, better than nothing, but not very good; airmail Daily Telegraph was the best.

I can't remember how long I was at the Bean Camp but it was probably five weeks or so. I lived in a single room of a Korean house with my guard — just the two of us — with no exercise allowed at all other than a heads [lavatory] call, of which I made an excess number just to get some exercise. The interrogation went on spasmodically and from what I remember there seemed to be a greater bias towards political and general questions. Here it was, I think, that my interrogator claimed to be a graduate of the London School of Economics. Again there was no pattern to the interrogation in either frequency or style, neither was there any outside news. I think that throughout this period my morale remained about the same — still expecting that a PoW camp was around the corner and that I would be off next day.

Again during this period of interrogation I had just gone through, one almost developed a desire for interrogation to take place as this was one's only relief. No one to talk to for days on end, no exercise allowed, so to talk to someone who could speak fluent English was a relief. On the other hand, you dreaded interrogation as, during it, you were fighting a constant battle to keep your conversation down to non-essentials and similar to the answers you had given previously. Perhaps this did serve to keep one's wits sharpened up, as to try and score off the Chinese was always good. Basically, though you were in a void — no news, just trying to exist for a doubtful future.

Finally one day I was told to come along and I was ordered on to one of the mud guards of a jeep, with another prisoner the other side, a guard and a burp gun between us and an officer and a driver in the front — a cosy little touring party! However, no chance of conversation was allowed — but we were off.

We started northwards and travelled about 200 miles right up to the Yalu River. Had the vehicle and the circumstances been more pleasant then the journey would have been quite interesting. Rather rugged country and hills (one range as far as I could see of the order of 8-10,000 feet), over most dangerous passes and by precipices, the road covered in sheets of ice, and in places there were sheer drops of 3-4,000 feet if the jeep did not quite make the grade. We stopped at least one night on the way, and I did manage to exchange names with my fellow prisoner for future reference. I suppose the reason behind this was the childish thought that the more people who knew I was alive and a prisoner of war, the less likely it was that I would be killed. It sounds melodramatic but one only had one's thoughts to occupy one for 24 hours a day.

On we went to Pyoktong on the Yalu and we drove across the river in our jeep. The winter has its uses as the river becomes an ice road and a short cut for journeys which in summer, with the water flowing swiftly down the river, would have necessitated large detours and perhaps boat and ferry crossings.

Pyoktong itself was not a camp, but it was a large interrogation centre, and it was a reasonably large town. We the prisoners lived in terrace type rooms, that is solitary again. We had about one guard to every three or four cells. The cells were rooms roughly 6 feet square and with about 5 feet of headroom. Food was still the same, a bowl of rice twice a day, and occasionally it was a sort of rice soup, with a few vegetables in it, and one occasionally got water to drink with it too. Sometimes one saw groups of prisoners being marched through the town, and so the conclusion was that there must be a camp not too far away this time.

Again the routine was similar, more questioning, the same questions again and again, with no reference to what had gone before. It was here I had a pretty low period — occasionally at night one would hear screams, and these did nothing to ease one's peace of mind. Then after a week or so, 1 was called out one night and wondered what on earth was up. I was taken out to the back of the town in some foothills, and told to dig a hole, or at least I thought it was a hole. It was explained to me that this should be just big enough and deep enough to take me in a crouching position. I was at this project two hours or so, for two or three nights, and each night I heard shots and the odd scream, and then it dawned upon me that this was probably my grave to be, and this was the reason for shots and screams. Again probably a vivid imagination, but one had little else to think about at that time. Things looked pretty grim, and it seemed the end was near. I had found earlier on that prayer was a great help. I am not deeply religious — I go to church most Sundays but I had not thought deeply about religion — but I did find that prayer was a great comfort; perhaps this is rather hypocritical, anyway the praying did help!

At this time I was still being called a war criminal — common language for Chinese to prisoners — and we were treated to a minimum of facilities such as sugar and tobacco which I had been getting sometimes since my original Korea Headquarters Interrogation Centre days. I had no exercise other than to walk round a 6 feet by 6 feet cell. I calculated that to walk a mile I had to walk the diagonal 600 to 700 times, and this rather stooped for the room was low; this I tried to do daily, just to get exercise. Then I tried knee stretching and anything to try and keep me in condition. At times it was dreadfully easy to lull oneself into a sort of semi-coma — fitfully sleeping all day and all night except for meals. The guards tried to stop this and so one almost developed the art of sleeping sitting up with one eye open. One had no physical or mental exercise to do other than self imposed — and I used to prove geometrical theorems just to relieve the absolute boredom. I used to try and go to the head at convenient times when other prisoners would be about, so that you could see something of them, and hope there was someone you might recognise and conversely one who might recognise you. This was probably another sign of my low ebb at this time.

This grave business was just about the last straw and I told my interrogator to stop messing around, and if they wanted to shoot me then jolly well get on with it. The next evening I was called out, and I thought this is it, but no, on to a lorry and off again to Chang-ni, to the Chinese headquarters there, about ten miles eastwards. En route we passed many other trucks with groups of PoWs and I tried to call out to them but was restrained from doing so. I waited there most of the day and I saw another PoW go off to the heads and I hopefully asked to go as well. Strangely enough they had not apparently seen the first man go and so they also allowed me to go. We quickly exchanged names and outfits and then we went back to the headquarters — one minute's speech with another English speaking man, great relief! His name was Commander Maury Yerger USN. Shortly after this I was moved out to a further solitary cell on the banks of a river. Here again my life was much the same as before with one exception, now after six months or so I was given reading matter. The food was better and now, because of summer routine, three times daily and occasionally it included eggs and tea to drink. I was able to wash each day in the stream and was allowed to sit outside my hut by day and walk up and down outside for exercise. This was good as it enabled me to see the other prisoners in neighbouring houses and occasionally I saw parties of prisoners marching along the road nearby. I knew now that I was near a main camp.

I think that having got over my low ebb that my morale started to improve again, certainly it was a great relief to see other PoWs around from time to time. I tried to get fit again with permitted exercise and I also managed to exchange names with one of the other prisoners. This was in itself an interesting event. The other prisoner was wearing an RAF blue webbing belt and I thought 'Ah, RAF!' However I knew that there was little or no RAF involvement in Korea, so he must be RAAF who I knew were flying their Mustangs in Korea in 77 Squadron. A few days later a band of prisoners marched past our solitary cells, about a quarter of a mile away, and they were singing 'Sarie Marais' and the other prisoner pointed to himself and I thought 'Wrong again he must be SAAF' who were also out in Korea flying Mustangs. I learned later that he was born and raised in South Africa, had come over to join the RAF and had been seconded out to Korea and was in fact flying with the RAAF. His name was Flight Lieutenant Olaf Berg. Again this was all a big fillip to one's morale just to get one-up on one's captors and guards. Anything you could manage to do and get away with did you a power of good — even though the occasion itself was childish and of no importance.

My interrogation was continued as before, but I felt that conditions were more relaxed. I was in this village three months or so, and during this time I moved houses two or three times, generally for no apparent reason but once for a flood. I was given such magazines as the Daily Worker and various communist books — surprisingly including David Copperfield — but anything to read was welcome relief. There did seem to be an air of excitement gradually pervading the area. One night I heard low flying aircraft, but no firing, and this again seemed very strange. A few days later I was allowed to watch a Chinese cinema show — it was very funny, Russian men with high pitched dubbed Chinese voices.

Two or three days later two of us were called out and put on the back of a mule cart and we moved off. My fellow prisoner was Maury Yerger whom I had met before. We were allowed to talk — wonders! We did so and discussed everything we could think of in our short journey, but still we did not know the truth — we knew something important had happened. After a two or three hour journey we came to a main camp and saw all the other prisoners. They swiftly told us that the war was over, and peace had been signed ten days previously. Relief — glorious relief! This was apparently the explanation of the low flying aircraft. We learned later that these aircraft had been ordered to fly low over all PoW camps and they had been specially equipped with loud speakers to broadcast to the prisoners that the war was over and peace had been signed. Unfortunately, the aircraft microphone went unserviceable just as it arrived overhead in my particular village. We stayed in this main camp for two or three weeks and every so often a party of prisoners would move off southwards, until my turn came and I moved off in one of the last groups. During this period conditions were much easier, obviously, than

I had had beforehand. I met some of the prisoners with whom I had originally been in the Korean headquarters at Pyongyang. I learnt from them that one of the negroes, the one with the two frost-bitten fingers, had been medically repatriated some three or four weeks earlier, when the Operation Little Switch exchange of medical repatriates had taken place.

During this time I started to get to know a little bit better some of the other prisoners and met Colonel 'Fred' Carne of the Gloucestershire Regiment, and once again, as I have found at other times, I realised that amongst the privates and ordinary troops of the various services the world over, there was a tremendous amount of illiteracy. To help to counteract this in some of the men we set up classes; we tried to give some of these people elementary lessons in reading, in English, in grammar and in basic mathematics. In these people, I think we sparked off a desire for learning which had been apparently non-existent up to this time.

When I left this camp, I left by truck and went to the head of the railway, and there entrained on a cattle train which was to take us down to. This was an interesting journey and for it we had been given extra cigarettes, (Chinese), most of which we threw away to villagers who came and watched the train passing through the countryside, all the way down. Some chaps even threw most of their clothes as well, wanting to be rid of any last evidence of this unforgettable time of their lives.

At Panmunjon we stayed two weeks or more, and again each day or so some were called out for the actual repatriation. In due course my time came and we went by truck to a transfer point where we dismounted and got into a United States Army vehicle and were driven on into Freedom Village. I crossed with one of the last parties with many of the Glosters Officers whom I met in this repatriation village. The date was 2nd September 1953.

We crossed the front line and went into an enormous marquee style of tent and were welcomed back to the United Nations forces by Senator Knowland, a Senator for California. Each prisoner was then directed according to his nationality to his own troops and there the routine was very similar, clothes were removed and burnt, we were sprayed with DDT and given clean uniforms, in my case British Army uniform, as there had only been four Naval prisoners of war and it was not considered necessary to issue them with Naval clothing, and thus have yet another supply problem! I then moved down to British Headquarters. I was met at the front line by the Signals Officer of HMS *Ocean*, Lieutenant Commander Hugh Sargeant who had been in *Ocean* with me a year previously and was out once again with *Ocean*. That evening I met some other friends at the British HQ and saw a film of the Coronation, which of course was also news to me. Then the following day we moved off down towards Seoul where we took an aircraft back to Iwakuni and then by boat across to Kure where I saw *Ocean* moored alongside the jetty. It was very moving to be welcomed back by the Royal Marine Band who were fallen in on the jetty waiting for our boat to arrive. There I met many old faces, people I had served with in *Ocean* a year earlier, and others of my friends whom I had known from other years in the Navy. Because of my association with *Ocean* I was offered a cabin on board, as well as the official accommodation which had been provided for us PoWs. Time in Kure was spent in interrogation by the Royal Marines — perhaps a more accurate description of this would be de-briefing or de-interrogation — and eventually we were all assigned to a troop ship to come back to the United Kingdom. However, luckily for me there was another carrier also in Kure, HMS *Unicorn*, and I was offered a passage in her down to Hong Kong by Commander Barney McHugh where I could then get in four days leave and shopping and catch the troopship as she went through on the way home. This I did and I had a very enjoyable time in Hong Kong and then joined the *Empire Orwell*, the troopship to which I had been assigned. Then there was the months long journey home to England and once again to be re-united with my family at Southampton Docks.

Fortunately for me I was very fit when I was originally captured, and I believe this stood me in very good stead, and I went through my time as a PoW with hardly any illness at all. It was only on the troopship coming home that I found I had a mild attack of beri-beri or 'Happy Toes' which was caused by a lack of vitamins in the diet and merely meant that circulation became impaired at the extremities of the system. When I was re-united with my family, I found out the extent to which the Communists had been prepared to go. Officials of the Daily Worker newspaper came to visit my parents and told them they understood that their son was a prisoner of war in China, and that if they cared to write a letter, they, the Daily Worker, would see that it was delivered to me as a prisoner. Fortunately I may say that my parents kicked them out of the house and told them that when the Admiralty told them their son was alive, then they would believe it and they would take action accordingly. The Admiralty in their turn duly turned up trumps, as, when they first got positive information that I was alive from Sam Massenberg who was a medical repatriate in Little Switch in April, they immediately cabled home to England and my parents were rung up in the early evening with a minimum of delay.

In summary, though one can, and does, learn from such experiences, there are other ways which have more to recommend them. I did not have any chance to evade capture or later on to escape. These things are difficult, particularly to remain free if you do escape, because of your facial characteristics. My only advice would really be to try to avoid the initial capture at all costs.

At his first camp, the Korean Headquarters Interrogation Centre, Lieutenant Mather refers to his being accused of being a war criminal and therefore not being subject to the Geneva Convention. In 1955 the Ministry of Defence published a booklet — Treatment of British Prisoners of War in Korea — the first chapter of which is entitled 'The "Lenient Policy"'.

The entry of the Chinese troops into the war brought to its full pitch the conflict of ideologies. It was in the prison camps set up by the Chinese and North Koreans that the battleground for this war of minds emerged. British troops who fell into enemy hands found that for them the battle with Communism had not ended when they were captured.

They were unprepared for this ordeal; they had expected hardship and foresaw rough or even brutal treatment. But they did not think of themselves as students of politics under the tutelage of their, mostly Chinese, Communist guards. In past wars those who have captured British soldiers have not concerned themselves with the politics of their prisoners. The UN prisoners soon learned that their treatment as prisoners of war depended upon how far their political convictions pleased their captors.

It gradually became clear that the Chinese aimed to convert at least a minority of prisoners to Communism and then to use this minority to undermine the confidence of the remainder, thus rendering them in turn susceptible to Communist indoctrination. This aim was embodied in what the Chinese called their 'Lenient Policy' towards prisoners of war. It was based on the lie that the war in Korea was one of American aggression and part of the conspiracy of the capitalist world against peace. The Chinese claimed that all United Nations prisoners taking part in this unjust war were war criminals, and that if they were captured their captors had the right to kill them. But, the Chinese argument went on, the soldiers of the 'aggressors' were, after all, ordinary working men who had been duped and misled by their reactionary rulers. Therefore prisoners would not be summarily executed (hence the 'leniency') but would be given the opportunity to reach a state of remorse and repentance for their crimes.

Thus the Chinese allowed themselves to claim that, whether conditions in the prison camps were good or bad by normal standards, they were treating their prisoners generously and well — far better, in fact, than they deserved or were entitled to expect. This was not true in the early days.

So far as the major camps were concerned, it was substantially true from late 1951 that the conditions in the prison camps were as good as those enjoyed by the local population and the Chinese troops themselves, but supplies of food and medicine and standards of accommodation still depended to a large extent on the degree of co-operation with their captors that the prisoners showed. In addition the Chinese used physical violence, solitary confinement and other 'incentives' to persuade prisoners to co-operate with them. This discrimination they justified by arguing that prisoners were only entitled to the full benefits of the 'Lenient Policy' if they accepted and observed certain rules and regulations, particularly those dealing with 're-education'. Until the end of 1951 're-education' was compulsory, but thereafter the Chinese abandoned compulsory 're-education' in favour of more subtle techniques. The principle of compulsory study was fundamental to the 'Lenient Policy'.

This theory was based on certain assumptions, namely: that the Communists had a monopoly of the truth; that the prisoners accepted that they had been dupes of their capitalist rulers; that they were willing to learn the 'truth'; and that they welcomed their 'liberation' by the Chinese.

If a prisoner would not accept these assumptions the Chinese considered that he was not entitled to the benefits of the 'Lenient Policy'. They argued that any reasonable man will accept the chance of improving his education, and since the 'truth' must be obvious once the veils of 'capitalist propaganda' have been removed, a refusal to see the light could be due only to malice. If a prisoner refused to be educated and to see the 'truth', he was voluntarily aligning himself with the forces of reactionary capitalism and imperialism and with the enemies of ordinary men and women throughout the world. He was therefore a criminal, outside the protection of the 'Lenient Policy', and the treatment he received in consequence vitas his own responsibility.

Communist propaganda was repeatedly claiming that all the Chinese were doing was offering their prisoners the opportunity to learn the truth; there was no obligation to accept it and punishment was not meted out to prisoners for holding opinions which differed from those of their instructors (nor even for expressing those opinions publicly), but only for 'reactionary' activity. But since the Chinese continued to regard the expression of anti-Communist opinions as a reactionary activity, as an attempt to influence others, as a slander of the Chinese forces, or as evidence of a hostile attitude, it was clear that the opinions of prisoners had to be 'progressive' if they were to go unpunished.

It was a natural accompaniment to this policy to classify prisoners according to their political convictions, to treat the 'progressives' better than the 'reactionaries'. The 'progressive' prisoner was the one who accepted the political, economic and social gospel of Marx, Engels, Lenin and Stalin — even if he was not quite sure what this was. In order to be fully accepted as a 'progressive' the prisoner had to do more than passively accept Communism. He must become a Communist propagandist and assist the Chinese, not only by giving them all the military information he had, but also by acting as an informer, revealing the plans and thoughts of his fellow prisoners and helping to spread Communism among them and among his family and friends at home. Thus he would show that he had become politically conscious'. Prisoners who did not co-operate in any of these ways were classed as 'reactionaries' and regarded as criminals not entitled to the mercy of the 'Lenient Policy'.

The four Royal Navy prisoners were: Lieutenant (E) D.G. Mather, Sub-Lieutenant D. Lankford RNVR, Pilot 3 R.H. Johnson, Naval Airman Penman.

CHAPTER 13

HMS OCEAN

807 and 810 Squadrons
17th May 1953 to End of Hostilities

In May, enemy attention turned to two partisan held islands, Hachwira and Sangchwira, in the Chinnampo estuary. Over 600 rounds were fired at the two islands in two weeks, but the partisans suffered few casualties and remained in possession. *Morecambe Bay* and RoK LSL *107* were also fired on, the latter receiving two hits. On 25th May, *New Jersey*, wearing Vice Admiral Clark's flag and accompanied by Rear Admiral Clifford in *Newcastle*, arrived on the scene. Admiral Clark had arrived at Inchon on one of his periodical visits to the west coast on 23rd May, to be met by Admiral Clifford. After lunch on board *New Jersey*, the two Admirals called on President and Mrs. Syngman Rhee and on the US Ambassador in Korea, followed by a visit by helicopter to the presidential mansion in Seoul.

New Jersey fired 32 x 16 inch rounds at Amgak and batteries on the north side of the River Taedong, while *Newcastle*, further inshore, neutralised enemy batteries with 6 inch guns, and stood by to engage AA batteries which might interfere with spotting aircraft. After the bombardment, *New Jersey* left for the east coast, after Admiral Clark had transferred to *Ocean* to witness flying operations. Next day guns on the northern shore were again engaged by *Newcastle* and *St. Bride's Bay* and HNethMS *Johann Maurits van Nassau,* who came under fire from 105 mm and 76 mm guns, being repeatedly straddled but not hit. Air spot was provided by aircraft from *Ocean*; several hits were obtained on the enemy gun positions which were also attacked from the air. *Newcastle* went on to the Paengyong-do area where, on 28th May, she carried out a concentrated bombardment of a particularly active battery sited in caves.

There was little of interest in the Haeju area. The enemy seemed to have been expecting an amphibious attack, he had doubled his forces on the west coast, with 36,000 Chinese around Haeju and 4,500 Chinese and North Koreans in the Ongjin area. This reinforcement greatly increased the difficulties of partisan operations. The fishing season in the vicinity started at the beginning of May, but with fewer than 800 fishing craft instead of the 1,200 expected, the careful arrangements made with the RoK Government and Navy worked well.

The Han estuary was visited twice in May: from the 17th to the 20th by

HMNZS *Kaniere* and from the 24th to the 26th by *Sparrow*, bombardments of the mainland north of Kyodong-do were carried out.

Throughout this period there were persistent rumours that the enemy was about to operate submarines in the Yellow Sea and special vigilance was ordered; although there is no evidence that any had been present.

Sea Fury 1320 RATOGed from HMS *Ocean* at anchor in Sasebo.   *(Mather)*

On the east coast, enemy gun activity was confined mainly to the Wonsan area but no US ships were damaged nor were any casualties caused. Increased use of gunnery radar by the enemy led to much greater interest in electronics counter measures by the US authorities. The naval effort was mainly concentrated on fitting search and direction finding receivers in ships and in a regular programme of 'window' dropping exercises by all US carriers was initiated.

British Commonwealth ships continued to operate in turn in the Songjin area and to the north: *Comus, Cockade, Charity, Consort, Cossack, Crusader, Haida and Anzac* all took part from January to June. Their main preoccupation was the security of Yang-do; that and the shortage of US destroyers for TE 95.22 in the early part of the year limited the range of operations on this part of the coast, even though the enemy showed little sign of activity. Commander Gatehouse described *Charity's* patrol from 27th February to 14th March as 'intensely disappointing … no enemy activity whatsoever … and in consequence not a shot fired in anger.'

As spring wore on, there was slightly more activity: *Consort* captured a sampan on 6th April which was presented to the garrison in Yong-do.

Considerable successes were gained in 'train busting' at night by the Train Busters Club of TF 95. Each ship in the club received a certificate signed by CTF 95 for their prowess giving the number of trains credited: *Crusader* four, *Endicott, Orleck, Haida,* and *Athabaskan* two each, and one to each of *Porter, Jarvis, Boyd, Traten, Eversole, Kyes, Chandler, McCoy Reynolds, Carmick, Maddox and Piet*

Hein. Crusader achieved a record of three trains in 24 hours on 15th April which was equalled shortly afterwards by *Endicott.* On 2nd May *Cockade* destroyed one large sampan and badly damaged two others on the beach to the north of Yang-do, and on the 6th destroyed three rail boxcars south of Songjin. The enemy opened fire on her with 105 mm and 75 mm guns. *Cockade* was steaming down the edge of a fog bank lying two miles to seaward and into which she promptly withdrew. She was under fire for three-and-a-half minutes during which time 45-50 rounds fell within 100 yards of the ship, some as close 20-30 yards, and she was straddled continuously; fire ceased at 6,000 yards range in the fog, having caused no damage.

First Patrol

Ocean arrived in Sasebo from Hong Kong at 0630 on Sunday 17th May 1953 with 807 Squadron (Lieutenant Commander T.L.M Brander DSC) and 810 Squadron (Lieutenant Commander A.W. Bloomer) embarked; *Glory* arrived an hour later from Iwakuni. *Ocean* was to take over the duties of Commonwealth carrier on the west coast of Korea for her second tour, from *Glory* exiting from her third. During the next two days aircraft and stores were embarked in *Ocean,* while the aircrew attended lectures and films on Escape and Evasion.

On passage to the operational area next day, pilots prepared their flying gear and maps, and during the afternoon carried out sten gun practice from the after end of the flight deck. That evening *Ocean* took over from USS *Bairoko* as CTU 95.1.1.

Operations were to be mainly against enemy communications, stores, troops, guns and buildings; CAS for the British Commonwealth Division and for the partisans on demand; and bombardment spotting for *New Jersey* and *Newcastle.*

To the disappointment of all on board no flying was possible on the 22nd, the first day of operations; low cloud, rain and fog persisting until about 1630 when it lifted, but not enough to allow the first strike to take off. Fog was to be a constant source of anxiety throughout the patrol. Flying was possible next day from 0500 to 1830 with a standing CAP of two Furies. Strikes were launched against Changyon-ni, Sosa-ri, Ullyul, Taetan, Haeju and the Ongjin Hang areas. At least one gun position and a transformer were hit, and damage was caused on other targets. Photo reconnaissance was carried out of the Haeju to Sariwon and Haeju to Yonan areas, of Ongjin and Changyon-ni. One Fury entered the barrier after engaging number ten wire.

On the 24th vehicle shelters, fuel dumps, stores and a road bridge were bombed in the Ongjin area and a rail bridge near Haeju. Next day air spot was provided for *New Jersey* bombarding the Amgak peninsula. Three rail bridges were attacked at Haeju and two sluice gates at Yonan and Ongjin. One Fury entered the first barrier after the main wheels bounced over the wires. Vice Admiral Clark and Rear Admiral Clifford visited the ship and watched flying on 25th May.

After replenishment on the 26th, operations continued next day until fog descended at 1530. The CAP and strikes airborne had to divert to K.16 (Seoul) for the night. Three TARCAP missions were flown in co-operation with *Newcastle* who was being shelled by enemy shore batteries. One gun position was claimed by the Furies. Early morning fog delayed the start of flying on the 28th, the four aircraft which were launched on the first detail having to return in a hurry. During the day one rail and three road bridges were knocked down. Six aircraft returned from Seoul during the forenoon, a seventh later in the day after repair to a tail oleo. Another Fury entered the barrier.

In reasonably good weather on the 29th another rail bridge was knocked down in the Haeju area. On the 30th, the last day of the patrol, the Furies knocked down a rail bridge and blocked the entrance to a tunnel on the Haeju to Sariwon line with 1,000 lb. bombs and strafed troops on the coast near Ongjin. 560 sorties had been flown on seven flying days at an average of 80 per day, and no aircraft were damaged by enemy action.

On 30th May Admiral Clifford transferred his flag from *Newcastle* to *Ocean* for passage to Sasebo, and that evening she left the area. It had been intended to disembark fourteen Sea Furies to Iwakuni on the 31st during passage to Sasebo, where she arrived that afternoon, so that they might carry out a fly-past over the Commonwealth Division on Coronation Day, but this had to be cancelled owing to low cloud, short visibility and heavy rain. However, at 1630 on Monday 1st June, thirteen Furies were RATOGed from the deck whilst the ship was still at anchor — an almost unique evolution.

During the harbour period until 7th June, apart from those officers at

Reconnaissance photo by Lieut. Anson, 30 May 1953.   *(FAAM)*

Iwakuni, others went to the front line and one to *Philippine Sea* off the east coast.

June 1953 opened with a festive occasion for the Commonwealth forces, which came as a welcome change from the drudgery of the west coast — the celebration with fitting ceremonial and rejoicings of the coronation of Her Majesty Queen Elizabeth II.

Arrangements had been made for all Commonwealth ships that could be spared from the operational area to be disposed between Sasebo, Kure and Tokyo. Present at Sasebo from TG 95.1 were *Tyne* wearing Rear Admiral Clifford's flag, *Ocean*, *Cossack*, *St. Bride's Bay*, *Telemachus* (to take part in A/S exercises) and *Johann Maurits van Nassau*. The Commander, 7th Fleet, Vice Admiral Clark, brought his flagship, *New Jersey*, there for the occasion, and Rear Admiral Olsen was also present in *Dixie*.

The CO of 807 Squadron, Lieutenant Commander T.L.M. Brander tells the story of the Coronation Day fly-past:

'RATOG was the only way we could get off without taking the ship to sea, it produced more speed than the catapult which would have been quite inadequate in the hot, no-wind conditions prevailing. Provided the correct drill was followed there was only a little sink at the bows. A tug had to point the ship in a safe direction so that the aircraft did not have to fly straight at a hill or another ship. After forming up in an "E" and passing over the ship, we flew in a downpour to Iwakuni and had to leave our Furies outside in a tropical deluge which went on all night. As a result when we wanted to take off for Seoul on the following day they were full of water and reluctant to start, radios were unserviceable, and the continuing downpour was daunting. Twelve aircraft reached the Commonwealth Division because one or two had to return to Iwakuni with radio or other unserviceability. The North Koreans had awarded the Brits a day's holiday from the war so we were able to fly over the front line and there was no flak. The weather was nasty with complete cumulonimbus cover and pouring rain. I think I was lucky to find Korea at all and I am sure the American radar put us right. We flew over the front above the Commonwealth Division in the form of a rather thin "E" owing to the aircraft shortage, we could not manage the R at all. We beat up the right place and there were rumours of a staff car going off the road as a result. At Seoul the cloud was broken for our landing but that did not solve everything because one of us could not get his wheels down, the electric's were probably still full of water. The pilots went to a cocktail party in the evening given by the officers of the Commonwealth Division Maintenance Area. We flew back to Iwakuni on the following day and to the ship on the 8th. 810 Squadron's Fireflies took no part in that pantomime at all because they did not have the range of the Fury, they were going to be too short of fuel for safety.'

On Coronation Day — 2nd June — ships of all nations were dressed overall from morning until evening colours. A parade and service, in which representatives from all HM ships present took part, was held in *Ocean*; the United States and Netherlands ships also sent contingents. It had been hoped to hold the parade on the flight deck, but — as in London that day — wet weather prevailed, and the hangar had to be used instead. The Vice-Governor of Nagasaki, and a number of Japanese authorities and senior United Nations officers, with their wives, attended. Admiral Clark accompanied Admiral Clifford on his inspection of the parade. A royal salute was fired by *Ocean*, *Tyne* and *St. Bride's Bay*, and by US ships *New Jersey and Dixie*. Afterwards, Admiral Clifford had a luncheon party in *Tyne* for the principal guests, while the remainder were entertained in *Ocean*.

In the evening, by order of Admiral Clark, a searchlight display was given by all ships, and at a reception attended by some 200 guests in *Tyne*, it was he who proposed the health of Her Majesty. There were celebrations, too, in the Chief Petty Officers' and Petty Officers' Club and the Fleet Canteen, where bands played and members of the US and Dutch forces were entertained; at each the royal toast was honoured.

Great interest and goodwill was shown by the Americans in everything connected with the Coronation. Special relays of radio programmes were made by the Armed Forces Radio Service, and news of it figured largely in their forces newspaper; of their genuine willingness to participate and co-operate there was no doubt. Japanese interest, too, was most marked. Banners with the royal crown and inscription 'Long live Queen Elizabeth II', appeared in the main streets of Sasebo. Many gifts of flowers were sent to Admiral Clifford and *Tyne* by the Governor, the Mayor, and leading Japanese business organisations. The local Chamber of Commerce erected a bar which served free drinks to UN personnel on Coronation Day and the day after, and the Mayor gave a dinner to Admiral Clifford, his senior staff officers, and the commanding officers of all British Commonwealth ships.

At Kure and Tokyo there were similar celebrations on a smaller scale. At the former, *Athabaskan*, *Hawae, Kaniere* and *Sparrow* represented the Commonwealth Navies. Platoons from all four ships were landed to take part in a parade organised by HQ, British Commonwealth Forces, Korea, the salute being taken by Lieutenant General H. Wells, Australian Army.

At Tokyo, *Mounts Bay* and *Anzac* berthed alongside Shibaura Pier, and occasioned much interest among the Japanese on this, the first 'goodwill' visit of HM ships since World War II. Parties from both ships attended a Coronation drumhead service ashore, followed by a parade. Later, a combined official

HMS *Modeste*.   *(Cox)*

reception was held by the two ships. HBM Ambassador subsequently described their visit as an outstanding success.

The ships in the war area, too, celebrated the occasion as far as circumstances permitted. HM ships were dressed with masthead flags and US ships flew white ensigns at the masthead as a courtesy. At Chodo, *Newcastle* and *Morecambe Bay* held services and the former fired a royal salute to the accompaniment of 90 mm fire from Sok-to. The main brace was duly spliced later in the day. Captain Schanze USN, Chief of Staff to Admiral Olsen, who was visiting the area, together with the garrison commanders of Chodo and Sok-to, and three USAF officers were entertained in both *Morecambe Bay* and *Newcastle*. At Paengyong-do, *Modeste*, and *Wave Knight* dressed ship with masthead flags and spliced the main brace. After a short service in *Modeste*, some of her ship's company landed at Paengyong-do with £10 worth of sweets for the orphanage there — the result of a collection on board (equivalent to more than £125 in the 1990s). Her officers and men felt that this gift was the best they could do to accord with the spirit of the day, in the somewhat limiting circumstances in which they were spending it.

Except for short bombardments of Hachwira in the River Taedong and Mahap-to in the Paengyong-do area the enemy took no part in the celebrations; but during the next few days things were more lively in the Chodo area. Frequent bombardments of gun positions and troops were carried out by the ships of TU 95.1.4 — *Morecambe Bay,* USS *Cocopa* and LSMR *409,* by *Johann Maurits van Nassau* on her return from Sasebo, and later by *Crusader*. The enemy retaliated. On 3rd June *Morecambe Bay* was fired on and had to slip her cable in her night anchorage west of Sok-to to get clear. After dark, three low flying aircraft made four attacks on

Chodo dropping light fragmentation bombs from 500 feet. No damage resulted. On each of the next three nights these aircraft visited the area, but made no attacks. On 5th June, LSMR *409*, on completion of a bombardment with rockets and 5 inch gunfire, came under fire herself; 30 rounds fell around her and two hits were scored, which caused some damage and five casualties.

A week after the Coronation Day celebrations the Commonwealth naval forces were faced with a large scale operation of a very different nature — the evacuation of all operational islands north of a line drawn in a direction south-west from the Han estuary, excluding Yong Pyong-do, Udo, Paengyong-do, Techong-do and Sochong-do which were to remain in UN hands. Those to be evacuated included the garrisoned and fortified islands of Chodo and Sok-to and seventeen minor islands held by partisans; in many cases these contained inhabitants who were anxious to leave before the Communists took over. The armistice terms required the evacuation to be completed within five days of their signature.

The armistice terms forbade any civilian to cross to the UN side of the armistice line who had not been resident south of it prior to 25th June 1950. Operation Pandora had been prepared for the evacuation, and it now had to be modified to allow for this residential restriction; all the inhabitants who so wished, refugees, partisans and their dependants would have to be evacuated before the armistice was signed; it therefore became essential that Admiral Clifford should receive notice several days before the signature date. The task to be completed in the five days following signature would be greatly facilitated, as only the military forces, installations and equipment in Chodo and Sok-to would remain to be dealt with.

The operation was planned to be conducted in two phases. First all evacuees were to be collected in staging areas before moving to their final destinations, the Partisan Infantry Regiments (PIRs) to the islands of Taemuido and Yong Yu-do west of Inchon and to Anmyong-do north of Kunsan. All civilian refugees were to be transported to reception centres on the South Korean mainland.

The signing of the prisoner-of-war agreement on 8th June seemed to bring the armistice very near indeed, and on the night of 9th/10th June evacuation of the outer islands started. Some of the PIRs and civilians left in their own boats, others were moved by the three logistic LSTs already on the coast whose routine movements were suspended. Captain Greening in *Birmingham* was CTU 95.1.2 with Commander Ritchie in *Modeste* as CTU 95.1.4 at Chodo, Commander Davis-Goff in *Hawea*, CTU 95.1.5, at Paengyong-do and Commander Ellis in *Sparrow*, CTU 95.1.6 in the Haeju area. On 15th June the assault transport USS *Lenawee* arrived on the west coast on loan from TF 90 carrying 26 assorted landing craft that were to be of the greatest value in the later stages of the evacuation.

On 12th June Admiral Clifford was informed that the armistice was considered imminent. *Newcastle*, though she had only just reached Sasebo from patrol, was sailed for Yong Pyong-do to take charge as CTU 95.1.6 in the Haeju area, and that evening, after taking a not inconsiderable number of hands from ships in Sasebo to get her to sea, *Tyne* sailed for Paengyong-do with Admiral Clifford and his staff to assume the duties of Officer in Tactical Command, West Coast, *Birmingham* going to Chodo as CTU 95.1.4.

During this period there was a marked change in the attitude of the RoK vessels under Admiral Clifford's command and on occasions there was reluctance to co-operate, but no serious incident or interference with planned operations took place. On 18th June came President Syngman Rhee's dramatic release of the anti-Communist prisoners-of-war and the prospect of an early armistice immediately faded, but evacuation of the islands continued, though certain islands had to be reoccupied by reduced partisan forces to avoid their falling into enemy hands prematurely.

Military activity continued at much the usual level during these operations. Single-engined enemy aircraft visited the Chodo area periodically at night and on 10th June included Paengyong-do where they dropped eight small bombs, killing and wounding a few villagers. Allied ships kept up the usual counter-battery and harassing fire and engaged targets of opportunity, but the enemy guns were only occasionally active, and his interference with the evacuation was negligible.

By 22nd June the evacuation movements were over except for the onward lifts of some refugees to the mainland, for which there was no hurry. *Birmingham* was sailed for Sasebo that day and at midnight on 23rd/24th Admiral Clifford followed in *Tyne* leaving *Newcastle* as CTU 95.1.2 in control of the west coast.

Between 10th and 30th June, more than 40,000 persons had been moved, in addition to large quantities of personal belongings and partisan equipment. Well over 17,000 were moved in *Lenawee* and the LSTs. Except for a lift of the 6th PIR weapons in *Kaniere* it was not necessary for combatant ships to be employed as transports.

> 'The evacuation,' remarked Admiral Clifford,' proceeded remarkably smoothly considering the attitude of none co-operation of the RoK Government ... and the fact that an immediate armistice vanished during the process. Although hostilities had to continue during the evacuation, anxieties about the time limit became less acute as the prospect of an early armistice receded...

'Much outstanding work was done by ships on the coast during this period. Improvisation, initiative, and infinite patience were the main ingredients of the operation; planning, accurate timing, and disciplined movement are things outside the comprehension of the people with which the Task Group had to deal.'

The Admiral gave great credit to the Island Defence Commanders and the CTUs — Captain Greening, Commander Ritchie, Commander Davis-Goff and

Commander Ellis — immediately prior to the evacuation, who between them made the final plans which laid such a sound basis for what was actually done.

> 'Perhaps the most outstanding services,' he added, 'were performed by Commander H.D. Ellis, R.N., and the officers and men of H.M.S. *Sparrow*, as in their area around Yong Pyong-do were by far the largest numbers of refugees, and due to the shallow water and numerous islands a great deal of movement had to be improvised in native craft with utterly undisciplined people, and in the face of negligible landing facilities, language difficulties and critical tide conditions.'

Admiral Clifford also commended the excellent work of *Lenawee* and the LSTs:

> 'The people which they carried were completely without knowledge of hygiene or sanitation. On each voyage the ships were rendered foul, but they reported back for more work, clean, zealous, and cheerful. The landing craft carried by *Lenawee* were invaluable for this type of operation. It is a matter for regret that this well-equipped and highly efficient ship could not be offered cargoes of people more nearly approaching her own standard ... All who saw her at work were impressed with her enthusiasm.'

While these exacting operations were taking place, it had fallen to the lot of a British officer to supervise a small evacuation at Yang-do, the only island on the east coast affected at that time. Captain Adair had arrived in *Cossack* to relieve *Haida* on 8th June, just as the evacuation problem came to the fore, and automatically became CTU 95.2.2, which then consisted of USSs *Buck*, *Chandler* and *Endicott*. The usual patrols and train-busting activities continued, but *Cossack* remained in the vicinity of Yang-do. The evacuation was on a very small scale compared with those on the west coast, but it was complicated by persistent fog and other difficulties, such as that the island commander had no crypto system, a problem overcome by landing an officer and a communication rating with a Fleet Code, a signal lantern and a portable wireless set.

HMS *Cossack* gives covering fire to LSU making her way to HMS *Unicorn* from Paengyong-do.   *(Kellaway)*

The evacuation took place successfully between 12th and 16th June.

Second Patrol

Meanwhile the carrier force had not been idle during the evacuation of the islands. *Ocean* sailed from Kure at 0645 on 8th June, the day of the signing of the prisoner-of-war agreement, to relieve *Bairoko*. Twelve Furies were flown on board from Iwakuni during the afternoon, Sub-Lieutenant Hayes having to make a successful forced landing at Iwakuni shortly after take-off due to his engine cutting. *Crusader, Athabaskan, Cockade, Anzac, Thomson, Chevalier, Preston* and *Southerland* served in the screen at different times.

The pattern of operations on this patrol vitas changed, a high proportion of sorties were employed son CAS for the army. The Chinese were exercising increased pressure on the main line of resistance at this time, which culminated in a heavy attack on the eastern central sector on 11th June, and by direction of Admiral Clark both TF 77 and TU 95.1.1 devoted much of their effort to providing close support for the troops. The organisation for dealing with this large number of aircraft proved unsatisfactory and a large number of missions were not controlled on to targets. *Ocean*, too, flew many more sorties than usual for TARCAP to cover withdrawals from the inshore islands, or to assist in silencing shore batteries. The usual attacks on enemy communications, supplies, troops, guns and buildings were therefore on a reduced scale.

The weather on the 9th was too bad for CAS with the 1st Commonwealth Division. Road bridges were attacked in the Anak area, of which two were knocked down. Thick fog next morning prevented flying until 1100, but the weather again was not suitable for CAS, so bridges in the Anak and Yonan areas were attacked by the Furies. Two more aircraft returned from Iwakuni and Lieutenant Halliday's division spent the night at K.16 (Seoul) having run short of fuel over Korea.

Fog prevented the first detail getting off on the 11th, but then a full day's flying was possible, the weather permitting successful CAS missions. Two Fury divisions did MPQ bombing for the first time. This was radar controlled for occasions when the weather was unsuitable for visual bombing. Normally in a fingertip formation of four aircraft, or sometimes in two fingers of eight aircraft, American radar controlled them at a steady heading and at a steady height until they were told to drop their bombs without seeing land or a target. Formation flying in cloud was always a strain, but this was worse because the pilots could usually tell when they were over enemy territory by the colour of the cloud — it went black from bursting flak! No aircraft or pilots were lost, but the aircraft got somewhat pockmarked since flying at a steady height, heading anal speed made it easy for the enemy gunners. It was a new technique in 1953 and the Americans said it was a very accurate system, later reporting all sorts of damage that had been achieved, but 807 Squadron never saw the targets or the damage for themselves. The Fireflies did not indulge in it because they were more suited for, and concentrated on, rocket attacks.

A full day's flying was possible on the 12th although low cloud over land meant that all Fury CAS missions were done by MPQ bombing again. Late in the afternoon, *Sparrow* requested support in evacuating partisans from two islands south of Haeju. Twelve sorties were flown attacking enemy troops and gun positions. Lieutenant Hands made the 1,000th deck landing for 807 Squadron since embarking in *Ocean* from Hal Far the previous December. Lieutenant Mulder's aircraft was twice hit by small-arms fire during the afternoon.

After replenishment on the 13th a full day's operations were again possible on the 14th. Most of the Fury sorties were CAS obtaining good results with the aid of spotter aircraft. Sub-Lieutenant Breakspear made a successful forced landing on the beach at Chodo when his oil pressure dropped after the return pipe from the engine to the oil tank had fractured. CAS with the Commonwealth Division was again possible next day, with good results — troop positions, trenches, caves and gun positions were the main targets. One rail bridge was destroyed on TARCAP.

On the 16th the first detail took off on time but by land-on fog was closing in which prevented any further flying until 1030. The rest of the day's programme was uninterrupted with CAS over the front line and strikes. During the evening Chodo called up for TARCAP and two divisions strafed and bombed gun positions on the mainland.

Bad weather interfered with flying on the last day of the patrol. The first take-off was at 0630, and three CAS missions were flown, the last one having to jettison their bombs due to the weather. Flying was cancelled at 1400, *Ocean* turned over the duties of CTU 95.1.1 to *Bairoko* and proceeded to Kure. A total of 539 sorties had been flown during the patrol.

Bad weather on passage next day prevented the CODS aircraft from making their routine visit to the ship from shore so that none of the aircrew could visit the front line or the east coast carriers.

Ocean arrived in Kure on the 19th, embarking AVGAS before going alongside. Lieutenants Mitchell and Anson left 807 Squadron to return to the UK. Sub-Lieutenants Wanford and Green joined the Squadron, having flown out from the UK by BOAC Comet; they had just completed OFS 2 at Culdrose as National Service Midshipmen and were the first National Service pilots to volunteer to serve in Korea.

Third Patrol

Ocean sailed from Kure at 1630 on 25th June and after a very foggy passage took over as CTU 95.1.1 in the evening of the 27th. *Cockade, Huron, Tobruk, Preston, Buck and Chevalier* formed the screen at various times. Considerable effort was again expended on CAS operations over the front line, and attacks continued on the usual targets.

Fog on the 27th, the first day of operations, reduced flying to one event of two Furies on CAP. Next day the weather around the ship was better but was bad over land. Most Fury missions were MPQ bombing over the front line, but strikes were also launched against gun positions in the Changyon area, and against shipping and a road bridge near Chinnampo.

On the 29th there was an improvement in the weather. Seven MPQ missions of CAS were flown as well as strikes on gun positions in the Pungchon area, on a road bridge near Anak, and on barges and railway trucks at Chinnampo. A Firefly, piloted by Lieutenant Bacon, which had been hit by small arms fire, was forced to ditch, the pilot being speedily rescued by the US SAR helicopter from Paengyong-do.

Another full day's flying was possible next day in good weather. On the CAS missions road and rail bridges were attacked in the Haeju, Yonan and Changyon areas and a rail tunnel near Haeju was blocked. While bombing a bridge near Changyon, Sub-Lieutenant Hick had an overspeeding engine in his Fury and headed out to sea. He tried to reach Paengyong-do beach, but the engine failed and he successfully ditched about two miles north-west of the island. The efficiency of the search and rescue organisation was again demonstrated, when the helicopter promptly picked him up and took him to Paengyong-do whence he was taken to the ship in the rear seat of a Firefly piloted by Lieutenant Smith.

Sea Fury flown by Lieut. Hagdoorn, RNethN., in barrier accident.   *(IWM)*

Sub-Lieutenant Whitfield, the third National Service pilot, joined 810 Squadron when the CODS Avenger came on board during the afternoon. He, Green and Wanford had all been on the same course at Culdrose before joining *Ocean*.

After replenishment on 1st July, flying recommenced on the 2nd, but was restricted due to weather. Only three CAS missions were flown, but a rail bridge on the Haeju to Sariwon line was attacked with success. Lieutenant Van Crusten brought a replacement Fury from Iwakuni, and Lieutenant Commander Brander and Sub-Lieutenant Sheppard escorted a Firefly to Paengyong-do where it had to make a wheels-up landing as a result of a complete hydraulic failure.

Due to low cloud and driving rain next morning there was no flying before 1100 when the first CAP was launched. Five divisions carried out CAS with MPQ bombing, the first landing-on at 1400. The target area was clear, and as a result of heavy flak at 12,000 feet Sub-Lieutenant Hayes received three shrapnel hits but brought his aircraft back safely to the ship.

Better weather next day permitted all but one detail of the programme to be flown. The Haeju to Sariwon railway line took a heavy pounding again, eight bridges were destroyed, Lieutenant Hagdoorn himself getting two. The CAS missions encountered heavy flak, one aircraft being hit at the base of the cockpit hood on the starboard side.

On the 5th weather again affected the programme, four CAP and four MPQ sorties of CAS were flown in very poor weather during the forenoon before flying was finally cancelled at 1430. In all 474 sorties were flown during the patrol, a daily average of 86 when a full programme was possible. *Bairoko* took over on completion of flying and *Ocean* proceeded to Sasebo where she arrived after a fairly rough passage at 1630 on 7th July.

During the week of routine maintenance and storing in harbour, divisions were held on the flight deck on the 12th.

With the preliminary evacuation of the islands completed at the end of June, things settled down to their usual routine for what was to be the few remaining weeks of the war. On the west coast the enemy was unusually quiet; his guns did not take any UN ships under fire, nor did he show any activity in the coastal area, apart from occupying the islands of Yuk-to and Sunwi-do near Paengyong-do after their evacuation by the partisans in mid-June. After a small partisan reconnaissance patrol had failed to return from Yuk-to, a stronger patrol was landed on the night of 1st/2nd July in search of them. This patrol ran into heavy opposition and had to withdraw. *Ocean's* aircraft bombed the enemy in the island on the 2nd, and that night another patrol landed to be greeted with fire from enemy mortars and 76 mm guns. Again the patrol had to withdraw, but on this occasion extremely accurate supporting fire was provided from *Johan Maurits van Nassau*.

In the Chodo area a considerable number of bombardments of enemy gun positions was carried out by UN forces during the first three weeks of July *Morecambe Bay*, *Cossack*, *Crane*, *Cockade*, *Kaniere*, *Johan Maurits van Nassau* and LSMR *409* taking part. A particularly successful shoot was carried out by *Cossack* (who had returned from the east coast) on the 13th July, who approached to within 2,800 yards of the gun caves on the north of Wolsa-ri peninsula at first light. Complete surprise was achieved and major damage was inflicted.

Johan Maurits van Nassau visited the Han estuary between 9th and 11th July, and at the request of the local PIR bombarded mortar positions on the mainland.

There was no activity in the Haeju area, apart from a bombardment by *Athabaskan* on 20th July, and a small PIR raid, supported by *Ocean's* aircraft, on the 21st.

On the east coast, in contrast to the west, the Chinese shore offensive was accompanied by increased activity and intensity of coastal gun-fire. Several US ships were hit at Wonsan and elsewhere. The US ships gave as good as they got. *New Jersey, St. Paul, Bremerton, Manchester* and destroyers of TG 95.2 and 7th Fleet operated at the bomb-line during this final period. During the last two months of the war, 1,774 rounds of 16 inch, 2,800 of 8 inch, 700 of 6 inch and 13,000 of 5 inch were fired at the enemy positions.

During this period, *Athabaskan* and *Huron* operated in the Songjin area. *Huron's* war service came to an unfortunate end when she grounded in clear weather on the south-west tip of Yang-do at 0100 on 13th July. The ship struck rocks at twelve knots and sustained very heavy underwater damage from the stern to about station 30. She succeeded in re-floating before dawn and was towed by US rescue tugs to Sasebo at five knots, where she arrived tour days later and was taken in hand for repairs.

Tobruk took Huron's place on the east coast and remained there for the rest of the war.

Fourth Patrol

A new commitment was undertaken during this patrol at the request of 5th USAF. A small unit consisting of three Firefly aircraft, seven officers and sixteen ratings sagas disembarked on 16th July to K.6 airfield (Pvongtaek, 40 miles south of Seoul) for use as night fighters against the slow, low-flying enemy aircraft — the 'bed-check Charlies' — that were sent on nuisance missions and were doing considerable damage to American ammunition dumps well behind the UN side of the lines. The American jet night-fighters had had very little success as they were much too fast and, on one occasion, an aircraft was lost when it flew straight into the raider. A relatively slow, piston-engined aircraft was urgently needed and the Firefly fitted the role perfectly, and having previously been fitted with APX-6 (IFF Mk 10) loaned by the Far East Air Force. A total of 21 hours day and eight hours night training, and 26 hours night operational flying was successfully carried out. Though no 'kills' were achieved in the 31 missions before the signing of the armistice, some of the raiders were chased away which deterred others. After the truce was signed the aircraft were switched to police duties patrolling the demarcation line throughout the night to prevent any violation of the demilitarised zone by any aircraft. Captain Logan wrote:

'The success of this venture, laid on at short notice and with little material backing, reflects great credit on the aircrew concerned and in particular on Lieutenant Commander Bloomer, Commanding Officer,

810 Squadron, who carried out all the initial flying tests and inspired
the whole unit with enthusiasm by his own personal example.'

Ocean sailed from Sasebo at 0615 on 14th July, and during the forenoon
Lieutenant Woods flew on a replacement Fury from Iwakuni. She carried out her
last war patrol between 15th and 23rd July, screened by *Cockade, Cossack,
Southerland, Buck, Preston* and *Chevalier* at various times. Once again the weather
was most unfavourable. In spite of fog, rain and low cloud, either in the vicinity of
the ship or over the whole target area, seriously interfering with flying on five of the
eight flying days, a total of 434 sorties were flown, and the standard of deck-landing
in these difficult conditions was very satisfactory.

The first detail on the 15th was cancelled due to poor visibility. The second was
launched, but with aircraft due to land on, the ship found herself in an extensive fog
patch which developed suddenly without warning. The Furies were diverted to K.14
(Kimpo) airfield, but one of them, piloted by Sub-Lieutenant Sheppard, was short of
fuel and a CCA landing was attempted. At the end of the second attempt, Sheppard
found himself on the port beam of the ship; realising that if he did not land then he
would have to ditch, he circled the ship from starboard and made a successful
landing from that quarter after only an occasional glimpse of her until the last
moment. He had some six gallons of fuel remaining.

The catapult went unserviceable during the afternoon, and since 8th Army had
asked for all possible air support at the time it was important to keep to the flying
programme, so the next mission of four Fireflies and four Furies was launched by
RATOG. The pilot of the second Fury to take off, Lieutenant Mulder, fired his
rockets too soon; he failed to gain flying speed and hit the water just ahead of the
ship, whence he was recovered by helicopter. Except for his pride, he was not
hurt, but he was very wet.

The remaining Furies took off satisfactorily, but the first Firefly, after some of its
rockets had failed, crashed into the sea and sank immediately, taking with it the
observer, Lieutenant K.M. Thomas. The pilot, Lieutenant A.J.D. Evans, was promptly
picked up by USS *Southerland*, but despite prolonged artificial respiration, failed to
regain consciousness, and died on board her. On completion of the flying programme
that evening a combined memorial and burial service for Lieutenants Thomas and
Evans was held in *Ocean*. In the gathering dusk the ships of the screen — *Buck,
Southerland* and *Cockade* — closed in astern and on the quarter to take their part. 'We
all appreciated their courtesy and sympathy deeply', recorded Captain Logan.

After this unfortunate start, things went better. There were no more losses, and
subject to the weather, CAS was provided for the army, and the usual offensive
sorties were flown against enemy communications, troops, guns, and so on.
Photographic reconnaissance once more paid good dividends.

Weather again disrupted the programme on the 16th when fog caused the second event to be cancelled. The Furies carried out CAS missions both with Mosquito aircraft and by MPQ bombing. Strike missions attacked road and rail bridges, knocking down two. Sub-Lieutenant Hick had total brake failure while taxying up the deck and his aircraft crashed into Lieutenant Bawden's and two Fireflies, badly damaging all four.

Due to the losses and unserviceability, the first event on the 17th was reduced by four aircraft. In spite of the maintenance crews doing their best to keep the aircraft in the air, serviceability remained low all day. However CAS missions, photographic reconnaissance and strikes on bridges were flown.

CODS Avenger accident – normally the aircraft caught No. 1 wire but this one floated into the barrier.   *(Neep)*

Serviceability again was low next day, and with very little wind launches and recoveries were delayed by up to ten minutes each event. In spite of these problems strikes and support were provided to meet a reduced programme. Lieutenant Crosse and Sub-Lieutenant Hick were flown ashore in the CODS Avenger to collect replacement aircraft from Iwakuni.

After replenishment on the 19th, a full day's flying was possible on the 20th. One replacement Fury landed-on from Iwakuni, and on the first event Sub-Lieutenant Breakspear made the ship's 1,000th accident-free deck-landing. A strike was launched late in the day against targets in the Yonan peninsula in support of a landing by 2nd PIR that would take place the next morning.

The landing took place on the 21st against gun positions, and the first twelve Fury strike sorties carried out bombing and strafing of enemy positions on the Yonan peninsula in support of the early morning raid by 2nd PIR. Low cloud and fog over the target area caused the last two events of the day to be cancelled. Next morning fog and low cloud prevented any flying other than CAP until the afternoon, when bridges in the Anak and Chaeryong areas were attacked, knocking down two.

Fog and low cloud prevented any flying before noon on the 23rd, and during the afternoon flying was restricted until the final land-on at 1810. *Bairoko* took over the duties of CTU 95.1.1 that evening and *Ocean* proceeded to Kure, where she arrived during the morning of the 25th, to refuel during the forenoon before securing alongside in the afternoon. The squadrons disembarked unserviceable aircraft to await *Unicorn's* arrival on the 29th with serviceable replacements.

The armistice was signed at on the 27th.

Since President Rhee's release of the prisoners of war on 18th June the Chinese had been preparing a punitive offensive against the South Koreans. On 13th July they struck with 40,000 men against the RoK east-central front. The South Koreans withdrew in good order inflicting heavy casualties on the enemy. For some days there was bitter fighting, but the attack was held. TF 77 concentrated their air effort on support of the army in the threatened sector, and by 19th July counter-attacks were restoring the situation. On that day, the Communists agreed to begin preparations for the actual signing of the armistice. Thereafter, negotiations proceeded apace and their final stages were completed quicker than had been expected.

Vice Admiral Sir Charles Lambe, CinCFES, arrived at Iwakuni on 24th July to visit Japan and the war area. He was met by *Birmingham* in which he took passage to Sasebo. Barely five minutes after his arrival there, information was received that the armistice would probably be signed very shortly. *Birmingham* at once proceeded to the west coast to take over the duties of CTU 95.1.2 from *Crane*, and Rear Admiral Clifford, accompanied by the CINC, followed in *Tyne*. On this occasion the additional ratings required to man *Tyne* were very willingly provided by the Royal Canadian Navy from *Huron*. Admiral Clifford remarked that with a ship's company comprising British, Canadians (one or two of whom could speak only French), and Chinese it was a tribute to the patience and common sense of the ship's officers, chief petty officers and petty officers that the ship worked so smoothly.

While on passage, a signal was received from the Supreme Commander, General Mark Clark, desiring the attendance of Admiral Clifford at the signing of the armistice. As the message was sent only an hour before the ceremony, it was quite impossible for him to comply. Vice Admiral Briscoe, COMNAVFE, and Vice Admiral Clark, Commander 7th Fleet, both expressed their regret that more notice had not been given to enable Admiral Clifford to attend, and added that had they known that Admiral Lambe was on board *Tyne* a similar invitation would have been extended to him. The armistice was signed at 1000 local time (0200 BST) on 27th July 1953, and became effective twelve hours later at 2200.

So far as the Commonwealth naval forces were concerned, the final evacuation of the west coast islands then became the main consideration. *Tyne* arrived at Paengyong-do on 28th July where Admiral Lambe left her to take passage to Kure in *Charity* while *Tyne*, wearing Admiral Clifford's flag, went on to Chodo. The task of evacuation this second time was considerably easier. The small PIR garrisons on the outer islands could use their own transport and only disciplined men, under proper leadership and with their own food supplies, remained to be dealt with by the four LSTs that had been retained on the coast. The period allowed for the evacuation had been increased from five to ten days, to 6th August.

By 29th July all the PIR elements had withdrawn from the outlying islands, and dismantling of the equipment on Chodo and loading of petrol, oil and lubricants had been completed by the 30th. The only hitch in the evacuation plan occurred on the 29th. The Tactical Air Direction Centre had been dismantled when information was received that 5th USAF required it to resume operations. It was then not practicable to re-erect it, so some of the TADC personnel embarked in *Birmingham* and she provided the radar coverage up to the River Yalu required by the air force.

At 2100 on 31st July the flag on the headquarters of the Island Defence Commander was struck, and the following morning *Iroquois* embarked the Commander and the demolition party. Save for ten elderly civilians who resolutely declined to leave, Chodo was deserted. Having provided them with provisions for six weeks and a few simple medicines, *Iroquois* sailed for Paengyong-do at 0950 on 1st August. Admiral Clifford reported the evacuation of the west coast islands complete.

Admiral Clifford remained at Paengyong-do in *Tyne* for a few days where on the evening of 3rd August he was joined by *Ocean*. The Admiral held a short press conference on board *Tyne*, attended by all the island commanders, for a group of correspondents who had been brought by *Ocean*, having been flown on board from Seoul earlier in the day. Next day Admiral Clifford sailed for Sasebo in *Tyne*, leaving Captain Greening in *Birmingham* as OTC, West Coast.

On 6th August, the end of the ten-day period, *Iroquois* was withdrawn, and TU 95.1.4 ceased to exist; *Birmingham* left the operating area for Hong Kong and

HMS *Birmingham* – CinC FES Sir Charles Lambe transferring by jackstay accompanied by a helicopter for safety.
(Author)

Captain Logan in *Ocean* took over as Officer in Tactical Command. Surface and air patrols were continued outside the three-mile limit of the North Korean coast for most of August, in order to remind the Communists that UN forces were still on the alert. Things were much more comfortable for the ships' companies, as from the moment of the cease-fire various relaxation's had been permitted. Ships were no longer darkened at night and scuttles and blackout screen doors were opened, a great relief in the hot and humid conditions of the Korean summer. Watchkeeping duties, too, were reduced, as instant readiness of full armament was no longer necessary.

On 25th August the surface patrols were discontinued, but British and US carriers continued to work in a nine-day cycle carrying out flying training off the west coast till the middle of September. Gradually this was extended to a six-week cycle with one carrier at 24 hours notice for operations, and the other at not more than a week.

Fifth Patrol

Ocean remained in Japanese and Korean waters until 31st October with flying consisting of exercises at the low intensity of between twenty and thirty sorties per day. On passage to her fifth patrol, at 0600 on 1st August, she had grounded on an uncharted shoal in Shimonoseki Strait; no damage was sustained except to the bottom log, and she got clear in half an hour but had to anchor for 10 hours to effect repairs to the main condensers that were choked with sand.

On 6th August, event Baker was to have been launched by free take-off, but Lieutenant Pugh who was first to go, in a Fury, crashed into the sea just ahead of the ship after the aircraft's hook had dropped whilst going down the flight deck and catching number two barrier. The barrier was dragged out and the port stanchion half-raised, then the hook pulled out of the aircraft which stalled into the sea, breaking in half on impact. He was brought back to the ship considerably shaken, having consumed quite a large amount of the Yellow Sea before managing to grab hold of the hook lowered by the helicopter.

Another accident occurred five days later on the 11th. *Unicorn* had joined *Ocean* for one patrol and was keen to exercise her deck. She had no aircraft, so for several days Lieutenant Halliday led a flight of four Furies on fighter interceptions from *Unicorn*. A different ship and a strange deck sometimes produces some variations in landing performances, and there had always been some doubts concerning certain pilots. Halliday was on the receiving end of a very bad error of judgement from the pilot landing behind him onto *Unicorn* deck. The conditions were normal and he landed and taxied clear of the barriers, which were then raised again in preparation for the next to land.

The Sea Fury was a superb aircraft for deck landing, but just a little too much speed could result in a wheeler and, if unlucky, the hook failing to engage a wire, with the inevitable result of a barrier crash — one of the facts of flying life that every pilot had to accept once the batsman (LSO) had given the mandatory 'Cut'. Whatever the circumstances, the throttle had to be closed and kept in that position. Normally in a Sea Fury at the correct deck landing approach speed, the aircraft's tail came down for a good arrestor wire engagement by the hook if the control column was snapped into the stomach. Too much speed and the aircraft floated, with the hook clear of the wires, into the barrier.

LSO + Teller + Talker; Sea Fury 'Roger' just before 'Cut'. *(Corkill)*

In this incident, the aircraft landing behind Halliday bounced after the 'Cut' and came clear of the deck without hook engagement, the pilot opened the throttle to go round again and cleared number one barrier, but then his hook caught number two barrier and the aircraft stalled onto the deck, crashing into Halliday's aircraft and severely damaging its fuselage, wings and empennage. When he was struck Halliday would have been handling the throttle and everything would then have been forced forward. Consequently it went roaring round the flight deck with the throttle jammed open, damaging the main plane of a spare aircraft, knocking a Clarkat (a small aircraft towing tractor) over the side, going up onto its nose and eventually crashing into the Jumbo mobile crane, after which it caught fire. He had subconsciously operated the brakes as the aircraft rushed to the deck edge and thus swung away. His instincts for survival were also apparent as he slipped his straps when the aircraft turned up on its nose and caught fire, but he was unconscious when the fireman and Lieutenant Blunden, the LSO, completed his rescue.

He had sustained severe head and face injuries and was taken by a USN destroyer to Inchon and was then transferred to the UN Danish Hospital Ship *Jutlandia*. The fact that within a year he was back flying jets and playing rugger was a tribute to the fine Danish doctors and nurses aboard *Jutlandia*.

Meanwhile the other aircraft fell over the side and crashed into the sea upside down and on fire. Its pilot was picked up by *Ocean's* helicopter unhurt.

Ocean sailed on a further four patrols before returning to the United Kingdom: the sixth was from 20th to 30th August, the seventh from 6th to 17th September, the eighth from 3rd to 9th October and the ninth — and final -patrol was from 12th to 16th October. She hoisted a paying-off pennant at colours on 31st October at Sasebo prior to sailing for the last time, for home.

During September the American carrier *Point Cruz* spent a number of days at Inchon, acting as a staging platform for Indian troops destined for the demilitarised zone in Korea. On arrival of the troop transports, the troops were moved to *Point Cruz* and lifted thence by helicopters of the US Army and USMC direct to the demilitarised zone, thus avoiding any unfriendly demonstrations that might have attended their movement overland. Over 6,000 troops were moved in this way. *Ocean* acted in a similar capacity during her eighth patrol when she was in Inchon on the 6th October helping with her helicopters in the transfer of 120 Indian troops. Whilst there, Lieutenant Derek Mather, who had been taken prisoner on 5th January when a member of 801 Squadron in *Glory*, was released. He came on board *Ocean* before going home to UK, described by one of the ship's officers as 'a poor emaciated shrimp'.

An aircraft carrier, cruiser and ships of the destroyer and frigate squadrons of the Commonwealth Navies were kept within easy reach of Korean coastal waters for some time longer, but though no peace treaty succeeded the armistice as had been expected, there was no recurrence of hostilities. Rear Admiral Clifford, after a farewell visit to South Korea and Japan, hauled down his flag as Flag Officer, 2nd in Command, Far East Station, at Hong Kong on 18th November 1953 — and with this event the participation of HM Naval Forces in the Korean War could be considered at an end.

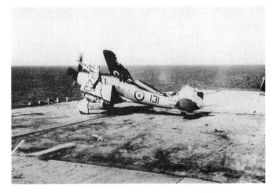

Accident to Lieut. Halliday on HMS *Unicorn*. As the aircraft swung away from the edge of the flight deck, obviously in a violent arc, the tail smashed over the side of the deck and ripped off, dropping over the side into the sea.

(Halliday)

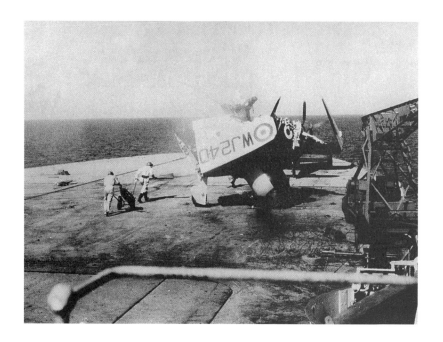

CHAPTER 14

HMS UNICORN

REPAIR and FERRY CARRIER
June 1950 to October 1953

HMS *Unicorn* left the UK for the Far East on 22nd September 1949, and at the outbreak of war in June 1950 was under orders to return home in the autumn. The important, if unspectacular, contribution she could make to the war effort was speedily recognised and she was retained on the station for the whole three years of hostilities. As Captain J.Y. Thompson commented:

'Though her activities did not hit the headlines at home, *Unicorn* made a name for herself on the station, and in wider circles too, and those who served in her can take pride in her achievements, without which the "fighting carriers" would not have been able to operate at all.'

She paid off and re-commissioned at Singapore in October 1951, the relief crew being sent out in Warrior. She eventually returned to Devonport in December 1953.

Unicorn's main functions were to carry replacement aircraft and stores from Singapore to Japan, where she replenished the operational carrier either by flight delivery or by direct transfer, or to the advanced air base at Iwakuni, and she acted as aircraft repair ship. Time expired aircraft or duds were transferred to *Unicorn*, on the return of the operational carrier to harbour. In addition, she provided a reserve of aircraft and air stores when in the forward area. But this was by no means the limit of her usefulness. Her two large hangars and facilities rendered her very suitable for carrying all types of cargo, stores, ammunition, RAF equipment, troops, and passengers between Singapore, Hong Kong, Japan and the forward area. In the anxious days of August 1950 one of the first two British battalions took passage in her from Hong Kong to Pusan.

Unicorn supported all five of HM light fleet carriers, on several occasions accompanying the operational carrier to the forward area, flying her own aircraft and acting as a spare deck. On one occasion she engaged enemy positions with her 4 inch guns, and thereby became more closely engaged than any of the other carriers.

During her four years' service in the Far East, *Unicorn* steamed over 130,000 miles (110,000 during hostilities), spent over 500 days at sea, carried more than 6,000 troops and passengers, and handled some 600 aircraft.

In general, the support given by *Unicorn* and the Naval Air Base at Singapore was essential to the conduct of these operations. The pipeline for the supply of aircraft was a long one, 12,000 miles from the UK to Korea, with *Warrior* ferrying replacement aircraft from the UK to Singapore. For all practical purposes, Royal Naval air operations were conducted without the support of airfield facilities closer than Singapore, about 1,500 miles away.

The question of replacement and upkeep of *Triumph's* aircraft had been considered soon after the outbreak of the war. It was proposed either that *Unicorn* should move to a forward air station (probably Iwakuni) to act as the aircraft repair ship, or that the Aircraft Repair Department with its workshop equipment and stores should disembark to HMS *Simbang* (the air station ashore at Sembawang, Singapore) and that *Unicorn* should act as replenishment ship only. The second proposal was adopted.

On Tuesday 20th June 1950 *Unicorn* arrived at the Singapore Naval Base. It had been decided that, before her imminent return to the UK, she would disembark aircraft and stores, and transfer the major part of the air personnel to Sembawang. During the next few days a start was made with these moves and preparations were made for a short docking and self-refit prior to sailing for the UK.

But on Sunday 25th June the North Koreans invaded South Korea.

That incident was to change the future for everyone. They were informed that it was probable that the ship would have to make one or two more trips with aircraft and stores for *Triumph*. The ship's company were accommodated for five days in Terror, during which time there was much activity with the re-embarkation of stores, ammunition and aircraft.

On 11th July *Unicorn* sailed for Okinawa with guns crews being drilled regularly on passage. However, the ship was diverted to the American Naval base at Sasebo, where she arrived on 20th July with seven Seafires and five Fireflies for *Triumph*. The total of fourteen Seafires *Triumph* was to receive from *Unicorn* were the oldest and least satisfactory of reserves and would prove to be difficult to maintain.

As time progressed it became obvious that there was little likelihood of the ship returning to the UK whilst the Korean War lasted. She sailed for Iwakuni on 24th July to collect aircraft and spares, and from there sailed for Hong Kong arriving on the 30th, leaving again on 2nd August. Close range firings were carried out on the way south at smoke bursts and meteorological balloons. Singapore was reached on 5th August where a very heavy storing programme was carried out. On 11th *Unicorn* went to sea to enable two newly joined pilots to get in some deck-landing practice, on completion of which she returned to the Naval Base, finally sailing once more for Hong Kong on 13th August. During this week of storing, three months victualling and naval stores had been embarked for *Triumph*, and with stores for other ships she had almost sufficient in the ship on sailing to open a small naval armament and victualling yard of her own. Hardly an inch of space remained in the lower hangar, whilst the upper hangar was crammed with aircraft. Amongst the stores embarked were 300 barrels of rum, and hundreds of cases of milk, tea, and bags of sugar for Hong Kong Victualling Yard, whilst stored below were many tons of flour.

Hong Kong was reached on 16th August where stores, provisions and ammunition were disembarked and re-embarked for ships up north. The ship sailed in company with *Ceylon* on the 18th for Sasebo. At 2100 that evening orders were received to return to Hong Kong where both ships arrived the next morning. She was to remain at one hours notice for steam, no leave was given and the following day orders were received to clear the lower hangar of all stores.

The mystery of all this unusual activity was disclosed when the local press headlined the news that the Middlesex Regiment and the Argyle and Sutherland Highlanders — to become universally known in Korea as the Agile and Suffering Highlanders — together with a Brigade Headquarters from other units were to be transported to Korea in HM Ships *Unicorn* and *Ceylon*.

On the afternoon of Saturday 25th August the troops, brigaded as the British 27th Brigade, embarked: *Unicorn* taking the 1st Middlesex Regiment and Brigade Headquarters, *Ceylon* the 1st Argylls. Army vehicles of every kind except tanks were tightly packed, virtually wheel to wheel, in the lower hangar — the skills of the Army transport drivers in these manoeuvres was much admired by the sailors. Farewell speeches were given by the Commissioner General the Right Honourable Malcolm MacDonald, the GOC Troops Far East, Lieutenant General Harding, and the Brigade Commander, Brigadier Coade, before the ships, escorted by *Warramunga*, sailed for

Pusan on a glorious but very hot evening at 1800. The troops were kept busy with weapon training, physical exercises and lectures, while on Sunday a combined religious service was held on the flight deck, the address being given by the Chaplain of the Middlesex Regiment.

Middlesex regiment embarking in HMS *Unicorn.*   *(Kellaway)*

At 1130 on 29th August *Unicorn* led the way into Pusan. This was another historic occasion, as these were not only the first British troops to arrive in Korea but were the first UN ground troops, other than US and South Koreans, to reach Korea. Two American Negro Bands were playing and a male choir and a South Korean children's' choir awaited them on the jetty. They sang, amongst other songs, their own and the British National Anthems. Shortly afterwards *Ceylon* entered harbour with the Argyles. The 'Jocks' had brought their pipe band and drums with them, causing a minor sensation when they played stirring Scottish marches and airs. A very touching incident was the presentation of a bouquet of flowers to Brigadier Coade by a small South Korean girl. Banners were everywhere, welcoming the troops to Korea, mostly in the name of the United Nations.

The remainder of the day and most of the following night were spent disembarking stores and equipment. At 1700 on the 30th the two battalions entrained for destinations in Korea, and a few days later were in action against North Korean attacks to the south-west of Waegwan, some 70 miles from Pusan. At 1000 the following morning

Argyle and Sutherland Highlanders disembarking from HMS *Ceylon*.

(Kellaway)

Unicorn and *Ceylon* sailed for Sasebo, escorted by HMASs *Bataan* and *Warramunga*, arriving at 1930 that evening. The disembarkation of *Triumph's* stores commenced the following morning.

On 2nd September *Unicorn* sailed for Singapore for a refit, arriving on the 8th when arrangements were made for the ship's company to be accommodated in *Terror* again. During this refit period the opportunity was taken by a number of the ship's company to take some leave in the Federation (now Malaysia) at leave centres. All service personnel travelling in the Federation at that time had to be armed. Several were in trains that were attacked by bandits, and in one in particular, that was derailed, the sailors quickly adapted themselves to the situation by assisting in removing the wounded when not actually using their weapons.

During this stay in Singapore, *Theseus* arrived from the Mediterranean to relieve *Triumph*, and *Triumph* passed through en route for the UK.

The refit ended on 17th October, the ship's company returned, and *Unicorn*, loaded with stores, ammunition and aircraft, sailed again for Sasebo, where she arrived on 1st November. Commander W. Elliott, DSC, was relieved at Sasebo by Commander J. Mayling, CBE, who had flown to Iwakuni from Singapore, completing his journey to Sasebo in the ship's Sea Otter piloted by Commander M.P. Francklin DSC.

During the passage to Singapore the ship ran into the edge of typhoon Clara on 10th November, during which a gust of 55 knots, which lasted for 20 minutes, was recorded, and it was estimated that there were short gusts at times of 80-90 knots. On Sunday 12th November a Remembrance Day service was held on the flight deck, and on the 14th Singapore was reached.

On 27th November Captain H. Hopkins, CBE, was relieved by Captain J.Y. Thompson.

On 2nd December *Unicorn* sailed north again, with 400 passengers, the largest body of which were Army personnel. They consisted of units for the Royal Ulster Rifles, Gloucesters, Devons, Wiltshires, Green Howards, CMP, and REME; there were about 50 RAF, and a small number of Naval personnel. It was a rough trip, with several boats being damaged. On arrival at Hong Kong the Wiltshires and the RAF contingent disembarked, the rest of the Army personnel remaining on board until arrival at Sasebo on the 10th.

After only a few hours, *Unicorn* sailed again, this time to rendezvous with Th*eseus* on the west coast of Korea to deliver five Sea Furies and one Firefly to her, the pilots being brought over by *Athabaskan*. After flying off the aircraft and transferring stores to *Constance*, course was set for Sasebo where she arrived on the 12th. Stores and the remaining passengers were disembarked, and the following day she sailed for Iwakuni. The purpose of this visit was to enable some newly arrived pilots for *Theseus* to get in some ADDLs ashore to be followed by DLP at sea. Lieutenant Beavan had an accident on the runway at Iwakuni, and on another occasion the engine of his Sea Fury cut at 7,000 feet and he had to make a glide approach.

The stay at Iwakuni lasted from 14th to 27th December, when she sailed for Kure where she stayed until 5th January 1951. During the period at Kure she provided working parties for *Theseus* and the small ships who were celebrating their Christmas, having been at sea on operations on Christmas Day.

Leaving Kure, *Unicorn* arrived at Hong Kong on 9th January, embarked cargo, and left for Singapore on 11th where she arrived on the 15th.

Ten days later on the 25th 400 troops were embarked, mainly replacements for the Middlesex and the Argyles; AVGAS was embarked, and next day *Unicorn* sailed for Hong Kong. On passage the soldiers were kept busy with small arms firing and PT, while the sailors also carried out a number of exercises — rigging gear for oiling and provisioning at sea.

She arrived at Hong Kong on the 27th, and on the following day, Sunday, a ceremony took place on the quarter-deck when a plaque was presented to the ship on behalf of the Middlesex Regiment to commemorate their association with *Unicorn*. The troops were landed, cargo was exchanged and on 31st January she sailed again for Sasebo.

Once clear of the harbour a splash target was streamed, to enable RAF pilots from Kai Tak to engage in firing practices. Several good hits were registered, and the last aircraft disposed of the target completely. The hands principally relieved when this happened were the Sea Boat's Crew, it was one less job for them to do — 'Recover splash target'.

Having discharged some cargo in Sasebo on 3rd February, *Unicorn* sailed next day for Kure, arriving on the 4th. The troops disembarked for further training at Hiro Camp before being sent on to Korea. *Unicorn* again provided working parties for *Theseus* and the small ships. She left for Sasebo on the 14th, and then followed a series of interruptions. First, due to a heavy fall of snow, visibility was reduced to such an extent that it was decided to anchor for the night near Iwakuni. The ship got under way at 0700 next morning, but at 1130 had to turn about and head at full speed for Kure to land an urgent surgical cot case.

Kure was reached at about 1630, the patient transferred to HMHS *Maine*, and at 1700 *Unicorn* could proceed again to Sasebo. It was decided to make the passage via the Shimonoseki Strait, a comparatively narrow and shallow strait between the main island of Honshu and the large western island of Kyushu. A notable feature of this strait is an overhead electric cable which the ship just missed when passing underneath. *Unicorn* was the largest RN ship to have passed through these straits.

Sasebo was reached at 1800 on the 16th February and after a ten day stay she proceeded to Singapore arriving on 5th March where she carried out some deck-landings before securing to her familiar Number 8 berth in the Naval Base. Storing and provisioning during the week was particularly memorable for the heavy rainfall, it being the monsoon season, with widespread flooding. Some more Middlesex, Argyle, RA and RAF personnel were embarked on the 12th prior to sailing. On the flight deck were a number of Meteors for No. 77 Squadron RAAF at Iwakuni.

Unicorn arrived in Hong Kong on 16th March to embark stores as usual, and also, this time, the band of the Middlesex Regiment for Kure where it was scheduled to provide musical entertainment for Army personnel at Hiro camp and other places. She sailed for Sasebo on the 17th arriving on the 21st to disembark cargo, sailing for Iwakuni on the 22nd to deliver the Meteors to 77 Squadron over the Easter weekend, and sailing for Sasebo on the 27th.

She was destined to remain there, on and off, for the next three months being used for a number of jobs, mainly as accommodation for officers and ratings awaiting the arrival of their respective ships. The monotony was relieved to some extent by occasional short trips to Kure, Iwakuni, Yokosuka and Pusan, on the latter two wearing the flag of Admiral Scott-Moncrieff.

The trip to Pusan was very different from the earlier one; the weather was very foggy and the ship was anchored outside the breakwater — little could be seen of Pusan itself. One of the Admiral's many official functions was to attend a memorial service and the dedication of a cemetery to be used for the burial of UN troops killed in action in Korea.

During the long stay in Sasebo, the officers and ship's company had, to a large extent, to provide their own entertainment. Not much football or hockey could be played since playing fields were available on very few occasions. Trips were organised to beauty spots and places of interest, including two to Nagasaki, the city on which the second atom bomb was dropped in August 1945. A pulling regatta was arranged for whalers, won by the Wardroom 'A' over-30s crew who beat the Electrical Division in the final. A boxing match was held against *Theseus* in the Fleet Canteen, won by *Theseus*. As a result of the Tote run on Greyhound Racing, collections, charity tombolas and other activities, £250 was sent to the HMS *Affray* Disaster Fund, an amount which would today (1992) be more than £3,000.

During a visit to Kure the ship was dry-docked from 8th to 16th April. Advantage of this stay was taken to grant 72 hours leave to the ship's company, and again trips were arranged to places of interest. A day was spent at sea after the docking period to carry out a flying programme.

It was with a feeling of great relief that the ship took her departure from Sasebo for Hong Kong on 17th June, which was reached on the 21st. The customary two days were spent there before moving off for Singapore to arrive at the Naval Base on the 27th.

In addition to the usual stores, more Meteors and a couple of Vampires were embarked, together with some RAF personnel, before *Unicorn* again left for the north on 4th July. Hong Kong was reached on the 8th where six Auster aircraft with their associated transport and personnel were embarked, sailing for Sasebo on the 10th to arrive on the 13th. On the 16th she sailed for Iwakuni where the Auster team was landed, together with the Meteors. Three days later she moved on to Kure where stores and aircraft were transferred to *Glory* who had relieved *Theseus*.

On 24th July she made her way south again to arrive at Hong Kong on the 28th, leaving on the 30th for Singapore for refit. She arrived at her old berth at the Naval Base on 3rd August and a salute of 21 guns was fired in honour of the Queen's birthday on Saturday 4th.

Admiral Sir Guy Russell, CinC FES, inspected the ship's company at divisions next day, and on Monday the ship entered the King George V dock, the ship's company once again being accommodated in *Terror*. Full advantage was taken of the availability of soccer, rugger, hockey and cricket pitches, as well as of the swimming pool. The re-organised concert party of 36 officers and ratings, under the management of the padre, the Reverend J. Fulton, put on shows at various establishments, often at short notice.

The refit ended on 3rd September and *Unicorn* sailed for Hong Kong on the 5th arriving on the 10th and sailing the same day for Kure to arrive on the 13th. After two days secured to a buoy, she left for Iwakuni where she stayed until sailing for Sasebo on the 17th.

On the 22nd September the two aircraft from *Glory* that had been stranded on Paengyong-do were salved. An LSU, borrowed from the Commander, Fleet Activities, at Inchon, arrived at the island escorted by *St. Bride's Bay* on the 20th. Both aircraft were successfully embarked next day, and transferred to *Unicorn* who arrived on the 22nd escorted by *Cossack* and *Comus*. This date chanced to be the anniversary of *Unicorn's* departure from the UK; to celebrate the event, as well as the visit to the operational area after many months of hard and monotonous ferry work, she then proceeded north across the 38th parallel and carried out a couple of short sharp bombardments against Chopekki Point, thereby becoming the first aircraft

HMS *Unicorn* off Kure – Firefly 1s and Seafire 47.   *(Wood)*

carrier to carry out a direct bombardment in the war. One target was a watchers hut, and of sixteen salvoes fired three were known to have hit the target. After the bombardment, *Cossack* refuelled alongside while passengers were exchanged by jackstay, on completion of which they sailed for Sasebo, arriving on the 23rd.

On the 27th, wearing the flag of Admiral Scott-Moncrieff, *Unicorn* sailed for Kure arriving and securing to a buoy the following day. Whilst at Kure the Admiral presented the Pentathlon Trophy to *Unicorn's* team that had won it — at short notice — when at Sasebo the previous week. The opportunity was taken to meet *Sydney* for the first time who was in the process of taking over from *Glory*. At a three cornered boxing evening, the Captain, in a short speech before the boxing started, said it was a fitting occasion to welcome *Sydney* and to say farewell to *Glory* before she left for three months rest and refit in Australia.

On 1st October *Unicorn* sailed in company with *Concord* and *Alert* to return to Sasebo via the Shimonoseki Strait arriving on the 2nd. A week later she sailed again for Iwakuni via the Shimonoseki Strait. Charts had been studied, the state of the tide had been taken into account, and it was calculated that *Unicorn* would safely pass under the power lines stretching from Honshu to Kyushu. It was however a very cold day and the power lines were covered in snow. The inevitable happened, as the ship passed under the wires, the radar on top of the tallest mast in the Fleet snagged the power lines one of which carried away giving a splendid firework effect as it struck the sea. The sudden overload tripped all the power stations in Kyushu, and the island (about the size of Wales) was without power. It took some time to get some limited power back and it was a matter of weeks before the lines were replaced. Thereafter when going between Sasebo and Kure she always went south-about round Kyushu, an extra 300 miles. She stayed until the 12th before returning to Sasebo, Hong Kong and Singapore.

At 0900 on 14th October *Unicorn* was ordered to sail from Sasebo to avoid typhoon Ruth heading for Japan. Ruth hit Japan at 1800 that day, by which time *Unicorn* was sea; she encountered the force of the typhoon from 1500 on the 14th to 0100 on the 15th, the maximum strength being felt at 2100 when she was 120 miles from the centre where winds of 130 knots were blowing. *Unicorn* experienced winds of 85-90 knots, gusting to 100 knots. The wind coupled with the swell created waves of 45-50 feet; the maximum roll recorded was 16° and pitch 8°, making the stern move a through vertical distance of 60 feet.

At Hong Kong on 18th October the key ratings of the new commission joined, those who were relieved left at Singapore on 1st November.

Unicorn sailed for Hong Kong on 1st November arriving at 0700 on the 5th, thence on the 7th to Kure where she arrived at 0730 on Sunday 11th November. A Remembrance Day service was held on the quarter deck that morning. After exchanging serviceable for unserviceable aircraft, the ship left for Sasebo at 1400 on the 12th, arriving the next day for 24 hours. She sailed for Hong Kong flying a paying-off pennant at 1800 on the 14th, arriving at 0945 on the 17th.

The advance party of the new commission joined on 18th November. Since this was the last Sunday on board for the old commission, a special service was held on the quarter deck. As she sailed for Singapore during the afternoon, she left to the strains of the band of the Middlesex Regiment playing from a tug.

She arrived in Singapore on the 22nd when the CinC, Admiral Sir Guy Russell inspected divisions and said farewell to the old ship's company. By the 24th cargo and aircraft from Japan had been

HMS *Unicorn*, cruiser USS *Juneau*, and two Essex class carriers at Sasebo.   *(Kellaway)*

disembarked and the whole of the new commission was on board.

The old commission left on the 24th of November in *Warrior* for the United Kingdom where they arrived on 20th December in time for Christmas.

On 29th November 1951 the ship's company moved into *Terror* again during *Unicorn's* refit period, which included a period in dry dock from 9th December to 2nd January 1952. The ship's company returned from *Terror* on 16th January, and the refit ended on the 20th. Christmas had been celebrated in *Terror* in true naval tradition, and with a carol service in the cinema. *Terror* had been a pleasant spot with its cool, airy dormitories, playing fields and swimming bath.

At 0730 on the 21st *Unicorn* slipped from the refitting berth and anchored in the stream to embark ammunition and AVGAS, after which she sailed round to Singapore Roads to join the troopships *Empire Halladale* and *Dunraven* who were taking home, amongst others, the old ship's companies of *Comus*, *Consort* and *Morecambe Bay*. The French carrier *Arromanches* (ex HMS *Colossus*) had been lying in the Roads for the previous week, visiting Singapore for a rest between her operations off Indo-China, and during the evening of the 23rd *Glory* arrived from Australia, having been escorted by *Warramunga* who had entered harbour during the afternoon. The three carriers made an impressive sight.

On the 24th *Unicorn* embarked five Vampires for the RAF at Kai Tak (Hong Kong) and eight Meteors for the RAAF at Iwakuni.

Glory and *Warramunga* sailed for Hong Kong on the 26th, to be followed on the 28th by *Unicorn*, all three ships arriving on 2nd February, preceded by *Sydney* who had earlier rendezvoused with *Glory* to transfer some aircraft. While *Glory* was taking over from *Sydney*, *Unicorn* took the opportunity to play rugger, soccer and hockey matches and to hold a shooting match against the Middlesex Regiment, winning the rugger and hockey.

On 5th February *Unicorn* sailed for Iwakuni. At noon on the 7th a 56 one-minute gun salute was fired to mark the 56 years of the late King George Vl's life. A short memorial service was held during the forenoon on the quarter-deck, for which lower deck had been cleared. At 1100 on 8th February a 21 gun salute was fired to mark the Accession to the throne of Her Majesty Queen Elizabeth II.

The ship arrived at Iwakuni at 1115 on the 9th with the American seaplane tenders *Suisun* and *Floyds Bay* in company. That evening Lieutenant (E) P.J. Rugg left to relieve Lieutenant (E) R.B.L. Foster in charge of the Aircraft Holding Unit ashore, which was inspected by Captain Thompson on the 11th.

On February 15th at Sasebo a memorial service was held on the quarter-deck, preceded by a 56 gun salute, to mark the funeral of the late King which was held in London on the same day. The service was attended by several American officers, including Rear Admiral G.C. Dyer, Commander of the UN Blockade and Escort Forces.

The following day, *Concord* entered harbour, followed by *Glory* who had completed her first patrol, needing three aircraft to replace losses. During the next few days *Unicorn* went to sea accompanied by *Concord* to carry out DLP for replacement pilots for *Glory*, during which one aircraft ended up with a wheel over the deck edge in a pom-pom sponson, two broke their tail wheels, one burst a tyre and another damaged a propeller in a barrier engagement. One evening during these exercises *Unicorn* achieved, what was for her, the record time of 20 minutes between passing the boom and shackling-on to No. 20 buoy, the ship's usual mooring which was about two-and-a-half miles from the Fleet Landing. On the 25th Admiral Scott-Moncrieff inspected Divisions and afterwards attended Church.

On 1st March the ship left Sasebo for Hong Kong, arriving on the 4th having carried out a full power trial en route. On the first night out she exercised boarding parties by storming *Cockade* in Exercise Formosan Fantasy. For the next four days she took part in Exercise Vortex, having borrowed four pilots from *Glory*. The fleet tug Encore was practically useless as plane-guard, *Unicorn* having to manoeuvre into a position to suit the tug when she launched and recovered her aircraft.

On the 15th she sailed for Sasebo with an Army draft of about 40 men and a large number of Naval personnel taking passage north, arriving on the 18th to secure to a buoy close to *Bairoko*. At 0645 on the 22nd *Bairoko* left harbour to relieve *Glory*, and during the forenoon launched an impressive strike on the ships still in harbour. *Glory* and *Piet Hein* entered harbour next day, *Glory* with one damaged Sea Fury for exchange.

The usual gunnery firings accompanied *Unicorn's* passage through the Bungo Suido en route for Iwakuni, arriving next day 1st April, to transfer stores and aircraft, and to embark aircraft damaged beyond the capacity of the Iwakuni unit to repair. It was here that the regatta was held, for which the crews had been training for some time past; it was won by the Gunroom after an exciting finish with a crew of Electricals. On the 7th she sailed for Kure to disembark ammunition, and where she was joined by *Glory* on the other side of the jetty on the 11th. Four aircraft were

Sea Fury of 801 Squadron (HMS *Glory*) on the beach at Paengyong-do.   *(Dixon)*

transferred to *Glory* and one received from her. On the 13th divisions were held on both ship's flight decks, *Unicorn* enjoying the musical accompaniment of *Glory's* Royal Marine Band. The following day she slipped at 1100 and proceeded for Hong Kong where she arrived on the 18th.

On 20th April, at a special ceremony, the presentation of the Regimental Marches of the Middlesex Regiment was made to *Unicorn*. Officers and other ranks of the Regiment, together with wives and families, started to arrive on board at about 1030, and lower deck was cleared at 1045. The ship's company fell in on either side of the flight deck facing inboard. The band of the Middlesex Regiment fell in forward of the island facing aft, and the ship's officers together with the officers of the Middlesex Regiment fell in aft facing forward. A Sea Fury, which had been specially selected and cleaned, was parked forward of the band facing aft.

At 1100 the bugler sounded off the Regimental Call and Major W.P.M. Allen MC, who was deputising for Lieutenant Colonel R.A. Gwyn, stepped forward to the microphone. Having described the bond that had grown up between the 1st Battalion the Middlesex Regiment and HMS *Unicorn*, which had started when the former took passage in *Unicorn* to Korea in August 1950, he read the Order of the Day conferring on *Unicorn* the honour of playing these marches.

'1. In memory of the close alliance between HMS *Unicorn* and the 1st

Battalion, the Middlesex Regiment (the Duke of Cambridge's Own), the Colonel has the honour to ask that on suitable occasions the Regimental March shall be played in HMS *Unicorn* to commemorate this friendship.

'2. This march includes both the original marches of the 1st and 2nd Battalions (57th and 77th Foot), namely "Sir Manley Powers and "Paddy's Resource".

'3. The Regiment will ever remember with both pride and gratitude the unfailing co-operation and friendship displayed during the Korean War to all ranks of the Battalion by the Captain and members of HMS *Unicorn*.

'4. Also, whenever the march is played all ranks present will remember all members of the Royal Navy in HMS *Unicorn* and pray for their honour, safety, welfare and success.

Signed: Maurice Brown Colonel
The Middlesex Regiment'

The Regimental Band then played the two marches, after which Major Allen presented the Regimental Marches and the Order of the Day to Captain Thompson on behalf of the Battalion. In his speech the Captain said he knew of only two other ships that had been honoured with the privilege of playing Regimental Marches — HMS *Vanguard* with the march of the Royal Regiment of Artillery and HMS *Excellent*, the Gunnery School at Whale Island, with the march of the Queen's Own Regiment. Having thanked the Regiment on behalf of the officers and ship's company, the Captain gave the March to Lieutenant (S) D.W.M. Feuerheed and the Order of the Day to Stoker Mechanic Hollis, they being two of only four officers and men left in the ship who were on board when the lift to Korea took place. The March and the Order of the Day were subsequently mounted and displayed in the centre of *Unicorn's* Battle Honours on the quarter-deck.

The Regimental Band then marched down the flight deck playing 'A Life on the Ocean Wave' and counter-marched with Feuerheed and Hollis to the tune 'Hearts of Oak'. The ceremony ended with the playing of the National Anthem, after which the Captain announced that the ship was open to visitors from the Middlesex Regiment.

Next day, being the Queen's Birthday, a 21 gun salute was fired at noon by all ships present. During the day two Hornets were embarked from Kai Tak for RAF Seletar. Two polo ponies were also embarked for passage to Singapore, being placed in the port pinnace space, the pinnace being secured on the flight deck. *Unicorn* sailed for Singapore on the 22nd, arriving three days later, having passed *Ocean* in the Johore Straits who was on her way to relieve *Glory*.

Four Vampires for Kai Tak were embarked, in addition to several service lorries and other items of stores and armaments during the ten days alongside. Captain J.Y. Thompson was succeeded by Captain R.R.S. Pennefather on the 5th May.

Next day, after refuelling with AVGAS whilst at anchor in the stream, the ship sailed for Hong Kong with eight Army officers and 230 other ranks, arriving on the 10th May. Two days later she sailed for Kure, arriving on the 15th. She left for Iwakuni early on the 20th, leaving there in the evening for Sasebo where she arrived next afternoon to join *Ocean*.

After a stay of eight days during which sailing races were held against *Ocean*, *Ladybird* and HMAS *Bataan*, and a boxing tournament was held in the Fleet Activities Gymnasium, the ship sailed on 31st May having embarked cargo for Hong Kong. Departmental evaluations were carried out during the three day passage.

At Hong Kong cargo was disembarked and embarked on the 4th; the Middlesex Regiment beat *Unicorn's* cricket and shooting teams; ships dressed overall for the Queen's Official Birthday on 5th June; and the ship sailed for Singapore on the 6th where she arrived on the 11th.

On 15th June Admiral Sir Guy Russell, CinC, inspected Divisions and attended Church. During her stay at Singapore large quantities of stores were embarked including ammunition, 30 drums of paint for *Ocean*, a 7 ton tracked crane for salvaging aircraft at Paengyong-do and two lengths of propeller shaft for *Constance* who had run aground and seriously damaged one shaft. After embarking aircraft, an Army draft of eight officers and 62 other ranks, and two RN officers and 20 ratings, *Unicorn* sailed for Hong Kong on 20th June where she arrived on the 24th.

After disembarking cargo and exchanging army drafts, she sailed on 26th June for Sasebo where she arrived on the 29th to join *Ocean* and *Bonne Homme Richard*.

The ammunition was disembarked on the 29th and three Fireflies, together with a large quantity of stores, were transferred by lighter to *Ocean* next day. Because the floating crane was unequal to the task of off-loading the mobile crane and the propeller shafts, *Unicorn* moved into the dockyard on 1st July where better craneage was available, returning to her buoy the same evening.

On the 3rd *Unicorn*, in company with *Ocean*, *Nootka* and HMAS *Bataan* sailed for the operational area. Flying Stations were sounded off at 0440 on 4th, and the ship remained at 10 minutes notice for landing-on throughout the day during which 54 landings were made by two Furies. Next morning a Firefly from *Ocean's* first strike made an emergency landing on *Unicorn* due to a fuel leak. A replacement aircraft was provided and the pilot returned to *Ocean* at 0730. *Belfast*, wearing the flag of FO2FE and carrying the CinC as a passenger, joined the Element for a while during the forenoon. *Unicorn* provided CAP for four events during the day. In the evening, due to the unserviceability of *Unicorn's* catapult, Lieutenant (E) Bingham and his catapult team joined *Ocean* for the remainder of the patrol to gain operational experience. On the 6th *Unicorn* joined *Belfast* off Paengyong-do where

Admiral Sir Guy Russell embarked with some of his staff for passage to Sasebo where the ship arrived next morning and the CinC left to visit ships in harbour, and to inspect *Ladybird* and the new shore offices, finally leaving for Tokyo on 9th July.

From Sasebo *Unicorn* sailed for Iwakuni on the 8th, passing through the Shimonoseki Strait — at night and in a rain storm — and managing to clear the low overhead cables with room to spare. After transferring aircraft to and from the Aircraft Holding Unit she moved on to Kure on the 10th. Next morning *Constance's* old propeller shafts were embarked and 20 mm ammunition was disembarked.

After embarking 200 x 500 lb. bombs, *Unicorn* slipped and sailed from Kure for Sasebo on the 15th taking the southern route through the Bungo Suido. At about 1800 she ran into a tropical storm with maximum winds of 34 knots and continual rain squalls. The weather improved during the night and the sea was calm again next day for the remainder of the passage to Sasebo where she arrived at 1815 on the 16th.

During this harbour period, *Newcastle* sailed for her first spell of duty on the west coast of Korea, having relieved *Ceylon* in Hong Kong.

On the 21st *Unicorn* sailed for Hong Kong where she arrived three days later having experienced rough weather and frequent rain squalls for 24 hours which put the flight deck out of action for deck hockey and other forms of recreation during the dog watches. The weather calmed down during the night of the 23rd to allow the long awaited Pentathlon to take place. Ten teams competed in a variety of races and contests, won by the Officer's team with the Stokers second and the Supply and Secretariat third.

Unusually three troopships were together in harbour when *Unicorn* arrived in Hong Kong — *Dunera, Empire Pride and Devonshire* — and HM Ships included *Morecambe Bay, Whitesand Bay, Amethyst* and *Charity*. A variety of stores was embarked during the next few days including a Vampire for Singapore, six cars, and a prefabricated crane whose total weight was 30 tons and which took 44 lifts of the ship's crane to get on board.

Unicorn sailed at 1000 on 27th July for Singapore where she arrived at 0900 on the 31st in the Johore Straits to embark AVGAS. Aircraft for return to the UK were transferred to *Vengeance* during the forenoon, after which the ship proceeded alongside No. 8 berth in the Dockyard. Aircraft for Sembawang were disembarked the next day together with a quantity of RAF bombs and miscellaneous cargo.

On the 2nd August the remains of *Unicorn's* flour was disembarked. Six weeks earlier a new stock of flour had been received that had been added to the old stock which had become 'lifeless', this in an attempt to improve the taste of the bread being baked in the bakery. It appeared that this new Australian flour had been kept too long before being issued to ships, had gone hard, and had been broken up and repacked. The ship was then on dockyard bread which, although not up to the standard of the best ship's bread, was a great improvement on that which was being provided with the old mixture. A new consignment of flour was embarked later that was hoped would be an improvement.

On Monday 4th August the ship dressed overall in honour of Her Majesty Queen Elizabeth the Queen Mother's birthday, a Royal Salute was fired at noon by the RN Police Battery. By the 9th the flight deck was almost fully taken up with Meteors for 77 Squadron RAAF to be taken to Iwakuni and with aircraft from *Simbang*. *Unicorn* sailed, direct for Kure, on 13th August.

As a result of the success of her short spell in the operational area in July, it had been decided that she would spend a further period in company with *Ocean* during her next trip to the north. Provision of CAP by *Unicorn* not only released more aircraft for strikes, but more important was the availability of a spare deck. In the event of an emergency landing during refuelling and re-arming, the flying programme and flight deck routine of the strike carrier would not be disrupted by having to move aircraft forward and then re-spotting them after the emergency which often increased the time between launches by half an hour or more. In addition to the value to the operational carrier of *Unicorn's* presence was the marked effect on the morale of her ship's company by these short spells in the operational area which undoubtedly increased everyone's faith in *Unicorn's* capabilities.

On 1st September *Unicorn* joined *Ocean* in the operational area and was responsible for CAP using pilots loaned by *Ocean*. Next day the force ran into rough weather at the edge of typhoon Mary, *Unicorn* having to heave-to and rejoining on the 5th.

Ocean and *Unicorn* returned in company to Sasebo. After replenishing *Ocean*, *Unicorn* sailed for Iwakuni, arriving on the 10th. Five days later she was in Kure for a four week maintenance period. During this stay, leave was granted to both watches; some went to Tokyo, some to Matsuyama on the nearby island of Shikoku, and some to enjoy the hospitality of the Army. On 1st October the Royal Marine detachment was landed for three days at the Hara Mura Battle School. On 6th October Ted Ray and his company gave a performance on board — saying on the radio later that *Unicorn's* audience was the cleanest he had ever faced, they were all dressed in white! On the 8th an Olympiad was held against the local military forces.

On 10th October *Unicorn* had the honour of embarking the First Sea Lord, Admiral Sir Rhoderick McGrigor, GCB, DSO, and the CinCFES, Admiral the Hon. Sir Guy H.E. Russell, KCB, CBE, DSO, to be joined later in the day by the new FO2FES, Rear Admiral E.G.A. Clifford CB, who arrived in *Constance*. *Unicorn* had been selected by the CinC as flagship during the First Sea Lord's visit to Japan. On the 11th Admiral McGrigor inspected Divisions, addressed the ship's company, and walked through the hangars. That evening the Admirals gave a dinner attended by Lieutenant General W. Bridgeford, CB, CBE, MC, Commanding British Commonwealth Forces, Brigadier R.H. Batten, DSO, OBE, his Chief of Staff, and the Captains of ships in company.

Unicorn sailed for Iwakuni with the CinC still on board on the 13th, and, on arrival, he carried out a brief tour of the RN Aircraft Holding Unit. On the 15th *Unicorn* was in Sasebo where, for three days, she was occupied with Admiral McGrigor's visit.

The First Sea Lord left on 19th October, and the ship sailed for Hong Kong arriving on the 23rd, to berth alongside the North Arm in the dockyard. On the 25th the Middlesex Regiment was engaged in various sports, and in the evening their band Beat Retreat on the flight deck. A passing typhoon delayed her departure for two days until the 27th.

She arrived in Singapore on 3rd November. During her stay she bade farewell to *Ocean* who was passing through en route to the Mediterranean, having been relieved by *Glory* a week or two earlier. On the 14th *Unicorn* sailed again with the usual Army drafts, arriving in Hong Kong on the 18th, sailing again on the 20th to arrive in Sasebo on the 24th.

On the 25th, wearing the flag of FO2FES, she sailed for Pusan where Admiral Clifford was to visit the Chief of Staff of the RoK Navy, British Ministers and the other authorities. The Army and other units ashore rose to the occasion and entertained the *Unicorn* surprisingly well in view of their somewhat drab wartime billets. Vice Admiral and Mrs. Sohn gave a dinner dance to the officers in the RoK Navy's floating club.

On the 29th *Unicorn* sailed for Kure via Shimonoseki, to secure alongside on the 30th. During the passage Admiral Clifford carried out mess-deck rounds. She moved to Iwakuni on the 3rd December, and on the 5th sailed for the south, arriving in Hong Kong on the 8th and Singapore on the 15th to start preparations for the annual refit.

On 19th December the ship's company moved to Terror, the Air Department going to Simbang. The only incident of note was a Dockyard strike from 29th December to 9th January 1953. The ship's company moved back on 28th February to start a fortnight's storing, ammunitioning, and generally getting ready for sea. On 16th March *Tyne* arrived in Singapore on her way to Sasebo to relieve *Ladybird* as flagship and depot ship at Sasebo. *Unicorn* sailed for Hong Kong, arriving on 21st March. After a three day stay she sailed for Kure arriving there on the 28th. On the 31st a memorial service was held for Her Late Majesty Queen Mary and a salute of 40 minute-guns was fired. *Glory* was replenished, and *Unicorn* returned to Singapore via Iwakuni, Sasebo and Hong Kong, to secure alongside her usual berth on 22nd April.

Unicorn's next commitment was to prepare for the forthcoming Coronation celebrations in Malaysia and Singapore. A ceremonial platoon of sixty seamen, stokers, and electrical ratings was formed and trained for the Coronation and Queen's Birthday parades. Visits were paid with the CinC, Admiral Sir Charles Lambe, KCB, CVO, (who had succeeded Sir Guy Russell), to Port Dickson, Penang, Port Swettenham, and Malacca before returning to Singapore.

On 30th May *Unicorn* moved round to take up her anchor berth in Singapore

Roads for the Coronation celebrations. A parade was held on the Padang during the forenoon, ships were dressed overall and a royal salute of 21 guns was fired. The mainbrace was spliced, and Sunday routine was worked for the remainder of the day. *Glory* had been relieved in the Korean theatre by *Ocean* and was also

HMS *Glory* coming alongside the jetty at Kure with HMS *Unicorn* ahead.   *(Neep)*

in the Roads. All ships were illuminated either by floodlight or by outline lights and a firework display was given that night.

After a period in the Dockyard, *Unicorn* sailed for Japan on 17th July with a load of Furies and Fireflies that had been prepared by *Simbang* and the ship's Air Department, leaving Hong Kong on 25th July, bound for Kure.

The armistice was finally signed on 27th July.

It was on Sunday forenoon on 26th July, and *Unicorn* was in position fifty miles from Ockseu Island, course 055 degrees, on passage from Hong Kong to Kure, at a speed of thirteen-and-a-half knots. At about 1000 a signal from SS *Inchkilda* was intercepted saying that she was being attacked by gunboats five miles east of Ockseu Island. *Inchkilda* was a Dutch vessel of some 1,900 tons owned by Williamsons of Hong Kong, and was employed mainly in running timber from Foochow to Shanghai.

Shortly afterwards an amplifying signal from *Inchkilda* was intercepted giving the number of gunboats as three, and reporting that she had suffered no damage or fire. On receipt of these signals and of a further one from Commodore, Hong Kong, speed was increased to 22 knots, at the same time *Unicorn's* expected time of arrival at Ockseu was broadcast to *Inchkilda*.

It was a beautiful morning with bright sunshine and a cloudless sky which gave extreme visibility. *Inchkilda* was sighted at 1130, at a range of 17 miles, heading westwards, escorted by three gunboats, one about five cables ahead, and the other two about a mile astern. Whilst the ships continued to close rapidly, the ship's company closed up to action stations and an armed boarding party was made ready.

To appear more aggressive, four aircraft were ranged on the flight deck.

The gunboats were then ordered by light and international flags to stop. At first this had no effect, and course was therefore altered to cut across *Inchkilda's* bows as close as possible without risk of collision. All gunboats were kept permanently covered by *Unicorn's* long range and close range weapons throughout the incident.

When the range closed to about 3,000 yards, *Inchkilda* and the leading gunboat were observed to stop. *Unicorn* then reduced speed to 20 knots and passed across *Inchkilda's* bows, whereupon the leading gunboat turned sixteen points and scuttled away into the lee of *Inchkilda*.

Unicorn then swung to starboard under full rudder, which must have been an impressive sight from the low decks of the gunboats, and crossed the line between *Inchkilda's* stern and the rear escorts.

As the circle continued, the leading gunboat went alongside *Inchkilda*, whereupon the Chinese boarding party left the bridge and scattered in disorderly confusion, finally ending up in the gunboat. *Inchkilda* was then ordered to steam at her best speed away from the vicinity. *Unicorn* altered course to head off the two rear escorts. All three gunboats then headed about 245 degrees and made off at about nine knots. *Unicorn* escorted them for twenty minutes making a complete circle of the three to ensure that they continued in the required direction. *Inchkilda* was closed and ordered to stop, when a boat was sent over to bring off the Master and his charts.

It appeared that *Inchkilda* had left Hong Kong in ballast on 24th July for Foochow. At about 0715 on Sunday the 26th three Nationalist gunboats which had been observed at anchor off a fishing village, got under way steaming toward *Inchkilda*. Five minutes later they opened fire. The Master altered course to 090 degrees and steamed at his best speed until 0755 when, observing the large number of overs, he decided that discretion was the better part of valour and stopped engines.

Some two hundred rounds were fired by the gunboats, but only six hits were made causing little damage and no fires or casualties. The gunboats closed and the Master was ordered by loud hailer, in Chinese, to send a boat. This he refused to do, and the Chinese then sent

Chinese Nationalist gunboat.   (Nicholls)

a sampan with a load of toughs armed to the teeth with tommy guns, pistols, and rifles. Some went below to take over the engine room, and some others went to the radio room, while the remainder took over the bridge at the point of a tommy gun.

Meanwhile, the 'Admiral' remained in the leading gunboat and directed operations by loud hailer. The Master was then ordered to steam to Ockseu.

When within about a quarter of a mile from the shore the Master refused to go any further and prepared to anchor. The Chinese refused to allow him to do this, and cleared all the officers off the bridge. The Master refused to leave and was allowed to remain being well covered by a tommy gun.

The Master sighted *Unicorn* shortly after 1130, guessed she was a warship, and hoped fervently that she was. The Chinese, who the Master described as a Harry Tate collection of louts, kept no look out, and did not notice *Unicorn* until she had approached to within a mile or so. There followed much shouting and arguing between the gunboat and the boarding party which eventually ended in their hasty departure from the bridge and other compartments back into the gunboat.

After returning the Master to his ship, *Unicorn* set course for Kure.

On 30th July *Unicorn* sailed for the operational area in company with *Ocean* on a patrol that lasted until both ships returned to Sasebo on 12th August. During this patrol she operated four aircraft in roughly every other event, the pilots being transferred from *Ocean* by helicopter as necessary. On the 11th the accident occurred in which Lieutenant Halliday was involved, described in the previous chapter.

She carried out one more patrol in company with *Ocean* from the 25th to 29th August before sailing from Kure on the 31st. After leaving Hong Kong she had to take avoiding action around typhoon Susan, and arrived in Singapore on 21st September.

Unicorn was finally released from the Station to sail for England on 15th October 1953.

SS *Inchkilda*.   *(Nicholls)*

CHAPTER 15

HMS UNICORN

Shore Support
Iwakuni, Suwon and the Offshore Islands

The author is grateful to Commander R.B.L. Foster OBE, RN, who was from June 1951 to February 1952 Lieutenant (E)(A/E) in charge of the RN Aircraft Holding Unit at RAAF Iwakuni, for providing material in this chapter.

When *Unicorn* arrived at Singapore in October 1949 Lieutenant R. Hallett, the Test Pilot, disembarked with about 30 aircraft maintenance ratings to the half-completed airfield at Sembawang — HMS *Simbang* — some five miles from the Dockyard. It had one short Pierced Steel Plate runway, one large and four small hangars with adequate workshops, and good living accommodation. They established a test flying facility and an aircraft holding unit for some of the embalmed aircraft to provide space in *Unicorn's* hangars in order to bring forward replacement aircraft for *Triumph* and to repair damaged ones, mainly the result of barrier accidents.

It soon became apparent that to try to use *Unicorn* as a factory to repair aircraft whilst alongside in the Dockyard was extremely inefficient. Maintenance ratings tended to be used for ship's domestic tasks to the detriment of the repair programme; the flight deck was not always available for running engines, and if an engine did have to be run for any length of time there were complaints from other departments or from the dockyard. In addition, the heat in the hangars coupled with poor ventilation was not conducive to aircraft maintenance. When an aircraft was ready for test flight it had to be towed the five miles to Sembawang. Since it was not known what defects would be thrown up by the test flight and therefore what tradesmen would be needed at Sembawang to rectify them, the tendency was to play safe and have men under-employed at the airfield when they could have been used in the ship. Productivity was about 3376 compared with carrying out the same task ashore in an airy hangar and with no interruptions.

By June 1950 it was realised that the afloat support concept in peace time did not work and it was decided that the entire Air Engineering Department would be landed to Sembawang and the ship would return to the UK and pay off. *Unicorn* was in Singapore and had nearly completed unloading when North Korea invaded the South. *Unicorn's* return home was countermanded and she sailed at short

notice for Hong
Kong to transport the
Middlesex Regiment
and the Argyle and
S u t h e r l a n d
Highlanders   to
Pusan.

Although   a
failure as an Aircraft
Repair Ship, she
proved herself as a
Ferry Carrier. Her
routine then became
established as she
ran backwards and

LSU coming alongside HMS *Unicorn* with a Firefly and Sea Fury, from
HMS *Glory,* aboard.   *(Foster)*

forwards from Kure or Sasebo via Hong Kong to Singapore on a cycle of six to
eight weeks to collect spare aircraft for *Triumph* that had been brought forward at
Sembawang.

In October 1950 the Air Engineering Department at Sembawang was:
Commander (E)(A/E) P. Blake, Lieutenants (E)(A/E) D. Hiscock, R. Foster, R.
Hallet and S. Aldridge, Lieutenants (AL) J. Carey and L. Oliver, Commissioned Air
Engineer (O) Brown, and Commissioned Air Electrical Officer J. Coker.
Commissioned Air Engineer J. Atkinson remained on board *Unicorn* with a team of
about 15 ratings to look after the aircraft in transit.

In October *Triumph* was replaced by *Theseus* which involved a change of
aircraft from Seafire 47s to Sea Fury 11s, and Firefly 1s to Firefly 5s.

In January 1951 *Unicorn's* AED complement was increased by transferring
Lieutenant Foster and about 25 ratings from Sembawang. The plan was that in
addition to acting as a ferry a limited amount of aircraft repair would be done.
Experience had shown that quite a number of aircraft rejected by *Theseus* required
14 to 21 days work and it was uneconomic to send them on a 14 day passage to
Singapore, have the work done and the aircraft then wait four to six weeks for
Unicorn's next round trip.

It was at about this time that the pattern of the ship's routine changed. Rather
than continual ferry work back and forth, a lot more time was spent at anchor in
Sasebo acting as Depot Ship with occasional trips to Kure.

In the middle of March 1951 *Theseus* had to divert two aircraft ashore — a
Firefly with one wing shot up and a Fury with half one propeller blade missing — to
Suwon (K13), a USAF air base about 30 miles south of Seoul. *Theseus* could not

spare the manpower to carry out the necessary repairs so Robin Foster with a team of five ratings, a mainplane, a propeller and some tools were despatched, and told to get on with the job, having been assured that all arrangements had been made at Suwon including accommodation and loan of a crane.

They went by barge from Kure to Iwakuni with all their gear and by midday they were embarked in a USAF C-110 Flying Boxcar with the Firefly wing sticking out at the back. They arrived at Suwon about an hour before dark, in bitter cold. Being totally unsuitably dressed in normal naval uniform and raincoats, they stood out like sore thumbs amongst the Americans in full winter combat gear. To add to their joys no one appeared to be expecting them or had even heard of them. The one bright cloud was that about a mile away on the far side of the airfield they could see a Firefly and a Fury. At least they were at the right airfield.

The American Air Force were absolutely charming and they were offered coffee non stop, but as far as practical help was concerned the Americans all wanted to see 'Your orders'. In true naval fashion the orders had been verbal, to the effect 'There is a problem, go and sort it out and come back when you are finished'. Eventually the C-110 pilot rustled up a crane and low loader. It would be nice to think he did it to help, but it is probable that his motives were personal as he wanted to get back to the civilisation of Japan that night. With the wing and the propeller on the low loader the reluctant driver was persuaded to deliver them to the Limey aircraft, followed by the crane, and the items were unloaded. The American drivers disappeared while the party was looking at the aircraft (had they brought the right wing?).

It was dark, they were very cold, had no food and felt unloved and unwanted. They hailed a passing jeep and the driver told them there was one 'Britisher' on the base and kindly delivered them to his tent. He was a Lieutenant of the 8th Hussars and was the resident UK Air Movements Officer. He seemed to have vaguely heard of their impending arrival but pointed out that with one small tent he had no room to accommodate them. He did volunteer that the British FMA (Forward Maintenance Area, the last base before the actual fighting troops) was about five miles away, and had them driven there in his jeep.

On arrival at the FMA the CO, a Major of Grenadiers, provided the first ray of sunshine for some hours — he had heard of the party but had no idea of what they needed. After listening to an explanation of their problems he said he would feed them, provide clothing more suitable for the climate and show them to the appropriate Messes — further embarrassment, they had brought no bedding. Next day a routine was arranged with the Major who undertook to deliver them to the aircraft with 'one-man-one-day' food packs and collect them at dark. Next day, leaving the team to get on with the work on the aircraft, Foster walked over to what appeared to be the hub of the airfield to try to negotiate the loan of a crane. Again 'Where are your orders?', and it did not help that he was wearing an army parka and winter cap with no badges or anything to show that he was a Naval Officer. He returned for lunch, having got nowhere. While they were eating, an American Staff Sergeant appeared and the gist of his conversation was that the American had a crane and no grog, but he understood that the Brits had some grog and needed a crane. They hadn't any, but the solution to the current and future problems became plain.

Theseus had been sending aircraft to Suwon on a daily basis to collect mail and Intelligence photographs for some time. By lunchtime that day the Americans knew that there was Royal Navy representation on the base and the next aircraft ashore was sent to their corner of the airfield for refuelling and turnaround. It was arranged that the next aircraft coming ashore would bring a couple of bottles of whisky. Next day the team was ready for the actual mainplane change, a bottle of whisky changed hands, a crane appeared and they were in business.

Whilst in residence at Suwon they did a number of minor tasks for *Theseus* such as freeing a stuck hook and releasing hung-up armament in addition to becoming the reception point for the CODS aircraft. After about a week the two original aircraft were flown back to *Theseus* and the team flew out to Japan to rejoin *Unicorn*.

By the 24th January 1951 the Communist New Year offensive had pushed the UN forces to a line running roughly north-east across the peninsula and from a point about 35 miles south of Seoul. The UN launched an offensive during the last week of January that took them to a line along the Imjin River and north of the 38th parallel by the third week in April. On 14th March Seoul was re-occupied by UN forces, for the second time. Lieutenant Foster can claim to be the first RN officer into the city after its capture, visiting when it was in complete desolation four days after liberation. In his own words:

> 'In the Navy we are very much shielded from the horrors of war. At that time, before it was televised into our homes nightly, I for one didn't realise the total despair imposed on innocent civilians and also the unspeakable stench of no running water, no drainage, unburied bodies and rats everywhere.'

The river Nishiki, in southern Honshu, before it enters the Inland Sea, splits and forms a delta. On a flat and featureless island in the delta there is an airfield. It had been built for the Imperial Japanese Navy as a training place for its naval fliers. It had a concrete runway, steel hangars and extensive wooden quarters. If you stand on the slipway at Iwakuni and look northwards you will see, rising mysteriously out of the fogs and rain clouds that so often shroud the Inland Sea in summer-time, the island of Miya Jima. Here the young Kamikaze ('divine wind') suicide pilots of the Imperial Navy, who exercised and learned to fly at Iwakuni, would go for a last pilgrimage to the Shinto shrine there, and rest for a brief space in the delightful island setting before going off to give their lives in battle for the Emperor. The Allies' Pacific

Fleets had suffered much from Kamikaze attacks during the Second World War.

Miya Jima was the sacred island of eternal life. To ensure its 'divinity' no one was ever born there, and no one was permitted to die there either. If some inconsiderate person showed a tendency towards expiring, they were quickly moved off the island to the mainland of Honshu.

Early in June *Unicorn* was required to make another round trip to drop off aircraft damaged beyond her capability to repair, to collect another load of replacements from Sembawang, and for general stores from Singapore and Hong Kong. The trip would take six weeks and during this time *Glory* (who had relieved *Theseus*) would require new aircraft on a couple of occasions.

It was decided to land Lieutenant Foster in charge of a party consisting of Chief Aircraft Artifices O'Flaherty, four Petty Officers and 20 junior ratings, to establish an aircraft holding unit at Iwakuni. This was the other side of Hiroshima Bay from Kure, only

LSU alongside.   *(Foster)*

some 25 miles by sea but more than 50 miles by land. It was an RAAF establishment, commanded by a Group Captain, with the RAAF running the airfield and domestic services, but there were a number of lodger units. The largest was about 80 USAF B-26 Invaders, some USN Neptunes and a flight of four RAF Sunderlands. It was a staging post for QANTAS, US Military Air Transport Service (MATS) and RAF Transport Command. Of base units there were initially 77 Squadron RAAF undergoing their conversion to Meteors, of which there were 20, and the invaluable RAAF Dakota flight which daily sent two or three aircraft to Suwon or wherever the British Air Head was situated.

The airfield boasted adequate runways and living accommodation but only four rather small hangars. The RN unit was very small beer, and whilst they and their 24 aircraft were made very welcome, there were no facilities for them. They took over a piece of rutted hard-standing using as their office, store and crew room the back of their three ton lorry. When it rained it became a little crowded. By courtesy of the USAF, a large tent was loaned which was much improved once some old engine crates had been acquired and broken up to make a dry floor.

With the 20-day carrier operating cycle, the work load varied considerably. One Firefly and one Fury were always kept at 24 hours notice, and other aircraft would then be brought forward as required through reading A25 (accident) Signals. The biggest delivery of new aircraft was eleven and the smallest was three. If all went well, on the first day in harbour the carrier would send some pilots to test fly the aircraft and inevitably there would be other pilots who needed ADDLs or armament practice. For four or five days they would run, what to their limited numbers, was an intensive flying programme. The replacement aircraft would be delivered by lighter across the bay to Kure and the carrier, and any wrecks brought back. They could relax while the carrier returned to station and started generating more A25s. They worked a fairly predictable 20-day cycle but their high and low spots were six days later than those of the carrier.

801 Squadron Sea Fury arrested.					*(Cook)*

The formal organisation was non-existent; there were no Standing Orders or regular working hours. Lieutenant Foster gave a verbal briefing on arrival to the effect:

1. There is a job to be done that comes first, after that we can play.
2. We are guests of the RAAF and will conform to their rules.

It worked well due, perhaps, to a piece of luck. After only a few weeks, one of the Petty Officers decided to put his convenience before the job. He very foolishly chose the day that *Unicorn* returned from Singapore with a fresh load of aircraft. He and Foster both went on board as soon as she had anchored — the difference being that he stayed. The rest learned the lesson.

The jeep and a three-ton truck were used for runs ashore, banyans and sightseeing trips during slack periods. One useful carrot at Foster's disposal concerned QANTAS. They had a twice weekly scheduled service from Sydney to Tokyo which passed through Iwakuni in both directions. Under IATA agreements they were not allowed to pick up fare-paying passengers in Japan. Inevitably on each flight to and from Tokyo there were empty seats. The QANTAS Station Officer lived in the RAAF Officer's Mess, as did Foster, and the old saying 'It is not what you know but who you know' was proven once again. Thus for any of the Air Mechanics that Foster particularly wanted to reward, he could send them off to Tokyo and they would return with glazed eyes, weary but happy three or four days later. The other main carrot was to be sent over to join the Forward Party for which there was never a shortage of volunteers.

One problem was one that has always been associated with large numbers of young men many miles from home. Like many large towns next door to military bases, brothels abounded. During the peak periods there was no difficulty in keeping the sailors out of them, but during the slack periods, with the price of a girl at less than a dollar, it was inevitable that some succumbed. Primarily that was their business, but it produced the secondary problem of venereal diseases (one girl in Iwakuni was known as the 'Jackpot' as she was reputed to have five different types of VD, including what in those days was the dreaded penicillin-resistant variety).

Some of the sailors caught the disease along with the men from other services and other nations. On the basis that prevention was better than cure, on *Unicorn's* next visit Foster went to the Sick Bay and asked for a gross of contraceptives. He was asked to call back when they had been brought up from the store, but unbeknownst to him he had stirred up a hornet's nest. He was sent for by the Commander who told him, supported by the Padre, that his moral standards were those of the gutter, and that he was unfit to do practically anything; his request was refused. In the ambience of today this 1951 response may seem very old fashioned, but for the day it was not all that surprising.

When he got back ashore he told the CAA of the problem who then, in his inimitable Irish brogue, said 'Can I borrow the jeep, Sor?'. An hour later a box containing not one gross but two were on Foster's desk. These were issued to the senior leading hand with strict instructions that before anybody went ashore, in lieu of a leave card, he was physically to show that he had one in his wallet. Thereafter there was not one single new case of VD. In practice the two gross lasted more than 25 young men nearly a year — they were not quite so morally degenerate as the powers-that-be might have thought.

Fairly early after their arrival the CAA adopted as a drinking chum a USN Stores Petty Officer, which turned out to be a very wise choice. Every aircrew was issued with a multi-language leaflet saying that he was flying on behalf of the United Nations and if he was shot down he would only give his name and number. In the RN this was an unclassified document and for some reason the unit had a packet of about 200 of them. In the USN it was treated as a CB (Confidential Book) and one day the PO came along in some distress saying that he was due for stocktaking and had lost about 25 of them. He was given fifty for good measure.

The petrol used for the jeep and the truck was drawn against a signature from the RAAF, and although the amount used on actual duty was small, no more than three or four gallons a week, due to being out on a limb considerably more than this amount was used on recreational trips. Eventually some clerk in Singapore sent a request via *Unicorn* asking to see the vehicle logs to justify the petrol usage. This was difficult as no logs were kept, there were more important things to do. After a little discussion, the CAA came up with what became almost his catch phrase 'Borrow the jeep, Sor' and this time he took the trailer as well. An hour later he was back with a 45 gallon drum of petrol, saying 'I have arranged for one of these every month but he says if we run out we can always have some more'. Who 'he' was not divulged, but it was not difficult to guess.

During the Japanese summer there is nothing more pleasant than working out of doors, but with the onset of autumn it was obvious that if any sort of production was to be maintained during the forthcoming Japanese winter, then some form of undercover work space was essential. After persistent lobbying of the RAAF, permission was given to use half a hangar which held up to four aircraft with wings folded. It was the carrot of the fact that the wings would fold that got the unit in. The initial request was turned down out of hand as four spread aircraft would occupy almost a whole hangar. Three small offices were also obtained to act as office, store and crewroom.

The next drama was a typhoon, flooding the low-lying airfield to a depth of about a foot. All electric power failed, and a group struggled around the hangar with the aid of a couple of torches trying to lift up everything of any value or which could be damaged by water out of harms way. Eventually the waters receded and on taking stock the losses were small.

The devastation in the local area, particularly up the valleys into the hills, was horrific. As luck would have it the first Dragonfly SAR flight was staging through Iwakuni at the time and there were no other helicopters in the area. The two pilots kept up a non-stop dawn to dusk flying programme, firstly rescuing people cut off and then delivering medicines, food and blankets to isolated hamlets. Something which is now almost routine helicopter work received much favourable comment from the Japanese.

About this time the senior hand of the three Japanese labourers said he was leaving. This was unfortunate as he was a hard worker and had a reasonable command of English (the reason he was the leading hand). When asked why, he said he was going back to his pre-war job — Purser on a liner. It was no wonder his English was quite good. Another surprise awaited one Sunday afternoon when three of them had taken the jeep up a valley as far as they could go and decided that they would climb to the top of the nearest hill. There was a very bent and ancient coolie in his paddy field, and when an attempt was made to try to explain to him in sign language what they were about, and would he keep an eye on the jeep for the next couple of hours, he replied in a perfect Oxford accent 'Certainly I will look after it and I would be delighted if you will have a cup of tea with me when you come down.' It turned out that he had been the Assistant Naval Attaché in London in the twenties.

In February 1952 the unit was dealt a bitter blow. After 77 Squadron and the B-

25s had left, the activities on the airfield were much reduced. Someone at UN Command decided that it would be economic to move a large US stores depot from the Tokyo area to Iwakuni to save the delay in delivering items to the Korean airfields. The unit would have to surrender its hangar and offices, but they obtained a reprieve and handed the problem over to the Staff in *Ladybird*. A unit remained at Iwakuni until the end of the war.

Returning to Korea and going back in the time scale, in June 1951 it was decided to establish a full time Forward Party at Suwon consisting of one Chief or Petty Officer and two junior rates. The primary duty would be to turn round CODS aircraft and to carry out minor repairs for other aircraft which might otherwise have made deck landing unnecessarily hazardous. On average each man did six weeks in Korea before returning to Iwakuni. One man was rotated every fortnight to give plenty of continuity.

The first team took their bedding and, for good measure, a tent. It was also arranged that one of *Unicorn's* two jeeps would be shipped to Pusan for onward delivery to Suwon by train. Two ratings travelled with it on the flat topped rail car for security reasons, since in addition to the tent and their own gear they had a number of tools and ready-use spares. While they were on their way Foster flew to Suwon to make arrangements with the FMA for them to be looked after. The train journey took about four days for 400 miles and the two men were fairly relieved when they were met at Suwon. Cheerful as only sailors can be, they were rather tired of army one-man-one-day packs and of trying to brew up on a moving open flat-top railway wagon.

As the front line moved forward towards the Imjin River so the British Airhead and the Dakota flights moved forward to Kimpo (K14). At the same time the FMA moved into Seoul, 30 miles from Kimpo. The Party could not commute that distance and new accommodation had to be found. About this time, the 77 Squadron pilots had finished their conversion to Meteors and the Squadron was deployed to Kimpo. At first sight it appeared logical to lodge the Party with 77 Squadron, but this turned out to be a mistake. The USAF Air Traffic Controllers would not send visiting aircraft to anything other than the designated visiting aircraft park, which was at the other side and end of the airfield from 77 Squadron. Thus the Party were quite often not around when an aircraft landed, and turnaround, which had to be associated with meeting deck-landing slot times, was delayed which produced the inevitable and legitimate complaints. In addition Foster, at Iwakuni, lost the close touch he had developed with the Party.

He shared a cabin at Iwakuni with one of the Dakota Flight's Navigators which made contact possible by means of hand written messages carried by aircrew of the Dakota flight — another case of who you know! These aircraft used the visiting aircraft park at Kimpo and the Party could send a message by the last aircraft to leave for Iwakuni at about 1600 daily and it would be received at Iwakuni at about 1900. The duty rating would dig out the necessary spare or tool and have it delivered to the Dakota Flight Office before 0500 next morning when it would catch the first Dakota and arrive at Kimpo at about 0800. Extra manpower could also be sent at short notice. Officially the passengers on these flights were cleared through the UK Army Movements Staff at Kure. They were always approached first but if there was no room a seat could usually be arranged as supplementary aircrew. The official aircrew of a Dakota was two pilots, a navigator and a wireless operator. Almost invariably they only flew with three aircrew so there was a spare seat.

The Party was moved to the other side of the airfield and lodged with the British Army Movements Officer. This was beneficial to both parties: when the carrier was off station the sailors could help the Army and they in turn reciprocated — it was not unusual to see an Army corporal refuelling a Sea Fury.

The next step which occurred about September 1951 was when Yongdongpo Airfield (K16) was opened just west of Seoul. All transport aircraft were then banned from Kimpo which became a 100Sc fighter base. The Airhead and Dakotas moved so the Party followed suit. At about this time Foster ran into an old friend who was running a unit known as 444 Forward Delivery Squadron. They were doing to Centurion tanks what Foster's unit was doing to aircraft at Iwakuni. This unit, about 25 strong, was located in a prison a mile or so from K16, and with winter coming on Foster accepted his offer to accommodate the sailors, since tents and mid-Korean winter are not a good mixture. The Junior rates were delighted, it was the first time since they had joined the Navy that they had been given a single cabin. The windows were a bit small and positioned so high that they could not see out, but they were infinitely better off than in a tent. The gatehouse was used as a combined Officers and Sergeants Mess. A further attraction of 444 was that it was only 300 yards from the main NAAFI depot.

When *Theseus* left the area in March, Lieutenant P. House, Senior Observer of 810 Squadron, remained to act as one of the four Naval Officers (the other three being USN) at the JOC. Until about July 1951 this had been at Taegu, 150 miles south of Seoul and there had been no liaison between JOC and the RN Party, but after JOC moved to Seoul a strong liaison developed. When the Party wanted anything Paul House would arrange to have their 'Orders cut' by the USN. Since most of the liaison was with the USAF it is probably being tactful to say that USN orders were not treated with all the respect they deserved. Thus for most requirements the old fashioned barter system was re-introduced.

This worked out in that four bottles of Scotch would be bought from the NAAFI. Whilst the carrier was off station the CPO would drive eastwards from Seoul until he considered he was behind the American portion of the front line; he would then turn north and when he began to feel frightened he would stop. An American would inevitably appear, negotiations would take place and one bottle would be sold for about four times the purchase price. One bottle would be contributed to the Gatehouse Mess and the remaining two used for barter, mainly for the use of cranes and common spares, and also to keep the bowser pool and Air Traffic sweet. For the transport aircraft using K16 their turnaround time and thus take-off was of no vital significance, but with RN aircraft having to meet slot times, to have a bowser on call and rapid take-off clearance was essential.

On another occasion a frantic message was received from the carrier to say they had run out, of all things, of eighth-inch split pins. The local friendly neighbourhood USAF store, when approached, said that the shortage was not just local to the RN, but was affecting most squadrons in Korea. This put the team on their mettle and eventually a box containing a gross was obtained — but the price was high, being two bottles of whisky. About this time the slightly odd way of getting things done reached the ears of Higher Authority and Lieutenant Foster was threatened with disciplinary action. When Authority was asked if the split pins had solved a problem, and after being told how they had been obtained, nothing further was heard. After a while the long-suffering and hard working jeep was taking more man-hours to maintain than the aircraft (and costing a lot of grog for spares), but a replacement was acquired for three bottles — next trip the CPO had to go right up to the sharp end before getting rid of his cargo!

Shortly after this episode a new CPO lost his way. He was driving up a valley when he was stopped by an American patrol and was asked where he was going. His answer was vague as he knew that to say he was on a whisky flogging trip would not go down very well. So he mumbled and then to his horror was politely informed that he was in No Man's Land and that there was a gook outpost round the next bend. He was reported to have driven backwards for over a mile, and when seen two days later he was still shaking! Had he not been stopped it would have taken an awful lot of explaining!

Off the south-west corner of North Korea are a number of small islands which remained in South Korean hands when the North Koreans advanced in the winter of 1950. They were used by the Americans for various nefarious purposes and one, Paengyong-do, had a picture-postcard sandy beach which at half-tide down provided an excellent landing strip. It was used by the RN as an emergency diversion for aircraft that had been damaged or had insufficient fuel to get to K16 or the carrier. On four occasions Paul House arranged for Robin Foster and some of the Forward Party to visit the island to service RN aircraft that had been forced to land on the beach.

On the first occasion two of the Party flew over in a USN Expeditor, serviced the aircraft, spent the night with the US Army and flew back next day. The second occasion was similar but three of them went in a Dakota, taking with them, amongst other things, a 20-pack of one-man-one-day rations. When they walked the mile or so from the beach to the US Army camp the first evening, the Major in charge asked how much food they had brought with them. When told, he smacked his lips and asked if they would share it with his men. It appeared that when their last supply LCT had arrived, there were sacks of rice for the Koreans but no good solid food for the Americans. He said the LCT was due the following day and if they shared their rations he would feed them for the remainder of their stay. It sounded a fair deal and they agreed.

Next day an LCT arrived at the other end of the beach from where they were working and started unloading. From a distance the load looked very like white sacks and not cardboard cartons as might be expected for tins and the like. When they arrived at the camp for supper, a very long faced Major approached and sadly informed them that the logistics were still up the creek, the only food to have arrived that day was rice — and more rice. For the next few days the party lived on rice boiled, fried, burnt, even raw. With the carrot of no return to normal food until the job was completed, the aircraft repairs were finished in record time.

Towards the end of September a unique combined operation was mounted involving the RN, USN, US Army and RoK Navy. Lieutenant Foster and three ratings together with an American Army mobile crane and driver embarked in a USN LSU at Inchon and were then escorted by *St. Bride's Bay* to Paengyong-do, arriving at about midnight. They lay at anchor for the night and then beached next morning. The crane was landed and they set about recovering the two aircraft from *Glory* that had been stranded on 2nd September — a Firefly that had done a belly-landing and a Fury that had caught one undercarriage leg in soft sand during landing and had wrenched it off. The Firefly was no problem, when it had been hoisted by courtesy of the US Army, they had only to pump the wheels down, fit undercarriage locks and it was mobile.

The Fury presented more problems: it was raised, a jury leg was fitted, the aircraft was lowered on to it, and the jury leg promptly collapsed. It was bodged and then, taking most of the weight on the crane and towing the Firefly (in the absence of a tractor) they reached the LSU. Getting the Fury into the LSU was accomplished with no real problems and it was blocked up. When it came to the Firefly's turn it could not pass through the bow door so it had to be lifted over the side. The crane was driven alongside the beached LSU and with all the manpower available the Firefly was pushed alongside the crane, the sling and crane hook were fitted and the signal given to hoist. The crane engine stalled and then ensued the longest 30 minutes trying to get the engine to start as the tide relentlessly rose. It first lapped the tyres, then the wheels and was just reaching the aircraft's underbelly when their prayers were answered and the engine started. The aircraft was hoisted inboard and the crane driven out of the sea only just before the tide flooded its engine. It was parked above the high water mark for the night while the LSU was un-beached and anchored.

Next morning *Unicorn* appeared over the horizon and after she had anchored the LSU went alongside to deliver the cargo. The landing craft then returned to Inchon, ostensibly escorted by the RoK Navy, but the LSU could only do a maximum of eight knots and as the escort set off at about twelve he was soon hull down, leaving his charge feeling very lonely with the enemy coast some five or six miles to port.

Lieutenant Foster's final trip to the islands was in early December 1951, described in his own words:

> 'We had a report of a Sea Fury force-landed at Paengyong-do and a rather vague report of a Firefly at another island, Taechong-do, 15 miles further south. Four of us flew over and spent the first day sorting out the Sea Fury. The island now sported a USN helicopter and I arranged with the pilot that he would fly two of us over to Taechong-do the following morning and collect us in the afternoon. Next morning a young Naval Airman called Ball and I embarked in the chopper. It was a lovely day and from four or five miles away we could see that the Firefly that we had come to inspect was near the high tide mark and half awash. I debated whether it was worth looking at as it had by this time been half submerged for at least five, if not six, tides. However having come so far, I decided to continue and the pilot landed us 50 yards from the aircraft. As I disembarked his last words were "I'll collect you at 3 o'clock".

> 'There wasn't much worth saving on the aircraft but we took out the guns and radios and placed them in a deserted fisherman's hut. Three o'clock came and went with no sign of the chopper as did 4 and by 4.30 it was getting dark and it was obvious we were marooned. We saw a light about a mile away so set off and found of all things two American airmen and a tent. They told us that on the top of the hill behind us was a Shoran (i.e. short range Loran) transmitting station in the charge of a Master Sergeant. It was a long flog up to the top of the hill but sure enough there were some eight airmen, a transmitter and four tents. They were very hospitable and fed us. After supper I asked if they could send a signal to the next door island to enquire about our chopper. They were amazed to discover that the next door island was even inhabited, let alone by Americans. But the answer concerning my signal was No. They did send a signal to their USAF base which was somewhere near Pusan, and in it I asked for Paul House at JOC to be informed of our whereabouts. (I later discovered that he never received it).

> 'Having done all we could, the Sergeant asked if we would like to see a film. We then saw "Samson and Delilah" with Rita Hayworth, this 12

days before the film was generally released in Tokyo! The next day the weather was clamped so Ball and I had a lazy day and saw more films. Our third day was bright and clear and we kept looking northwards to no avail. We tried sending more signals. I discovered that the USAF crew would not be rotated for another four weeks and unless I did something we were liable to have to wait until then to get off the island. The fourth

Sea Fury being hoisted aboard HMS *Unicorn.*   *(Foster)*

morning was bright but it was blowing a gale and at about 0800 I saw what appeared to be an RFA tanker come into the southern lee of the island and drop anchor about five miles away. Shortly afterwards a destroyer secured alongside to refuel. One of the Americans told us that on that side of the island there was a small fishing harbour. A plan germinated that we might be able to get a fishing boat to take us out to the tanker.

'Off we set and after a two hour hike we arrived at a small harbour about the size of Polperro. There were some six small dories which did not seem to be very practical for the heavy seas which were running, but there was what appeared to be an RoK HDML. I went on board and was met by a Petty Officer who could not speak English. In sign language I explained what we wanted and asked for his CO. It appeared that the Captain and his First Lieutenant were ashore. I asked to be taken to them, and after much hesitancy we were led to what appeared to be the local pub. When the door was opened there was much giggling and again a reluctance to take us to the Captain. At last a door was opened and the reason for the giggling, reluctance and hesitancy was obvious. The Captain, believing in the old sailor's adage "a wife in every port", was in bed with one of the local lovelies. His

First Lieutenant was being equally accommodated in the other bed. The Captain's command of English was limited but I made him understand what we wanted. He showed extreme reluctance to get up and dressed, making excuses that the weather was too rough.

'It was at this stage that Ball pulled his master stroke. Everybody who visited Korea carried a personal firearm, and when working on aircraft a rifle gets in the way so we all wore revolvers. Before they left for Korea all the sailors did a session on the RAAF range at Iwakuni to show that they knew how to handle, and could be safe with, their revolvers. I would not say that Ball failed, but for our own safety I considered it prudent if his revolver was not loaded and thus I had not issued him with any ammunition but had kept it in my pouch. Whilst I argued with the Captain, Ball was standing just inside the door, and out of the corner of my eye I observed him do a very creditable impression of John Wayne. He slowly drew his revolver, ostentatiously cocked it and then started spinning it round his forefinger, simultaneously whistling. The effect on the Koreans was electrifying, they leapt out of bed, dressed and were onboard their vessel in no time flat.

'We had a fairly hazardous trip out to the RFA, indeed I had considerable sympathy with the Captain's view that the weather was too rough, but we wanted to get home. We had by this time seen all the American's films twice, and it was only five days to Christmas. Jumping from the HDML to the pilot ladder lowered by the RFA was distinctly hairy, but it was very nice to be amongst ones own, and a hot bath was extreme bliss. We transferred to the next destroyer which came up for replenishment. This took us out to sea and we were transferred by breeches buoy to *Sydney*, who was on the last day of her cycle. We left the area that evening and arrived in Sasebo two days later. After an overnight train journey we arrived back at Iwakuni on Christmas Eve.'

At the end of February Lieutenant Foster was relieved by Lieutenant P. Rugg who was in turn succeeded about six months later by Lieutenant A. Peglar who was an (A/E)(P) and an obvious choice for the job as he could test-fly the aircraft before the carrier returned and if necessary could ferry spare aircraft up to K16 for onward collection.

CHAPTER 16

FINALE

The Korean War occupies a unique place in history, as the first superpower essay of the nuclear age in the employment of limited force to achieve limited objectives.

In the years that followed the Korean War, as the immediate sense of frustration and stagnation that attended the armistice faded, soldiers and politicians became disposed to think more favourably of its value as a demonstration of the West's commitment to the arrest of Communism. If the United Nations failed to achieve re-unification of Korea, they had prevented the North from imposing its will by force upon the South.

North Korea exists today in pitiful isolation, a society dominated by poverty and the cult of Kim Il Sung; whereas South Korea has become one of the great economic and industrial powers in Asia. The harshest price it has paid for the war is that even today it remains a country under siege. The threat from the North has never receded. Pyongyang maintains a constant propaganda war, and a military capability that cannot be ignored.

Today, the people of South Korea have achieved a prosperity and fulfilment that gives them immense satisfaction. The simple material satisfaction is very deep, for people who have come such a long way in nearly forty years. They look back upon the war as a nightmare for their nation. But they reveal a real gratitude for the campaign waged by the United Nations, that enabled their society to retain its independence, that made possible everything they have today. Few Westerners, looking upon the respective circumstances of North and South Korea today, can doubt that the West's intervention in 1950 saved the Southerners from a tragic fate, and indeed opened the way to a future for them infinitely better than anything attainable under Kim Il Sung. If the Korean war was a frustrating, profoundly unsatisfactory experience, more than thirty years later it still seems a struggle that the West was right to fight.

For the Royal Navy, participation in the Korean War was a timely and stimulating jolt. It threw into relief the faults which had crept into the Navy's most potent striking force since the end of the Pacific War — the aircraft-carrier arm. The consequential spell of close co-operation with the US Navy off Korea was of the first importance in enhancing British naval co-operation in the NATO alliance.

Above all, the Korean War restated the ancient truth that sea power is Britain's most timely gift to her allies in time of war.

Without her ocean-going Navy, Britain would have been reduced to making noises on the touchline during the only joint military intervention against naked aggression ordered by the United Nations.

So far as the British Commonwealth naval forces were concerned, the most conspicuous role was played by the light fleet carriers. Their performances were admitted on all sides to be outstanding, but this was rendered possible only by the virtual absence of enemy air activity. Had there been opposition on an appreciable scale, so much effort would have been required for fighter defence and escort that offensive operations would have been severely curtailed; in any case, the effect of these from one light carrier on the war as a whole could be but negligible. Nor, as things were, were they achieved without extremely hard work, much improvisation, the driving of machinery to the limit on occasions, and the acceptance of other calculated risks. Admiral Andrewes was careful to stress that it would be

'wrong to regard the single light fleet carrier as an adequate representative of naval aviation in any theatre.'

He went on to list the shortcomings of the class:

1. low maximum speed,
2. susceptibility to weather damage in head seas,
3. liveliness in swell conditions,
4. the single catapult with only one month's operating endurance,
5. inadequate accommodation for crew and air group, let alone a flag-officer and operational staff,
6. structural weakness, e.g. both *Triumph* and *Theseus* suffered stern-gland trouble.

The general pattern of operations carried out by the Fleet Air Arm in the different stages of the war has already been recorded, but a word should be said on one or two special points. Photography was used extensively, being particularly useful for harbour reconnaissance in the enforcement of the blockade, and for assessing the results of the interdiction missions. In the middle of 1952 a photographic interpretation officer was appointed to the operational carrier. His services were described as invaluable and the hundreds of photographs taken when expertly interpreted, revealed many ingeniously camouflaged targets.

The value of the helicopter as a short-range rescue aircraft was amply demonstrated both on land and sea. As a plane guard it was unrivalled for efficiency and economy. This was as much due to its ubiquity as to its peculiar capabilities. For instance, at different times RN aircrew were rescued by helicopters operating from bombarding cruisers at Wonsan and Inchon, from the LST mine-sweeping tender, and from USAF airfields, as well as those operating from their own carriers. Their actual and morale value in the sea/air rescue work was very great, and for general utility purposes, such as mine spotting, guard mail, and personnel transfers they were invaluable.

The USN were operating Sikorsky HO3S-1 (S-51) and HO4S-1 (S-55), (the Dragonfly and Whirlwind respectively to the RN), while the RN carriers had only Dragonflies.

However the helicopter suffered from several limitations, which had to be appreciated. Radius of action over the sea was affected by one or all of the following factors. A 30-knot head wind reduced the cruising ground speed to little more than that of a surface vessel. Dead-reckoning navigation was subject to large errors, and instrument flying capabilities were nil. VHF communication ranges were not at all good. It is for these reasons that ubiquity was an important factor, and there is little doubt that some of the aircrew rescued by helicopter would not have been recovered if only the carrier-borne helicopter had been available.

There were reports, though muted, from some US Naval Air Squadrons of the difficult task for air group and squadron commanders of maintaining high morale. Commander Marshall V. Beebe, AGC *Essex* Air Group 5, commented that because of the unchanging routine of interdiction missions, of the danger and often of the lack of visible results, it made it difficult to convince the pilots that what results were being achieved were worth the risk. He considered that the Korean war demanded more competence, courage and skill from naval pilots than did World War II; they needed to know more (search and rescue points, recognition signals, primary and secondary targets), the flying hours were longer, days on the firing line were more, and the anti-aircraft hazards greater, added to which the weather was worse. Every attempt was made to work Air Groups into as many different missions as possible in order to provide some variety and to combat boredom.

Lieutenant Commander P.H. London, CO of 802 Squadron in *Ocean* a year later in 1952, made the comment, that because they were operating under the UN in a war they could not 'win', that it was not worth losing a pilot on behalf of the UN. The Squadron's tactics were adjusted accordingly: either you flew at a safe height, over 4,000 feet, or, if attacking, you got down on the deck — tactics were therefore used to reduce danger, although they could not eliminate it. Flak was a problem, because the Chinese were so good at camouflage. One could not see where the fire was coming from — therefore 'Don't attack a target you cannot see'. Boredom was another problem on what were mainly interdiction missions, (most sorties were bombing attacks on bridges), and because the Chinese were experts at keeping their heads down, pilots rarely saw anything moving to shoot at.

Most of the squadron's operations were in flights of four aircraft, which meant that the squadron could not work as a team. London thought about a squadron attack with twelve or sixteen aircraft on a suitable target as a morale booster. Captain Evans approved and asked the Staff to come up with a target. They produced the Communist Party HQ in the middle of Pyongyang, complete with photographs, flak positions, and so on. London and his Air Weapons Officer Lieutenant Illingworth went into it together, but he concluded that it was altogether too dicey and went back to the Captain and turned it down. To be ordered to do it was one thing — to volunteer was another. This episode shows that morale was constantly a consideration but there were limits.

In another attempt to liven things up, to boost morale, and to make their strikes more effective, London hit on the idea of the pre-dawn take-off. The object was to be over the target area just as it was getting light, and to catch the Chinese with their trousers down. All armies stand-to at dawn, and the Chinese were no exception. The results were spectacular. They had no problems with take-off or forming up in the dark, and they arrived over the target to find camp fires blazing and the enemy's road transport still on the move; many lorries were destroyed in this way. It was only in the half-light that it was possible to see how much small-arms fire was coming up at them, but the tables had been turned — they could see the Chinese but they could not be seen. It was a tremendous boost to confidence, and therefore for morale. The enemy was not slow to react, however, and *Glory's* aircraft, later, though achieving some success at first, were soon having difficulty owing to a simple but effective air-raid warning system. A low approach was then tried to deceive the enemy radar, but the foggy season intervened before the effectiveness of this method could be gauged.

The pilots had not been trained in night deck-landings and there were therefore risks involved that were considered worth taking, so a procedure had to be evolved for ditching in the event of engine failures. Initially, *Ocean* had stationed one destroyer directly ahead showing a yardarm group as a horizon when doing pre-dawn take-offs. As finally developed by *Glory*, two destroyers of the screen, burning three lights in a triangle, were stationed each at 3,000 yards, 15° on either bow of the carrier. If forced to ditch immediately after launching, the pilot transmitted 'ditching ahead', and the destroyers illuminated the sea between them. If the necessity to ditch was not urgent, the pilot transmitted 'delayed ditching'. The port-hand destroyer then illuminated the sea on her port bow, the aircraft ditching in this area. The starboard-hand destroyer was then available to come round and back up the other in the rescue.

London, and many other Squadron COs, made it a practice to be on the flying bridge to watch launches and landings and to de-brief returning flights; in that way, too, faults could be corrected, even though it may have been resented by some.

Morale is one of those intangible things which it is hard to define, but you know it, or the lack of it, when you see it. It all boils down to leadership and discipline, which itself comes from the word 'disciple' meaning a willing follower. Though the matters referred to by Commander Beebe existed in the RN, there is no evidence that they were allowed to develop into major problems.

Throughout the war CAS missions were controlled either by the USAF method of an airborne Mosquito controller or by the USN/USMC system of direct ground control. The latter was the more efficient and less likely to be aborted. The USAF were caught with no suitable aircraft for ground support; they had only 0.5 in guns rather that 20 mm cannon; they had de-emphasised both pilot training and photo-reconnaissance for army support. In short the new service was obsessed with strategic air and, five years after the end of World War II, had forgotten the lessons of north-west Europe. Thanks probably to the influence of the USMC, the USN had cannon, insisted on ground support pilot training, had appropriate aircraft for the job, and had maintained the system of operational target intelligence based on daily photographic coverage that had been developed in World War II.

The RN carriers on the west coast were operating in the USAF zone and were therefore Mosquito controlled. Captain A.J. Leahy, in 1953 a Flight Leader in 801 Squadron in *Glory*, recalls that the ship would hand the flight over to an American marshaller who would then record the type and number of aircraft together with their weapon load. The standard weapon load was four Furies each with 2 x 500 lb. bombs delivered in a 45° dive. (All very embarrassing if a Skyraider flight was inbound at the same time — each aircraft seemed to carry twice the ordnance of a whole flight of Sea Furies). After checking in, the flight would be held back until an airborne controller came up with a target and they would then go in. The target would often be marked with a white phosphorus (Willie Peter) rocket by the Mosquito. On the way out the flight always got a flattering damage assessment from the American controller. Leahy's five CAS missions destroyed trenches, a gun position, five mortar positions and three shelters, and damaged a gun position, four caves and a shelter.

Ocean Saga, the story of HMS *Ocean's* commission from May 1951 to October 1953, compares the Korean War with World War II:

> '...quite unlike the Second World War in which so many of *Ocean's* crew had fought...[where] an aircraft carrier would make her maximum effort when a target came her way and there were... times of intense action followed by lulls of mere watchfulness. But in this Korean War, things were very different, the target was always there and whilst on patrol there was no lull, it was nine days — and nights — of solid, unabating, action, with no lulls, no variation, no let-up from the

daily round of landing-on and taking-off, repairing and checking, loading and firing, and all the thousand and one tasks throughout the ship, whether actively concerned with the aircraft or not, until the time came to return to harbour, and even then, the repair work and maintenance took up all the time that was available in harbour, with only brief chances for desperately needed rest and relaxation.'

Frequent reference has been made to the UN interdiction campaign against Communist supplies. Complete interdiction of the battlefield has always proved difficult; but circumstances in Korea seemed to offer special opportunities. The total blockade enforced by the overwhelming UN naval forces entirely ruled out supply by sea; the meagre rail and primitive road communications of North Korea seemed very vulnerable to the almost undisputed UN air power, and in addition important communications centres on the east coast were open to naval bombardment. The vulnerability of the railways seemed enhanced by the large number of bridges and tunnels forced on them by the mountainous terrain of North Korea; for example, the eastern network (destined to be the scene of the navy's long interdiction effort) included 956 bridges and causeways, and 231 tunnels in 1,140 miles of track.

So after the situation produced by the Chinese intervention had been partially stabilised, the main effort of the UN air power was concentrated on interdiction; and from January 1951, except on occasions when the course of fighting on land or other reasons dictated other employment of aircraft temporarily, this policy was maintained for twenty months. Immense damage was unquestionably inflicted on the enemy communication system, and all movement by rail or road was confined to dark hours, but interdiction of the battlefield was never achieved, and throughout the campaign the enemy always had strength to launch an offensive if he wished to do so.

The causes of this failure were partly due to inhibitions voluntarily accepted by the UN for political reasons, and partly to tactical and operational conditions. In the former category the ban on attack on sources of supply in Manchuria robbed the aircraft of targets which many well qualified to judge thought might have been decisive; and the static war, accepted during the long drawn-out armistice negotiations, enabled the Communists to keep their strongly fortified front lines sufficiently supplied in a way they never could have done in a war of movement. General Van Fleet stated:

'If we had ever put on some pressure and made him fight, we would have given him an insoluble problem. Instead we fought the Communist on his own terms, even though we had the advantages of flexibility, mobility, and fire power. We fought his way, which was terrible...'

The use of the atomic bomb — at that time held by the United States alone among nations — was vetoed; and what its effect might have been cannot be certainly known.

The result of these self-imposed limitations was to confine the interdiction attacks virtually to railways, roads, and rolling-stock. Great damage was inflicted and the enemy was forced to restrict movement to the hours of darkness. But at night, and in thick weather, the aircraft could not find and attack the small, individual targets they were able to destroy by day. And the Communists possessed unlimited manpower, which they exploited to the full. They moreover proved themselves to be adept in the arts of camouflage and all sorts of tricks to mitigate and impede the attacks, and in affecting repairs to any damage with incredible rapidity. As an example, 400 feet of railway track near Wonsan were destroyed on 4th April 1952, yet on the 5th April the track was repaired and in operation. Cuts made in the morning would frequently be repaired by the same afternoon.

In order to cope with maintenance of highways and railroads permanent organisations existed. Units of these organisations were assigned to various sections of North Korea, special provision being made at important points. At key bridges and tunnels, in emergencies, local labour, including women and children, would be drafted to reinforce their efforts. Special equipment, such as welding apparatus, jacks, levers, and cranes were kept at key repair points, and prefabricated wooden bridges, metal spans, as well as building material, were stock-piled, much of it kept in tunnels and the thousands of caves with which the country abounds. When bridges across rivers were too badly damaged for repair, they frequently laid a temporary bridge across the bed of the stream itself, or if this was not feasible, constructed a lengthy bypass to cut out the bridge altogether. They also adopted a shuttling system of rail traffic at night between the many breaks in the line.

Every possible trick of concealment, deception, and camouflage was employed. If a truck convoy had to be left exposed it would be covered with straw or foliage, in winter with white canvas, or concealed in caves or tunnels. Damaged trains and trucks were left in plain view, often brightly painted to invite attack; operating trucks carried oily rags that, in the event of an attack, the drivers would light to give an impression of destruction. Rail breaks were simulated by strewing debris, mud, and straw across the tracks, or sections of rails would be hidden in tunnels during daylight hours, leaving gaps that appeared from the air as unrepaired breaks.

In addition to their organised repair schemes, their clever use of concealment and camouflage, and the other factors referred to, the Communist anti-aircraft fire steadily increased. By August 1952, practically all the interdiction targets in North Korea were heavily defended, and CTF 77 directed that attacks south of Wonsan should not be carried out from an altitude of less than 3,000 feet. It became the rule, too, for aircraft to include the AA guns themselves with the interdiction targets.

It remains to consider how far this prolonged effort at interdiction was justified. When initiated in January 1951 with the object of impeding the advance of the Communist armies and their supplies while the UN forces were reorganising to cope with the situation created by the Communist intervention, it was doubtless worth trying, though from the first it had its opponents. Admiral Struble was strongly of the opinion that the carrier borne aircraft of TF 77 would be better employed in providing close air support for the army, but he was overruled by General Ridgway, acting on the advice of Major-General Partridge, commanding FEAF.

But its continuation throughout the procrastinated armistice negotiations savoured dangerously of trying to win the war by air power alone, while the army and navy were relegated to comparatively static and defensive roles. It is difficult to resist the conclusion that this strategy (which suited the Communist book) was persisted in far too long, and that better results would have been obtained by the adoption of a more aggressive strategy — such as large-scale landings behind the enemy front-line positions, as advocated by General Van Fleet — implemented by the three services working in the closest co-operation in support of each other. It would seem in retrospect that the exertion of mobility and flexibility — conferred on the UN by their command of the sea and air — to enforce a war of movement on shore, might well have compelled the Communists to accept more satisfactory armistice conditions, and at an appreciably earlier date.

Defensive minefields were laid by the North Koreans at the entrance to all the major ports. On the west coast the only form of offensive mining that occurred was the discharge of floating mines, which followed the tidal streams round the coasts. In a period of about two weeks in September 1950, fifteen mines were laid each night. They proved to be no particular menace to ships by day, provided lookouts were placed, but by night they were undetectable, and achieved a certain measure of success in forcing the ships to keep a respectful distance from the coast, which thereby relaxed the close blockade in some areas.

They were destroyed by either single shots with a 40 mm Bofors in hand-training and elevation, or by rifle fire using armour-piercing ammunition. Air patrols established to spot the positions of mines were often able to destroy them by their own machine gun fire, and the Americans employed their helicopters as scouts ahead of their ships with great success. But it was unfortunate that the sea abounded with jelly-fish that looked exactly like mines just under the surface.

After these initial mining operations, the enemy seemed to realise the futility of laying moored mines in the strong inshore tides of the west coast, with their large rise and fall, and except for some defensive lines close in to Chinnampo, their minelaying was devoted to the east coast.

On the west coast, check-sweeping of the route Cigarette was carried out by two RoK AMSs fitted with wire-sweeps, until the defence of the strategic islands became the major commitment. The areas around Chodo, Sok-to and Yong Pyong-do were known to be dangerous, and they were cleared by part of US Mine Squadron Three.

The signing of the armistice at on 27th July 1953 brought to a close hostilities which had lasted 1,128 days, and involved many nations. Naval forces had been contributed by Australia, Canada, Columbia, France, Great Britain, the Netherlands, New Zealand, the Republic of Korea, Thailand and the United States of America. By far the largest contribution was of course that of the USA, but the Commonwealth effort was by no means insignificant.

During the war, a total of 76 ships of the Commonwealth Navies and the Fleet auxiliary services served in the war area for varying periods. These comprised 32 warships of the RN, nine of the RAN, eight of the RCN, six of the RNZN, two headquarters ships, one hospital ship, sixteen RFAs and two merchant fleet auxiliaries. Some statistical information will indicate the scale of the contribution made by these forces to the United Nations cause.

Taking the Royal Navy first, the warships steamed a total of 2,100,550 miles while the auxiliaries steamed more than 300,000 miles. During the operations, 23,000 rounds of 6 inch, 148,000 of 4.7 or 4 inch shells were fired in bombardments; 15,200 bombs of varying weights were dropped and 57,600 3 inch rocket projectiles and 3,300,000 rounds of 20 mm ammunition were fired from aircraft in nearly 23,000 operational sorties.

Casualties suffered by the Royal Navy and Royal Marines amounted to 182, made up as follows:

Casualties	Officers			Ratings and other ranks			
	RN	RM	Total	RN	RM	Total	Total
Killed	25	1	261	15	17	32	58
Died of wounds	–	–	–	1	1	2	2
Died in captivity	–	–	–	1	9	10	10
Missing	1	1	2	-	1	1	3
Wounded	5	3	8	14	63	77	85
PoW	2	-	2	2	20	22	24
	33	5	38	33	111	144	182

More than half these casualties were suffered by the 41st Independent Commando in the operations between Hagaru-ri and Hungnam after the Chinese intervention in November 1950. Air operations in the carrier-borne aircraft accounted for a large proportion of the remainder; 26 aircrew of the Fleet Arm and 1 RAF officer lost their lives in attacks on troop concentrations and various targets, and during operational sorties, and a further 7 lost their lives in accidents. Considering that the ten squadrons involved flew nearly 23,000 operational sorties, these losses were mercifully light.

Decorations for distinguished services against the enemy were awarded to 165 officers and men, and a further 289 were mentioned in dispatches.

Turning to the other Commonwealth Navies, *Sydney* and the eight Australian destroyers and frigates steamed over 419,000 miles during the hostilities.

Ammunition expended amounted to over 25,000 rounds of 4.7, 4.5, and 4 inch shells, 50,000 40 mm and 9,900 2 pounder shells. In addition, *Sydney's* aircraft fired 269,000 20 mm rounds of cannon and 6,300 rocket projectiles, and dropped 800 bombs on the enemy. Casualties amounted to three aircrew officers killed, and one officer and five ratings wounded. Fifty seven officers and men received decorations for their war services.

The eight Canadian destroyers steamed 724,000 miles and fired 50,000 rounds of main armament and 70,000 rounds of close range ammunition. The only operational casualties suffered were in *Iroquois* when she was hit by shore batteries near Songjin; one officer and one rating were killed, one died of wounds, and ten were wounded. Nineteen officers and men received awards.

All six of New Zealand's frigates in eight tours of duty steamed 340,000 miles and fired 72,000 rounds of ammunition. The only casualty sustained was one rating killed. Awards to personnel included seven DSCs and two DSMs.

Particularly fine work was carried out by HM Hospital Ship *Maine*. She was at Kobe when the war broke out, and proceeded to Pusan in July 1950, to assist in the evacuation of casualties. She was then the only hospital ship on the scene of operations. Eight trips entailing 700 hours steaming and over 7,600 miles were made between Pusan and Japan in those early days, and 1,849 casualties — all but four of whom were United States officers and enlisted men — were evacuated and treated by the medical staff under Surgeon-Captain T.B. Lynagh between 16th July and 16th August.

HMAS *Sydney,* off Iwakuni, with deck cargo ready to depart for Australia.   *(Zammit)*

During the years of hostilities that followed these ferrying trips, 2,900 persons were treated in *Maine*, 1,100 of whom were wounded in action. Over 1,000 operations were performed in the ship's operating theatre. Those treated included personnel of the Commonwealth navies and RFAs, Royal Marines, and Commonwealth and US armies. On 21st May 1953, HMHS *Maine* was awarded the United States Presidential Citation for her good work.

A satisfactory aspect of the Commonwealth effort lay in the fine morale maintained throughout. Despite long periods at sea, the drudgery of patrols, escort work, anti-submarine screening, and the monotony of the island defence measures continued through the tropical heat of the summers and the extreme cold in the winters, the morale of the ship's companies never wavered or flagged.

The seal of royal approval was set on the Commonwealth effort two days after the armistice was signed when the following message from Her Majesty the Queen to the Board of Admiralty was signalled to the Fleet:

> Please express to all serving in Commonwealth Fleet my deep appreciation of the splendid service they have given throughout the fighting in Korea.

> (Signed) ELIZABETH R.

APPENDIX A

Abbreviations

A21	Aircraft defect report
A25	Aircraft accident report
AA	Anti aircraft; also Aircraft Artificer (depending on context)
ADDL	Aerodrome dummy deck landing
ADR	Aircraft Direction Room
AGC	Air Group Commander
AMS	Auxiliary motor minesweeper
A/P	Armour piercing
AR	Armed reconnaissance
A/S	Anti submarine
ASH	Firefly A/S radar
ASPRO	Anti-submarine patrol
AVGAS	Aviation gasoline
CAA	Chief Aircraft Artificer
CAP	Combat air patrol
CAS	Close air support
CBGLO	Carrier-borne Ground Liaison Officer
CCA	Carrier controlled approach
CCRAK	Covert, Clandestine and Related Activities Korea (US)
Cd Pilot	Commisioned Pilot
CinCFES	Commander in Chief Far East Station
CO	Commanding Officer
CODS	Carrier on-board delivery service
COMNAVFE	Commander Naval Forces Far East (UN commander in Korean waters)
CSO	Chief Staff Officer
CTE	Commander Task Element
CTF	Commander Task Force
CTG	Commander Task Group
CTU	Commander Task Unit
CVA	Fleet carrier (US) — 90 aircraft
CVE	Escort carrier (US) — 24-28 aircraft
CVL	Small carrier (US) — 24-28 aircraft
DLCO	Deck landing control officer (Batsman) (see LSO)
DLP	Deck landing practice
DMZ	Demilitarised zone
EinC	Engineer in Chief of the Fleet

EM(A)	Electrician's Mate (Air)
EUSAK	Eighth United States Army in Korea
FB	Fighter bomber aircraft
FFO	Furnace fuel oil
FIR	Front line immediate replacement
F02FE	Flag Officer second in Command Far East — RN
FMA	Forward Maintenance Area
FR	Fighter reconnaissance aircraft
HDML	Harbour duty motor launch
IFF	Identification friend or foe
JCS	Joint Chiefs of Staff
JML	Motor launch — Japanese built
JOC	Joint operations centre
LCM	Landing craft mechanised
LCVP	Landing craft vehicle and personnel
LSD	Landing ship dock
LSMR	Landing ship medium rocket
LSO	Landing Signals Officer (batsman) (see DLCO)
LSU	Landing ship utility
ML	Motor launch
NA(A) or (E)	Naval Airman Mechanic (Airframe) or (Engine)
NKPA	North Korean Peoples Army
NKPR	North Korean Peoples Republic
NNRC	Neutral Nations Repatriation Committee
OFS	Operational Flying School
OTC	Officer in tactical command (on west coast)
POAF(A) or (E)	Petty Officer Air Fitter (Airframe) or (Engine)
PPI	Plan position indicator, radar presentation
PT	Motor torpedo boat (US)
QRB	Quick release box
RATOG	Rocket assisted take-off gear
RCT	Regimental combat team
REM(A)	Radio Electrician's Mate (Air)
RESCAP	Rescue CAP
RFA	Royal Fleet Auxiliary

RoK	Republic of Korea (South)
RP	Rocket projectile
RPC	Request the pleasure of your company (to drinks, a meal, party)
	MRU (Reply) — much regret unable
	WMP (Reply) — with much pleasure
R/T	Radio Telephone — voice communication
S	Serviceable — of aircraft or item of machinery or equipment (see U/S)
SAP	Semi-armour piercing
SAR	Sea air rescue
SO	Senior Observer
SP	Senior Pilot
TADC	Tactical Air Direction Centre
TARCAP	Tactical Air Reconnaissance and Combat Air Patrol
TE	Task Element
TF	Task Force
TG	Task Group
TSR	Torpedo spotter reconnaissance
TU	Task Unit
U/S	Unserviceable — see 'S'
USAF	United States Air Force
USMC	United States Marine Corps
VMT	Very many thanks — see RPC
W/T	Wireless Telegraphy — non voice communication

APPENDIX B
HM Ships

Royal Navy

Aircraft Repair and Ferry Carrier
Unicorn	Captain H.S. Hopkins OBE
	Captain J.Y. Thompson
	Captain R.R.S. Pennefather

Cruisers
Belfast	Captain Sir Aubrey St Clair-Ford, Bt, DSO
	Captain A.C.A.C. Duckworth DSO, DSC
Birmingham	Captain J.D. Luce DSO, DSC
	Captain C.W. Greening DSC
Ceylon	Captain C.F.J. Lloyd-Davies DSC
	Captain G.A. Thring DSO
	Captain J.C. Stopford OBE
Jamaica	Captain J.S.C. Salter DSO, OBE
Kenya	Captain P.W. Brock
	Captain T.E. Podger
Newcastle	Captain W.F.H.C. Rutherford

Destroyers
Charity	Lieutenant Commander P.R.G. Worth DSC
	Commander J.A.C. Henley
	Commander R. Gatehouse DSC
Cockade	Lieutenant Commander H.J. Lee DSC
	Commander J.T. Kimpton DSC
	Commander H.S. Hayes DSC
Comus	Lieutenant Commander R.A.M. Hennessy
	Commander C.E. Pollock

	Commander W.J. Parker DSO
Concord	Lieutenant Commander J.D. McLaughlan DSC
	Commander C.P. Mills DSC
Consort	Commander J.R. Carr
	Commander G.B. Rowe
	Commander P.E. Yonge DSC
Constance	Commander A.G.L. Seale DSC
	Commander A.V. Lyle
	Commander P.U. Bayly DSC
Cossack	Captain R.T. White DSO
	Captain V.C. Begg DSO, DSC
	Captain W.A. Adair OBE, DSO

Frigates
Alacrity	Commander H.S. Barber
	Lieutenant Commander N.R. Turner
	Commander H.A.I. Luard
Alert	Commander R.de L. Brooke DSO, DSC
	Commander J.R.L. Moore DSC
Amethyst	Commander P.E. Fanshawe
	Commander A.R.L. Butler
Black Swan (F3)	Captain A.D.H. Jay DSO, DSC
	Captain G.A.F. Norfolk DSO
Cardigan Bay (F4)	Captain W.L.M. Brown OBE, DSC
	Captain H.C.B. Coleridge DSC
Crane (F3)	Captain R.L.H. Marsh DSO
Hart	Commander H.H.H. Mulleneux DSC
Modeste	Commander R.D. Ritchie MVO

Morecambe Bay	Commander C.C.B. Mackenzie
	Commander J.J.E. Farnol DSC
Mounts Bay (F4)	Captain J.H. Unwin DSC
	Captain J.B. Frewen
	Captain A.F.P. Lewis
Opossum	Commander J.C. Cartwright DSC
St. Bride's Bay	Commander A.H. Diack DSC
	Commander W.G.C. Elder OBE
	Commander J.G.T. Western
Sparrow	Commander W.J.P. Church DSO.DSC
	Commander H.D. Ellis
Whitesand Bay	Lieutenant Commander J.V. Brothers
	Commander A.N. Rowell OBE
	Commander M.W.B. Craig Waller DSC

Headquarters Ships, Sasebo

Ladybird	Commander A.H. Diack DSC
	Commander N.H. Pond
	Commander D.G. Clark
Tyne	Captain A.J.F. Milne-Home

Hospital Ship

| *Maine* | Master, Captain S.G. Kent OBE |
| | Master, Captain W.W. Peddle |

Royal Australian Navy

Destroyers

Anzac	Commander J. Plunkett-Cole
	Captain G.G.O. Gatacre DSO, DSC
	Captain J.S. Mesley DSC
Bataan	Commander W.B.M. Marks DSC

	Commander W.S. Bracegirdle DSC
Tobruk	Commander R.I. Peek OBE, DSC
	Commander I.H. McDonald
Warramunga	Commander O.H. Becher DSO, DSC. Promoted Captain 31st December 1950
	Commander J.M. Ramsay DSC

Frigates

Condamine	Lieutenant Commander R.C. Savage DSC
Culgoa	Lieutenant Commander D.A.H. Clarke
Murchison	Lieutenant Commander A.N. Dollard DSC
Shoalhaven	Lieutenant Commander I.H. McDonald

Royal Canadian Navy

Destroyers

Athabaskan	Commander R.P. Welland DSC, CD
	Commander D.G. King DSC, CD
	Commander J.C. Reed DSC, CD
Cayuga	Captain J.V. Brock DSO, DSC, CD
	Commander J. Plomer OBE, DSC, CD
Crusader	Lieutenant Commander J.H.G. Bovey DSC, CD
Haida	Commander D. Lantier
Huron	Commander E.T.G. Madgwick DSC, CD
	Commander R.C. Chenoweth MBE, CD
Iroquois	Captain W.M. Landymore CD
Nootka	Commander A.B.F. Fraser-Harris DSC, CD
	Commander R.M. Steele DSC, CD

Sioux	Commander P.D. Taylor DSC, CD

Royal New Zealand Navy

Frigates

Hawea	Lieutenant Commander F.N.F. Johnston DSC
	Captain G.R. Davis-Goff DSC
Kaniere	Lieutenant Commander L.G. Carr
Pukaki	Lieutenant Commander L.E. Herrick DSC
Rotoiti	Commander B.E. Turner DSC
	Lieutenant Commander G.O. Graham DSC
Tnupo	Lieutenant Commander K.A. Craddock-Hartopp MBE, DSC
Tutira	Lieutenant Commander P.J.H. Hoare RN

Ships of the Fleet Train

Tankers

RFA	Master
Birchol	Captain W.H.S. Hine
Brown Ranger	Captain S.W. Camamile DSC
	Captain W.H.S. Hine
	Captain W.R. Holt OBE
Echodale	Captain G.S. Perry
Green Ranger	Captain E. Payne
	Captain F.G. Evans
Oakol	Captain H. Oakley
Wave Chief	Captain R. Grimes
	Captain F.A. Shaw RD
	Captain A.E. Curtain OBE, RD
Wave Conqueror	Captain R.D. Almond
Wave Knight	Captain H.W. Flint
	Captain B. Smith
Wave Laird	Captain R.K. Hill OBE
Wave Premier	Captain J.M. Humphrey OBE, DSC

Wave Prince	Captain H. Jolly
	Captain H.F. Colbourne
Wave Regent	Captain R.V. Boodle
Wave Sovereign	Captain H.F. Colbourne
	Captain F.C. Holt
	Captain D.J.S. Newton

Stores and Victualling

MFA *Choysang*	Captain J.S.G. Fotheringham
	Captain D.E. Reeve
Fort Charlotte	Captain D.B.C. Ralph OBE, DSC
	Captain F.G. Edwards
MFA *Fort Langley*	Captain H. Mackinnon
Fort Rosalie	Captain S.C. Kernick
	Captain A.R. Wheeler RD
Fort Sandusky	Captain R.K. Hill

APPENDIX C
Carrier Officers and Aircrew

HMS TRIUMPH
25/6/50-29/9/50

Ship's Officers

Captain	A.D. Torlesse DSO
Commander	A. Davies
Commander (P)	M. Bruce (Air)
Lieut.Cdr.(P)	J.C.N. Shrubsole (Lieut.Cdr. (Flying))
Lieut.(P)	P. Cane (SAR Sea Otter Pilot)
Acmn.l	G. O'Nion (Sea Otter)
	K.L.J. Sims (Sea Otter)

13th Carrier Air Group

Lieut.Cdr. (P)P. B. Jackson AGC
Lieut.Cdr.(E)(A/E)(P) R.L. West AEO
Lieut.(E)(A/E) S. Buck

800 Squadron		**827 Squadron**	
Lieut.Cdr.(P)	I.M. MacLachlan (CO)	Lieut.Cdr.(P)	B.C. Lyons (CO)
	T.D. Handley (SP)	Lieut. (F)	M.J. Baring
	(CO 29/8/50)		J.H.B. Bedells
Lieut.(P)	R.C. Fluker	(P)	R.A. Thurston
	D.I. Berry		H.M.A. Hayes
	P.M. Lamb		N.D. Bridgman
	J.D. Treacher		W.D. Lawrence
	G.J.C. Hanchard-Godwin		S.A. Mearns DSC
	R. Von T.B. Kettle		D.T. Andrews
	H.J. Abraham		R.D. Forrest
	A.A. Reid		J.P. David
	A.J. Tallin		D.P. Norman
Cd. Pilot	D.R. White		J.M.H. Ogden
	R.A. Peters	(O)	L.P. Dunne DSC (SO)
	A.R. Warren		P.R. Hartley
	F. Hefford		V.B. Hawes
	D.F. Fieldhouse	Cd.Pilot	D.F. Wright
	M.I. Darlington		D.L. Collingwood
		Cd.Obs.	H.J. Lambert
		Acmn.l	K.A. Creer
			J.W. Churlish
			E.R. Ripley
			E. Waterson
			H. Cottis

HMS THESEUS
29/9/50-23/4/51

Ship's Officers

Captain	A.S. Bolt DSO, DSC
Commander	F.W.R. Larken (Executive) (Promoted Captain 31/12/50)
	R.W. Mayo from 28/2/51
(P)	F.H.E. Hopkins DSO,DSC (Air) (Promoted Captain 31/12/50)
(P)	A.F. Black (Air) from 22/1/51
Lieut. (P)	P. Cane (SAR Sea Otter pilot)
Acm.	I K.L.J. Sims (Sea Otter)
CPO	Fndley USN (Helicopter pilot)

17th Carrier Air Group

Lieut.Cdr.(P)	F. Stovin-Bradford DSC (Promoted Commander 31/12/50)
	M.P. Gordon-Smith DSC (12/1/51)
(E)(A/E)	G.A. Thompson (Promoted Commander 31/12/50)
Lieut.(E)(A/E)	R. Saxby-Soffe

807 Squadron

Lieut.Cdr.(P)
M.P.Gordon-Smith
DSC (CO)
A.J. Thomson DSC
(CO 15/1/51)
B. Bevans
Lieut.(P) A.T. Green
D.P.W. Kelly
N.R. Williams
J.M. Pinsent
A. Ford
S. Leonard

G.C. Debney
T.C.S. Leece
W. Noble
S.H. Borthwick
C.J. Lavender
K.G. Shirras
A.C. Beavan
F.P. Curry
R.T. Highett RM
P.J. Young
A. Fane
P.L. Keighley-Peach
J.S. Humphreys

I.L. Bowman
T.R.S. Hamilton
R.C. Stock
R.J. Rickord
Lieut. (E) (A/E)(P)
H.G. Julian
J.I. Checketts (AEO)
Cd. Pilot P. McKerral
F. Barker
Pilot 3 H. Johnson
P. Lines

810 Squadron

Lieut.Cdr.(F)
K.S. Pattisson
DSC (CO)
G.R. Coy
Lieut. (F)
D.W. Winterton
(P) G.H. Cooles
G.F. Birch
D.J.H. Davis
W.E. Cotton
J.D. Nunn
R.G.D. Williams

D.A. Hook
F.D. Stanley
D.L.G. James
(O) B.M. Tobey
P. House
A.G.B. Phillips
D.E. Johnson
J.R. Fraser
F.K. Steele
Cd. Pilot I. McKenzie
F.D.B. Bailey
G.A. Andrews
R.B. Young

Pilot 3 R.C. Grant
F.E. Bottomley
Acmn.1 F.H.Shiel
C.F. Beeton
S. Ball
A. Wilson
J.J. Hayball
J. Loveys
H.C.G. Griffon
H. Cottis (loan)
K.L.J. Sims (loan)

HMS GLORY
23/4/51-30/9/51

Ship's Officers
Captain	K.S. Colquhoun DSO
Commander	R.L. Alexander DSO, DSC
	(P) S. Keane DSC (Air)
Lieut.Cdr.(P)	N.A. Bartlett (Lieut.Cdr. (Flying))
Lieut.	P. O'Mara USN (SAR Helicopter pilot)
CPO.	Fridley USN (Helicopter pilot)

14th Carrier Air Group
Lieut.Cdr.(P)	S.J. Hall DSC (AGC)
(E)(A/E)(P)	I.F. Pearson (AEO)
Lieut.(E)(A/E)	R.M. Fillery

804 Squadron
Lieut.Cdr.(P)
- J.S. Bailey OBE (CO)
- M.A. Birrell

Lieut.(P) R.H. Kilburn
- I.W. Campbell
- G.W. Bricker
- K. Whitaker
- J.A. Winterbotham
- W.R. Hart
- R.C.B. Trelawney

D.A. McNaughton
P.G. Young
R.F. Hubbard
P.S. Davis
J.R. Fraser
E.P.L. Stephenson
A. Fane

Lieut. (E) (A/E)(P)
- P.A.L. Watson
- P. Barlow

Sub-Lieut.(P) J.R. Howard

Cd.Pilot F. Hefford
P. MacKerral
W.A. Newton
R.E. Collingwood
B.J. Potts
T. Sparke
C.E. Mason
P.O. Richards
M.I. Darlington
D.F. Fieldhouse

812 Squadron
Lieut.Cdr.(P)
- F.A. Swanton DSC* (CO)
- R.H.W. Blake

Lieut. (P)
- T.V.G. Binney
- R.A.L. Smith
- W.H. Gunner
- P.G.W. Morris
- T.G. Davies
- R.E. Wilson
- J.K. Arbuthnot
- P.A. Jordan

J.H. Sharp
R. Williams
D.E. Johnson
(O) J.G.C. Harvey
G.E. Legg
W.J. Carter
A.D. Hooper

Sub-Lieut. (P)
- J.S. Tait
- I.R. Shepley
(O) R.J. Bates
- R.G.A. Davey

Cd.Pilot J.A. Neilson
J.P Hack

J.T. Griffiths
M.H.C. Purnell
R.G. Clarke
W.F. Cockburn
J.H. Eagle
C.B. Sleight
Pilot 3 S.W.E. Ford
Acmn. I K.L.J. Sims
G.B. Wells
G. Mortimer
D.E. Jackson

HMAS SYDNEY
30/9/51-27/1/52

All RAN unless shown otherwise

Ships Officers

Captain	D.H. Harries CBE,
Commander	V.A. Smith DSC,
	(P) L.J. Kiggell RN (Air)
Lieut.Cdr. (P)	R.H. Hain (Lieut.Cdr. (Flying))
Lieut.(P)	C.W. Perry (SAR helicopter pilot)
Lieut. P.	O'Mara USN (SAR Helicopter pilot)
Lieut.	Barfield USN (SAR helicopter pilot)
Ensign	Dixon USN (SAR helicopter pilot)

Ch. Aviation Pilot A.K. Babbitt USN (SAR helicopter pilot)

Airman	A.C. Gooding USN (SAR helicopter)

21st CAG (Disbanded 30/6/51 but still operating as such)

Lieut.Cdr. (P)	M.F. Fell DSO DSC RN (Air Group Commander)
	(E)(A/E)(P) R.J. Tunstall RN
Lieut. (P)	E.T. Gene
Lieut. (E)(A/E)	C.A.R. Wendt

---

805 Squadron	P.W. Seed	R.P. Sinclair
Lieut.Cdr.(P)	A.G. Cordell	R.J. Coleman
W.G. Bowles (CO)	Sub-Lieut.(P)	A.J.B. Smith RN
Lieut.(P) K.E. Clarkson	I. McDonald	A.G. Powell
DFM (SP)	F.T. Lane	
G.McC. Jude	E.I. Webster	

---

808 Squadron	R.A. Wild DFC	G.F.S. Brown DFC
Lieut.Cdr. (P)	J.H.G. Cavanagh	N.W. Knapstein
J.L. Appleby	G.A. Beange	A. Rickell RN
RN (CO)	D.C. Johns	J.R.N. Salthouse
Lieut. (P)	P. Goldrick	Sub-Lieut.(P)
T.A. Rickell (SP)	P.B. Cooper	A.R. Wright
J.G.B. Campbell DFC	C.M.A. Wheatley	

---

817 Squadron	J.M.W. Brown		A.H. Gordon DFC
Lieut. Cdr. (F)	M.H. Simpson		D. Christley RN
R.B. Lunberg	Sub-Lieut. (P)		G. Cable
RN (CO)	C.E. Champ		B.G. O'Connell
(P) M.W. Wotherspoon	A.J. Roland		Obs.1 P.H. Hancox
RN (SP)	N.D. MacMillan		G.C. Hughes
Lieut.(P) J.A. Gledhill DSC	N.E. Lee		L. Kenderdine
W.E. Dunlop	Lieut. (O)	Obs.2	K.Bunning
A.L. Oakley DFC	J.T. Williams		S.J. Chalmers
H.E. Bailey	J.S. Williams		G. Morris
D.J. Robertson	J.S. Hickson RN		M.A. Clarke

HMS GLORY
27/1/52-5/5/52

Ship's Officers

Captain	K.S. Colquhoun DSO T.A.K. Maunsell
Commander	R.L. Alexander DSO, DSC
(P)	S. Keane DSC (Air)
Lieut.Cdr. (P)	N.A. Bartlett (Lieut. Cd r. (Flying))
Lieut.(P)	E.S. Taylor (SAR helicopter pilot)
Lieut.(P)	C.W. Perry (SAR helicopter pilot)

14th Carrier Air Group

Lieut.Cdr.(P)	F.A. Swanton DSC (AGC) (E)(A/E)(P) I.F. Pearson
Lieut.(E)(A/E)	R.M. Fillery C.M. Caldecott

804 Squadron

Lieut.Cdr.(P)
  J.S.Bailey OBE (CO)
  M.A. Birrell
  (SP to 22/3/52)
Lieut.(P) J.R. Fraser
  (SP 22/3/52)
  K. Whitaker
  D.A. McNaughton
  P.G. Young
  P.S. Davis

N.E. Peniston-Bird
R.J. Overton
M.E. Scott RAN
A.G. Cordell RAN
Lieut.(E)(A/E)(P)
  P.A.L. Watson
  P. Barlow
  P.I. Normand
Sub-Lieut.(P)
  J. R. Howard
  D.L.G. Swanson

C.E. Haines
P.H. Wyatt RAN
A.G. Powell RAN
Cd.Pilot M.l.
  Darlington
D.F. Fieldhouse
F. Hefford
W.A. Neveton
R.E. Collingwood
B.J. Potts
A.F. Griggs

812 Squadron

Lieut.Cdr. (P)
  J.M. Culbertson(CO)
Lieut. (F)
  J.R. Hone (SP)
Lieut. (P)
  T.J. Kinna
  P.B. Reynolds
W.LeG. Jacob
  E.J. Meadowcroft
  J.G. Pope

(O) R.C. Hubbard
     A.D. Hooper
     C.J. Fursey
Sub-Lieut. (P)
     J.M. Wood
     J.S. Tait
     J.S. Cotgrove
     R. Cox
(O) R.J. Bates
     M.C.S. Apps
     J.S. Kendall

M.J. Jenvey
Cd.Pilot R.G. Clarke
     J.T. Griffiths
     M.H.C. Purnell
     C.B. Sleight
Cd.Obs. G.G. Gibbs
Acmn.1 T. Leigh
     A. Japp
     L.M. Edwards
     L.J. Stevens

HMS OCEAN
5/5/52-8/11/52

Ship's Officers

Captain   C.L.G. Evans DSO, DSC
Commander   T.N. Catlow
(P)   A.F. Black DSC (Air) (Promoted Captain 30/6/52)
Lieut.Cdr.(P)   O.N. Bailey (Flying) ((Promoted Commander 30/6/52)((Air) 9/9/52)
(P)   S.G. Orr DSC**, AFC ((Flying) 9/9/52)
Lieut.Cdr.(E)(A/E) P.L. Luby
Lieut.(P)   W.P. Powell (SAR helicopter pilot)
                 C.W.Perry (SAR helicopter pilot)
Lieut.(E)(A/E)   F. Ireland

---

802 Squadron

Lieut.Cdr.(P)	D.T. McKeown	Sub-Lieut.(P)
S.F. Shotton	M.L. Brown	C.F. Haines
DSC (CO)	J.R. Fraser	B.E. Ellis
R.A. Dick DSC (SP)	A.G. Crosse	R.A.C. Mallace
(CO 13/7/52)	I.A. Oldham	D.L.G. Swanson
P.H. London DSC	I.E. Jones	R.M. Carter
(CO 14/8/52)	R.M. Crosley DSC*	Lieut. (A)(P)
Lieut. (P)	A. R. Graham	J.C.R. Buxton RNVR
P. Carmichael	(F) W.W. Illingworth	T.O. Adkin RNVR
J.L. Treloar	(P) M.E. Scott RAN	R.J. Clark RNVR
R.H. Hallam	(E)(A/E)(P)	Sub-Lieut. (A)(P)
N.E. Peniston-Bird	C.M.Jenne	B. H . Randall RNVR
P.S. Davis	K. MacDonald	N. Cook RNVR
H.M. McEnery	D.G. Mather	Lieut.(E)(A/E)
	P.I. Normand	M.J. Button (AEO)

---

825 Squadron

Lieut.Cdr. (P)	W.R. Heaton	Cd. Pilot
C.K. Roberts (CO)	A.L.L. Skinner	R.B. Wigg
T.J.C. Williamson-	W.R. Sherlock	M. Kent
Napier(SP)	(O) S.R.A. Taylor	R.M. Brand
Lieut. (O)	T. Clancy	Cd.Obs. E. Beynon
W.J. Cooper (SO)	R.C. Hubbard	Acmn.1 C.P. McCullagh
(P) S.S. Gandey	C.J. Fursey	L.S. Dunmore
P. Watkinson	Lieut.(E) (A/E) (P)	J.P. Potter
R.C. Hunter	D.F. Robbins	C. Hearnshaw
R.G.D. Williams	Sub-Lieut. (P)	T.E.StJ. Vaughan
R.D.R. Hawkesworth	P. Millett	L.M.E. Edwards
P.B. Reynolds	D.A. Hanson	Cd. Air Eng.
W.LeG. Jacob	J.R.deB. Wailes	F. Fowler (AEO)
T.J. Kinna	P.K. Arbuthnot	
	(O) A. Bishop	

HMS GLORY
8/11/52-19/5/53

Ship's Officers

Captain	T.A.K. Maunsell (to 30/11/52)
	E.D.G. Lewin DSO, DSC (from 14/12/52)
	D.E. Bromley-Martin (Acting 1/12/52 to 14/12/52)
Commander	D.E. Bromley-Martin
	(P) J.W. Sleigh DSO, DSC (Air)
Lieut.Cdr. (P)	J. K. Cannon (Lieut.Cdr. (Flying))
Lieut.Cdr.(E)(A/E)(P) I.F. Pearson (AEO)	
Lieut.(P)	A.P. Daniels DSM (SAR helicopter pilot)
Cd.Air Eng.	S. Jones BEM Acmn.1 E.R. Ripley (Helicopter)

---

801 Squadron

Commander (P)
    B.C.G. Place VC, DSC
Lieut. Cdr. (P)
    P.B. Stuart (CO)
Lieut. (P)
    J.H.S. Pearce (SP)
    P.D. Handscombe
    R.J. McCandless
    A.J. Leahy
    J.H. Fiddian-Green
    A.R. Graham
    R. Nevill-Jones
    P. Wheatley
    J.R.T. Bluett

P.A.B. Wemyss
E.R. Anson
V.B. Mitchell
J.A.S. Crawford
C.A. McPherson
J. Bawden
J.T. McGregor
(E) (A/E)(P)
    D.G. Mather
Sub-Lieut.(P)
    B.E. Rayner
    R.D. Bradley
    M.B. Smith
    D.McL. Baynes
    W.J.B. Keates

G.B.S. Foster
J.F. Belville
M. Hayes
A.R. Pearson
Lieut.(A)
    T.O. Adkin RNVR
    J.C.R. Buxton RNVR
Sub-Lieut.(A)
    J.M. Simmonds
    RN-VR
Cd.Pilot P.R. Lines
Lieut.(E) (A / E)
    R.A. Langley (AEO)

---

821 Squadron

Lieut.Cdr.(P)
    J.R.N. Gardner (CO)
Lieut. (P)
    P. Cane
    (SP to 13/1/53)
    P. Dallosso
    (SP to 18/3/53)
    G.D.H. Sample
    (SP 18/3/43)
    R.E. Barrett
    R. Garvin
    W.R. Sherlock
    A.L.L. Skinner
    J.M. Bacon
    J.F. McGrail

J.G. Marshall
W.R. Heaton
P. Spelling
H.J. Smith
B.V. Bacon
A.G. Hamon
P.G. Fogden
P.R. Banner
P. Millett
(E) (A/E)(P)
    D.F. Robbins
(O)   J.M. Hunter (SO)
    J.S. Agnew
Sub-Lieut.(P)
    J.R.De B. Wailes
(O)   J.R. Coleman

R. Harrison,
D.J.R. West
Cd.Pilot M. Kent
Lieut.(E)(A/E)
    J.R.P. Lansdown
    (AEO)

HMS OCEAN
9/5/53-31/11/53

Ship's Officers

Captain	B.E.W. Logan
Commander	T.N. Catlow
(P)	O.N. Bailey (Air)
Lieut.Cdr.(P)	W.C. Simpson DSC (Lieut. Cdr. (Flying))
(E)(A/E)	P.L. Luby (AEO)
Lieut. (P)	P.R.W. Earl (SAR Helicopter pilot)
	R. Hooker (SAR Helicopter pilot)

807 Squadron

Lieut. Cdr. (P)
  T.L .M . Brander
  DSC (CO)
Lieut. (P)
  I.J. Brown (SP)
Lieut. (F)
  D.G. Halliday
(P) W.H. Whant
  J. Bawden
  V.B. Mitchell
  E.R. Anson
  J.W. Ayres

A.E. Lane
A.R. Pearson
J.A.S. Crawford
W.H. Hands
N. Woods
C.D.W. Pugh
G.B. Cross
Sub-Lieut.(P)
  R.W. Breakspear
  P.R. Sheppard
  C.C.B. Hick
  M. Hayes
Cd.Pilot T.C. Martins

Sub-Lieut.(A)(P)
  D.W.B. Wanford
  RNVR
  D.S. Green RNVR
  F. Whitfield RNVR
Lieut.   A.H. Hagdoorn
  RNethN
  E.C. Van Crusten
  RNethN
  J.J. Mulder RNethN
Lieut. (E)(A/E) R.H. Leeson
  (AEO)

810 Squadron

Lieut.Cdr.(P)
  A.W. Bloomer (CO)
  J. Elliott AFC (SP)
Lieut. (P)
  P.R. Banner
  M.S. Boissier
  J.O. Ealand
  H.J. Legate
  P.J. Spelling
  H.I. Smith
  B.V. Bacon
  J.F. Hollingworth

A.J.D. Evans
(E) (A/E)(P)
  L.G. Locke
(O) R. Greenshields (SO)
  J.A. Howell
  K.M. Thomas
  T.G. Butler
Sub-Lieut. (P)
  P.J.W. Broadhurst
  C.F.J. Chresta
  M.H. Coles
  G.S. Fawkner
  R.J. Noyes

(O) D.W. Ashby
  P.L. Moranne
  R.K. Simmonds
  T.J. Penfold
(A) (O) F.P. Carson RNVR
  C.A. Risso-Gill
  RNVR
Lieut. (E)(A/E)
  R.H. Streatfield
  (AEO)
T.A. McCrossan (AEO)

APPENDIX D

Aircrew Casualties

	Date
HMS *TRIUMPH*	
Lieutenant Commander I.M. McLachlan	29th August 1950
HMS *THESEUS*	
Lieutenant A.C. Beavan	26th January 1951
Lieutenant G.H. Cooles	13th March 1951
Flight Lieutenant D.W. Guy, RAF	13th March 1951
HMS *GLORY*	
Lieutenant E.P.L. Stephenson	26th April 1951
Pilot 3 S.W.E. Ford	5th June 1951
Lieutenant J.H. Sharp	28th June 1951
Aircrewman G.B. Wells	28th June 1951
Lieutenant R. Williams	16th July 1951
Sub-Lieutenant I.R. Shepley	16th July 1951
Commissioned Pilot T. Sparke	18th July 1951
Sub-Lieutenant R.G.A. Davey	22nd July 1951
HMAS *SYDNEY*	
Lieutenant K.E. Clarkson RAN	5th November 1951
Sub-Lieutenant R.P. Sinclair RAN	7th December 1951
Sub-Lieutenant R.J. Coleman RAN	2nd January 1952
HMS *GLORY*	
Lieutenant R.J. Overton	15th March 1952
HMS *OCEAN*	
Lieutenant (E) K. McDonald	14th May 1952
Lieutenant Commander T.J.C. Williamson-Napier	20th May 1952
Aircrewman L.M.E. Edwards	20th May 1952
Lieutenant R.C. Hunter	4th July 1952
Lieutenant Commander R.A. Dick DSC	24th July 1952
HMS *GLORY*	
Lieutenant R. Neville-Jones	18th November 1952
Lieutenant A.P. Daniels	15th December 1952
Aircrewman E.R. Ripley	15th December 1952
Lieutenant P.G. Fogden	20th December 1952
Lieutenant R.E. Barrett	25th December 1952
Sub-Lieutenant B.E. Rayner	5th January 1953
Sub-Lieutenant J.M. Simmonds	5th January 1953
Lieutenant C.A. MacPherson	11th February 1953
Sub-Lieutenant R.D. Bradley	11th February 1953
Lieutenant J.T. McGregor	25th April 1953
Sub-Lieutenant W.J.B. Keates	25th April 1953
HMS *OCEAN*	
Lieutenant A.J.D. Evans	15th July 1953
Lieutenant K.M. Thomas	15th July 1953

APPENDIX E

Honours and Awards
Royal and Commonwealth Carriers

Flag Officers Second in Command, Far East Fleet

Vice Admiral William Gerard Andrewes	KBE
	Silver Star Medal (USA)
	Commander of the Legion of Merit (USA)
Rear Admiral Alan Kenneth Scott-Moncrieff DSO*	CBE
	CB
	Mention in Despatches
	Commander of the Legion of Merit (USA)
Rear Admiral Eric George Anderson Clifford	CBE

HMS TRIUMPH

Captain Arthur David Torlesse	Mention in Despatches
	Legion of Merit (USA)
Commander (P) Martin Bruce	Mention in Despatches
Commander (E) Peter Francis John Trollope	Mention in Despatches
Lieutenant Commander (P) Thomas Denley Handley	Mention in Despatches
Lieutenant Commander (P) Ian Murray Maclachlan	Mention in Despatches
Lieutenant (P) Peter Melville Lamb	DSC
Lieutenant (P) Peter Cane	Air Medal (USA)
Aircrewman 1 Kenneth Alwyn Creer	DSM
Aircrewman 1 Gilbert Charles Edward O'Nion	Mention in Despatches
Chief Aircraft Artificer Christopher Turner	BEM
Chief Petty Officer (Tel) Edward George Leonard Nash	Mention in Despatches
Petty Officer Airman Arthur Jack Prior	Mention in Despatches

HMS THESEUS

Captain Arthur Seymour Bolt DSC**	DSO
Commander Robert White	08E
Commander Francis Wyatt Rawson Larken	Mention in Despatches
Commander Frank Henry Edward Hopkins	Mention in Despatches
Commander Peter Maxwell Compston	Mention in Despatches
Commander (E) George Allen Thompson	Mention in Despatches
Lieutenant Commander (P) Frederick Stovin-Bradford DSC	DSC*
Lieutenant Commander (F) Geoffrey Rolfe Coy	DSC
Lieutenant Commander (P) Major Patrick Gordon-Smith DSC	DSC*
Lieutenant Commander (P) Bernard Bevans	DSC
Lieutenant Commander (E) Allan Frederick Budden	MBE
Lieutenant Commander Alaric Hubert St. George Gore-Langton	Mention in Despatches
Lieutenant Commander (F) Kenneth Stuart Pattison DSC	Mention in Despatches
Lieutenant (P) Peter Lindsey Keighley-Peach	DSO

Lieutenant (P) Charles James Lavender	DSC
Lieutenant (P) William Noble	DSC
Lieutenant Anthony John Austin	Mention in Despatches
Lieutenant (P) Geoffrey Hammond Cooles	Mention in Despatches
Lieutenant (P) David John Holmes Davis	Mention in Despatches
Lieutenant (P) Albert Ford	Mention in Despatches
Lieutenant Gerald Young Temple	Mention in Despatches
Lieutenant (P) Neville Richard Williams	Mention in Despatches
Lieutenant (F) David Willoughby Winterton	Mention in Despatches
Lieutenant (E)(A/E)(P) Harry Graham Julian	DSC
Lieutenant (E)(OE) Melville Ruan Hocken	Mention in Despatches
Commissioned Pilot Francis Dominic Bailey	Mention in Despatches
Commissioned Pilot Ian MacKenzie	Mention in Despatches
Pilot 3 Frank Edward Bottomley	DSM
Pilot 3 Raymond Charles Grant	DSM
Pilot 3 Peter Ronald Lines	DSM
Aircrewman 1 Charles Frederick Beeton	DSM
Aircrewman 1 Frederick Henry Shiel	DSM
Bandmaster Ernest William Buckingham RM	Mention in Despatches
Chief Petty Officer Airman (AH) George Short	BEM
Chief Mechanician Leslie Madden	BEM
Chief Electrician (Air) Clarence Frederick Headon	Mention in Despatches
Chief Radio Electrician (Air) David Stephen Chapman	Mention in Despatches
Chief Radio Electrician Douglas Craig Davidson	Mention in Despatches
Chief Aircraft Artificer (O) Ewart Leslie Hornbuckle	Mention in Despatches
Chief Engine Room Artificer Thomas Henry Smith	Mention in Despatches
Aircraft Artificer 2 Ronald Frederick John Gatrell	Mention in Despatches
Radio Electrical Artificer 3 Brian Anthony De La Pain	Mention in Despatches
Leading Seaman Albert Lindley Rich	Mention in Despatches
Leading Airman (O) Alfred John Russell	Mention in Despatches
Leading Airman (E) Brian Warwick Smith	Mention in Despatches

HMS GLORY

Captain Kenneth Stuart Colquhoun DSO	CBE
Captain Edgar Duncan Goodenough Lewin DSO, DSC*	CBE
Commander (P) James Wallace Sleigh DSO DSC	OBE
Commander Robert Love Alexander DSO, DSC	Mention in Despatches
Commander (S) William Hugh Field	Mention in Despatches
Lieutenant Commander (P) Sidney James Hall DSC	DSO
Lieutenant Commander (P) Francis Alan Swanton DSC*	DSO
Lieutenant Commander (P) John Savile Bailey OBE	DSC
Lieutenant Commander (P) James Robert Nigel Gardner	DSC
Lieutenant Commander (P) Reginald Howard Watson	DSC
Lieutenant Commander (P) Peter Basil Stuart	DSC
Lieutenant Commander William Thomas Rutherford Smith	MBE
Lieutenant Commander (E)(A/E)(P) Ian Francis Pearson	MBE
	Mention in Despatches

Lieutenant Commander (O) Philip Reginald Spademan	Mention in Despatches
Lieutenant (O) John Gabriel Cavendish Harvey	DSC
Lieutenant (P) Alan John Leahy	DSC
Lieutenant (P) Douglas Arthur McNaughton	DSC
Lieutenant (P) Robert John McCandless	DSC
Lieutenant (P) Paul Millett	DSC
Lieutenant (P) James Henry Silvester Pearce	DSC
Lieutenant (P) Geoffrey David Hutton Sample	DSC
Lieutenant (P) Thomas Victor Giles Binney	Mention in Despatches
Lieutenant (P) Robin Christopher Beaumont Trelawney	Mention in Despatches
Lieutenant (P) Kenneth Whitaker	Mention in Despatches
Lieutenant (P) Robert Williams	Mention in Despatches
Lieutenant (P) Roi Egerton Wilson	Mention in Despatches
Lieutenant (O) Anthony Desmond Hooper	Mention in Despatches
Lieutenant (E)(A/E)(P) Peter Barlow	DSC
Lieutenant (E)(A/E)(P) Derek Graham Mather	Queen's Commendation (PoW)
Lieutenant Paul O'Mara USN (and HMAS *Sydney*)	Hon. MBE
Commissioned Pilot Frederick Hefford	DSC
	Mention in Despatches
Commissioned Pilot John Alexander Neilson	DSC
Commissioned Pilot Maurice Henry Charles Purnell	DSC
Commissioned Pilot Michael Ian Darlington	Mention in Despatches
Commissioned Pilot Derek Frederick Fieldhouse	Mention in Despatches
Commissioned Air Engineer Jones BEM	Mention in Despatches
Commissioned Air Engineer (O) James Henry Freeland	Mention in Despatches
Bandmaster Walter James Spencer RM	Mention in Despatches
Chief Aircraft Artificer Arthur Charles Fooks	BEM
Chief Engine Room Artificer George Jack Turp	BEM
Chief Air Fitter (E) Ronald Cater	BEM
Aircraft Artificer 2 Leslie Green	BEM
Aircraft Artificer 3 John Stanley Abbott	BEM
Aircraft Artificer 3 Jerrold Peter Chisholm	BEM
Chief Yeoman of Signals Kenneth Charles Youngjohns	Mention in Despatches
Chief Petty Officer (Tel) Thomas Edward Carlow	Mention in Despatches
Chief Petty Officer Airman Albert Sadler	Mention in Despatches
Chief Engine Room Artificer Michael Conheeney	Mention in Despatches
Chief Aircraft Artificer (O) Gerald Wright Jones	Mention in Despatches
Chief Engine Room Artificer Alfred James Brett	Mention in Despatches
Aircraft Artificer 3 Leonard Mathew Mitchell	Mention in Despatches
Aircraft Artificer 3 Harold Sydney Tuffin	Mention in Despatches
Chief Electrician (Air) Ronald Albert Edward Morris	Mention in Despatches
Petty Officer Charles McKiddie	Mention in Despatches
Petty Officer Air Fitter (A) Horace Dowler	Mention in Despatches
Petty Officer Air Fitter (A) James Saunders Leitch	Mention in Despatches
Petty Officer Stoker Mechanic John Smith	Mention in Despatches
Leading Airman Alexander Jones Law	Mention in Despatches
Leading Airman Pilot's Mate Kenneth Arthur McMichael	Mention in Despatches

Leading Air Mechanic (A) Albert Mark	Mention in Despatches
Leading Air Mechanic (E) Peter Ernest Jones	BEM
Leading Air Mechanic (O) Ronald Daily	Mention in Despatches
Electrician (Air) Herbert Geoffrey Brice	BEM

HMAS SYDNEY

Captain David Hugh Harries RAN	CBE
	Legion of Merit (USA)
Commander (P) Launcelot John Kiggell DSC, RN	Mention in Despatches
	Legion of Merit (USA)
Lieutenant Commander (P) Michael Frampton Fell DSO, DSC, RN	DSC*
Lieutenant Commander (P) Walter George Bowles RAN	DSC
	Legion of Merit (USA)
Lieutenant Commander (E) Robert Joseph Tunstall RN	MBE
Lieutenant Commander (P) John Leslie Appleby RN	Legion of Merit (USA)
Lieutenant Commander (P) Ronald Bruce Lunberg RN	Legion of Merit (USA)
Lieutenant Commander Brian Stewart Murray RAN	Mention in Despatches
Lieutenant (P) Harold Edwin Bailey RAN	DSC
Lieutenant (P) Guy Alexander Beange RAN	DSC
Lieutenant (P) George Firth Spencer Brown DFC, RAN	Mention in Despatches
Lieutenant (P) Edward Thomas Genge RN	Mention in Despatches
Lieutenant (O) Alexander Hughie Gordon DFC, RAN	Mention in Despatches
Lieutenant (P) Peter William Seed RAN	Mention in Despatches
Lieutenant (E) William John Rourke RAN	Mention in Despatches
Sub-Lieutenant Armand John Roland RAN	Mention in Despatches
Petty Officer Observer I Gordon Hughes RAN	DSM
Chief Air Fitter (E) Clifford Frank Dubber RAN	Mention in Despatches
Chief Petty Officer Eugene Elderfield Fernandez RAN	Mention in Despatches
Chief Airman William Daniel Gardner RAN	Mention in Despatches
Chief Electrical Artificer James Patrick Whelan RAN	Mention in Despatches
Chief Air Fitter (E) Arthur Winstanley RAN	Mention in Despatches

HMS OCEAN

Captain Charles Leo Gandore Evans DSO, DSC	CBE
Captain Brian Ewen Weldon Logan	Mention in Despatches
Lieutenant Commander (P) Cedric Kenelm Roberts	DSO
Lieutenant Commander (P) Andrew William Bloomer	DSC
Lieutenant Commander Richard Arnold James Lea	MBE
Lieutenant Commander (E)(A/E) Philip Leslie Luby	MBE
Lieutenant Commander (P) Donald Arthur Dick DSC	Mention in Despatches
Lieutenant Commander (E) Ronald Albert Harcus	Mention in Despatches
Lieutenant (P) Peter Carmichael	DSC
Lieutenant (P) Peter Steel Davis	DSC
Lieutenant (P) Richard Denison Rowan Hawkesworth	DSC
Lieutenant (P) Michael Lawrence Brown	Mention in Despatches
Lieutenant (P) Robert Henry Hallam	Mention in Despatches

Lieutenant (P) David Thomas McKeown	Mention in Despatches
Lieutenant (P) Norman Edmund Peniston-Bird	Mention in Despatches
Lieutenant (P) John Lewis Treloar	Mention in Despatches
Lieutenant (P) Peter Watkinson	Mention in Despatches
Lieutenant (O) William James Cooper	Mention in Despatches
Master at Arms Ivor George Howells	Mention in Despatches
Aircrewman 1 Charles Patrick McCullagh	DSM
Aircrewman 1 James Patrick Potter	DSM
Chief Yeoman of Signals Jack Stephens DSM	BEM
Chief Air Fitter (E) Ronald Brighton	BEM
Chief Engine Room Artificer James Poolev Rowe	Mention in Despatches
Chief Aircraft Artificer Ian Ivor Basil Pearce Hamon	Mention in Despatches
Chief Aircraft Artificer Frank Webb	Mention in Despatches
Chief Aircraft Artificer David William Wynne	Mention in Despatches
Chief Engine Room Artificer Douglas Perrin BEM	Mention in Despatches
Aircraft Mechanician 1 Thomas Lewin Sampson	Mention in Despatches
Radio Electrical Artificer (Air) 3 John Edwin Lucken	Mention in Despatches
Chief Air Fitter (O) Stanley Reid	Mention in Despatches
Chief Petty Officer Airman Alan Dixon	Mention in Despatches
Supply Chief Petty Officer (S) Henry Roy Ronald Williams	Mention in Despatches
Leading Airman (O) Reginald Arthur Fountain	Mention in Despatches

HMS UNICORN

Captain John Yelverton Thompson	Mention in Despatches
	Legion of Merit (USA)
Commander James Kenneth Hamilton	Mention in Despatches
Lieutenant (E)(A/E) Robin Beadon Lisle Foster	Mention in Despatches
Commissioned Airman Dennis Raymond Mottram	Mention in Despatches
Chief Petty Officer Cook (S) Henry George Barnett	Mention in Despatches
Aircraft Artificer 3 Gerald O'Brien	Mention in Despatches
Petty Officer Air Fitter (E) Edward Lockhart	BEM

APPENDIX F
The Carriers and their Aircraft

Development of Colossus Class Light Fleet Carriers

The loss of *Prince of Wales* and *Repulse* to Japanese bombers on 10th December 1941, made it painfully obvious that fighter carriers would be indispensable for future operations within range of enemy land-based aircraft. At the same time, Britain lacked the capacity to build new fleet carriers quickly. 'Woolworth' carriers were attractive, if the cost and complexity could be kept down.

In a quick Staff study, three possibilities were examined: to build existing *Audacity* type escort carriers; to build a merchant ship type to operate TSR, small bombers and land-type fighters; and to build a fighter type to protect the battlefleet. The basic requirements were for a flight deck long enough for the latest high performance fighters (for fleet protection), a hangar for 15-24 fighters, and speed comparable with the King George V class battleships, a few low-angle guns, and a maximum AA battery. Conversion of existing hulls (cruiser, fast minelayer or liner) was not considered feasible.

An outline requirement was raised on 26th December, and DNC was instructed to design an unprotected carrier with a speed of 25 knots, to carry at least 15 fighters, as a battleship escort. Though it was not stated, it appears that the fighters envisaged were Spitfires and Typhoons. Quick construction was the most important consideration; the hull was to be to merchant ship standards with cruiser machinery (half the plant designed for the suspended *Bellerophon*) of 40,000 shaft horse power. There was to be little armament and no armour. The 'intermediate aircraft carrier' was estimated at £1.75 million, less than half that of a fully armoured fleet carrier. In the event, the final cost averaged £2.5 million as they got more sophisticated during the early design phases.

The result was an outstanding success — the *Colossus* Class.

Vickers, who had experience in building both merchant and warships, produced a first sketch design on 14th January 1942, stating that it would take 21 months to build, which seemed long. The Staff required additions, and a new sketch design was produced nine days later. In the de facto Staff Requirement of July 1942, the flight deck was to be long enough for free (rolling) take-offs for Typhoons, and a catapult was included.

The carrier was essentially un-armoured, except for splinter protection for exposed personnel; and had no conventional side protective system. A torpedo hitting amidships would flood one, or probably two, compartments. To limit the effect of such a hit, better subdivision was provided than for a merchant ship. Structurally, the light fleets followed merchant ship practice; the flight deck was the strength deck. The machinery was of the unit system in two large machinery spaces, each containing two boilers at a working pressure of 400 lbs per in^2, one geared Parsons turbine main engine set, one 500 kW turbo-generator and a set of evaporators; these spaces were separated by two spaces, 24 feet long, containing auxiliary machinery and petrol tanks. In addition there were two 200 kW diesel generators on the centre line; a third 180 kW diesel generator was later fitted.

One BH 3 pneumatic/hydraulic catapult was fitted; two safety barriers; and initially eight arrestor wires on four Mk 8 units, but after trials in the first ships to complete this was found to be inadequate and another two-wire unit was fitted as ships became available.

Standard armament consisted of six quadruple 2 pounder pom-poms and up to 19 single power worked 40 mm Bofors guns. In 1949 the radar fit consisted of two 277Q sets, one 293Q and one carrier controlled approach set.

All ships of the class suffered from vibration, strongest just abaft the after lift. In an effort to minimise vibration, *Theseus* was fitted with one three bladed and one four bladed propeller.

HMS *Unicorn*

The experience of the Abyssinian crisis in 1935 showed that the fleet required mobile support in order to achieve true strategic mobility. The construction of *Unicorn* can be seen as the forerunner of the much larger effort required when the fleet went to the Pacific in 1944-45.

The requirement for a depot ship to carry out aircraft repairs amp overhauls made it possible for the astute Controller, Admiral R.G.H. Henderson, to secure a ship which could and did function in wartime as an emergency carrier. He was painfully aware of the need for carriers and yet was severely limited by both finances and by the resistance of the Air Ministry. He argued that a ship limited to aircraft maintenance would be a poor peacetime investment, and that it would need a landing-on deck in order also to be used as a training carrier.

The ship was laid down in 1939, and was built with an upper hangar to accommodate seven spread aircraft (324 x 65 x 16 ft 6 in), with workshops forward and component stowage aft; and with a lower hangar for 20 folded aircraft (360 x 62 x 16 ft 6 in); 16 ft 6 in was accepted as the hangar height sufficient for normal maintenance, anything more could be done on the flight deck using cranes. She could also carry 14 or 15 crated aircraft. As a training carrier the ship would have sufficient stowage for 30 aircraft. Parts stowage was about four times that built into the large fleet carrier *Ark Royal*, and included 50 spare engines.

The design showed two self-propelled lighters, one in a recess under the after round-down, lifted by a gantry and one which could be lifted onto the flight deck by the port (15 ton) aircraft crane. The starboard (7 ton) crane plumbed the after lift, and so could place aircraft with damaged undercarriages onto it. The unusual hull form aft, to accommodate the lighter, required special wind tunnel work.

EinC called for four generators, two steam units in the engine rooms and two diesels at the ends. The Staff Requirement reduced this to four steam generators, two of which were to be as far as possible from the engine rooms (for survivability). Four 400 kW turbo-generators were fitted.

	Unicorn	*Colossus*
Date	1943	1945
Displacement		
standard tons	14750	13190
deep tons	20300	18040
LOA ft	640	693
Beam WL ft	90	80
extreme ft in		112-6
Depth ft in	74-10	62-6
Freeboard ft	50-10	39-3
Draught deep forward ft in	23-1	23-1
aft ft in	24-10	23-5
Flight deck length ft	600	665
Shaft horsepower	40000	40000
Speed kts	24	25
Oil fuel tons	3000	3196
Petrol galls	36500	80000
Lifts ft	33x45, 24x46	2 — 34x45
Catapults	1 x BH 3	1 x BH 3
Guns	8x4 in HA	11x1, 10x2
		40 mm Bofors
	4x4 barrel	6x4 barrel
	2lb pom-pom	2lb pom-pom
	4x2, 5x1	
	20 mm	

Name	Builders	Laid down	Launched	Completed
Glory	Harland & Wolff Ltd., Belfast	28/2/42	27/11/43	2/4/45
Ocean	Alex. Stephen & Sons Ltd., Govan	8/11/42	8/7/44	30/6/45
Theseus	Fairfield S.B. & Eng. Co. Ltd, Govan	6/1/43	6/7/44	9/1/46
Triumph	R & W Hawthorn Leslie & Co. Ltd., Hebburn	27/1/43	2/10/44	9/4/46
Sydney	Royal Dockyard, Devonport (Ex Terrible)	19/4/43	30/9/44	5/2/49
Unicorn	Harland & Wolff Ltd., Belfast	29/6/39	20/11/41	12/3/43

Flight Deck Machinery
BH 3 Catapult

The gear for launching an aircraft in a tail-up attitude resting on a cradle attached to a trolley was said to be a 'catapult', a practice discontinued in the light fleet carriers before the start of the Korean War; when the aircraft was launched tail-down, on its own undercarriage, it was from an 'accelerator'; though this is the correct nomenclature, they are always generically referred to as 'catapults', and will be so called here.

The towing hook was attached to a trolley towed along a twin-track by a rope led round pulleys to the mechanism below in the catapult room (Fig. 1). This consisted of a cylinder and piston unit whose speed was multiplied eight times in transmission to the towing hook. The piston was driven forward by compressed air which had to accelerate the mass of piston, piston rod, pulleys, ropes, hook and aircraft. This assorted ironmongery was brought to rest at the end of the run hydraulically, the piston forcing water out of a cylinder through a narrow annulus. To return the trolley for the next aircraft, water would be forced back by a pump recompressing the air, which was used as a spring.

In designing a catapult particular attention must be paid to the maximum acceleration and to the way in which it is built up in order to avoid damage to the aircraft or its crew. The rules which govern the acceleration are:

1. The maximum acceleration must not exceed 1.25 times the average acceleration.
2. The acceleration must build up smoothly to the maximum value in the first 10 feet of run (0.4 seconds).
3. The acceleration must diminish steadily from the maximum to the

end of the run. For a launch speed of 66 knots reached in 96 feet, the mean acceleration would be 2g with a maximum of 2.5g. The maximum designed retardation of the towing hook was 11.5g. The track length was 140ft 9ins.

A condensing steam turbine drove a multi-stage centrifugal pump discharging water at a pressure up to 2,000 lbs per in^2 into the power cylinder. This water armed the catapult by forcing the main ram to the air end of the cylinder, compressing air (through a manifold) into twelve vessels, and holding the ram in that position until launch. A piston rod at each end of the main ram was connected to a crosshead carrying the multiplying sheaves for the acceleration and retardation ropes; the fixed crossheads were attached to the ship's structure.

At launch, the control worker in the control position at the edge of the flight deck operated the control lever; this caused a pilot valve to operate a relay valve which then admitted water pressure to the opening cylinder of the launching valve (Fig. 3), allowing the closing cylinder at the other end to exhaust its water to the tank, and thus permitting the launch valve to open. As soon as the launching valve began to open it allowed water to be discharged from the power cylinder annulus, causing a drop in the pressure. The difference in pressure between the air on one side of the piston and the water pressure on the other created a load on the piston, which pushed it along the cylinder; the trolley was drawn forward by the accelerating rope, while the retarding rope was 'paid off' by its crossheads at the same rate.

The second design requirement, of a rapid but smooth build up of acceleration, was met by controlling the rate at which the launching valve opened. This rate was controlled by the rate at which the hydraulic fluid could escape from the closing cylinder: a spindle attached to the closing piston of the launching valve carried a 'rate-of-opening control' sleeve, which in conjunction with a choke ring formed in the closing cylinder, provided an annular orifice through which the water in the cylinder could escape during the opening stroke. The sleeve was profiled so that when pressure was admitted to the opening cylinder and acted on the opening piston, there was an adequate escape to permit initial rapid opening to carry the valve through the 'lap' stroke; the sleeve had then entered the orifice and the rate of opening slowed dramatically. The slow rate of opening was maintained until the area through the launching valve was such that the trolley had reached its maximum acceleration; then the orifice was increased, and the valve allowed to complete its travel to full open at a higher speed. By this means the rate of opening of the launching valve was rigidly controlled; it was not dependent on the human factor in operation, and could only be modified by dismantling the valve and machining a new profile on the sleeve; it had no moving or wearing parts and was therefore consistent and reliable in operation.

When the launching valve was fully open the water (Fig. 2) had a free escape from the cylinder, and the water pressure in the cylinder annulus due to its expulsion was negligible, so that the force exerted by the whole air pressure acting on the piston became available to accelerate the ropes and sheaves, the trolley and the aircraft. In this condition the third design requirement — that the acceleration should diminish steadily from maximum — is met automatically by the expansion of the air, as the rate of pressure drop during the stroke is related to the swept volume of the piston and the capacity of the air vessels.

At the retarding end of the power cylinder, i.e. on the water side, a heavy bronze ring was screwed into the cylinder at the end of the piston's stroke. The main piston had an extension on its fluid side of diameter larger than the piston rod and having a slight taper, the larger end being towards the piston and of such a diameter that it had a clearance of 0.005 inches between itself and the bronze choke ring — this was the retardation profile.

The accelerating stroke continued until the retardation profile entered the choke ring; as soon as it did so the escape of fluid from the annulus between the piston rod and choke ring was checked, and it was forced through the small annular orifice between the choke ring and the retardation profile. The orifice was designed so that the expulsion of the water through it at a rate corresponding to the velocity of the piston created a high pressure in the fluid in the annulus. This pressure exerted a force on the piston which not only balanced the force due to the air pressure, but also resisted further movement of the piston. The inertia of the trolley, the ropes and the sheaves, acting through the retardation piston rod of the main ram, pulled the piston along against the resistance of the fluid pressure, and in so doing their kinetic energy was absorbed and they were brought to rest.

As soon as the trolley (Fig 1) came to rest at the end of the stroke the control worker closed the launching valve and by a remote control opened the drawback valve. Water under pressure from the pump entered the cylinder and drove the piston back to the air end of the cylinder, recompressing the air into the vessels, and drawing the trolley back to the after end of the track ready for the next aircraft. The drawback valve was then closed and the gear was in the hydraulically locked condition.

The cycle can be summarised thus:

1. The air drives the piston forwards, accelerating the mass of the piston, piston rods, sheaves, ropes, trolley and aircraft.

2. The water absorbs the energy of the piston, piston rods, sheaves, ropes and trolley.

3. The pump forces the piston back and recompresses the air.

The air was therefore used as a spring, and was not expended; the pump gave to the air energy which it imparted to the moving parts and the aircraft, and as the

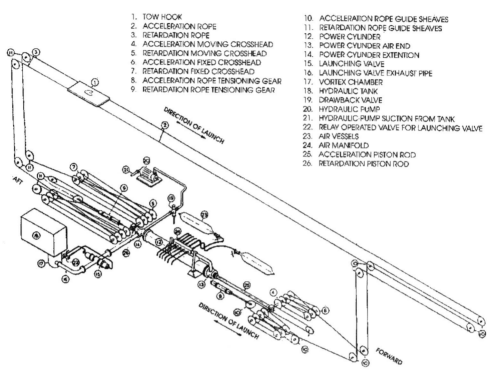

1. TOW HOOK
2. ACCELERATION ROPE
3. RETARDATION ROPE
4. ACCELERATION MOVING CROSSHEAD
5. RETARDATION MOVING CROSSHEAD
6. ACCELERATION FIXED CROSSHEAD
7. RETARDATION FIXED CROSSHEAD
8. ACCELERATION ROPE TENSIONING GEAR
9. RETARDATION ROPE TENSIONING GEAR
10. ACCELERATION ROPE GUIDE SHEAVES
11. RETARDATION ROPE GUIDE SHEAVES
12. POWER CYLINDER
13. POWER CYLINDER AIR END
14. POWER CYLINDER EXTENTION
15. LAUNCHING VALVE
16. LAUNCHING VALVE EXHAUST PIPE
17. VORTEX CHAMBER
18. HYDRAULIC TANK
19. DRAWBACK VALVE
20. HYDRAULIC PUMP
21. HYDRAULIC PUMP SUCTION FROM TANK
22. RELAY OPERATED VALVE FOR LAUNCHING VALVE
23. AIR VESSELS
24. AIR MANIFOLD
25. ACCELERATION PISTON ROD
26. RETARDATION PISTON ROD

FIG 1. CATAPULT GENERAL ARRANGEMENT

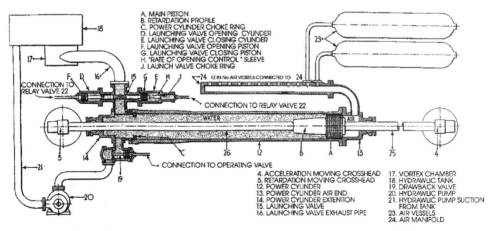

A. MAIN PISTON
B. RETARDATION PROFILE
C. POWER CYLINDER CHOKE RING
D. LAUNCHING VALVE OPENING CYUNDER
E. LAUNCHING VALVE CLOSING CYLINDER
F. LAUNCHING VALVE OPENING PISTON
G. LAUNCHING VALVE CLOSING PISTON
H. "RATE OF OPENING CONTROL " SLEEVE
J. LAUNCH VALVE CHOKE RING

CONNECTION TO RELAY VALVE 22

24 12 IN No AIR VESSELS CONNECTED TO   24

CONNECTION TO RELAY VALVE 22

WATER

AIR

CONNECTION TO OPERATING VALVE

FIG -DIAGRAM OF ACCELERATOR MACHINERY

4. ACCELERATION MOVING CROSSHEAD
5. RETARDATION MOVING CROSSHEAD
12. POWER CYLINDER
13. POWER CYLINDER AIR END
14. POWER CYLINDER EXTENTION
15. LAUNCHING VALVE
16. LAUNCHING VALVE EXHAUST PIPE
17. VORTEX CHAMBER
18. HYDRAWLIC TANK
19. DRAWBACK VALVE
20. HYDRAWLIC PUMP
21. HYDRAWLIC PUMP SUCTION FROM TANK
23. AIR VESSELS
24. AIR MANIFOLD

FIG 2. DIAGRAM OF ACCELERATOR MACHINERY

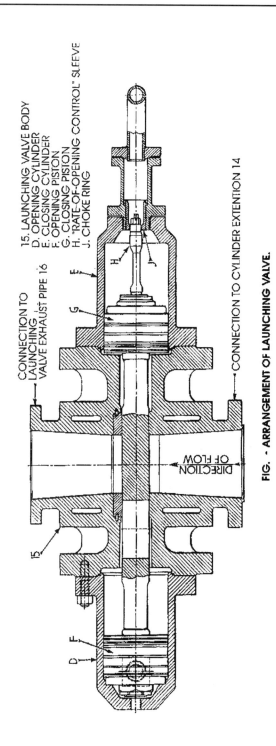

CONNECTION TO LAUNCHING VALVE EXHAUST PIPE 16

15. LAUNCHING VALVE BODY
D. OPENING CYLINDER
E. CLOSING CYLINDER
F. OPENING PISTON
G. CLOSING PISTON
H. "RATE-OF-OPENING CONTROL" SLEEVE
J. CHOKE RING

DIRECTION OF FLOW

CONNECTION TO CYLINDER EXTENTION 14

FIG. - ARRANGEMENT OF LAUNCHING VALVE.

FIG 3. ARRANGEMENT OF LAUNCHING VALVE

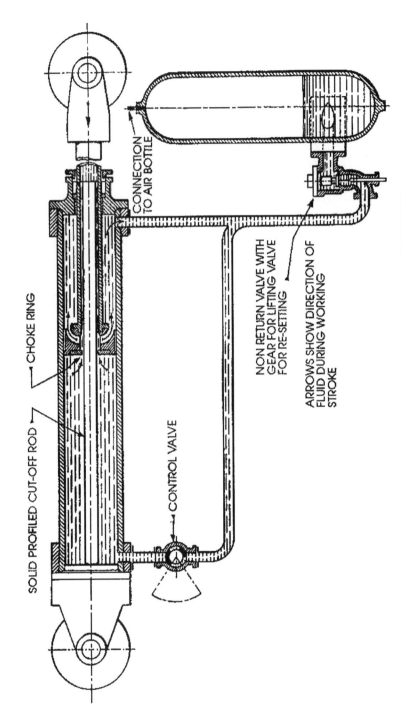

CHOKE RING

SOLID PROFILED CUT-OFF ROD

CONTROL VALVE

CONNECTION TO AIR BOTTLE

NON RETURN VALVE WITH GEAR FOR LIFTING VALVE FOR RE-SETTING

ARROWS SHOW DIRECTION OF FLUID DURING WORKING STROKE

FIG 4. ARRESTING GEAR - DIAGRAMMATIC ARRANGEMENT

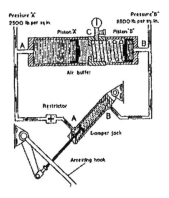

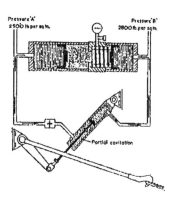

Static and Lowering. *Pressures at A, B and in the air space were 2,500lb per in ². Piston B is held by the spring and remains at the end of the cylinder. The hook is retained in line UP position by a mechanical lock and is released by the pilot when required. When the lock is released, pressure B, acting on the larger surface area at the top of the damper jack piston, and assisted by the weight of the piston, overcome pressure A acting on the smaller surface area, and the hook lowers.*

Arresting. *When the hook picked up a wire, the hook travelled very quickly upwards and backwards and engaged the lock, retracting the damper jack piston which forced the fluid in the space above the piston along the pipeline to move piston B inwards against the combined action of the coil spring and air pressure. The increased air pressure in the centre compartment moved piston A outwards and forced fluid through the restrictor to the underside of the jack piston. The extra fluid in the B end of the air buffer was released when the UP selector valve was depressed.*

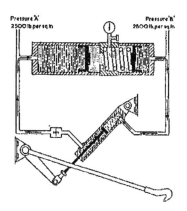

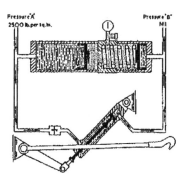

Bounce and recoil. *The speed of upward travel of the jack was so rapid that fluid was not able to pass through the restrictor quickly enough, and partial cavitation occurred beneath the piston. There was thus no resistance to the action of the high pressure fluid B which instantaneously forced the hook downwards to engage the nearest wire.*

Raising. *When the plunger of the spring loaded selector valve is depressed, pressure B is cut off and the fluid from the damper jack is diverted to the reservoir. Pressure A then retracts the jack and raises the hook which engages the lock.*

Fig. 5

pump was driven by a turbine, the accelerator was in effect steam operated — it could go on operating for an unlimited number of cycles, at as high a rate as the size of the pump would permit.

Throughout the Korean operations, the life of the catapult wires was 900-1,000 heavy shots, heavy in this case meaning aircraft 'bombed up' at an all-up weight of up to 16,000 lbs. About 400 heavy shots were launched in each operational period of eight flying days, the normal length of a patrol. Thus it was necessary to re-reeve both ropes at the end of every second patrol.

This had always been a major dockyard job until, necessity being the mother of invention, *Theseus* did the job in 38 hours. Most of the time was taken up by 'rat-tailing', but when old and new wires were joined by welding, the time was considerably shortened, *Ocean* achieving an average of $10\frac{1}{2}$ hours, with an optimum of $7\frac{1}{2}$ hours.

The packing rings of the main rams also required renewal after about 1,000 launches, another job initially taking about 24 hours, but reducing to 16 with experience; combined with re-reeving.

The next generation of aircraft was to take the hydraulic/pneumatic catapult with its wires and sheaves to its limits in the BH 5. The steam catapult was conceived by Mr. (later Commander (E)) C.C. Mitchell in 1936, was developed for trials in 1951, and entered service as the BS 4. Boiler steam acted directly on a piston in a slotted cylinder. The piston carried an arm projecting outside the cylinder through the slot, and the arm pulled the towing bridle to launch the aircraft; the only moving part was the piston. The slot was sealed by a hinged longitudinal valve opened and closed by the arm as it passed along the cylinder.

Mark VII (Modified) Arresting Gear (Fig. 4)

The design requirements for arresting gear were:

1. A smooth build-up of retarding force when the hook on the aircraft picks up the transverse wire deck span.
2. The maintenance of the maximum retarding force which can be applied to the aircraft as long as possible, subject to 3 below; and
3. The steady diminution of the wire tension as the velocity of the aircraft approaches zero, in order to allow the tail of the aircraft to settle on to the deck.

The desired performance could be obtained by a simple hydraulic system consisting of a fixed cylinder and a moving piston. The wires were rove 12/1 round pulleys on two crossheads, one on the cylinder, the other on the piston rod end.

The arresting gear fitted in the light fleet carriers was a simplified version of those in the *Illustrious* class fleet carriers, initially designed for *Unicorn* in 1940 to accept aircraft of 20,000 lbs weight entering at 60 knots and with a maximum retardation of 1.5g. To reduce costs the cylinder and ram were fabricated from solid drawn steel tubes and other components were of welded steel construction rather than forgings.

Fixed axially along the centre of the cylinder was a solid rod whose outer surface was profiled. Fitting over this cut-off rod was the piston and hollow piston rod with an annular clearance between the piston and the cut-off rod. The piston was a bronze casting with a choke ring fitted to the piston head providing a restriction to the flow of fluid between itself and the cut-off rod as the unit compressed. Large ports in the piston from the wake of the choke ring allowed the fluid to pass to the annulus side whence a small quantity flowed through a non-return valve into the base of an accumulator. Since there was no occasion when there was a static pressure difference between the two sides of the piston, no U-leathers were employed, light bronze piston rings only being fitted. The accumulator consisted simply of an air-bottle, housed vertically, the fluid expelled from the unit entering tangentially near the bottom of the bottle, and the normal level being about one-quarter full. Compressed air was introduced above the fluid and no piston was employed; since glycerine and water was the working fluid no aeration occurred, with the submerged tangential entry assisting in its prevention, as entering fluid caused a vortex without breaking the surface.

As the piston is pushed into the cylinder, the fluid in front of it has no exit other than through the annular orifice between the piston choke-ring and the cut-off rod. This creates a fluid pressure which resists the motion of the piston, and creates a tension in the wire: the kinetic energy of the aircraft is converted into pressure energy in the fluid, which in turn becomes velocity energy in the orifice and this is dissipated in heat. A small amount of the aircraft's energy is stored in the accumulator which is returned in resetting the wire. The profiling of the cut-off rod varies the rate of flow of fluid between itself and the choke ring as the piston moves into the cylinder by altering the area of the annular orifice, so that the retarding force on the aircraft matched the desired characteristics, namely:

- build up of retardation gradual, over about 60 feet;
- maximum retardation about 1.5g;
- reduction of retardation gradual.

To allow for different weights of aircraft some fluid was allowed to flow directly to the accumulator from the cylinder through a variable control valve, bypassing the choke ring. The unit was re-set by pneumatically lifting the non-return valve, the air pressure in the accumulator expelling the fluid back into the main cylinder, driving out the piston rod, and pulling in the wire.

Ten cross-deck spans were rove in pairs to five arresting units; in order that the hook on the aircraft could pick up the deck span, each span was held at least four inches above the deck by bow-springs which were themselves eight inches above the deck. The bow springs were retracted to deck level pneumatically at all times except when landing-on. Double reeving in this fashion provided a self-centring action to aircraft landing off-centre by swinging the tail outboard and the nose towards the ship's centre line.

Ocean reported renewing fourteen arrestor unit reevings and 124 centre spans. The highest number of arrests obtained from one unit was 2,220; and an average of 250 arrests was achieved from each centre span.

The barriers operated on a similar principle to the arrestors, but the pull-out was restricted to about 40 feet, and the retardation was therefore greater.

The Aircraft
Supermarine Seafire

The Seafire IB entered naval service in 1941 as converted Spitfire VBs fitted with a V-frame arrestor hook and catapult spools, but non-folding.

By the end of World War II, the Merlin engined Seafires II and III were being superseded by Griffon engined Mark XVs with sting arrestor hooks mounted in the tail under the rudder; they in turn being replaced by the Mark XVII with a bubble canopy and a cut away rear fuselage.

The last Seafire in squadron service was the Mark 47 featuring contra-rotating propellers on the up-rated Griffon 88. Captain Eric Brown CBE, DSC, AFC, RN reported it as being the easiest of all the Seafires to operate from a deck. Full power up to +18 lbs per in^2 boost could be applied for take-off with the rudder neutral and the aircraft running straight. It was a delightful machine; variations of power no longer demanded alterations to trim, and the contra-prop gave very powerful braking on cutting the throttle. The control column had to be pulled back as the throttle was cut because the nose otherwise pitched down sharply. The supreme feature of the Mark 47 was its superlative control harmony, which, combined with its performance, rendered it an outstanding combat fighter.

Hawker Sea Fury
The single seat Sea Fury was probably the finest piston-engined all-purpose aircraft (fighter and ground strike) to enter operational service. It was descended from the RAF Tempest, the specification, N.7/43, being for a smaller and lighter version.

Experimental Furies were powered by a Napier Sabre VII; a Rolls-Royce Griffon 85 with contra-propellers; and two marks of Bristol Centaurus, the XII and XXII. The Griffon was a 12-cylinder, Vee, liquid cooled, poppet valve engine; the Sabre was a 24-cylinder, H, liquid cooled, single sleeve engine; and the Centaurus was an 18-cylinder, two row, air cooled radial, single sleeve valve engine. The Sabre was discontinued because of unreliability and limited development potential of the engine; the Griffon powered development ceased when the RAF contract was cancelled; and the Centaurus XII gave trouble due to a defective lubrication system.

The Sea Fury prototype had a pronounced swing to starboard on take-off, so that rudder control was critical. It was also directionally unstable during the landing run. These two faults were corrected by enlarging the area of the fin and rudder, and fitting a tailwheel lock. Hook bounce, encountered during the early deck-landing trials, was cured by modifications to the hook and by improved pneumatic damping. Lubrication problems with the Centaurus XII were solved in later Marks.

Production of the Sea Fury started with the F.X powered by a 2,560 hp Centaurus 18 with a Rotol five-bladed propeller. The early aircraft were mainly used for further development, and were soon superseded by the FB.11 that met the fighter bomber role, with the ability to carry a wider range of armament stores.

Fairey Firefly

In 1939, the Griffon engine was being developed by Rolls-Royce primarily for the Royal Navy. The N.5/40 specification was approved by the Board as a multi-purpose two seater aircraft with fighter capabilities that became the Firefly.

The Mark I with the beard radiator was powered by a Rolls Royce Griffon IIB engine developing 1,730 hp. It possessed good low-speed handling qualities necessary for a carrier aircraft, due largely to the Fairey Youngman flaps, extending from the ailerons to the centre-line of the fuselage. In addition to the fully retracted or housed position, these flaps had three positions: extended at near-zero incidence beneath the trailing edge to improve low speed manoeuvrability; moved aft and lowered to improve take-off; and moved further aft and rotated through a maximum angle for landing

Major changes appeared in the Mark 4. A 2,250 hp Griffon 74 engine with a two-speed two-stage supercharger drove a four-bladed propeller; radiators were fitted in forward extensions of the centre-section; and the wings were square-clipped, giving it an improved rate of roll. The Mark 5 was a sub-variant of the Mark 4, which included hydraulic wing folding.

A major fault with the Firefly at touch-down was a tendency for the hook to bounce over all the wires and for the aircraft to enter the barrier. It was cured by Mod.1210 introduced in 1951 (Fig. 5).

The arresting-hook damper mechanism consisted of a jack operating in conjunction with an air buffer cylinder. These two components lowered the hook, maintained it in the fully down position until a wire was engaged, and then damped its resulting upward movement.

The damper jack was of the conventional double-acting type, connected in parallel with the air buffer to the aircraft hydraulic system. The jack body was anchored to the aircraft structure, the piston rod to the hook. The air buffer comprised a double-ended cylinder containing two opposed floating pistons, one of which was spring loaded towards one end of the cylinder. The air space between the pistons was initially charged to a pressure of 1,250 lbs per in^2. Both ends of the cylinder were connected to the hydraulic system.

Vickers-Supermarine Sea Otter

The Sea Otter was a carrier-borne or shore-based amphibian carrying a crew of three or four, for SAR and communications squadrons. It was constructed from wood and metal with a hydraulically retracting undercarriage, and was powered by a single Bristol Mercury XXX radial engine.

Westland Dragonfly

In 1947 Westland acquired a licence to build the Sikorsky S.51 two-seat helicopter, designated the Dragonfly HR.1, HR.3 and HR.5, powered by an Alvis Leonides 50 radial engine, and intended for utility and SAR roles.

	Sea fire 47	Firefly 1	Sea Fury 11	Firefly 5
Power Plant	Griffon 88	Griffon 12	Centaurus 18	Griffon 74
horse power	2350	1990	2560	2250
Dimensions				
span ft in	36-11	44-6	38-5	41-2
length ft in	34-4	37-7	34-8	37-11
height	12-9	13-7	15-11	14-4
wing area ft²	244	328	280	330
Weights				
empty lb	7625	9750	9240	9674
max. all up lb	11250	14900	14650	16000
Performance				
max. speed kts	398	278	405	340
at ft	20500	14000	18000	14000
cruising speed kts				194
range miles	400	1300	700 at 30000ft	660
Landing				
max. weight lb	9500	12200	12400	13000
speed kts	85	85	90	90
Armament				
gun	4x20 mm	4x20 mm	4x20 mm	4x20 mm
RP lb	8x60	8x60	12x60	16x60
or bombs lb	3x500	2x1000	2x1000	2x1000

	Sea Otter	Dragonfly
Power Plant	Mercury	Leonides
	XXX	50
horse power	855	550
Dimensions		
span ft ins	46-0	
rotor diameter ft ins		49-0
length ft ins	39-5	57-7
height ft ins	16-2	12-11
wing area ft^2	610	
Weights		
empty lb	6805	4397
gross lb	10000	5870
Performance		
max. speed kts	132	91
at ft	5000	
cruising speed kts	88	71
ceiling ft	16000	13500
range miles	725	
Armament	3xVickers	
	K mc/gun	

APPENDIX G
LSO SIGNALS

Every deck landing was an individual aerobatic under the benevolent charge of the Landing Signals Officer (Deck Landing Control Officer or batsman).

On the axial-deck light fleet carriers, the landing area was approximately 300 feet long by 60 feet wide; the carrier was steaming into wind so that there was a relative wind speed of 30 knots along the deck; the Sea Fury was flying at 95 knots and the Firefly at 92 knots (just above stalling speed), at a high angle of incidence (attitude), and with considerable power on. When over the deck, the batsman instructed the pilot to cut the throttle; the aircraft then dropped to the deck with a forward velocity of 60+ knots to engage an arrestor wire and was brought to rest in a distance of 60 feet at a retardation of 1.5g. If the aircraft failed to pick up a wire, it entered one of the safety barriers, erected amidships to prevent errant aircraft from ploughing into the others parked at the forward end of the flight deck; so much damage was caused by a full barrier entry that a replacement aircraft was required from *Unicorn* or Iwakuni. Aircraft catching numbers 9 and 10 wires almost always entered the barriers gently, suffering a minimum amount of damage that could be repaired on board.

Not infrequently, after a good approach and touch-down, Fireflies would engage the barrier because their hooks had bounced over all the wires. This was prevented by Mod. 1210 to the hydraulic system, introduced in 1952. A description of the installation and operation of this modification is given in Appendix F (The carriers and their aircraft).

The standard technique was to fly a 150 feet circuit flying into an imaginary box with the pilot being given the 'cut' as the aircraft 'flared' 30 feet above the deck. The batsman usually aimed to bring the aircraft along a path such that it would engage number three wire. Pilots tended to have personal idiosyncrasies — one might always approach high, another might delay closing the throttle after being given the 'cut' — and the batsman would adjust for this. He would have a copy of the flying programme, would know who was airborne, and therefore the members of each flight as they joined the circuit.

The batsman stood on a platform projecting from the port side of the flight deck at number two wire with a wind-break shield behind his back. Around and beneath the platform was a net into which the batsman could jump if the approaching aircraft was likely to hit him. With him were two ratings, the Teller and the Talker — the Teller watching the approaching aircraft through binoculars, checking and reporting to the batsman that the wheels, hook and flaps were down; the Talker watching events at the forward end of the deck, reporting the position of aircraft, the wires had been reset, and the barriers erected.

The batsman had two paddles — or bats — of yellow or pink fluorescent material. How he held them told the pilot of the approaching aircraft his position and speed relative to the landing area. The attached sketches illustrate the advice being offered to the pilot. Only two of the batsman's signals were mandatory — the Cut and the Wave-off — all the others were advisory in that the responsibility for acting on them rested with the pilot, he was responsible for making a successful landing.

On a pitching deck, in bad weather, the batsman had some difficulty in coping with the horizon, and in allowing for the arrival of the aircraft to coincide with the movement of the deck.

Roger.   Speed, attitude and position correct; continue as you are. Arms horizontal and outstretched.

Cut.   Instruction to close the throttle and land. The right paddle cut across the front of the batsman's chest, the left one behind his body.

Wave-off.   Instruction to abandon the approach and landing, to go round again and make another approach. Paddles crossed and re-crossed above the batsman's head.

Too High.   Both arms held above the shoulders at 45°.

Too Low.   Both arms below the shoulders at 45°.

Too Slow.   Paddles moved together in front of the batsman from outstretched

Too Fast.   Right paddle moved up and down from shoulder to ground, left paddle held horizontal.

Starboard wing too High. Left paddle up, right down, both at 45°.

Port wing too High.
         Right paddle up, left down, at 45°.

Undercarriage not Down.
         Both paddles held on right hand side of batsman's body, rotated together in a vertical circle.

Hook not Down.
         Both paddles on right hand side, moved up and down in opposite directions.

Commander Fiddian-Green's three photographs taken with cameras mounted in a modified drop tank — Approach, Lined Up and Arrested — show how a landing should be performed: where the pilot wanted to be and what he saw during his landing.

The other series of four Sea Fury photographs — how it should not be done — illustrates a classic torque stall, starting from having got dangerously low and slow towards the end of the approach and perhaps having been waved-off a little late. This wave-off is unusual in that normally the pilot would go to port for two reasons — a) the airflow down-wind of the island was turbulent and included funnel gases, and there were the physical obstructions of the crane, the mast and the bridge, and b) another flight of aircraft would probably be thundering down the starboard side prior to breaking off to join the landing circuit. In the first photograph the wave-off has already been given and the aircraft going into the torque stall, which is itself caused by applying full power at a very low airspeed, and pulling back on the stick to gain height at the same time. The result of this is to increase the wing incidence to a point where all lift is lost and the aircraft tries to rotate around the engine. The aircraft is already out of control and the starboard wheel has hit the deck (which slows it down even more). It is probable that both wheels hit the deck causing the aircraft to bounce over the gun sponsons before, in the second photograph, the aircraft is totally stalled, despite being the right way up, and is falling seaward. In the third photo the aircraft has hit the water wheels first with some forward speed resulting in the inevitable nose-over. In the last of the series, the pilot has surfaced along side the fuselage and the attendant destroyer is taking rescue action.

Most of the straight-deck problems were

– Approach at 90-92 knots.   (Author)

– Lined up.   (Author)

– Arrested.   (Author)

resolved with the introduction of Commander D.R.F. Campbell's angled deck and Commander H.C.N. Goodhart's mirror landing sight. Both these officers subsequently achieved Flag rank.

The pilot made a steadily descending approach along a light beam, stabilised at 3° to the horizontal, onto a clear deck without barriers, angled at 10° to the left of the ship's centre line, which allowed him to make a 'touch-and-go' landing if he missed the wires, taking off to port while the aircraft in the deck park were over to starboard. The mirror sight overcame the human factor in that a batsman became nearly redundant.

Another factor which may have been coincidental, but which was just as vital, was the introduction into service at about the same time of jet and turbo-propeller aircraft. At long last the pilot, by sitting in front of, or in the case of the Gannet on top of, the engine(s) could see where he was going. The mirror sight gave a flight path in the vertical plane, but in the horizontal plane the pilot had to rely on the 'Mark I Eyeball' to line himself up with the centre line of the deck (both by day and by night). However, landing the single engined Sea Fury or Firefly type of aircraft on an angled deck was not easy, and in order to line himself up the pilot had to rely heavily on the batsman for horizontal position even if he used the mirror sight for height.

APPENDIX H
IMMERSION SUITS
and
MAE WESTS

Mark 6 Immersion Suit

Prior to World War II no protection was given to aircrew against the hazards of cold water immersion. In water temperatures of one or two degrees above freezing an average person fully clothed is unlikely to survive for more than half an hour, though remarkable feats of endurance and survival have been recorded. Ordinary clothing will reduce heat loss from a body to the surrounding water by limiting circulation of water around the body, and retaining a layer of warm water next the body, but body heat is nevertheless conducted away by the water.

The first immersion suits were designed by Squadron Leader Pask at Farnborough, for RAF pilots flying Hurricanes on convoy protection who were accommodated in Catapult Merchant Ships. There was no means of recovering the aircraft after launching, the pilot had to ditch or bale out and wait to be picked up, a particularly hazardous undertaking on north Atlantic and Russian convoys.

The first suit was made of soft leather with rubberised fabric socks, attached helmet, rubber wrist seals and a gusset neck. Leather was not an ideal material, but it was the only suitable fabric available, which was sufficiently ventile, a poor conductor of cold and had a slow rate of water absorption. The suits were very successful and did a lot to improve the morale of the pilots.

The task of providing air cover for the convoys transferred to the Navy when escort carriers became available, and the RN Air Medical School took over development of immersion suits. At that time the textile industry had developed fabrics which had the property of being ventile and yet, when immersed, were highly resistant to water penetration. It would be simple to design a water-tight suit in rubber or rubberised fabric but it would not be acceptable for aircrew. Rubberised materials will not ventilate and for normal flying conditions such suits would be unacceptably hot and sweaty. Suits were made to a design similar to Pask's in these new materials which were popular and saved the lives of many aviators.

Interest in these suits flagged after the war, and development was slowed in consequence. A one-piece suit underwent trials for several years, closed by a zip from crutch to behind the right ear. The zip, or later a slide fastener, could not be made watertight and the neck seal was never satisfactory.

At the end of 1929 it was suggested that the easiest and best way of sealing an immersion suit was to make a two-piece suit with a rolled rubber sleeve at the waist. A prototype was made and displaced, and was received with acclaim. An early trial in the swimming bath showed encouraging results, though the fastening of the urination tube was unsatisfactory and needed redesigning. Flight trials were also encouraging; after a trial in a Vampire at 38,000 feet the suit was pronounced to be as comfortable to wear as a lightweight flying overall.

By July 1950, the suit was designated the Mark 6, and twelve suits were ordered for service trials later in the year which, on the whole, proved the suit to be acceptable. Adverse comments were:

1. The belly seal could be felt in the small of the back; the roll was too bulky. (Overcome by reducing the thickness of the rubber and by reducing the length.)

2. The belly roll did not keep in place. (Press-stud connection added between jacket and trousers.)

3. The neck seal was uncomfortable. (The thickness of rubber was reduced; the size varied by marking neck sizes and then cut down to the appropriate level.)

4. Difficulty in putting the suit on, rubber sticks to the skin. (Nylon sleeves were fitted inside the neck and wrist seals, the extremities slid through, and the sleeves then tucked back.)

5. Urinating arrangements unsatisfactory. (Difficult to achieve without sacrificing watertight integrity of the suit.)

6. Boots need to have ventilating properties and to be strong enough to permit walking long distances under escape and arctic conditions. (Improved boots with ventile uppers were developed .)

7. Need for a glove to insulate the hands between the time of leaving the aircraft and getting into the dinghy.

The suit went into production in 1951 and was issued to front line squadrons. From an American report on the US Naval Immersion Suit in Korean waters, it appeared that the RN Immersion Suit had overcome the majority of the criticisms aimed at their own suit.

Protection of the hands had long been a difficult problem. Hands become rapidly useless as a result of cold and thus a very limiting factor in survival. If enclosed in rubberised fabrics the ventilation is unacceptable for everyday flying; if designed of ventile fabrics they are too clumsy for flying aircraft with numerous button and switch controls.

The problem was attacked from another quarter and a glove supplied — to be donned after immersion. Initially the down-filled glove had a rubber wrist seal that proved impenetrable to water but made donning difficult. The rubber seal was replaced with one inflated by mouth through a small valve on the back of the glove.

Flotation Waistcoat — Mae West

In late 1947 trials of a new waistcoat designed by the Safety Equipment School and the Air Medical School proved unsuccessful — in a choppy sea the subject developed a pendulum motion, where his head was immersed every ten or so swings. Modifications were made to the jacket to increase the volume of air behind and at the sides of the head, and above the chest, to maintain the self-righting moment. It then became known as the Naval Life Saving Jacket and was accepted for general naval use, subject to modification to the harness.

When the single flotation chamber over the chest was divided down the mid-line, the same jacket ultimately replaced the existing Mae West. Its advantages were that it was very much less bulky lichen deflated, and had remote controlled gas release. The CO bottle was tucked away at the back, to the right, with a release toggle at the end of a Bowden cable at the front. One pilot accidentally inflated the waistcoat during take-off, resulting in the release toggle being housed in a definite pocket inside the toggle cover.

The Mark 2 (later Mark 3 after some modifications) as designed by the Air Medical School and RAE, Farnborough, met the following specification:

1. General. The waistcoat was worn with the front lobes of the stole and the fabric cover folded and fastened with durable baby dot fasteners. When inflated the gas pressure would force the fasteners apart allowing the stole fully to inflate.
2. Fastenings. Heavy weight zip or button.
3. Waist Adjustment. Made in one size with adjustable slides at the sides.
4. Stole. Contained 18 litres of gas. Was to be of a size and shape to give the necessary stability and head support as a result of trials.
5. Gas inflation. Release by giving the gas bottle cap a sharp pull or tug.
6. Mouth Inflation. By gripping the mouthpiece in the teeth and pushing down. To be fitted with an automatically closing valve.
7. Equipment carried:
a) Fluorescent pack in the folded portion of the front lobe.
b) Pocket for sea-cell battery and torch.
c) Whistle, in the folded portion of the right hand lobe.
d) Life-line anti toggle in a pocket on the left hand side of the wearer.
e) Lifting loops or beckets in the folded portion of the front lobes to be one continuous length of webbing under the arm holes and round the back.

They were to be of a length such that when hooked onto the helicopter hook, the subject could hold the hook as well.

f) Quick release hooks to be provided for attachment of dinghy lanyard and survival pack.

The jacket filled a much needed requirement for a lighter and less bulky item with greatly improved flotation and self-righting properties. It made a great difference to pilot comfort in hot weather flying and was designed to integrate with other articles of flying clothing. It was space saving and allowed easy egress from the cockpit, and was suitable for ejection seats.

SOURCES and BIBLIOGRAPHY

The following works have been consulted in compiling this book, and grateful acknowledgement is made to the authors, contributors, reporters, and publishers.

A Unpublished Sources

Naval Staff History	*British Commonwealth Naval Operations, Korea, 1950-1953*, MOD, 1967
Commander D.C.V. Isard	Midshipman's Journal, HMS *Ocean* Sept. 1951 — Oct. 1952
Lieutenant Commander F.T. Lane Ph.D RAN	*HMAS* Sydney *in Korea: The Sea Furies* — Lecture to Australian Naval Historical Society April 1990
Rear Admiral Peter N. Marsden	Midshipman's Journal HMS *Unicorn* Oct. 1951 — Aug. 1952
Captain HMAS *Sydney*	Report on Typhoon Ruth 22nd October 1951 — Department of Defence (Navy Office) Canberra Reports of Proceedings 29th October 1951, 15th November 1951, 1st December 1951, 20th December 1951, 11th January 1952, 26th January 1952 — Australian War Memorial Canberra
HMAS *Sydney*	Deck Log October 1951 — Australian Archives, Sydney, NSW.
Squadron Records, Diaries and Line Books	Nos. 800, 801, 804, 805, 807, 810, 812, 821 — Fleet Air Arm Museum, Yeovilton
	Nos. 808, 817 — RAN Fleet Air Arm Museum, Nowra, NSW, Australia

B Published Sources and Bibliography

Anon

'British Commonwealth Naval Operations during the Korean War — I to VII'

Journal of the RUSI Vol. XCVI No 582
584
XCVII No 586
XCVIII No 589
590
592
XCVIX No 593

'Logistic Support of Carrier Operations' — *Journal of Naval Engineering* Vol. 5 No 3 — Admiralty 1951

'Catapult HMS *Theseus*' — *Journal of Naval Engineering* Vol. 5 No 4 — Admiralty 1952

'Post-War' Wars of the Fleet Air Arm — *Fly Navy* – Journal of the Fleet Air Arm Officer's Association — Summer 1987.

Treatment of British Prisoners of War in Korea — HMSO 1955

Norman Bartlett (Editor)

With the Australians in Korea — Australian War Memorial, Canberra 1954

Commander (E) E.C. Beard

'Development of Wire Rope for Aircraft Catapults' - *Journal of Naval Engineering* Vol. 4 No 3 — Admiralty 1950

Paul Beaver

The British Aircraft Carrier — Patrick Stephens 1982

Encyclopaedia of the Fleet Air Arm — Patrick Stephens 1987

Bentley

'HMS *Belfast* in Korea' — *Naval Review* Vol. XXXVIII No. 4

Captain A.S. Bolt DSO, DSC**

'*Theseus* in the Korean War' — *Journal of the RUSI* Vol. XCVI No 584

General Omar N. Bradley and Clay Blair

A General's Life — Sidgwick and Jackson 1983

D.K. Brown

'Ship Assisted Landing and Take Off' — *Flight Deck* January 1986

Neville Brown

The Future of Air Power — Croom Helm 1986

Malcolm W. Cagle and Frank A. Manson

The Sea War in Korea — United States Naval Institute, Annapolis, Maryland 1957

Carrier Commissions Record Booklets

HMS Triumph	*— Record of Second commission*
HMS Theseus	*Goes East*
HMS Glory	*— 1951-1953*
HMS Ocean	*— Ocean Saga — The Story of the Commission May 1951 to October 1953*
HMS Unicorn	*— Far East Station 1949-51 — CPO* Logie DSM
HMS Unicorn	*1951-53*
John Chartres	Fly for their Lives
Captain W.W.F. Chatterton Dickson	Seedie's Roll of Naval Honours and Awards 1939-1959 — Ripley Registers 1989
A.K. Chesterton MC	'General MacArthur and the Far East' — *Journal of the RUSI* Vol. XCVI No 582
General Mark W. Clark US Army	*From the Danube to the Yalu* — George Harrap 1954
James Cotton and Ian Neary (Editors)	*The Korean War in History* — Manchester University Press 1989
Commander R. Mike Crosley DSC	*They Gave Me a Seafire* — Air Life Publishing Ltd. 1986
S.J. Davies, MBE, MA, CF	*In Spite of Dungeons* — Hodder and Stoughton 1954
General Sir Anthony Farrar-Hockley	*The British Part in the Korean War Vol. 1* — HMSO 1990
W.S. Farren CB, MBE	'Naval Aircraft Design' — *Journal of Naval Engineering* Vol. 1 No 4 — Admiralty 1948
Rosemary Foot	*The Wrong War* — Cornell University Press 1985
Norman Friedman	*British Carrier Aviation* — Conway Maritime Press 1989
Mike Gaines	'Own Goal' — *Aeroplane Monthly* November 1988
G.H.S.	'Naval Operations in Korea' — *Naval Review* Vol. XXXVIII No 4
	'The Korean War' — *Naval Review* Vol. XXXIX No 1
Ross Gillett	*Wings across the Sea* — Aerospace Publications (Australia)
A.A.C. Griffith, Lt. S.M. Tennant, D. Wyllie	'Hydraulic Fluids in Arresting Gear' — *Journal of Naval Engineering* Vol. 11 No 1 — Admiralty 1958

Eric J. Grove	*Vanguard to Trident: British Naval Policy since World War II* — The Bodley Head 1987
Richard P. Hallion	*The Naval Air War in Korea* — The Nautical and Aviation Publishing Co. of America 1986
Robert Debs Heinl Jnr. USMC	*Victory at High Tide* — Leo Cooper 1972
Commander (E) D.S. Holt-Wilson DSO	'Recent Aircraft Catapult Developments' — *Journal of Naval Engineering* Vol. 2 No 3 — Admiralty 1948
Robert Jackson	*Air War over Korea* — Ian Allan 1973
Lieutenant Denis Lankford RNVR	*I Defy* — Allan Wingate 1954
Callum A. MacDonald	*Korea: the War before Vietnam* — MacMillan 1986
Douglas MacArthur	*Reminiscences* — Heinemann 1964
Commander (E) C.C. Mitchell OBE, RNVR	'Flight Deck Machinery — Accelerators' — *Papers on Engineering Subjects* — Admiralty 1946
	-'Arresting Gear' — Admiralty 1947
Lieutenant C.F. Motley R.N.	'Naval Air Power in Korea' — *Aviation News* 4-17/8/89
Rear Admiral D.S. Murray RAN	'The Sea War in Korea' — *Naval Historical Review* June 1976. (Naval Historical Society of Australia)
Edgar O'Ballance	*Korea 1950-53* — Faber and Faber 1969
Observer	'The Commonwealth Navies in the Korean War' — *Naval Review* Vol. XXXIX No 4
George Odgers	*Across the Parallel* — William Heineman Ltd. Melbourne 1952
The Royal Australian Navy;	*An Illustrated History* — Child and Henry (Australia) 1982
Chapman Pincher	Traitors: The Labyrinth of Treason — Sidgwick & Jackson 1987
Dr. Alfred Price	*Spitfire at War 3* — Ian Allan 1990
David Rees	*Korea: The Limited War* — Macmillan and Co. 1964
David Rees (Consultant Editor)	*The Korean War: History and Tactics* — Orbis Publishing 1984
Matthew B. Ridgway	*The War in Korea* — Barrie and Rockliff, London 1967
Robert Smith	*MacArthur in Korea — the Naked Emperor* — Simon and Schuster, New York 1982

James L. Stokesbury   A short history of the Korean War — William Morrow
                                        and Co. Inc. — New York 1988

Ray Sturtivant   The Squadrons of the Fleet Air Arm — Air Britain
                                        (Historians) Ltd. 1984

British Naval Aviation: *The Fleet Air Arm 1917-1990* — Arms and Armour
                                        Press Ltd. 1990

H.A. Taylor   *Fairey Aircraft since 1915* — Putnam 1974

Major R.C.W. Thomas OBE   *The War in Korea* — Gale and Polden 1954

Duane Thorin   *A Ride to* — Henry Regnery Company, Chicago 1956

Commander (E) J.F. Tucker DSC   'A commission in a Light Fleet Carrier' — *Journal of
                                        Naval Engineering* Vol. 7 No 3 — Admiralty 1954

John Frayn Turner   *Hovering Angels*

Ray Williams   'The Sea Fury' — *Aeroplane Monthly* Dec.1985,
                                        Jan. and Feb. 1986

John Winton   'One Man's War' — *Seascape* March 1988

                                        Air Power at Sea 1945 to Today
                                        — Sidgwick & Jackson 1987

Wing Commander
P.G. Wykeham-Barnes
DSO, DFC, AFC   'The War in Korea with special reference to
                                        the difficulties of using our air power'
                                        — *Journal of the RUSI* Vol. XCVII No. 586

Alan Zammit   'Ruthless Attack' — *The Sun*, Melbourne 27/3/84

'Korea Revisited'   — *The Sun*, Melbourne 17/10/85

'I'm Jesus, Canteen Manager'   — *Naval Historical Review* June, October 1982 (Naval
                                        Historical Society of Australia).